Dangerous Energy

Dangerous Energy

*The archaeology of gunpowder and
military explosives manufacture*

Wayne D Cocroft

ENGLISH HERITAGE

Published by English Heritage at the National Monuments Record Centre,
Great Western Village, Kemble Drive, Swindon SN2 2GZ.

Copyright © English Heritage 2000

Images (except as otherwise shown) © Crown copyright NMR.
Applications for the reproduction of images should be made to the
National Monuments Record.

Crown copyright material is reproduced under licence from the
Controller of Her Majesty's Stationery Office.

English Heritage is the Government's statutory advisor on all aspects
of the historic environment.

The National Monuments Record is the public archive of English Heritage.
All the research and photography created while working on this project is
available there. For more infomation contact NMR Enquiry and Research Services,
National Monuments Record Centre, Great Western Village, Kemble Drive,
Swindon SN2 2GZ. Telephone 01973 414600.

First Published 2000

ISBN 1 85074 718 0

Product Code XC10854

British Library Cataloguing in Publication Data
A CIP catalogue record for this book is available from the British Library

Edited by Susan Wright, Ellen McAdam, and Val Kinsler
Indexed by Veronica Stebbing
Designed by Val Kinsler
Edited and brought to press by David M Jones and Andrew McLaren,
Academic & Specialist Publications, English Heritage

Printed by Snoeck-Ducaju & Zoon, Gent

Contents

9 Survival and reuse

Illustrations

Tables

Foreword

Defence of the realm has been a prime responsibility of the modern nation state. Securing efficient supplies of weaponry is fundamental: yet, while the development and manufacture of artillery and rifles has its own extensive literature, the same is not true for the manufacture and handling of the explosives that acted as propellants and charges. The dangerous and occasionally exotic installations that produced gunpowder in early times and, latterly, an increasingly wide and increasingly specialised range of chemical explosives for military use have an erratic history of abandonment and mothballing that reflects the extremes of capacity required by times of war and the redundancy brought by peace. Such redundancy has accelerated recently as a result both of the peace dividend following the end of the Cold War and of the globalisation of the explosives industry.

Although the Royal Commission on the Historical Monuments of England (RCHME) had already recorded characteristic gunpowder manufacturing sites at Oare (near Faversham in Kent) and at Postbridge, Cherry Brook (in Devon), it was fieldwork in 1993 on the former RGPF at Waltham Abbey – surplus to requirements and up for disposal – that brought home the paucity of archaeological and architectural information about the military explosives industry available in the public domain. That survey provided the basis upon which recommendations for statutory protection could be made and the foundations upon which a secure and viable future for the site could be established (for which see Chapter 9). The further result was this groundbreaking study undertaken by the RCHME and its publication as a cooperative venture between the Royal Commission and English Heritage, extending the excellent partnership of the two agencies at Waltham Abbey. It is fitting that *Dangerous energy* is the first major academic publication to emerge from the Royal Commission and English Heritage after the two bodies were amalgamated in April 1999.

This book sets out to achieve five objectives:

- to increase our understanding of the unusual and problematic buildings and site types associated with the gunpowder and military explosives industry
- to help planners, local authority archaeologists, conservation officers and others working in the field to identify individual buildings and sites and to place them in a national context

- to promote greater appreciation of these remarkable sites and encourage sensible, well-informed, and sensitive management
- to promote further study, especially at a local level: and, not least,
- to tell a fascinating and important story

This joint publication forms part of a wider programme of work on the defence estate being carried out by the RCHME and English Heritage. This includes the Royal Commission's earlier work on the Royal Naval Dockyards (Coad 1989), current work on MoD disposals, concentrating especially on installations of the Cold War (also intended for publication), and English Heritage's surveys of barracks, of dockyards of the steam navy, and of aviation structures and airfields, which are aimed primarily at protecting the most significant buildings through listing and scheduling but are also being published in a series entitled *Themes in military architecture and archaeology*. In parallel with the continuing work of the Monuments Protection Programme, these publications will transform our understanding of the infrastructure of the defence establishment over the last 300 or so years.

Many of the sites recorded in this book were the wartime workplaces of men and women who still vividly remember them – places where strong friendships were forged and the stresses and personal sacrifice of working with dangerous energy were endured. To them, these sites mean more than this book can convey.

The Royal Commission and English Heritage acknowledge the generous financial help received from British Aerospace towards the publication of this book. Above all, it is a pleasure to acknowledge the exceptional energy, research, and interpretive skills of the author, Wayne Cocroft of the RCHME's survey staff, in investigating all the sites and presenting the results gleaned from a remarkably rich and hitherto almost untouched body of documentary material.

March 1999

Sir Jocelyn Stevens
Chairman
English Heritage

Lord Faringdon
Chairman
Royal Commission on the Historic Monuments of England

Acknowledgements

Many individuals and institutions contributed to the investigation of sites and buildings described in this book, and to the documentary research supporting it. Chapters 1–4 on early gunpowder production have built on the very solid foundations laid by the Gunpowder Mills Study Group; their friendship and free exchange of information, exemplified in the outlook of their chairman, Professor Alan Crocker, afforded vital support to the project. Individuals among them gave particular help: René Amiable in Paris, David Ashton, Dr Brenda Buchanan, Professor Alan Crocker, Glenys Crocker, Malcolm McLaren, Malcolm Tucker, and Dr Jenny West. Dr Brenda Buchanan's efforts in bringing gunpowder scholars together under the auspices of the International Committee for the History of Technology (ICOHTEC) have greatly advanced the international dimension of the subject, and promoted productive contact with overseas colleagues, pre-eminently Dr Patrice Bret of the Académie des Sciences in Paris, Professor Ian Rae of the Victoria University of Technology, Melbourne, and Professor Seymour Mauskopf of Duke University, North Carolina.

The project's fieldwork could not have been undertaken without the assistance of many landowners, both public and private. Throughout, staff of the Royal Commission on the Historical Monuments of England (RCHME) enjoyed practical support from Royal Ordnance plc, especially through the staff of its Environmental Services Group, including Ian Barrow, Dr Gordon Bulloch, Chris Delahunt, Kerry Green, Dr Malcolm Green, Bryan Hughes, Roger Neal, Tom Smith, and Graham Vincent. The Ministry of Defence, Defence Estate Organisation, and the Defence Evaluation and Research Agency arranged access to many formally restricted areas of the defence estate through their local offices and officials. At the former RGPF at Waltham Abbey, practical assistance and encouragement throughout the project was received from members of the Waltham Abbey Royal Gunpowder Mills Project, its steering committee, and their advisers, in particular Dan Bone of CIVIX, Steven Chaddock, Dr David Prince, and David Stanners.

Staff of the Royal Commissions in Scotland and Wales – respectively, Dr Miles Oglethorpe and Miriam Macdonald (RCAHMS), and Medwyn Parry (RCAHMW) – collaborated in fieldwork, exchange of information, and checking the gazetteer entries.

Most of the historical research was carried out at the Public Record Office at Kew, but also drew upon many other libraries and institutions and the knowledge of their staff. These included: Bolton Central Library, Carlisle Library, Epping Forest District Museum (Kate Carver and Susan Dalloe), Falkirk District Council Museum (Geoffrey Bailey), Guildford Muniment Room, Hampshire Record Office at Winchester, Imperial War Museum Library, Keele University Library (Martin Philips and his staff), Leeds Central Library, Morecambe Library, Northamptonshire Archaeology (Iain Soden), Northamptonshire County Council (Graham Cadman), the Royal Armouries Library (Sarah Barter-Bailey and Nicholas Hall), Royal Artillery Institution (Brigadier and Mrs Timbers), the Science Museum (Dr John Becklake, Dr Robert Bud, Dr John Griffiths, and Douglas Millard), the Science Museum Library, West Yorkshire Archaeology Service (Ian Sanderson and Dr R E Yarwood), and Whaley Thorns Heritage Centre, Derbyshire.

Established museums of the explosives industry also provided useful information, through Robert Howard (Curator of Technology and Industry at the Hagley Museum and Library, Delaware), Brendan Kelleher (Royal Gunpowder Mills at Ballincollig, Cork), and Dr Arthur Percival (Honorary Director of the Faversham Society).

Other individuals who freely provided information or advice were Dr Malcolm Airs, Mrs Margaret Arbon (Gainsborough and District Historical Society), Dr Bjorn Ivar Berg, Norway, Stewart Chamberlain (formerly MoD Procurement Executive), Arthur Clark of Kirkby, Susan Edlington, Lt Brian O'Flinn (United States Air Force), Dr Peter Gaunt (University College, Chester), Wesley Harry, Lesley Hayward, Bernard Lowry, Fred Nash, Norman Paul, Gordon Routledge, Stanley Thomas, Alan Turner (President of the Royal Arsenal Woolwich Historical Society), and Keith Ward.

Many contributions were made by present and past Commissioners and staff of the RCHME. In addition to the team who delivered the survey of RGPF Waltham Abbey (listed in RCHME 1994, 7), fieldwork and site assessments by Tony Calladine, Jo Donachie, Peter Guillery, Hazel Riley, Nicky Smith, Roger Thomas, Andrew Williams, Mike Williams, and Robert Wilson-North were incorporated in the book. Staff of the National Monuments Record's Public Search Room carried out aerial photographic cover searches, and Nigel Wilkins efficiently supplied bundles of historic maps. Ground photographs were taken by Sid Barker, Keith Buck, Steven Cole, Keith Findlater, Leonard Furbank, Michael Hesketh-Roberts, Derek Kendall, Dank Silva, Roger Thomas, and Peter Williams; aerial photographs by Roger Featherstone and Peter Horne. Responsibility for co-ordinating photographic printing lay with Diane Kendall, supported by the RCHME darkroom staff. The majority of the drawn illustrations were prepared by Philip Sinton; additional illustrations by Bernard Thomason, Tony Calladine, and Barry Jones. Administrative and editorial support came from Elizabeth Smith, Dr Diane Williams, Dr David M Jones, and Dr Robin Taylor. The overall supervision of the project lay with Paul Everson.

Dr Marilyn Palmer, Paul Everson, and Keith Falconer saw the text through several drafts on behalf of the RCHME, providing comment and specialist advice. Dr Martin Cherry and Professor Angus Buchanan (as consultant) read it for English Heritage, and many of their wise suggestions have been incorporated.

This project, from its origins in the RCHME's survey of the RGPF at Waltham Abbey in 1993, has enjoyed a close working relationship with English Heritage and its officers, notably Dr Martin Cherry and David Stocker. They have contributed the section on conservation issues as exemplified at Waltham Abbey that forms the substance of Chapter 9.

Final thanks go to John Whitbourn, who inspired the title.

Wayne D Cocroft

Summary

The sites and monuments associated with gunpowder and military explosives production in Britain have often been cloaked in secrecy. In consequence, they have been poorly documented in archaeological and conservation literature and ill understood.

This book describes the physical remains associated with the industry and places them within a historical and technological context. A variety of historical sources has been used to identify the sites in Britain associated with military explosives manufacture and these are presented as a gazetteer. A glossary of terms and a bibliography are also included. Standing buildings, earthwork remains, and wider landscapes have been surveyed or more selectively recorded to illustrate what survives. The study's focus is explicitly military: sites connected with the supply of explosives to the mining industry are excluded, although it often proves difficult to draw a distinct line between the two areas. Sites engaged in commercial firework manufacture are also omitted, although again many of the principles of site and building design apply.

There is clear historical evidence for the introduction of gunpowder manufacture in the Middle Ages in Britain, but few early sites or structures survive as field monuments. Remains of gunpowder works established by the late seventeenth century can be identified archaeologically: most are overlain by later developments, but site layouts and the organisation of water supplies to power mills commonly perpetuate early arrangements. The late eighteenth and nineteenth centuries saw a transformation of the industry, initially by a more standardised preparation of raw materials and latterly by production on a truly industrial scale, harnessing steam and hydraulic power, and with increasing technological refinement. This was promoted by state ownership of key factories, notably the Royal Gunpowder Factory at Waltham Abbey and associated establishments, which pioneered change and set standards for the commercial industry. These developments, reflected in sites, buildings, and processes, form part of an international picture with parallels in continental Europe and in America.

The description of the development of the chemical explosives industry in the late nineteenth century, with special emphasis on gun propellants, also draws heavily on the Royal Commission on the Historical Monuments of England's fieldwork at the state factory at Waltham Abbey; however, the scope of the study is broadened by consideration of the remains of other contemporary factories, many of which survive as field monuments.

The urgency and large-scale demands of the two World Wars in the first half of the twentieth century again brought state-directed or state-led solutions and a series of distinctive buildings and site types. In the First World War, the technology of explosives manufacture and handling influenced the form and architecture of the factories and is reflected in the field remains and their chronology. Standard Royal Ordnance factory types with modular layouts and specialised functions were developed throughout the 1930s rearmament period, and increased in number and scale to meet calculated need. Inter-war technological developments influenced factory design in identifiable ways. The location of the factories was distinctive, a matter of conscious choice rather than of inherited capacity, and was related to integrated supply and transport networks, labour, and safety. The social history of the industry becomes more prominent in twentieth-century wartime conditions, with provisions for the employment of women, for accident prevention, and off-site housing, all of which are reflected in surviving field remains as well as contemporary images.

The main text concludes with a section on the sites and structures associated with handling explosive rocket propellants, which, after 150 years of intermittent development, dominated post-war military strategy until the 1960s. Finally the book includes a gazetteer, a glossary of terms, and a bibliography.

This comprehensive national study provides a framework for identification, interpretation, and conservation of sites and remains of the military explosives industry. It also provides a foundation for specific, detailed local investigations and a structure for international comparisons.

Résumé

Les sites et monuments concernant la production de poudre à canon et d'explosifs militaires en Grande-Bretagne ont souvent été entourés de mystère. Ils ont été, par conséquent, pauvrement documentés dans les parutions archéologiques et traités de conservation et donc peu compris.

Le livre décrit les vestiges associés à cette industrie et les replace dans un contexte historique et technologique. Une variété de sources historiques a été utilisée pour identifier les sites de Grande-Bretagne relatifs à la manufacture des explosifs militaires et ceux-ci sont présentés sous forme d'un répertoire. Des édifices toujours sur pied, des restes de terrassements et des sites plus étendus ont été inspectés ou recensés plus sélectivement pour illustrer ce qui survit. L'accent de cette étude est explicitement militaire: les endroits liés à l'approvisionnement en explosifs pour l'industrie minière sont exclus bien qu'il s'avère souvent difficile de tirer un trait distinct entre les deux sujets. De même, ne sont pas représentés les sites dediés à la manufacture commerciale de pièces d'artifice, bien que la plupart des principes d'emplacement et de concept de construction s'appliquent ici aussi.

L'évidence historique démontre clairement que la production de poudre à canon en Grande-Bretagne fut introduite au Moyen-Age, cependant peu d'anciens sites et de structures ont survécu sous forme de ruines. On peut identifier archéologiquement les vestiges de poudreries établies avant la fin du 17ème siècle; la plupart sont recouverts par des constructions ultérieures mais la disposition des sites et l'organisation de l'approvisionnement en eau des moulins perpétuent de façon générale les aménagements précédents. La fin du 18ème et le 19ème siècle virent une transformation de cette industrie; initialement, la préparation des matières premières fut plus standardisée et plus tard la production se fit à une échelle véritablement industrielle, en domestiquant l'énergie à vapeur et l'énergie hydraulique, et en accroissant les perfectionnements techniques. Ceci fut encouragé par l'acquisition des usines clef par l'État, notamment la Manufacture Royale de Poudre (à canon) à Waltham Abbey et des établissements associés, provoquant des modifications et établissant des standards pour l'industrie commerciale. Les développements, reflétés dans les sites, constructions et procédés techniques, font partie d'une image internationale avec des parallèles en Europe continentale et en Amérique.

La description des changements affectant l'industrie des explosifs chimiques vers la fin du 19ème siècle, avec un accent spécial sur les propuleurs à canon, s'inspire fortement de l'étude sur le terrain entreprise par la Commission Royale des Monuments Historiques d'Angleterre à l'usine d'État de Waltham Abbey; cependant, l'ampleur de cette étude est accrue du fait que les vestiges d'autres usines contemporaines sont passés en revue, la plupart survivant sous forme de ruines.

Les besoins pressants et l'échelle importante des demandes durant les deux guerres mondiales du 20ème siècle engendrèrent à nouveau des solutions proposées et dirigées par l'État et une série de constructions et de types de sites distinctifs. Durant la première guerre mondiale, la technologie dans la manufacture et la manipulation d'explosifs influença la forme et l'architecture des usines; ceci se reflète dans les bâtiments en ruine et leur chronologie. Les types d'usine correspondant au standard de l'Artillerie Royale aux tracés modulaires et fonctions spécialisées furent adoptés tout au long de la période de réarmement dans les années 30, se multipliant en nombre et en importance pour répondre à des besoins précis. Les développements technologiques de l'entre-deux guerres influencèrent la conception des usines de façon identifiable. Les emplacements de celles-ci étaient distinctifs, le reflet d'un choix conscient plutôt que la réutilisation d'une fonction préexistante, lié à l'intégration de l'approvisionnement et des réseaux de transport, de la main d'oeuvre et des mesures de sécurité. L'histoire sociale de cette industrie devient encore plus remarquable avec les conditions de temps de guerre du 20ème siècle. Les dispositions quant à l'emploi de la main d'oeuvre féminine, la prévention des accidents, et les cités ouvrières se reflètent dans les édifices qui ont survécu de même que dans les représentations de l'époque.

Le livre s'achève par une section sur les sites et structures associés à la manufacture des explosifs pour propulsion par fusées, qui, après 150 ans de développement intermittent, domina la stratégie militaire d'après-guerre jusque dans les années 60.

Un lexique des termes employés et une bibliographie sont inclus.

Cette étude d'ensemble réalisée au plan national fournit un système d'identification, d'interprétation et de conservation des sites et des vestiges de l'industrie militaire en explosifs. Elle forme, de même, une base pour des recherches détaillées locales et une structure pour des comparaisons internationales.

Traduction: Christine Bedeschi-Smith

Zusammenfassung

Die Standorte und Monumente in Großbritannien, welche mit der Produktion von Schießpulver und militärischen Sprengstoffen in Zusammenhang gebracht werden, sind oftmals geheim gehalten worden. Auf Grund dieser Geheimhaltung sind sie schwach dokumentiert in der Archeologie- und Konservierungsliteratur und falsch verstanden worden.

Dieses Buch beschreibt die noch bestehenden Überreste verbunden mit dieser Industrie und stellt sie im historischen und technologischen Zusammenhang dar. Zur Indentifizierung der britischen militärischen Sprengstoffproduktionsstandorte wurde eine Vielfalt von historischen Quellen benutzt, welche in einem Namensverzeichnis angegeben sind. Ein Erklärung der gebrauchten Umgangsformen und eine Bibliographie sind auch enthalten. Noch existierende Gebäude, Erdwerke und Landschaftsgebiete wurden vermessen oder mehr selektiv dokumentiert, um zu illustrieren was noch erhalten ist. Der Brennpunkt der Studie ist rein militärisch. Standorte der Sprengstofflieferung an die Bergwerksindustrie wurden ausgelassen, auch wenn es häufig schwer ist eine klare Trennung der beiden Gebiete zu erreichen. Kommerzielle Feuerwerksproduktion ist ebenso nicht enthalten, selbst wenn die gleichen Prinzipien für Standort- und Gebäudeplanung zutreffen.

Es gibt klare historische Beweise für die mittelalterliche Einführung von Schieüßpulverproduktion in Großbritannien doch nur wenige der frühesten Standorte und Strukturen überlebten als noch sichtbare Monumente. Rückstände der Schießpulverwerke vom späten 17. Jahrhundert können archeologisch indentifiziert werden, auch wenn später überbaut, da Standortlage und die Organisation von Wasserzufuhr und -mühlen zur Energielieferung Ihren früheren Verwendungszweck erkennen lassen. Das späte 18. und 19. Jahrhundert brachte eine erhebliche Veränderung der Industrie mit sich, anfangs mit der standartisierten Vorbereitung der Rohmaterialien und später mit der Produktion in wahren industriellen Ausmaßen, durch die Nutzung von Dampf- und Hydraulikkraft und mit ständig wachsenden technologischen Verbesserungen. Voran getrieben durch die staatliche Besitzerschaft von Schlüsselfabriken, wie der Königlichen Schießpulverfabrik in Waltham Abbey und verbundenen Einrichtungen, welche Veränderungen einführte und neue Standarte setzte für die kommerzielle Industrie. Diese Entwicklungen, reflektiert in Standorten, Gebäuden und Produktionsprozessen, sind Bestandteil eines internationalen Gesamtbildes mit Parallelen im kontinentalen Europa und Amerika.

Die Beschreibung der Entwicklung der chemischen Sprengstoffindustrie im späten 19. Jahrhundert, mit speziellem Gesichtspunkt auf Kanonenmunitionspulver, lehnt sich im Wesentlichen an Praxisuntersuchungen der Königlichen Kommission für Historische Monumente in England (Royal Commission on the Historical Monuments of England) in der staatlichen Fabrik in Waltham Abbey. Der Rahmen der Studie wird außerdem erweitert durch den Einbezug von den Rückständen anderer gleichalteriger Fabriken, welche als Monumente erhalten blieben.

Die Notbedärfe und Großraumansprüche der beiden Weltkriege in der ersten Hälfte des 20. Jahrhunderts bringt wiederum staatlich geleitete Lösungen und eine Serie von unterschiedlichen Bauwerken und Standorten. Im ersten Weltkrieg wurde die Form und Architektur der Fabriken durch die Technologie der Sprengstoffproduktion beeinflußt, und spiegelt sich eindeutig in den Rückständen und ihrer Chronologie wieder. Königliche Feldzeug (Royal Ordnance)-Fabriktypen mit Modularplänen und spezialisierten Funktionen wurden in den 30-er Aufrüstungsjahren entwickelt und wuchsen in Anzahl und Größe nach vorher kalkuliertem Bedarf. In der Zwischenkriegszeit wurden Fabrikplanungen klar von den technologischen Entwicklungen gekennzeichnet. Die Lage der Fabriken war eher von von klaren Überlegungen als von überlieferten Fähigkeiten gekennzeichnet und direkt mit den Zufuhr- und Transportstrukturen, Arbeitskräften, und Sicherheitsbedürfnissen verbunden. Die Sozialgeschichte der Industrie wird deutlicher sichtbar in den Kriegsbedingungen des 20. Jahrhunderts, mit der Provision für die Anstellung von weiblichen Arbeitskräften, der Vorbeugung von Arbeitsunfällen sowie der Entstehung von Wohngelegenheiten außerhalb der Fabriken, welche alle noch sichtbar sind in den überlebenden Rückständen sowie in Bildern aus dieser Zeit.

Der Haupttext schließt mit einem Absatz über die Standorte und Strukturen verbunden mit der Herstellung von explosiven Raketentreibstoffen, welche, nach 150 Jahren von zwischenzeitlichen Entwicklungen, die Militärstrategie bis 1960-er Jahre bestimmt. Und wie schon erwähnt das Buch enthält am Ende eine Nahmenserwähnung, eine Erklärung der Umgangsformen und eine Bibliographie.

Diese umfangreiche nationale Studie gibt einen Rahmen für die Indentifikation, Übersetzung, und Konservierung der jeweiligen Standorte und Überreste der militärischen Sprengstoffindustrie und eine Struktur für internationale Vergleiche.

Übersetzung: Gillian M Stewart

Introduction

Gunpowder, along with the compass and printing, has been regarded as one of the defining inventions of the modern, in contrast to the medieval, world. It provided a controllable and portable form of energy which changed the world by encouraging trade, exploration, mining, and civil engineering. But especially and persistently it served the military purposes of conquest and defence that have preoccupied modern states. In this, gunpowder was followed and replaced by latter-day chemical-based explosives and propellants, which continued the same functions and were produced under much the same considerations of effective processing and safe handling – so much so that they can be regarded as part of the same industry.

Scope

This study adopts an archaeological approach to the industry: it examines the extant remains and the evidence for the earlier physical forms – the buildings, the site layouts, the manufacturing flowlines, the supply, power, and transport networks – for the manufacture of these important commodities. This requires an awareness of historical context in both a political and economic dimension and, for example, in the intimately related developments of weaponry and weapons platforms, but the result is not a history of the industry in a traditional sense. It requires an outline of technological change and scientific developments. But this is not a history of technology, which for this industry is best represented in the production manuals listed in the bibliography. The focus is archaeological – on buildings and landscapes and on what they reflect and uniquely convey about the explosives industry and its development.

The study's geographical core is England, and this is reflected in the detailed treatment. But the organisation of military explosives and propellants production in the national interest (ie that of Britain) means that more than passing reference must be made to sites in Ireland, Scotland, and Wales, either because of their intrinsic importance or because they formed part of production networks which, in the twentieth century particularly, were deliberately geographically dispersed. This wider view is the more desirable, since sites such as Ardeer in Scotland, Ballincollig in Ireland, and Caerwent in Wales afford exceptional surviving field remains for examination. Fortunately, the active interest and cooperation of colleagues in all three countries, with similar concerns for recording and for informing conservation or management decisions, has promoted a mutually beneficial exchange of information and understanding.

The chronological scope of the research extends from the earliest times to the sophisticated military rocketry of the post-war era, described in Chapter 8. The cancellation of Blue Streak in 1960, and with it Britain's pretensions as an independent military power, has been taken as an emblematic terminal date. The inclusion of rocketry, with its development for military applications in the eighteenth century and perhaps earlier, legitimately reflects the fact that until comparatively recently the propellants involved, and their manufacture, have differed little from those used to propel projectiles from guns. The recent differences then serve to sharpen perception about the distinctiveness of the resulting structures and sites developed for manufacture and testing. For the earliest period, before the mid-seventeenth century, identifiable buildings and field remains are extremely rare: an attempt has nevertheless been made to provide a full chronological framework of understanding from available sources, within which new discoveries might be recognised and placed.

Research, fieldwork, and the preparation of the text of this book were completed before the RCHME and English Heritage were merged into a single organisation in April 1999. Accordingly, reference is made throughout to each body separately.

Previous work

Any substantial study builds on existing literature. This one has at the same time a vast amount – of a historical and technical nature – and rather little, in that it has itself very much pioneered the study of buildings and sites. Relatively little has been written about the archaeology of gunpowder and explosives manufacture. From the eighteenth century onwards, summaries of the history of gunpowder (and later of chemical explosives) and the practice of its manufacturing are found in contemporary encyclopaedias. The most useful of the early works is Diderot's *Encyclopédie, ou dictionnaire raisonné des sciences, des arts et des métiers* (1771). General nineteenth-century encyclopaedias continue to be a source of valuable information, especially when supplemented by others devoted specifically to trade and industry (Rees 1819; Horner nd).

In the nineteenth-century literature, a historical perspective was provided almost in passing in the introductions to works by practitioners – who were primarily concerned with contemporary manufacture and research – or as part of treatises on artillery. Short historical surveys of the development of explosives gradually became a feature of War Office manuals. The most significant and influential books on the subject were published by the Hungarian, Oscar Guttmann, one of the leading chemical engineers of his day. In *The manufacture of explosives* (Guttmann 1895), he introduced a study of contemporary practice with a short historical preface of great interest; but his most notable historical work was *Monumenta pulveris pyrii* (Guttmann 1906), in which he reproduced many early engravings relating to the industry. A significant study of the situation in Britain took the form of a collection of essays entitled *The rise and progress of the British explosives industry* (Hodgetts 1909), which provides an important survey of the contemporary industry, and Arthur Marshall's works on explosives published during the First World War also contain useful historical summaries (Marshall 1915 and 1917). It is a series of important technical manuals produced before and during the Great War, however, that although rarely containing a historical perspective, describe the contemporary manufacturing process of new chemical explosives (eg Guttmann 1909; Quinan 1912; Weaver 1917; Colver 1918).

A handful of local studies, published both before and after that war, made useful contributions: one, a survey of the gunpowder industry in Surrey, where some of the earliest powder-mills were situated, was produced as part of *VCH Surrey* (1905), and this was followed at long intervals by studies of the Battle Mills in Sussex (Blackman 1923) and of the government charcoal works, also in Sussex (Dickinson and Straker 1938). Few people were employed in the industry between the wars and few historians were interested in the subject. During the Second World War, Pelican Books published a popular paperback on explosives which also contained some brief historical notes (Read 1942) and an officially sanctioned account of the Royal Ordnance Factories appeared in 1949 (written under his pen name, Ian Hay, by J H Beith), a work whose value is reduced by having been compiled under security restrictions. More useful are the official civil histories of the war published during the 1950s, especially *Labour in the munitions industries* (Inman 1957) and *Factories and plant* (Hornby 1958), although these also suffered from contemporary security constraints.

The beginning of modern scholarly interest in the subject can be dated to 1960 with Partington's *A history of Greek Fire and gunpowder*. Pioneering studies in the industrial archaeology of the gunpowder industry began with Wilson's (1963–4) account of the gunpowder mills of Westmorland and Furness, published by the Newcomen Society, and Arthur Percival's (1968) study of the Faversham explosives industry in *Industrial Archaeology*. The Faversham Society, although at first concerned primarily with the excavation and preservation of a single mill building, has continued to contribute to the wider debate and published a number of studies of more than local significance (Percival 1986; Patterson 1986a and b; 1995a; 1995b; Cocroft 1994; Crozier 1998).

The 1970s saw the publication of only a small number of important papers (Warner 1975; McLaren 1975; Buchanan 1976), but this belied a considerable groundswell of interest in the subject among a diverse and as yet unconnected group of individuals interested in economic history and the history of technology. In the mid-1980s they were brought together under the auspices of the Society for the Protection of Ancient Buildings (Wind and Water Mills Section) to form the Gunpowder Mills Study Group. This decade saw a significant shift of gear in terms of the excavation and publication of several individual mill sites. A major role was played by Glenys Crocker, whose popular account of the industry (Crocker 1986) provided one channel for the wider understanding and appreciation of the industry, and her editing of the *Gunpowder mills gazetteer*, an essential source, is another (Crocker 1988a).

Substantial monographs also began to appear, with Joseph Needham's epic history of Chinese military technology blazing the trail (Needham 1986). An important analysis of the state's involvement in the industry in the eighteenth century was provided by Jenny West in her *Gunpowder, government and war in the mid-eighteenth century* (West 1991), while the industry was located securely in its private and commercial context in Brenda Buchanan's study of gunpowder production and technology in the Bristol region (Buchanan 1996c). All aspects of the industry – the role of the state and of private investors and the diffusion of technology – were placed on a broad canvas following an international conference held at Bath in 1994, which was published as a collection of essays entitled *Gunpowder: the history of an international technology* (Buchanan 1996a). The early 1990s also saw the first systematic conservation initiatives in the gunpowder industry in England, when in 1993 English Heritage's Monuments Protection Programme commissioned David Cranstone to produce a comprehensive national review of the sites of this industry (Gould 1993; Stocker 1995). The summary report, passed on as formal advice to the Secretary of State in 1996, was the first detailed policy statement about the conservation of this class of industrial remains (Chitty 1996).

There are far fewer studies of the chemical explosives industry and of the industrial archaeology of individual sites. General histories of the chemical industry contain some information on explosives manufacture and related industries (Hardie and Davidson Pratt 1966; Reader 1970; Haber 1971). Studies of individual factories or of the industry in a region, like Earl's on Cornwall (Earl 1978) and Kelleher's on Ireland (Kelleher 1993), have relied principally on historical sources, while noting the survival of structures or using them for illustration. A notable exception in its archaeological approach through fieldwork is Garrad's account of the Bellite factory on the Isle of Man (Garrad 1980). The short monograph reporting RCAHMS's work at Ardeer, in Ayrshire, forms an important complement to the present publication (Dolan and Oglethorpe 1996). Elsewhere in the world, too, relatively modern explosives factories are being regarded as important cultural resources. At the Albion explosives factory in Melbourne, Australia, assessments of structures and recommendations for retention of historic features were made in advance of proposed demolition (Yelland 1989; Vines and Ward 1988).

Objectives

Responding to the limitations of available information, the objective of the study and of the book is to set a framework of understanding for the field remains of the military explosives industry, within which the typically fragmentary remains of most former sites and installations may be placed and become capable of evaluation in terms of function and importance. In this, at a national level, it complements the assessment completed for gunpowder production by English Heritage's Monuments Protection Programme and affords support to any future assessment of chemical explosives sites and other specialist military and industrial facilities, and to the Thematic Listing Programme with its associated series of monographs, *Themes in military architecture and archaeology* (English Heritage and the Ministry of Defence, to be published by The Stationery Office). At a regional and local level, it provides a background to inform conservation decisions on a topic where information has previously been limited, partial, and unreliable, and where decisions may be difficult or weighted against the superficially unprepossessing sites and structures of this industry. Much potential lies in the further local study and documentation of sites which a project

at this national level has only been able to identify: this study provides the context for that local work.

Wow!

In September 1992, four experienced staff from RCHME and English Heritage made a reconnaissance visit together to the recently redundant site of the RGPF at Waltham Abbey. It was a day in which unparalleled excitement – as discovery followed discovery in the leafy jungle of the northern half of the site – was combined with profound puzzlement. The form, function, and interrelationships of structures stumbled over were wholly novel and completely unclear; these were the remains of an industry – indeed of a whole world – previously little considered by archaeological and architectural scholarship and statutory heritage activity. The consequence of that visit directly affected the solutions found for the Waltham Abbey site. The importance of these solutions in the development of sustainable conservation practice, and in the involvement of partners to exploit the unprecedented resources made available through the Heritage Lottery Fund, are set out in Chapter 9. To a large extent the origins of this book also lay in that visit. The international importance of the Waltham Abbey factory was to become abundantly clear through its own history, its exceptional preservation, the excellence of its surviving documentation, and the level of understanding that could be achieved there. Nevertheless, it was only by obtaining a grasp of the wider framework of the production facilities of gunpowder and explosives in Britain that Waltham Abbey's role and importance at each stage from the seventeenth century to the present day could be more roundly perceived. For the mass of strange sites and installations elsewhere that do not survive in such a remarkably complete state, this framework (to which they contribute) simultaneously provides a context and a means of understanding.

The understanding and developments now documented in England, and more widely in Britain, invite comparison on an international front, not least with the circumstances of other western European states that were the military allies and rivals of Britain over the centuries.

Public interest in military and industrial remains of the recent past is high, and growing. It is to be hoped that this, too, may be served, both directly and indirectly, through the contents of this book.

1
'Success to the Black Art!'[1]

Origins

Gunpowder or 'black powder' is a mechanical mixture of saltpetre, charcoal, and sulphur. From the time of its discovery, it held a fascination as a source of destructive energy. When harnessed as a source of propellant energy it transformed warfare. These twin foci remained the driving forces in the search for an improved understanding of its properties and advances in manufacturing methods, and, ultimately, its replacement by chemical-based explosives.

In the Middle Ages, the combination of its power to maim and terrify and its association with alchemy led to its manufacture being regarded as one of the black arts. Conversely, the names associated with the early introduction of this devilish knowledge are those of monks in the great centres of learning and scholarship in Europe. Unlike other medieval industries engaged in the extraction of raw materials or primary manufacturing, no archaeological evidence has yet been discovered relating to its early manufacture. Its close association with seats of learning and governments has, nevertheless, ensured that its early history is better documented than many of the solely artisan-based industries.

The date at which a substance recognisable as gunpowder appears is obscure and its origins are made more uncertain by difficulties in understanding the contemporary terminology. The development of a proto-gunpowder took place in China in the late first millennium AD, though parallel origins may lie in areas of central Asia or the eastern Mediterranean where naturally occurring substances with incendiary uses are found, but where the contemporary documentation is lacking. As significant were the methods developed for recognising and refining saltpetre in China and central Asia. In China toxic fumes were used in warfare from the fourth century and were the subject of Taoist alchemists' experiments, ironically searching for the elixir of life. References describing a proto-gunpowder occur there by the ninth century, more as warnings to unwary alchemists than describing any practical use. Yet by the tenth century incendiary compositions were in use in fire lances and for filling bombs and grenades, and by the end of the twelfth century the earliest rockets had been developed.[2] These early substances may be characterised as being deflagatory and incendiary rather than explosive.

This knowledge was probably transferred to the west through Arab traders and scholarship, and increasingly from the thirteenth century by direct contact between Europeans and China. The first true gunpowders with a high nitrate content were recognised by the early thirteenth century. Early accounts of gunpowder appeared almost simultaneously in the Islamic world and Europe.[3] In the late thirteenth century, the English Franciscan monk Roger Bacon described the thunderous phenomenon which gunpowder could produce,[4] but recognising also its destructive potential he encrypted its preparation (Fig 1.1). Other formulae appeared in Europe at this date: by the German Dominican, Albertus Magnus, and at the end of the century in the *Liber ignium ad comburendos hostes* ('Book of fires for the burning of enemies'),

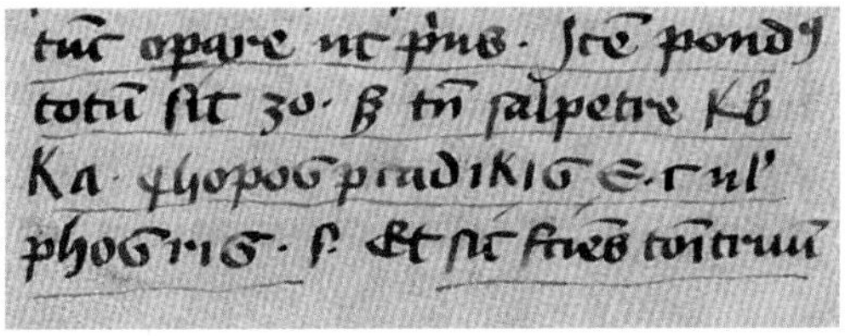

Figure 1.1 Copy of Roger Bacon's encrypted description of gunpowder recipe c 1249. (By permission of The British Library, Sloan MSS 2156).

1

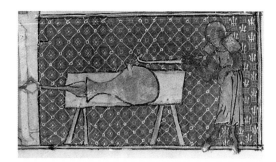

Figure 1.2 The earliest illustration of a gun, from De officiis regum *by Walter de Milimete, 1326. (Christ Church Oxford, MS 92, fol 70v).*

a collection of pyrotechnical recipes put together under the perhaps fictitious name 'Marcus Graecus'.[5]

Black powder's use as a propellant force, as opposed to a bursting charge in a grenade or bomb or as an incendiary composition, evidently originated at the end of the thirteenth century. Early cannons or bombards are independently dated in China from around the 1280s onwards and are known at almost the same time in the Arab world.[6] In the west, the idea of using black powder as a propellant is generally attributed to another semi-legendary figure, Berthold Schwarz of Freiburg, in the early fourteenth century.[7] The earliest illustration of a gunpowder weapon shows a flask-shaped cannon firing an arrow-like projectile (Fig 1.2). Imprecision in the dating evidence makes it impossible to tell whether the idea moved from east to west or vice versa, or if it was simultaneous invention. In any case, it created a regular demand for gunpowder and the beginnings of the industry.[8]

Ingredients

Gunpowder is an intimate mixture of charcoal, sulphur, and saltpetre. The actual proportions varied through time and between countries. In Britain by the late eighteenth century military powder was manufactured in the proportions of 15% charcoal, 10% sulphur, and 75% saltpetre.[9]

Production of charcoal was a widespread and important forest industry throughout the Middle Ages. The technique of charcoal burning depicted by Diderot towards the end of the eighteenth century (Fig 1.3) differed little from that used during the Middle Ages. The method was to clear a circle of ground and at its centre to place a vertical pole; this was used as the focus for a stack of cut poles and billets shaped like a wigwam. The stack was covered with turves and earth, and the clamp was fired and left to burn for a number of days. At the end of firing the clamp was dismantled and the charcoal removed.

Charcoal burning is widely documented in both place-names and family names. In some localities the stances for clamps remain as earthworks or are visible as soilmarks in arable fields which were formerly afforested. By far the largest consumer of charcoal during the Middle Ages and early post-medieval period was the metalworking industry. In comparison, the amounts used by the early gunpowder makers were very small. Charcoal's ready availability meant that its supply for gunpowder is little documented. It was unlikely to have played a critical role in the location of early gunpowder manufacture, and certainly the group of early gunpowder makers centred on London had convenient sources in the major charcoal-burning areas of the Sussex/Surrey Weald and Essex. Nevertheless, as early as the sixteenth century, treatises refer to the advantages of employing different types of wood in charcoal for gunpowder, recommending, for example, willow for heavy guns and hazel twigs for hand guns.[10]

The value of sulphur is the low temperature at which it inflames and gives out great heat, which facilitates the ignition and accelerates combustion.[11] The powder-makers were probably largely dependent on foreign sources for this ingredient, though a little may have been available as a by-product of copper mining.[12] The principal sources in Europe lay in Italy and Sicily. Curiously, despite this reliance on foreign merchants few documentary references refer to the supply or transportation of sulphur. This may reflect the fact that quantities were relatively small and were readily available through merchants.[13]

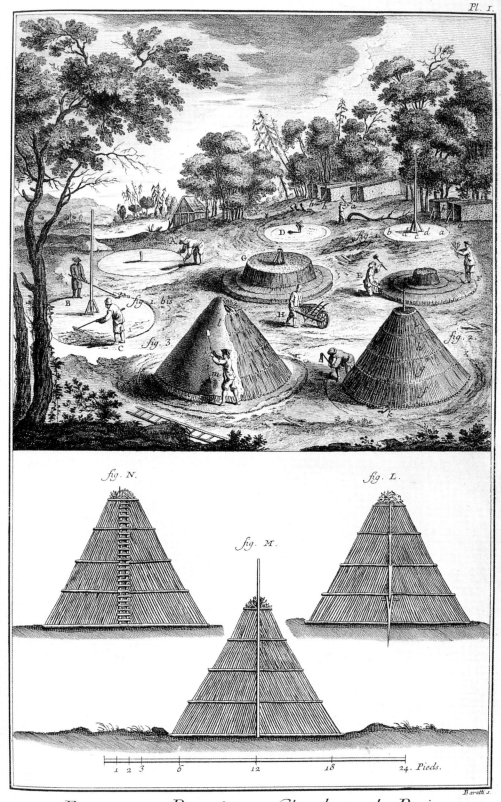

Pl. 1.

56   *Economie Rustique, Charbon de Bois.*

Barath s.

Figure 1.3 Charcoal burning, from Diderot Encyclopedie, ou dictionnaire raisonne des sciences, des arts et des metiers, *1771.*

3

Figure 1.4 (left) Ipswich, drawing of a saltpetre works in 1593. (© Suffolk County Record Office Deed C9/13/4.31).

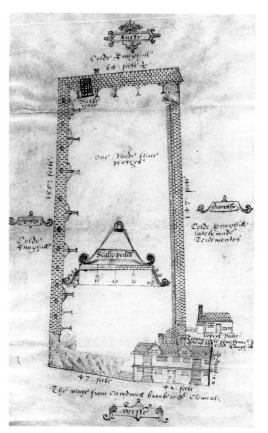

Figure 1.5 (right) Saltpetre House at Ashurst, Hampshire. The earthworks occupy a rectangular area, 140 × 70m, on ground gently sloping from north to south: their limits are unclear owing to later woodland banks. The area is divided into a series of irregular rectangular zones by banks varying in height between 0.4m to 2.2m and in width from 3m to 10m: in the north-west corner of the enclosure a level platform (A), measuring 38 × 11m, may mark the position of a number of structures. (© Crown copyright. NMR).

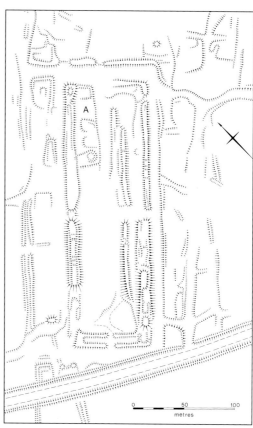

Saltpetre, a fine crystalline substance, is by volume the largest ingredient of gunpowder. Its function is to provide oxygen for the rapid combustion of the two fuels, charcoal and sulphur.[14] Some domestic production of saltpetre had begun by the late fifteenth century but the small English gunpowder industry remained heavily dependent on imported supplies.[15] The Low Countries and Antwerp were the most important supply centres. As a great trading city, Antwerp was an entrepot for goods arriving from all over Europe, and it is likely that the origin of much north European saltpetre was the Baltic states through the Hanseatic ports.[16]

Continental writers of treatises knew of naturally occurring deposits of saltpetre;[17] none are found in Britain. Attempts were made in the 1580s to extract saltpetre from the cliffs at Fulstone in Yorkshire, but appear to have come to nothing.[18]

Two alternative sources were available for indigenous raw materials – collection of nitre-rich earth and manufacture in compost-like heaps. Both entailed processes of refinement and purification. Together, in circumstances where political necessity demanded a reliable supply which was vital for national security, they gave rise to a distinctive saltpetre industry that is almost archaeologically invisible and remains largely unexplored historically. Its growth appears to have been stimulated by knowledge acquired from continental experts. This may have occurred as early as 1545 when Stephanus de Haschenpergk petitioned Henry VIII that he had invented 'a way of making saltpetre, otherwise called black vitriol, in one place without going about the realm searching for it'.[19] Little probably came of this bargain for in 1561 the German Gerrard Honrick was paid £300 by Elizabeth I for a 'statement of the true and perfect art of making saltpetre grow'.[20]

The most commonly used source for saltpetre involved the collection of earth around human habitations. The foul places where nitre-bearing earths might be found included the bottom of dovecotes, byres, cesspits, old burial grounds, fallen plaster in derelict buildings, and all places where decaying organic matter had been mixed with earth. As with gunpowder makers, the activities of the saltpetremen were in principle regulated by the Crown through patents. The patentees in turn appointed saltpetremen to dig for saltpetre in the counties allotted to them; in some cases the powdermakers might also hold the authority to dig for saltpetre. These rights, which included that of demanding the movement of their goods by any available cart, often brought them into conflict with the local populations. Their arrival in a district might also spark conflict with potash or soap makers, who also required good supplies of fuel and wood ash.

Once a quantity of suitable earth had been collected, it was necessary to extract the saltpetre from it. A common method involved placing the earth in a large tub with a tap hole at its base, alternating with layers of wood ash; the tub was then filled with water, which was allowed to percolate through and was collected in another vessel. This liquor, termed the 'mother liquor', was boiled in either a large cauldron or large rectangular copper pan, similar to that used in salt production; this was next placed in a tub to allow any earthy impurities to settle and the liquor was then reboiled. It was then poured into a long open wooden vessel to crystallise and any remaining liquor was recycled. The remaining earth from the tubs was saved to be recycled also.

The recycling formed part of the manufacturing process of 'making saltpetre grow'. In some accounts it was advised that earth heaps should be formed under cover (see Fig 1.4). Horse dung and other excrement might be added; the heap was watered with waste liquor, and the urine of men, and horns, claws, and hooves could also be added. Estimates varied between two and seven years for the formation of good nitrous earth, which would imply that a large area was required for heaps in different stages of decay. A petition to the King in 1630 spoke of the need for an open field of 4 acres (1.6ha) 'to multiply and make saltpetre'.[21] Though not as capital-intensive as some industries, saltpetre production clearly did require the construction of boiling furnaces, and of sheds or buildings to cover them, and perhaps also of large sheds to cover beds of artificial saltpetre. These structures amounted essentially to small factories. The equipment of the saltpetremen might comprise spades, tubs, cauldrons, and barrels for moving the finished product.

Honrick's instructions in 1561 for wholly artificial saltpetre imply greater intensity and shorter time-scales. He stated[22] that mounds should be created of black earth, horse dung (especially of those horses fed with oats – rich in potassium), lime made of plaster of Paris (the best of which was made from oyster shells), and all this to be mixed with urine (especially from those who drink wine or strong beers – rich in ammonia). Over a number of months this heap was turned until a satisfactory amount of salt had formed; it was then refined in the same way as if it had been extracted from nitrous earths. Lazarus Ercker's mining treatise, first published in Prague in 1574, shows a contemporary saltpetre works.[23] A central workshop, comprising a leaching house and adjacent building where the solution was boiled down, is surrounded by a group of long, free-standing heaps of decaying vegetation, from which the nitrous deposits were scraped.[24] Recent research has argued that medieval saltpetre was composed of a mixture of calcium, sodium, and potassium nitrates, the calcium nitrate giving rise to a very hygroscopic gunpowder.[25] It was probably not until the sixteenth century that refining processes evolved sufficiently to produce pure potassium nitrate for black powder.

Exceptionally for this period, archaeological earthworks at Ashurst in the New Forest may give some indication of the form of one of these establishments (Fig 1.5). The site was identified as 'Saltpetre Bank' on an eighteenth-century map and may probably be equated with an early seventeenth-century account describing 'certain place for making saltpetre called Saltpetre House'.[26] The remains correlate poorly with the details of manuscript illustrations of saltpetre production and demonstrate how difficult on solely archaeological grounds it might be to detect saltpetre works.[27]

This rural site was situated conveniently close to the coast to acquire oyster shells for liming the heaps and also perhaps for importing coal, which was often preferred to wood for boiling.[28] Wood ash for the refining process was also readily available. Urban locations are, nevertheless, more commonly documented from the late sixteenth century. The privilege of making saltpetre in London was granted as early as the 1580s,[29] and works are recorded in Ipswich in the 1590s (Fig 1.4). Saltpetre works are known from documentary sources to have formed part of the townscapes at Gloucester, Oxford, and Reading in the 1620s, and later at Thornbury north of Bristol, in Bath, Salisbury, Sherborne, Stamford, and on the Isle of Wight.[30] Documentary evidence indicates that these works probably handled part-refined saltpetre liquor brought in barrels from the surrounding rural area.[31] The towns would also form an abundant source of decaying organic matter to make saltpetre grow. If this was part of the works' activity, their sites might be expected to be located on the urban periphery, along with other noxious trades, where sufficient land was available to lay out the heaps of decaying material without presenting a nuisance. Detailed documentary or topographic research into the structure of post-medieval towns may be able to locate some of these works, but their size and form might vary depending on what combination of refining natural saltpetre, gathering nitrous earth, and growing artificial saltpetre they employed.

From the saltpetre works around the counties, the saltpetremen were required to deliver their product to the king's storehouse at Southwark. Later, the Surrey powdermakers also had a store at Kingston-upon-Thames, and later again, in the seventeenth century, important saltpetre storehouses were located at the Tower, the Minories, and Woolwich.[32]

Notwithstanding this evidence of a widespread and expanding industry (much of it provided by the increasing level of complaints it generated), it was never large and it produced insufficient saltpetre for the needs of the royal powdermakers.[33] Imported saltpetre remained vital and from the 1620s was increasingly provided by the East India Company from India (Fig 1.6); this source was supplemented by supplies from European merchants and the Barbary coast.[34] Though as late as 1666 a contract was made with 11 contractors to make saltpetre and an imprest of £200 issued to each to erect workhouses and furnaces, and for the purchase of boiling coppers, they were unable to compete with the East India Company in terms of price. In 1670 the contractors were allowed to keep their imprest though the contract lapsed, effectively bringing to an end the manufacture of saltpetre in England.[35]

The beginnings of manufacture in England

Knowledge of gunpowder resided in England from the mid-thirteenth century, and its impact is indirectly witnessed by the increasing sophistication of gun ports, artillery fortifications, and cannon throughout the later Middle Ages.[36] Its manufacture, however, remains archaeologically invisible until far later. One of the difficulties is that it was a small industry operating on few sites and supplying essentially one customer, the Crown. Though a specialised and hazardous task, it required no particularly distinctive apparatus beyond a hand pestle and mortar nor was it conducted in specialised buildings. Much early gunpowder may also have been prepared on the field of battle. This removed the risks involved in its carriage, and ensured that the ingredients were well mixed before use. For, with simple hand incorporation of the ingredients, there was a tendency for them to separate if agitated during transport.

The calendared surviving documentation reflects increasing royal interest throughout the fourteenth century in

Figure 1.6 Free Trade Wharf, The Highway, Tower Hamlets. The East India Company's saltpetre store 1797. (BB95/16611)

obtaining powder and saltpetre supplies. Knowledge of the manufacturing process appears to have lain in the hands of the artillerists. Contemporary treatises on the art of gunnery show that a gunner was more than a man who fired the gun.[37] In the sixteenth century he was supposed to possess the knowledge to make and refine saltpetre, refine sulphur, produce charcoal, and to be able to restore unserviceable powders.[38] The earliest manuscript illustrations date from the fourteenth century and show rudimentary techniques of manufacture focusing on mixing with a hand pestle and mortar.[39] The mid-fifteenth-century German *Firework Book*[40] describes and illustrates the whole range of an artillerist's expected knowledge: the greater part is devoted to types of ordnance and their carriages and deployment, but it includes manufacture of powder, filling of grenades, and fire arrows.[41] Ingredients are shown being prepared by hand, by weighing then pre-mixing in a trough (Fig 1.7). Incorporation is in a row of fixed mortars, within a frame using pestles attached to sprung or counter-balanced poles – a hand (ie, hand-powered) stamp mill (Fig 1.8). A liquor was evidently added, which may imply some provision for

a drying process, however rudimentary. All operations were supervised by an artillerist or knightly overseer and operatives apparently wore a distinctive skull-cap similar to a military arming cap (see Figs 1.7 and 1.8). Even with this larger scale of manufacture, few archaeological traces would be left in the fabric of a building. Such rows of mortars are depicted elsewhere as a large free-standing block,[42] and the holes left by the overhead beam (as illustrated in the *Firework Book*, see Figs 1.7 and 1.8) could not be regarded as diagnostic of a hand stamp mill.

Royal accounts in the calendars of state papers suggest that powder manufacture remained in the hands of the artillerists in royal strongholds until the early part of the sixteenth century. As early as 1346 powder was being manufactured at the Tower of London and by 1461 there was a 'powder-house'.[43] In 1515 Hans Wolf was appointed as one of the king's gunpowder makers there.[44] The Tower remained one of the most important gunpowder stores in the kingdom until the seventeenth century. The peril of this activity in the centre of London was clearly demonstrated in 1548 when one of the towers was wrecked by an accidental explosion.[45]

Figure 1.7 Mid fifteenth-century German manuscript, the Firework Book, preserved in the Tower of London. This illustration perhaps depicts the initial weighing and hand mixing of the ingredients, in a box which was later known as a Mingling Trough. Alternatively it may show the incorporation of gunpowder by hand, which is known to have persisted in eastern Europe until the seventeenth century. (© Royal Armouries, A8/419).

Figure 1.8 Mid fifteenth-century German manuscript, the Firework Book, preserved in the Tower of London. This illustration depicts a hand stamp mill. Note the use of a spring beam attached to the pestle and the handles to draw the pestle down; also the hour glass to time the operation and the bucket perhaps containing water to dampen the powder during stamping. (© Royal Armouries, A8/420).

Elsewhere in the country there are frequent references to gunpowder stores in royal castles, though few allusions to its manufacture. Payment was made in 1512 for the manufacture of powder at the royal stores at Portchester Castle in Hampshire.[46] References to the supply of saltpetre along with gunpowder may also suggest local manufacture was a fairly regular occurrence. In 1541 it was reported that 'workmen at Edinburgh Castle have long been making guns and other ordnance and they have a mill there that has made six barrels of gunpowder within three weeks since Easter'.[47]

Even by the reign of Henry VIII the industry was poorly developed. His invasion of France and the capture of Boulogne in 1544 were dogged by shortage of gunpowder. Though he ordered that 'all gunpowder makers are to be set to work to make a great proportion',[48] a great deal of powder needed to be imported. The most important source was the Low Countries, mainly through the port of Antwerp, where the orders were handled by the king's agent William Damsell.[49]

Throughout the sixteenth century such documentary evidence reflects the close interest the state took in this industry because of its crucial role in the defence of the realm. State papers, though essentially concerned with the control and administration of the industry, nevertheless, begin to help us locate some of the earliest manufacturing sites and give some insight into the current state of gunpowder manufacturing technology.

Gunpowder in the later sixteenth and early seventeenth centuries
An incipient industry

To Renaissance writers gunpowder formed one of the triad of inventions, along with printing and the compass, which distinguished the modern world from the medieval.[50] Although its manufacture had been practised in the Middle Ages, in England it was one of the 'new industries' which grew in importance and became more technologically complex during the reign of Elizabeth I.[51] Though scarcely consumer goods on a par with stockings, soap or oilseed, gunpowder, saltpetre, and sulphur shared the same economic climate of projects and projectors, of patents and commissioners, and of skilled foreign refugees, that aimed in part to lessen a traditional costly reliance on imports.[52] Powder manufacture evidently transferred from the artillerists to a small group of entrepreneurs, whose operations were characterised by the use of water mills. This growth coincided with increased production of cannon, including the earliest manufacture of cast iron cannon in the Weald, and with Elizabeth's recruiting of German miners to exploit copper sources for ordnance. Two monopoly companies were formed as a direct result.[53] A further factor stimulating growth of the home gunpowder industry was the strained diplomatic relations with many countries in Europe throughout Elizabeth's reign. Spanish control over the Low Countries interfered with the source on which England had traditionally relied for supplies of powder and saltpetre. Periods of actual warfare, such as the war with Spain after 1586, generated massive government demand for the munitions of war, including guns and gunpowder, and government closely controlled both industries.[54] The wider economic background against which to set the development of the gunpowder industry (and of the chemical industry producing saltpetre) in the sixteenth and seventeenth centuries can be found in, for example, Thirsk[55] and Clay.[56]

By 1554 Henry Reve had erected a gunpowder mill at The Crenge at Rotherhithe; since the complaint was that sluices and floodgates had weakened the bank, the mill may by then have been in operation for some time.[57] From the 1560s the supply of gunpowder became more formalised as a small group of contractors undertook to supply all the powder needs of the kingdom. In 1561, Brian Hogge, Robert Thomas, and Francis Lee stated that they had erected at great expense five new powder mills. Their locations are uncertain, but Francis Lee is known to have been associated with Rotherhithe and may have taken over Reve's mill and around the same date a gunpowder mill was operating at Ratcliff on

the opposite bank of the river Thames.[58] An early predominance of mills lying south and south-west of London in Surrey was also established at this period, when in 1589 George Evelyn, his son John, and Richard Hills were granted letters patent to dig saltpetre and supply the queen with powder. Such grants do not necessarily date the origins of the mills that these men established. For example, Evelyn had associations with an estate at Tolworth, where he had mills from the 1560s, many years prior to the patent. During the late sixteenth century the Evelyn family established other gunpowder mills at Godstone and Wotton in Surrey, while their co-patentee Richard Hill probably operated powder mills at Abinger. It is likely that the mills at Rotherhithe also continued in operation, for a powdermaker was recorded there in 1600. All the new mills were located in stream or river valleys and may be presumed to have used water as

Figure 1.9 The gunpowder industry prior to 1640.

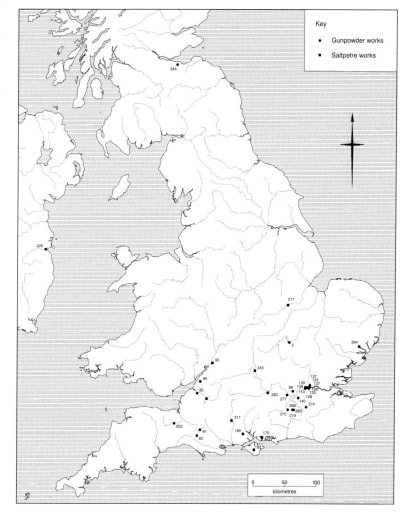

their primary source of power, thereby tapping into a long-established technological context with a tradition of diverse applications.[59]

The extent of manufacture was clearly wider than the patentees alone would suggest (Fig 1.9). In south-east England, manufacture was recorded at three different mill sites in the Stratford area in Essex (now Greater London) in the late sixteenth and early seventeenth century; whether they were regarded as illegal operations or tolerated to make up the shortfall in supply for other customers besides the Crown remains uncertain. Powder mills established in the early seventeenth century at Bedfont, in Middlesex, by 1630 had been converted to sword mills.[60] Gunpowder 'houses' in the city at Fleet Lane and Fetter Lane may have been store houses rather than places where gunpowder was made.[61]

Such documentary evidence also hints at a wider distribution of gunpowder manufacture, without allowing the sites of any of the specific works yet to be identified (Fig 1.9). In 1580 the Dublin Corporation paid Robert Poynter, a master gunner, to dig saltpetre and make gunpowder.[62] In the 1620s and 1630s references are found to gunpowder makers in Bedford and in Devon, and at Taunton in Somerset.[63] In 1625 the king's prohibition of anyone from making 'gunpowder or any saltpetre for service against any enemy or for sale but by his majesty's warrant' brought further examples of illegal manufacture to light. In 1627 three or four horse mills were reported in Bristol, and water mills at Battle in Sussex and in Dorset, and later a horse mill at Bankside in Southwark and a mill at Hocknell near Chester.[64] Attempts at suppression appear to have been half-hearted, for during the 1630s two powdermakers were reported operating in Bristol and by the end of the decade a powdermaker in Bristol called Parker had formally obtained a licence to manufacture powder.[65] When the activities in Dorset were investigated, Walter Parker of Stockwood claimed he had been making powder since 1588 in ignorance of the king's command.[66] Further attempts to control the trade after 1636, when Samuel Cordwell and George Collins of the Chilworth mills in Surrey became the only authorised gunpowder makers in the kingdom, may have resulted in the loss of a number of mills.[67]

Throughout this period the mills operated by the Evelyn family remained dominant. This dominance survived the reorganisation of powder supply in the 1620s and the appointment of Commissioners for Saltpetre and Gunpowder, for John Evelyn received the contract to supply the Crown with powder.[68] But during the 1620s an important rival emerged, as the East India Company tried to establish its own mills, presumably to exploit its role as importer of saltpetre. By 1625 the company had converted a former corn mill at Thorpe in Windsor Forest, but was forced to stop work as it was causing annoyance to the deer; the company was subsequently allowed to erect mills at Chilworth.[69] Between 1635 and 1641, and again after 1664, the Crown agreed with the East India Company to buy all the saltpetre it imported, thereby preserving its control of the powdermakers.[70]

The primary factors controlling the location of the industry throughout this period were the royal patent and the Crown's resulting control over the industry, along with the exclusive use of powder for military purposes. This resulted in a marked concentration of the legal powder trade in the London area. The tributaries of the Thames estuary also provided the powdermakers with the necessary motive power, and gave them a safe and convenient method of transport to and from the government stores and to the proof yards at the Tower and Greenwich (Fig 1.10). It was also an industry dependent on imported raw materials which could be supplied through the London merchants. In choosing a site for a powder works the makers often selected a pre-existing mill site, thereby avoiding or reducing the cost of large-scale water engineering. Both their locations and the documents indicate that most of the mills were water-powered; only the illegal mills at Bristol and Southwark are known to have been horse-powered. The geographical spread of other documented mills, however, shows that the supply of raw materials was not a constraint on the location of the industry. If economic factors had

been the sole consideration, an expanding shipping centre such as Bristol might have been expected to provide an ideal location for an unrestricted powder industry.

Early mills and technology of manufacture

Documentary sources give a picture of no more than a handful of gunpowder works operating in England at any one time during this period. They name places but rarely if ever furnish precise locations. If water power was employed it is as likely that an existing mill was converted or at least an existing mill site reused, which may point to specific locations though not necessarily distinctive sites, since early powder works were often short-lived and their sites reverted to other milling processes. Indeed, some examples suggest the presence of more than one contemporary production process in the same building or complex, either of which might take precedence at any given time. These alternatives would most likely be other forms of military equipment (see Fig 1.11), and might create an arrangement particularly responsive to

the notoriously uneven demand for gunpowder. Other forms of power – human muscle and horse – could have reused unspecialised buildings and left hardly any distinctive physical traces. Throughout this period there may be a terminological distinction to be drawn between gunpowder *making* sites, employing entirely muscle power and relatively simple equipment in buildings and locations that were not distinctive, and gunpowder *milling* sites. But such a distinction remains elusive on the basis of the surviving evidence and may be illusive in fact (eg Fig 1.12).

The oldest form of power available to the powdermakers was human muscle, which had been used from the Middle Ages to pound mortars with pestles, turn hand cranks, use sprung poles, or walk in treadmills, as depicted in later continental manuscripts. Where any form of rotative power was required animals could also be employed, and horse mills are recorded in documentary sources and worked alongside water power in the production of gunpowder until the nineteenth century. Early depictions show an arrangement of drive

Figure 1.10 Greenwich powder magazine, nd, perhaps 1733. In the foreground, the building with the tall conical roof may be a proof house or stove. (BB96/7925; © Greenwich Local History Library, Martin Collection 1182).

11

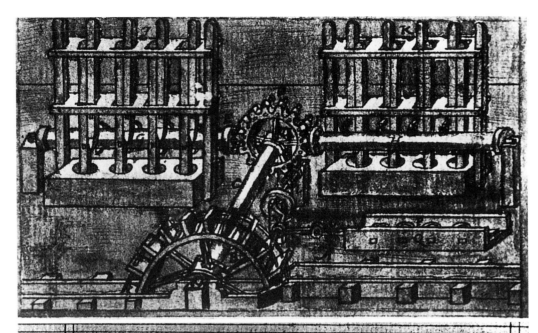

*Figure 1.11
Sixteenth-century
English water
powered stamp mill,
from Hodgetts 1909
fig 5 taken perhaps
from a more general
treatise on millwork.
'This mill is also for
making of powder,
and goeth double,
and serueth where
commoditie of water
is to be had. The
water running
thorow the case A
falleth on the wheele
B turning the said
wheele B the axle
tree C and the
wheele D The Wheele
D turneth the
lanternes E and F
and also the axle
trees G and H whose
cogges moveth the
stampers J and K
which stampers beat
the powder. The
whole D in his
motion moveth the
lanterne L the whole
M which assisteth
the facility of the
motion, it moveth
consequently the
wrest N and the
branches O whereon
the sives P stand in
the case Q by which
meanes the corne is
powdred. The wheele
M serveth to glaze
sworde blades and
knives when the mill
standeth idle.'
(BB97/3429 and
BB97/3430).*

machinery little different from that applied to a variety of industrial tasks (Fig 1.12). Muscle power had the advantage of being flexible in its application but tired easily if required in large quantity, especially in the protracted mixing and milling processes that were found to be most effective in gunpowder production. Archaeologically this phase of development is virtually impossible to detect, as the machinery was timber and as yet relatively unspecialised and probably free-standing within a building. From the middle of the sixteenth century water increasingly became the prime mover in the industry (see below, Gazetteer). It could offer the sort of steady, inexhaustible power that was required, but imposed greater financial penalties, as it employed more complex machinery and presumed control of the water rights to a mill.

At this period, power was applied to two or three processes or stages of powder production – preparing and mixing the ingredients, their incorporation into an intimate mixture, and sieving or corning the resulting substance – but principally to incorporation. For the reasons discussed above, the physical remains of this developing technology remain elusive. Continental treatises supply some insight (eg Fig 1.12); accounts begin to appear in English from the late sixteenth century, though few contain any illustrations.[71] These sources need to be used with care, as many of the treatise writers borrowed freely from earlier works and may not necessarily have been describing current English practice. Two such woodcuts purporting to show late sixteenth-century gunpowder mills in England were published from an unacknowledged source (perhaps a more general treatise on mill work) by Hodgetts[72] (fig 4, p 15 and fig 5, p 17, the latter reproduced here as Fig 1.11). The first depicts a single hand-cranked stamp mill with three mortars for incorporating powder, with the motion of the mill apparently controlled by a regulator. Also powered through a series of drives and cogs was a small shaking frame which contained the parchment sieves used to corn the powder (see below). The second illustration (Fig 1.11) shows a similar stamp mill, but here the water wheel powered a double mill, each mill with four mortars. Here, too, the drawing shows corning of powder taking place in a mechanised shaking frame. Extraordinarily, this drawing depicts a grinding wheel adjacent to the stamp mills 'to glaze sword blades and knives when the mill standeth idle', perhaps indicating not foolhardiness or a lack of knowledge about gunpowder on the part of the author but rather the diversification associated with the early industry.

In the absence of surviving remains, the documentary material described above indicates the typical features of a works during this period. At its core was perhaps a single mill building housing water-driven stamps and a mechanised shaking frame. A single frame was probably sufficient to corn the relatively small output from the stamps. It is uncertain to what extent the ingredients were prepared or refined within the works. Saltpetre for the royal powdermakers came from the royal store, some as double refined while other supplies may have required further refining on site. Sulphur was acquired from merchants and charcoal was perhaps obtained through dealers or was manufactured by the powdermakers themselves. From the available evidence it appears that the ingredients were pulverised and pre-mixed either by hand or beneath stamp mills, though this process may have seen early use of edge runners as shown in continental illustrations (for example, see Fig 1.12). Other specialised buildings are unlikely to have been required, other than perhaps a drying shed and some general store buildings. A powder works at this date probably comprised no more buildings than any other mill needing to store its raw materials and products. The willingness of the Crown by the early seventeenth century to issue an imprest or advance of money of £2000 to the royal powdermakers for equipping the mills may nevertheless indicate that, by contemporaries, they were regarded as unusual and costly enterprises.[73]

This development of relatively complex and capital-intensive works did not preclude gunpowder manufacture by far simpler methods. For in 1639 Robert Davies of Thames Street in London was reported for storing all the ingredients necessary to make powder in his house. Perhaps the information was supplied to the Office of Ordnance by his fearful neighbours, as his previous house in Whitechapel had blown up by accident. In his possession were four mortars of wood and pestles, two brass pans, and one searcher or sieve, 'all things necessary' to make powder, and his guide was 'a book...in English'.[74]

Gunpowder – the product

In studying the origins of the gunpowder industry archaeologically, the lack of any closely identified manufacturing sites is compounded by the absence of the contemporary product. Only in exceptional circumstances have residues of powder been found. Even in, for example, such cases as the sealed breeches of guns recovered from shipwrecks, residues will invariably be affected by submersion and chemical reaction with the metal of the gun. On land, a bucket of early gunpowder was found, extraordinarily, in the roof of Durham Castle;[75] shells filled with powder might produce contemporary samples of powder, but again post-depositional chemical reactions are likely to have affected the composition.[76] What chemical analysis of well-preserved samples might in principle

Figure 1.12 Seventeenth-century continental powder-mills, from Hassenstein 1941, bild 30.

do is to define the percentage of the ingredients used and their purity. Without samples of early powder, it is from documentary material that information has to be sought for the changing nature of powder, and its complex relationship with the development of ordnance during this period.

Similarly, we are dependent on indirect evidence to date the introduction of another crucial process, corning. Loose powder which had been incorporated simply by mixing, with no other working, was commonly termed serpentine powder. It suffered from the disadvantages of producing a lot of dust and was also likely to break down into its constituent parts if roughly handled during transport. If calcium nitrate was present in the saltpetre it was also likely to be highly hygroscopic. A solution described in the mid-fifteenth-century *Firework Book* was to mould the gunpowder into *Knollen* or dumplings, which would be broken into

crumbs before use.[77] Corning was the process, in use by the late fifteenth century, whereby incorporated powder was formed into distinct grains by forcing the moist mixture through holes in a parchment sieve. Corned powders were more durable and were also found to be far stronger than serpentine powders.

By the sixteenth century a sophisticated, if empiric, understanding of the different powders was evident, with different size grains used for different weapons. This is confirmed by contemporary accounts which record delivery of fine corn, coarse corn, and serpentine powders.[78] In material terms this elaboration of the manufacturing process added nothing more to the inventory of the powder-maker beyond a wood and parchment sieve. Its effect is reflected indirectly through developments in cannons throughout the sixteenth century, as these became more robust to withstand the increased strains created by a more powerful charge.

The Civil War 1642–9

In 1642 the distribution of the gunpowder industry was firmly centred on London (see Fig 1.9). Although the royal patent regulating gunpowder manufacture was repealed in August 1641, it took time to loosen the industry's domination by the small coterie of existing manufacturers. The clustering of powder mills around the capital placed them within the territory controlled by the Parliamentary forces. Yet by the mid-seventeenth century powder was an essential munition of war; although pikes and swords remained in service, it was the cannon which became particularly important in determining the outcome of sieges. For either side to prosecute the war successfully, they needed to control munitions manufacture or to have access to imported materials.[79]

Little archaeological evidence is available about gunpowder manufacture during the Civil War or the form of mills employed. The difficulty of supplying besieged cities and towns was even greater than supplying the field armies. In many the solution was to establish local powder mills (Fig 1.13), since from their traditional training the

Figure 1.13 Distribution map of gunpowder works operating during the Civil War.

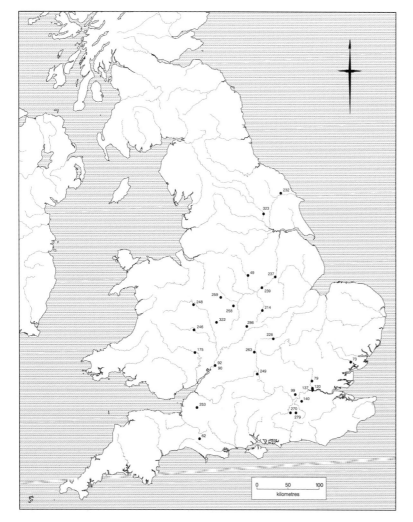

artillerists employed by both sides probably possessed the knowledge to make gunpowder. Saltpetre and charcoal were readily available in most areas: indeed in many of the larger towns saltpetre works may already have existed. Sulphur was the one ingredient which could not be produced locally, and both sides were reliant on importing and moving it around England.

The stamp mills used in powder manufacture were relatively unspecialised, easy to make or move, and were widely used in other industries, while other parts of the process might be improvised in surrounding buildings. Where suitable water mills existed they could readily be converted for powder production, though in some cases there was a competing need to use them for manufacturing ordnance. At Oxford, the king's principal stronghold and ordnance store, a Bristol powdermaker, William Baber, converted a former fulling mill at Oseney and other mills for powder production, while the cloister of New College was used as a powder magazine.[80] At Banbury the royalist garrison was reported to be digging saltpetre and making gunpowder at a house specially built near the town.[81] The royalist garrison at Newark-on-Trent converted the water mills below the castle for powder production.[82] In York the castle mills were set to grinding gunpowder, but did not work for long before they were destroyed by fire and explosion.[83] At Lichfield payments of £87 for a corn mill and gunpowder mill, and a further payment in 1645 for a mill horse, reflect the operation of these small war-time mills. The royalist garrison also paid £18 for a saltpetre furnace and for setting it up. Charcoal and saltpetre could be manufactured locally, coal was brought from Cannock Chase for the saltpetre refinery, and they acquired Sicilian sulphur at £32 a ton.[84]

Parliamentary garrisons adopted similar strategies. When Bristol fell in July 1643, Gloucester became the only Parliamentary garrison in the west of England. The loss of Bristol may also have resulted in the loss of powder mills, for peace-time mills were active in the city as late as 1640, and William Baber later claimed to have furnished the King with large quantities of powder at Bristol.[85] At Gloucester only 40 barrels of powder were available at the beginning of the siege; there were mills in the cathedral precinct and probably one on the quay, and payments were made for the manufacture of powder and saltpetre.[86] In Northampton a powder works was in operation from 1643 to 1646. Barns on the south-east side of the town were adapted as saltpetre refineries and a water-powered powder mill established.[87] At Coventry the besieged troops had three 220lb brass pans for making gunpowder amongst their equipment.[88] These may have been simple hand mortars or the bases of stamp mills, or even boiling pans for saltpetre such as were recorded at Stafford. Powder mills are documented at Colchester, Derby, Hereford, Ludlow, Nottingham Castle, Shrewsbury, Stockwood, Wells, and Worcester, and there is potential for further discoveries at this level; however, little can be gleaned about their form.[89] Smaller and even more transient mills may have left no documentary record. An example was revealed, only through chance archaeological discovery, attached to the southern end of North Allerston Manor House in North Yorkshire (Fig 1.14) and illustrates the archaeological remains which such a gunpowder mill might leave.[90]

This wider spread of gunpowder manufacture was a temporary war-time phenomenon, and had few discernible effects on the longer-term development of the industry. At the close of hostilities the majority of the mills were either demolished or converted to other uses. Some war-time mills were evidently free-standing structures which could be broken down and readily transported at short notice, perhaps with a level of complexity shown in contemporary continental manuscripts (see Fig 1.11). For example, Parliament commanded the committee of Leicester 'to deliver the materials of a demolished powder mill to Sir Arthur Hesilrigge for use in the north'.[91] Gunpowder manufacture on a domestic scale was certainly practised with deadly consequences in one documented instance: in 1643 Edward Morton of Cheshire 'was drying some powder in his house' when he was killed along with four of his children and his house and goods destroyed.[92] In such cases of extreme need powder might be manufactured by

Figure 1.14 Allerston Manor House, North Yorkshire, plan of the excavated remains (after Rimington 1966). This mill was built with cut and cemented stone walls, 3ft (0.91m) thick, and comprised in excavation an L-shaped stone-lined channel, controlled by sluices in the eastern wall. A mill building covering the sluices would give an internal working area of no more than 15ft 6in (4.7m) by 11ft (3.4m). On the floor of the hall three pieces of roll sulphur 4in (100mm) long were found, each weighing 4oz (113.4g). To its north lay a small store-room in which was found a layer of charcoal 4in to 6in (100mm to 150mm) thick and overlain by wall plaster. Pottery associated with the charcoal layer and the mill was dated to the early seventeenth century.

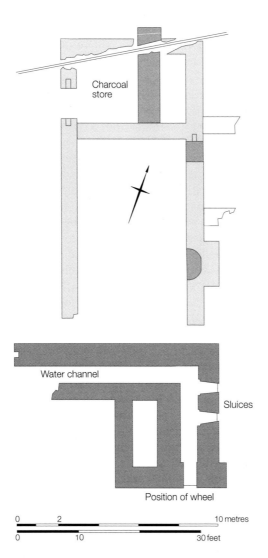

pestle and mortar, a technique reported as late as 1639, and any archaeological trace is even less likely to exist.

The second half of the seventeenth century and the eighteenth century

During the period of the Commonwealth, following the execution of Charles I in 1649, a number of important powder mills are documented for the first time, though their foundation may lie a few years earlier. The reasons for this increase, which became more marked in both number and scale of enterprise through the second half of the seventeenth century, are complex.[93] An obvious factor was war: war with both France and Spain in the later 1620s, repeated conflict with the Dutch (1651–3,

1664–7, 1672–4), and war against France after 1689. But colonial activities in themselves also brought a demand, and gunpowder was an essential trading commodity of the transatlantic slave trade, in which British shipping had a leading role. While government attitudes to the industry are examined by, for example, Tomlinson and West,[94] the commercial, entrepreneurial, and business history of the industry for this period needs substantial further work. Aspects of seventeenth- and eighteenth-century gunpowder technology have been the subject of recent research,[95] and the publication of documentary sources for Surrey, one of the major centres of the industry, will surely prove invaluable.[96]

Of particular importance in the longer-term consolidation of the manufacturing industry was the introduction in England of gunpowder's application in mining. Shot firing in mining was reputedly first employed in a Venetian mine in the late sixteenth century, and the technique spread across continental Europe in the early seventeenth century.[97] Despite this, demand for this purpose appears to have remained at a fairly low level and did not become a significant locational factor for powder mills until the end of the eighteenth century. In England the earliest documented use was before 1685 at the Ecton copper mines in Staffordshire, where the introduction was ascribed to Dutch or German specialists.[98] Despite the notorious difficulty of identifying and dating many mining features, fieldwork carried out there in 1995 has discovered traces of early shot holes.[99]

In the 1650s the growth in the number of powder mills along the river Lea in Essex resulted in one of the densest concentrations in the country. Mills established at Leyton and Sewardstone in the 1640s were two of the few mills established in the Civil War to survive subsequently, and they were joined by mills at Enfield, Hackney, Tottenham, and Walthamstow. By the 1660s Dr Thomas Fuller, curate of Waltham Abbey, commented that 'more [gunpowder] is made by the mills of late erected on the river Lea, betwixt Waltham and London, than in all England besides'.[100] Mills were established at Carshalton (now in Greater London) and East Molesey in Surrey, and powder mills were founded at Faversham in Kent which were to become some of the most important in the country.

After the Restoration of 1660, new mills at Maidstone in Kent and North Feltham in Middlesex swelled the number, and at Bedfont the powder mills were re-established. In Essex, too, further mills were established in the Enfield area, and around 1664 the powder mills at Waltham Abbey were founded. The monopoly of gunpowder maker to the king was temporarily restored, but was abolished in 1664.[101] By the end of that year the Crown's commissioners had contracts with seven powdermakers and this rose to 16 by 1667, accounting for all the known powder mills at this date.[102] Away from the Thames basin an important group of mills was established on the rivers Asten and Brede near Battle in Sussex (see below, Gazetteer). Of the mills at Crawford and Wandsworth operating in the late seventeenth century very little is known.[103]

Contemporary inventories and descriptions of the processes are still the prime sources for information about the physical form and component parts of a typical powder works of this date. Though many of the mill sites continued in use, they are known only from later mapping after substantial alterations; or, if powder production ceased, most were reused for alternative milling processes, thereby erasing the evidence. One of the most important accounts of English gunpowder production in this period was a paper read to the Royal Society by Thomas Henshaw in 1662 and published in Thomas Sprat's *History of the Royal Society* (1667). It described current English practice, whereas contemporary artillery treatises were still heavily dependent on earlier continental sources. Henshaw portrays a typical late seventeenth-century works in terms of a scatter of small, probably timber, buildings each dedicated to one process. Sulphur and charcoal were bought ready-processed from middlemen, obviating the need for a sulphur refinery or charcoal burning within the works. He does suggest that the saltpetre should be boiled, though more to soften it than as a further refining process. The initial pulverisation of sulphur and charcoal took place under what we would term an edge runner in a horse mill (cf Fig 1.12). After

sieving in a bolting mill or through coarse cloth, sulphur and charcoal were mixed with saltpetre in a mingling trough by men with shovels. Henshaw states that the powder (ie incorporating) mills 'are seldom made to move with anything but water power' and goes on to describe stamp mills of a form where each mill had two troughs and 16 pestles, while his contemporary, Nathaniel Nye, also mentions the use of horse mills.[104] From the mills the powder was removed for corning; whereas earlier illustrations (see Fig 1.12) showed this took place adjacent to the stamp mills, the process was now carried out in a separate building, though the sieves might have been shaken by hand or mechanised. Powder was next taken to a drying stove, which from Sprat's description was of a form later termed a gloom stove, perhaps in use since the 1640s.[105] After drying it was sieved to separate large grains for cannon powders and smaller grains for pistols, and to remove any dust. Sprat's account corresponds remarkably with an inventory of the buildings and contents of the Carshalton mills in Surrey (now Greater London) made in 1661, which identified a boiling house with a horse mill, three trough mills, corning house, stove house, stables, watch house, kitchen hall with a chamber over, and a house.[106]

Few contemporary travellers and writers in search of the novel and ingenious inventions of their age appear to have considered powder mills worthy of recommendation to their readership. One exception was John Aubrey, who visited the Chilworth powder works in Surrey in 1673. Here he found 16 water mills which powered 18 powder mills, though five had recently blown up. He described the remainder of the works as comprising 'a nursery of earth for the making of saltpetre: there is also a boiling house, where the saltpetre is made and shoots [ie crystallises], a corning house and separating and finishing houses and very well worth the seeing of the ingenious'.[108] County maps of the period, even if they locate the sites of powder mills, rarely show sufficient detail to make the scale or plan form of a works intelligible. One of the best early depictions of a powder works nevertheless actually shows the Chilworth works around 1690 to some effect (Fig 1.15).

Processes

Contemporary descriptions indicate that a late seventeenth-century works might be a fairly sizeable establishment, perhaps comprising up to seven distinct process buildings along with unspecified ancillary buildings. Combined with inventories, they show that by the turn of the century all the principal components of a powder works were in place. These included refineries for the raw materials, the use of edge-runner incorporating mills, corning houses with presses, glazing houses, drying stoves, and some form of finishing house for final sieving and packing (see Table 1.1). For example, the recent discovery by Keith Fairclough and Glenys Crocker of deeds dated 1708 and 1713 relating to the Sewardstone mills has identified 'In the new mill. One large bedstone, two large runners...In the corning house. One large wooden press...'.[107]

What is also clear from contemporary sources is that at this stage of the industry's development considerable diversity in the production machinery and variation in the production techniques are to be expected. The recent identification of pressing at such an early date through documentary sources also illustrates the difficulty in detecting technical change by studying the plan form or cartographic sources when a process was not allocated its own building in a works. For pressing was carried out in the corning house, a characteristic which appears to have persisted throughout the eighteenth century (see Fig 2.5). Pressing was carried out after incorporation and before the powder was corned, and it endowed the powder with many qualities, the most important of which was to increase its specific density. It also helped to compact the grains further, which made the constituents less likely to separate if roughly handled during transport. Additionally, pressing made the powder less hygroscopic and less likely to produce dust during corning; it also ensured that a greater volume of inflammable gases was produced from a given weight of powder.

Fourteen mills are indicated schematically, all either situated at the head of ponds or on leats along the Tillingbourne river. For all the map's necessarily simplified form, their division into three groups, named as the Upper, Middle, and Lower Works, is clear. The topographical relationships to Chilworth Manor and Weston Place in Albury together with the distinctive depiction of the water features encourage identification of the Upper Works with Postford Brook Great Pond, the Middle Works with Chilworth mill pond, and the Lower Works with the mill sites based on a header leat below that mill dam.

A detailed estate map of 1728 of Chilworth allows changes to be traced that appear in many ways characteristic of the industry (Fig 1.16). By that date the mills of both the Lower and Middle Works had switched from gunpowder to paper manufacture in the hands of one group of lessees. Alongside them to the south, within a large rectangular plot bounded on the south and east by roads, still stood a saltpetre earth-house and saltpetre boiling shop – perhaps those seen by Aubrey – together with a 'workhouse', cooper's shop, stove 'where they dry powder', and substantial dwelling house with a compartmentalised ornamental garden. The stove was sited within a circular tree-covered earthen embankment, perhaps the earliest traverse yet identified in

Figure 1.15 The Chilworth gunpowder works around 1690 (after John Sellers).

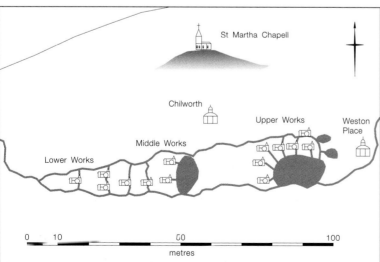

Table 1.1 Summary of the development of gunpowder technology in the most advanced works by the late seventeenth century

PREPARATION OF INGREDIENTS
Stack or 'pit' burnt charcoal, imported part refined sulphur and saltpetre, further refined by middlemen or within the works

INITIAL CRUSHING
Edgerunner mills – probably animal powered
Charcoal and sulphur pulverised before incorporation

MIXING
Bolting mill and mingling trough
The ground and refined ingredients are first sieved, perhaps using a bolting mill, and then loosely combined in the correct proportions in a mingling trough

INCORPORATION
Stamp or edge-runner mills – usually water powered
Intimate mixing and grinding of the ingredients

PRESSING
Hand operated presses
Powder is pressed to compact the grains together further and to increase its specific gravity

CORNING
Shaking Frames – water powered
Process whereby the pressed powder is reduced to corns or granules of approximately even size

GLAZING
Tumbling barrels – water powered
In this process the corned powder is tumbled in a barrel to remove any sharp edges and to impart a glaze to the grains by friction

DRYING
Gloom stove
The powder is laid out on trays and dried by heat radiated from a cast-iron fireback or gloom

FINISHING
The powder may be sieved according to size and packed for dispatch

England. It may have been a recent innovation, for a 'Stove Plot' without extant building lay immediately on the northern side of the mills and 'Old Stove Coppice' a few hundred metres upstream.

While some preparation and process buildings therefore remained unchanged, the principal innovation at Chilworth by 1728 was what amounted to a purpose-built works lying just upstream of the old mill pond and based on a valley-side header leat known as the 'New River Cut'. Four incorporating mills (with provision for adding a fifth), a 'coal and brimstone' (ie charcoal and sulphur) mill, and a corning house, all driven by water-wheels off the leat, were spaced out below it over a distance of some 438yd (400m) and evidently separated by blocks of woodland (Fig 1.16). The complex also included a charcoal house (presumably a store building) and watch house. With the buildings of the old Lower and Middle Works not transferred to paper manufacture, these works were in the hands, as lessee, of Francis Grubert alias Grueber, a member of a Huguenot family

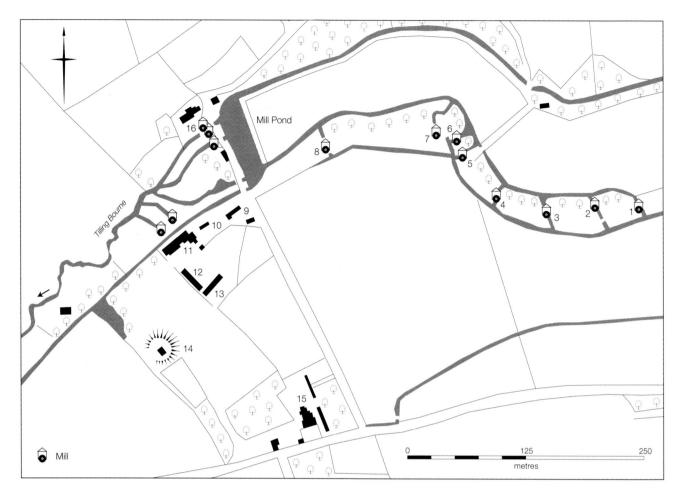

Mill Pond

Tilling Bourne

Mill

0   125   250
metres

Figure 1.16 The Chilworth gunpowder works in 1728 (redrawn from British Library, Althorp Papers P4).

with interests in powdermaking at Faversham as well.[109]

Little is yet known about the composition of the workforce or the working practices in the gunpowder mills during this period. It might be imagined that a large works such as Chilworth would employ many hands, but the numbers involved would partly be regulated by the level of demand and by working practices in the factory. If, for example, gunpowder was manufactured a batch at a time with the men passing from building to building and process to process, the workforce might be comparatively small, whereas if all the mills were working each might require a number of workers. It is difficult, too, to assess the housing associated with a powder works of this date. Most were owned or more typically leased by partnerships or by individuals with an interest in a number of mills. Under such arrangements few of the owners lived adjacent to their mills, unless, like the Evelyn family at Godstone and Wotton,

they owned a house at a place where they also established a powder mill. In some arrangements one partner might act as the work's manager, as at Carshalton in the 1650s, though no house has been identified.[110] At Chilworth the mills were leased – first from the Randyll family who lived in the nearby Chilworth Manor and then from the Duchess of Marlborough's estate. The only directly associated residential property was the 'Dwelling home with garden and orchard', later 'Powder Mill House', whose scale and style was suitable for a works manager. There was no distinctive housing for the workforce at the works.

Through the eighteenth century, production at Chilworth concentrated on the new facilities. The former mills at Postford Brook Great Pool that had made up the Upper Works were completely removed by 1787 or perhaps much earlier. An estate map of that date shows the overall stability of the new complex, but (without ascribing functions to buildings) hints at detailed changes.[111] The fifth mill projected earlier in the century was in place; of more general significance, small detached structures, square or rectangular in plan, depicted adjacent to the stove and to at least two of the mills were probably expense magazines, reflecting the provisions of the 1772 Act (which restricted the amount of powder that could be kept in a process building: see below, this chapter, The 1772 Act).

This story was repeated elsewhere. The distribution of powder mills in the early eighteenth century remained essentially static. Where new mills were established, as at Balham in Surrey and the Oare Works at Faversham in Kent, they were in areas long associated with gunpowder manufacture. The most notable losses were the mills along the river Lea. Many disappeared from the record in the late seventeenth century, often modified for other uses, like the mills at Tottenham and Walthamstow which were converted to paper mills. Those at Sewardstone survived until the early eighteenth century, when they too were probably converted to another use. This left the mills

at Waltham Abbey as the only operating powder works on the river Lea. Outside the traditional powder-producing areas, mills were established at Water of Leith in Scotland and at Woolley in north-east Somerset. The Woolley mills were the first of a small regional group and represented a break from the dominance of the mills of south-eastern England. Despite the use of many technologically innovative features, the fortunes of this group of mills were linked, not to the military, but to the merchants of Bristol and to a local mining industry.[112]

Waltham Abbey

Of the mills established during this period, those at Waltham Abbey provide a good example of the development of a successful powder works. Characteristically they were established at a pre-existing mill site. They occupied the head of a man-made leat nearly 2km (1/ miles) long, already shown on a map of 1590.[113] Then it served a fulling mill, which, with the leat, was probably monastic

Figure 1.17 The Waltham Abbey powder mills in 1735, from Farmer 1735: 1 a horse mill; 2 the corning and glazing engine; 3, 4, 5 horse mills; 6 the stables; 7 the coal mill and composition house; 8 the carpenters and millwrights work house; 9 the clerks counting house and the watch house; 10 the loading house; 11, 12 stamping mills; 13, 14 two dumb mills; 15 the charging house; 16 the old composition house; 17 the store house; 18 the dusting house; 19 the little stove; 20 three sun stoves or drying leads; 21 the great stove. (BB94/8020)

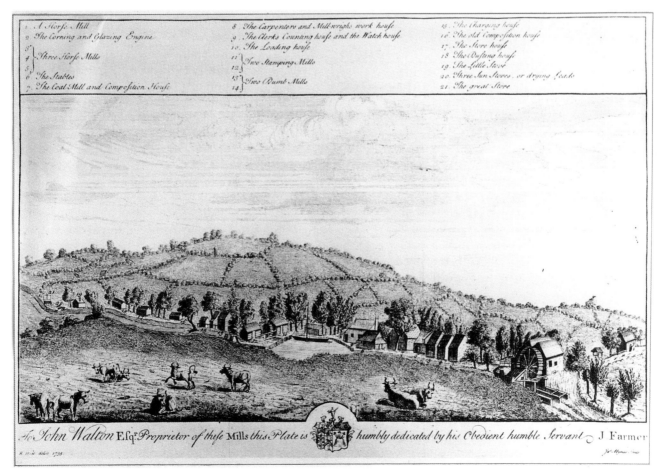

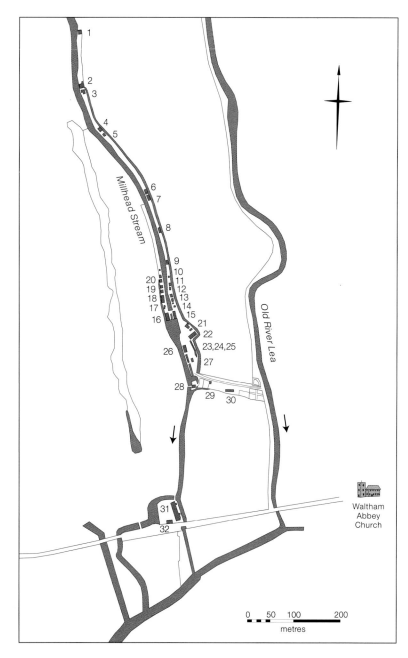

Figure 1.18 Extract from 1783 plan of Waltham Abbey (after PRO/MR 593).

their valley-bottom location, but more importantly by the necessity of providing a number of mills dedicated to specific processes with independent power sources, at a safe distance from their neighbours. A clear manufacturing flow-line from south to north had been established. At the southern end the ingredients were probably prepared in the horse mills (Fig 1.17 [3–5]) before the powder passed northwards through a succession of buildings to the drying stoves [19–21] at the northern extremity. In this arrangement the corning and glazing engines [2] lay out of sequence, perhaps through pragmatic adaptation of an earlier structure. It is also evident from this engraving that to establish such a works required considerable capital investment, even when the water courses were already in place.

By 1783[115] the plan form of the Waltham mills had altered little (Fig 1.18) except for considerable infill within the Millhead area. Also, additional centrally powered mills built along the western side of Millhead indicate a significant technological development (see below, Mill types). The manufacturing flow-line appears to have been rationalised, too, with the construction of a hand-powered corning house and tumbling room (which may equate to a glazing house) north of the incorporating mills. Designation of the mill which formerly carried out these functions as 'Old Engine house' may suggest its disuse. The map shows a long rectangular building at the southern end of the site, which was later described as a saltpetre refinery. There is also a proliferation of small buildings described as 'Charge Houses', which later emerge as expense magazines, where powder was stored between processes. As at Chilworth, these were probably constructed as a direct result of the 1772 Act.

Nearly all these building sites were occupied by a succession of later structures. This highlights the problem, characteristic in this industry, of each generation destroying the archaeological evidence of the preceding technology.

Water systems

For the developing powder works of the later seventeenth and early eighteenth centuries, the most distinctive physical remains are the

in origin. A deed of 1669 described the mills as 'all that heretofore an Oyle Mill and now lately converted into two powder mills...with all the necessary boylinge corninge and drying of powder', and they were probably founded a few years previously in 1664.[114] An engraving of 1735 (Fig 1.17) – the earliest topographical view of an identified English powder works – provides a topographical and technological snap-shot of a contemporary powder works. The mills by this date present the characteristic form of a small powder works, with a linear straggle of buildings. This was partly imposed by

networks of leats, ponds, and dams that supplied and controlled the water power on
which they depended. These are also their
most substantial physical survivals. Though
many works had their origins in earlier water
mills, the scale and detailed arrangements of
the larger factories set them apart as field
remains. This arose from the multiplication
of mills that became typical of a developed
factory, resulting not solely from the sheer
scale of production but from the application
of water power to increasing numbers of
specialist stages in the production process,
and from the reliance on water power which
led to efforts to secure and diversify the
supply. These stages typically included initial milling of the ingredients, followed by
the intimate mixing of the powder, and (as
the industry developed) mechanised corning, glazing, and dusting houses; they all
tended for reasons of safety to be conducted in separate mill buildings, each with an
independent requirement of only a few
horsepower. Commonly these water systems became the fossilised infrastructure of
later site layouts. In most works they also
served as a relatively safe and efficient
method of moving the partly finished powder between process buildings.

Several strategies may perhaps be discerned in the physical remains and site layouts; they are not necessarily clear-cut or
mutually exclusive, and they were evidently
influenced by local topography and ownership, and by the common factor that most
early sites were in south-eastern England at
low elevation and in relatively flat terrain.
One is the multiplication of leats and ponds,
generally with one set of mills to each. The
Home Works at Faversham adhered to that
form, since its origins lay in sewing together
several pre-existing mills (cf Chapter 2).
Hounslow was similar in this respect (see
Fig 3.44). A second strategy was the creation
of a large head of water, typically with some
form of more-or-less massive dam. Whether
in any given instance this was an inherited
resource is often not clear. An excellent
example is the site at Albury/Chilworth in
Surrey, which equates with the Upper Works
of Figure 1.15. There, as mapped in 1728,[116]
Postford Brook Great Pond extended to
over 6 acres (2.5ha) and there were four mill
sites below the dam and another on an

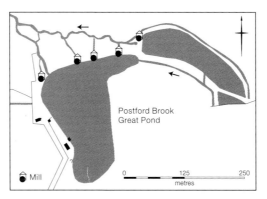

Figure 1.19 Postford
Brook Pond, extract
from 1728 map of
Chilworth gunpowder
works (redrawn from
British Library,
Althorp Papers P4).

adjacent leat (Fig 1.19). All these mills had
gone by 1787[117] but the dam survives as an
impressive field monument performing its
original function. The large pond at the core
of the Oare Works at Faversham, formed by
damming the shallow valley, similarly had a
series of process buildings along or immediately below the dam.[118] At Oare, too, there
was a valley-side leat of a form that could
provide the sort of modest head of water
required to power a series of process buildings at intervals along or below its downslope embankment. Typically, in those
circumstances water was drawn off through
spill-ways to drive a vertical wheel set at
right-angles to the leat and disgorge into a
water-course below. At Oare, the leat as
encountered now acts as a canal leading to a
mid-nineteenth-century corning house, and
evidence for its origin as a header leat is
slight. By contrast, at Chilworth the exploita-
tion of the leat as a power source is clear,
both in the field remains and in the early
mapping, which shows a layout developed
and functioning by 1728 and with provision
for an additional process building to draw on
its capacity (Fig 1.16). A less elaborate and
apparently earlier variation on this existed
also below the lowest dam at Chilworth, and
formed the Lower Works there, latterly occupied by paper mills (Figs 1.15 and 1.16). As
Chilworth shows, such header leats did not
necessarily have a mill at their end-point in
the way a conventional mill leat would. The
'Millhead stream' at Waltham Abbey did
have such head mills, which reflects the
chronology of this works' development. But
at least by the early eighteenth century it
came to conform more closely to the distinctive form of a developed gunpowder
works through a tailrace that flanked the
eastern side of the leat (see Fig 1.17),

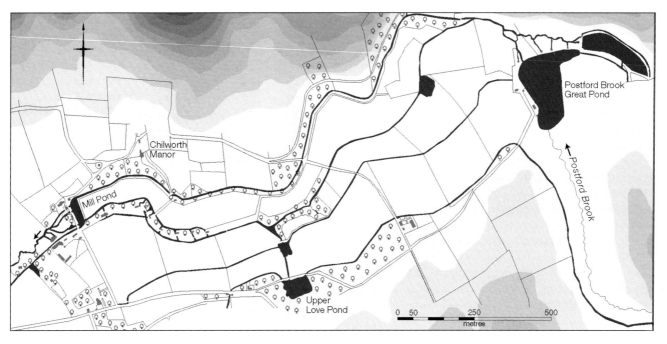

Figure 1.20
Diagram of the
Tillingbourne valley
at Chilworth showing
systems of supply
leats and header
ponds (redrawn from
British Library,
Althorp Papers P4).

which was mirrored later in the century by another along its western side, and through the straggle of water-powered process buildings spaced along them (see Fig 1.18).

A further aspect of the larger factories is the extent and elaboration of the water systems created to secure the head of water. The Millhead stream at Waltham Abbey is 1¼ miles (2km) in length and a considerable engineering feat in itself. But more impressive still is the multiple network of channels and ponds supporting the Chilworth works, that operated at several levels and drew water off both the Postford Brook and the Tillingbourne River (Fig 1.20). It was already in place by 1728 (Fig 1.16), controlling the drainage of the valley over a distance of well over 2km and ensuring the factory's water supply and therefore capacity to operate.

Mill types

Discussion of the types of mills in use until the early eighteenth century relies on documentary sources to reconstruct the different milling operations in the industry. However, from this date, former mill sites can be recognised as archaeological field monuments, and a few of them have been the subject of archaeological excavation. At Waltham Abbey in the 1960s a pair of

circular brick foundations were found during building work and recorded as 9ft (2.74m) in diameter, with their centres spaced at 18ft (5.48m).[119] They were mills [3] and [4] from the 1735 engraving (Fig 1.17). Though this casual intervention produced no dating evidence, it confirmed the use of horse-powered edge-runner mills in Britain, probably for initial milling of ingredients rather than for incorporating powder. By contrast, extensive topsoil stripping under archaeological supervision during decontamination of the area in 1994 revealed no trace of the mill depicted as number [1] in 1735, which illustrates the elusive nature of this type of mill.[120]

In the early eighteenth century the adoption of the most characteristic monument of the industry, namely the edge-runner incorporating mill, powered by a central water wheel with mills located to either side, also took place. This form of mill, and the broken and abandoned edge-runner stones resulting from its use, are the most distinctive features encountered on all abandoned powder works. Documentary evidence[121] suggests that horse-powered edge-runner mills were in use in Britain for pulverising ingredients from the late seventeenth century, as on the Continent (Fig 1.12). By the end of the century water-powered edge-runner mills had evidently been applied to incorporation.[122] The technology occurred in other industries, such as clay grinding, pulverising bark for dyeing, metal ore crushing, and cider making, but its early transfer to gunpowder production proved to be one of the defining characteristics of the British industry, in contrast to that in France and its derivatives like the American mills. Its benefits included the efficiency of rotary motion and improved safety. Though most commonly associated with incorporation, this type of mill with a central wheel-pit was used to power other kinds of process machinery, which in a powder works generally needed a low level of power but one which could be reliably sustained for many hours. Its use persisted throughout the nineteenth century and until the end of production on most sites.

The evolution of this distinctive mill type is a question which archaeological excavation should be well placed to answer. The sites of these process buildings are easy to recognise in the field in comparison with other structures that were built of timber, since the mill foundations are very substantial. This factor, coupled with the symbolic nature of the water-powered edge-runner mill for the industry as a whole, has indeed resulted in its being the principal monument type within gunpowder works to have been subject to excavation. But none of the excavations has yet produced independent dating evidence for the phasing within the structures, and perhaps it is unlikely that finds made on mill sites would produce refined chronologies. Furthermore, excavations at Bedfont, Dartford, and the Chart mills in Faversham (see Fig 2.9) were conducted with a view to leaving remains visible for public display, which constrained the complete dismantling of the mill structures.[123]

Mills required very substantial footings, as they were often built on man-made ground at the side of a mill race or dam. Such foundations had to support the edge-runner mill as it turned, and such mills generally comprised a bedstone and two edge runners which could weigh up to around ten tons (10.16 tonnes). A design drawing of 1771 for the mill at Waltham Abbey shows brick foundations extending down for 14ft (4.3m) below the mill floor, with the brickwork resting on timber piles

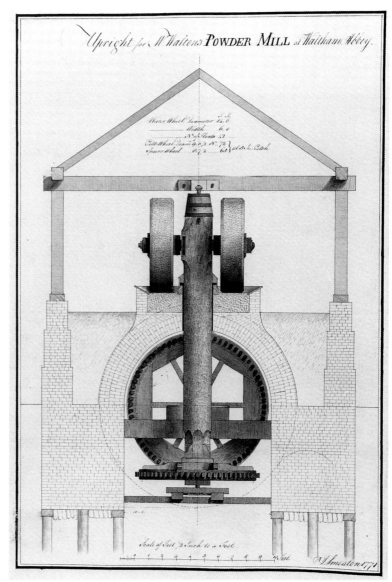

(Fig 1.21). In some of the later buildings, the mill beds themselves rested on deep brickwork foundations, while in the one mill excavated at Waltham Abbey elm posts, with a cross-section of 7 × 5fiin and 6ft 5in in length (0.18m × 0.14m and 2m in length), were found beneath a machinery base.[124] Given the waterlogged nature of most powder mill sites, dendrochronological analysis has great potential for refining the dating of individual mill structures and for providing an independent date for the introduction of timber piling employed beneath mill bases.

The superstructure of a typical powder mill consisted of a timber-framed building clad in loosely fixed boards that could easily blow away in the event of an explosion.

Figure 1.21 (Design drawing for an underdriven powder mill for Mr Walton's Waltham Abbey powder mill. (© Royal Society).

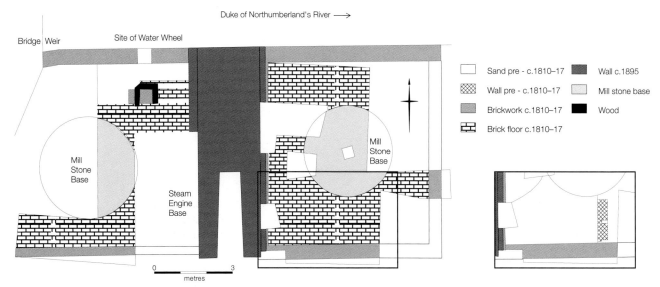

Duke of Northumberland's River ⟶

Bridge Weir   Site of Water Wheel

☐ Sand pre - c.1810–17	▨ Wall c.1895
▨ Wall pre - c.1810–17	☐ Mill stone base
▨ Brickwork c.1810–17	■ Wood
▦ Brick floor c.1810–17	

Mill Stone Base

Steam Engine Base

Mill Stone Base

0 ———— 3
metres

Figure 1.22 Lower Mills, Bedfont, Greater London, plan of the excavated incorporating mill (after Philo and Mills 1985).

The restored Chart mill at Faversham (Figs 2.9–2.11) corresponds with the evidence from contemporary manuscript illustrations[125] and gives some idea of the appearance of one of these mills. This mill is additionally important as it retains overhead gearing, which was normally removed for scrap while the timber element was fired or left to rot.

Excavation of the Lower Mills at Bedfont[126] demonstrated the complexity of phasing which may be encountered within a single mill building (Fig 1.22). Continued renewal of the mill's foundations also showed how the evidence of the earlier phases was swept away by each later rebuilding. The mills were originally a free-standing pair, each mill building measuring approximately 26ft 3in × 23ft (8 × 7m); a similar pair lay to their north on the opposite side of the mill race known as the 'Duke of Northumberland's River'. The mills sat at the head of the weir, and each pair was powered by a breast-shot water-wheel approximately 16ft (5m) in diameter and 8ft (2.5m) wide, supported by a central pier in the middle of the stream while the other end entered the mill to drive the machinery. The arrangement of the mill gearing was probably similar to that shown in a design drawing for Bedfont, prepared for Mr Walton at Waltham Abbey by John Smeaton around 1770 (Fig 1.23).

Indeed, the prosperity of some of the powder mills close to London in the late eighteenth century is illustrated by their

Figure 1.23 Design drawing by John Smeaton for Mr Walton at Waltham Abbey c 1770, showing the possible configuration of the mills at Bedfont. (© Royal Society).

owners' ability to employ the great civil engineer and mill improver, John Smeaton, to provide designs for powder mills.[127] Designs were executed at Waltham Abbey in Essex, Hounslow in Middlesex, and at Worcester Park (Tolworth) in Surrey, where Smeaton also drew up a design for a steam drying house.[128] Drawings also survive for two mills at Waltham Abbey. One was apparently intended for the head of Millhead stream and proposed two mills to one side of the wheel, connected by overhead gearing.[129] The other was designed to sit on the west side of the stream. It was to be a conventionally driven mill with a central wheel, 14ft (4.3m) in diameter and 6ft (1.8m) wide, but was evidently to use a novel form of underfloor gearing, at this date still entirely made from large timbers (Fig 1.21). Though Smeaton records that he executed one or two mills at Waltham Abbey,[130] it is uncertain if either of the designs illustrated here (Figs 1.21 and 1.23) was carried out. A mill marked on the Waltham Abbey map of 1783 as 'Smeaton's Mill' sits on the opposite side of the stream compared to the drawing, but two mill groups marked as the 'new mill' may represent mills built to Smeaton's design a decade earlier.[131] It is therefore uncertain whether the extraordinary below-the-floor gearing of the design (Fig 1.21) was employed. But the foundations of these mill groups survive and the waterlogged ground should have ensured good preservation if the gearing was left in place when the mills were rebuilt.

The 1772 Act

By the late eighteenth century the distribution of the gunpowder industry had changed little (Fig 1.24). Though during the century mills closed and others were founded, they tended to be in areas of established gunpowder production. The wider use of powder in mining had, however, stimulated the beginning of its manufacture in the Lake District and Scotland. The number of operating mills had also risen little, from 16 in 1700 to 25 in 1800. It is perhaps surprising, therefore, to find that an Act was passed in 1772 to regulate what was a very small industry.[132] The scale of production had changed, however, and the effect of an accident in any mill or magazine, or to any district when powder was being carried through, could potentially be devastating.

The importance of the 1772 Act was that it marked the beginning of state interest in regulating the industry in an attempt

to make it safer. This had an impact on the physical remains of the industry. For the act operated partly by governing the layout and building materials to be employed within powder works and partly through regulating working practices, which also had an indirect effect on the structure of a powder works.

A primary effect of the legislation was to restrict gunpowder manufacture to sites in use for that purpose when the Act was passed. It also concerned itself with details. It outlawed the use of pestle mills. Only the mills in the Battle area of Sussex were allowed to retain them for producing a fowling powder known as 'Battle Powder'. This ban may also have brought an unforeseen technological benefit. Milling of gunpowder under heavy stone edge runners was recognised as one of the reasons for British powder superiority to continental powders, where *moulins à pilons* and *moulins à tonneaux* remained in use until the latter

Figure 1.24 Map of the eighteenth-century gunpowder industry.

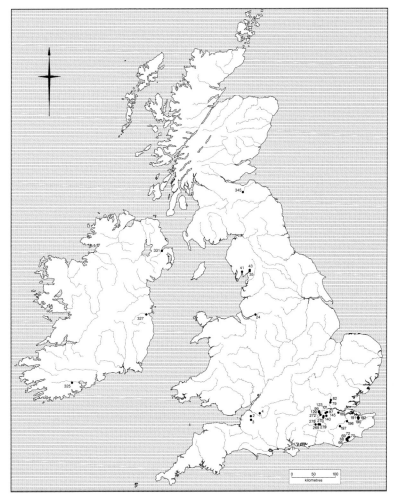

half of the nineteenth century.[133] It restricted to 40lb (18kg) the amount of powder that could be incorporated in one batch, and the amount of powder that could be dried in a stove to 40cwt (2032kg). In other buildings, such as corning and dusting houses, no more powder was to be stored than was needed for the work in hand. The legislation also began to affect the physical form of gunpowder works by stipulating that gunpowder magazines or storehouses were to be built of stone or brick and that they were to be situated at least 50yd (45.7m) from mill buildings. Charcoal stores were to be 20yd (18.3m) from any process building or magazine. The passing of this Act also increased the documentation of the industry, for any new mills required a licence from the local Justices of the Peace, who were also given the duty of designating land suitable for new magazines.

The industry that came under this regulation was made up of a series of capital-intensive enterprises of factory-like form. An increasing number of processes were housed in separate buildings, typically with timber superstructures but in the case of the mills involving costly groundworks and machinery. Technological innovation occurred with little scientific understanding of either the powder or how it could be improved through different manufacturing methods. It was partly concern about the resultant variable quality that persuaded the government in the late eighteenth century to become directly involved in powder manufacture.

Endnotes

1   A favourite toast of the powdermakers noted by William Congreve, 1788.
2   Needham 1980.
3   *Ibid* 1980, 39.
4   Needham 1986, 39–50; BL, Sloan MSS 2156.
5   Needham 1980, 39, 41; *ibid* 1986, 39–41, 50.
6   Needham 1980, 40; *ibid* 1985, 14–16; *ibid* 1986, 289–94.
7   Kramer 1995.
8   Hogg 1963a, 41–3; West 1991, 8.
9   Hogg 1944, 179.
10 Biringuccio [*c* 1540], 413.
11 Admiralty 1905, 6.
12 Ruhmann 1996, 158; Buchanan 1996c, 128.
13 Amsterdam was the chief source of sulphur as well as of saltpetre and gunpowder: see Edwards 1995, 111, 121–2.
14 Patterson 1995b, 10.
15 Williams 1975.
16 *LPFD Henry VIII*, 1539, 14(1), 207, 393; *ibid* 1544, 19(2), 63, 382; *ibid* 1545, 20(1), 205.
17 'W T' 1672, 9; Partington 1960, 322.
18 *CSPD*, 1581–90, 112.
19 *LPFD Henry VIII*, 1545, 20(1), 16.
20 *CSPD*, 1547–80, 172; *Engineering* 1894.
21 Hodgetts 1909, 259.
22 *CSPD*, 1547–80, 172.
23 G Crocker 1986, 4.
24 Cf the similar processes and facilities in the production of alum in north-eastern England; Marshall 1995.
25 Hall 1996, 90–4; Hall 1997, 74–9; Kramer 1996, 51–2.
26 Wrey 1953.
27 For contemporary accounts of saltpetre refining, see Agricola 1556, 558–64; Norton 1628, 142–4; 'W T' 1672, 9–15; see also *VCH Surrey*, 1905, 307–10.
28 Nef 1932, 1, 210–11.
29 *CSPD*, 1581–90, 607.
30 *Ibid* 1627–8, 377; ibid 1628–9, 546; *ibid* 1635, 236; *ibid* 1636–7, 148, 322; *ibid* 1639–40, 176; Ferris 1964, 159; Buchanan 1996c, 130.
31 Ferris 1964.
32 Nef 1932, 1, 211.
33 For examples of concern over the assured supplies of saltpetre and measures to increase supplies, see *CSPD*, 1626, 170–1; *idem* 1627, 303, 391.
34 *Ibid* 1627, 391.
35 *CSPD*, 1670, 374, 377.
36 Saunders 1989, 15–19.
37 Barter Bailey 1996.
38 Hogg 1963b, 124–5.
39 Greener 1910, 16; Hassenstein 1941, 10 fig 7.
40 Royal Armouries Library, London, Anon, Firework Manuscript, 1–34.
41 Barter Bailey 1996.
42 Hassenstein 1941, 103.
43 Hodgetts 1909, 183; Hogg 1944, 184.
44 Hodgetts 1909, 185.
45 *Ibid*; Colvin *et al* 1975, 270, 291.
46 Hodgetts 1909, 184.
47 *LPFD Henry VIII*, 1540, 16, 456.
48 *LPFD Henry VIII*, 1544, 19, 101.
49 *LPFD Henry VIII*, 1546–7, 21, 257–8.
50 Wolper 1970.
51 Nef 1934.
52 Thirsk 1978, esp 47, 54–5.
53 Nef 1932, 1, 170, 241.
54 Clay 1984, 2, 214–16.
55 Thirsk 1978.
56 Clay 1984, esp 2, 61–4.
57 *VCH* Surrey 1905, 310; Crocker 1988a, 24.
58 Hodgetts 1909, 215; Fraser 1996, 122–3.
59 Eg Gimpel 1977, 15–40.
60 *VCH* Surrey 1905, 306–21; Crocker 1988a, 16; Barron 1990.
61 Crocker 1988a, 54; Barron 1990.
62 Kelleher 1993, 6.
63 Hodgetts 1909, 256, 274, 341, 303.
64 *CSPD*, 1627–8, 493; *ibid* 1628–9, 118, 544; *VCH* Surrey 1905, 319.
65 *CSPD*, 1640, 523.
66 *Ibid*, 1635, 2.
67 *Ibid*, 1635–6, 390; *ibid*, 1637, 187, 498.
68 *Ibid*, 1621, 248.
69 *Ibid*, 1625–6, 90, 93, 109, 376, 407.

70 Clay 1984, 2, 216.

71 See, for example, Whitehorne 1562, 135; Norton 1628.

72 Hodgetts 1909, 15.

73 *CSPD*, 1635–6, 390; ibid 1639–40, 424.

74 *CSPD* Charles I, 1639–40, 369–70; Hodgetts 1909, 288–9.

75 Presumed to be of Civil War date, Silberrad and Simpson 1906.

76 Personal communication W S Curtis with specific reference to samples of French powder recovered from a shell fired during the siege of Paris in 1870–1.

77 Hall 1996, 89; Kramer 1996, 47; Hall 1997, 69–80.

78 Eg *LPDG Henry VIII*, 1542, **17**, 367; *ibid* 1544, **18**, 113.

79 Edwards 1995, 111.

80 Roy 1964, 28–32; Toynbee and Young 1973, 31–2; *VCH* 1979, 81.

81 *VCH* 1979, 64.

82 RCHME 1964, 30, 53.

83 Wenham 1970, 188.

84 Clayton 1992, 62.

85 Hodgetts 1909, 298.

86 Atkin and Howes 1993, 32–3.

87 Foard 1995, 16.

88 City of Coventry 1992.

89 *CSPD*, 1660–1, 547; Roy 1964, 37; Snape 1989; *Gunpowder Mills Study Group News* 1989a and 1989b; Pluck 1989; Carlton 1992, 223; Edwards 1995, 116.

90 Rimington 1966.

91 *LPFD*, 1649–50, 566.

92 Barlow 1855, 166.

93 West 1991, ch 1 *passim*.

94 Tomlinson 1979, and West 1991.

95 Crocker and Fairclough 1998.

96 Crocker *et al* forthcoming.

97 Wild 1996.

98 Plot 1686, 165; Hollister-Short 1985, 48 n 41.

99 I am grateful to John Barnatt, Peak District National Park Archaeology Service, for a report of his recent discoveries, August 1995.

100 Fuller 1662, 165.

101 PRO WO 55/425, Warrants 1660–8.

102 Tomlinson 1979, 114–15.

103 *Ibid*, 117.

104 Nye 1670, 19.

105 Roy 1964, 30.

106 A Crocker 1986.

107 See Crocker and Fairclough 1998; Crocker *et al* forthcoming.

108 Aubrey 1718, 56–7.

109 West 1991, 150, 206–8.

110 *VCH Surrey* 1905, 323.

111 BL, Althorp Papers, P12.

112 Buchanan and Tucker 1981; Buchanan 1996c.

113 Essex Record Office, T/M125.

114 Fairclough 1985, 14.

115 PRO MR 593.

116 BL, Althorp Papers, P4 1728 map of Chilworth gunpowder works.

117 BL, Althorp Papers, P12.

118 Cocroft 1994.

119 WASC 176.

120 Essex County Council Planning Department 1994.

121 Crocker and Fairclough 1998.

122 Buchanan 1976, 78–9; *ibid* 1996b, 242–3; *ibid* 1996c, 142–6.

123 Philo and Mills 1985; Philp 1984; Percival 1968; Cherry 1974.

124 WASC 1479; WASC 106.

125 Hodgetts 1909, 24 fig 10.

126 Philo and Mills 1985.

127 Wilson 1957.

128 Royal Society folio John Smeaton Volume II, fos 33v–39v (Waltham Abbey), fos 40–1 (Hounslow Heath), fos 41 v–47Av (Worcester Park).

129 Royal Society folio John Smeaton Volume II.

130 Wilson 1957, 39, 41.

131 PRO MR 593.

132 Statutes at Large 1772, **12 George III, c. 61**.

133 Smith 1868, 106–33.

2
The royal factories 1759–1850

Introduction

The historian Paul Kennedy views the Seven Years War (1756–63), which had its origins in the struggle between Britain and France for supremacy in North America and Europe, as having 'claim to the title of the first world war' in respect of its geographical extent.[1] The war soon highlighted the deficiencies in the quantity of gunpowder supplied by the trade and its quality, demonstrated by the amount failing proof at the Greenwich magazines. Early attempts in 1756 to control the gunpowder and saltpetre trade by statute failed.[2] In an effort to overcome these problems the government purchased a group of mills at Faversham in 1759 to undertake the manufacture of powder directly.[3]

State involvement was crucial in the development of improved production methods, for in the closing decades of the century it provided a nucleus of scientifically minded officers and the necessary finance to remodel the government's powder works. The late eighteenth century was notably a period of increased scientific experimentation, and a better understanding of the properties of gunpowder was another factor which allowed the industry to progress beyond the procedures of a craft.

Similar trends were evident on the Continent. Problems with the supply and quality of privately manufactured gunpowder during the Seven Years War prompted the French government in 1775 to place control of saltpetre and gunpowder production under the *Régie des poudres*, which included among its number Antoine Lavoisier (1743–94) – arguably the most influential chemist of the late eighteenth century.[4] In Britain, change was brought about under the leadership of the deputy comptroller of the Royal Laboratory at Woolwich, William Congreve (Fig 2.1). During his tenure of office the royal powder works became model factories, and private contractors were encouraged to emulate the improvements carried out there, 'for which purpose they have access to the King's works whenever they please'.[5] The improved government powder was then set as the standard against which the trade powders were tested at proof, which acted as the stimulus for the trade to improve its methods.

Figure 2.1
Lieutenant General Sir William Congreve, 1st Baronet, died 1814. (WASC 559)

The first royal gunpowder factory – Faversham

The necessity, of quickly acquiring a group of powder mills, forced on it by war, dictated that the Board of Ordnance should purchase an existing group of mills which could in the first instance be devoted to reworking unserviceable powders. The Faversham mills, established in the mid-seventeenth century, were well known to the Board as one of their most important suppliers and the works were in easy seaward reach of the government establishments along the river Thames. Their final selection may, however, have been a pragmatic decision by the Board prompted by the owner's willingness to sell.[6]

The mills (Fig 2.2) were situated immediately to the west of the town and comprised a straggle of ponds and buildings stretching for over a kilometre and across four parishes. They were referred to as the 'Faversham mills', but were made up of a number of individual estates and groups of mills. Later they were referred to as the 'Home Works' to distinguish this group from the other powder works around Faversham. Today most of this area is lost beneath modern housing estates, and we are reliant on a combination of historic maps and documentary sources to reconstruct the development of the works.

The mills as acquired in 1759 split into three sections, which were linked to contemporary land holdings. They were close to sea level and relied on a sequence of stepped ponds to power the mills, falling from Ospringe in the west towards Oare Creek. The creek was vital for importing raw materials and exporting finished powder. To the south-west were the Ospringe Mills, a leasehold property; they comprised a long mill pond and at its head a large mill with a side wheel and a second mill apparently centrally driven. The middle section of the works was a freehold property comprising a series of sub-rectangular ponds and leats to drive the single central water wheel of the Chart Mills (Fig 2.2, and see Figs 2.9–2.11). The largest section of the works was the leasehold estate of Kingsmill manor to the north-east. This included the King's Mill, a water-driven corn mill and an associated mill house and grounds. Below these were a series of finger-like ponds which stored water for the lowest set of powder mills. A further group of mills to the north-west of the town, the Oare Works, was developed from the early eighteenth century but remained outside government control.[7]

The poor organisational layout of the Faversham mills was the consequence of its low-lying position and numerous large header ponds. This was compounded by the different land holdings across the site, which probably reflects its development from a number of individual corn mills. It led to greater numbers of barge movements compared to the more efficiently organised mills at Waltham Abbey (Fig 1.17). The majority of the incorporating mills were water powered, though a number of horse mills were retained. As late as 1784 a centrally driven pestle or stamp mill was

Figure 2.2 RGPF Faversham 1784. The Ospringe Mills appear bottom left, the Chart Mills in the centre, and the King's Mills above them, with storage ponds and the lower powder mills beyond again. Note north lies to the top left; cf Fig 2.8. (BB95/11938; © PRO, MR 914)

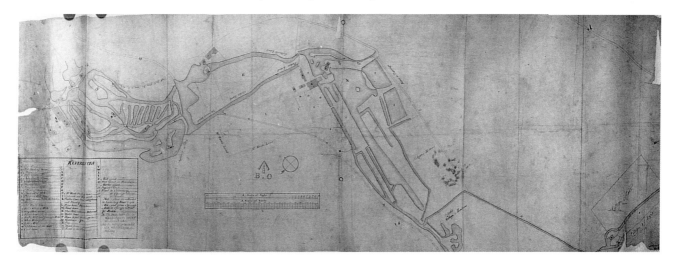

recorded, perhaps operating under government exemption to the 1772 Act. As elsewhere, separate mills were provided for the different processes and sufficient space allowed between mills to reduce the effects of accidental explosion.

Though the plan illustrated in Figure 2.2 was made 25 years after the government's purchase, little had changed physically to distinguish it from its private origins or its trade rivals. Contemporary accounts also indicate that the Board was unsuccessful in improving either the quality or the quantity of powder compared to its contractors. Nor can provision of extra facilities for reworking unserviceable powders be detected in the layout of the works, in the form of dusting houses and drying stoves over and above the normal requirements of manufacture. Though considerable sums of money were spent on the factory they had little effect on its plan form. For where mill machinery was renewed or a mill replaced, it tended to sit on the site of its predecessor, and therefore presents no discernible change on a map.

Until the early 1780s most of the manufacturing was carried out in a small part of the works at its north-eastern end. Here was the densest concentration of buildings within the works. It contained buildings associated with the preparation of ingredients – an earth house, a saltpetre mill, charcoal mill, an unspecified refining house, and a mixing house – but also, since incorporated powder was moved back to this area for finishing, corning houses, a glazing house, and drying stoves located perilously close to the town centre.[8] By contrast the factory magazine was positioned adjacent to Oare Creek, on a site later to be developed as the Marsh Works (see below, Faversham).

Reorganisation of the royal powder works under William Congreve

In the first 20 years or so of government ownership, therefore, little progress was made in addressing the problems of the quality or quantity of powder produced at Faversham. During the American War of Independence (1775–83) the rottenness of British powder in terms of strength and durability was notorious.[9] In appearance, too, the works lacked the scale of the contemporary continental powder works, depicted by Diderot in his *Encyclopédie* (1771), and they did not exhibit the grand planning evident in royal arsenals and analogous state manufactories abroad. Yet from this seeming impasse in the early 1780s, British powder by the end of the century was regarded as a world standard.

The factors which brought about this change were complex. They included organisational change, as well as an increased understanding of the nature of gunpowder and its ingredients through scientific experimentation, particularly through the work of Charles Hutton (1778), Benjamin Thompson (Count Rumford), and Ingenhousz (1779), building on the earlier work of Robins (1742).[10] These gentlemen experimenters were concerned with the force of fired gunpowder rather than its composition or how a scientific study of manufacturing techniques could improve its quality. Innovation was also unlikely to come from the powder suppliers, whom Congreve described as being 'too indolent to go into the dirty work of their mills and have generally left the superintendence thereof to artful but ignorant foremen'.[11] Perhaps most importantly, there was a need for more effective powder, as unrest in Europe in the wake of the French Revolution threatened Britain's security. This external threat persuaded a previously reluctant Treasury to invest in the expansion of the royal powder works and more readily to commit itself to new technology.

Of central importance in improving the quality of British powder were the military officers who, through their scientific knowledge, could direct the state powder works to vary the composition and/or manufacturing processes and to investigate their effects on the finished powder. Such experiments at Faversham began in 1782 under the short-lived Comptroller of the Royal Laboratory, Colonel George Napier.[12] The practical effect of organisational change in April 1783 was to place the responsibility for manufacture and proof of gunpowder in the hands of Major William Congreve, at that time deputy comptroller of the Royal Laboratory but in practice its acting comptroller.

In Congreve the Board had a man with the necessary organisational, scientific, and technological abilities, who was able to transform the manufacture of gunpowder within the government establishments and reorganise the supply from the trade.[13] His experimental work gave him both authority and a central position as Comptroller of the Royal Laboratory, so that he could effectively bridge the gap between experimenter and manufacturer, which had earlier been a distinction of social class as well as function.

That experimental work had two foci – research to 'establish a proper mode of proof' (see below, Proof) and practical improvement of methods of manufacture. A bewildering range of experiments were initiated at Faversham in 1783, including comparative trials of foreign powders and manufacture of powder based on foreign compositions. The differences between glazed and unglazed powder and between rounded and angular grains, were tested to determine which was stronger. Later trials at Waltham Abbey in 1789 compared the effects of the time the powder spent beneath the runners in incorporation and how many revolutions the runners made per minute.[14]

Congreve also had to battle politically to retain gunpowder production in government hands. The prime minister, William Pitt, proposed putting the sale of the Faversham mills before Parliament, after lobbying by the private merchants who claimed they could supply better powder more cheaply than the royal mills. Congreve refuted these claims by showing that the royal mills made a profit, and argued that if some of this profit was expended on the mills a far stronger powder could be produced. His case was so convincing that he was later able to secure the purchase of an additional set of mills at Waltham Abbey.[15] The effect of his reforms was such that shortly before the end of his period in office he was able to claim that 'so great a quantity of powder is manufactured by the Ordnance themselves, that they are enabled to keep the contractors in order, both as to price, and to the quality of the powder'.[16]

While strength was obviously vital in military gunpowder, it was equally important that a given charge of powder had a consistent and reproducible effect, in nineteenth-century parlance an 'equal' powder. Powder's durability could be vitiated by impure ingredients. It was alleged that sulphur bought directly from the merchants might be adulterated with flour, leading to fermentation in warm climates.[17] To achieve consistent results it was necessary to assure the purity of the ingredients and to ensure that the manufacturing process was replicated in every instance. These priorities are reflected in the rebuilding campaigns of the late 1780s at Faversham and later at Waltham Abbey, and in the provision of large and up-to-date refineries to secure quality of ingredients, while the replication of process is implicit from the early nineteenth century in the standardisation of building types.

Faversham

The immediate impetus for the remodelling of the Faversham works came in April 1781 when a corning and dusting house blew up, devastating large areas of the works and the town. Instead of rebuilding on the same site, as hitherto, the Board sought to identify land further away from the town. As early as June 1781 a remote area of marshland was earmarked as a possible site for the more dangerous process buildings. It was situated to the north-west of the town in Luddenham parish adjacent to Oare Creek (Fig 2.3), and the resultant Marsh Works eventually covered 62 acres (24.8ha).[18]

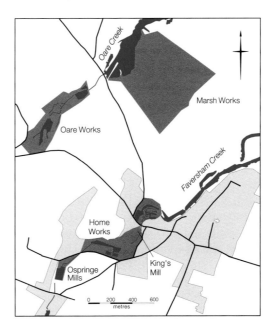

Figure 2.3 Location map of Faversham factories, extract from first edition OS, Canterbury, Sheet 3, 1-inch, published 1819 railways revised to 1889.

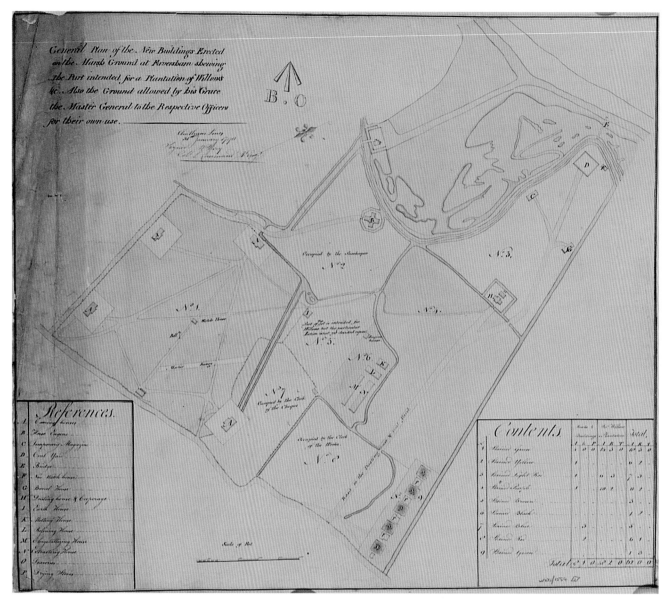

Figure 2.4 RGPF Faversham, Marsh Works, January 1790. (© PRO MPH 426)

It is unlikely that any work began until Congreve had satisfactorily resolved the political future of the mills. However, by 1786 work was under way. Initial plans show that it was to comprise three corning houses, a dusting house, stove, two watch houses, and stables for the corning house horses. It was a model site laid out on flat, virgin ground with well-spaced buildings connected by canals and trackways. By 1790 four corning houses had been constructed (Fig 2.4). In plan they were large rectangular buildings, probably with a loading porch to one side. The internal arrangement and combination of processes carried out in these buildings are clearly illustrated in contemporary sketches (Figs 2.5 and

2.6), which provide some of the earliest evidence about the types of machines used in English factories.[19] Such buildings contained a breaking-down table, a hand-powered press and a shaking frame containing the corning sieves. The press was hand-operated and consisted of a wooden handle attached to a brass screw which fitted into a wooden saddle. The millcake, roughly broken by wooden malls on the bench, was placed in layers between sheets of copper or hardened leather in a wooden trough; the saddle was then lowered into the trough and a pressure of around 113 tons per square foot applied. After pressing, the powder – now termed presscake – had a hard slate-like appearance and was once again broken

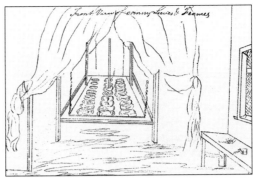

Figure 2.5 (left) RGPF Faversham 1798, sketch of Corning House. Hodgetts 1909, fig 13. (B97/3431)

Figure 2.6 (right) RGPF Faversham 1798, sketch of Corning House. Hodgetts 1909, fig 14. (BB97/3432)

up using wooden malls in preparation for corning. On the opposite side of the building was the corning frame (Fig 2.6). This consisted of a heavy frame suspended from the roof by ropes, onto which were placed the corning sieves. It was apparently shrouded by a cloth while working. The frame was made to oscillate by the pole set at its centre; this in turn caused the 'runners' to oscillate, thereby forcing the powder through the sieves.

Corning assumed greater importance under Congreve, as he had shown through experimentation the advantages of using large-grain powder in cannons and fine-grain powders in small arms and for priming, in contrast to the Board's policy in the middle of the century of using one size for all purposes.[20] Corning sieves were made up of two parchment skins, the upper with holes of the required size and the lower with smaller holes to catch the grains and let the dust pass through. The broken millcake was placed on the top sieve and a circular 'runner' of *lignum vitae* or other hard and heavy wood placed on top of it. To ensure a uniformity of grain size, the parchment skins for the sieves were either supplied from the Tower of London or manufactured within the factory by a designated sieve puncher using punches supplied from the Tower or to its specification.[21] Some contemporary writers suggest a further sieving operation was then required to sort the powder into different sizes.[22]

The layout of the Marsh Works suggests a renewed desire to carry out the original intention for the Faversham mills to rework unserviceable powders, instead of selling them back to the trade for reworking or for the recovery of saltpetre. Partial reworking of damp powder from ships' holds could restore the powder to a serviceable quality.[23]

The Marsh Works formed a self-contained unit, which could carry out all the necessary processes for this, although its provision of no less than four corning houses was far greater than the manufacture of powder alone would require. The numbers may suggest that the powder was corned before it was dusted and dried. The works were also adjacent to the creek so powder could be delivered directly, without interfering with the manufacturing process at the Home Works.

Drying stoves were located in the eastern corner of the site, each separated from its neighbour by an earthwork traverse. Surprisingly, although Congreve was clearly abreast of all contemporary developments in gunpowder manufacture, he chose to persist in the use of gloom stoves in preference to steam drying stoves. Gloom stoves had been in use since the seventeenth century. They consisted of at least two rooms (Fig 2.7): one contained a series of drying racks while the other housed a fire, its cast iron back protected by a copper cover projecting into the drying room. Sometime around 1770 the new method of drying

Figure 2.7 RGPF Faversham 1798, sketch of the interior of a gloom stove. Hodgetts 1909, fig 17. This shows the cast-iron fireback or gloom and racks for drying gunpowder. The drawing and the others in this series (2.5 and 2.6) were probably made by apprentices or officers during their initial training course. (BB97/3433)

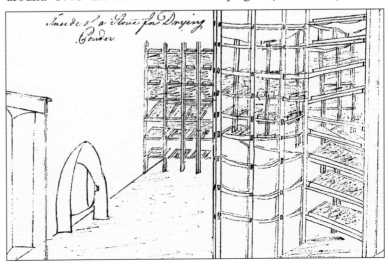

gunpowder by steam pipes was introduced. Steam stoves were regarded as less likely to overheat, thereby reducing the risk of accidental explosion or of causing the sulphur in the powder to sublimate.[24] Early examples include a design drawing by John Smeaton prepared for the Worcester Park (Tolworth) mills at Long Ditton in 1772, and a steam stove was functioning at the Oare Works from 1776.[25] By contrast, gloom stoves continued to find favour with Congreve and were later employed at Waltham Abbey, where they remained in use well into the nineteenth century.

In the Home Works, too, some changes were implemented in the early 1780s. New drying stoves were added at the extreme north-western corner of the site, partly dug

into the valley side and separated from one another by an earthwork traverse. To the east of the Chart Mills and St Ann's House, new horse mills were erected along with various storehouses and workshops. Below these mills the King's Mill, formerly a corn mill, was converted to gunpowder production.

Further developments in the late 1780s demonstrate a programme under Congreve's leadership aimed at radically improving the processing facilities for raw materials. Dated drawings in the Public Record Office indicate that a major building campaign was under way early in 1789.[26] A new piece of land was purchased at the eastern end of the Home Works (Fig 2.8) and the buildings within it were entirely dedicated to preparation of ingredients.

Figure 2.8 RGPF Faversham 1790. Note addition of ingredients preparation complex at the east end of the Home Works; cf Fig 2.2. (BB95/11943; © PRO, MPH 189)

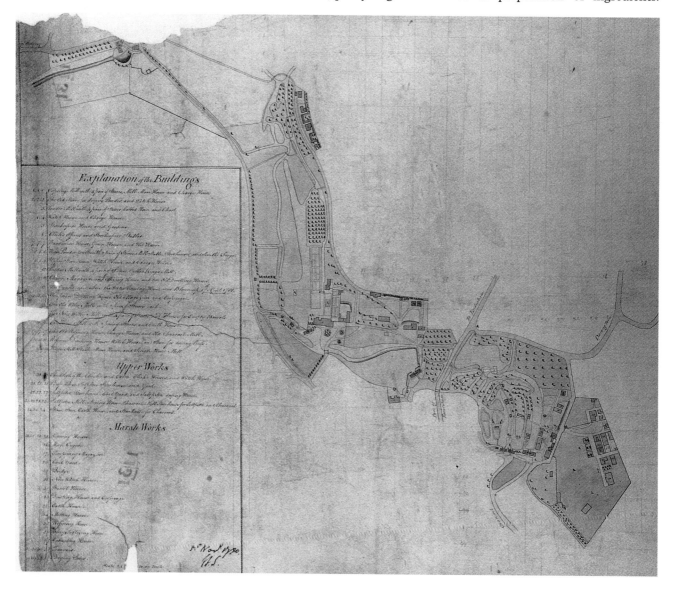

They included a brick-built saltpetre and sulphur storehouse measuring 60ft (18.3m) × 31ft (9.5m), a sulphur refining house and subliming dome – the first time a sulphur refinery may be identified as a named structure in a gunpowder factory.[27] There were six mills for grinding saltpetre, charcoal, and sulphur, probably all horse-powered, and a mixing house, where the ingredients were mixed prior to incorporation. Charcoal was stored in this area, but it is uncertain if charcoal-burning retorts were established as early as 1790 (see below, cylinder power and the charcoal houses at Fernhurst in west Sussex). So great was Congreve's concern about the purity of the ingredients that by 1796 over one-third of the workforce at Faversham was engaged in the processing of ingredients.

During the 1790s attempts were also made to increase the capacity of the Home Works. The header pond at the Ospringe mills was redug to form a larger rectangular pool. On its dam were placed a pair of centrally driven mills with a further mill on an outlet to the north. Sited in the middle of the works, the Chart Mills were originally centrally driven with stones to either side. At sometime during the 1780s they were enlarged so that the wheel was used to move two pairs of edge runners to either side. This method of increasing capacity appears to be a feature of the Faversham mills at this date, for similar arrangements were also found at the King's Mills and in the Lower Mills. In another group, the mills were arranged with two wheels turning three pairs of stones. The Chart Mills were badly damaged in an explosion in February 1792 and were later rebuilt as a separate pair of mill buildings, each with a central wheel which powered a pair of stones either side of the wheel (Fig 2.9).[28] In this configuration (which still survives) a central wheel house covered a cast-iron-framed low breast-shot wheel running in a stone-lined wheel pit (Fig 2.10). In the pair of stone edge runners to either side, each stone weighed some 3 tons (3.05 tonnes) (Fig 2.11). The superstructure was timber-framed and covered by loosely pegged boards; the interior was lit by removable shutters. It is uncertain whether the brick

Figure 2.9 RGPF Faversham, Home Works, the Chart Mills. To the rear is the mill rebuilt by the Faversham Society in the 1960s. The displayed remains are at least the third group of mills known to have occupied this site and were probably established in this configuration during the 1790s. (BB94/13780)

blast wall alongside the easterly mill is contemporary with the 1790s reconstruction.

At the Marsh Works, Congreve's concern about the purity of ingredients was manifest in the construction of a new saltpetre refinery at the centre of the works (Fig 2.4). Maps date this phase of development with remarkable accuracy to the latter half of 1789.[29] As initially laid out, the refinery consisted of four buildings: a melting house (K in Fig 2.4), refining house (L, and Fig 2.12), crystallising house (M, and Figs 2.13 and 2.14), and extracting house (N), with an 'engine house' nearby and a small square earth house (J) at a distance to the west.

Figure 2.10 RGPF Faversham, Home Works. Mill wheel at the Chart Mills. (BB94/13782)

The principal source of saltpetre was the East Indies, and as imported the partly refined or 'grough' saltpetre contained organic and inorganic impurities which needed to be removed to make it fit for gunpowder manufacture. The process involved triple refining. Initially 35cwt (1718kg) of saltpetre was boiled in a 500 gallon (2273 litres) copper with 270 gallons (1227.42 litres) of water for three-and-a-half to four hours; impurities were skimmed off the surface and cold water thrown in to precipitate the chlorides and salts. At the end of the boiling the furnace doors were thrown open, which caused the chlorides and salts to fall to the bottom. A brass pump moved the cooled liquor via a wooden trough with four or five brass cocks, and through canvas filter bags into 36 gallon pans. It was allowed to crystallise and the remaining 'mother liquor' was drained off for reprocessing. The saltpetre obtained was known as 'once refined' and was refined twice again using the same process.[30]

This refining process required large clear floor areas for laying out the pans and troughs and for manoeuvring the large cast blocks of saltpetre. It also required waterway access for importing the bulky grough

Figure 2.11 RGPF Faversham, Home Works. Restored early nineteenth-century edge-runner mill; note how the runners are set asymmetrically from the centre post. (BB94/13788)

Figure 2.12 RGPF Faversham, Marsh Works. Saltpetre refining house c 1790. (BB94/13805)

Figure 2.13 RGPF Faversham, Marsh Works. Saltpetre crystallising house c 1790, showing louvred ventilation. (BB94/13803)

saltpetre and coal for the refineries. All the buildings in the refinery were large single-storey structures open to hipped roofs with stout, through bolted, king-post trusses with expanded feet and heads and raking struts. The surviving crystallising house (Fig 2.13) is typical of a process that carried no fire risk in being a long timber shed, 147ft × 22ft 4in in plan (44.8m × 6.8m), originally consisting of 13 bays, now reduced to 12. The underside of its roof was boarded and the exterior clad in weather boards; one side retains louvre vents placed to aid the air circulation within the building and promote crystallisation (Fig 2.14). This building was in use as stores in 1923 towards the end of powdermaking at Faversham (see Chapter 4); it apparently owes its survival with such detailing intact, like some early farm buildings, to its adaptable utility.

The refinery also had an extracting kitchen for recovering saltpetre from powder which was too damaged to be restored. The form of this building was similar to the melting house within the saltpetre refinery at Waltham Abbey (Fig 2.37). A later drawing shows it as a large rectangular building open to the roof with a vented clerestory. Around the edge of the central room were furnaces for boiling bags of powder. After boiling, the bags were squeezed between two side plates in a screw press to extract nitre in solution from the powder. A press was specially devised by Congreve in 1785

for this operation, which was carried out at the Marsh Works and also at Woolwich until at least the 1790s.[31]

Also in the late 1780s building campaign an additional pair of drying stoves was built, as was a coal yard (D on Fig 2.4) adjacent to the creek to supply the boilers and probably also the furnaces in the saltpetre refinery. A dusting house (H) and a cruciform structure (B) identified as a horse engine were also built. The precise function of the latter is unclear. Later it was described as a reel house, and may have contained a central horse 'engine' powering four dusting reels in the arms of the building.

Figure 2.14 RGPF Faversham, Marsh Works. Interior of saltpetre crystallising house with louvre vent and boarded ceiling, c 1790. (BB94/13806)

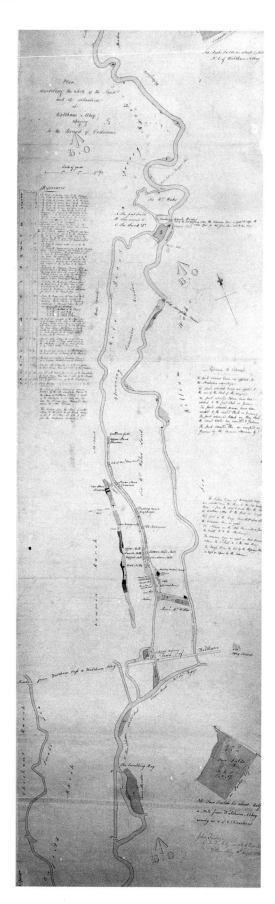

*Figure 2.15 RGPF
Waltham Abbey,
map of 1801.
(BB95/11931;
© PRO, MR 80/2)*

Royal Gunpowder Factory (RGPF) Waltham Abbey – the first 15 years

At the same time as work commenced on the Marsh Works at Faversham negotiations were starting for purchase of the gunpowder mills at Waltham Abbey. Though Congreve had begun to improve the quality of the powder produced at Faversham, its constricted site and the proximity of the town forced him to look elsewhere if he wished to increase the capacity of the government controlled mills. The mills chosen at Waltham Abbey were, as the Faversham mills had been, an important private supplier to the Board of Ordnance. They were well structured and organised with a distinct south-to-north flow line (Fig 1.17); in the hands of the Walton family they had also expanded since the beginning of the century with the construction of new buildings and replacement of old process buildings. Yet as one of a number of trade factories supplying the Ordnance they did not stand out as being exceptional in either size or their application of new technologies (Fig 2.15). The decision to buy them was probably founded on a pragmatism like that which is thought to have led to the acquisition of the Faversham mills, for these mills had recently come into the possession of a distant member of the Walton family, who perhaps had little interest in the business.[32]

The mills at Waltham Abbey were purchased in 1787 for £10,000, but before manufacture was resumed an extensive programme of repairs and improvements was undertaken.[33] The impact of the first decade of government ownership on the plan form of the factory as a whole appears to have been negligible as new buildings replaced old.[34] In contrast to the investment in the new refineries at Faversham, preparation of the ingredients at Waltham Abbey appears to have followed the practice employed prior to the government's purchase of the factory. Immediate demands for new equipment fail to show any re-equipping of the existing saltpetre works, which remained isolated at the southern end of the site. Contemporary documents also do not reveal any evidence for a sulphur refinery, which might suggest that sulphur was supplied by the refinery at Faversham.

Figure 2.16 RGPF Waltham Abbey. Mixing House (left) and Saltpetre Melting House (right) constructed soon after the government's acquisition of the factory in 1787. (BB92/26066)

Wood for charcoal was collected over a wide area of East Anglia to augment the coppices of alder, dogwood, and willow with which nearly all parts of the factory were planted. Charcoal burning at this date needed no fixed facilities, but did require large open areas for stack yards and clamps, and these were found to the north and east of the main mill area. In the 1790s two charcoal burners were recorded on the factory's complement.[35]

Two of the surviving buildings of this phase do, nevertheless, reflect Congreve's concern with preparation of ingredients – a saltpetre melting house and a mixing house (Fig 2.16). They are situated in the area south of Millhead traditionally used for the preparation of ingredients (Figs 1.17 and 2.31), on the site of an earlier composition house. The architectural treatment of these buildings was similar to the refining house built on the Marsh Works at Faversham around the same date (Fig 2.12). Both were of red brick with flat arched windows; internally they were open to the roof with similar stout king-post roof trusses. In a later drawing, the mixing house is shown as a large open room with a single mixing table, apparently with storage bins for the ingredients in the small rooms to either side.

The saltpetre melting house had a partition wall composed of four chimney shafts at its northern end serving four melting vats. The remainder of the interior was clear except for two low benches and a table. Adjacent to these buildings were others involved in processing ingredients, including horse-powered saltpetre, charcoal, and sulphur mills, and a coal yard (probably for charcoal) and stabling for the horses.

Government purchase of the factory also brought a structured hierarchy of officials and bureaucracy. The principal officer, James Wright, was titled the 'Storekeeper'; his principal administrative officer was the 'Clerk of Cheques', with junior clerks beneath him. To house them a purpose-built office was put up soon after the government acquired the factory (Fig 2.17). Built of red brick and with a hipped roof with carpenter's marks for assembly, it was similar in style to the other buildings erected at this date. As constructed it was two-storeyed and rectangular, two bays by one bay, with two rooms on each floor and a staircase on its eastern side.

The extent of remodelling in the remainder of the factory at this time is unclear, as later development or demolition has removed other contemporary features.

Figure 2.17 RGPF
Waltham Abbey.
Walton's House,
named after the last
private owner of the
works but built as
offices soon after the
government pur-
chased the works in
1787.
(BB92/26067)

Figure 2.17 RGPF
Waltham Abbey.
Walton's House,
named after the last
private owner of the
works but built as
offices soon after the
government pur-
chased the works in
1787.
(BB92/26067)

Figure 2.18 RGPF
Waltham Abbey.
Gloom stove con-
structed in the 1790s
at the northern end
of Horsemill Island;
note the use of brick
traverses and light-
ning conductor poles
(from Illustrated
London News 25,
11 November 1854,
478).

The relatively long period between the purchase of the mills in 1787 and the resumption of production on 10 February 1789
may suggest the work was fairly extensive,
perhaps on watercourses as well as buildings and machinery, before manufacture
could begin.

When production did commence six
pairs of runners were in use, the same
number as in 1783. Cartographic evidence
shows mills in the same positions as 1783;
what the maps do not convey is whether
the mills were the same structures and if
the same machinery remained in place. It is
uncertain whether the presses introduced
at this date were a technological innovation
introduced by the Board of Ordnance, or
were replacing earlier machines, perhaps
invisible to us if the process, as at
Faversham, was carried out in the corning
house.[36] Contemporary demands for
equipment show that most of the small
equipment was replaced, in many cases to
a Faversham pattern.[37] From the resumption of manufacture in 1789 Faversham
and Waltham Abbey may be seen to be
working in tandem, employing identical
manufacturing processes, and with much
of the skilled labour and know-how initially provided by the mother factory at
Faversham.

The layout of the Waltham Abbey works
remained unaltered throughout the 1790s.
Frequent accidental explosions during the
decade necessitated rebuilding of the affected
mills but had no effect on the ground plan
of the factory, nor probably on the sub-sur-
face archaeology. One addition at the end of
the decade was a new gloom stove at the
northern end of what was to become
Horsemill Island (Fig 2.18). The transient
existence of some powder buildings is

illustrated by a new horse-powered corning and glazing house constructed to the south of this gloom stove. It, too, was erected sometime during the late 1790s, but it was destroyed by an explosion in 1801 with the loss of nine men and four horses and it was not rebuilt.[38]

France declared war on Britain in 1793 and the advent of Napoleon brought Britain to the verge of defeat, but the tide turned from 1797, with Nelson in command of the fleet. As a lull in hostilities with France developed in 1801, and peace was offered, it appears that production at Waltham Abbey was reduced as men were discharged or transferred to Faversham,[39] though with no discernible effect on the factory layout.

Cylinder powder and the charcoal houses at Fisherstreet and Fernhurst in Sussex

Despite the many improvements made since the early 1780s, a letter dated June 1795 from HMS *Triumph* moored at Plymouth still complained about the quality of British powder, describing it as 'notoriously unequal to that employed by the French'.[40] This was soon to change with the introduction of 'cylinder powder' in the royal factories during the 1790s.

In 1785 Congreve initiated, and took a close personal interest in, a series of experiments at Faversham into the uses of different types of wood and methods of charring for preparing charcoal.[41] In the following year he entered into correspondence with Dr Watson, Bishop of Llandaff and a noted chemist, about the ways in which the strength of gunpowder might be increased. Watson suggested that charcoal, the most variable of all the ingredients, should be made in sealed iron retorts or cylinders after a method earlier proposed by George Fordyce. Congreve's experiments with such cylinder powder at Hythe in 1787 demonstrated a marked improvement in performance of the gunpowder.[42] Despite these clear advantages, it was not until April 1794 that the first consignment of charcoal produced by this method arrived at Waltham Abbey.

To supply the proven need, a government cylinder works was established at Fisherstreet in West Sussex in May 1795,

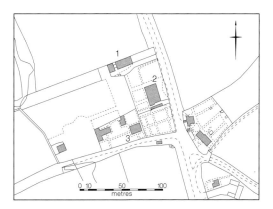

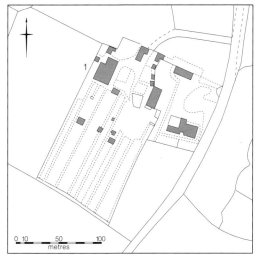

followed by a second works 3fl miles (6km) to the south-west at Fernhurst in August 1796 (Fig 2.19).[43] The presence of the charcoal retorts is betrayed by the local placename 'Cylinders' at both sites. Both works were apparently administered by Waltham Abbey RGPF. They were located in Sussex to take advantage of the ready supply of coppice woodland previously managed to serve the iron industry. Each establishment occupied a rectangular roadside enclosure of around 2 acres (0.8ha) in extent, with large open areas to stack wood before firing. A deed of 1880, probably citing an earlier document, described the Fernhurst works as comprising two cylinder houses, cooking house, charcoal store, stable, coal yard, mortar shed, building for reducing the wood acid, tankhouse, and other buildings.[44] At Fernhurst (Fig 2.20) the retort or cylinder house still survives as a row of cottages. It is a substantial brick building 42ft (12.8m) square with walls two-and-a-half bricks thick; annexed to this was a second building measuring 33ft (10m) × 21ft (6.4m).

Figure 2.19 Plans of the charcoal factories at Fisherstreet (above) and Fernhurst (below) in the Sussex Weald. OS, Sussex, Sheet XI.7, 25-inch, first edition, 1875, OS, Sussex, Sheet X.16, 25-inch, first edition, 1874. Fisherstreet: 1 Fisher Hill Cottage; 2 Fisher Hill House; 3 Cylinders Cottages (retort house). Fernhurst: 1 Former retort house. Note how the land is divided into narrow strips in the area of the old stackyard.

*Figure 2.20
Fernhurst, Sussex,
view of former retort
house converted to
modern cottages.
(BB96/3726)*

*Figure 2.21
Fisherstreet, Sussex.
Drawing of roof
truss in former retort
house. (© Crown
copyright. NMR)*

*Figure 2.22
Fisherstreet, Sussex.
View of former retort
house converted to
modern cottages.
(BB96/3742)*

On one of the outer walls of the square building are four bricked-up arched openings 6ft (1.8m) wide, and one 3ft wide (0.9m) wide; blocked openings are also visible on the other walls. Close by, another building has a characteristic hipped roof, but because of its extensive alteration, it is not possible to tell if this was built as a process building or cottage. Other buildings, though built on the sites of their nineteenth-century predecessors, have been so altered as to disguise their original functions.

The works at Fisherstreet (Figs 2.21 and 2.22) were described by the contemporary agricultural improver, Arthur Young.[45]

The cylinder room is 60 feet [18.3m] in length and proportionately high and wide: three sets of iron cylinders are placed in a very thick wall, or bed of brickwork, built nearly along the centre of the house; each of them contains three cylinders, each being six feet [1.83m] long and two feet [0.6m] diameter. To prevent every possibility of air being admitted, iron stops are contrived, 18in [0.46m] in length, and the size of the inner circumference of the cylinder, which are placed in the mouth, and are filled and rammed down with sand: besides which sand doors (as they call them) are made to project obliquely over the front or opening of the cylinder, and are entirely filled with sand, and stops covered with it. At the back part of the building are copper pipes projecting seven feet

[2.13m] in length, communicating at one extremity with the far end of the cylinder, and at the other extremity immersed in half-hogshead barrels. These pipes serve to draw off the steam or liquid, which flows in large quantities into the tar barrels during the process of charring.

At Fisherstreet the obvious retort house is Cylinders Cottages; it is rectangular in plan, 44ft 6in × 31ft 6in (13.6m × 9.6m), and has similar blocked openings to the building at Fernhurst. It has a double hipped, king-post roof with incised numeric assembly marks; the roof timbers are blackened by the retorts and there are traces of a former ventilation dormer. The dimensions given by Young more closely correspond with the length of Fisher Hill House, however.

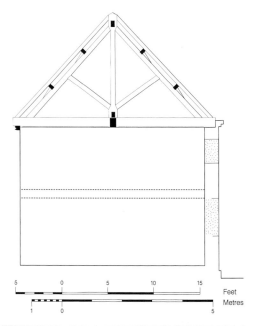

This outwardly appears to be a large Georgian-style house, but it, too, has a hipped roof and may originally have been arranged like the later cylinder house at Waltham Abbey (Fig 2.54). The use of hipped roofs might imply some standardisation of building types, but the retort houses' brickwork is in a Flemish bond with decorative grey headers characteristic of the local vernacular architecture.

In addition to production of 79 tons (80.58 tonnes) of charcoal annually by each cylinder works, the destructive distillation of wood also created by-products including wood spirit (mainly methyl alcohol), pyroligneous acid (crude acetic acid), and wood tar and pitch. These were collected and used, but at this date were potentially a commercial embarrassment.[46]

Though some charcoal was supplied from the Sussex works, the Home Works at Faversham was also equipped with its own cylinder house, perhaps as early as 1790. Contemporary sketches (Fig 2.23) of the Faversham cylinders show an arrangement similar to that described by Young in Sussex. At Faversham the wood acid was disposed of by evaporation; the tar was stored in a cylinder. A typical day in the operation of these cylinders was described on a contemporary diagram. 'The wood is cut to about seven inches long before introduced to the cylinders, the cylinder is then loaded, and fire lighted at 6 o'clock in the morning, kept until 2pm, when it is allowed to decrease gradually until 5 o'clock in the evening at 5 o'clock the following morning the charcoal is taken out and put into sheet iron receivers to cool.'[47]

The introduction of cylinder charcoal was recognised by contemporaries as the single most important factor contributing to the excellence of English powder.[48] The new cylinder powder had a strength expressed as a ratio five to three compared to traditional pit powders. By 1796 it was found that charges in most ordnance pieces could be reduced by one third, bringing tactical, logistical, and financial benefits to the British forces. Ever conscious of the wisdom of emphasising the financial savings which these new technologies could bring, Congreve stated in 1803 that the adoption of cylinder charcoal represented a saving of

£100,000 per year to the government.[49] Further experiments also confirmed that it produced the strongest and the most durable powder. After its introduction a clear distinction was made between 'cylinder powder' and 'pit powder' and their barrels were marked accordingly. It was also found that old powders or 'prize' powder removed from the holds of enemy ships could be strengthened by mixing them with equal quantities of new cylinder powders.[50] Some pit powder continued to be used for fuzes and pyrotechnic compositions where a

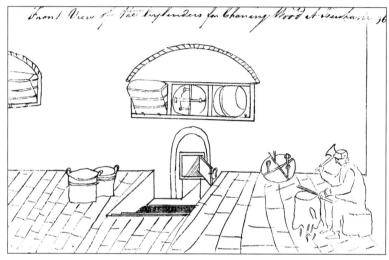

Figure 2.23 RGPF Faversham 1798, sketches of charcoal cylinders in the retort house. Hodgetts 1909, figs 6 and 7. The upper view (a) shows the front of the range of cylinders with the furnace door at the bottom and the three openings for the cylinders above. The right-hand one is open, the central one is sealed by a metal plate and in the left-hand one the 'sand door' is in place. The lower view (b) shows the 'horns' projecting from the rear of the cylinders; copper pipes joined these to the receiving barrels. ((a) BB97/3434, (b) BB97/3435)

slower burning rate was required. Private works if they wished to retain their government contracts probably had quickly to adopt cylinder-burnt charcoal. Documented examples include the Ballincollig mills near Cork, which had a cylinder house by 1804, and the Chilworth mills, which had one by 1813 (see below, RGPF Ballincollig).

Waltham Abbey RGPF continued to rely on the Sussex works or Faversham for its cylinder charcoal until 1830. A detailed drawing by Frederick Drayson in 1830 of the proposed or newly built cylinder house at Waltham, clearly illustrates a system unaltered from the 1790s (Fig 2.54). In the developed form of this process adopted at Waltham Abbey, however, the by-products were directed into the furnace beneath the retorts to reduce fuel consumption.

Proof

Though government powders had been subject to proof since the seventeenth century, increased scientific understanding of the nature of gunpowder and ballistics was achieved through the pioneering experiments in Britain of Benjamin Robins (1707–51), and later by Benjamin Thompson (Count Rumford).[51] Soon after becoming Deputy Comptroller of the Royal Laboratory in April 1783, Congreve was advised by the Master General of the Ordnance, Viscount Townsend, 'that the first object in any trial is to establish a standard to try by'.[52] His initial concern was to determine 'a proper mode of proof', which he documented in a series of pamphlets from 1783.[53] In these experiments he used the vertical *éprouvette* or 'powder trier' (Fig 2.24), the most common method of proof during the eighteenth century, though the accuracy of its results was questionable. Through his work he determined that a surer procedure was the method preferred by the French using a mortar and shot.

The government magazines along the Thames had long been associated with the proof of powder before it was accepted into military service (see Fig 1.9). In the construction of the Purfleet magazines in the early 1760s a purpose built proof house was provided. It is a cubical building of 30ft (9.14m) side (Fig 2.25), seemingly of two storeys, but in fact internally a single space open to the roof, probably with a gallery. It was alternatively called the flashing house, since powder was flashed on copper plates with a hot iron. In 1785–6 a new mortar proof house was built south of the

Figure 2.24 Equipment used in the proof of gunpowder, from Drayson 1830. Above is a vertical éprouvette or 'powder trier'. In this device a measured amount of powder was placed in a tray and on firing it raised a small weight in a vertical column to a given height depending on the strength of the powder. Below is a gun éprouvette, which was designed to measure the recoil of a gun produced by given weight of powder. It was devised by Charles Hutton, professor of mathematics at the Royal Arsenal Woolwich. (BB92/26521; © PRO, MP 11/15)

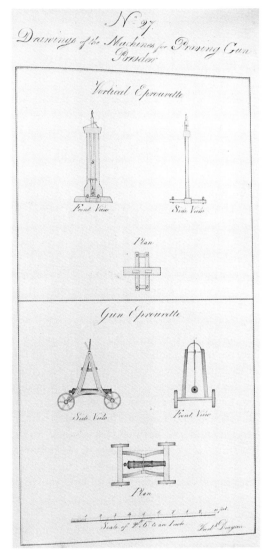

Figure 2.25 Purfleet, Essex. Proof or 'Flashing' House, c 1760. (BB94/8149)

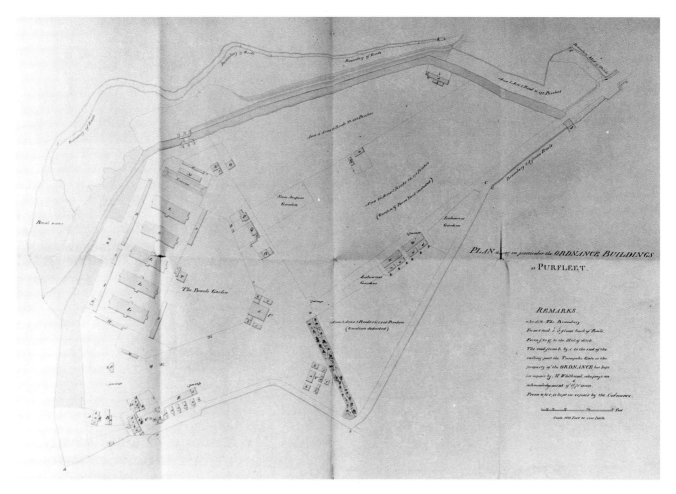

Figure 2.26 Purfleet, Essex. Plan of Ordnance complex, including Magazines (L), Flashing House (T). (BB96/7909; © PRO WO55/2425)

magazines, and in 1796 a carbine proof house was added for testing fine-grain powders (Figs 2.26 and 2.27). A new flashing house was also added at this time.[54] These later developments in the proof facilities may be directly connected to Congreve's improvements in the methods of proof, linked also to the adoption of large-, small-, and fine-grain powders by the Board of Ordnance.

Congreve's recognition of the importance of testing powder was reflected in the wider provision of proof facilities. Though one building was used for proving powder at Faversham in the early 1780s, the earliest formalised range at a powder works was laid out at the Marsh Works in the latter half of 1789 (Fig 2.4). This mortar range consisted of a simple cleared strip down which a shot could be projected with a measured charge of powder. It was not until the first decade of the nineteenth century during the factory's refurbishment that the proof house itself was constructed (Fig 2.28). It is a

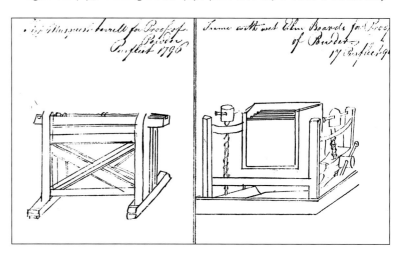

Figure 2.27 Apparatus used in the proof of powder at Purfleet in 1796. Hodgetts 1909, fig 18. In this method of proof, a carbine or musket barrel was mounted in a frame placed 39ft 10in (12.14m) away from a frame holding seventeen wet elm boards. The boards were each ½in thick (12.5mm) and placed ¾in (19mm) apart. To pass proof, a steel ball had to pass through fifteen or sixteen of the boards. (BB97/3436)

small square building with a pyramidal roof surmounted by a lantern, partly to let in light but also perhaps to disperse the sulphurous fumes of the powder. Adjacent to the Marsh Works proof house at the head of the range stood the proof mortar (Fig 2.29). At Waltham Abbey a demand in 1788 for utensils for proofing included provision of copper plates for flashing powder, copper measuring thimbles, firing irons, and other more general utensils.[55] Though there are accounts of proof by mortar and carbine as early as 1789, the first dedicated proof houses were not built until after 1804.[56]

The date at which proof facilities appeared in the trade factories is less certain. In many instances, ranges are difficult to detect where they consisted simply of a cleared strip. The range at the mid-nineteenth-century works at Cherry Brook in Devon is marked by the proving mortar which remains in place, while at the Oare Works (Fig 4.3) a terraced range lined with Wellingtonia trees was laid out in the second half of the nineteenth century.[57]

Expansion of state involvement in gunpowder supply in the early nineteenth century

The Peace of Amiens concluded between Britain and France in March 1802 secured peace for just over a year. The resumption of hostilities in the following May (which would only end at Waterloo in 1815) brought with it a heightened threat of French invasion. So great was the perceived risk that the Board of Ordnance embarked on a costly scheme of coastal defence, including the string of Martello towers and other defence schemes around the south coast.[58] It also provoked a new phase in the Board's involvement in the supply of gunpowder (see Fig 2.30). As already discussed, by the 1790s improvements in the manufacturing process chiefly involving purity of ingredients had been achieved; the problem now was to increase the output from the royal mills. By expanding the amount of powder directly manufactured, the Board gained advantages in an assurance of quality and quantity of supply.

Figure 2.28 RGPF Faversham, Marsh Works. Early nineteenth-century proof house. (BB94/13801)

Figure 2.29 RGPF Faversham, Marsh Works. Early nineteenth-century standard military pattern mortar bed, probably for an eight-inch mortar used in the proof of powder. In this test, the mortar was charged with two ounces of powder and loaded with a shot weighing sixty-six pounds twelve ounces. The strength of the powder was determined by how far the shot travelled down the range. (BB94/13800)

This could in turn be used as a check on the trade for the quality of powder they supplied and the price they charged.

Waltham Abbey

At Waltham Abbey RGPF, where the field remains are best preserved, it is possible to recognise the effects of this expansion programme in a standardisation of building types between the factories. The structures represent deployment of identical technologies and working practices within the state factories.

The potential for expansion of the factory at Waltham Abbey was severely constrained by the available head of water and by the rights of the adjacent Cheshunt and Waltham Abbey corn mills to take water from the river Lea. These were purchased in 1805 and 1809 respectively, thereby freeing that potential.[59] To address the immediate problem, however, the construction of nine horse-powered incorporating mills on a narrow island on the western side of the factory, Horsemill Island, was authorised in autumn 1804 (Figs 2.31 and 2.32).[60] Horse mills had other advantages than independence from water supply: they were quicker and cheaper to build, they dispensed with the need for the excavation of water channels, and each mill required less gearing than a comparable water mill. In construction, the mills were 31ft (9.45m) square, set on earth-filled brick foundations, and their superstructures were timber-framed and boarded in wood with gabled ends.[61] They were reported to be equipped with iron beds and runners.[62]

The Board was able to increase the number of water-powered mills to some extent by taking advantage of the fall in the water level below the Tumbling Bay (Fig 2.31). To the north and above the Tumbling Bay a new canal and head race were dug to supply and power the new group of mills. This became known as the Lower Island Works. They consisted of a press house, corning and reeling house, the buildings separated by oval brick traverses, and at the northern end two powder mills; all were water-driven. Further proposals to increase the capacity of the factory by cutting a channel between Cheshunt Mill to the west

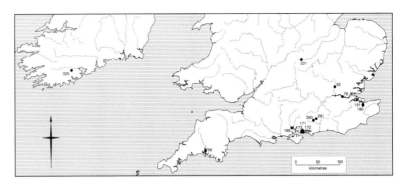

Figure 2.30 Location map for the Board of Ordnance establishments mentioned in the text.

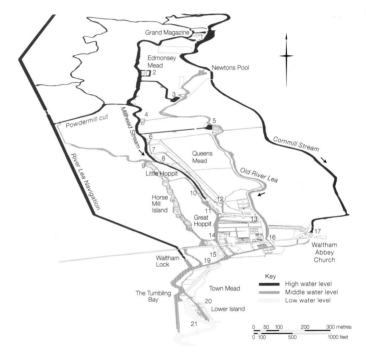

Figure 2.31 RGPF Waltham Abbey, 1827. Principal buildings (redrawn from PRO MPHH/271): 1 Grand magazine; 2 Steam drying stove (Figs 2.34 and 2.35); 3 Site of horse corning house (Fig 2.33); 4 Press house and corning house (Fig 2.54); 5 Site of horse corning house (Fig 3.27); 6 Press house and corning house; 7 Glazing mill; 8 Gloom stove; 9 Gloom stove (Fig 2.18); 10 Incorporating mills; 11 Saltpetre, charcoal and sulphur mills, mixing house (Fig 2.16); 12 Deputy storekeeper's house (Fig 2.49); 13 Engineers yard; 14 Saltpetre refinery (Fig 2.37); 15 Old refinery; 16 Storekeepers house; 17 Corn mill; 18 Stores; 19 Sulphur refinery (Fig 2.38); 20 Incorporating mills; 21 Press, corning and reel house (Fig 2.51).

and Mill Head Stream, and by erecting additional mills south of Lower Island, were never carried out.[63]

In the main (northern) part of the site there was a determined campaign of building between 1803 and 1806. New process

POWDER MILLS, WALTHAM ABBEY.

Published by J. Stratford 112 Holborn Hill, March 26th 1808.

Drawn and Engraved by Ellis.

For Dr Hughsons Description of London.

Figure 2.32 RGPF Waltham Abbey, 1808, View from the west. ERO Mint Binder. The nine horse mills are visible; to the left is the gloom stove at the northern end of Horsemill Island (Fig 2.18) and to the right a stable block later used a sulphur store.

Figure 2.33 RGPF Waltham Abbey. Early nineteenth-century corning house traverse. To the left stood the corning house and to the right the press house, both light timber structures not surviving. The barge sits in the former canal basin. (BB92/26157)

buildings included two horse-powered corning houses constructed on the eastern side of the factory (3 and 5 in Fig 2.31; Fig 2.33). These comprised a central oval, earth-filled brick traverse, 49ft 2in × 14ft 7in and 19ft 7in tall (15m × 4.45m and 6m tall), with timber-framed buildings set on brick foundations to either side. To the south of the traverse was a hand-operated press, in the larger rectangular building to the north was the corning frame and perhaps also a glazing reel. They were linked to Millhead Stream by two new canal cuts with a turning basin in front of the building. These canals represented the beginning of an elaborated factory canal system taken off the artificial channel of Millhead Stream (Fig 2.31). Since the latter was raised above the surrounding flood plain to give a 6ft (1.83m) head of water at its southern end, such new canals were a considerable undertaking in embankments alone. Surviving sections of the canal to the southern corning house have vertical sides revetted in wood. Later canals had battered sides to

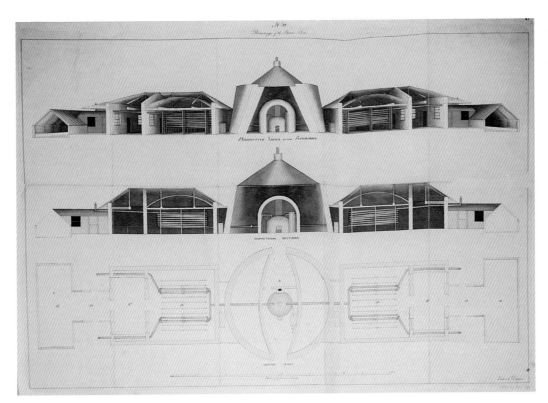

Figure 2.34 RGPF Waltham Abbey. Early nineteenth-century steam drying stove. Drawing by Frederick Drayson 1830. (BB92/26541; © PRO, MP 11/15)

dispense with the need for a continuous revetment, and a timber walkway was laid along their sides to allow the factory barges to be hauled between the buildings (see Chapter 5).

Further north a steam drying stove was erected against Millhead Stream (2 in Fig 2.31; Figs 2.34 and 2.35). It comprised a central boiler encased in an elliptical brick traverse and in turn enclosed in a circular brick traverse, 40ft (12.2m) in diameter. To either side were rectangular brick drying rooms, 40ft (12.2m) by 29ft (8.8m), with hipped slated roofs. Each room was given a domed curved ceiling perhaps to prevent build-up of powder dust and to aid circulation of warm air. From the boiler room a steam pipe passed to each of the drying rooms onto a labyrinth of pipes between the drying shelves for the powder. On the outside of the drying rooms were rooms for 'unheading' and 'heading', where the powder barrels were opened and sealed, and covered barge porches. The whole complex was surrounded by a canal connected to Millhead. As noted above, though steam stoves were in use from the 1770s, the stoves erected during this period represent their first deployment in the state factories.

Provision of a 'Grand Magazine' for the factory (1 in Fig 2.31) was perhaps a reflection of the increasing amounts of powder which needed to be stored on site before it could be moved down the river Lea to the government magazines at Purfleet. The surviving brick-vaulted structure is the third magazine to sit on this site and was probably constructed around 1867. The first 'Grand Magazine' constructed in the early

Figure 2.35 RGPF Waltham Abbey. Foundations of the steam drying stove temporarily uncovered during 1994. (BB94/7997)

Figure 2.36 Purfleet, Essex. Powder magazines 1973. Magazine number 5 in the foreground is the sole survivor of this group of magazines. (BB73/6403)

nineteenth century was rectangular in plan, measuring 68ft (20.7m) × 35ft (10.7m), and was described as boarded with brick foundations. It was replaced within 20 years by a T-shaped magazine, 80ft (24.4m) × 20ft (6.1m). This was a single-storey brick-built structure, with a slated hipped roof and single doorways on its long sides. Internally it was divided into eight storage bays served by a central passageway and was lit by windows at either end.[64] The function of any magazine is not primarily to contain an accidental explosion within it, but rather to protect its contents from any external threat, mainly the weather but also from bombardment or an accidental explosion in the vicinity. Board of Ordnance magazines, often sited close to naval installations, were commonly designed to withstand bombardment, as evidenced in the massive constructions at Purfleet (Fig 2.36). Where there was little threat from attack, Ordnance practice in the early nineteenth century favoured slighter structures in brick and wood with slated roofs, of which the near-contemporary magazines at Marchwood are examples.[65] The remoteness of the 'Grand Magazine' at Waltham Abbey, both from the threat of attack and from the remainder of the factory, allowed the Board to opt for this cheaper form. To obviate the need for fully laden powder barges to travel the full length of the factory

from the newly built 'Grand Magazine' at its northern end to the river system southwards, a new channel called Powdermill Cut was made between Millhead Stream and the Lea Navigation.

In addition to the 'Grand Magazine', small expense or charge magazines, measuring 10ft (3m) × 15ft (4.6m), were scattered around the site to store powder between processes. In contrast to the 'Grand Magazine' these were entirely brick built, with a brick-vaulted roof covered in slate. The magazines had a single door in their end walls and buttresses to prevent the vault spreading. Internally many had suspended wooden floors and match-lined wooden walls. The floors in at least their porches were lined in spark-proof leather hides fixed with copper nails, and other fittings such as door hinges and locks were made of bronze.

The expanded factory was provided with an engineers' yard off Powdermill Lane, which had developed as its principal landward entrance. This service area developed around a rectangular central courtyard with long single-storey sheds to the north and south with king-post truss roofs identical in form to other Board buildings, and offices along Powdermill Lane. The buildings originally housed carpenters' and millwrights' stores and shops, a plumbers' shop, and bricklayers' store, and in the yard a covered saw pit. On Powdermill Lane an

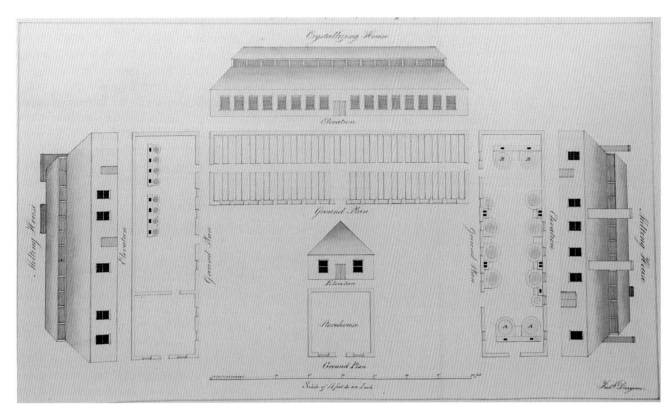

Crystallizing House

Elevation

Malting House

Elevation

Ground Plan

Ground Plan

Ground Plan

Elevation

Malting House

Elevation

Storehouse

Ground Plan

Scale of 18 feet to an Inch

Figure 2.37 RGPF Waltham Abbey. Layout of the early nineteenth-century saltpetre refinery. Drawing by Frederick Drayson 1830. (BB92/26542; © PRO, MP 11/15)

impressive two-storey building with an attic and basement was added, originally comprising four bays with single-storey bays to either side. It was divided between offices for the Engineer's Department and apartments for the Clerk of Works. Additional stores were constructed along High Bridge Street and also, since barrels were vital for the safe transport and storage of powder, a cooperage.

Congreve's continuing concern about purity of ingredients was reflected during this building campaign by increases in the capacity of the refineries. The saltpetre refinery inherited from the private factory apparently remained unaltered in the first decade of government occupation. Now the old refinery was demolished and a new saltpetre refinery was built against Highbridge Street, the main east–west road across the valley linking Waltham Cross to Waltham Abbey. The rebuilt refinery comprised seven buildings: saltpetre refineries, melting houses, and a crystallising house. It was itself soon superseded by a new saltpetre refinery (Fig 2.37) to the north-east. The buildings were similar in form to those installed at the Marsh Works in Faversham, namely large rectangular buildings open to the roof with extensive open floor areas for the refining process. The importance of ventilation either to disperse the heat from the furnaces or to aid crystallisation was reflected in large wooden clerestory vents and window openings with wooden louvres. Its predecessor on Highbridge Street appears to have been converted to the recovery of saltpetre from unserviceable powder.

Probably at the same time that the new refinery was constructed, a sulphur subliming kiln was built at the northern end of the Lower Island Works. It is difficult to assess how technologically advanced the royal factories were in their adoption of sulphur domes; though they were in use on the Continent in the late eighteenth century, no other examples are known from archaeological evidence in England. Only the foundations of this unusual building survive, but contemporary accounts enable this technically advanced process to be understood (Fig 2.38). The best quality sulphur or brimstone for use in the government mills was called 'Licara firsts' and was imported from Sicily. As purchased, the 'grough sulphur' contained around 3–4% of earthy impurities. The simplest method of removing them was to heat the 'grough sulphur' and skim the impurities off the top. This technique remained in use until the more sophisticated method using a subliming furnace or kiln was introduced.[66]

The large size of the government refineries and cylinder works with capacities above the needs of the royal mills reflects another

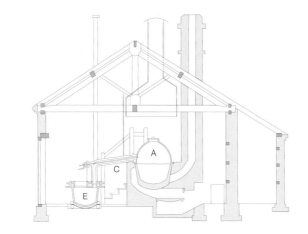

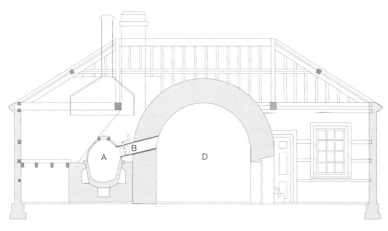

Figure 2.38 RGPF Waltham Abbey. Sections through the sulphur refinery; (A) iron pot or retort, (B) outlet to subliming dome, (C) outlet to casting pot, (D) subliming dome, (E) casting pot. After Smith 1870. To purify the sulphur, around six hundredweight of once refined sulphur was placed in the iron pot or retort (A) and heated. Connected to this pot were two outlets, one leading to the sulphur dome (B) and the other (C) to the casting pot. As the sulphur was heated a yellow vapour was given off and the outlet (B) to the subliming dome opened. Inside the dome (D) the sulphur sublimed on to the walls forming a fine pale yellow powder known as 'flowers of sulphur'. This was too acidic for use in gunpowder and was either sold or returned to the retort. After about three hours the vapour turned to an iodine colour; the outlet to the dome (B) was closed and the outlet to the casting pot (C) opened. This vapour passed through pipes jacketed by cold water to be distilled, which caused the sulphur to condense and run into the casting pot (E). After cooling it was ladled into wooden tubs to set; it was later turned out in the form of a solid cylindrical block.

innovation introduced by Congreve, whereby the trade was supplied with ready-refined ingredients.[67] By this policy Congreve was able to assure the purity of ingredients used in government powder. A further advantage in the case of saltpetre was that less needed to be supplied to the trade, since its guaranteed purity did away with the amount formerly allowed for wastage during refining.

Faversham

At Faversham there was less opportunity to expand the capacity of the works because of its proximity to the town. The Home Works appears to have remained essentially static in plan from about 1790 (Fig 2.8), though individual groups of mills were remodelled in the 1790s and a cylinder works was constructed at its eastern end.

At the Marsh Works, however, a fairly extensive building programme was perhaps designed to increase the amount of unserviceable or prize powder which could be reworked (Fig 2.39). A development sequence may be put forward for this site (Fig 2.40), although its precise dating depends on a map series with confused dating. In the first decade of the nineteenth century the saltpetre refinery at the centre of the works was enlarged by the addition of a small brick-built melting house (20 in Fig 2.40). Adjacent to it a timber-framed and -boarded crystallising house was added. Its roof truss was similar in form to those found earlier at Faversham and Waltham Abbey (Fig 2.41). In the new melting house a slight variation of this form was employed, where a strut from the tie beam between the king-post and end wall supported the principal rafter of the hip (Fig 2.42). Other additions were a store, two small boat houses, and a watch house, and away from the central buildings a long rectangular structure identified as an earth house that replaced a much smaller predecessor in the same location. This part of the complex was further expanded after 1810 by the addition of further earth houses. The fenestration of the surviving example (5 in Fig 2.40; Fig 2.43) suggests it may have been used for more than a simple store, perhaps an office or workshop, but without further documentary

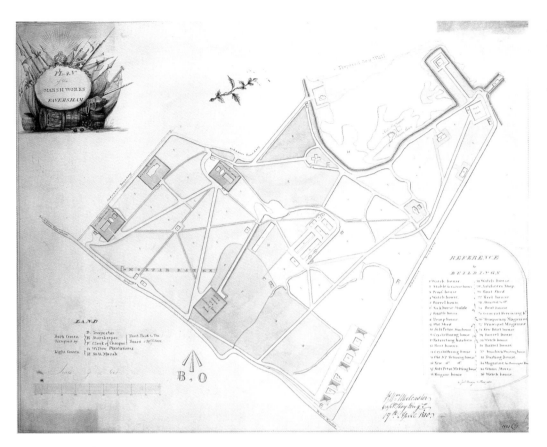

Figure 2.39 RGPF Faversham, Marsh Works, 1810. (BB95/11941; © PRO, MPH 189)

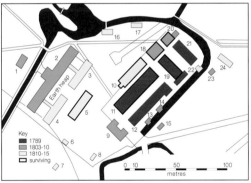

Figure 2.41 RGPF Faversham, Marsh Works. Detail of early nineteenth-century roof truss in a saltpetre crystallising house. (BB94/13809)

Figure 2.40 (above) RGPF Faversham, Marsh Works. Layout and suggested development of the saltpetre works: 1 Stable for corning house horses; 2 Earth house; 3 Earth house; 4 Earth house; 5 Earth house (Fig 2.43); 6 Earth house; 7 Pump house; 8 Earth house; 9 Saltpetre storehouse; 10 Pump house, offices, store and cottage (Fig 2.44); 11 Crystallising house (Fig 2.13, 2.14); 12 Extracting kitchen; 13 Boat house; 14 Boat house; 15 Watch house; 16 Old shed; 17 Old shed; 18 Crystallising house (Fig 2.41); 19 Refinery (Fig 2.12); 20 Melting house (Fig 2.42); 21 Melting house; 22 Unidentified; 23 Watch house; 24 Watch house.

Figure 2.42 RGPF Faversham, Marsh Works. Roof truss of early nineteenth-century saltpetre melting house. (BB94/13817)

Figure 2.43 RGPF Faversham, Marsh Works. Early nineteenth-century earth house in saltpetre works. (BB94/13810)

Figure 2.43 RGPF Faversham, Marsh Works. Early nineteenth-century earth house in saltpetre works. (BB94/13810)

Figure 2.44 RGPF Faversham, Marsh Works. Pumphouse, offices, stores and cottage, c 1810–20. (BB94/13816)

research the precise functions of these buildings are uncertain. The most likely original function was as large sheds for storing government stockpiles of saltpetre. Nevertheless, such long sheds are also known from contemporary European factories covering artificial nitre beds.[68] Though Britain had a ready supply of saltpetre through the East India Company, there may have been financial benefits to be gained from using refinery waste to activate beds of decaying vegetable matter. The map annotation, 'Earth heap', may lend some weight to this idea. This complex was completed, probably in the second decade of the century, by the addition of a range containing a

pumphouse, store, and small cottage (10 in Fig 2.40; Fig 2.44).

Probably also after 1803, the corning houses at the Marsh Works were rebuilt on a similar model to those at Waltham Abbey (see Fig 2.33). Each structure comprised a central oval traverse with rectangular danger buildings to either side. If the arrangement at Waltham Abbey was followed, on one side, in the smaller building, would have been a press and on the other the corning machine. The original north-western corning house was left in unreconstructed form and was later described as a reel house, suggesting it was used as a glazing house. A third corning house on the new pattern was added after 1810 on the rectangular site shown vacant on the plan of that date (Fig 2.39). That plan also shows the position in the creek for a proposed steam stove of the design adopted at Waltham Abbey. This proposal came to nothing, however, and the Marsh Works apparently retained gloom stoves until the end of government control in the 1830s. It was also during this period that the proof house described earlier was built (Fig 2.28).

RGPF Ballincollig

To increase the capacity of the royal mills still further, steps were taken in 1804 to purchase a relatively newly established powder works at Ballincollig, 5 miles (8km) to the west of Cork (Fig 2.45). As at Faversham and Waltham Abbey, the precise reasons why the Board chose these in preference to other mills are unclear. It was, indeed, a fairly up-to-date factory laid out in 1794 by Charles Henry Leslie and John Travers; it covered 332 acres (133.6ha) and stretched for over 1fi miles (2.5km) along the river Lea, which provided power for the mills and ready access to Cork harbour, with its British naval base.[69]

As a supplier to the government, the plant and processes within the works probably closely matched those of the royal factories. As a result of their relative isolation the works were self-sufficient in the refining of ingredients, possessing when purchased a sulphur refinery, saltpetre refinery, and – remarkably at this date – a cylinder house. The only immediate improvement in the refineries made by the Board of Ordnance was to construct an additional cylinder house.

Management of the new works was placed in the hands of a long-standing employee of the Board, Charles Wilks. He began his career at Chatham in 1780, and had served as Clerk of Works at Faversham and Waltham Abbey before he was promoted to Superintendent at Ballincollig. On acquisition the Board immediately began a building campaign aimed at increasing the capacity of the works and providing standardised facilities comparable with the other two state factories. Work probably began soon after 1804 and passed through at least one plan of intended works before a decision was taken on their final form.[70] By 1806 many of the new facilities were in use. A new canal was dug in a series of loops extending the whole

Figure 2.45 RGPF Ballincollig, 1825. (BB95/11935; © PRO, MPH 311)

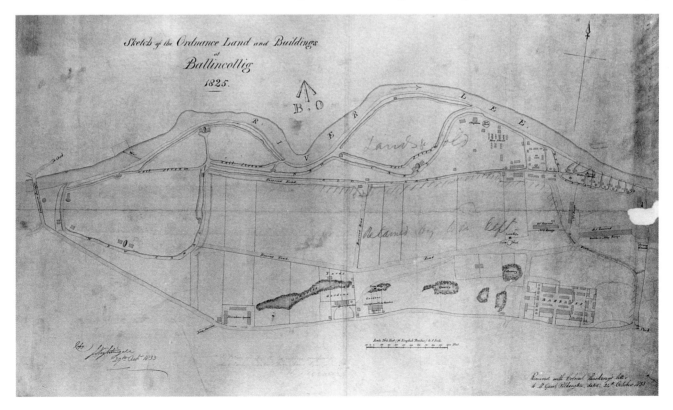

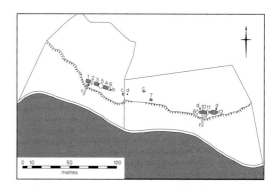

*Figure 2.46
Plymouth Royal
Powder Works, St
Budeaux, 1811
(redrawn from PRO,
MPH 677 H/12).
No scale on original;
contemporary desig-
nations of buildings
from PRO
WO55/2331:
1 Receiving house;
2 Traverse; 3 Stoves
for drying powder by
steam; 4 Stoves for
drying powder by
steam; 5 Circular
traverse enclosing
boiler; 6 Traverse;
7 Guard house;
8 Traverse; 9 Dusting
house; 10 Cooperage
near dusting house;
11 Traverse;
12 Mixing houses;
a Sheds for work-
men; b Engine
house; c Cooperage;
d Shed for covering
proof mortar;
e Office; f Jetties.*

*Figure 2.47
Portsmouth Royal
Powder Works on
Stampshaw Point
near the Tipnor
Point magazine,
1811 (after PRO
MPHH 590):
1 Dusting house;
2 Traverse; 3 Dusting
house; 4 Traverse;
5 ?Guard house;
6 Proof house and
house for mortar;
7 Mixing house;
8 Mixing house.*

length of the site, both to supply the head water for four new pairs of incorporating mills at the eastern end of the site and to link the new process buildings.[71] Following Board of Ordnance practice in other areas, standard building types already in existence were utilised for new process buildings. Central oval traverses separated new dusting and press houses at the west end of the site. The corning houses were simple rectangular buildings without traverses, similar to those used in the first phase at the Marsh Works. The existing gloom stove was augmented by a steam stove of standard form, with a central circular brick boiler house and drying rooms to either side. Innovations in the manufacturing process included a glazing house and proof house. The standardisation was reinforced by importation of framed and prepared carpentry and of machinery from England. The factory retained a character of its own, however, with the widespread use of local stone in contrast to the red brick of southern England. It was also unique in having small, circular, stone charge magazines, 21ft 4in (6.5m) in diameter and 12ft 6in (3.8m) tall with an entrance porch and conical slated roof.

The royal powder works at Portsmouth and Plymouth

In addition to the building campaigns carried out at Faversham, Waltham Abbey, and Ballincollig in 1804, the state's capacity to supply the fleet with powder and munitions was further enhanced by creation of outposts of the Royal Laboratory at Portsmouth in Hampshire and Plymouth in Devon. The prompting to establish these new laboratories lay in concern about the threat from attacks by French incendiaries on the Royal Arsenal Woolwich, and also in operational efficiencies which could be made through having the laboratories close to the major dockyards. Both establishments were relatively small: in 1810 the Portsmouth works employed 41 people and the Plymouth works employed 28. Approval for construction to begin was granted by the Board of Ordnance on 15 June 1804.[72]

The laboratories were established to assemble and pack various types of munitions including small arms cartridges and grape shot. Also attached to them were specialised powder works. The function of the latter was to 'restore' damaged powder returned to the magazines from ships' holds, through sieving, re-dusting, and drying. Additionally the powder might be restored by mixing weaker powders made from pit charcoal or prize powders with the stronger cylinder powders. This limited range of tasks was reflected in a restricted range of building types, though of a standardised pattern found in the other works.

The powder works at Plymouth were situated at St Budeaux to the north of Devonport, connected to the other naval installations by the stretch of water known as the Hamoaze. As initially laid out the works covered just over 14 acres (5.67ha) excluding the adjacent mud flats (Fig 2.46). They consisted of two well-spaced groups of buildings, the drying stoves to the west and the corning and mixing house to the east; each group was served by its own barge jetty. The form of the gunpowder drying stoves was identical to contemporary stoves constructed in the other royal factories (eg Figs 2.34 and 2.35),

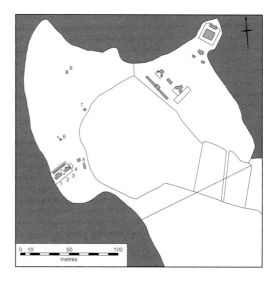

differing only in the extra oval traverses at either end. The other group of buildings comprised a corning house with oval traverse to either side and mixing house to its east.[73] The establishment was also provided with a proof mortar which was housed in a shed.

The powder works at Portsmouth, split as they were between two sites, were less efficient in layout than Plymouth. The dusting houses, mixing houses, and a proof range were sited at Stampshaw Point (Fig 2.47), on the opposite side of a peninsula to the 'Grand Magazine' at Tipnor Point. The re-stoving powder works were situated a barge journey away on Little Horsea Island opposite Portchester Castle. They comprised a stove house of standard form, shifting house, guard house, cooperage, store, shoe house, and a heading and unheading house. The method of working was for the powder for restoring to be deposited at the Tipnor magazine; it was taken to Stampshaw Point, where it was unheaded, sieved, and dusted, and from there it was transported by barge to the stove houses on Little Horsea Island. It was then either returned to the Tipnor magazine or taken back to Stampshaw Point for mixing before it was returned to the magazine.[74]

Safety

Before the government's direct involvement in powder manufacture accidental explosions were regarded as one of the hazards of the trade about which little could be done. Government ownership brought not only men with some scientific training, with a belief that a scientific understanding of the causes of accidental explosions could be determined, but also a bureaucracy to draw up and enforce regulations.

Even before the government became directly involved in manufacture of gunpowder it is possible to recognise features which would later be regarded as good safety practice, but it is uncertain whether they were deliberately conceived or were present for other reasons. For example, the majority of the powder mills were sited in wooded valleys; woodland was later recognised as an effective flexible blast screen, but had originally been planted at many mills as a source of charcoal. At Chilworth in 1728 there

were blocks of woodland between the mill buildings along the newer, valley-side leat (Fig 1.16). Later evidence from the Oare Works at Faversham suggests some intentional and careful tree planting, with remnants of yew hedges close to danger buildings and Wellingtonias used to line the test range. Poplar trees were also recommended as a good screen. Most mill buildings were relatively flimsy wooden structures, but so were many other water mills in south-eastern England. It is also difficult to recognise when the use of traverses as protective screens around buildings first became prevalent. At Chilworth a tree-planted earthen mound is shown around a stove in 1728 (Fig 1.16). At Faversham and Waltham Abbey cartographic evidence suggests traverses were not introduced until the late 1780s. At Faversham the stoves were separated from one another by earthwork traverses, while at Waltham Abbey brick traverses filled with earth were deployed from the 1790s (Fig 2.18). The distinctive type of oval brick traverse with an earth core (Fig 2.33) found on all the royal powder works sites was a feature associated with the 1804 expansion campaign. Also at this date the use of a protective circular brick traverse around boiler houses was introduced (Figs 2.34 and 2.35).

Another trend during this period was the multiplication of buildings, as processes which had formerly been carried out under one roof were allocated to separate buildings. The necessity of providing an independent power supply and a safe distance between the buildings caused the areas occupied by factories to expand while the density of buildings within them remained low. A feature of government control was the instigation of an investigating committee to look into the more serious explosions. Following the destruction of the press and corning house on Lower Island at Waltham Abbey in 1811 there was considerable discussion about how it should be rebuilt.[75] In the event, an additional traverse was constructed and on the recommendations of the investigating committee Bramah hydraulic presses were installed (Fig 2.51). This allowed the workers to operate the hand pumps shielded from the presses by a brick traverse. An argument against further subdivision of the process was that the men might carry grit between the buildings, and elsewhere in the factory old-fashioned screw presses survived until the 1840s. It was indeed after the explosion which destroyed the last of these presses that Michael Faraday, an eminent member of the Royal Society, was asked to comment on the likely sources of danger within the manufacturing process.[76] It was another 30 years, however, before an official inspectorate was established to investigate the causes of accidental explosions and disseminate their findings for the benefits of the industry.

Many of the measures introduced to improve safety practices at the royal works are not evident in the archaeological record. In the demand made in 1788 for material are lists of clothing, which included leather aprons, canvas frocks and magazine shoes, and painted floor cloths. In specifying other items of equipment the lists are careful to list the non-ferrous materials from which they were to be made – brass, copper, leather, and wood.[77] At the Faversham factory the formulation and regulation of working practices began in October 1785 with the issue of a set of factory rules.[78] These were the forerunners of individual factory rule books, which supplemented the controlling legislation in the safe management of the industry.

Transport

Water was one of the prime locating factors for powder mills as a source of power. In the early post-medieval period water was also the only effective means of bulk transport in England, and remained the prime method of transport for powder and its bulky raw materials even after the improvement of the roads in the eighteenth century. This was partly through inertia, as the powder mills were all located on waterways, but it also brought advantages of safety and convenience as all the large magazines and naval installations were either coastal or located on inland waterways. The trade in raw materials was conducted through the major ports, where they were either transhipped directly into smaller river-going barges or stored in dockside warehouses.

Water was also the principal method of moving powder between the process buildings within the royal works. At Waltham Abbey in 1788 there were four punts; by 1814 this had risen to a small flotilla comprising five barges, nine powder boats, two ballast barges, and six punts.[79] Within the factory the powder barges were either punted or pulled by men or boys; horses appear to have been used only on the river sections, where greater distances were involved.

The canal network put in at the Marsh Works at Faversham at the end of the 1780s and developed thereafter (Fig 2.4 and 2.39) was notable for its elaboration and – perhaps uniquely among manufacturing sites – for not acting simultaneously as a source of power, as the works was laid out on flat marshland with no scope for engineering a fall. The canal-based arrangement of the central arms and ammunition storage depot at Weedon Bec in Northamptonshire, and at Marchwood in Hampshire, shows similar thinking by the Board of Ordnance.[80]

Larger river-going or coastal barges served all the royal powder works, delivering the raw materials to the factories and connecting them to the wider network of government establishments. The river barges were larger at around 72ft (22m) in length; from Waltham Abbey they were pulled by horses the 24km (15 miles) or so south to the Thames and moved under sail once they entered the Thames estuary.[81] Only rarely might the factories need to resort to road transport if the rivers and canals were frozen.

Housing

In comparison with many emerging industries, the royal powder mills employed comparatively few people. When production began at Waltham Abbey in 1789 the workforce was 79. This rose to around 250 at the height of wartime production in 1813, but was still far smaller than the Faversham factory, which at its peak employed nearly 400.[82]

The works at Faversham and Waltham Abbey were both close to their respective town centres, where the workmen might find accommodation. Housing was specially provided for the officials in charge of the

establishments and the senior workmen. These men might expect to have a number of postings during their careers, as in the example of Charles Wilks at Faversham, Waltham Abbey, and Ballincollig, and would occupy an official residence according to their rank.

At Faversham the Storekeeper's residence lay at the centre of the Home Works (see Fig 2.2); known as St Ann's House, it was a large Georgian building with dormer windows, which survived until the 1960s. The Clerk of Cheques lived in a detached house above the refineries at the eastern end of the works and other clerks were accommodated in three official houses in the town.[83] Besides these houses for the senior officials only three cottages were attached to the factory; two were occupied by millmen (Fig 2.48) and the third by the Storekeeper's servant.

At Waltham Abbey the only accommodation on site was the Master Worker's house, which stood adjacent to Walton's house and is now demolished, and a former public house called the Turnpike and Chequer Inn at the northern end of the factory. This was occupied by the Master Worker from Faversham named William Newton, who gave his name to the nearby pool. By the second decade of the nineteenth century a considerable number of dwellings were constructed along Highbridge Street, while others close to the abbey were acquired when the abbey mill

was purchased.[84] Several were substantial residences for the senior officers; only one residence survives, that initially built for the Clerk of Cheques (Fig 2.49). When by the 1820s the number of workers fell to just 34, there was probably enough housing attached to the factory to accommodate the entire workforce.

In contrast, Ballincollig was located in the remote Irish countryside. When those works were purchased, there was a dwelling house and two rows of buildings comprising two foremen's houses and 20 cabins for labourers attached (Fig 2.45). Soon after acquisition the government built a new range called Feversham Square. It was intended to be arranged as an enclosed courtyard to house 40 labourers; ultimately only three sides were constructed to house 30 labourers. At the eastern end of the works a new row known as the Waltham Abbey range was added to house 32 labourers. This development was 306ft 4in (93.37m) long and comprised 14 two-storey cottages, 17ft (5.18m) × 14ft (4.27m), with larger foremen's houses at either end. Larger individual three-storey houses were also provided for the senior officials along the southern boundary of the site.[85]

Retrenchment

From a peak in 1813 the amount of powder manufactured at Waltham Abbey was reduced, rising only in 1815, the year of

Figure 2.48 (left) The White House, Lower Road Faversham; late eighteenth-century millman's house. (BB94/10457)

Figure 2.49 (right) RGPF Waltham Abbey. Early nineteenth-century house built for the Clerk of Cheques. (BB92/26069)

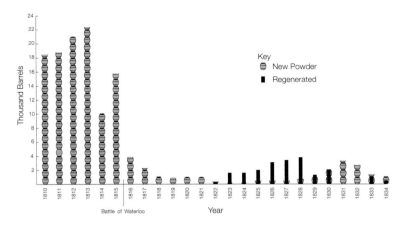

Figure 2.50 Graph to show the output of new and regenerated powder at RGPF Waltham Abbey in the period 1810–33. (Figures after Winters 1887).

Waltham Abbey (Fig 2.50). The effect on the physical layout of the factory was less marked, however, as buildings were shut up and mothballed or used less intensively. Though there were losses, these principally fell on the recent wartime additions. In 1814 the use of horses in gunpowder manufacture ceased, though they were probably retained for initial milling of ingredients. The mills on Horsemill Island were pulled down, and the two horse-powered corning mills dismantled and later sold. This probably did not represent a great fall in the capacity of the factory for two water-powered incorporating mills were added to the Lower Island Works and its pressing, corning, and dusting house was rebuilt (Fig 2.51), while on

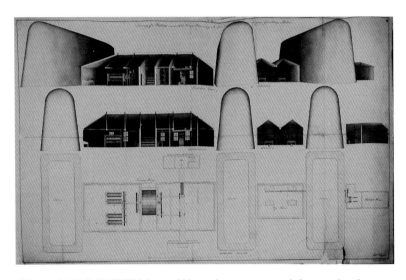

Figure 2.51 RGPF Waltham Abbey. Arrangement of the corning house using the Congreve machine installed in 1816. At the extreme right is the wash-up house and adjoining it the hand-operated pumps for the Bramah hydraulic presses, separated from it by the brick traverse. The corning house is driven by a central waterwheel with brick traverses to either side. The corning machine lies to the right of the wheel, enclosed in a wooden cabinet, with buildings to either side to house the powder hoppers. To the left of the wheel are dusting reels. (Drawing by Frederick Drayson 1830; ©PRO, MP 11/15)

Figure 2.52 Charlton, St Luke's Church, monument to William Congreve. The epitaph reads 'He had the happiness of having saved to His Country more than one Million Sterling yet died unenriched himself...' (BB96/7132)

Millhead Stream two groups of buildings were built comprising a press house and, separated from it by a traverse, a corning and dusting house powered by a central water wheel.

On 30 April 1814 William Congreve, created a baronet in 1812, died (see Fig 2.52). He was succeeded by his son, also William (1772–1828), in the title and as 'Comptroller of the Royal Laboratory'. The period of tenure of the younger Congreve (better known today for his invention of the Congreve rocket: see Chapter 8) coincided with the marked downturn in British military expenditure after Waterloo.[86] At Waltham Abbey, production remained low and throughout the 1820s there was increased emphasis on reworking old powders (Fig 2.50). Nevertheless, in the early years of office Congreve turned his inventive talent to improvements in the manufacturing process, which he patented in 1818.[87] These included a machine for mixing the ingredients of powder in their correct proportions, and a breaking-down machine for the press house. This comprised a pair of toothed rollers between which the mill cake was fed, and ensured cake was finely broken to give a uniform mass of powder between the press plates. His most enduring contribution to gunpowder technology was the granulating machine to replace the shaking frame and corning sieves (Fig 2.53; cf Fig 2.6). It was similar in principle to his breaking-down machine, using toothed rollers to granulate the powder and filter it through a series of sieves which graded the grains according to size. The machine was first installed in the corning house in the Lower Island Works in 1816. It was widely adopted throughout the industry and the American powdermaker Lammot du Pont on a later visit to the factory commented that Congreve's granulating machine was 'decidedly the best in England and Europe'.[88] In the late 1820s there was concern over the quality of powder supplied from Waltham Abbey. It may have been this problem which prompted the Board to commission from Frederick Drayson a treatise with illustrations, perhaps with a view to restructuring the factory as one of Drayson's diagrams showed a scheme to construct additional water mills.[89] The treatise

contained a detailed description of all the processes carried out in the works and was illustrated with fine colour-washed drawings of all the principal process buildings and the equipment used within them. None of the suggestions implicit in this report seems to have been acted upon.

One of the few buildings constructed during this period at Waltham Abbey was a charcoal cylinder house (Fig 2.54), the wisdom of which had been mooted by William Congreve senior some 20 years earlier. The new building was positioned in an unoccupied meander of the old river Lea on the eastern side of the factory. A new canal was

Figure 2.53 RGPF Waltham Abbey. Congreve-type granulating machine (redrawn from Smith 1870).

Figure 2.54 RGPF Waltham Abbey, Cylinder House. (BB92/26499; drawing by Frederick Drayson, 1830; © PRO, MP11/15)

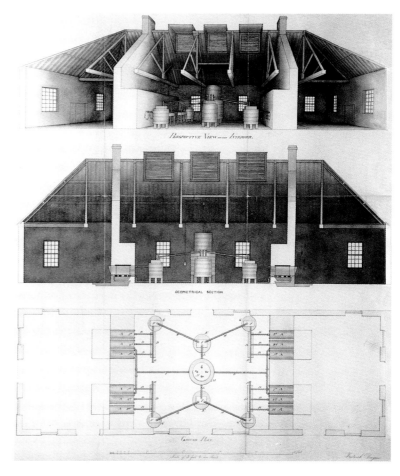

Figure 2.55 RGPF Waltham Abbey. Explosion of no 2 corning house on Thursday 13 April 1843 (from Illustrated London News *2, 22 April 1843, 275)*

dug to link it to the canal network, causing an earlier brick bridge to be replaced by a cast iron bridge dated 1832 beneath which barges could pass (Fig 3.37). Four cylinder-house men were transferred from Faversham, but it is uncertain whether the cylinders were also moved.[90] Alongside this facility a barge repair yard was established, perhaps to make use of the tarry by-products of the wood distillation.

At Faversham, the Home Works were leased to John Hall of Dartford, and then in 1825 sold to him. The Marsh Works, which were more up-to-date and ideally equipped for the current policy of reworking old powder, were retained until 1832. Then they, too, were leased to John Hall, who finally acquired the site and control of all the Faversham mills in 1854.[91] Powder production at Ballincollig ceased in 1815, though the works were retained on a care and maintenance basis. Surveys of their condition were carried out in 1822 and 1828, and in October 1832 the Board finally decided to dispose of the Ballincollig mills. They were eventually sold in 1834 to a partnership called Horsfall, Tobin and Company, which later changed its name to the Ballincollig Royal Gunpowder Mills Company.[92] The life of the Portsmouth and Plymouth powder works was probably limited to immediate

needs, while the cylinder works at Fisherstreet and Fernhurst were later adapted for use as dwellings.

By the 1830s Waltham Abbey remained the sole government gunpowder factory, but with a much reduced workforce often working a short week. Though during the 1830s there was a slight revival in production of new powder, no new building or technological innovations resulted, beyond actions necessary to reconstruct buildings and machinery after minor explosions. From around 1840 the beginnings of new investment were seen at the Royal Small Arms Factory Enfield, the Royal Arsenal Woolwich, and at Waltham Abbey, though at a low level. Many of the minor works carried out at this period are virtually undetectable and often only the chance survival of design drawings allows any insight into developments. In 1843 a serious explosion in a press and corning house, where old-fashioned corning sieves and hand-operated presses were still in use, resulted in the loss of seven lives (Fig 2.55) and the destruction of the corning and press house at a distance of about 60m (197ft).[93] Rebuilding proposals were drawn up during the following year and in 1845 a new granulating machine was built at the Royal Arsenal Woolwich at a cost of £2000. Owing to the greater efficiency of the Congreve design, the two old-fashioned corning houses were replaced by a single machine. It was probably this machine or a similar one constructed around 1856 with its cast gunmetal parts (Fig 2.53) which prompted the enthusiastic comment of the American powdermaker Lammot du Pont.[94] Though this machine was capable of granulating and sorting varying sizes of powder, it was often restricted to granulating one size as a more careful distinction came to be made between the types of charcoal used in cannon and musket powders.

Other correspondence in the 1840s refers to the erection of five incorporating mills and the installation of hydraulic pipes perhaps for replacement presses. The location of these five mills and a new iron mill called the Iron Duke, erected in 1847, is unknown and it is probable that they occupied the sites of earlier mills rather than representing an increase in capacity.[95]

The long-term future of the factory continued to remain in doubt, for in October 1845 an order was received to close the factory for three years, but it was apparently never carried out.

Conclusion

From the 1780s manufacture of gunpowder within the royal factories underwent a profound change, with the result that British gunpowder came to be regarded as a world standard. The measures that achieved this, largely enacted by the elder William Congreve by the late 1790s, were based on an empiric understanding of gunpowder manufacture, in particular his careful attention to the refining of ingredients, his introduction of cylinder powder, and new methods for the proof of powder. This stood in contrast to the more overtly scientific, academy-based study of the problems of gunpowder supply favoured by the French.[96] At the royal powder works these changes are reflected in improved production facilities; other innovations, such as the production of different grain sizes for different weapons, are difficult to detect archaeologically. Congreve was also able to show that between 1783 and 1811 the Board of Ordnance had made a direct saving of £1,045,494 10s and 6/d through supplying raw materials to the trade and direct manufacture and reworking of powder.[97]

Waltham Abbey's standing as one of the world's leading gunpowder factories was further reflected in the number of foreign manufacturers who came to inspect its facilities. Many of them left valuable accounts of the factory. One of the earliest in English was by J Braddock, who was sent to

Waltham Abbey in 1812–13 to learn the art of powdermaking before embarking to manage the Honourable East India Company's powder works at Madras.[98] In the 1820s, with their recent experience of the potency of British powder, a group of French military engineers visited England. One of the most significant consequences of their visit was the adoption of distilled wood charcoal, and cylinder houses were set up at the new model powder works at Le Bouchet near Paris and at Angoulême.[99] In the 1830s Waltham Abbey was visited by Antoine Bidermann from the du Pont powder mills near Wilmington in Delaware, a factory laid out on French principles.[100] He, too, devoted a large part of his account to the manufacture of cylinder charcoal. Any assessment of the influence of the improvements carried out at Waltham Abbey on the continental and American factories awaits comparable archaeological studies in those quarters.

By the late 1840s the layout and technology employed at Waltham Abbey was still essentially that resulting from Congreve's improvements and influence. In contrast to other European countries, little research was conducted into armaments technology in Britain during the long period of peace after Waterloo. The factories controlled by the Board of Ordnance were also beginning to lag behind the private manufacturers in all sectors in the adoption of new manufacturing practices and technology, notably in the application of steam power. Only in circumstances of urgent external pressure did Waltham Abbey again from the 1850s develop as one of the few truly industrial gunpowder manufactories in Britain, in competition and partnership with the other great powder factories of Europe.

Endnotes

1 Kennedy 1976, 98.
2 *Statutes at Large* 1756, c.16; see Bibliography, Selected legislation.
3 West 1991, 162–6.
4 Bret 1994 and 1996; see also Mauskopf 1990.
5 Royal Artillery Historical Institution

Library (RAHIL), Woolwich, Congreve 1811, 27.
6 Percival 1986, 2–3.
7 Cocroft 1994.
8 West 1991, 149–62; PRO MPH 250.
9 PRO Supp 5/870. See also RAHIL Woolwich, Congreve 1788.

10 Thompson 1782. See also West 1991, 178–83; Steele 1994.
11 PRO Supp 5/870; RAHIL Woolwich, Congreve 1788.
12 Napier 1788.
13 West 1991, 178.
14 PRO Supp 5/65 Faversham In-Letter

Book 6 Feb 1778–25 May 1785; PRO Supp 5/866.

15 RAHIL Woolwich, Congreve 1811, 9–10.
16 *Ibid*, 27.
17 Napier 1788, 102.
18 PRO MPH 250.
19 Hodgetts 1909, 20–5, 30–5; Crocker G, 1986, 14, 18–19, 21; Crocker 1989.
20 RAHIL Woolwich, Congreve 1811; West 1991, 180; PRO Supp 5/866.
21 Winters 1887, 32; PRO WO 47/60.
22 Rees 1819, 142.
23 RAHIL Woolwich, Congreve 1811, 32.
24 Rees 1819, 143.
25 West 1991, 171.
26 MPH 189 [10]; MPH 409, MPH 426, MPHH 597.
27 PRO WO 78/1533; MPHH 597 1790.
28 WASC 1375; WASC 1376.
29 PRO MR 909; MPH 426.
30 Coleman 1801, 355; Baddeley 1857, 3–4.
31 PRO Supp 5/868.
32 West 1991, 210.
33 RAHIL Woolwich, Congreve 1811, 15.
34 See PRO MR 593; MR 580 [2].
35 Winters 1887, 41, 99; *VCH* Essex 1907, 448.
36 West 1991, 171; WASC 1396.
37 WASC 1396.
38 Winters 1887, 57–9.
39 *Ibid*, 60.
40 PRO Supp 5/866.
41 West 1991, 180–3; PRO Supp 5/65.
42 Watson 1818, 240–3.
43 See RCHME architectural survey

reports, Fisherstreet (NMR 94771) and Fernhurst (NMR 94772).
44 Dickinson and Straker 1937–8, 61–2.
45 Young 1808, 432.
46 Dickinson and Straker 1937–8, 65.
47 PRO MPH 555.
48 Rees 1819, 142.
49 RAHIL Woolwich, Congreve 1811; Watson 1818, 242.
50 PRO Supp 5/866.
51 Thompson 1782; see also West 1991, 178–83; Steele 1994; Mauskopf 1996.
52 PRO Supp 5/866.
53 Congreve 1783 and 1785, RAHIL Woolwich.
54 Congreve 1783 and 1785, RAHIL Woolwich; Hodgetts 1909, 36–9; Guillery and Pattison 1996; PRO Supp 5/866; WO 55/2334.
55 WASC 1396.
56 PRO Supp 5/866.
57 For proof at the government factories, see West 1991, 179–82; WASC 540.
58 Saunders 1989, 141–5.
59 RAHIL Woolwich, Congreve 1811, 16; Winters 1887, 66, 68.
60 Winters 1887, 62.
61 PRO WO 55/2351.
62 Winters 1887, 62.
63 PRO MR 580 [3].
64 PRO WO 55/2351; WO 55/2694.
65 Coad 1989, 263.
66 Coleman 1801; Baddeley 1857, 8–9; Smith 1870, 22–5; PRO MP 11/15.
67 Winters 1887, 81.
68 Bret 1994, 304–5 figs 3–4.
69 For more detailed accounts of the

Ballincollig works, see Kelleher 1993, 13–37, and 1996.
70 PRO MPH 206 [5].
71 PRO MPH 206 [6].
72 PRO Supp 5/869.
73 PRO WO 55/2331; MPHH 677 [12].
74 PRO WO 55/2425; MPHH 590.
75 PRO Supp 5/867.
76 WASC 557.
77 WASC 1396.
78 Percival 1986, 9–10.
79 Winters 1887, 78; WASC 1396.
80 SAVE 1993, 235–7.
81 See Wood 1977.
82 Winters 1887, 77–8; Simmons 1963, 28–9; Percival 1986, 10; WASC 518 Notes on the records of the RGPF.
83 PRO MPH 410.
84 PRO WO 55/2351.
85 WASC 791.
86 *Gentleman's Magazine* 1828; DNB 1930, 934.
87 RAHIL Woolwich, Congreve 1818.
88 Wilkinson 1975, 94.
89 PRO MP 11/15.
90 Winters 1887, 102.
91 Percival 1986, 11.
92 Kelleher 1993, 35–7, 45.
93 *Gentleman's Magazine* 1843; Winters 1887, 106–8.
94 Wilkinson 1975, 40.
95 Winters 1887, 106–9.
96 Mauskopf 1990; Bret 1996.
97 RAHIL Woolwich, Congreve 1811, 9.
98 Braddock 1829.
99 Bret 1996, 271.
100 WASC 540.

3

Gunpowder manufacture in the second half of the nineteenth century

Trends and influences: competition and rivalry

The second half of the nineteenth century was a period of profound change in the gunpowder industry. Between 1850 and the end of the century the number of gunpowder mills in Britain was reduced by a quarter. But this conceals an exceptional surge of increased production that reached a peak in the 1870s, followed by a steep decline as new chemical explosives were introduced and usurped gunpowder's supremacy as the only practical explosive (Chapter 5). It also conceals changes in the scale of production, and in the diversity of specialised factories, for ammunition, fuzes, fireworks, and other explosive stores. Although lying outside the scope of this book, these specialised manufacturers were also subject to control under the explosives legislation and exhibited many similarities in factory layout and building design.

By the time of the 1875 Explosives Act the industry had become established in a restricted number of locations (Fig 3.1). A total of 28 continuing certificates were issued to gunpowder works under the Act; 18 of these factories remained active at the Armistice in 1918, along with a further four factories licensed since the Act came into force. Some – in south-western England, Wales, the Lake District, and Scotland – resulted from the industry's expansion during the late eighteenth and early nineteenth centuries in supplying blasting powder for mining and civil engineering. A few of these proved to be commercial failures and lasted only a few decades, while other losses prior to the 1875 Act included the long-established mills in Somerset and Sussex. In addition, many of the colonies relied on British gunpowder: Australia, for example,

had no powder mills during the nineteenth century. The worldwide spread of factories manufacturing Nobel's dynamite from the 1870s was a further factor in the decline of domestic production. By the end of the nineteenth century nearly 50% of the remaining private manufacturing capacity of gunpowder had been acquired by one company, Curtis's and Harvey of Hounslow in Middlesex.[1]

It was, however, in the manufacture of gunpowder for military use that the most

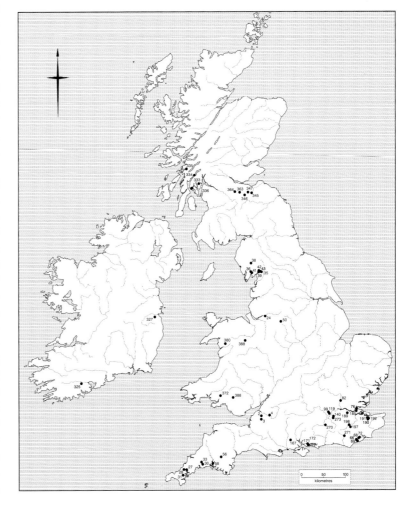

Figure 3.1 Map of gunpowder works operating during the nineteenth century.

innovative developments took place during this period. This was driven by leapfrogging technological innovation in the armaments industry, as the manufacturers of armour plate vied to keep pace with the development of ever larger guns and more effective armour-piercing projectiles. Latent popular concerns about France's belligerent intents, echoed by politicians, also created a climate in which it was possible to justify spending huge sums of money on defence. In actuality, the second half of the nineteenth century, and up to 1914, was an exceptionally peaceful period for Britain, only briefly punctuated by major wars and those fought at some distance – with Russia (1854–6), and in South Africa during the Boer War (1899–1901).

International competition and imperial rivalries propelled the development of military gunpowder production in Britain. Whereas British practice, and in particular that at Waltham Abbey RGPF, had in the first half of the nineteenth century been seen as exemplary, as the century progressed the British powdermakers increasingly looked abroad for solutions to their problems, especially to Germany. Technological diffusion was aided by increasing numbers of official manuals detailing manufacturing processes, and manufacturers' details of machinery were published in trade catalogues or books,[2] or in engineering journals.[3] The rise of the international trade fair in this period also hastened the dissemination of new ideas. This was consolidated by engineering firms' speedy dispatch of up-to-date machinery around the globe. As the greatest industrial powers in Europe, Britain and Germany were the largest exporters of gunpowder manufacturing machinery, their position underpinned by the high reputations of their respective powder manufacturers. Technological transfer in the armaments industry was not left entirely to the vagaries of free trade, however, but was partly controlled by changing diplomatic and imperial rivalries. The routes of transmission were further complicated by the end of the century with the emergence of international companies, whose commercial ties often cut across political boundaries.

In a declining market for gunpowder few powder mills in Britain developed into factories producing gunpowder on a truly industrial scale. In state hands the mills at Waltham Abbey RGPF were exceptional in their size and level of investment during this period. In the private sector, it was only the largest producers, also serving government contracts at home and abroad, that needed and could afford to keep pace with the international developments in gunpowder technology. It was also characteristic that much of the 'new technology' introduced into powdermaking was already well tried and tested in other industries.

Stimuli to change: the race begins

The Crimean War (1854–6) acted as the catalyst to stimulate state spending on all three royal munitions factories – the Royal Small Arms Factory (RSAF) at Enfield, Waltham Abbey RGPF, and the Royal Arsenal Woolwich. Though committees had met intermittently since the end of the Napoleonic Wars to discuss the manufacture of munitions, little progress had been made. Some modernisation was begun at Woolwich in the 1840s, and plans were already well advanced at Enfield for the total reconstruction of the factory along American lines at the outbreak of war.[4] For Waltham Abbey, the war itself and the widespread criticism of the organisation and supply of the British army prompted by it marked the beginning of a period of almost continual expansion and development over the next three decades. Inadequacies in state capacity to manufacture sufficient powder formed just one complaint. For example, it was stated in Parliament that of the 100,000 barrels of gunpowder used at Sebastopol 32,000 barrels had been imported from America and Belgium.[5]

Administratively, management of Waltham Abbey RGPF was changed as the autonomy of the Board of Ordnance was dissolved and from May 1855 the Ordnance Department was brought under the control of the Secretary of State for War.[6]

Fears about French aggressive intentions – encapsulated in Palmerston's earlier comment that 'the channel is no longer a barrier..., nothing more than a river passable by a steam bridge' – were whipped up into an anti-French scare in 1859–60, and further fuelled by reports of the laying down of the steam-powered ironclad *La Gloire* and large French orders for rifled cannons and iron plating.[7] These concerns led to the establishment of a Royal Commission on the Defences of the United Kingdom, followed by construction of the string of fortifications along the south coast pejoratively known as 'Palmerston's Follies'; and the wooden walls of England were superseded by the new ironclad battleships led by HMS *Warrior* in 1860.

As the century progressed, the increased scale and specialisation of gunpowder manufacture directly linked to the phenomenal growth in charge sizes that took place after the Crimean War. At the close of that war in March 1856 the largest gun in British service on land or sea was a smooth-bore 68-pounder (Fig 3.2). Within 30 years the largest gun in service weighed 110 tons (111.76 tonnes) (Fig 3.3) and fired a charge of prismatic powder weighing up to 960lb (436.36kg) to propel a projectile of 1800lb (818.2kg) – a sixty-fold increase in charge size.[8] In production terms this represented 19.2 mill loads, each weighing 50lb (22.7kg), each of which required incorporating for around three-and-a-half hours. The 110-ton guns were exceptional in their requirements, but a whole range of medium-sized guns had also been developed requiring charges weighing many hundreds of pounds.

It is against this international political, military, and technological background, together with developments in gunpowder manufacture abroad, that the growth of Waltham Abbey RGPF should be placed. The evolution of that factory's layout responded to the twin demands of increased output and then of production of more specialised powders.

Expansion at Waltham Abbey RGPF

The exceptional growth of Waltham Abbey RGPF from the later 1850s was emulated by few other explosives factories in Britain. The quality of buildings and plant there are in many ways typical of the remainder of the

Figure 3.2 A smooth-bore muzzle-loaded 68-pounder cannon. (© The Royal Artillery Historical Trust). This weapon fired an 18lb black powder charge with a projectile weighing some 66lb; it represented the largest gun in British service during the Crimean War, seen here in a coastal defence role.

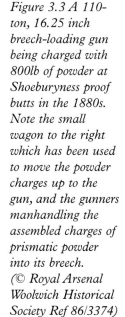

Figure 3.3 A 110-ton, 16.25 inch breech-loading gun being charged with 800lb of powder at Shoeburyness proof butts in the 1880s. Note the small wagon to the right which has been used to move the powder charges up to the gun, and the gunners manhandling the assembled charges of prismatic powder into its breech. (© Royal Arsenal Woolwich Historical Society Ref 86/3374)

industry, but they illustrate some of the most technologically advanced production methods used in Britain. Their remarkable survival as field monuments within a factory setting is matched by the wealth of their documented history. Such detailed evidence is particularly important in documenting the adoption of new technology or building types, which is often lacking in private sector factories. As the pre-eminent British powder factory, the site is also the most significant exemplar of gunpowder manufacture in Britain, against which state factories of other nations may be compared.

At the outbreak of the Crimean War in 1854, Waltham Abbey RGPF was essentially the same factory which had served Britain during the Napoleonic Wars. Small-scale improvements had affected individual buildings rather than altering the character of the whole factory (see Chapter 2). The power source for the majority of process buildings was water, whose reliability in all seasons could not be guaranteed, especially as the valley of the Lea became ever more heavily exploited for water transport, manufacturing, and utilities such as reservoirs to serve the expanding eastern sprawl of London. Incorporation was crowded along Millhead, with each water wheel limited in traditional fashion to a pair of mills.

The developments of the late 1850s, beginning in the spring of 1856, marked a radical departure, both in the adoption of

Figure 3.4 RGPF Waltham Abbey. Group A mills; Engine House and Mechanics' Shop: foundation stone 1856, erected 1857. (BB92/26077)

steam power for incorporation and in a break away from the linear thread of Millhead Stream onto previously unoccupied land, which transformed the factory's layout, appearance, and functional flow lines.

Steam-powered gunpowder incorporating mills

With few exceptions, powdermakers were slow to take full advantage of a centralised steam-driven power source. The additional risks of heat and fire compared with traditional water power are obvious. But in addition the wide dispersal of the manufacturing processes dictated by safety requirements would have resulted in high capital costs, if many small process buildings had to be provided with individual engines. As traditionally organised, too, the power needs of the majority of process buildings were small, generally not more than a few horsepower per machine. This combination of factors, coupled with traditions and the inertia inherent in established factories, ensured that water power remained the preferred prime mover in the industry to the end of gunpowder production in England.

The foundation stone of the new steam-driven Group A gunpowder incorporating mill was laid east of Millhead at Waltham Abbey RGPF in March 1856, the closing month of the Crimean War. The contrast between this new mill, with its round-arched Italianate style openings and the application of modern mill technology to gunpowder making, and the old water-driven, timber-framed incorporating mills could not have been more striking. The architectural form of the central engine house is reminiscent of the great northern textile mills (Fig 3.4), and its embellishment with polychrome brickwork reflected the influence of the Ordnance Department, as in contemporary buildings at the RSAF at Enfield and the Royal Arsenal Woolwich.[9]

The connection with the technology of the northern millwrights was reinforced when the Ordnance Department placed its contract for the compound steam engine of 30 horse power, along with six pairs of edge runners and other ironwork, with one of its

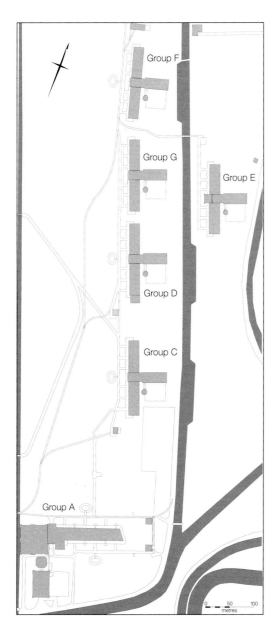

Figure 3.5 RGPF Waltham Abbey. Developed layout of the steam-driven gunpowder mills at the end of the nineteenth century (redrawn from contemporary factory plan): Group A 1856–7; Group C 1861; Group D 1867–8; Group E 1877–8; Group F 1878; Group G 1888–9.

Figure 3.6 RGPF Waltham Abbey. Steam-powered gunpowder incorporating mills 1861–88. (BB92/26175)

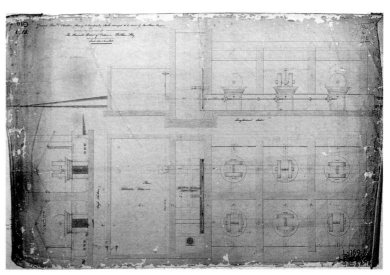

Figure 3.7 RGPF Waltham Abbey. Undated plan showing the proposed arrangement of the Group A incorporating mills, signed B Hick and Son. (© PRO WASC 901/106)

principal suppliers – Benjamin Hick and Son of the Soho Iron Works of Bolton.[10] As they were successively added to over the next three decades, the Italianate mills at Waltham Abbey RGPF formed not only the largest grouping of steam gunpowder mills in Britain but also the grandest (Figs 3.5 and 3.6).

As originally conceived, the Group A mills were to consist of a central engine house, a mechanics' shop to the west, and six incorporating mills to the east arranged in two parallel rows (Fig 3.7).[11] The mills were to be powered by two parallel drive shafts housed in separate under-floor drive-shaft alleys, in a similar arrangement to the

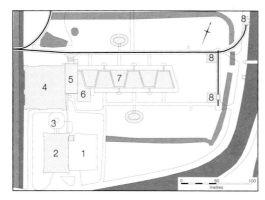

Figure 3.8 RGPF Waltham Abbey, Group A mills, 1856. Block plan digitised from 1:500 factory plan: 1 Coal yard; 2 Boiler house; 3 Chimney; 4 Mechanics shop; 5 Engine house; 6 Lathe house; 7 Incorporating mills; 8 Expense magazines. Note the oval foundations of traverses to north and south of the mills; cf Fig 2.33 and 3.26; the toned bands surrounding the complex on all sides indicate the location of former hedged screens.

contemporary Etruscan bone and flint mill in Stoke-on-Trent.[12] Such a system had the advantage of removing the mill gearing from the powder-laden atmosphere of the mill room and eliminated the risk of over-head gearing becoming detached and falling onto the bedplate. Though not a common means of power transmission, this method had been used in the textile industry since the beginning of the century.[13]

As built (Fig 3.8), the mills comprised an engine house, a mechanics' shop to its west, and a single row of six incorporating machines to its east. The boiler house was detached to the rear and an elegant 150ft (45m) high octagonal chimney on an octagonal plinth was placed between it and the mechanics shop. Design drawings specified a 30 horse power engine, with a flywheel 18ft (5.4m) in diameter. This was connected to a single drive shaft, 129ft (39.5m) in length and 5.25in (0.13m) in diameter,

housed in a cast iron-lined drive-shaft alley running beneath the mill bays. Instead of being set in parallel rows as had originally been suggested, the mills were grouped in opposed trapezium-shaped bays, separated by brick walls 3ft (0.9m) thick. The fourth wall of each bay was clad in corrugated iron and the roof was covered with galvanised sheets in an attempt to minimise the danger caused by flying debris in the event of an explosion. Suspended above each of the incorporating machines was a copper drenching tub, which would tip around 40 gallons (182 litres) of water on each of the mills should one 'blow'. The effects of such an explosion in June 1861 were graphically illustrated in an engraving in the *Illustrated London News*[14] (Fig 3.9). At this date potentially lethal unprotected glass windows were still in use.

Up-to-date construction techniques for fireproofing were also used in the construction of these mills. The roof of the mechanics shop was supported by cast iron pillars and beams and, like its boiler house, was composed of angle irons, rolled irons, and decorative cast iron compression members. These roofs were fireproof and could survive minor 'blows'. Other innovations introduced in the operation of these mills included a tramway with hand-propelled bogies for moving the gunpowder to and from two small detached expense magazines adjacent to the mills (Fig 3.9).

Figure 3.9 RGPF Waltham Abbey, explosion at the Group A mills, 1861 (from Illustrated London News **38**, *8 June 1861, 519). On the extreme left is an Expense Magazine and adjacent to it a hand-propelled powder bogie.*

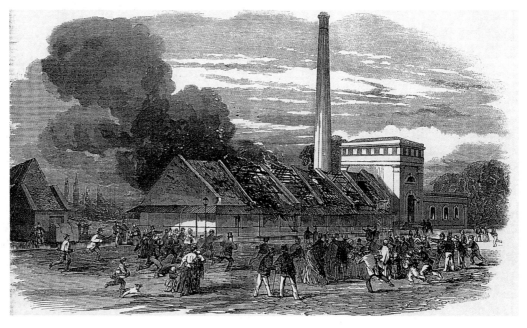

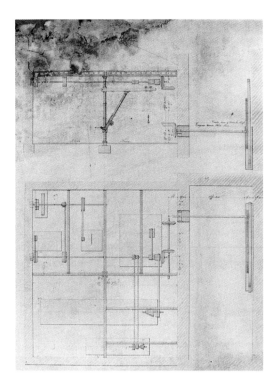

Power for the mechanics shop was supplied by a second motion shaft from the engine house, which in turn powered a series of belt drives. Mounted on the central pillar of the shop was a 4 ton (4.06 tonne) crane, that was able to lift the heaviest edge runners in use at Waltham Abbey RGPF (Fig 3.10).[15] This shop, and particularly its boring mill capable of turning the large iron runners and bedplates of the incorporating mills, was of especial interest to the American powdermaker, Lammot du Pont, who visited the mills shortly after their completion.[16] It made such an impression that he initiated construction of a new machine shop in du Pont's Hagley Yard on his return home.

The single long drive shaft of the Group A mills, with the engine placed at the end of the mills, was found to be 'an objectionable arrangement'.[17] Trapezium-shaped bays, that might seem to have some benefit in directing the scatter of debris away from the building, were also not widely used. The only other English example of their use in an incorporating mill was at Sedgwick Gunpowder Company's works in Cumbria in the Lake District, constructed about the same time. Though also using under-floor drive shafts, these mills were powered by a water wheel.

Group B mills were erected at the end of the 1850s on the Lower Island Works. The constricted area of land available and the pragmatic benefits of combining water and steam as power sources probably influenced their form, but in other respects they represented a transitional development to the evolved form of late nineteenth-century gunpowder mills at Waltham Abbey RGPF. They consisted of a central wheel house holding a water wheel 14ft (4.27m) in diameter, with two mill bays to either side powered by an under-floor drive shaft. The bays were rectangular in plan and were divided by brick walls, with the open sides and roof covered by match boarding supported on an iron frame. A steam engine placed next to the water wheel was held in reserve for times of drought. A detached boiler house stood to the north, embodying within it an octagonal chimney 75ft (22.86m) in height. The auxiliary steam engine may have been supplied by Benjamin Hick and Son; the water wheel and edge runners were supplied by one of the most illustrious northern firms of machinery manufacturers, W Fairbairn and Sons of Manchester.[18]

With the construction of the Group C mills in 1861, the form for the steam-powered gunpowder incorporating mills became standardised in a T-shaped plan (Fig 3.11), perhaps reflecting the arrangement of the 1814 rocket factory at the Royal Arsenal Woolwich (see Fig 8.3).

Figure 3.10 RGPF Waltham Abbey, Group A mills, 1856. Internal arrangement of the mechanics shop, fitted out by Benjamin Hick and Son, Soho Ironworks, Bolton. (AA94/5619; © Bolton Central Library)

Figure 3.11 RGPF Waltham Abbey. Reconstruction of the Group C steam-powered gunpowder mills as built in 1861. (© Crown copyright. NMR)

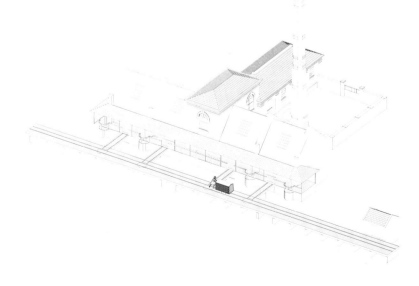

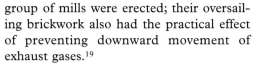

group of mills were erected; their oversailing brickwork also had the practical effect of preventing downward movement of exhaust gases.[19]

The central engine houses were open, brick-built structures designed to house a single beam engine. Those of the 1860s mills – Groups C and D – were entered from open verandas through a double door with semi-circular head. The interior was lit by four semi-circular arched windows, one on each elevation, with walls covered by cement render and scored to represent ashlar. The hipped roof was of slate. The side elevations of the rear boiler houses were divided into four bays by brick pilasters, separating what were originally sash windows with a cambered head and a rectangular blind panel beneath. The boiler houses were entered from the rear through a double door with a round-arched head, and were spanned by iron trusses covered with slate and ventilated by a raised central ridge. The engine and boiler houses had similar denticulated cornices in the same buff-coloured brick as the rest of the building. The later mills – Groups F (1878) and G (1888–9) (discounting the converted pellet powder house) – differed only in details, principally a pair of semi-circular headed windows on the upper front and rear elevations (Fig 3.12) and contrasting red bricks used in the heads of the windows and the cornice. The continued use of the tall central engine house until the late 1880s maintained the architectural integrity of the group but also implies that beam engines continued to be installed, an implication confirmed by design drawings from the late 1870s.[20]

Figure 3.12 RGPF Waltham Abbey, Group G mills, erected 1888–9. (from glass plate in WASC). Photographed after explosion in 1902; in front is the raised platform of the tramway. (BB97/3437; © MoD)

Figure 3.13 RGPF Waltham Abbey, Group G mills, 1888–9. Note the iron framing, drenching tub and lamp box.

In this layout the beam engine house was placed at the centre of the mill, with a boiler house attached to its rear and a coal yard adjacent. Each group of mills was served by an ornate chimney 75ft (22.86m) in height standing detached from the boiler house. Design drawings and contemporary photographs (Figs 3.12, 3.19, 3.32) show octagonal chimneys on panelled plinths constructed in polychrome brickwork; light-coloured bricks were used on the quoins, with bands and diamond shapes picked out in darker bricks on their shafts. The caps of the chimneys were treated in a variety of decorative styles reflecting a period of almost 30 years over which the whole

To either side of the engine house were the bays in which the incorporating mills were housed. The practical efficiency of the mills gave them their symmetry while the architectural detailing of the central engine and boiler house contrasted with the functionalism of the mill bays. In the earliest of the T-shaped steam mills, as illustrated in the reconstruction drawings (Figs 3.11 and 3.14), two bays were placed either side of the engine house; this was later extended to three, which became the standard form Access into the mill bays was from an open-fronted veranda supported by cast iron columns. A foot board marked the division

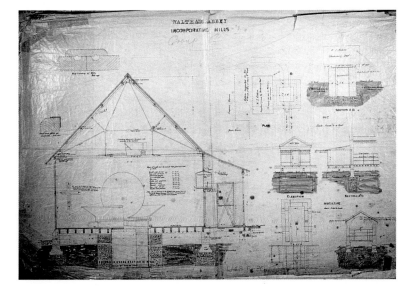

between the tramway, a 'dirty' area, and the veranda, a 'clean' area (see below, Safety). The bays were separated from one another by a brick wall, 2ft 3in (0.68m) thick, laid in English bond. Their walls and roofs were supported on a frame of angle- and T-irons, their floors were laid in deal, like the veranda. The external walls were infilled with light wooden panels and McIlwraith's patent non-inflammable felt, and were pierced at the front by a self-contained lamp serviced from the outside of the building (Fig 3.13). Supported on the tie beams above each of the mills was a copper drenching tub set to douse all the mills within the group should one 'blow'.

How the steam incorporating mills at Waltham Abbey worked

The fittings and operation of each group of mills were similar (Fig 3.14). Steam for the engine was raised in two Lancashire boilers in the rear boiler house. The beam engine in the central engine house was mounted on massive brick and ashlar piers, and fixed by vertical mounting bolts. The suspended metal grating floor of the engine house was supported on cast iron beams over a basement, which was lined with cast iron plates bolted together to keep the compartment watertight on this low-lying site. The drive shaft, placed slightly off centre to the mill, was housed at basement level in a drive-shaft alley lined with cast iron plates bolted together; a plate laid across the top of the alley formed the floor of the mill room above. Exceptionally, in Group D of 1867–8, the drive-shaft alley was a brick-vaulted tunnel (Fig 3.15). The shaft was made up of segments joined together to form a single horizontal shaft, 69ft (21m) in length, and was supported in the tunnel by cast iron shoulders, with central brass bearings through which the shaft passed (Fig 3.16).

In operation, a connecting rod joined to a crank on the horizontal shaft to convert the reciprocating motion of the engine into the circular motion required to drive the mills. Either side of the crank were a pair of spoked, heavy-rimmed cast iron

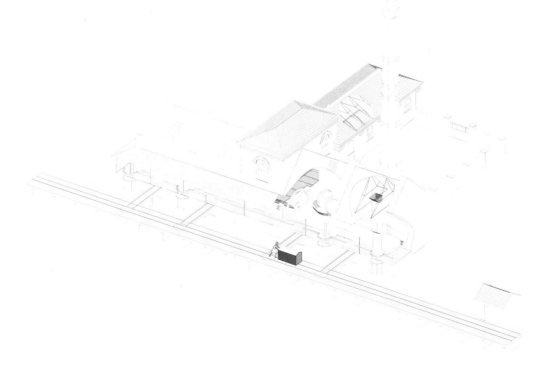

Figure 3.14 RGPF Waltham Abbey. Reconstruction of Group C steam-powered gunpowder mills as built in 1861, showing method of power transmission. (© Crown copyright. NMR)

Figure 3.15 (top left) RGPF Waltham Abbey. Brick-vaulted drive-shaft alley beneath the Group D mills built in 1867, showing the large bevel wheel beneath the incorporating mill and pinion wheel attached to the friction clutch. (BB92/26188)

Figure 3.16 (bottom left) RGPF Waltham Abbey. Drive shaft abandoned in cast-iron drive-shaft alley beneath the Group E mills, as reconstructed in 1877. (BB92/26183)

Figure 3.17 (top right) RGPF Waltham Abbey. Chamber and drive-shaft alley beneath one bay of the Group C incorporating mills with the floor removed. Visible are the central bearing, where the vertical spindle sat, and behind it the pinion wheel attached to the friction clutch. The mill gear and cast iron tanks were made by Benjamin Hick and Son at the Soho Ironworks, Bolton. B93/27088)

Figure 3.18 (bottom right) RGPF Waltham Abbey. Cross-section showing arrangement of incorporating mill gearing, Cavendish c 1878.

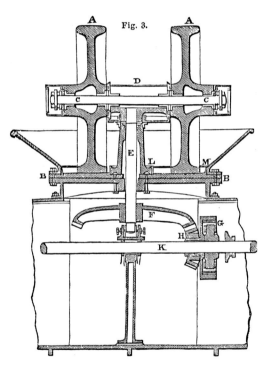

segmental flywheels, 14ft (4.27m) in diameter, to ensure the smooth running of the mills. Beneath each of the bays the drive-shaft alley opened out into a circular chamber 7ft (2.13m) in diameter (Figs 3.17 and 3.18), to house a 5ft (1.52m) bevel wheel with 75 teeth. This wheel was engaged and disengaged by means of a friction clutch attached to a solid casting consisting of a drum and pinion wheel with 33 teeth. During the operation of the mills the main horizontal drive shaft was continuously spinning. To engage any of the mills, two copper edged segments keyed onto the shaft were made to expand into the drum, thus transferring motion to the pinion wheel. The friction clutch was remotely controlled by a rod passing up through the ceiling of the alley and connecting to a wheel on the veranda. From the centre of the bevel wheel a vertical spindle, supported at its base in a brass stuff box, passed up through the bed of the mill and was connected via a crosshead to a horizontal spindle passing in a brass bearing through each of the edge runners. The edge runners in the new steam mills were of cast iron, with a flat surface bevelled at the edge, turning on a cast iron bed. Each was 6ft 6in (1.98m) in diameter, and weighed around 4 tons (4.064 tonnes). The runners were set at slightly different distances from the central spindle so a greater area of the bed was covered, and mounted so that they were able to rise and fall within the crosshead depending on the thickness of the charge on the bed; the powder was spread evenly on the bedplate by a plough attached to the crosshead.

During incorporation, between two and eight pints of distilled water (the amount depending on the time of year) were added to ensure an intimate cohesion of the particles. The milling time for a charge of powder, set by the 1875 Act at 50lb (22.68kg) for government powder, varied according to the power of the mills and the type of powder being milled. Cannon powder, for example, required 3fi hours working under stone runners weighing 3fi tons (3.556 tonnes) at 7fi revolutions per minute, but only 2fi hours under iron runners of 4 tons (4.064 tonnes) at 8 revolutions per minute. Powder for small arms required 5fi hours in the former mills and 4 hours in the latter. It was calculated that a pair of water mills working night and day all year, excluding Sundays, could produce 660 barrels of cannon powder or 330 barrels of small arms powder; steam mills could produce 950 barrels of cannon powder or 473 barrels of small arms powder under the same conditions.[21]

Technological change – pellet, pebble, prismatic, and brown powders

Profound changes beyond those of scale affected gunpowder production at Waltham Abbey RGPF in the second half of the nineteenth century. They are to do with the finished form in which gunpowder was produced, and the search for efficient combustion of charges for weapons of increasingly large calibre.

The technology of combustion – an international problem

In order to understand the significance of the development of different forms of powder it is necessary to unravel the complex technological background against which they were set. It is an international story, and serves to emphasise the role played by Waltham Abbey RGPF in the development of gunpowder technology and its importance in maintaining Britain's position as a great power.

As the principal supplier to the Services, Waltham Abbey RGPF produced a very narrow range of powders, in contrast to other government contractors who were also supplying blasting and sporting powders. In the mid-nineteenth century there was a range of grain sizes in Service use, the finer grains for muskets and rifles and the larger grains in cannons and mortars.[22] During the Crimean War the sole output of the RGPF was cannon powder, whose quality enjoyed a world-wide reputation.[23] On his visit to European gunpowder mills in 1858, Lammot du Pont made particular efforts to gain access to Waltham Abbey RGPF, 'where they manufacture nothing but cannon powder.'[24] He took away a sample of the new large-grained powder developed for use in Mallet's 36in (0.91m) calibre mortar, which he had watched undergoing trials at Woolwich.[25]

The difficulty of devising a suitable powder for large mortars and guns of ever-increasing calibres faced the powdermakers in all the state arsenals of Europe and America.

As charge sizes increased, two basic problems were presented to the powdermakers. First, if a large charge was ignited in the breech of the gun it could literally blow the gun to pieces. Secondly and conversely, complete combustion of a large charge of tightly packed powder might fail to occur if the igniting flame was not carried to the centre of the charge, thereby leaving some of the charge to be blown from the barrel unconsumed. The way in which the problem was addressed was to control the area of the burning surface, that is, the surface area of a grain of gunpowder in relation to its mass. Empiric knowledge had always favoured larger grain sizes for cannon powders. A scientific understanding of how a propellant burns was provided by the French scientist Guillaume Piobert; his law formulated in 1839 recognised that the burning surface of a discrete piece of explosive recedes in consecutive layers, comparable to those of an onion.[26]

Towards the end of the 1860s, with the adoption of Armstrong's breech loading guns, it became standard practice also to glaze the large grains with graphite to inhibit combustion.[27] How the powder was packed within a charge was also important in ensuring that enough interstices remained between the grains for the flame to pass almost instantaneously through the whole charge. The aim was to assure an increasing evolution of gases as the projectile travelled up the barrel of a gun, so that it reached its maximum velocity as it left the gun, while exerting the least pressure on the barrel.

It has been argued that Lammot du Pont's tour of Waltham Abbey RGPF and associated discussions may have sown the seeds of ideas that led to the development of his 'mammoth powder'.[28] In America, du Pont renewed his collaboration with Captain Thomas J Rodman, a soldier-technologist with the United States Ordnance Bureau. Rodman saw his research into large, 15in (0.38m), coastal and other large calibre guns as the study of an integrated system comprising the gun, the projectile, and the propellant. He conducted experiments in the 1850s to reduce the pressure exerted on the barrel by using circular, perforated cake cartridges of gunpowder of the same calibre as the gun. He found that such discs presented a minimum burning surface at the beginning of combustion, which increased as the holes enlarged with combustion and produced a greater amount of gas. Rodman's co-worker General Doremus later proposed large pellets of prismatic form, known as hexagonal cake cartridges, each perforated with cylindrical holes.[29] Elsewhere, Paoli di san Roberto experimented with compressed cartridges as early as 1852, by utilising the low melting point of the sulphur to bind the grains together. In other countries solutions such as sugar or gum arabic were employed to produce cartridges for use in large guns, while the Italians devised 'Fossano powder' or *poudre progressif*, which was regarded as extremely efficient.[30]

A parallel development, first introduced by the Belgians, was pellet powders, cylindrical in shape, $5/8$in (20mm) in diameter and height, and with a slight hollow or indentation in their upper surface.[31]

The technology of production

Pellet powders

In 1858 a committee was set up at Waltham Abbey RGPF under the then Superintendent, Colonel W H Askwith, to investigate the problems of suitable powders for large calibre guns.[32] The discs or cakes produced by Doremus were evaluated but the results were irregular and unsatisfactory and this line of research was abandoned.[33] Instead, this committee advocated the use of pellet powders for large guns, and its final report in 1866 recommended systematic and extensive experiments with that form. Small-scale production was started with an experimental hydraulic press, constructed at the Royal Laboratory at Woolwich. Meanwhile, a new explosives committee under the new Superintendent, Colonel C W Younghusband, continued to deliberate over the rival merits. In May of 1869 Younghusband visited the state factories at Spandau in Prussia and Wetteren in Belgium to study machinery in use for pressed powders. He saw no advantage in adopting prisms rather than pellets; cylindrical pellets were chosen for the practical reason that they were regarded as being easier to press. Spurred on by the progress made by the continental powers, plans for a new engine and hydraulic accumulator house to serve the pellet press to be erected at Waltham Abbey RGPF were ready by December 1869 (Fig 3.19). A larger press than the one currently in use at the Royal Arsenal Woolwich was designed by John Anderson, Inspector of Machinery, and was installed and operational at Waltham Abbey RGPF by 1870.[34]

Even while these new facilities for manufacturing pellet powder were being installed, the explosives committee decided that the simpler form of pebble powders were to be adopted for use in large calibre guns. Whether through an administrative or a technical volte-face, pellet powders were apparently manufactured for less than two years at Waltham Abbey RGPF. This explains the conversion of the newly built pellet powder house (L149) into the Group E T-shaped incorporating mill in 1877–8. In 1870–1, 1451lb (658.17kg) of pellet powders were supplied to the magazines at Purfleet; in the following year only 370lb (167.83kg). Additional supplies of pellet powders may have been acquired from Curtis's and Harvey, who were manufacturing it by late 1869, but an enquiry to the magazines at Purfleet in 1881 revealed that no pellet powder was in stock.[35] Unsuccessful experiments were also conducted with pressed powder of a similar size but with hemispherical ends and a flat central band.

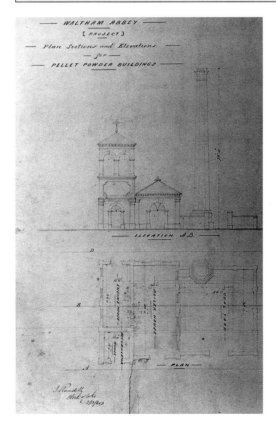

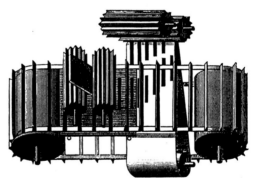

Figure 3.19 (left) RGPF Waltham Abbey. Design drawing for a Boiler, Engine and Accumulator House to serve a Pellet Powder Press, 1869; drawn up under the supervision of I Randell, Clerk of Works at the Royal Gunpowder Factory. (BB92/26360; © MoD)

Figure 3.20 (top right) Morgan's Pebble Powder Cutter, 1872. (Guttmann 1895, 244)

Figure 3.21 (bottom right) Models of pebble powder. (WASC 263)

Pebble powders

Pebble powders at their simplest were little more than lumps of gunpowder cake. The earliest and simplest way of forming them was by breaking press cake with copper hammers and passing the broken pieces through sieves of the required size. In 1870 a system was introduced at Waltham Abbey RGPF whereby the square slabs of press cake were cut into strips and then into cubes with a copper knife. Using this method, it was estimated that a man could produce 150lb (68.04kg) of pebble powder per day. This process was improved on by a system, introduced by the Assistant Superintendent, Captain Smith, where a series of knives were arranged around a roller and cut a number of strips simultaneously. Smith's successor, Major S P Morgan, had by 1872 invented a machine consisting of two pairs of phosphor bronze rollers that first cut the powder into strips and then into cubes (Fig 3.20).[36] Pebble powders were classified as Class B or 'cut' powders, sometimes referred to as 'cubical' powders (Fig 3.21). Different sizes were experimented with, related to the calibre of the gun, and were assigned identification codes – 'P' powders were $\frac{5}{8}$in (20mm) cubes, while 'P2' powders were cubes of between 1–2in (30–50mm). The larger 'P2' types were hand cut, using a hinged blade similar in form to an old-fashioned paper guillotine.[37] After cutting the cubes were placed in glazing machines to remove their sharp edges, which might flake during transit.

Prismatic powders

In the wake of the Civil War in America there was little desire to engage in costly military research. The initiative in exploiting Rodman's important innovations passed to the Old World. A Russian military commission visited America during the Civil War and was introduced to Rodman's compressed powders. By 1866 Professor Wischingratzki had developed a cam press for manufacturing prismatic powder at the Russian state factory at Okhtinsky near St Petersburg. Subsequent trials at the Krupps' factory alerted the Prussians to this new type of powder, and after further trials in 1868 at the Tegeler range near Berlin confirmed the improved ballistic results that could be obtained from prismatic powder, it was adopted for use by the Prussian artillery.

Like pebble powder, prismatic powder varied in size according to the calibre of the piece it was to be used in or according to contemporary thinking on the optimum size. By the late 1870s a typical hexagonal prism might measure 40mm from corner to corner. It stood 25mm high and was pierced by a single central channel, 9.5mm in diameter at its base and 9mm at its summit (Fig 3.22). In the older forms it was pierced by seven holes, each 4.7mm in diameter at its base and 4.2mm at its summit. Large charges could be assembled by carefully packing the prisms so that the holes lined up with one another, ensuring the flame travelled in a consistent manner through the charge. This would not occur in a loosely packed charge. It was also found that all of the charge was consumed, whereas in pebble powders a large percentage would be blown out of the gun unconsumed. With their large initial burning surface, pebble powders created an initial violent jolt to the projectile, but subsequently a smaller burning surface reduced the available gas with an attendant fall in pressure; the converse was true with prismatic powders.[38]

Britain persevered with pebble powders. In a major rebuilding campaign at Waltham Abbey RGPF in the late 1870s, nothing suggested an imminent intention to introduce prismatic powders. The extra capacity acquired at this time was entirely consistent with increased demands for pebble powders, including, for example, the construction of an additional drying stove (see Fig 3.60) to cope with the longer drying times required by pebble powders. But the explosives committee, now under the presidency of Colonel W H Noble (later to become Superintendent of Waltham Abbey RGPF), was set the task of enquiring into 'the production of powder which shall develop the maximum power of heavy guns with the least detriment to their endurance' and was clearly convinced by the widespread adoption of prismatic powders by the continental powers that Britain ought swiftly to follow suit.39 Samples of prismatic powders were requested from continental producers in Germany and Belgium, including Otto Heusser of Roensahl Pulverfabriken near Wipperfurth, Max von Duttenhofer of Rottweil Pulverfabriken near Hamburg, and F N Heidemann of Vereingte Rheinische-Westphalische Pulverfabriken at Cologne. Samples were to be delivered to the government magazines at Purfleet. In 1879 Colonel Hay, Superintendent at Waltham Abbey RGPF, also visited the factories at Wetteren in Belgium and Roensahl, Cologne, and Spandau in Germany. Prismatic powder manufactured in England by Curtis's and Harvey was also delivered to Purfleet for testing.[40] In 1885 they installed 'very heavy and expensive machinery' in their Leigh Mills at Tonbridge in Kent to manufacture government prismatic powder.[41]

Initially large quantities of prismatic powder were imported from Germany and this probably was the cause of the six-fold increase in the amount of powder imported between 1884 and 1885.[42] It became vitally important that Waltham Abbey RGPF should have the capability to manufacture prismatic powder, both as a producer and to provide government contractors with a specification and samples by which to judge their powders. In 1881 Duttenhofer and Heidemann were asked to undertake the manufacture of prismatic powder at Waltham Abbey RGPF for instructional purposes.[43] By 1882 new construction work and adaptation of pre-existing buildings show that preparations were being made to manufacture prismatic powder at Waltham Abbey RGPF. This work included construction of a wooden moulding house surrounded by a mass concrete traverse (Fig 3.23). This was perhaps in itself an experimental design, as another moulding house of this date was surrounded by a more conventional brick and earthwork traverse. It was probably also at this time that a press house constructed in 1879 (Fig 3.34) was converted to a moulding house.

Two types of press were adopted at Waltham Abbey RGPF to produce prismatic powders, hydraulic and cam presses. Those on the northern part of the RGPF were hydraulically operated and powered by the centralised hydraulic system. A variety of moulding machines were installed including one manufactured by Taylor and Challen of Birmingham, who had supplied a similar machine to China in the 1870s, and another by an unidentified manufacturer (Fig 3.24).[44] These machines moulded 64 prisms in one pressing, forming the perforations in the prisms by phosphor bronze rods which passed through the lower plunger. The cycle of charging, pressing, and unloading took about two minutes. The complexity of this press illustrates another factor in the advance of powder technology, namely a greater precision in machinery design as iron and steel replaced timber in their construction.

Figure 3.22 (bottom left) Models of prismatic powder and part of moulding machine. The annular ring on one prism distinguishes EXE prismatic and the circular hollow SBC prismatic. (WASC 257)

Figure 3.23 (bottom right) RGPF Waltham Abbey. Mass concrete traverse formerly enclosing two free-standing timber-framed gunpowder moulding houses. That on the left dates from 1882; the less well finished right-hand bay with its timber shuttering still visible was added in 1884. (BB92/26220)

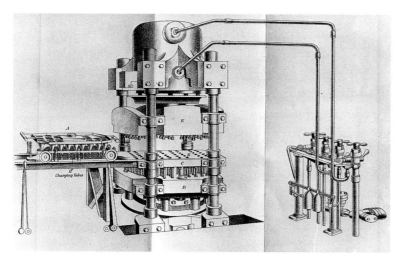

Figure 3.24 (left) Hydraulic prismatic powder moulding machine. From Wardell 1888. (BB94/8014)

Figure 3.25 (right) RGPF Waltham Abbey. Cam presses photographed after an explosion on 13 December 1893 in which nine men lost their lives. (BB94/8012; © MoD)

Cam presses for moulding prisms were first installed at Waltham Abbey RGPF in 1887. Compression in this type of machine was applied by means of a cam or eccentric on a shaft driven by water or steam power (Fig 3.25). This was similar to that devised by Professor Wischingratzki in Russia and had been widely used in continental factories since the mid-1860s. Such presses worked automatically, and very rapidly, pressing six prisms at a time. It was claimed that they produced a superior prismatic powder, because the eccentric generated an enormous pressure in a very short space of time. The resulting prisms displayed a very hard, smooth finish, which had the practical effect of reducing the initial pressure on ignition compared to prisms with a rougher finish from hydraulic presses.[45] Elsewhere in Britain cam presses were little used. Enquiries by the Explosives Inspectorate after an explosion in 1893 at Waltham Abbey RGPF revealed that only six manufacturers were using them, in three cases for pressing mining cartridges. John Hall and Son reported that they had been the first to use the principle about 20 years earlier at their Oare Works at Faversham; the works at Chilworth had been using four since 1886. Curtis's and Harvey at Hounslow, after investing £2000–£3000 in 1890 on two cam presses, considered them too dangerous to operate and abandoned them shortly afterwards.[46]

Brown powders

The early prismatic powders manufactured in England in the early 1880s used traditional black powder to form the prisms. The leading German manufacturers J N Heidemann and Max Duttenhofer, in seeking to mitigate the effects of large explosive charges on the breech mechanism of the guns, altered the composition of the gunpowder used in the prisms by substituting lightly carbonised rye straw for traditional wood charcoal. The resulting powder was termed brown or 'cocoa' powder from its reddish brown hue. In addition to securing a slower evolution of gases, a further important characteristic of brown powder was that it produced little smoke, which dispersed very quickly. This was a significant military benefit for the comparatively large quick-firing guns and machine guns that were being introduced specifically to combat small and swift-moving motor torpedo boats. The new slower burning powders were themselves also a factor in a return to breech-loading guns in British service in the 1880s.

The British Government was aware of these developments from 1882 and the Superintendent of RGPF secured details of manufacture on condition of secrecy.[47]

In 1884 trials took place with brown powder supplied to the British government by the Rottweil and Rheinische-Westphalische factories. It was reported early in 1885 that the Russians were also experimenting with brown powders supplied from Germany, and full-scale manufacture of brown prismatic powders began at Waltham Abbey RGPF later in 1885.[48]

No major changes of buildings or layout at the RGPF accompanied this important development. Ensuring an adequate supply of rye straw was a considerable concern. Throughout the summer of 1885 advertisements were placed in the agricultural press. One in *The Field* in July of 1885 asked 'which are the largest rye growing districts near London, and in which towns could information be obtained as to supply and cultivation, also any names of local persons or officials to whom inquiries might be addressed, also foreign sources of supply?'. The enquiry was hidden under a cloak of secrecy by the signature 'SALIX', no doubt a witty allusion on the part of the Superintendent to the fact that willow had previously been the preferred source of charcoal for large calibre guns.[49] This may have been an attempt to conceal Britain's interest in brown powders from rival powers, although it was common knowledge in Germany and indeed some rye straw was imported through Rotterdam. Alternatively, it may have been a commercial ploy to prevent a sharp rise in the price of rye straw. In 1886 the specification for formal government acceptance of prismatic brown powder stated that the prisms should be 24.8mm in height with a hole 10mm in diameter. The proportions for the ingredients were also varied so that it contained 79 parts saltpetre, 3 parts sulphur, and 18 parts charcoal. Special forms known as EXE and SBC, distinguished by an annular ring and a circular hollow, were manufactured using mixtures of carbonaceous substances that at the time were not divulged (Fig 3.22).[50]

The development and manufacture of brown prismatic powders brought some additional requirements for hydraulic pressing. Yet this represented the final evolutionary form of gunpowder technology as applied to propellants. Despite the advantages of significantly reduced strain on the breech of a gun and reduced smoke that brown powders had brought, gunpowder was now an outmoded technology. The technological breakthrough made with chemical explosives within the next decade would almost replace gunpowder as a source of propulsive energy (see Chapter 5).

Hydraulic power

Hydraulic power in the form of Bramah hand-operated presses was in use for pressing gunpowder at Waltham Abbey RGPF from around 1812.[51] Hydraulic power offered the powdermakers a method of operating presses remotely, and hence more safely. Pressing mill cake was recognised as one of the most important manufacturing processes, but it was also one of the most dangerous. Of the 30 most destructive explosions that occurred between May 1858 and June 1870, no less than 9 originated in press houses and cost 44 lives.[52] The application of a mechanical means of generation also presented a method in which greater pressures could be achieved.

Cartographic evidence at the Oare Gunpowder Works at Faversham suggests that water power may have been harnessed as early as 1846 to power an hydraulic pump.[53] At Waltham Abbey RGPF two presses powered by a water-driven pump were certainly in use by late 1854[54] (Fig 3.26). These press houses reused the sites of two former horse-powered corning houses at the termini of canal branches on the high level water system. The corning houses were dismantled about 1818, but their oval brick traverses were left standing and were reutilised to separate the press house from the pump house. In the surviving example, the pump (Fig 3.27) was driven by a low breast-shot iron water wheel, but could also

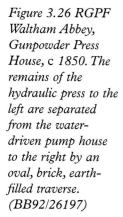

Figure 3.26 RGPF Waltham Abbey, Gunpowder Press House, c 1850. The remains of the hydraulic press to the left are separated from the water-driven pump house to the right by an oval, brick, earth-filled traverse. (BB92/26197)

Figure 3.27 (top right) RGPF Waltham Abbey. Remains of hydraulic pump attached to water wheel within the pump house of Fig 3.26. (BB92/26200)

Figure 3.28 (bottom right) RGPF Waltham Abbey. Hydraulic gunpowder press from Press House in Fig 3.26. (BB92/26264)

be operated by hand levers should the water level fall too low. The press (Fig 3.28) consisted of a cast iron (or by the end of the century cast steel) hydraulic ram (C in Fig 3.29) with four round columns supporting the head stocks. Water under pressure was introduced through a narrow pipe at its base to raise the ram. Powder for pressing was brought from the breaking down house where the mill cake from incorporation had been crushed between rollers to form meal powder. It was loaded into a stout oak box measuring 2ft 6in (0.76m) square and 2ft 9in tall (0.84m) with opening sides, between 46 copper plates each 2ft 5fiin (0.75m) square (Fig 3.30). During packing with 800lb (362.88kg) of gunpowder the box was turned on its side and the plates separated by spacers. Once filled, the spacers were removed and the sides secured before it was righted and manoeuvred onto the table of the ram beneath the press block (B in Fig 3.29). The press was then operated remotely from a room on the opposite side of the traverse adjacent to the pump house, exerting 70 tons (71.12 tonnes) per square foot for a quarter of an hour. The most reliable method for ascertaining when the correct degree of compaction had been achieved was simply to measure how far the block had penetrated into the box. The box was opened and the powder removed,

sometimes with the assistance of a wooden mallet and copper chisel, or spud[55] (Fig 3.30). As in earlier processing (see Chapter 2), the resulting press cake was then roughly broken by hand and allowed to harden further before granulation. Many private manufacturers dispensed with the press box, and simply formed a layer cake of plates and gunpowder. This had the disadvantage of allowing powder to spill out at the sides and producing a less densely pressed powder at the edges, which had to be cut away. Against this stood the hazards of chipping powder away from the box sides, and by the end of the century the box

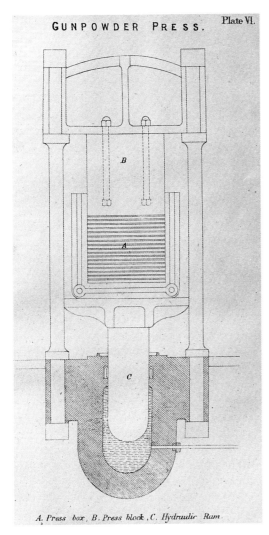

GUNPOWDER PRESS.   Plate VI.

B

A

C

A. Press box, B. Press block, C. Hydraulic Ram.

was no longer used.[56] Also by this date copper plates had been superseded by ebonite in many private factories. Circumstantial evidence suggests that the machinery for this hydraulic press house was supplied by William Fairbairn and Sons of Manchester.[57]

Around the same time as the two water-driven press houses were installed at Waltham Abbey RGPF, William Armstrong developed the weight-loaded hydraulic accumulator.[58] His innovation was to use a steam engine to pump water into the accumulator, which raised a weight-loaded ram and thereby increased the pressure of the water within the system (Fig 3.31). When water in the system was used the ram would fall and reactivate the pump to restore pressure. Such systems were used at large ports from the 1850s.[59] The problems facing the dock owners were similar to those confronting the large powdermakers, namely large dispersed sites where mechanical linkages were impractical and concern about the fire risks that many small steam plants might present. Centralised systems offered the additional advantages of being able to store power against demand and to serve a number of different machines, as well as removing the cyclical variation that was experienced where only pumps were used.

The increased scale of production at Waltham Abbey RGPF brought scope for application of these advances (see Fig 3.35). A weight-loaded accumulator was first introduced in the late 1860s, when a boiler, engine, and accumulator house (Fig 3.19) was constructed to power a pellet powder machine. The low elevation of the engine house indicates installation of a horizontal engine. The abandonment of pellet powders left this new plant idle, and in 1877–8 it was remodelled to form a standard T-shaped steam-driven gunpowder mill, with the central engine house serving

Figure 3.29 Section through hydraulic gunpowder press, similar to Fig 3.28. From Wardell 1888. The press illustrated has a fixed press block (B), which in earlier examples was moveable. (BB94/8017)

Figure 3.30 RGPF Waltham Abbey. Copper press plates and copper chisel (or spud). (BB94/7985)

Figure 3.31 The principle of the hydraulic press: a small force acting on a plunger (p) of small area over a long travel will create a large force on a ram (r) of large area over a short travel.

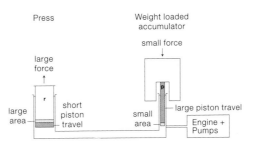

Press   Weight loaded accumulator

small force

large force

large piston travel

large area   short piston travel   small area

r   p

Engine + Pumps

Figure 3.32 RGPF Waltham Abbey, remodelled accumulator tower of the Group E mills, 1877. Note the mill bays to either side and the header tank on top of the tower. Photograph taken after an explosion in the adjacent Group G mills on 15 December 1902. (BB92/26115)

three mill bays to either side (Fig 3.32). The hydraulic accumulator was retained, with a cast iron header tank replacing the hipped roof of the tower. This then formed the centre of a centralised hydraulic system for the factory, with at least one receiver or remote accumulator to act as a storage device and regulator within the system (Fig 3.33) serving new presses over 600m away from the accumulator (Fig 3.34).

Use of hydraulic power became increasingly important as new forms of moulded and pressed powders were introduced. A traversed moulding house was added close to the remote accumulator. With the introduction of prismatic powder, a further moulding house was built in 1882, and another was added next to it in 1884 (Fig 3.23). Hydraulic presses also remained important in the manufacture of new chemical explosives (see Chapter 5); as early as the 1860s presses for guncotton were introduced and were followed in the 1890s by presses for extruding cordite. To meet these increased demands a new accumulator was constructed shortly before or at the outbreak of the Great War.

Elsewhere in the gunpowder industry screw presses remained in use until the late nineteenth century. The larger manufacturers installed hydraulic presses worked by pumps, powered by water wheels, turbines, and steam engines, for use both in the normal course of manufacture and for pressing blasting cartridges and more specialised

cannon powders for government contracts.[60] Hydraulic accumulators were installed only by the major suppliers of powder to the government, at factories where presses were in regular use for the manufacture of prismatic powders. These included Curtis's and Harvey's Hounslow Works and the Chilworth Gunpowder Company's main factory.[61]

Consolidation of the factory landscape

The changes of power systems and technology thus outlined may be shown to have had a direct influence on the factory landscape at Waltham Abbey.

The break with Millhead

Before 1850 Millhead, as the prime power source, dictated the layout of Waltham Abbey RGPF in a characteristic way; developments away from it were limited (see Chapter 2). The systematic and large-scale application of steam power to gunpowder incorporation brought about a decisive shift in the factory layout away from the Millhead. The Group A mills and workshops, significantly located at right-angles to and due east of the water-powered facilities crowded on Millhead, defined the southern side of a new and formally arranged development onto the low-lying land between Millhead and the old river Lea that was previously occupied only by the 1830s gas and charcoal plant. Its eastern side was defined by the north–south line of near-identical groups of mills, beginning with Group C of 1861 at the southern end and continuing to Groups F and G of 1878 and 1888–9 at the north of the alignment that on completion extended for 240m (see Fig 3.5). The uniformity of form of the mill groups, their repetitive symmetry betokening organised and purposeful industry, and their well-built and finely detailed Italianate style together added up to a visually expressive grouping that was undoubtedly deliberate. It compares in conception with the grand architectural treatment of the French government's new powder factory laid out at Sevran-Livry to the north of Paris in the early 1870s, and more generally with contemporary industrial developments in England such as Armstrong's new works at Swindon of 1869–77.[62]

The ranges of incorporating mills were serviced on their rear, eastern side by a new north–south canal sprung off the canal branch serving the gas works on the site's lower level. This in turn dictated the location and orientation of buildings on its eastern side. These included the pellet powder house with its accumulator (Fig 3.32), so that, when converted to a set of incorporating mills, it shared the same alignment as well as detailing with the mills to its west.

The network that this accumulator served – of ancillary hydraulic accumulator and press houses – was scattered through the southern end of the former coppiced woodland to the north of Queen Meads (Fig 3.35). They took locations alongside the newly extended canal network, for ready transportation of products, but integrally with that network they effectively extended the factory across a much larger consolidated area.

The increased capacity of the steam mills imposed pressures on other sections of the factory concerned with finishing, and those processes themselves became more elaborate. These needs were met similarly by expansion into low-lying areas between the Millhead Stream and Cornmill Stream, north of Queen Meads. At first, expansion in the early 1850s was piecemeal, with the

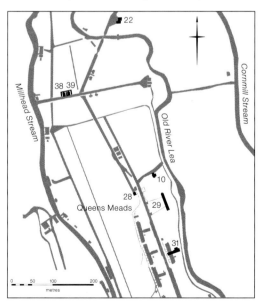

Figure 3.33 RGPF Waltham Abbey, remote accumulator tower, 1878. It was converted into offices after 1945.

Figure 3.34 RGPF Waltham Abbey, facade of Press House no 4, 1879. Note contraband box on wall. (BB92/26106 (DS))

Figure 3.35 (left) RGPF Waltham Abbey, introduction of centralised hydraulic power. Redrawn from OS, Essex, Sheet XLIV.14, 25-inch, second edition, 1897. OS, Essex, Sheet XLIV.10, 25-inch, second edition, 1897. Power: 28 Remote hydraulic accumulator tower 1878–9 (Fig 3.33); 31 Pellet-powder buildings 1869, remodelled as Group E incorporating mills 1877–8 (Fig 3.19 and 3.32). User: 10 Moulding house 1860s; 22 Hydraulic press house 1878 (Fig 3.34); 29 Guncotton press house 1870s; 38 Moulding house no 4 1882–3 (Fig 3.23); 39 Moulding house no 4 1884–5 (Fig 3.23).

Figure 3.36 RGPF Waltham Abbey, no 4 steam stove, 1885. (BB92/26171)

construction of new hydraulic press houses on the sites of earlier facilities. But as it progressed, principally through a greatly extended high level canal system (see below, Tramways and canals) providing both power and transport networks in a traditional way, a much increased site area away from the overcrowded Millhead was brought into occupied use. This allowed new large process buildings to be constructed with an adequate space between, and the need for increased capacity of the works to be met. These included a new press house (Fig 3.34) and a new steam stove further north (Fig 3.36), both alongside the new canal. The extended possibilities for water power were used to power a dusting house and a breaking down house, perhaps dating to the 1860s. The developed high level canal essentially created a new flow line for powder manufacture parallel to the facilities along Millhead.

These developments had their effects on the established parts of the site. In the Lower Island section the most significant change was the construction of the Group B mills in the late 1850s. The sulphur refinery was also extended and a new proof range constructed. Along Millhead change was piecemeal as mills were reconstructed or underwent change of use. Northwards an additional water-powered granulating house was added in 1874, and in 1885 another steam stove (see Fig 3.36), coinciding with the introduction of prismatic powders.

Figure 3.37 (facing) RGPF Waltham Abbey, expansion in the late nineteenth century (redrawn from OS, Essex, Sheet XLIV.14, 25-inch, second edition, 1897. OS, Essex, Sheet XLIV.10, 25-inch, second edition, 1897). ***1850s****: 1 Granulating house 1857; 2 Granulating house expense magazine 1857; 3 Hydraulic press house* c *1856 (Fig 2.33); 4 Hydraulic press house* c *1856 (Fig 3.26–3.28); 5 Group A incorporating mills and expense magazines 1856 (Fig 3.4 and 3.8–3.10).* ***1860s****: 6 Grand magazine rebuilt 1867–8 (Fig 3.42); 7 ?Box store 1861; 8 Expense magazine* c *1865; 9 Breaking-down house and magazine 1862; 10 Moulding house 1860s; 11 Group D incorporating mills and expense magazine 1867–8; 12 Group C incorporating mills and expense magazine 1861 (Fig 3.11); 13 Pellet-powder buildings 1869 (Fig 3.19).* ***1870s****: 14 Watch house* c *1870; 15 Unidentified 1870s; 16 Aqueduct 1878–9; 17 Unidentified ?1879; 18 Dusting house no 4 1879; 19 Expense magazines 1879; 20 Granulating house no 4 1874; 21 Stove 1879 (Fig 3.60); 22 Hydraulic press house 1878 (Fig 3.34); 23 Aqueduct 1878–9 (Fig 3.38); 24 Bridge 1878–9; 25 Bridge 1878–9 (Fig 3.37); 26 Magazine 1874; 27 Expense magazine 1879; 28 Hydraulic accumulator tower 1878–9 (Fig 3.33); 29 Guncotton press house and expense magazines 1870s; 30 Group F incorporating mills 1878; 31 Group E incorporating mills 1877–8 (Fig 3.19 and 3.32); 32 Water-wardens house 1878–9;* ***1880s****: 33 Magazine 1880s; 34 Dining room 1880s; 35 Stove 1885–6 (Fig 3.35); 36 Moulding house expense magazine 1883; 37 Moulding house expense magazine 1885; 38 Moulding house no 4 1882–3 (Fig 3.23); 39 Moulding house no 4 1884–5 (Fig 3.23); 40 Tray magazine 1882; 41 Expense magazine 1880s; 42 Group G incorporating mills 1888–9 (Fig 3.12–3.13); 43 ?Charcoal store 1889; 44 Charcoal store 1887; 45 Gas and charcoal works 1830s–80s.*

Overall, these were decisive changes in area and layout and functional connections. The last were more diverse and more flexible than the factory flow line based solely on Millhead. It was because of that diversity and flexibility, created by gunpowder production on a truly industrial scale which developed in the second half of the nineteenth century, that Waltham Abbey RGPF was able to adapt and accommodate the far-reaching developments of chemically-based explosives production in the last two decades of the century (see Chapter 5).

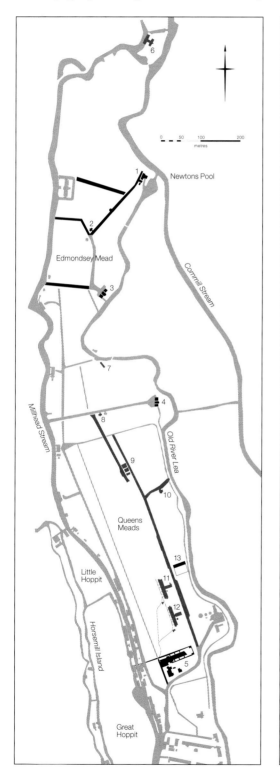

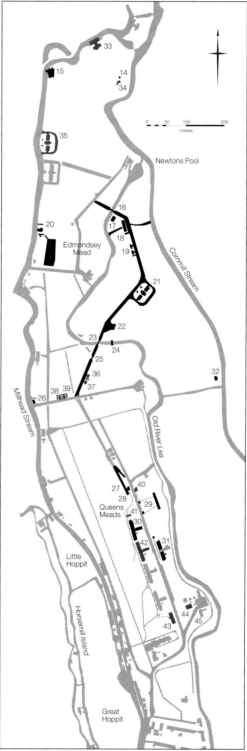

Tramways and canals

As the pattern of steam-driven incorporating mills on Queen Meads developed from the 1850s, they were linked to the Millhead and to each other by tramways. Powder was brought from the mixing house on Millhead to the expense magazines or mills in hand-propelled bogies. The 2ft 3in (0.69m) gauge tramway, of flat-bottomed rails nailed directly to timber decking supported on brick piers (see Fig 3.12), was raised to approach the mills at the level of the verandas along their western sides and to keep them above the flooding to which Queen Meads was liable.[63] Entrance doors on the contemporary expense magazines were, therefore, also at a similar elevated level. While the mills or other danger buildings were working a red signal was raised as a sign that no powder bogie or barge was to approach. At least from the later 1870s the powder moved northwards after incorporation to an interchange point with the developed high level canal network.

A great increase in the factory's canal system underpinned the expansion away from Millhead (Fig 3.37). After initial piecemeal reuse of the existing infrastructure for two hydraulic press houses, a short length of canal was excavated to create an extension to a new granulating house added in 1857 adjacent to Newton's Pool, and thereby link it to Millhead. By the mid-1860s, too, a further branch on the high level system was dug southwards in a raised embankment towards the steam mills. It certainly served a new breaking down house and perhaps continued south to create an interchange with the tramways of the steam mills and, thus, a direct flow line to the new process network away from Millhead.

At the lower end of the old river Lea the network was extended by the canal dug to the rear of the steam mills. Perhaps added in the 1860s to supply the mills with coal, it also linked the new guncotton press house to the guncotton factory at the southern end of the site (see Chapter 5).

The key to exploiting the under-utilised eastern half of the factory was to create a new north–south arterial canal system to provide passage independently of Millhead. This was achieved in a single building campaign in 1878–9 and is securely chronicled by date stones on buildings, aqueducts, and bridges (Fig 3.38). The new high level canal system to the north linked together and extended the existing spurs off Millhead. Where it crossed the old river Lea it was carried in cast iron aqueducts (Fig 3.39). Pedestrian access between the process buildings was improved by raised causeways with a wood-block surface in places. New bridges carried them over the canal and the old river Lea (Fig 3.38). A lock on the branch towards

Figure 3.38 RGPF Waltham Abbey. Footbridge over canal, built in 1878. (BB92/26104)

Figure 3.39 RGPF Waltham Abbey, cast iron aqueduct dated 1878–9. As it crosses the old river Lea, the height difference demonstrates the fall between high and low level systems. (BB92/26168)

Figure 3.40 RGPF Waltham Abbey, canal lock, 1878. (BB92/26206)

the steam mills linked the high and low levels (Fig 3.40); though undated, it is built with bricks by Joseph Hamble of West Bromwich of the same type as in the dated bridges of 1878. Until its construction the upper and lower canal systems were closed systems, linked only by a circuitous route through Powdermill Cut and the river Lea Navigation. This whole development entailed engineering works and investment of a significantly different order from the earlier canal works in the factory. It increased the capacity of the works, but the pace of manufacture remained unaltered, conditioned by the time it took men or boys to haul the powder barges or tramway bogies between process buildings.

Barges

By 1907 the factory canal network comprised around five miles of navigable waterways.[64] Two types of barges plied this network: the larger were up to 34ft 5in (10.5m) in length with a pointed prow at either end (Fig 3.41) and the smaller were flat or swim-ended up to 28ft 2in (8.6m) in length (Fig 3.42), each about 6ft 6in (2m) in beam. These barges were carvel built and incorporated many of the safety features of the buildings, including use of copper nails, bronze fittings, and internal leather-lined decks. The form of the powder boats appears to have altered little from the earliest illustrations in the mid-nineteenth century to the latest boats built in the twentieth century.[65] The central section of the barges was covered by a barrel-shaped wooden cabin with canvas flaps in the centre through which the powder was loaded; at either end of this cabin doors communicated to the open prows. More specialised boats also existed. The remains of a small ice breaker were recovered during clearance of the canals; and in the late 1880s a barge called *The Spark* was used by Colonel Noble, the Superintendent, for internal communication.

Around the developed waterway network at Waltham Abbey there were a number of boat houses, large enough to accommodate a single vessel. These brick-built structures had vaulted brick and concrete roofs and may have functioned as a form of expense magazine for loaded barges.

Figure 3.41 RGPF Waltham Abbey, factory powder barge. (BB92/26163)

Figure 3.42 RGPF Waltham Abbey, Millhead in October 1897, showing barge porches and swim-ended barge, perhaps in this instance used as a maintenance boat. (BB97/3439; © MoD)

Engravings and photographs show powder punts were a common feature of other powder works in the south of England, as at Chilworth and Hounslow and Oare, where the mills were linked by slow-moving leats or ponds. At Faversham and the former Littleton powder works in Somerset (now Bath and North East Somerset Unitary Authority) small flat-bottomed boats have been recovered from ponds.[66] But only at Waltham Abbey were multi-level waterways so fully developed and integrated for transport as well as power.

Magazines

As new process buildings were added to the expanded factory, so too were associated expense magazines to hold powder against use. These were a bomb-proof type of magazine, identical in form to those erected at the beginning of the century. They took the form of a simple rectangular building, 9m × 5m and standing to 4m at the gables, with the roof a solid brick vault covered by slates. In those cases where buildings were on the canal network, barges were unloaded and loaded under a covered porch over the canal.

The factory's 'Grand Magazine', located at the extreme northern tip of the site since 1804 (see Chapter 2), was rebuilt in 1867–8 (Fig 3.43). Its substantial brick-vaulted form was more reminiscent of the late eighteenth-century bomb-proof magazines at Purfleet than the flimsier Board of Ordnance magazines of the early nineteenth century.[67]

Figure 3.43 RGPF Waltham Abbey, Grand Magazine as rebuilt in 1867–8. (above) design drawing (BB92/26330); (below) interior in 1993 (BB92/26226)

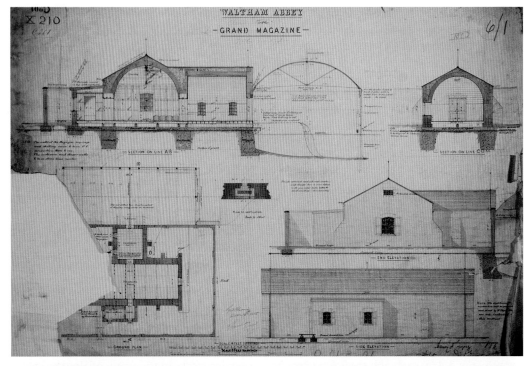

Parallels and imitators

Steam power at home and abroad

In the application of steam power the mills at Waltham Abbey were by no means unique. As early as 1806 a Boulton and Watt type engine was supplied to Mr W G Harvey, owner of the Sedlescombe Mills near Battle in Sussex.[68] By the early 1820s the French engineer Maguin on his visit to England noted steam engines in operation at four powder works.[69] Commonly they were installed to form a backup for the water mills in times of low water. It was the scale of the steam mills at Waltham Abbey which set this site apart. The only other producers who could justify this large-scale investment were a small number of large powder producers, whose volume of production would be badly hit by a water shortage. Steam power was principally applied to the incorporating mills but elsewhere in powder factories water power remained the prime mover.

One of the most important private producers was Curtis's and Harvey's Hounslow powder works in London (Fig 3.44). In addition to the many water mills on the site, the presence of three large T-shaped steam-powered incorporating mills may be identified by the late nineteenth century. One group was powered by a 50 brake hp 'Robey' horizontal engine and the other by a 45 brake hp 'Simpson's' incline steam engine. They were described as 'each consisting of six mills, three on either side of an engine house, and all driven from overhead shafting'.[70] A third group of seven incorporating mills was powered by a 50 brake hp 'Hick's Corliss' horizontal steam engine and a water wheel[71] (Fig 3.45). At Curtis's and Harvey's Bedfont works, also in Greater London, a single engine powered a group of six mills; by the end of the century an auxiliary engine was added to a pair of water mills (see Fig 1.23).[72] The group of six offer a close parallel to those at Waltham Abbey RGPF, but were housed in detached buildings and again were powered by overhead drive shafts. A similar configuration was installed at Chilworth in Surrey, where steam-driven mills with under-floor gearing

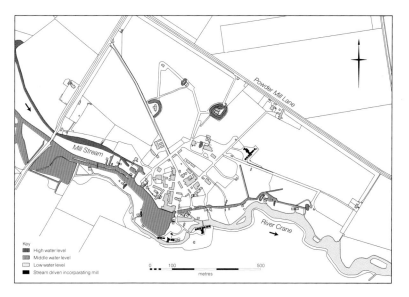

Figure 3.44 Curtis's and Harvey's Hounslow Gunpowder Mills, 1898; though now occupied by Crane Park, many of the leats may still be traced. Redrawn from OS, Middlesex, Sheet XX.14, 25-inch, second edition, 1898.

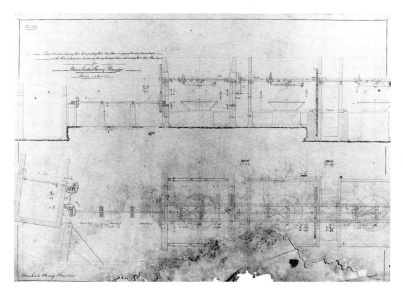

Figure 3.45 Hounslow Gunpowder Mills. Design drawing for the southerly group of mills showing dual use of water and steam power, 1860; machinery supplied by B Hick and Son, Soho Ironworks, Bolton. (AA94/5659; © Bolton Central Library)

were in operation during the 1870s, with the engine between two groups of mills.[73] In these examples the runners were turned by the drive shaft. At the Worsborough Dale gunpowder factory in South Yorkshire, exceptionally, an engine powered the

Confederate Powder Works
Augusta, Ga.

Figure 3.46
Augusta, Georgia,
USA Confederate
Powder Mills.
(© Library of
Congress, Washington
B8184–5307)

under-floor drive shaft, which turned the bedplate of the mills while the runners remained fixed.[74]

The clearest example of the influence of the Waltham Abbey RGPF and the rapid diffusion of new technology by the published word was in the establishment of the new confederate powder mills at Augusta, Georgia (USA). At the outbreak of the American Civil War in April 1861, the southern confederate states had no independent facilities for gunpowder production to match the large mills of the north, notably those of du Pont at Wilmington, Delaware. The option of importing large quantities of gunpowder was also ruled out by blockade of its ports. In directing the construction of the new confederate powder mills, Colonel George Washington Rains stated that he had the 'singular good fortune' to come into the possession of Major Baddeley's pamphlet on the *Manufacture of gunpowder as carried on at*

the Government Factory Waltham Abbey, published in 1857.[75] Rains recognised that the process and machinery employed at Waltham Abbey RGPF were 'the best existing in any country', and, though this pamphlet lacked illustrations, found the descriptions sufficiently detailed for the form of the mills to be reconstructed. In this, he had the assistance of a man named Wright, who had worked at Waltham Abbey RGPF. Though described as being 'sadly defective in a certain way', Wright may have been able to supplement the pamphlet's descriptions with his firsthand knowledge.[76]

The mills constructed at Augusta were monumental in scale and architectural conception (Fig 3.46). They measured 296ft (90.2m) in overall length, with a central engine compartment flanked by six mill bays on both sides. The drive shaft matched the building in length, with a diameter of 10–12in (0.25–0.31m) tapering to 8in (0.20m) at the extremities. Power was supplied by a 130hp steam engine with a 14 ton flywheel, designed to power a flour mill before the war. As at Waltham Abbey RGPF, the main shaft turned continuously and the drive was engaged using a remotely controlled friction arrangement. As in the Group A mills, the mill bays were arranged facing alternately: in place of trapezium-shaped bays, Rains used what he described as a 'mortar-shaped' bay measuring 17ft (5.2m) wide by 24ft (7.3m) long with separating walls 28ft (8.5m) high. The roof and fourth wall of each bay were constructed from light materials. Each of the cast iron runners weighed 5 tons (5.08 tonnes) and revolved on an iron bed; suspended above each pair was a water-filled drenching tub.

Rains introduced production refinements, one of which was to reduce the ingredients to a 'semi-liquid slush' after initial refining. This mud was transferred as a solid cake in 60lb (27.22kg) charges to the incorporating mills. This process was similar to one described by Baddeley as in use at a large unnamed powder factory in England, and was claimed to reduce the time the charge was under the runners from four hours to one hour. Rains also found that with 5 ton (5.08 tonnes) edge runners he was able to dispense with the necessity of pressing powder to achieve the desired density.

An international industry

The influence of the German manufacturers on the English industry went beyond a transfer of ideas and was most evident in the formation of the Chilworth Gunpowder Company Limited. By the late nineteenth century, Chilworth was one of the oldest gunpowder factories then operating in England. It was acquired in 1881 from Samuel Sharp by Marcus Westfield, and was managed as a going concern by Westfield. It was a relatively up-to-date factory that included among its plant a number of steam-driven incorporating mills and a hydraulic press powered by a water turbine.[77]

Early in 1885 a company was established to supply the British government with brown or 'cocoa' powders. Its directors included J N Heidemann and Max Duttenhofer, who had recently developed this product in Germany, along with Eugen Ritter, also of the Rheinische-Westphalische Pulverfabriken, and their London agent, Edward Kraftmeir, and Carl Duttenhofer of the Duneburg Pulverfabriken. The board was chaired by Lord Sudeley, one of the largest shareholders in the British armaments firm of Armstrong and Mitchell and Company Limited.[78]

Marcus Westfield retained a place on the board as managing director. The share prospectus spoke of the difficulty other manufacturers had experienced in producing brown powders and gave the reassurance that the managers at Chilworth had been instructed 'in the process of manufacture, with terms for ensuring secrecy'.[79] The commercial security was such that not only German machinery but German personnel were imported.

The factory was at once modernised. New buildings included a range of incorporating mills divided into six self-contained bays each 20ft 8in (6.32m) in width and divided by walls 5ft (1.53m) thick (Fig 3.47). These were powered by a detached boiler and engine house located to the rear, with a drive shaft running along the rear of the building to power the gear rooms beneath the mills probably via a belt drive (Figs 3.48 and 3.49). The transmission of power from the engine house to the drive

Figure 3.47
Chilworth, Surrey.
Range of six
Incorporating Mills
constructed in 1885
for incorporating
Brown Powders.
(BB94/10118)

Figure 3.48
Chilworth, Surrey.
Piers at rear of the
incorporating mills
which formerly
supported the drive
shaft.
(BB94/10121)

Figure 3.49
Chilworth, Surrey.
Mill bay. Note
under-floor gear
room and the beam
which supported the
drencher tub; this
was formerly inter-
connected with the
other bays by the
mechanism surviv-
ing along the wall
tops. (BB94/10119)

Figure 3.50 Incorporator made at Grusonwerks Buckau-Madgeburg and installed by the Chilworth Gunpowder Company in the late 1880s. (© Hagley Museum and Library TP270 A12D9 vol 35, 5)

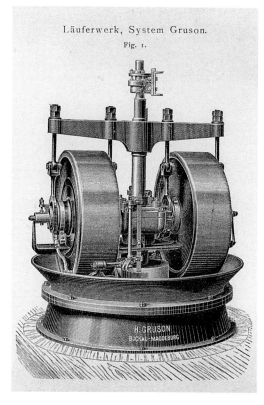

shaft may provide a rare British example of the use of a rope drive, a feature found in contemporary continental and American gunpowder works. The mills were all operated independently from tunnels between the bays or outside the end walls; instructions painted on their walls included the commands 'SLOW', 'FAST', and 'CLUTCH'. The mills, although built partly from local brick, included rolled steel I-section girders marked 'BURBACH 1884'. Machinery was also imported from Germany, including modern Grusonwerk suspended edge-runner incorporating mills (Fig 3.50). After modernisation the mills were regarded as among the finest in the world and by the 1890s were the chief supplier of gunpowder to the British and colonial governments, after Waltham Abbey RGPF.[80]

Housing and work force

By the standards of many late nineteenth-century industries, the explosives industry employed comparatively few people. In 1885, the earliest year for which reliable statistics are available from the Explosives Inspectorate, 934 people were employed in

the danger buildings and a further 1236 in non-danger buildings, giving a total of 2170 in 29 explosives factories. Including all workers employed in explosives handling (gunpowder and newer chemical explosives) in ammunition and firework factories, the total almost doubled from 7484 in 1885 to 14,567 in 1905. But this is lower than the true total because these figures excluded managerial and clerical staff and the other employees servicing these factories. They also exclude around 500 employees at the state factory at Waltham Abbey RGPF and the staff in the ammunition filling departments at the Royal Arsenal Woolwich.[81]

At Waltham Abbey RGPF the working day was from 7am until 5.30pm during the summer, with an hour for lunch. Saturday was a half-day with work until 1pm; no work was carried out on a Sunday during peacetime. The millmen worked 12-hour shifts from 6am to 6pm. Other departments might work slightly different hours to suit their particular needs.[82]

At the majority of powder works little provision was made for housing the workforce beyond that for the more senior staff. At the Oare Works, Faversham, a large house was provided for the manager, a bungalow for the foreman (Fig 3.51), and a couple of attached cottages for the workers. At Waltham Abbey the majority of the workers lived in private accommodation in the town or at nearby Waltham Cross. Little extra provision was made for the workforce beyond the dwellings erected at the beginning of the century, except a row of cottages (now demolished) at the entrance to

Figure 3.51 Oare Gunpowder Works, foreman's bungalow on site. (BB91/27281)

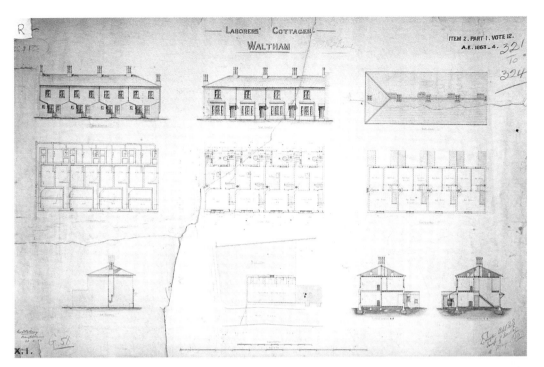

Figure 3.52 RGPF Waltham Abbey, design drawings for labourers' cottages in Powdermill Lane. (BB92/26466; © MoD)

Figure 3.53 (left) Chilworth, Surrey. The Old Manor House. This was the home of the Prussian work's manager, Captain Otto Bouvier, his wife and six children in the period 1887–1906. (BB94/10124)

Figure 3.54 (right) Chilworth, Surrey. Longfrey. This housed the foreman, Heinrich Wirths, his family and a lodger, Theodor Fischer, who was also a foreman at the factory. The remainder of the terrace was occupied by factory workers and their families. (BB94/10114)

Powdermill Lane (Fig 3.52) and opposite to them on Highbridge Street. In the allocation of the tied factory housing, preference was given to the older foremen: additionally a barracks in Powdermill Lane housed 13 constables and sergeants of the Metropolitan Police.[83]

At Chilworth the Old Manor House (Fig 3.53) was traditionally linked to the powder mills and was occupied by the works manager, Captain Otto Bouvier, from the late 1880s. By the end of the century the workforce at the factory had risen to between 300 and 400, many of whom were ex-soldiers, but little accommodation was provided. Alongside the factory, a terrace of five houses named Longfrey (Fig 3.54) was home to the German foremen

and other workers.[84] A small group of cottages, known as 'Magazine Cottages' was also added in the 1890s. Some of the German families became thoroughly assimilated into the local community and were christened at the local church: the son of one of the foremen, Heinrich Wirths, died serving in the Royal Flying Corps, and Edward Kraftmeir became naturalised and assumed the name Edward Kay.

Legislation and safety

Manufacture of gunpowder created inherent dangers for those working within the industry and for its immediate neighbours. The size of the industry and the number of people employed within it stood in inverse

Figure 3.55 Major, later Colonel, Vivian Dering Majendie, Her Majesty's Inspector of Gunpowder (© H&S Executive)

relationship to the havoc that an explosion might wreak on its surroundings. By late eighteenth-century standards the 1772 Act made an important contribution to promoting greater safety in gunpowder manufacture (see Chapter 1). By the late nineteenth century, however, the Act's inability to regulate manufacture of types of ammunition unknown in the 1770s and new explosive compositions was becoming apparent (for a general discussion of the circumstances leading up to the drafting of the 1860s and 1875 explosives legislation, see Majendie 1874). It was the loss of 21 lives in 1859 at Mr Pursall's ammunition and percussion cap factory in Whittall Street, Birmingham, just such an unregulated enterprise, that led to the new Act of 1860.[85] While principally drafted to govern manufacturers of percussion caps, ammunition, fireworks, and fulminate of mercury, it spelt out in greater detail the conditions under which gunpowder was to be produced. It allowed an increased charge under any pair of runners to 50lb (22.68 kg) for government and sporting powders and 60lb (27.22kg) for inferior powders; in contrast to previous vagueness it laid down the permitted quantities to be

worked and stored in designated danger buildings; it required provision of small expense magazines to prevent illegal storage of powder within process buildings.

Deficiencies in the 1860 Act were addressed by no less than four further Acts within the decade, but the defects of such piecemeal legislation were well known to those who had to administer it or deal with the consequences of the mishandling of explosives.[86] A series of disastrous explosions in 1870, again associated with the Birmingham ammunition industry, and in particular an explosion at Ludlow's ammunition factory where 53 lives were lost, prompted an investigation, instigated by the Home Secretary and undertaken by a professional army officer, Major Vivian Dering Majendie of the Royal Artillery (Fig 3.55).[87] Three main conclusions were drawn; firstly, that the 1860 Act was frequently infringed in ammunition, cap, and similar factories; secondly, that even where it was enforced it was inadequate to afford protection to the workpeople and general public; and, thirdly, to enforce the observance of any Act a system of government inspection would be required. Majendie backed up his findings by requesting permission to draw up an abstract of the present law for circulation to all explosive makers and handlers, and powers to visit all relevant premises in Britain to make an assessment of how the present law was working and how it might be amended.

From 1870, when Major Majendie was appointed as Her Majesty's Inspector of Gunpowder Works, until his report was presented in 1874, 409 places were visited. He was assisted by Captain F M Smith, late of the Royal Gunpowder Factory, and after his death by Major A Ford. Over three-quarters of the places visited were magazines, and of the factories only 26 manufactured gunpowder, although one of these subsequently ceased such manufacture.

The enquiry was carried out within a ruling spirit of free trade and abhorrence of government restriction, encapsulated in an earlier guiding principle that 'legislative restrictions upon trade are only to be justified by the necessity of providing for the public safety'. Yet Major Majendie's report made sobering reading.[88] In the 25 working gunpowder factories inspected, all permitted dangerous practices or omitted important safety precautions, and in 18 factories violations of the law also occurred.

The result was the 1875 Act.[89] Its single most important result was the establishment of the Explosives Inspectorate. Provision had been made in the 1860 Act to appoint inspectors of explosives, but no formal body had ever been constituted. Establishment of the Inspectorate under the Act provided a regulatory organisation that could oversee implementation of the legislation. This addressed a frequent complaint from the leading manufacturers that disregard for the law by some producers put responsible operators at a commercial disadvantage. The Act also created a national licensing system, under which certificates were issued to pre-existing factories and magazines, while new works were controlled by licenses and amending licenses. Such licenses still required the assent of the local authority, but were issued by the Secretary of State on the advice of the Inspectorate. This had the effect of removing many of the inconsistencies of the old system, which relied on local Justices of the Peace, often with no knowledge or body of expertise to call upon. Continuing certificates were issued to 28 factories, the three factories at Faversham having perhaps been earlier counted as one.[90] The new Act also made it a requirement that any accident involving explosives or fires within registered premises had to be reported to the Inspectorate. As with previous legislation, factories, stores, and other places where explosives were kept or used belonging to the government were exempted.

The inspectorate was a small body consisting of two inspectors, Majors Majendie and Ford, with a third inspector being appointed in the 1880s. Yet it became a body with a fund of accumulated knowledge about best practice in the manufacture and handling of explosives across the country and abroad. This knowledge was communicated in its annual reports or special reports on specific explosions that aimed at preventing their recurrence. These reports, sometimes with accompanying plans and photographs, are among the most valuable sources of information detailing the technology and working practices within the industry.

It was in no small measure because of the care with which the 1875 Act was drafted that the expansion of the industry in the last quarter of the nineteenth century was not met with a commensurate increase in serious accidents. A crude index of its effectiveness may be obtained by comparing the years 1868–70, when on average 43 people per year were killed, with the period from 1885–1905, when the death rate reached double figures in only three out of those 20 years.[91] This was despite a three-fold increase in the size of the industry, handling far greater quantities of explosives, many of which were new and relatively untried. The principles on which the Act was based have also stood the test of time and the 1875 Act, with minor amendments enacted in 1923 and through Orders in Council, still remains in force to regulate the modern explosives industry.[92] Those principles, with additions from subsequent annual reports, were adopted by a number of continental countries and British overseas possessions in formulating their own explosives legislation.

Safety clothing

The 1875 Act went far further than previous legislation in regulating working practices within licensed factories, and, to a certain extent, the construction of buildings. Although its primary purpose was not social reform of working conditions, it did have a beneficial effect in making explosive factories safer places to work. For example, it stipulated that suitable clothing should be provided for workers in the danger buildings. Characteristic clothing consisted of a pocketless suit of wool, or other non-inflammable material, and a cap with pull-down ear flaps. Powder or magazine shoes were also provided for all those entering the danger areas. Typically these were either entirely of leather, or if shod a non-ferrous metal, usually copper, would be used. At Waltham Abbey RGPF, workers in the incorporating mills wore a suit of 'lasting' (a durable cloth) with bone buttons (to which powder did not adhere), gauntlets, and a cloth helmet, which gave some protection against fire (Fig 3.56). Concern for the workers was also manifest in deep wells

Figure 3.56 RGPF Waltham Abbey. Worker in gunpowder incorporator mills, late nineteenth century. He is wearing a 'lasting' suit, protective cap, gauntlets and magazine boots, and sits on a powder barrel! (BB94/8004; © MoD)

Figure 3.57 Faversham, Fleur de Lys Centre. Display of early twentieth-century explosive workers' clothing and tools. (BB94/10618

outside each danger building that 'the authorities have thoughtfully provided ... into which men who have been badly burnt may plunge'.[93] Use of ferrous tools in the manufacturing process or in repairing danger buildings was another hazard that was guarded against by restricting the materials

from which tools and fittings could be made to safe materials, including leather, wood, copper, or brass (Fig 3.57). At Waltham Abbey this policy even extended to the use of copper barbed wire. More formalised distinctions appeared between 'clean' and 'dirty' areas. 'Clean' areas were parts of the factory where loose explosives might be encountered; a foot board, sometimes painted red, often marked the boundary and acted as a physical reminder of the distinction. This may also have been visible as a change in flooring material. In larger factories changing or shifting rooms were built where the workers could change and wash, as at Waltham Abbey RGPF, along with police posts or search rooms. Changing areas were also provided in the lobbies of danger buildings, where workers could leave outdoor clothing and change into magazine shoes. A shoe box was often provided for this purpose. Workers were searched to prevent the introduction of 'contraband' items into the danger areas and to enforce the wearing of regulation footwear and clothing. Employment of young people continued, although persons under 16 were only allowed to work in danger buildings and magazines under adult supervision.

The archaeology of safety

The 1875 Act also went further in stipulating the distances that were to be maintained between buildings in explosives factories. Provision of a protective traverse generally halved the permitted distance. This had the effect of reinforcing the two most obvious characteristics of explosives works, their dispersed nature and the presence of traverses or blast banks and walls of a variety of forms. But until more work is undertaken to produce detailed archaeological accounts of gunpowder factories, supported by documentary sources, any fine assessment of the effect of legislation on plan form is difficult to make.

Building design

As with other areas where there was the risk of fire such as textile mills or large warehouses, new construction techniques and materials allowed these risks to be minimised. There was recognition that small 'blows' were inevitable even in the best regulated factories. As a consequence, the danger buildings of the gunpowder industry were usually relatively flimsy structures, with superstructures that were generally timber-framed, with a weather-boarded or canvas covering. In a small explosion the force of the blast would thus be dissipated outwards, leaving the machinery relatively undamaged. Their interiors were lined with match boarding or a gritless cement and any ferrous metal fittings were covered. An exception to this general rule were the mills of south-western England with their Cyclopean granite walls, where their weight was perhaps sufficient to contain any minor blow and direct the force upwards.

In operation the majority of danger buildings were thick with black powder dust. In an attempt to prevent a build-up of powder, the floors were often covered in leather, sometimes in elephant or possibly hippopotamus hide, fixed with copper nails, and were continually swept and kept damp. As a rule few people worked in any given danger building; later licenses restricted the number allowed in any one building. Potential casualties were also reduced by devices allowing remote operation of machinery from behind the safety of a traverse.

Considerations of safety, therefore, gave buildings within the industry some of their distinctive characteristics. Safety also increasingly dictated that only one process was carried out in any one building. The design of individual buildings accordingly remained closely tied to the machinery or plant they housed and to their function. At the same time, the later nineteenth century offered new challenges and opportunities to explosives manufacturers in the choice of building materials, as it did with power sources. Here, too, they appear to have been slow in adopting new methods and technological innovation; but some changes were aimed to make the manufacturing buildings safer.

Iron framing and iron roofs were used in the textile industry and naval dockyards as a method of fireproofing from the early decades of the nineteenth century.[94] It was

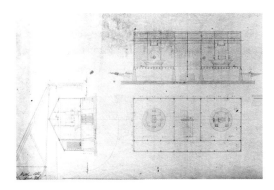

Figure 3.58 RGPF Waltham Abbey. Design drawing for an iron-framed gunpowder mill by B Hick and Son, Soho Ironworks, Bolton, 1856. (AA94/5649; © Bolton Central Library)

not until 1847, however, that a mill known as the 'Iron Duke' was documented at Waltham Abbey RGPF.[95] A design drawing (Fig 3.58) prepared a decade later shows a gunpowder mill of traditional design with underdriven incorporating bays on either side of a central, geared wheel, possibly steam powered. The mill sat on concrete foundations with an iron-framed superstructure, clad in corrugated iron, its roof covered by metal sheeting.[96]

Lightning conductors

The Act could not legislate against natural disasters, however. The most devastating of these to the industry could be lightning. It was the practice in the early part of the nineteenth century to erect a mast with a metallic rod attached to it at some distance from the building it was intended to protect (see Fig 2.18). Advances in scientific thinking showed this to be a false strategy and that to protect a building it was necessary to ensure an effective line of discharge to earth.[97] By mid-century the principle of lightning conductors, already common protection on warships, was applied to powder magazines. The 1860 Act made lightning conductors or thunder rods a requirement for store magazines. The 1875 Act was more specific in requiring lightning conductors for all factory and expense magazines and for every danger building if required by the Secretary of State. The loss of four lives when lightning struck the corning house of the Black Beck gunpowder factory in Cumbria, despite having a conductor fitted, illustrated the need to ensure that lightning conductors were adequately installed. As a result, it was recommended that the terminal should consist of three or four points

Figure 3.59
Chilworth Surrey.
Corrugated iron
cordite drying stove,
1890s. The stove was
warmed by an
underfloor heating
system.
(BB94/10102)

and be fixed to a copper strip directly on the wall of the building. All other metal fittings on the building and the machinery were to be connected to this strip, which was in turn attached to a copper earthplate or metal pipe preferably in damp ground.[98] In at least one example at Waltham Abbey RGPF the earthplate took the form of a copper spiral affixed to a timber crucifix and embedded in the bottom of a canal.[99] Workmen were also required to stop work during a thunderstorm and leave the buildings they were working in closed.

Corrugated iron and galvanised sheeting

Corrugated iron was one of the most revolutionary building materials introduced in the nineteenth century. It allowed robust prefabricated buildings to be erected virtually anywhere in the world. It was introduced in the 1820s and from the 1830s galvanising made it more resistant to corrosion.[100] To the explosives manufacturers it offered a relatively cheap, light and non-inflammable building and roofing material. One of its earliest uses at Waltham Abbey RGPF was for a charcoal store built between 1841 and 1851. While it is uncertain whether the 'Iron Duke' mill described above was built, corrugated iron was used to roof the hydraulic pump house known to have been constructed by 1854 (see Figs 3.26 and 3.27). It was noted that galvanised corrugated iron would provide an ideal protection against lightning, ensuring a rapid discharge to earth.[101] Despite these early experiments with corrugated iron at Waltham Abbey RGPF, its use later in the century was generally restricted to minor or ancillary buildings and for roofing.

Private manufacturers of gunpowder generally used corrugated iron only in a similarly limited way as a roofing material. But those producing the new chemical explosives used it in the same pioneering spirit as their customers used their products. A photograph taken in 1871 after a large explosion at the Patent Safety Gun cotton Company Limited in Stowmarket in Suffolk, constructed during the 1860s, shows corrugated iron from the buildings strewn over the factory site.[102] At Chilworth

Figure 3.60 RGPF
Waltham Abbey,
South Site.
Secondary zinc
lining in 1894
Cordite Mixing
House.
(BB92/26255)

during the refurbishment of the factory for manufacturing cordite in the 1890s, corrugated iron was used not only for roofing and infilling walls but for entire buildings. These included a pair of cordite drying stoves (Fig 3.59) constructed on an iron frame and clad in corrugated iron; the interior was insulated with hair secured by chicken wire and rendered in cement. Its widespread and distinctive use for constructing or revetting blast mounds at Chilworth gave rise to the familiar term within the industry for such mounds as 'Chilworth mounds', though the technique was widely used elsewhere, notably by Nobels at Ardeer in Ayrshire (Fig 5.16).

Flat galvanised metal sheeting was also employed as a roofing material. It was worked to form roof vents and other fittings, too, including guttering and drain pipes. It was even used to line buildings (Fig 3.60), especially those where loose dry guncotton might become lodged in the tightest of match boarding. Such metal lining allowed buildings to be easily washed out, and further reduced the chance of the dangerous build-up of dust.

Willesden paper

Willesden paper, sometimes referred to as Willesden cardboard, was chemically treated to render it tough, waterproof, and fire resistant.[103] It was cheap, and as a roofing material afforded a line of least resistance in case of an explosion and minimised injury from flying debris. At Waltham Abbey RGPF, in addition to roofing a number of buildings including a nitroglycerine washing house, it was also employed to form the walls of a guncotton stove built in 1884. Archaeologically Willesden paper is virtually impossible to trace, but the reports of the Explosives Inspectorate do refer to it, for example in connection with an accident at Roslin in 1890, and may suggest a more widespread use.[104]

Concrete

Concrete was first used in building foundations at Waltham Abbey RGPF in the 1850s. Though mass concrete was employed as a structural material in the Royal Commission forts from the 1860s onwards, it was only in the extensive reconstruction of Waltham Abbey RGPF in the late 1870s that a similar use was made of it in explosives structures. Even then it was hidden from view, for example behind the brick retaining wall of the traverse surrounding the no 4 press house (Fig 3.34), or to fill the void between the inner brick vault and the outer wall of the steam gunpowder drying stove (Fig 3.61), where in earlier traversed stoves earth was used (Fig 2.30). Only in 1882 was a freestanding concrete structure built, in the form of a U-shaped traverse to enclose a gunpowder moulding house (Fig 3.23). By the end of the century simple earthwork mounds were again regarded as the most effective means of absorbing blast debris. The dangers of

Figure 3.61 RGPF Waltham Abbey. Brick and mass concrete traverse enclosing a boiler house at the centre of a steam heated gunpowder drying stove, 1883–4. (BB92/26109)

Figure 3.62 Hayle, Cornwall. 1890s Mass concrete explosives magazine. (BB94/16165)

solid traverses themselves becoming flying debris had been clearly demonstrated when a brick traverse surrounding the nitroglycerine factory at Waltham Abbey RGPF was wrecked by an explosion in 1894.[105]

The explosives industry was, therefore, slow to exploit the potential of concrete as a cheap and fireproof building material for freestanding buildings. The Explosives Inspectorate reported in 1890 that it was inserting a clause in all new licenses that magazines were to be built of good Portland cement concrete.[106] Probably in response to this 1890 directive, the National Explosives Company at Hayle in Cornwall laid out the earliest known group of surviving concrete magazines (Fig 3.62). The personal involvement of the chemical engineer Oscar Guttmann may have been significant here. With his experience in the continental explosives industry, Guttmann had a long-standing interest in factory construction, and argued in a number of papers published around the turn of the century for the benefits of the use of ferro-concrete buildings.[107] It is also significant that in 1890 a continental company was responsible for the development of the bellite factory at

*Figure 3.63 RGPF
Waltham Abbey.
External Maxlume
electric lamp boxes
on Tetryl Magazine,
1940s. (B92/26165)*

Port Cornaa on the Isle of Man, which made extensive use of concrete in its buildings.[108] At Purfleet, Essex, in 1910 the new magazine was built only to floor level in ferro-concrete and the remainder in brick, as it was feared an entirely ferro-concrete magazine would provide too much resistance to an explosion.[109] Little enthusiasm was otherwise shown by the industry in Britain for concrete as a building material for factory buildings.

Lighting

Artificial lighting in powder magazines and explosives factories always presented a potential source of danger. In Drayson's drawings of Waltham Abbey RGPF of 1830, no provision for lighting of buildings appears to have been made beyond opening of shutters or large glazed windows, with the attendant risk of flying glass.[110] The use of wired-glass as opposed to glass merely shielded with wire was not generally adopted until the turn of the century.[111] Where artificial lighting was required a light was suspended on the exterior window shining inwards, a technique common to ships' magazines.

New sources of light in addition to oil lamps became available during the nineteenth century, namely gas and electricity. For the majority of powder producers remote from centres of population the expense of establishing an independent gasworks was beyond their means. At Waltham Abbey RGPF a substantial gasworks constructed in the middle of the century boasted three gasometers by its end. In the 1870s the incorporating mills at Waltham Abbey RGPF were lit by a lamp box set into their walls and vented to the exterior (Fig 3.14). A /in gas pipe led into the lamp, and special rules in the mills required the bases of the lamps to be constantly filled with 1in (25mm) of water.

Electricity

Electricity was introduced into explosive factories in the 1880s. The arrangements adopted for its use were designed to minimise risks from sparking and heat, especially in the most hazardous of the danger buildings designated as 'dusty' areas. The solution at Waltham Abbey RGPF was described in a paper by Jenkins (1891). Electricity was carried along overhead transmission lines to a fuse and switch box, at this date of teak, located 50yd (45.72m) from any dusty building. From this, continuous leads encased in wrought iron steam pipe were taken to lamp posts detached from the building. The lamp holder was screwed onto the end of the pipe to form an entirely closed system. The glow lamp was in turn protected by a glass dome or globe entirely filled with a water and glycerine mix, sealed with a layer of oil; it was secured by copper straps and in vulnerable situations protected by a wire cage. The Explosives Inspectorate later went further by prohibiting the use of electric lamp wire carrying current in any dusty area.[112] This instruction was not followed to the letter at Waltham Abbey RGPF, as electric fittings, as described in Jenkins's article, survive attached to the wall of the gunpowder press house (Fig 3.26). During the factory's restructuring in the 1890s to manufacture chemical explosives, more familiar cast iron switch and fuse boxes were introduced, along with the Cordeaux type porcelain insulators to carry the transmission lines. Perhaps because there were fewer risks of loose explosive dust, lights were inserted into the roofs of the nitroglycerine buildings, although the light was still housed within a glass globe (Fig 5.19). The pioneering principles for protecting electric circuits within explosives factories continued in use, with the wiring circuits and switch and fuse boxes fixed to the exterior of buildings and lighting either shining in through a window (Fig 3.63) or, more recently, contained in sealed bulkhead lights or specially shielded fluorescent tubes. Few attempts appear to have been made in the late nineteenth century to harness electricity to power gunpowder manufacturing machinery.

Endnotes

1   For an account of the English explosives industry in 1882, Guttmann 1883.
2   Eg Fairbairn 1861.
3   Eg *Engineering* 1878 gives an account of gunpowder manufacture and engravings of machinery made by Taylor and Challen of Birmingham.
4   Putnam and Weinbren 1992, 29–39.
5   Sweetman 1984, 152 n82.
6   *Ibid*, 125.
7   Francis 1852, 461–2; Guedalla 1926, 417.
8   *The Times* 1890.
9   Giles and Goodall 1992, 135–45; RCHME 1994.
10 Bolton Central Library (BCL), Benjamin Hick and Son Archive, 1856/9 Waltham Abbey, incorporating mills.
11 WASC 901/106.
12 Baker 1991, 74–7.
13 Falconer 1993, 21–4.
14 *Illus London News* 1861.
15 BCL, Benjamin Hick and Son Archive, Drawing 1857/95 Waltham Abbey, gearing and hoist.
16 Wilkinson, 1975.
17 Smith 1870, 40.
18 Fairbairn 1861, 55–9; BCL, Benjamin Hick and Son Archive, Drawing 1857/106 Waltham Abbey, crank and links.
19 Giles and Goodall 1992, 151.
20 Drawings collection at Waltham Abbey, New Incorporating Mills, Group F, L–145/2 dated 1877.
21 Smith 1870, 20.
22 Baddeley 1857, 30.
23 *Illus London News* 1854, 479.
24 Wilkinson 1975, 94.
25 Hogg 1963a, 756–60.
26 Bailey and Murray 1989, 22.
27 Smith 1868, 118.
28 Science Museum Library, London, Wilkinson 1975, 44. Unpublished typescript in MS 412.

29 Abel 1890, 328; *The Times* 1890; Mauskopf 1996, 285–9.
30 Abel 1890, 329; Guttmann 1895, **1**, 236–7.
31 Smith 1870, 75.
32 Morgan 1875, 1.
33 Smith 1868, 132.
34 Guttmann 1895, **1**, 258–9; Smith 1870, 75–80.
35 PRO Supp 5/510.
36 Morgan 1875, 6.
37 *The Times* 1879; Wardell 1888, 56–9.
38 *The Times* 1879.
39 PRO Supp 5/559.
40 PRO Supp 5/559.
41 Hodgetts 1909, 357.
42 Explosives Inspectorate 1906, 1907, 100.
43 Newbold 1916, 43.
44 Guttmann 1895, **1**, 253 fig 128; PRO Supp 5/559.
45 Wardell 1888, 62.
46 Explosives Inspectorate 1894, 127–9.
47 *The Times* 1886.
48 PRO Supp 5/577; MUN 7/555.
49 PRO Supp 5/595.
50 Wardell 1888, 63 and 110–17.
51 Smith 1870, 45; see Chapter 2.
52 *Ibid*, 49.
53 Cocroft 1994, 13 fig 2.
54 *Illus London News* 1854, 478.
55 Baddeley 1857, 13–15.
56 Guttmann 1895, 208.
57 Fairbairn 1861, 256.
58 Richie-Noakes 1984, 123.
59 *Ibid*, 122–8; Smith 1991.
60 Wilson 1963-4, 50; Explosives Inspectorate 1879, 6.
61 *Sporting Goods Rev* 1896, 63; a plan of Chilworth gunpowder works, late 1880s, in the possession of Alan and Glenys Crocker.
62 Cattell and Falconer 1995, ch 5.
63 Jenkins 1989, 385–415.
64 *VCH Essex* 1907, 455.

65 *Illus London News* 1854, 478.
66 *Gunpowder Mills Study Group Newsletter* 1989c, 13; Arthur Percival personal communication.
67 Guillery and Pattison 1996, 37–52.
68 Birmingham Central Library, Boulton and Watt Collection, portfolio 383.
69 Dr Patrice Bret personal communication.
70 *Sporting Goods Rev* 1896, 62.
71 Over 1984, 3 appendix 7; BCL, Benjamin Hick and Son archive, Drawing 1860/184 Curtis's and Harvey, Hounslow, incorporating mills.
72 Philo and Mills 1985, 101; Ordnance Survey 25 inch 1896, Middlesex XX.9.
73 Explosives Inspectorate 1879, 2; Explosives Inspectorate 1883, 4.
74 Explosives Inspectorate 1884, 4.
75 Rains 1882, 8; see Melton 1973 for a general account of the works.
76 Rains 1882, 8.
77 Explosives Inspectorate 1879, 1–6.
78 Newbold 1916, 33.
79 132/3 Guilford Muniment Room, Guildford, Guildford Municipal... Surrey Prospectus for The Chilworth Gunpowder Company Limited, 1885.
80 132/5/2 Guilford Muniment Room, Guildford, The Chilworth Gunpowder Company Limited, trade pamphlet for Royal Naval Exhibition 1891.
81 VCH Essex 1966, 164; Explosives Inspectorate 1905-6, 5.
82 PRO EF 5/18.
83 PRO RG 12/1715.
84 PRO RG 12/573(2).
85 Public General Statutes 1860, **23 and 24 Victoria, c. 139.**
86 Public General Statutes 1861, **24 and 25 Victoria, c. 130**; Public General Statutes 1862, **25 and 26 Victoria, c. 98**; Public General Statutes 1866, **29 and 30 Victoria, c. 69**; Public General Statutes 1869, **32 and 33 Victoria, c. 113.**

87 Sladen 1898, 552.

88 Majendie 1874.

89 Public General Statutes 1875, **38 Victoria, c. 17**.

90 Patterson 1986a, 13.

91 Majendie 1874, 13; Explosives Inspectorate 1906, 5.

92 Thomson 1941; Public Acts General 1923 **13 and 14 George V, c. 17**.

93 Fitzgerald 1895, 311.

94 Giles and Goodall 1992, 70–3.

95 Winters 1887, 109.

96 BCL, Benjamin Hick and Son Archive, Drawing 1856/74 Waltham Abbey, machine details.

97 Snow Harris 1858a and 1858b.

98 Explosives Inspectorate 1884.

99 Adam Ford personal communication.

100 Dickinson 1945.

101 Snow Harris 1858b, 130.

102 Double 1991, 45.

103 Malcolm Airs personal communication.

104 Explosives Inspectorate 1890, 4.

105 HMSO 1894b, 18.

106 Explosives Inspectorate 1890, 9.

107 Earl 1978, 184–5; Guttmann 1908; 1910.

108 Garrad 1980.

109 *Ferro-concrete* 1910.

110 PRO Supp 5/762, MP 11/15.

111 Guttmann 1908, 671.

112 Explosives Inspectorate 1906, 160.

4
The demise of gunpowder

The gunpowder industry in 1900

Adoption of cordite as the principal British service propellant in the 1890s (see Chapter 5) might be expected to have led to widespread closures amongst the powder producers. In the quarrying and mining industry, too, newer types of chemical explosives, in particular dynamite, had made serious inroads into the traditional black powder markets, both at home and in the export trade, as dynamite factories multiplied abroad. Another factor was commercial rationalisation, for by the turn of the century nearly 50% of the powder mills in the country were owned by one powder maker, Curtis's and Harvey of Hounslow. In a number of instances they had acquired unviable mills in order to reduce competition by closing them. The overall picture is, nevertheless, one of many old works struggling to survive in a declining market (Fig 4.1). The quarrying and mining industry remained an important user, for in some types of quarrying the heaving action of black powder was (and still is) preferred to the sharp crack of a chemical explosive. The only closure directly attributable to the change in military propellants was that of the Leigh Mills at Tonbridge in Kent – a factory modernised just over a decade earlier specifically to manufacture government prismatic powder.

It is therefore surprising, with overcapacity in the industry and a declining market, that some new facilities were created. A gunpowder section was constructed within the newly built explosives factory at Kynochtown in Essex in 1897.[1] It was probably electrically powered along with the remainder of the factory. Elsewhere, when there were close business ties between gunpowder firms and the new chemical explosives manufacturers, factories might be co-located, as at Chilworth, Dartford in Kent, and the government factory at Waltham Abbey. But, in general, large open waterside sites were preferred for the new chemical-based industry (see Chapter 5) rather than the cramped valley-bottom sites historically favoured for gunpowder production, reliant on water power. Exceptionally, the former Curtis's and Harvey powder works at Trago and Herodsfoot in Cornwall were converted

Figure 4.1 Location of early twentieth-century gunpowder production.

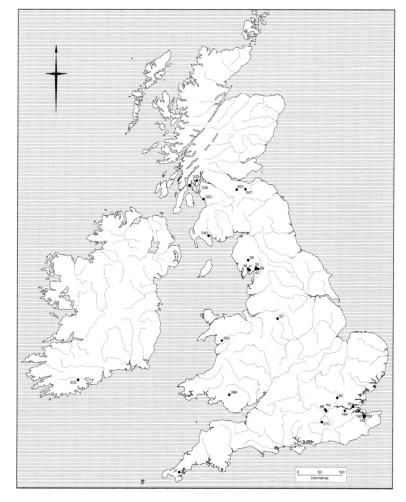

into works for manufacturing ammonal explosives, and these continued in operation until the end of the Great War.[2] They also closed the short-lived powder works at Cliffe on the Kent side of the Thames Estuary and developed the site into a large chemical explosives factory (see Fig 5.43 and 5.44).

RGPF Waltham Abbey

At Waltham Abbey, where gunpowder was manufactured exclusively for military consumption, the changes were especially complex. Some of the older gunpowder buildings had been converted and new buildings constructed as early as the 1860s, when the manufacture of guncotton started; but this had relatively little effect on the layout and functioning of the powder factory. Conversion to cordite was on a different scale. It not only did away with the need for production of gunpowder in volume, but also introduced a totally new technology. While some new buildings were constructed specifically to meet the needs of cordite manufacture, many other pre-existing gunpowder buildings were adapted. These were already constructed as danger buildings, with basic provisions to limit the effects of any accidental explosion. New machinery was generally installed with relatively slight alteration to the fabric of a building and often left little physical evidence of the conversion. In the gunpowder press and granulating houses the old machinery was replaced by tables for mixing cordite paste. Similarly, in the T-shaped incorporating mills the edge-runner mills were replaced by cordite incorporators and presses installed in their place. The vertical drive shafts of the earlier mills were simply cut off at floor level, and where the under-floor gearing was too difficult to remove it was left *in situ* (see Figs 3.16 and 3.18). The steam engines were retained for some time, but the drive was changed to an overhead line shaft and belts for the cordite incorporators, the line shafting passing through bearing boxes set in the partition walls. Therefore, despite introduction of a novel technology, the outward appearance of the mills (see Figs 3.6, 3.13 and 3.33) and much of the factory remained relatively unchanged.

The peacetime requirement of the services for gunpowder was less than 100 tons (101.6 tonnes) annually prior to the Great War. Despite the conversion to cordite there was still a small demand for prismatic powder charges for large-bore breech-loading guns still in service.[3] Though the trade factories had the capacity to supply this, the government perceived a need to maintain a small manufacturing capacity of its own. A number of water-powered mills within the Lower Island Works were kept in use for at least the first decade of the new century, including an incorporating mill, granulating house, and cam presses.[4] Some of the older water-powered mills along Millhead were also retained. This allowed government specialists to maintain their knowledge and act as a check on the trade on quality and price. Gunpowder continued to fulfil more specialised uses, including filling fuzes and within igniters for cordite charges (Fig 4.2). The latter led to the development of a distinctive sulphurless gunpowder, consisting of 70.5 parts of saltpetre and 29.5 parts of charcoal, as it was found sulphur had an injurious effect on cordite MK1.[5] Though the manufacturing process for fuze powders was almost identical to ordinary black powders, it had to be carried out with great exactitude to ensure a precise rate of burning.

The Great War 1914–18

For the majority of powder works the Great War brought a brief revival to an ailing industry, though this left few distinct or identifiable features on their sites. At the outbreak of war there were four factories producing gunpowder for military use: Waltham Abbey's annual production of 500 tons (508 tonnes) was specifically for fuze time rings, while Curtis's and Harvey's factories at Faversham and Cliffe (the latter perhaps with only finishing facilities), together with the Chilworth Gunpowder Company, had a combined annual output of 5750 tons (5842 tonnes).[6] It is not known if the remaining 19 or so active gunpowder works were also given military contracts, or served the war effort indirectly by supplying the quarrying and mining industry.

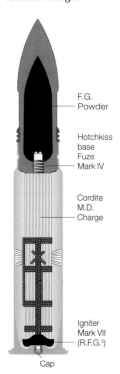

Figure 4.2 Section through 6-pounder quick-firing round. After Admiralty Handbook on Ammunition *1915. This shows the various uses to which black powder continued to be put; viz as an exploder in the shell, within the magazine of the base fuze and as an igniter for the main cordite charge.*

F.G. Powder

Hotchkiss base Fuze Mark IV

Cordite M.D. Charge

Igniter Mark VII (R.F.G.²)

Cap

Gun or black powder was required in large amounts for shell filling and cartridge igniters and in smaller quantities for use in primers, fuzes, gaines, and various Trench Warfare Department stores. The many specialised uses to which powder was put gave rise to a variety of different powders. Those meeting normal requirements were rifle and pistol powder, RFG2, black LG, Shell P, and RFG meal. So-called 'short milled' powders for use as bursting charges in shrapnel and common shell were also introduced to increase the output with a shorter milling time.

Archaeological evidence alone reflects but little the effect of the Great War on most powder works. There was, for example, no sudden increase in the number of buildings, as most of the factories had been operating below their total capacity before the war. Output could be increased by working longer hours or by bringing underused plant back into operation: neither action left a discernible effect on a factory's plan-form. One of the few sites with documented expansion was the Marsh Works at Faversham. Here, somewhat curiously, a small high explosives section was created, apparently within the middle of the still active gunpowder factory. A small fuze factory was also added, though this lay just outside the original factory perimeter.[7]

The private companies retained management of most powder works; but the Chilworth Powder Company was compelled to sever its German links, and in Cornwall the former powder mills at Herodsfoot, which were partly Austrian-owned, were seized and operated directly by the Ministry of Munitions.

Explosives filling factories (see Chapter 6) generally obtained the powder they needed directly from the trade, working to government specifications. This led later in the war to concerns about the lack of independent government checks on the quality of powder. Though not manufacturing gunpowder, some filling factories contained small gunpowder sections for blending fuze powders. Little is known about the activities of these sections or the types of buildings used to house them.

As firms with relevant skills and premises, many pre-war firework manufacturers were drawn into munitions work. They would otherwise have been idle and they had sites ideally suited to handling small quantities of explosives and to assembly work. These were controlled by the Explosives Inspectorate and were laid out according to the standard safety rules governing distance between buildings. 'Clean areas' were designated where explosives were handled, and buildings within a group were typically linked by timber walkways to reduce the dangers from grit. The buildings themselves were generally flimsier than those on military explosives sites, many having the appearance of small gabled garden sheds. The wartime work included the assembly of parachute flares, Verey lights, and signalling rockets, and other pyrotechnic stores. Well known firms such as James Pains and Sons at Mitcham in Surrey undertook this work. The weekly consumption of this one factory was around 10,000lb (4536kg) of meal powder and 750lb (340.2kg) of fine powder, manufacturing principally small trench rockets.[8]

Merger and Explosives Trades Ltd

As early as 1917 the private explosives manufacturers recognised that the peacetime market would be unable to sustain the number of explosives factories then in existence (see also Chapter 6). After the Treasury turned down an initial request for a merger as it feared diversion of money away from the war effort, the companies themselves merged to form Explosives Trades Ltd on 29 November 1918. This took the name of Nobel Industries Ltd in 1920, acknowledging Nobels as the leading company in the partnership; in 1926 it became the Nobel Division of the newly formed giant, Imperial Chemical Industries (ICI).[9]

With very low military demand for black powder and a declining civilian market, and as new chemical explosives continued to erode many of its traditional markets, exacerbating a pattern evident since the closing decades of the nineteenth century, the black powder factories were ripe for rationalisation. In this atmosphere little new investment had taken place in the industry in either plant or buildings. Any modernisation had been piecemeal. This not only allowed

Figure 4.3 Oare Gunpowder Works. Archaeological survey, 1991. Last known functions of buildings: 1 Packing room; 2 General stores and boiler house; 3 General stores and boiler house; 4 Engineers shop; 5 Saw mills, sulphur refinery and mill, smithy, engineers shop, carpenters shop, engine house and charcoal mills; 6 Magazine; 7 Tin shop, Japan shop and label shop; 8 Charcoal store; 9 Boiler house and stoves; 10 Barrel store; 11 Foreman's house (Fig 3.52); 12 Hoop store; 13 Packing rooms, workshop, office, boiler house; 14 Boiler house and stores; 15 Cooperage; 16 Box makers shop; 17 Oil store; 18 Store and timber shed; 19 Timber store and lodge; 20 Incorporating mills, saw mills, workshop and engine room; 21 Factory magazine; 22 Dusting house; 23 Hand press house and magazine; 24 Pump and engine house; 25 Glazing house; 26 Test range; 27 Press house; 28 Corning house (Figs 4.8–9); 29 Incorporating mills (Figs 4.5–6); 30 ?Expense magazine; 31 Expense magazine; 32 Grove Cottages; 33 Grove Bungalow; 34 The White House; 35 Incorporating mill; 36 Stables.

inefficient practices to remain but also permitted sites established before the 1875 Act to continue to operate, even though they did not fully meet all the safety provisions of the Act. Water remained the most widely used source of power, despite the introduction of steam and other independent power sources in place in the late nineteenth century.[10] Few factories had adopted electricity, as they were either too remote to draw on a public supply or could not justify the expense of erecting a generator house and converting all the machinery to a different power source.

In the immediate post-war rationalisation the black powder factories at Chilworth, Dartford, Fernilee in Derbyshire, Kames in Argyllshire, and Kynochtown in Essex were closed. Further reductions in the Nobel Division followed after 'an exhaustive study of black powder manufacture...' had been undertaken '... for the purpose of determining whether any of the existing factories are redundant and also as to the possibilities of effecting economies by means of concentration'.[11] In the south of England this review recommended that the mills at Bedfont and Hounslow should close, but that the lost capacity should be made up through expanding the Faversham works. A parallel policy in the north of England saw two of the six surviving Lake District mills closed. Wales was left with a single black powder mill, Scotland with two.

Refurbishment at Faversham

During the early nineteenth century the powder works around Faversham had come under the control of John Hall and Son of Dartford. They managed the Oare Works from 1812, and soon after acquired the lease to the Home Works section of the royal powder works and purchased them outright in 1825. In 1832 they obtained the lease to the Marsh Works and were able to purchase that site in 1854.[12] Though the Oare and Marsh Works were largely able to operate as independent factories, the Home Works relied on the Marsh Works to carry out the more dangerous manufacturing operations (see Chapter 2).

It was this sprawling group of works that Explosives Trades Ltd inherited after the war, with many buildings dating back to the late eighteenth century and an inefficient manufacturing process split between three sites. The oldest of the three works, the

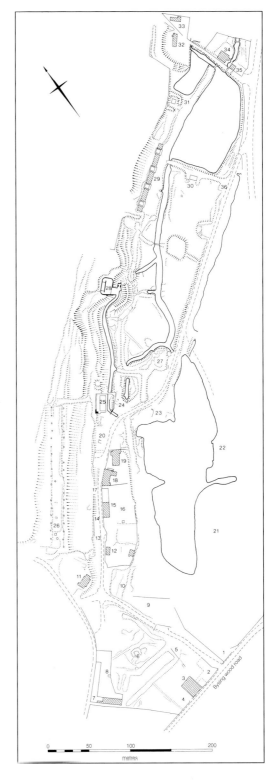

Home Works, appears to have fallen into disuse soon after the end of the war and certainly by the early 1920s. Following the recommendation that black powder capability within Nobel Industries should be concentrated on Faversham, the Oare and Marsh Works were selected for modernisation in the mid-1920s. Though Faversham enjoys the rare survival of a contemporary manufacturing method book explaining the manufacturing processes in operation, there are no contemporary factory plans and few building drawings showing the works after modernisation.[13] Archaeological survey of the Oare Works has been able to fill some of these gaps in knowledge about the last phase of use, though even here the less distinctive building types are difficult to identify by their field remains alone. By contrast, at the Marsh Works gravel extraction has removed large parts of the site. The Faversham factories nevertheless provide an important insight into the last phase of powder manufacture in England.

The Oare Works (Fig 4.3), in common with many other powder works which had grown organically on a physically constrained site, exhibited a relatively inefficient layout. This resulted in the powder and its ingredients being transported further than might have been necessary if the site had been created anew. The works also lacked an integrated transport system and materials were moved around variously by tramway, canal, and cart. Similarly, while most of the works had been converted to electricity the press house remained water powered.

During the nineteenth century many of the larger powder works were equipped with large refineries for the purifying of sulphur and saltpetre. The growth of the chemical industry during the late nineteenth century removed this need for self-sufficiency, as the powdermakers were now able to purchase refined ingredients. By the late 1920s at Faversham high-grade saltpetre (potassium nitrate) was bought in from Germany, while lower-grade material came from Nobel Industries' Gatebeck powder factory in Cumbria. Sulphur was also supplied in a refined state, a lower grade known as 'American crude' by Chance and Hunt, while a finer grade for government powders

was provided by Castner Alkali Company. Though the need for large refineries within the factories was dispensed with, the final grinding and sifting of ingredients took place on site and under the control of the powdermakers. By the late 1920s grinding and crushing of ingredients for both factory groups was concentrated in the buildings adjacent to the Bysing Wood Road entrance to the Oare Works. These mills were electrically driven; the saltpetre was crushed in a machine resembling a granulating machine, the sulphur beneath edge runners. Somewhat unusually for the industry, since in normal circumstances neither process presented any risk of accidental explosion, they were housed in a two-storey building.

Charcoal was the most variable ingredient used in gunpowder, yet its chemical properties had still in the 1920s to be defined by modern analytical methods.[14] Judgement of the optimum level of charring wood was still based on the empirical skill of the refinery staff. For this reason the charcoal works remained an important feature of the Faversham factories. Retort-burnt charcoal had been produced at the Home Works at Faversham since the 1790s, and from the early nineteenth century in a

Figure 4.4 Marsh Gunpowder Works, Faversham. Above (a) view of the building in the 1890s with the retorts in place (from Britain at Work, Cassell & Co, *no date). Below (b) interior of the charcoal cylinder house (BB94/13797)*

large charcoal works at the northern end of the Marsh Works adjacent to Oare Creek. The charcoal works in use there in the 1920s were housed in a large, late nineteenth-century double-bay structure, 99ft 5in × 82ft (30.3m × 25.8m), on the site of the earlier works (Fig 4.4a). It is of a fireproof construction with brick outer walls, each bay spanned by an iron roof just under 49ft 3in (15m) in width. A contemporary illustration (Fig 4.4b) and later accounts show that the large open space was occupied by three freestanding brick batteries each containing six retorts. Later floor surfaces have obscured any traces of their positions, but scars on the floor behind where the retorts stood may indicate the position of receptacles to collect the by-products. The Oare and Marsh Works also retained buildings for grinding and sieving charcoal.

From the initial processing area adjacent to the Bysing Wood Road, the ingredients were either moved by cart to the Marsh Works or to an unidentified mixing house at the Oare Works. The capacity of the Oare Works was greatly expanded during the refurbishment programme by the construction of a range of electrically powered incorporating mills (29 in Fig 4.3; Fig 4.5).

As one of the last groups of mills to be built in England, these represent the ultimate in design technology for incorporation and in the arrangement of their power transfer. They consist of a single range, 275ft 6in (84m) long, with a reinforced concrete basement: above, 12 mill bays are divided by brick walls. In four of these bays were motor compartments open from the basement to the ceiling (Fig 4.6), which contained electric motors powering the eight mills housed in the remaining bays. With brick walls on three sides, the front of each bay was weather-boarded, to blow out in the event of an explosion. Bolt holes and scars on the walls provide evidence for a series of belt drives and gears. In the compartments beneath the mills the openings for the drive shafts remain, together with the large concrete block with mounting bolts to hold the base plate supporting the bevel wheel and main shaft which passed vertically through a hole in the floor. A drawing of a similar mill installed later at Ardeer in Ayrshire illustrates the general arrangement of the mills at Oare (Fig 4.7). Powder was brought to the mills by an internal tramway system in hand-pushed bogies. At the southern end of the mills an earthwork embankment raised the tramway onto a trestle at the same height as the mills. Typically, little physical evidence survives for this important timber component, whose existence is confirmed by the chance survival of a contemporary and probably unofficial photograph (Fig 4.5).

The edge runners installed in these mills were of the most up-to-date design (Fig 4.7). In this evolved system, probably introduced from Germany into Britain in the late nineteenth century, the runners were suspended from a cross-head, which supported them at about 6–9mm above the bedplate while still allowing for some upward movement. Four of the new mills were referred to as the 'Chilworth' mills, however, and the others as the 'Kynoch' mills, which suggests they were brought secondhand from recently closed powder works controlled by Nobel Industries. The edge runners were of solid cast iron and had a diameter of 4ft 11in (1.50m) to 5ft (1.52m); they travelled on their beds at 9rpm. This system had the advantage of

Figure 4.5 Oare Gunpowder Works, Faversham, Kent. Electric-powered gunpowder incorporating mills soon after construction in the 1920s. Arthur Percival collection 23/27. (© The Faversham Society)

Figure 4.6 Oare Gunpowder Works, Faversham. 1920s incorporating mills. In the foreground is the motor bay and beyond is an enclosed compartment which housed a large bevel wheel beneath the incorporating mill. (BB91/27343)

removing the danger of frictional heat from the runners skidding on the bedplate, which was probably one of the greatest causes of explosions in incorporating mills. So dramatic was the improvement in the safety record of these mills that the Explosives Inspectorate raised the limit of powder that could be milled at Faversham beyond the 50lb (22.7kg) set by statute to 150lb (68kg). At Ardeer and Wigtown in Wigtownshire this was later raised still further to 250lb (113.4kg).[15] The effect of this improvement in technology was that far fewer mills were required to incorporate the same amount of powder, thereby further hastening the demise of factories with outdated plant. At the Marsh Works three of the four groups of incorporating mills appear to have been nineteenth century in date with a T-shaped plan. Two groups consisted of a central engine house with two pairs of detached mill buildings to either side, each group housing eight mills. The third group, also T-shaped in plan, was powered by a 85hp National Gas Engine with a detached mill building to either side, each housing three mills. These mills were limited to a 75lb (34kg) charge, which suggests they used an older design of runner resting directly on the bed. A new set of electrically driven mills (though unlocated) was added in the 1920s with suspended runners with a 150lb (68kg) limit.[16]

At the Oare Works, the mid-nineteenth century water-powered hydraulic press house remained in use housing two vertical presses. A concrete by-pass leat may indicate that the old building was partially refurbished at this date. At the Marsh Works there were two press houses, using presses manufactured by Kynoch's of Birmingham. Both were surrounded by earthwork traverses. The electric motors or oil engines that powered the hydraulic pumps were housed in a separate building outside the traverse. A new press house constructed during the 1920s measured 20ft (6.1m) by 28ft (8.6m) internally and stood 10ft (3m) to the eaves. It was timber-framed with a Belfast truss roof, the interior lined in uralite boarding and floored with linoleum.[17] Porches to either side of the building covered the canal and tramway serving it.

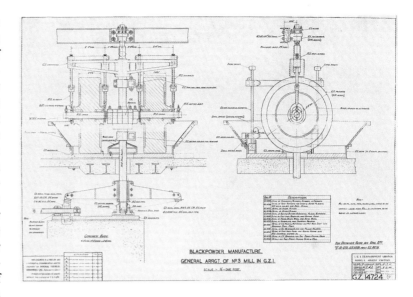

BLACKPOWDER MANUFACTURE.
GENERAL ARRGT. OF Nº3 MILL IN G.Z.I.

Figure 4.7 ICI Ardeer, edge runner mill. (AA96/3625; source RCAHMS)

During the reconstruction programme the corning house at the Oare Works was remodelled and an additional corning house was built at the Marsh Works. In the former case, the surrounding nineteenth-century brick traverse was retained while internally a mass concrete dividing wall, 22ft 4in (6.8m) high, was constructed (28 in Fig 4.3; Fig 4.8). Scars on this wall indicate that it supported the timber corning house and its machinery. The main beams of the machinery (Fig 4.9) and the drive shafts powering it passed through the wall, thereby separating the electrical motors from the dusty machinery and interior of the corning house. At the Marsh Works only the concrete dividing wall remains, with openings that indicate that it supported a similar machine to the one at the Oare Works. Documentary evidence describes them as being of a Nobel type.[18] Marks on the wall indicate the position of the timber-framed building that formerly enclosed the

Figure 4.8 Oare Gunpowder Works, Faversham. Corning house (28 in Fig 4.3). The mass concrete internal wall of the 1920s building sits within the massive nineteenth-century brick traverse. (BB91/27324)

Figure 4.9 Oare Gunpowder Works, Faversham. Interior of a corning house. Arthur Percival collection 23/74. This shows the complex timber-framed corning machine formerly supported by the concrete wall (Fig 4.8). The man at the centre is emptying powder onto a bucket elevator to take it up to the first set of cracker rollers. (© The Faversham Society)

machinery and smaller holes mark the position of batons to secure the match-board inner lining. Gravel extraction has removed any evidence for a surrounding traverse.

The glazing house at the Oare Works was similarly remodelled internally, while the earlier traverse was retained. Inside the building were eight glazing drums coupled in pairs and mounted on concrete bases; they were driven by an external 40hp electric motor via a system of drive shafts and belts. At the Marsh Works the glazing house underwent a more drastic reconstruction. It had an L-shaped concrete traverse wall on two sides, measuring 114ft 9in × 87ft 6in (35m × 26.7m), 6ft 6in (2m) wide at its base, and standing 23ft (7m) high. The third side was closed by an earthwork traverse, while the fourth facing the marsh was open. Internally any trace of the building has been removed by gravel extraction. Its engine or motor house was placed beyond an earthwork mound. Power was transferred by a horizontal drive shaft through an arched brick tunnel beneath the mound to the danger building.

At both sites demolition and later gravel extraction have removed all evidence of the process buildings involved in the finishing of powder.

The end of gunpowder at Waltham Abbey RGPF

Gunpowder manufacture at Waltham Abbey RGPF had continued throughout the Great War, using outdated plant with an overwhelming reliance on water power.

This dependency was one of the factory's principal weaknesses and seasonal water shortages on a number of occasions brought the factory to a standstill.[19] A report into the future of gunpowder manufacture at Waltham Abbey in the 1920s clearly revealed its inadequacies and need of immediate repair. The lack of water could have been solved by spending £4000 on independent power sources for the mills, but this would have been no more than a partial solution. For the layout of the factory was less than ideal: it was neither suited to efficient manufacture of gunpowder, nor was it laid out to modern safety requirements for spacing of buildings. Among other outdated features, it retained a saltpetre refinery far too large for its current requirements. Any attempted rationalisation along modern lines would have been constrained by the constricted nature of the site and by the active cordite factory within which the gunpowder section was located. The investigating committee was also of the opinion that the trade manufacturers could fully meet the peacetime and any wartime needs for service gunpowders, which amounted to a total of only 150 tons (152.4 tonnes) in peacetime and would rise to no more than 2000 tons (2032 tonnes) for a large-scale war. By contrast it was estimated that 6000 tons (6096 tonnes) were produced and consumed annually in mining and quarrying. Despite the overwhelming case for closure, it has widely been assumed that gunpowder production continued at Waltham Abbey until 1941, when the last standing mills were irreparably damaged by a German parachute mine.[20] Photographic evidence suggests rather that the manufacturing capacity was indeed removed earlier, for some mills were demolished (Fig 4.10) and others such as the press house (Fig 3.26) were derelict and inoperable by 1940.

What continued at Waltham Abbey, in addition to blending of fuze powders, was work in association with the Woolwich Research Department in developing experimental powders. One of the most important of these was a fuze powder, RD 202, developed for the time ring of long burning fuzes.[21] The technology involved in its manufacture was similar to that of gunpowder manufacture, since the ingredients of

Figure 4.10 RGPF Waltham Abbey. Demolition of No 3 mill on Millhead Stream in September 1936. (BB94/8010; © MoD WASC 139)

ammonium perchlorate, charcoal, and starch were milled under edge runners. Rather than adapt the old mills, a factory was laid out in the north-western quarter of South Site. This was essentially a new facility, powered by electricity and served by a tramway system, though perhaps remodelling a few existing buildings.

The end of black powder manufacture in England

The closure of the Hounslow and Bedfont mills followed shortly on that of the Black Beck and Elterwater mills in Cumbria. This left four working powder mills in Cumbria, however, namely Low Wood, Bassingill, Gatebeck, and New Sedgwick. As at Faversham, those remaining underwent piecemeal modernisation, including installation of suspended runner mills at the Gatebeck and Low Wood Works, which raised the explosive limit within these mills to 150lb (68kg). Other processes were modernised with new plant or conversion to electricity, in a programme that continued until a year before closure in 1935. In contrast, the plan form of the works altered little. Water remained the principal source of power within these factories, though at the Low Wood Works more efficient water turbines were installed in place of wheels in some mills. The original water mills were retained at Low Wood to power a single suspended

edge-runner mill, which replaced a pair of edge-runner mills, except in one mill where traditional edge runners were kept.[22]

Throughout this period ICI's explosives groups, with the exception of the black powder makers, increasingly concentrated on their principal manufacturing site at Ardeer in Ayrshire, where their main research laboratories for investigations into explosives also lay. In the recession following the 1929 Wall Street crash, the company again looked at the savings that could be made through further rationalisation and concentration of its activities. In 1931 the mills at Glyn-neath in Powys and Camilty in West Lothian were closed. By early 1934 design work began on the new works for black powder production at Ardeer and in the same year the Faversham mills were closed. In 1936, with the closure of the last remaining Lake District mills at Gatebeck High Works, Ardeer was left as the sole producer of black powder in Britain, though Roslin in Midlothian was kept as a reserve factory and retained limited production facilities until the early 1950s.

ICI Ardeer black powder factory

Ardeer, in a remote coastal location near Stevenston, north of Ayr, was the first black powder factory to be built in Britain for over 30 years and, given the more usual

Figure 4.11 Ardeer, Ayrshire; gunpowder incorporating mill, c 1935. Note the clean area marked by a low kerb joining the mills. (RCAHMS, B48304)

experience of the engineering division at Nobels, it is not surprising that the new facility assumed the character of a chemical explosives factory. Freed from the traditional constraints of an extensive system of watercourses to provide power and transport, it was laid out on a rectilinear plan. The process buildings were interlinked by an internal tramway system and independently powered by electricity. Nevertheless, despite the modern layout the black powder was transported for up to two miles during the manufacturing process. Following the practice established at Faversham, saltpetre and sulphur were bought in and elaborate on-site refineries dispensed with. Charcoal remained a scientifically undefinable ingredient, its quality dependent on the skill of the charcoal burners. Concern for its quality caused a carbonising plant dating back to 1893 to be retained on site. It was situated away from the black powder area surrounded by a large stock yard of debarked and well-weathered wood, and it remained in use until the 1970s.[23]

The buildings of the black powder section were well spaced according to current safety standards and all were surrounded by subrectangular traverses, a feature more typical of chemical explosives factories. Tramways between buildings within the factory carried hand-pushed powder bogies. Where they passed through tunnels through the traverse to the danger buildings, iron rails gave way to brass or gunmetal. The less dangerous processes were housed in timber-framed buildings, some with Belfast truss roofs; the more hazardous were contained in barrel-vaulted structures covered by a layer of earth, like the contemporary buildings employed at the Royal Naval Cordite Factory (RNCF) Holton

Heath in Dorset (see Chapter 7). Some features in the works drew on ICI's recent experiences in remodelling their English works. For example, the typical method of powering process machinery was by an external motor coupled to a drive shaft running through a tunnel beneath the traverse to the danger building, as in the glazing house at the Marsh Works at Faversham (see above, Refurbishment at Faversham).

The incorporating mills at Ardeer were housed in ranges made up of three freestanding structures, each housing a pair of mills with a central motor room. Each range had five mills and in the end bay was a cake breaking or breaking-down machine (Figs 4.7, 4.11 and 4.12). They were constructed from reinforced concrete with a buttressed rear wall; the front of the mills and the roofs were clad in wooden boarding designed to blow out in the event of an accidental explosion. In the earliest ranges (GZ 1–3) utilising machinery brought from England, the gearing beneath the mills was left open (Fig 4.7). In GZ 4, perhaps built some time later, the gearing beneath the mills was enclosed in a sealed metal box. Though the buildings' construction introduced many design features new to the black powder industry, not all the machinery was new. Design drawings reveal that the edge-runner

Figure 4.12 Suspended edge-runner mill at ICI Ardeer. The painted stripes allowed the mill men to check that the runners were revolving at the correct speed. (RCAHMS, B48308)

mills from Oare and Gatebeck were moved north for installation in the new factory.[24] If some of the mills at Oare had been acquired in turn from Chilworth and Kynochtown, these machines may have been 50 years old when they were installed at Ardeer.

The section at Ardeer introduced innovations into gunpowder production which hitherto had been little used in British mills and perhaps reflected Nobel's wide knowledge of international practice. Ball mills, for example, were employed to pulverise the charcoal and sulphur prior to incorporation. In addition to the traditional vertical presses, a horizontal press manufactured in America and colloquially referred to as the 'Yankee press' was used and, indeed, preferred owing to its greater throughput. At the next stage of production the press cake was first taken to a cracker house, where it was roughly broken before granulation. Further efficiencies were achieved during glazing, when a stream of hot dry air was blown through the drum, dispensing with any need for a separate drying stage.

The Second World War 1939–45

At the outbreak of war, five grades of gunpowder remained in use by the services for seven main purposes. These were blank charges, charges for firing paper shot, igniters for most cordite charges, fuzes and tubes, combustible compositions, bursting charges, and various other pyrotechnic stores.[25] The principal supplier by this date was the ICI factory at Ardeer, with its reserve factory at Roslin, supplemented to a lesser extent by gunpowder sections in a number of the new filling factories (see Chapter 7). The contribution of the Waltham Abbey mills was probably minimal. Thus a German parachute mine dropped in 1941 administered the *coup de grâce* to this venerable powder factory rather than seriously affecting British gunpowder manufacturing capacity.

As the main producer of black powder Ardeer played a vital role in the war effort; its loss through an accidental explosion or enemy action would have caused great disruption to the supply of munitions. Therefore, on the pattern of other important munitions factories, a shadow factory was established by the Ministry of Supply to take up production if the main factory was lost. This was constructed 55 miles (88.5km) away near Wigtown in south-western Scotland in 1940 and was closely modelled on Ardeer. It had 14 incorporating mills and, like Ardeer, was electrically powered.[26] It was run as an agency factory for the Ministry of Supply by ICI, and staffed by its own personnel.

A specialist role for gunpowder in the Second World War was in the timing rings of fuzes used in anti-aircraft shells. Before proximity fuzes were developed after the war, the height at which an anti-aircraft shell detonated was controlled by a spiral of gunpowder within the fuze, the length of which could be varied. For this purpose gunpowder had to be produced to a very high specification with a known burning rate. Before the war this specialist work was carried out at Waltham Abbey. In the late 1930s provision was made at the Royal Ordnance Filling Factory Chorley in Lancashire (see Chapter 7) for a small black powder section in the south-eastern corner of the complex. Saltpetre and sulphur were brought in ready processed, whereas the charcoal, made from alder buckthorn for these fuze powders, was prepared on site. Process machinery within this plant is known to have included edge-runner mills and presses, machinery for breaking down millcake, for granulating, glazing, polishing, and dusting. Almost certainly, all were electrically powered.[27] Gunpowder produced by this section was used in the Group 3 buildings dedicated to fuze filling (see Chapter 7).

The shadow factory at Wigtown was closed with the end of the war in 1945, followed by the Roslin factory in 1954, and after the war the gunpowder section at Chorley was demolished and its site redeveloped. Ardeer was left as the sole producer of black powder in Britain for both military and civil use. A declining market for the product forced the closure of the Ardeer works in October 1976 and brought the manufacture of gunpowder in Britain to an end. The small continuing demand for use in munitions and quarrying, along with powder used by historical re-enactment societies and black powder shooters, is today met by imported powder.

Endnotes

1 Kelway 1907.
2 Earl 1978, 264–73.
3 Admiralty 1905, 14.
4 WASC 1509, 42.
5 HMSO 1938, 165.
6 HMSO 1920–2, **X**(IV), 116; PRO MUN 5/159/1122.7/28.
7 Nobels Explosives Co Ltd, Plan of Oare and Marsh Works 15-7-20, Arthur Percival Collection.
8 PRO MUN 4/3186.
9 Reader 1970, 310–14.
10 Patterson 1986a, 21.
11 Reader 1970, 381.
12 Percival 1986, 25.
13 Patterson 1995a.
14 Gray *et al* 1982.
15 Patterson 1986a, 23–4.
16 Patterson 1995a, 16.
17 Nobel Industries Ltd, Drawing 1924, Arthur Percival Collection.
18 Patterson 1995a, 18.
19 War Office 1925.
20 Gray *et al* 1982, 3395.
21 HMSO 1938, 167.
22 Patterson 1995b, 16.
23 WASC 1482.
24 HMSO 1938, 161–9.
25 Nobel's Explosives Co Ltd Ardeer, Drawings GZ 7792 and 7794, held by RCAHMS.
26 Patterson 1986a, 12, 22; G Crocker 1988a, 50–2.
27 I am grateful to Mr Stanley Thomas, a wartime employee of the Research Department, for his recollections of research into the problems of charcoal production. Confirmation of the process machinery was provided by entries in a privately owned photographer's day-book.

5
The development of the chemical
explosives industry, *c* 1850–1914

Introduction

The chemical explosives industry of the second half of the nineteenth century was more science-based. Its early history had been beset by devastating explosions, as manufacturers and scientists had laboured to understand the new explosives and to develop novel solutions for the safe handling of these materials. Some promising ideas were slow to be taken up, while others proved impractical in production or ill-suited to the military requirements towards which they were directed.

Technologically, the industry represented an almost complete break with the gunpowder industry. This change was reflected in the distribution of the industry, which had new locational needs (Fig 5.1). In contrast to the powdermakers, the new factories required large open sites. In most cases, greenfield sites were chosen and, although water was no longer the primary power source, coastal and riverine sites were preferred. These sites potentially provided large level areas of sparsely populated land on which to space the factories' dangerous buildings. Waterways also provided good bulk transport links for moving coal for the factory power houses – to produce steam, gas, and, by the end of the century, electricity. Water also remained a significant means to move the finished products, although many sites were joined to the extensive late Victorian railway system. Copious amounts of water were also required in the acids sections of these factories.

The new factories required investment capital that was beyond most of the powdermakers. They also depended on skilled chemists to supervise their running,

supported by the developing science of organic chemistry. This knowledge was also beyond most traditional powdermakers. In order to operate successfully the industry was dependent on a whole new infrastructure of suppliers and acted as a stimulus to them. These included producers of acids, glycerine, and other chemicals, earthenwares used for acid handling, and machinery manufacturers. Whilst the norm for most businesses in the nineteenth century

*Figure 5.1
Distribution of chemical explosives factories prior to the Great War.*

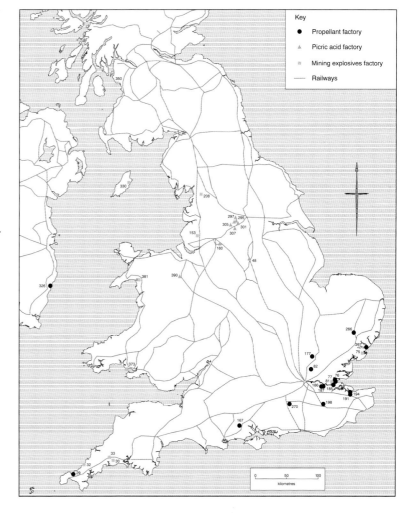

119

was still the family firm, many of the new explosives companies were established innovatively as limited liability companies, employing professional managers and tech- nicians. In bringing all these elements together, chemical explosives factories rep- resented one of the most sophisticated industries in Victorian Britain.

Definitions: explosives and propellants, high and low explosives

Gunpowder was not a homogeneous substance. By altering the ingredients and/or the manufacturing process various types were created to suit different functions and needs. For the greater part of its history of use, the military emphasis with gunpow- der lay with its utilisation as a **propellant**. In this role it was qualities of effective and controlled combustion that were particularly sought (see Chapter 3). By contrast, its use in mining, for example, was as a **disruptive explosive**, where the resultant shock wave was the objective.

With the introduction of chemical explosives, a much wider range of specific functions came to be developed for individual explosive substances, and they were increasingly used in combinations that exploited their particular qualities. In the military sphere, there was a dynamic interplay with advances in artillery design. New types of propellants were sought which could not only give the projectile a higher velocity, but also weigh less and give off less smoke in firing. Projectiles, too, became more sophisticated. Although black powder was until the turn of the century the only effective bursting charge for shells, more advanced fuzes were added to allow them to penetrate heavily reinforced defences or armoured warships before exploding. At the other end of the scale, self- contained rounds (Fig 5.2) burning smokeless propellants were developed for quick-firing guns. The assembly of these complex products consequently began to emerge as an increasingly important feature of the industry that is manifest in the prominence of the filling factories of the Great and Second World Wars (see Chapters 6 and 7).

Against this background, a more refined vocabulary was adopted to define the roles which the individual explosives fulfilled.

Explosives which are required to burn to liberate propellant gases are generally termed **propellants** and have historically been referred to as **low explosives**. These may be ignited by a **cap** or **primer** containing very sensitive explosives, sometimes via an intermediary **igniter**.

High explosives (HE) are designed to detonate. Detonation of a high explosive shell is usually through a shock wave generated by a smaller and more sensitive det- onating charge in a complex exploder system. An explosive train might comprise, for example, a **fuze** which sets off the **detonator** containing an **initiatory** or **primary** high explosive such as mercury fulminate or lead azide, which would detonate a slightly larger **intermediary** or **booster** explosive such as tetryl, in turn sending a detonating shock wave through the **main, bursting** or **receptor charge**.[1] The inter- mediary explosive was sometimes contained in a **gaine** or sheath passing down the centre of the explosive filling.

Like gunpowder itself, not all explosives fall into neat categories. Guncotton or nitrocellulose was in different circumstances used as either a propellant or a high explosive. Products initially developed for one function proved better suited for another, either immediately or in the context of subsequent research.

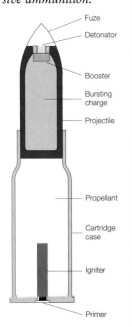

Figure 5.2 Section through typical round of high explo- sive ammunition.

- Fuze
- Detonator
- Booster
- Bursting charge
- Projectile
- Propellant
- Cartridge case
- Igniter
- Primer

What is guncotton?

Celluloses under the action of strong nitric acid (usually with sulphuric acid as a dehydrating agent) form nitric esters known as nitrocellulose; where cotton is the cellulose the result is guncotton. The term nitrocellulose is strictly a misnomer, as the compounds formed by the action of nitric acid on celluloses are nitrates or nitric esters and not nitro bodies. A more accurate term for these compounds would be cellulose nitrates; 'nitrocellulose' is enshrined in historic usage, however.

Nitrocellulose may be referred to as 'soluble' or 'insoluble'. Insoluble nitrocellulose contains more than 12.8% nitrogen and is only soluble to a limited extent in ether-alcohol. By contrast, the lower nitrates are entirely soluble in ether-alcohol.[2]

Explosives

Early history of guncotton

Research and development

At the very period when gunpowder production reached its zenith of industrial scale (Chapter 3), alternative propellants and explosives were being sought through scientific research. The sheer bulk of gunpowder deployed in single propellant charges made any less bulky, cheaper, and explosively more effective propellant highly desirable, especially if it could be relatively smokeless on combustion. Guncotton offered that potential.

Professor Christian Friedrich Schobein of Basle University is generally credited with its first announced discovery in 1846. He was only one of a number of workers active in the field, however. As early as 1813 a Frenchman, Braconnot, experimented with the action of nitric acid on starch, linen, and sawdust. In the 1830s his fellow countryman, Pelouze, investigated the effects of nitric acid on paper, noting its explosive properties. Shortly after Schobein's announcement, it was reported that Böttger in Frankfurt, Otto in Brunswick, and Fadeev in St Petersburg had all produced guncotton. They all noted the weight gained by cellulose substances when treated with nitric acid, and their high combustibility. In summer 1846, Schobein and Böttger visited England to demonstrate their discovery at Woolwich. John Hall & Son of Faversham were quick to obtain the British patent and in the same year established the first guncotton factory in the world at their Marsh Works. Nothing is known about this early enterprise or its manufacturing methods, as it was abruptly halted by a disastrous explosion on 14 July 1847, in which 20 people lost their lives.

As a consequence, and coupled with explosions in French factories at Vincennes and Le Bouchet, commercial interest in guncotton as an alternative to gunpowder declined. Research on the continent continued under the auspices of the Austrian government, whereby an artillery officer, Baron von Lenk, achieved some success in the use of guncotton as propellant. Interest was rekindled in Britain by an offer from the Austrian government in 1862 to pass on the process devised by von Lenk. The War Department chemist Frederick (later Professor Sir Frederick) Abel, along with Major Young, travelled to inspect the plant at

Figure 5.3 Royal Arsenal Woolwich 1864, Chemical Laboratory designed in accordance with the views of Sir Frederick Abel. (AA94/3213)

Figure 5.4 Guncotton manufacture at Stowmarket in the mid 1870s; process flowline and machinery (A). Reproduced from Cavendish c 1878. 'Fig 1 Clean cotton waste is picked to remove any foreign matter, then passed through a carding machine to bring it to a free and open condition, and rolled; Fig 2 Rolls of cotton, C, were dried by a combination of steam and blasts of air in jacketed driers. After cooling, the cotton was weighed in 1lb quantities and carried by a boy to the dipping vessels; Fig 3 It was immersed in mixed nitric and sulphuric acid for three to four minutes before being squeezed by the workman on the grating. In this saturated condition it was placed in a closed earthenware pot; Fig 4, where it remained for 24 hours in a shallow trough of water to keep it cool. The chemical process was now complete; the remaining stages were concerned with washing and pressing the guncotton; Fig 5 The guncotton was placed in a centrifuge to remove excess acid; Fig 6 It was washed and then stored in water tanks for up to three weeks and afterwards boiled in large vats to destroy all the less stable compounds; Fig 7 The beating engine reduced it to a pulp'. (AA96/3645)

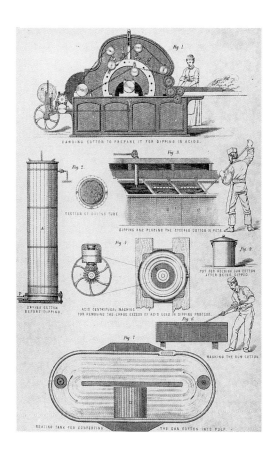

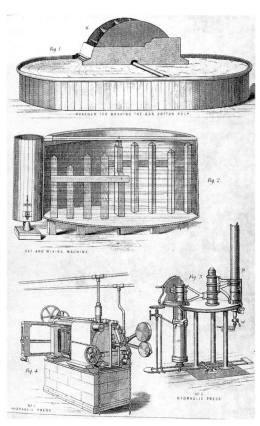

von Lenk's works at Hirtenburg near Vienna, which had been in operation since 1853. In the following year Abel was instructed by the Secretary of State for War to investigate the manufacture of guncotton and its composition when produced on an extensive scale. Small-scale manufacture was established at Waltham Abbey around 1863, while chemical analysis and testing of batches manufactured there was carried out at the Royal Laboratory at Woolwich (Fig 5.3).[3]

The instability of guncotton was its most acute problem. Abel's important innovation was to introduce guncotton's pulping after nitration. This facilitated thorough washing to remove all traces of the nitrating acids, whose residue was one of the major causes of instability. The machinery adopted for these processes was borrowed directly from the paper industry (Figs 5.4 and 5.5). It is probably significant in the transfer of this technology that Abel's laboratory at Woolwich stood adjacent to the paper cartridge factory and its rag pulping machines. The change allowed cotton waste to be employed as the raw material in place of expensive cotton skeins used previously.

Reducing the guncotton to a pulp also allowed it to be moulded under hydraulic presses and used as a high explosive filling in shells, mines, and torpedoes. Another important discovery made by Abel's colleagues, and patented in 1868, was that wet guncotton (which is more stable than dry) could be detonated using fulminate of mercury surrounded by dry guncotton as an initiatory explosive.

Due to the violent effects of granulated guncotton Abel failed in his original research aim to provide an alternative to gunpowder as a propellant. His work to solve the chemical instability of guncotton did, however, re-establish guncotton as a practical military explosive for demolition charges, mines, and shell filling. These innovations in the manufacturing process were of recognised international significance and were widely copied at home and abroad.

Waltham Abbey RGPF

The manufacturing capacity to support Abel's research work was established at Waltham Abbey in 1863. The Lea and its connections to the Thames Estuary now became a vital link for the supply of nitric and sulphuric acid moved from Mr Barnes's acid factory at Hackney, transported in carboys by barge, and for the supply of cotton waste from the Lancashire mills.[4] The buildings chosen for this new process were the old saltpetre refinery in Highbridge Street (15 in Fig 2.31). The requirements for the early guncotton factory were not unlike those for saltpetre, namely large open floor areas to set out acid vats and to provide sufficient working space to handle the nitrating pots. The existing well-ventilated buildings – open to the roof, with louvred vents and clerestories – share such features with later purpose-built acid handling facilities. In the early years the adjacent stream was used for final washing of the guncotton, which was dried on lines, perhaps on the large open area to the north of the refinery.[5]

In 1872 manufacture of compressed guncotton commenced for use in demolition and bursting charges. It remained centred on the old saltpetre refinery, while a guncotton press house was constructed to the north of the newly erected, but idle, pellet powder building (Fig. 3.35), possibly because of its ready connections to the hydraulic accumulator in the latter building (see Figs 3.19 and 3.32). It is, indeed, conceivable that the guncotton press house was originally intended to house the pellet powder presses. Its cartographic depiction apparently shows a rectangular building not divided into bays. Two small expense magazines were located on the adjacent canal to receive the guncotton by barge, and were in turn linked to the press house by tramway lines.

The work on guncotton illustrates two of the important functions of an explosives plant in state hands. Firstly, the plant was used along with the research facilities at Woolwich to develop plant on a manufacturing scale. Secondly, it was able to vary the manufacturing process at the request of the scientists to ascertain its effect on the product. There are clear parallels with the experimental work on gunpowder conducted by Congreve in the 1790s using the facilities of the state factory at Faversham (see Chapter 2).

Stowmarket

Closely associated with Abel's work, but in the private sector, was the Patent Safety Gun-cotton Company of Stowmarket in Suffolk.[6] It was established using the von Lenk system, independently of Abel's initiatives, around 1861 by the Prentice family, who had other business and chemical interests in the area. The works were split into two sections, the guncotton factory and a factory for filling sporting cartridges. It employed around 130 people, mainly men and boys. Manufacture began with the von Lenk system, but there was a serious explosion and in 1865 the factory was rebuilt using the process devised by Abel.

The works lay sandwiched between the Great Eastern Railway line between London and Norwich and the river Gipping, an important source of water for the guncotton factory. Two factors made this location acceptable. One was the lack of controlling legislation, for (by contrast) no gunpowder factory would have been permitted within one mile (1.6km) of a market nor adjacent to a railway line. The second, remarkably, was that during the initial stages of manufacture guncotton was deemed to be a non-explosive substance. The premise on which the factory had been designed and located was that any problem during manufacture would result in a severe conflagration rather than an explosion.

The imperfect understanding of the properties of guncotton, in part aggravated by the design of the factory, were shown up with devastating effect on 11 August 1871. On that Friday afternoon there was an explosion in one of the three magazines, which spontaneously destroyed its neighbours. It caused not only the destruction of surrounding factory buildings but also widespread devastation in the town; 24 people were killed and over 50 injured.

The accident report[7] shows that the magazines were small wooden buildings only about 14ft (4.3m) apart. They had been surrounded by earthwork traverses, but these were replaced by buttressed brick walls. Such flimsy construction was thought to have helped to dissipate the effects of the explosion. Solid brick bombproof magazines surrounded by earthwork traverses to

Figure 5.5 (facing, right) Guncotton manufacture at Stowmarket in the mid 1870s; process flowline and machinery (B). Reproduced from Cavendish c 1878. 'Fig 1 In the poacher it was washed again, a strainer at the base of the tank allowing the water to be changed. After testing, the pulp was mixed with other batches of pulp in the vat and mixing machine; Fig 2 With caustic soda added it was ready for pressing; Figs 3 and 4, when any excess moisture was also extracted. The resulting pressed slab or cylinder was then soaked in water until its water content was about 25% for safe storage and handling.'

*Figure 5.6 Uplees
near Faversham,
Kent. Dan's Dock
on the river Swale
belonging to the
Cotton Powder
Company.
(BB94/10463)*

*Figure 5.6 Uplees
near Faversham,
Kent. Dan's Dock
on the river Swale
belonging to the
Cotton Powder
Company.
(BB94/10463)*

*Figure 5.7 RGPF
Waltham Abbey,
South Site. Layout
of the guncotton
factory established
in 1885 and first
phase cordite factory
(after HMSO
1894). 1 Guncotton
factory (Figs 5.8,
5.9, 5.10, 5.11, and
5.13); 2 Guncotton
stove (Fig 5.26);
3 Proof range;
4 Nitroglycerine
factory; 5 Cordite
factory (Fig 5.37).*

absorb the impact might, nevertheless, the inspector thought, have provided more effective protection. The guncotton factory itself comprised a cluster of closely grouped, large single-storey buildings in the western corner of the site and along the Gipping. With fewer of the restrictions found elsewhere in the danger area, guncotton sections of most explosives factories are readily recognisable as this form of close grouping of large single-storey buildings accommodating the nitrating, washing, and press houses. Their compact disposition also had advantages in power transmission, as it allowed fewer and larger engines to power this section of the works.

Despite the devastation caused by the 1871 explosion, the factory was rebuilt and became one of the leading suppliers of explosives for naval, military, mining, and sporting purposes for home and export. In the early 1860s the company set up another factory at Penrhyndeudraeth in Gwynedd, North Wales, manufacturing an explosive composed of guncotton, starch, and india rubber.

Cotton Powder Company of Faversham

In addition to those at Waltham Abbey and Stowmarket, other trade factories were established to manufacture guncotton or nitrocellulose compounds. One of the earliest was the Cotton Powder Co Ltd at Faversham, established in 1873. Originally built to manufacture 'Punshon's patent controllable cotton gunpowder or guncotton', it came to dominate the market for civil blasting guncotton with tonite, a mixture of guncotton and barium nitrate. It was remotely situated on the Uplees Marshes

adjacent to the river Swale, away from the town and black powder mills. This location ensured the minimum of danger to its neighbours and provided a large area of flat ground to lay out the factory. The Swale afforded good links to bring in supplies of acid, cotton, and other raw materials, and a safe means of transporting its products into the Thames Estuary (Fig 5.6). One disadvantage of this site was its unsuitability for growing trees to act as protective blast screens around the buildings. In 1873 the company also acquired a factory at Melling in Lancashire for the manufacture of nitro-lignin and potentite, an explosive similar to tonite.[8]

Waltham Abbey RGPF

A new guncotton factory

By the 1880s the demand for guncotton prompted the decision to erect a new purpose-built factory at Waltham Abbey, and in 1885 a site covering 100 acres (40.49ha) was purchased on Quinton Hill Farm, south of the original works. The factory was laid out with the intention of bringing the whole manufacturing process into a single complex of up-to-date buildings (Fig 5.7). Within, there was a clear production flow from east to west, the process employed differing only slightly from that at Stowmarket (Figs 5.4 and 5.5). Contemporary photographs indicate at least five boilers in the factory to provide steam for heating and power for the teasing, pulping, and potching machines, the blending tanks, and the pumps for the hydraulic accumulator.[9] They may also have supplied electricity for lighting. Though an acid separating house was part of the new factory, it remained reliant on outside suppliers for acids and the recycling of waste products.

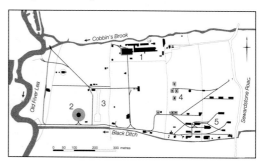

The buildings were constructed in a similar style to the other buildings in the factory in buff-coloured stock bricks with red facings and cast iron window frames. The roofs were of light metal construction, slated and partly glazed, with vents over the acid-handling sections. There, the floors were paved in blue acid-resistant bricks; elsewhere the floors were concrete. The principal elements of the factory comprised a two-storey building used as a machinery store and for teasing the cotton, an occupation reserved for nine women (the only women employed in the factory at this date).[10] In the end bays adjacent to this two-storey building were the drying (Fig 5.8) and weighing rooms (Fig 5.9). Next to this was the long single-storey dipping room (Fig 5.13), where the dipping tanks (Fig 5.10) stood along the dividing wall separating it from the weighing room. Above them, earthenware fume towers, supported by a timber latticework, rose through the roof of the building, though in reality they did little to alleviate the unhealthy atmosphere of this room. The remainder of its interior was covered by shallow cooling tanks to hold the

Figure 5.8 (top left) RGPF Waltham Abbey, South Site. Cotton waste drying oven, c 1909. (BB97/3440; © MoD)

Figure 5.9 (above) RGPF Waltham Abbey, South Site. 1880s guncotton factory. Guncotton weighing room (near section) and drying room (far end, abutting the two-storey teasing room and store); the demolished dipping room (Figs 5.10, 5.13) joined to the left of the weatherboarded wall. (BB92/26249)

earthenware pots, and the floor sloped gently to carry away acid spills. From the cooling tanks the cotton was taken to be spun in a centrifuge to remove excess acid; it was then rapidly immersed in fresh water before being spun once again in a centrifuge and taken from there to the vat house. In this long single-storey building at the rear of the factory, it was boiled for four or five days in large wooden vats. A covered way linked the vat house to the pulping and moulding rooms (Fig 5.11). At the eastern end of the building was an engine house to power the

Figure 5.10 (left) RGPF Waltham Abbey, South Site. Interior of dipping room on 1 March 1894 after a minor explosion. Note the earthenware pots in the foreground; cf Figs 3 and 4 in Fig 5.4. The fume towers to the rear were brought down by the explosion. (BB94/8013; © MoD)

Figure 5.11 (below) RGPF Waltham Abbey, South Site. Pulping and moulding rooms, 1888. (BB92/26251)

Figure 5.12 The Nathan-Thomson displacement process. Diagrammatic section through a guncotton displacement tank. In this method, the mixed acids were run into the earthenware displacement pans. A 20lb (9.09kg) charge of cotton was immersed in each, with the pans covered by the aluminium fume hoods. Perforated earthenware plates were then fitted over the charge and a film of water was run over the plates to prevent the escape of acid fumes. Since the water was lighter than the acid it remained as a discrete layer on top. After about 3 hours, cocks at the base of the pans were opened allowing the waste acid to drain off for recovery, while at the same time water was run into the top of the pan. As displacement proceeded, the acid became weaker to a point where it was no longer viable to recover it and it was run to waste. Following displacement, the guncotton was taken directly to be boiled. (BB972/3441; © MoD)

machinery and the pumps for a hydraulic accumulator for the presses. At the same end, raised on a platform, were the pulping machines to render the guncotton into a fine slurry. It was then run by gravity through a grit trap, blanket and magnet runs to remove any foreign bodies, and on into the poachers or potchers on the ground floor, where it was agitated in a large volume of water to remove any remaining traces of acids; thence to the presses. Ancillary buildings associated with the factory included a police hut, store (perhaps for cotton bales), stables, chemical laboratory, shifting room, dining room, and a small magazine.[11]

New methods – the Nathan-Thomson displacement process

Though the nitration process at Waltham Abbey was considered to make good guncotton, it was expensive. It was very labour-intensive; additionally a lot of power was required for the centrifuges and large quantities of water for cooling and immersing. Although none of the plant was individually expensive, items required frequent replacement. Spontaneous decomposition

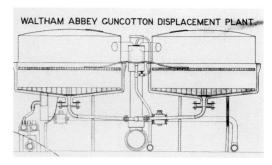

of treated cotton also led to losses. The commercial trade responded in different ways to similar factors. Nobel's factory at Ardeer, on the Firth of Clyde, introduced a direct dipping process, while Messrs Curtis's and Harvey at their Dartford guncotton works, built adjacent to their powder works, installed a nitrating centrifuge, a type of machine common in Germany. The system devised at Waltham Abbey by two of the factory's chemists, J M Thomson and W T Thomson, and implemented in 1905 was the displacement process (Figs 5.12 and 5.13). Displacement tanks replaced the stages of dipping, squeezing, digesting in pots, acid centrifuging, immersing, and water centrifuging. The new system was hailed as a great advance since it resulted in

Figure 5.13 RGPF Waltham Abbey, South Site. View of displacement tanks installed in 1905 in the former guncotton dipping room (Fig 5.10). The earthenware displacement tanks, 3 ft 6in (1.07m) in diameter, were arranged in groups of four. Note also the fume hoods and perforated plates in the tanks, and the acid-resistant brick floor. (BB97/3442 © MoD)

cost savings in labour and power, in greater acid recovery, and the less frequent need to replace plant; it also produced a more stable guncotton with an improved yield. It was widely adopted throughout the industry as the most efficient method of nitrocellulose production. Yet, though a major breakthrough in manufacturing technology, it had relatively little effect on the outward form of the factory, despite considerable reorganisation internally. The dipping room was converted to the nitrating room (Fig 5.13), with little modification beyond replacing the shallow cooling tanks with a brick floor for the displacement tanks to stand on. Other plant such as immersing tanks and centrifuges was removed, with a resulting fall in power requirements. New plant concentrated on the manufacture and recovery of nitrating acids.[12]

The new process also went some way to improving working conditions in the factory by reducing the amount of fumes in the building.

Schultze powder

Schultze powder was another form of nitro-compound produced from the action of nitric and sulphuric acid on wood pulp to form nitro-lignin, and, unlike guncotton, was in its form and handling qualities a direct replacement for gunpowder. It enjoyed success as a sporting powder, yet was not adopted for military use in Britain. It represents, therefore, an evolutionary dead end in the history of the industry. Nevertheless, it provides another instructive example of the close association between the British and continental explosives industries.

Captain Eduard Schultze, of the Royal Prussian Artillery, started manufacturing nitrated wood pulp at Potsdam in 1864.[13] In 1869 a company was established in England and located its factory at Eyeworth, Hampshire, on the site of a short-lived gunpowder factory. Schultze powder was regarded as a less hazardous material than other explosives, and liable only to burn and not to explode when unconfined. This was reflected in the factory layout (Fig 5.14) where all the initial processing buildings were grouped together, with a flow line of drying sheds, dusting house, press house, packing houses, rifle butts, and a long covered shooting gallery spread away from this core. Four storage magazines were located 590ft 6in (180m) to the north of the main factory buildings, each spaced at least 295ft 4in (90m) from its neighbour. Three had earthwork traverses while the fourth was freestanding. About 1898 the company was reformed as the New Schultze Gunpowder Co, and in the following decade the works expanded by adding new process buildings and storage magazines. Many of its 60 buildings may still be traced as earthworks.[14]

In addition to expansion at Eyeworth, the firm in 1898 acquired the Smokeless Powder & Ammunition Co Ltd at Barwick in Hertfordshire (Fig 5.15). This was established in 1889 as the Smokeless Powder Co in a factory designed and managed by Ernest Spon, formerly manager of the Pembrey dynamite factory (Carmarthenshire). It, too, manufactured a nitro-lignin compound and in layout was similar to Eyeworth. At its western end the closely grouped factory core was conveniently located next to a stream to provide wash waters for the nitration tanks. Other process buildings were scattered to the east, a number of which survive in agricultural use.

These are small rectangular single-storey buildings in a yellow stock brick. The roofs were slated and those identifiable as stoves were insulated internally with 'slag wool' covered in linoleum, and their roofs lined in varnished wood. Some of the buildings are freestanding while others – drying stoves and what were perhaps magazines in the wood to the east – are either dug into the hillside or surrounded by an earthwork traverse. A narrow-gauge tramway provided interconnections. The German links and perhaps working methods of the firm are reflected by Adam Seip, the factory foreman; described as a British subject, he was originally from Hessen.[15]

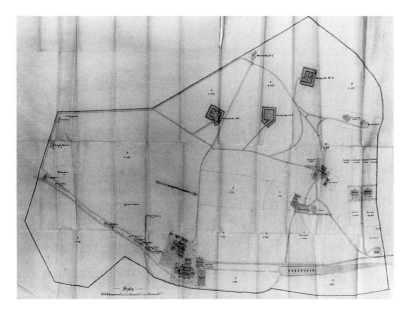

Figure 5.14 Eyeworth, Hampshire. The New Shultze Powder Company 1898. (BB95/11950; © PRO BT 7899/56909)

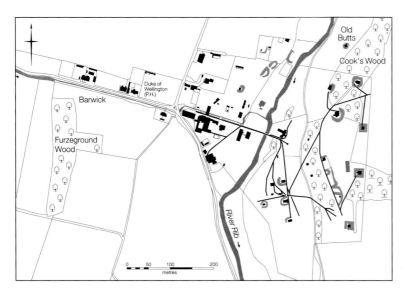

Figure 5.15 Barwick, Hertfordshire. Plan of the Smokeless Powder and Ammunition Co Ltd's factory, established in 1889 (drawn from OS, Hertfordshire, Sheet XX11.9, 25-inch, third edition, 1932; OS, Hertfordshire, Sheet XX11.10, 25-inch, third edition, 1932; OS, Hertfordshire, Sheet XX11.13, 25-inch, third edition, 1932; OS, Hertfordshire, Sheet XX11.14, 25-inch, third edition, 1932).

Nitroglycerine, Alfred Nobel, and Ardeer

Nitroglycerine was one of a number of explosive compounds, formed by treating organic substances with nitric acid, which were announced in 1847 by Professor Ascanio Sobrero of Turin. Yet because of its volatility no practical use could easily be found for this new and powerful explosive.

It was through the inventive genius of Alfred Nobel (1833–96) that nitroglycerine was mastered and manufactured as a commercial explosive. At this date it was used in a form known as 'blasting oil', with all the attendant dangers of handling it. His first breakthrough was the development of a mercury fulminate detonator, patented in England in 1864, which explodes with little gas but a violent shock sufficient to detonate nitroglycerine. His second requirement was a material which could absorb nitroglycerine effectively. This he found in a siliceous sediment known as *Kieselguhr*. The resulting mixture was 'dynamite', patented in England 1867. The combination of a safe method of handling and efficient means of detonation was the basis of this particular 'genius industry' and of Nobel's great influence and wealth. The timing of his discoveries also coincided with the inauguration of ambitious civil engineering projects in Europe, and the opening up of the Americas, Africa, and Australia by European settlers and mineral prospectors with an almost insatiable demand for his products.

One of the drawbacks of dynamite was the inert mass of *Kieselguhr*. Where a more powerful explosive was required, by 1875 Nobel was able to offer blasting gelatine, a mixture of nitroglycerine and nitrocellulose, followed later by gelignite and gelatine dynamite. In these substances a nitroglycerine syrup (containing 4% nitrocellulose) was absorbed in a mixture of saltpetre and woodmeal.

During the 1860s Nobel established factories around Europe but regarded Great Britain as pre-eminently important for access to its markets at home and in the colonies. However, he experienced the greatest difficulties in financing the enterprise and working around the constraints imposed by the recently passed 1869 Nitroglycerine Act.[16] By 1871 he was able to raise the necessary capital in Scotland and identified a site on the Firth of Clyde at Ardeer in Ayrshire (Figs 5.16 and 5.17). It was remotely set in coastal sand dunes which allowed for the statutory spacing of buildings and the construction of protective traverses. It was served by coastal shipping and the adjacent Glasgow and South-Western Railway. From these beginnings it became the largest dynamite factory in Europe, covering over 704 acres (285ha) by the end of the century.[17]

The Nobel Dynamite Trust and its competitors

For a decade the manufacture and sale of dynamite from Ardeer was protected by patent legislation. An early rival was the New Explosives Company of Stowmarket, through their dynamite factory set up on a 155 acres (62.75ha) site among the sand dunes at Pembrey Burrows, Carmarthenshire, in 1882. In recognition of competitive threats, the Nobel Explosives Company of Ardeer in 1886 joined with German dynamite makers to form the Nobel Dynamite Trust, a holding company which had control of the assets of the subsidiary companies.[18] Despite this move, a number of competitors attempted to break into this lucrative market, including the National Explosives Company at Hayle, Cornwall (see below, National Explosives Company, Hayle, Cornwall). Also in Cornwall, the British and Colonial Company Ltd established a factory at Perranporth in the early 1890s. This dynamite firm soon ran into financial trouble and was absorbed by Nobels in 1893. They expanded the works and introduced gelatinous explosives, though the soluble nitrocellulose was provided by Ardeer rather than manufactured on site.[19] Another rival emerged in the early 1890s in the British Explosives Syndicate Ltd of Pitsea in Essex. This company drew on the expertise of George McRoberts, formerly of Ardeer, who was later sued by Nobel's for breaking an agreement not to manufacture dynamite, and established a strong market for itself in Australia.

Manufacture of dynamite, blasting gelatine, and related explosives served the civilian market. The products were too sensitive to be used as shell fillings and too violent to be used as propellants. The adoption of smokeless explosives (discussed below, Propellants) based on a combination of nitroglycerine

and guncotton, however, blurred the distinction between the producers of blasting explosives and the makers of propellant or powder. The expertise of the Nobel companies in manufacturing nitroglycerine was vital to the propellant makers, while they in turn became rivals to Nobel's, since with nitroglycerine plants they were able to enter the market for blasting explosives.

Many other types of chemical explosives were also developed in the late nineteenth century but not for military use. Examples are the group of ammonal explosives based on ammonium nitrate for use in collieries.[20] Roth, an Austrian firm with its head office in Vienna, established factories in the disused gunpowder mills at Herodsfoot and Trago in Cornwall. Other companies built new factories at Gathurst, near Wigan in Greater Manchester and at Stanford-le-Hope in Essex. Though restricted to civil use at this date, ammonium nitrate was later an important filling for trench warfare munitions (see Chapter 6).

Propellants

Despite the success of the nitro-compounds as sporting powders or as explosives, none was able to demonstrate the stability or uniformity of action required for military propellants. The combination of tactical advantages of invisibility of a firing gun and clear visibility for the firer remained sought after. The search for so-called smokeless

Figure 5.16 Ardeer, Ayrshire, 1897. This engraving marvellously captures the atmosphere of a late nineteenth-century nitroglycerine hill. On the top of the hill are the tanks holding the acids and glycerine: below them is the nitrating house (A), protected by the red flag and lightning conductors. Below again are the separating and pre-washing houses (B) and below these the final washing and filtering house (C). The building (D) dug into the hillslope is protected by corrugated iron traverses filled with earth, so-called 'Chilworth mounds'. Also clearly visible are the gutters that conveyed the liquids by gravity from building to building.

Figure 5.17 Ardeer, Ayrshire, 1897. Final washing and filtering house, (C) in Fig 5.16. Nitroglycerine is being run from the raised tanks into a wooden, brass-lined box probably containing kieselguhr for dynamite. This was hand-mixed before being conveyed to the cartridging huts. Note the earth floor to absorb any spilt nitroglycerine. The factory licence restricted the number of operatives in this building to four, in addition to the superintendent and overlookers.

powders continued, therefore, and was accelerated as new types of weapons were developed, in particular small quick-firing guns and machine guns. In its turn the discovery of suitable smokeless powders provided new opportunities for the armaments manufacturers, as the new powders generated more energy for a given mass (see Fig 4.2).

'Poudre B', ballistite, and cordite

In the early 1880s, Paul Vieille in his Paris laboratory developed 'poudre B', nitrocellulose gelatinised with ether/alcohol in the form of small squares cut from thin sheets.[21] Nobel's own earlier work on blasting gelatine (a preparation of nitrocellulose and nitroglycerine) also had in it the basis of a successful propellant, though it was itself too violent. During Nobel's residence in France at Sevran-Livry to the north of Paris, he devised a method of blending together a greater proportion of nitrocellulose with nitroglycerine and camphor. The resultant horn-like substance could be pressed into grains or rolled into sheets and exhibited the stability and uniform action required. The new explosive, termed 'ballistite', was patented in France in 1887.

In England in the following year a War Office committee under Abel and Dewar was set the task of investigating smokeless propellants. Drawing on a wide range of

experts, including Nobel, within six months it developed an explosive consisting of 58% nitroglycerine, 37% guncotton, and 5% mineral jelly as a stabiliser. This was patented in 1889 as 'cordite', after the long cords it was extruded into (see Fig 4.2). It used a more highly nitrated 'insoluble' form of nitrocellulose than ballistite, using acetone as a solvent. The circumstances under which the committee came to its conclusions, essentially through the work of others, and the way in which the committee members were allowed to benefit personally from foreign patents of their invention achieved some notoriety in the 'cordite scandal'. In 1892 Nobels Explosives of Glasgow brought an action against the British government for infringement of patent. They lost because Nobels patent specified nitrocellulose 'of the well-known soluble kind', while Abel and Dewar specified the more highly nitrated 'insoluble' nitrocellulose.[22]

Waltham Abbey remodelled

With cordite quickly adopted for military use, the necessity followed of establishing enough manufacturing capacity to supply the needs of the services. The site chosen lay to the south of the newly erected guncotton factory (Fig 5.7) on the South Site at Waltham Abbey. As created, the cordite factory was self-contained, with its own supply of guncotton and nitroglycerine and all the requisite process buildings laid out to the south of the nitroglycerine section.

Though the officers of the RGPF were expert in producing guncotton, the technology of nitroglycerine manufacture was outside their experience. With establishing a facility an urgent priority, Colonel Noble, Superintendent of the factory, went to inspect a Nobel-type plant of the Rheinische Dynamitfabrik at Opladen near Cologne. A similar plant was ordered from Germany and by 1890 fitting out was under way. As built, the nitroglycerine factory comprised four rectangular brick traverses and at their centres wooden process buildings containing the acid separating house, two nitrating houses, and a washing house. Downslope of these were two nitroglycerine stores also surrounded by brick traverses and a guncotton stove. In operation, the nitroglycerine was run by gravity from the nitrating house to the washing house and then on to the stores. There, two leaden tanks could store 2200lb (1000kg) of purified nitroglycerine. Measured weights of nitroglycerine were drawn from the tanks to mix with guncotton to form cordite paste, in a process later carried out in mixing houses (see below, The rebuilt nitroglycerine factory 1894).

The remaining processes of the cordite factory were housed in long single-storey buildings, that comprised acetone stores, incorporating houses, press houses, reel houses, and drying stoves along with other ancillary buildings. Though of superficially uniform appearance, process buildings such as press and incorporating houses are distinguished by their bayed structure and screening concrete traverse, perhaps added later. The new factory operated safely until May 1894 when explosions in the nitroglycerine washing house and store brought production to a halt. The accident report was highly critical of the close spacing of the buildings within the factory, and of the practice of storing successive batches of nitroglycerine on site instead of absorbing each into guncotton – a procedure all private factories were required to abide by.[23] The three main remedial recommendations were that the buildings should be more adequately spaced, that working methods should be altered, and that a duplicate factory be established (see below, Edmonsey Mead nitroglycerine factory 1895–6). These changes were set against a recognition of the necessity of quickly bringing the factory back into operation.

The rebuilt nitroglycerine factory 1894

The rebuilt factory of 1894 provides a good example of the working of a late nineteenth-century nitroglycerine factory which may be illustrated through surviving field remains and contemporary documents.[24] The topography of the Quinton Hill site fortuitously lent itself to the construction of such a factory because the natural fall of the ground could be used to move the nitroglycerine from process to process by gravity. Because of nitroglycerine's sensitivity it can neither be pumped nor carried with safety.

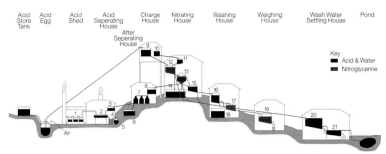

How this plant functioned can be illustrated diagrammatically (Fig 5.18). Acid from the store tank was let down into the acid egg, a closed iron or earthenware vessel. Before the development of acid-resistant metals and pumps, eggs were an important method for raising chemicals between processes. Compressed air introduced into the egg forced the acid into a tank (9 in Fig 5.18) in the charge house, which also housed the glycerine tank (10). Thence the mixed sulphuric and nitric acid was run down into the nitrating vessel (12); in later years, the glycerine was run into the store tank (11) in the nitrating house before being sprayed into the nitrating vessel (12). This was a lead-lined tank supplied with a compressed air supply to agitate the acids and glycerine. Temperature control during nitration was achieved by a ring of water-cooled coils within the vessel. If any problems arose during nitration the whole charge could be emptied into the drowning tank (14) at the bottom of the building. At the end of the nitration process, the nitroglycerine floated on top of the acids as an oily liquid. An earthenware cock at the base of the nitrator was opened and both nitroglycerine and acids were let down into the separating tank (13). Relying on the fact that the nitroglycerine floated on the acids, the main part of the nitroglycerine charge was run off to the prewash tank. The acids were then run off to separating houses for recovery and reuse, by the nitric acid being distilled from the sulphuric acid by gentle heat. A glass inspection window allowed the remaining nitroglycerine to be seen and run off into the prewash tank (15). In the prewash tank the nitroglycerine was run through water and a soda solution wash before it was sent down a gutter to the washing house to remove all traces of the nitrating acids (16, 17). The wash water

Figure 5.18 RGPF Waltham Abbey, South Site. Quinton Hill Nitroglycerine Factory (section redrawn from HMSO 1895 (Treatise on Service Explosives), plate XIV opposite p81): 1 Nitric acid receivers; 2 Acid still; 3 Settling tank; 4 Syphon tank and coil; 5 Sulphuric acid carboy; 6 Drowning tank; 7 Separating bottles; 8 Acid tank; 9 Acid tank; 10 Glycerine tank; 11 Glycerine tank; 12 Nitrating apparatus; 13 Separating tank; 14 Drowning tank; 15 Prewash tank; 16 Washing tank; 17 Filter tank; 18 Drowning tank; 19 Store tank; 20 Wash-water settling tank; 21 Labyrinth; Red shows the path of the nitroglycerine.

from all the tanks was run into the settling house (20), where it was run through a final labyrinth (21) to remove any remaining nitroglycerine. The purified nitroglycerine was stored in the weighing (or mixing) house (19), where measured quantities were drawn off to be mixed with guncotton. The filtered wash water was then drained into a pond, into which every Saturday a dynamite cartridge was thrown to blow up any residual explosive matter.[25]

In its rebuilt form the factory retained the solid brick traverses around the nitrating and separating houses. The washing and weighing houses destroyed in the explosion were replaced in a different form, however. The new washing house (Figs 5.19 and 5.20) was a timber round-house with an internal diameter of 23ft (7m). Its rafters joined to a central wooden crown piece to form a conical roof covered by galvanised metal sheeting, with a central vent. The interior of the house was lined in matchboard, and its floor was originally covered in lead sheeting. It was lit by roof lights and small windows around the top of the walls. Artificial light was provided by electric lights enclosed in spherical glass bowls protected by chicken wire; all the wires leading to these were contained in metal pipes on the roof. Steam heating pipes supplied the vital warmth to prevent the nitroglycerine freezing and becoming unstable when thawed. The building was designed to be served by two nitrating houses; for this reason a Y-shaped tunnel led to it from the nitrators. Two of the wooden nitroglycerine washing barrels, measuring 4ft (1.2m) in height with internal diameters of 3ft 3in (0.98m) and 3ft 2in (0.96m), form part of the remarkable surviving fittings. From the washing house the purified nitroglycerine was run down a lower gutter to the junction house and on to one of two mixing houses. The reconstructed and surviving mixing house was of a similar construction to the washing house. Each was surrounded by a circular concrete and brick retaining wall, which rose above the height of the building, the wall revetting an earthwork traverse. The operatives approached the building on foot along a single curving brick tunnel.

Edmonsey Mead nitroglycerine factory 1895–6

The recommendations following the 1894 explosion resulted in a second new nitroglycerine factory sited at the northern end of North Site at Waltham Abbey in the area known as Edmonsey Mead. Though it now lacks the standing buildings of the Quinton Hill factory, the manufacturing process may be traced through the footings and surviving earthworks (Figs 5.21 and 5.22).

The site was not ideal, for it occupied level flood plain rather than the falling ground favoured for nitroglycerine factories, where the nitrator is routinely located at the high point. Nevertheless, as originally built this factory used a similar manufacturing method to that used at Quinton Hill. It differed, however, in the novel way by which the acids and glycerine were raised to the charge house. Instead of using an acid egg and compressed air, they were transported from the acid factory in tramway bogies to a lift at the base of the nitrating house and raised to the charge house, where they were run into store tanks (1, 4, 16 in Fig 5.23; Fig 5.24).

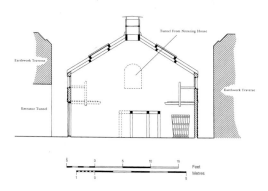

Figure 5.19 RGPF Waltham Abbey, South Site. Quinton Hill Nitroglycerine Factory, Nitroglycerine Wash House, 1894. Note the original washing barrel. In the foreground is a displaced steam heating pipe: to the rear the opening of the tunnel through which the nitroglycerine was run into the building (Fig 5.20) is visible. (BB92/26257)

Figure 5.20 RGPF Waltham Abbey, South Site. Quinton Hill Nitroglycerine Factory, section through Nitroglycerine Wash House; cf Fig 5.19.

The nitrating house and the washing houses were housed in similar structures to those adopted on Quinton Hill, but, because of the flat site, the gravity flow was engineered entirely by the relative heights of the built structures. Because of the structures' prominent hill-like form, the men working in this section were known as the 'hillmen'. The nitrating house was enclosed within a circular earthen traverse, 134ft 6in (41m) diameter and 18ft 8in (5.7m) in height. Its centre was revetted in brick and within stood the nitrating house itself, a timber round-house, faceted on its northern side.

From the nitrating house the acid nitroglycerine was run along covered lead gutters to one of two washing houses. Between the buildings the gutters were carried along wooden trestles over a canal and into the washing houses. The washing houses were of a similar construction to the nitrator, that is a circular timber round-house enclosed within a brick and earthwork traverse, though smaller at 95ft (29m) diameter and 12ft 4in (3.75m) in height. The floors of the buildings were lead-covered and the roofs lined with Willesden paper. In the washing houses all traces of the nitrating acids were removed and passed through a filtration process. From there the purified nitroglycerine was delivered by gutters to the mixing houses (see below, Mixing).[26] The wash waters were sent to the settling house where remaining acid and nitroglycerine was removed. Sludge from the settling house

Figure 5.21 RGPF Waltham Abbey, North Site. Aerial photograph of Edmonsey Mead Nitroglycerine Factory. (NMR 1857/29)

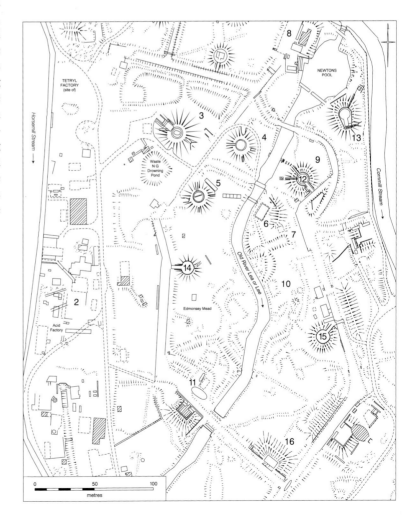

Figure 5.22 RGPF Waltham Abbey, North Site. Edmonsey Mead Nitroglycerine Factory, as surveyed in 1993: 1 Glycerine and acid shed; 2 Nitric acid factory; 3 Nitrating house (Fig 5.24); 4 Washing house; 5 Washing house; 6 Wash-water settling house; 7 Mud house; 8 Mixing house (former gunpowder granulating house); 9 Mixing house (built 1904 destroyed 1940); 10 Mixing house (built 1904 destroyed 1940); 11 Mixing house (former gunpowder Press House); 12 Mixing house (built 1940) (Fig 5.31); 13 Mixing house (built 1940); 14 Mixing house (built 1904) (Fig 5.32); 15 ?Mixing house (built 1940); 16 Mixing house (?1914–18). (© Crown copyright. NMR)

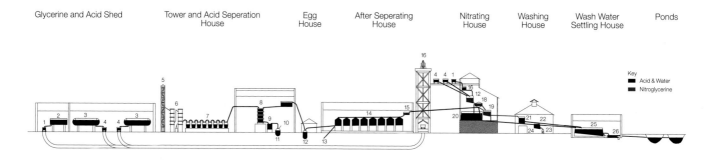

Glycerine and Acid Shed   Tower and Acid Seperation House   Egg House   After Seperating House   Nitrating House   Washing House   Wash Water Settling House   Ponds

Key
■ Acid & Water
■ Nitroglycerine

Figure 5.23 RGPF Waltham Abbey, North Site. Edmonsey Mead Nitroglycerine Factory (section redrawn from HMSO 1900, Treatise on Service Explosives, plate XX opposite p75): 1 Glycerine bogie; 2 Glycerine store tank; 3 Acid store tanks; 4 Acid bogies; 5 Fume shaft; 6 Condensing towers; 7 Nitric acid receivers; 8 Acid towers; 9 Syphon tank and coil; 10 To concentration plant; 11 Sulphuric acid egg; 12 Acid egg; 13 Drain to river; 14 Separating bottles; 15 Acid tank; 16 Bogie lift; 17 Glycerine tank; 18 Nitrating apparatus; 19 Prewash tank; 20 Drowning tank; 21 Washing tank; 22 Filter tank; 23 Scales; 24 Drowning tank; 25 Wash-water settling tank; 26 Labyrinth; Red shows the path of the nitroglycerine.

Figure 5.24 RGPF Waltham Abbey, North Site. Nitrating House E2 in Edmonsey Mead factory, showing acid bogie lift; photographed in 1897. Note the dip in the side of the mound to provide a line of least resistance in case of an explosion. (BB94/8007; © MoD)

Figure 5.25 RGPF Waltham Abbey, North Site. Recovered artefacts – waste nitroglycerine acid bucket, nitroglycerine acid container and acetone bottle from the incorporating section (BB94/7990)

was taken to the 'mud hut', where it was washed again to remove any lingering nitroglycerine. The small amount recovered was carried in a bucket back to the prewash tank in the nitrating house. The residues were mixed with paraffin and burnt.

Throughout these processes, great care was taken to prohibit any implements which might fall and set off an explosion. For necessary tools and equipment, malleable materials such as rubber, gutta-percha, and leather were preferred. Examples of artefacts found during site decontamination include gutta percha sample bottles and containers for waste nitroglycerine acids (Fig 5.25).

The Nathan-Thomson-Rintoul nitration process

A particular source of danger within this production process were the earthenware cocks used to discharge nitroglycerine from the base of the tanks, because of the frictional heat generated between the body of the cock and the key. A minor explosion in the No 2 nitration house on Quinton Hill in 1902 prompted an investigation into how this danger could be eliminated. The solution devised at Waltham Abbey was to dispense with the earthenware cocks and instead to discharge the nitroglycerine from the top of what was now termed a 'nitrator-separator'. At the end of the nitration process, waste acids from the previous batch were let into the base of the nitrator-separator, which caused the nitroglycerine floating on top of the acids to be pushed over a gutter and into the prewash tank. At the base of the prewash tank rubber tubes were substituted for the earthenware cocks. In 1903 one of the nitration houses on Quinton Hill was converted to the new process, as was the Edmonsey plant in the following year. After the latter was proved, the Quinton Hill plant was reduced to a reserve and the old Nobel type nitrator was dismantled. This shift coincided with a change in the composition of cordite: instead of cordite MK1 using 58% nitroglycerine, a modified form, cordite MD, used only 30%, thereby reducing by almost half the amount of nitroglycerine required.[27]

It was also probably at this date that the experiment with the acid bogie lift was abandoned and replaced by compressed air to raise the acid and glycerine to the charge house, now placed on the side of the mound. As with other innovations made at Waltham Abbey, this method of nitration was widely adopted by the trade.

Cordite at Waltham Abbey

By the end of the 1890s the adoption of cordite as the principal service propellant had rendered much of the gunpowder plant at Waltham Abbey obsolete. The heavy investment in buildings and the inherited infrastructure at Waltham Abbey, however, produced an inertia in the government's willingness to take a decision about where to locate its cordite factory. In contrast to the private producers, many of whom developed greenfield sites, on the North Site at Waltham Abbey novel manufacturing processes were shoehorned into former gunpowder buildings and onto an awkwardly configured site.

The impact of the new technology was first seen with the construction of the Edmonsey nitroglycerine factory. In this area the powder buildings were taken out of use; some were relegated to stores, while a press house and a granulating house were converted into cordite mixing houses. Further south, the steam-powered gunpowder incorporating mills, including the

Group G mills which were less than a decade old, were converted to new uses. This left a small group of water-powered mills along Millhead for the continued production of gunpowder (see Chapter 4).

Guncotton drying stoves

As the other main component of cordite, guncotton was produced, handled, and stored wet. Before mixing with nitroglycerine to form cordite paste it needed to be dried, in guncotton drying stoves. A small experimental stove was built on North Site in 1884 with a concrete wall to separate the stove and boiler from the drying rooms. The remainder of the building was timber-framed and covered by Willesden paper. When the cordite factory was established on South Site, two stoves were built, one square in plan surrounded by an earth-filled brick traverse, the other circular (Figs 5.7 and 5.26). Following experiments with the form of the stoves, in 1894 rectangular stoves surrounded by earthwork traverses were built at the northern end of North Site.

In order to match the production capacity of the Edmonsey nitroglycerine factory, between 1897 and the outbreak of the Great War in 1914, 21 guncotton drying stoves were built on North Site. They followed the design of the 1892 guncotton stove on South Site (Fig 5.26) and consisted of a timber round-house surrounded by an earthwork traverse. The earliest were built on Millhead Stream, and later on the largely unutilised land between the nitroglycerine factory and the 'Grand Magazine' (3–4, 23–30, 35–7 in Fig 5.27). In the period between 1908 and the Great War when the northern section of stoves was completed,

Figure 5.26 RGPF Waltham Abbey, South Site. Guncotton drying stove, 1892. (BB92/26252)

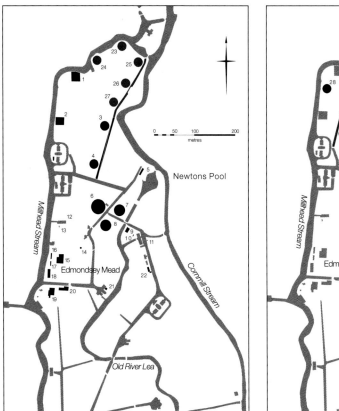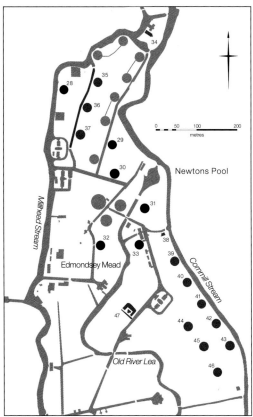

Figure 5.27 RGPF Waltham Abbey, North Site. Development of the guncotton drying stoves and canals in the Edmonsey Mead area prior to 1914 (based on Court of Enquiry plan 1940): **1890s:** 1–2 Guncotton drying stoves 1894; 3–4 Guncotton drying stoves 1897; 5 Mixing house converted 1895–6; 6 Nitrating house 1895–6 (Fig 5.24); 7 Washing house no 3 1895–6; 8 Washing house no 2 1895–6; 9 Wash-water settling house 1895–6; 10–11 Mud-washing houses 1895–6; 12 After-separating house 1895–6; 13 Egg house 1895–6; 14 Water tower 1896; 15 Nitric acid factory 1895–6; 16 Sulphuric acid concentration house 1895–6; 17 Denitrating house 1895–6; 18 Glycerine and acid store; 19 Boiler house 1895–6; 20 Engine house 1895–6; 21 Mixing house converted 1895–6; 22 Guncotton drying stove 1895; **1903:** 23–27 Guncotton drying stoves 1903; **1904:** 28–30 Guncotton drying stoves 1904; 31–33 Mixing houses 1904 (Fig 5.32); **1908–14:** 34 Wet guncotton magazine 1908–14; 35–37 Guncotton drying stoves 1908–14; 38 Guncotton weighing house; 39–46 Guncotton drying stoves 1908–14 (Fig 5.30); 47 Mixing house 1908–14.

a further group of eight was added to the south of the nitroglycerine factory against Cornmill Stream (39–46 in Fig 5.27).

The stoves were of a standard circular design (Figs 5.28 and 5.29) with an internal brick revetment wall 35ft 5in (10.8m) diameter, surrounded by an earthwork traverse, between 6ft 6in (2m) and 7ft 9in (2.4m) in height, the height of the eaves of the stoves. At the centre of each traverse was a timber-framed round-house, bolted to a concrete platform of 10ft 4in (9.25m) diameter. The circular form was probably chosen to improve the airflow and to eliminate potential cold corners. The low conical roofs were supported either by a wooden centre post or a group of four smaller posts. Internally the stoves were lined in zinc sheeting soldered together, and their floor covered in lead to prevent the build-up of guncotton dust. A ladder from the top of the traverse led down into the surrounding gully to give access to the lights on the outside of the windows and to removable vent boards in the stove walls to aid air circulation. The stoves were loaded and unloaded from a covered porch over the adjacent canal or tramway.[28]

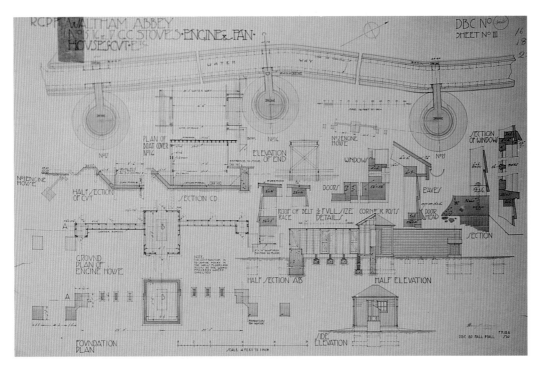

*Figure 5.28 RGPF
Waltham Abbey,
North Site.
Architect's drawing
for guncotton drying
stoves, c 1910 (by
Harry Balham
FRIBA of DBC,
80 Pall Mall).
(BB92/26336)*

Each pair of stoves was served by a central, electrically powered engine house (Fig 5.29) driving a pair of belt races which blew air over a heat exchanger and into the stoves. In later examples a building called a motor house was placed between the stoves, housing a warm air blower not unlike a large hair drier. From the heat exchangers air was blown into the stoves along a lagged pipe raised on wooden, and later concrete, stanchions. At the stoves there were two methods of introducing warm air. The first was via a flanged cast iron pipe, probably assembled from standard industrial fittings, set in the gully between the stove and the revetment wall. Joined to it were 12 flanged elbows connected to the base of the building. In the second method (Fig 5.29), a lagged sheet metal pipe, 1ft (0.30m) in diameter, was joined directly to the apex of the roof by a circular or octagonal roof plate. Whereas warm air if blown in at the bottom was thought to rise and pass out through the vents with limited effect, when introduced at the top it took up water vapour, cooled, and became denser, thereby sinking to the base of the stove to greater effect. The guncotton was dried on trays stacked in wooden racks with cross wires, each of which was earthed. The remains of metal racks in two of the stoves (Fig 5.30)

*Figure 5.29 RGPF
Waltham Abbey,
North Site.
Reconstruction of the
arrangement of a
pair of guncotton
drying stoves.
(© Crown copyright.
NMR)*

*Figure 5.30 RGPF
Waltham Abbey,
North Site.
Guncotton drying
stove with timber
roundhouse removed
but metal drying
racks in situ.
(BB92/26247)*

may be later adaptations. Each stove held 3500lb (1587.6kg) of guncotton, which was dried over a period of 60 hours.[29] The stove was then allowed to cool and the guncotton remained there in the stove until it was required.

Figure 5.31 RGPF Waltham Abbey, North Site. Mixing House built in 1940 on earlier pattern. Note imprints on the floor from the mixing tables and L-shaped hole where burette stood above; cf Figs 5.32 and 5.33. (BB92/26292)

Mixing

In a dried state guncotton was particularly sensitive to friction and very hazardous to handle. From the stoves it was taken to the weighing house to be weighed into waterproof canvas bags for carriage to the mixing or pouring-on house. The first mixing houses (see Fig 5.27) were converted from a gunpowder press house and a gunpowder granulating house. In 1904 three new mixing houses were added. They were of a similar design to the circular guncotton stoves but with concrete revetment walls in place of brick. They also differed from stoves, as a tunnel led through the mound carrying the nitroglycerine gutter from the washing houses (Figs 5.31 and 5.32). They were similarly lined in zinc sheet and had lead-covered floors. Inside, the nitroglycerine was stored in two lead tanks. It was run from these into a lead burette which held

Figure 5.32 (below) RGPF Waltham Abbey, North Site. Interior of no 3 mixing house around 1909. Note lead-lined floor, burette on left, mixing tables on right. (BB97/3443; © MoD)

Figure 5.33 Nitroglycerine burette, used to deliver a measured charge of nitroglycerine to mix with guncotton. A rubber tube was attached to the lower pipe; when not in use it was connected to the upper knob. (BB94/8027)

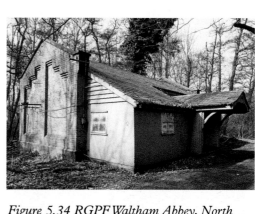

Figure 5.34 RGPF Waltham Abbey, North Site. Cordite paste store, c 1908–14. It formerly fronted onto a canal, which has been filled and surfaced as a road. (BB92/26211)

the exact amount required for each charge (Fig 5.33), and then into a rubber bag containing the dry guncotton in a special hollow in the floor beneath the burettes. This mixture was placed on one of the leaden mixing tables, where it was kneaded by hand, pushed through a coarse sieve, and bagged.

The mixture of these two sensitive explosives – guncotton and nitroglycerine – was known as cordite paste and was relatively safe to handle. From the mixing houses it was moved by barge to a cordite paste store. Some of these were former gunpowder expense magazines, but before the Great War three purpose-built paste stores were erected (Fig 5.34). Their design, of rectangular gabled buildings roofed in slate and lined internally with painted calico, contrasted with the earlier bombproof gunpowder magazines and reflects the relative safety of handling, though two of them were mounded.

Incorporation, pressing, and drying

From store the cordite paste was moved either by barge to a tramway interchange or directly by tramway to the incorporating mills. The former steam-driven gunpowder incorporating mills on North Site were converted to cordite incorporation. The edge-runner mills were removed, but the under-driven shafts and gearing were left in place, and replaced by belt-driven cordite incorporators, one per bay (Fig 5.35). These were modified bread dough mixers supplied by Werner Pfleiderer Perkins of Peterborough, and were widely copied and used throughout the industry. During incorporation the cordite paste was blended with the solvent acetone and with mineral jelly as stabiliser to form the 'devil's porridge', as Sir Arthur Conan Doyle later called it.[30] In place of the under-floor drive shafts, overhead shafts passing through bearing boxes in the bay walls were installed. For at least the first decade of operation the central beam engines remained in use, though they were probably converted to electricity by 1910.

Adjacent groups of gunpowder mills were stripped and cordite presses installed in their place (Fig 5.36). Hydraulic power came both from the accumulator in the former pellet powder building (Fig 3.32) and by an arrangement with the East London Water Company whereby the factory was supplied with higher pressure mains water.[31] The cordite dough was extruded into its distinctive cord-like strands. The thicker strands for large charges were cut by hand and placed on trays for drying, while the thinner strands for rifle cartridges were wound onto brass spools or reels.

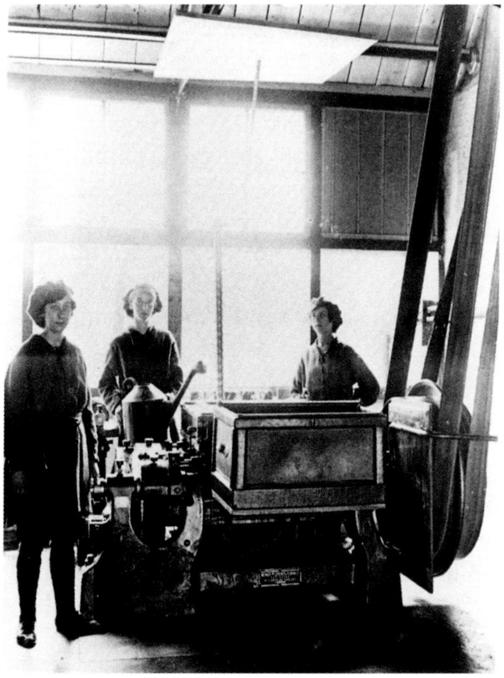

Figure 5.35 (left) RGPF Waltham Abbey, North Site. Cordite incorporating machine, photographed July 1917. (BB94/8018; © MoD)

Figure 5.36 (right) RGPF Waltham Abbey, South Site. Vertical cordite press in secondary location. (BB93/27114)

Figure 5.37 RGPF Waltham Abbey, South Site. Quinton Hill, interior of cordite reeling house after the explosion in 1894, with machinery in situ. Note the toe-boards defining the dirty area with tramway rails and clean areas. (BB94/8008 © MoD)

Figure 5.38 RGPF Waltham Abbey, South Site. Aerial photograph of cordite drying stoves of 1902–4 in the Cob Mead area. (NMR 4825/43)

Originally the cordite was dried in a building thought to have been erected in the later 1880s as a charcoal store. New stoves erected in 1904 included a method to recover the acetone during drying. Cordite was next taken to a reeling house (Fig 5.37), where different reels were wound together. Final drying took place in stoves on South Site, of which 40 were built between 1902 and 1904 (Fig 5.38). The large numbers probably resulted from the adoption in 1901 of cordite MD, with its lower nitroglycerine content, since that required a longer drying time than cordite MK1.

Factory layout and infrastructure

The manufacture of cordite brought a repolarisation of the production flow lines within the overall RGPF and integrated North and South Sites. Wet guncotton was moved from its South Site factory to the 'Grand Magazine' at the extreme northern point of North Site, which was converted into a wet guncotton magazine (34 in Fig 5.27).

The product flow was then generally southwards through North Site. Barges remained as the preferred method of transport between the process buildings. The stoves built on Millhead Stream had access to the high level canal system. For those added between the nitroglycerine factory and the 'Grand Magazine', two new canals were dug linking Millhead and the upper canal level (see Fig 5.27). The easterly one of around 1897 (Fig 5.39) served two new stoves (3–4 in Fig 5.27). It is uncertain whether at this date it was linked through the 'Grand Magazine' or if an extension was made northwards when five additional stoves were built in 1903 (23–7 in Fig 5.27). The westerly canal was added between 1908 and the Great War to serve three further stoves (35–7 in Fig 5.27). A canal loop was also dug to reduce the number of barge movements through the core of the nitroglycerine factory, on the canal between the nitrator and its washing houses.

The group of stoves against Cornmill Stream were served by a hand-push tramway system, an overhead electric supply, a fire-fighting hydrant system, and cast iron telephone pillar. In common with the other buildings in the factory they were heated by steam pipes, which were lagged in asbestos and tarred sheeting and carried on poles above the ground. The tramway linked to the canal system at two points: at its western side at a simple interchange (Fig 5.40), perhaps for delivery of wet guncotton, and at its northern end via a weighing house, where the dried guncotton was weighed into bags for transit to the mixing houses. At this date, too, a short dead-end canal cut was made to serve a new mixing house to the west of these stoves. In contrast to the circular form of the other newly built mixing houses, this was rectangular with a gabled roof and similar in form to the cordite paste stores built at this time.

Movement southwards through the flow line of processes was generally by barge and/or tramway on what by this date was an elaborate and integrated transport network (see Chapter 3), consolidated by the construction of a new canal lock at the southern end of Millhead in 1896–7 to give an additional link between high and low level water systems. From North Site, the return of the partly finished cordite to South Site was again by barge, and there a series of new canals served the battery of drying stoves on Cob Mead. Only later, during the Great War, was this link augmented by a tramway system that passed from the southwestern section of North Site under Highbridge Street to South Site (see Chapter 6). Then, too, the RGPF was connected to the standard-gauge railway network through exchange sidings in the south-western corner of South Site.

Cordite and the trade

The market for cordite, unlike gunpowder, was very restricted, with the British government the one dominant customer. From the outset it was intended that Waltham Abbey should manufacture only a proportion of the state's requirements. In order to make up the shortfall and to provide spare capacity for times of crisis, the government sought to encourage the trade to establish its own facilities with the lure of government contracts. 'We created the trade by giving contracts' stated the Director of Contracts in the War Office.[32] Waltham Abbey continued to play a central role in developing manufacturing technology, which was widely adopted by the trade, and its products were also the yardstick against which the quality and costs of the trade could be judged. Additionally, retaining a significant manufacturing facility in state hands allowed the government to exert a measure of control in a market otherwise dominated by Nobels.

Few companies could compete for the contracts because of the lack of either the necessary expertise or capital to establish new factories. In particular, few of the established gunpowder companies entered into this new market and the geography of the industry was very much influenced by those with pre-existing factories manufacturing dynamite and other nitroglycerine-based explosives.

In tendering for government cordite contracts, the trade factories adopted a variety of strategies to create the necessary plant. One option was to erect a new factory; another, and the preferred choice by many, was to extend a pre-existing factory where the necessary infrastructure was already in place. In order to spread the financial risk, few companies chose to rely entirely on government contracts and many also produced a range of other nitroglycerine-based explosives such as dynamite, gelatine dynamite, and blasting gelatine. In form such factories are complex, and are composed of factories within factories served by a diverse infrastructure to provide power, transport, and water, and to dispose of waste; structures within the larger factory may represent a series of overlapping manufacturing processes. The extent to which the raw materials were prepared on site also had a direct effect on the plan form and component mix.

Complex relationships developed between the cordite manufacturing companies. The Chilworth Gunpowder Company was able to acquire its cordite paste from the Nobel Explosives Company; in other cases guncotton pulp was moved between factories.

Figure 5.39 RGPF Waltham Abbey, North Site. Footbridge over canal in Edmonsey Mead area, dug around 1897 (see Fig 5.27). Note the timber boardwalk over the battered canal sides. (BB92/26287)

Figure 5.40 RGPF Waltham Abbey, North Site. Interchange between the canal system and tramway serving guncotton drying stoves on the east side of Edmonsey Mead. (BB92/26114)

The trade in part-finished explosives assumed particular importance after the destruction of the Waltham Abbey nitroglycerine factory in 1894. Guncotton from Waltham Abbey was transported to Ardeer, Faversham, Hayle, and Pitsea in Essex to be mixed with nitroglycerine and then shipped back to Waltham Abbey as cordite paste for finishing.[33] These linkages mean that factories varied greatly in size and complexity. They also emphasise the continuing importance of coastal transport to the explosives trade, and many of the industry's networks remained those of the gunpowder era, especially with the major dockyard magazines, all of which relied on water transport.

Kynoch's – Arklow (Ireland) and Kynochtown (Essex)

From the early 1890s the arms firm of Kynoch's were keen to expand their interests to include the manufacture of explosives. To this end they purchased the gunpowder works at Worsborough, near Barnsley (South Yorkshire), in 1893. They began to look for a site to manufacture cordite, and one of the directors, Arthur Chamberlain, entered into negotiations with Nobels to supply cordite pulp or paste. After initial agreement, it was clear by January 1895 that the deal had fallen through.

In the meantime Kynoch's was one of only two companies to secure a government contract for cordite and needed to establish a factory quickly to fulfil their commitments. Work began on the new factory early in 1895 on the site of a former chemical works at Arklow, Co Wicklow, on the eastern coast of Ireland, and on 10 July the first

batch of finished cordite was ready. The coastal location stretched for 1fl miles (3km) along the beach with a maximum width of 820yd (750m). It employed around 400 people. As in other areas of the company's business, Chamberlain was intent on being independent of outside suppliers, a concern reinforced by the strained relations with Nobel's. The former chemical works at Arklow had its own plant for manufacturing sulphuric acid; a nitric acid section was added along with a guncotton works, nitroglycerine factory, and cordite section. By the end of the century these were joined by an acetone factory and a picric acid plant to allow manufacture of lyddite, along with a patent commercial explosive kynite. Glycerine was manufactured at both Arklow and the company's main works at Witton in Birmingham, so that mineral jelly was the only ingredient of cordite not made directly by the company. Arklow had its own gas works, electricity generator, and tramway system.[34]

In order to meet its current obligations and in search of future contracts, Kynoch's began work on a second factory, situated south of Corringham in Essex. This, too, was designed to be self-sufficient with its own chemical plant and guncotton section. Within the danger area were sections for nitroglycerine, cordite, and smokeless sporting powders, as well as black powder, plus a .303 rifle cartridge factory linked to Kynoch's other interests.

The new site, named Kynochtown and covering 200 acres (80.97ha), was laid out on flat marsh fronting onto the Thames, Holehaven, and Shellhaven creeks (Fig 5.41). Despite its great size the factory was

Figure 5.41
Panoramic view of
Kynochtown c *1900.*
(AA95/5206; source
and © Mobil Oil)

later redeveloped as an oil refinery and most traces cleared. Contemporary photographs (eg Figs 5.41 and 5.42) show buildings of typical design, with the widespread use of corrugated iron and timber sheds in the non-danger area. In the danger area structures were more sturdily constructed of brick with corrugated iron roofs, and the magazines were surrounded by earthwork traverses to eaves height. The cordite ranges were of a familiar bayed form with brick dividing walls and corrugated iron roofs. The pride Kynoch's took in their new factory is evident in the gardens incongruously laid out and lovingly tended in front of the cordite ranges, evoking the air of almshouses despite the tramway serving them along their veranda (Fig 5.42).

Curtis's and Harvey – Cliffe (Kent)

One of the few gunpowder makers to take up manufacture of smokeless sporting powders was Messrs Curtis's and Harvey. In addition to absorbing several traditional gunpowder makers in the 1890s, they acquired a number of firms manufacturing chemical explosives, among them a guncotton factory adjacent to their gunpowder works at Dartford and, later, the War and Sporting Powder Syndicate's factory at Trimley in Suffolk. They later closed this and consolidated their manufacture of smokeless sporting powders at their former gunpowder works at Tonbridge in Kent. However, their most ambitious venture was a purpose-built explosives factory on Cliffe at Hoo marshes in Kent on the Thames, lying opposite Kynochtown, on the site of a shortlived powder works. It occupied a river frontage, nearly one mile (1.6km) in length, with two jetties and a loading bay (Fig 5.43). Though the field remains of this extensive factory survive relatively intact, the former functions of many structures are not readily identifiable from field evidence alone. Their interpretation is complicated by the interlinking of a number of manufacturing flow lines – for cordite, blasting gelatine, and gelatine dynamite. Among those that can be recognised are single-storey office buildings, the large concrete floor areas of the acid factory, and the mounds of the nitroglycerine factory to its north.

The nitroglycerine factory was closely modelled on that at Waltham Abbey. For example, it used a windlass to raise the glycerine bogie to the top of the nitrating house, but whether the acids were also raised in this manner is not known; after an explosion in 1904 in the nitrating house, this was rebuilt using a Nathan pattern nitrator. Cliffe also has the only other surviving examples of circular traverses on the Waltham Abbey pattern, albeit smaller, with an external diameter of 46ft (14m) and a single straight entrance leading into the mounds.

The location of the factory gave it the characteristic treeless and bleak air of many of these Thames-side factories (Fig 5.44).

Figure 5.42 (top) Kynochtown near Corringham, Essex. Cordite ranges. (AA95/5216; source and © Mobil Oil)

Figure 5.43 Cliffe, Kent. Aerial photograph of the site of Curtis's and Harvey's purpose-built explosives factory: on the centre right is the 1890s nitro-glycerine factory. (NMR 15033/46)

Figure 5.44 Cliffe, Kent. Open marshland location alongside the Thames estuary. BB94/8728

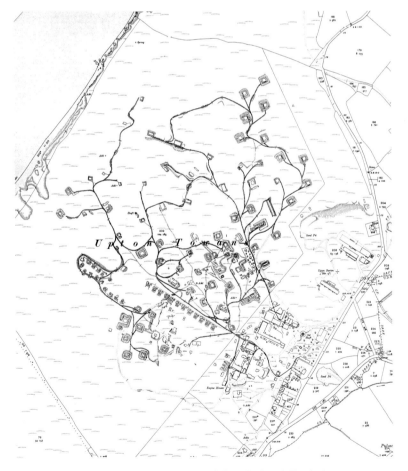

Figure 5.45 Hayle, Cornwall. Plan of the National Explosives Company's factory, established in 1889, extract from OS, Cornwall, Sheet LXII.10, 25-inch, second edition, 1907.

These flat marshland sites allowed them to be laid out in a more organised manner than the factory at Waltham Abbey. At Cliffe the only pre-existing features were a few gunpowder buildings and a criss-cross pattern of drains. Its danger buildings were characteristically small, including rectangular brick guncotton stoves, roofed with corrugated iron, lined with zinc sheeting, and floored in lead sheeting. Other buildings were wooden, also roofed in corrugated iron and floored in lead, but lined with varnished matchboards. They were connected by a 2ft (0.6m) gauge tramway system. Where traverses were used they were earthworks whose borrow pits were left as open ponds around the factory. [35]

National Explosives Company – Hayle (Cornwall)

One of the most successful independent explosives manufacturers was the National Explosives Company at Hayle (Figs 5.45 and 5.46). The factory was set up in 1889 by the Kennall Gunpowder Company, aware of the inroads that dynamite was making in the local mining industry. The site chosen was in the sand dunes at Upton Towans in Hayle, well served by coastal shipping and with a local railway line to bring in raw materials and distribute its finished products.

The factory was laid out in the most up-to-date manner by Oscar Guttmann, a Hungarian by birth and one of the leading consulting chemical engineers of his day (see Fig 5.57).[36] The dunes formed an ideal location for the falling levels of the nitroglycerine factory and for the wide spacing of other buildings, which were either dug into the dunes or surrounded by sand traverses. Guttmann divided the danger area of the factory on a continental pattern into a 'wet part' and a 'dry part'. In the wet part nitroglycerine was manufactured, purified, and stored, and in the dry part it was processed to form marketable explosives. In operation this differed from normal British practice by holding nitroglycerine in a store house before it was moved by tramway bogie to a mixing house, in contrast to Ardeer (see Fig 5.17) or Waltham Abbey, for example, where nitroglycerine was poured directly onto an absorbent substance. From the mixing house the explosive was removed by tramway to the cartridging huts (Fig 5.47), where three or four girls per small hut worked hand-operated cartridging machines to produce the familiar sticks of dynamite. The buildings in the factory were timber-framed, weatherboarded on the exterior, and lined internally with varnished wood, with a material described as 'breeze' between. Their pitched roofs were wooden with a felt covering. For the magazines Guttmann made extensive use of mass concrete, a feature also perhaps reflecting his continental background (see Chapter 4).

At the rear of the dunes a large area was levelled for the central services of the factory. These included steam raising facilities, air compressors, and engines to power pumps to extract water. Large acid handling plants, also designed by Guttmann, included sulphuric and nitric acid factories with denitrification and acid recovery sections. The factory was served by its own tramway and electricity supply.

At the outset the factory's primary product was dynamite; later, with the lapse of the gelatine patent, it secured licences to extend its activities. Before cordite production could commence, a guncotton section was constructed between the nitric acid section and the central services, close to the water supply and power for the guncotton manufacturing machinery.

Its capacity to manufacture cordite placed this modern factory in an ideal position to diversify its activities away from high explosives into propellants. The investment already made in the guncotton section was well placed, as it had adopted the Abel pot process and purification processes specified for government cordite contracts. The company's speculative development of a cordite factory in advance of government contracts was rewarded when in 1894 it was one of two firms, along with Kynoch's, to receive a contract. The buildings of the cordite section lay to the south and east of the first nitroglycerine factory on Jack Straw's Hill. Their field remains include the mounds of guncotton drying stoves, the long rectangular cleared areas of the cordite incorporating mills and press houses, and

Figure 5.46 Hayle, Cornwall. Aerial photograph of the National Explosives Company's factory from the seaward side, SW5740/2. (© Cornwall County Council CCR5130/34)

Figure 5.47 Hayle, Cornwall. View from Jack Straw's Hill overlooking the Mixing House traverse to the earthworks of the cartridging huts. (BB94/16166)

(indistinguishable from the mounds of the guncotton drying stoves) cordite drying stoves and storage magazines. The central services area was also extended, and pumps and accumulators were installed to provide hydraulic power. The factory by this date

Figure 5.48 (left) Chilworth, Surrey. Cordite kneading and press houses. (BB94/10109)

Figure 5.49 (right) Chilworth, Surrey. Bay wall of kneading and press house. (BB94/94/10107)

Figure 5.50 Chilworth, Surrey. Cordite drying stove. (BB94/10102)

employed around 200 people in about 100 buildings spread out over an area of 300 acres (121.46ha).

Continued cordite contracts not only ensured the financial security of the company, but also led to further extensions of the factory. Around 1905 an additional nitroglycerine factory was built to the west of Jack Straw's Hill. Set amongst the traverses of the cartridging huts, it was probably designed principally to serve the manufacture of commercial explosives. At the same time the factory adopted the Nathan-Thomson displacement method for guncotton manufacture and constructed a new plant adjacent to the nitric acid works close to the site entrance.[37]

Chilworth Gunpowder Company (Surrey)

The Chilworth Gunpowder Company was able to enter the cordite market with a far more modest investment owing to its close connections with the Nobel Dynamite Trust through Edward Kraftmeier. An agreement with Nobel's assured the company of a supply of cordite paste from Ardeer.[38] Hence all the company needed at Chilworth was a factory specialising in finishing cordite, without costly acid processing facilities, a guncotton factory, or the hazardous manufacture of nitroglycerine. The latter's absence had the additional benefit of allaying any commercial suspicion from the manufacturers of blasting explosives within the Nobel Dynamite Trust.

The new factory developed in the early 1890s lay on virgin ground away from and distinct from the gunpowder works and functioned as a separate unit. The restricted range of operations was reflected in the limited number of process buildings compared

with factories where the full manufacturing process was carried out. At its centre was the surviving kneading and pressing house (Fig 5.48), 165ft (50.3m) in length, where the imported cordite paste was incorporated to form cordite dough before it was pressed in adjoining bays. The bayed single-storey building is brick built; its corrugated iron roof was supported by rolled steel joists, whose German manufacture is indicated by the name 'BURBACH' visible on several. Between the bays, the steel-framed walls were clad in corrugated iron sheets and iron-framed windows glazed in clear unwired glass (Fig 5.49).

Other surviving buildings include two drying stoves. Single-storey two-roomed rectangular buildings, 52ft 6in × 33ft 2in (16m × 10.1m) (Fig 5.50), they were warmed by under-floor heating, and each had its own chimney or flue to aid circulation. They were largely iron-framed, clad in corrugated iron set on low brick walls in the centre and to the rear. They were insulated by a hairy material, possibly horse hair, secured by chicken wire and internally plastered and painted to produce a smooth washable surface. All the windows were double glazed.

As at Waltham Abbey, the drying process was later refined by the construction of an acetone recovery stove. The building is single-storey, brick and gabled, 31ft 6in × 22ft (9.6m × 6.7m), with its function stencilled on its southern wall, 'DRYING AND EXTRACTION OF SOLVENTS'. Its roof was lagged in a similar manner to the drying stoves; its windows were wooden with brass fittings, however. The factory's stoves and magazines were all protected by earthwork traverses partly revetted in corrugated iron, the so-called 'Chilworth mounds'.

As elsewhere, the cordite was moved between processes by tramway. There is no evidence for a central power house producing electricity or steam for power or heating. The two kneading and press houses were equipped with their own engine and motor rooms, and the stoves appear to be self-contained units all perhaps reflecting the modest investment in this factory. No evidence remains for the form of lighting in use during the 1890s.

Nobels – Ardeer, Pitsea, Stowmarket, and Uplees (Faversham)

Nobels Explosives Company of Ardeer did not receive a government contract until the Boer War (1899–1901), despite having been active in the trade through its subsidiaries.[39] In time, however, the remainder of the cordite trade came to be dominated by the Nobel Dynamite Trust Company, through its network of subsidiary companies. By the outbreak of the Great War they had acquired, often secretly, controlling interests in the British Explosives Syndicate at Pitsea, the New Explosives Company at Stowmarket, and the Cotton Powder Company of Faversham, as well as being closely associated with the Chilworth Gunpowder Company. Of the cordite makers only

Kynoch's, Curtis's and Harvey, and National Explosives remained independent.[40]

The British Explosives Syndicate established a factory on Pitsea Hall Island in Essex in 1891.[41] It was set back 2fi miles (4km) from the Thames and relied on a tidal creek for the import and export of goods by barge. The island it occupied also provided a slight eminence in the otherwise flat and remote marshland for the fall necessary for its nitroglycerine factory.

It was created to manufacture a range of nitroglycerine-based explosives including No 1 dynamite, gelignite, gelatine dynamite, and blasting gelatine. At the centre of the site, a large square earthwork mound with mass concrete tunnels can be identified as the nitrating house; other mounds falling away to the north are arranged in the classic configuration for handling nitroglycerine. The sites of other buildings are readily identifiable by the square traverses which formerly surrounded the danger buildings. Surviving buildings are brick built and all retain evidence of a covered tramway porch. Remarkably one of them has its internal matchboard lining intact, and its corrugated iron roof and porch. The lack of evidence for a large guncotton factory may suggest this raw material was acquired from elsewhere. In 1902 a cordite section was added; a group of buildings lying at an angle to the original nitroglycerine section may represent the cordite ranges. Early aerial photographs show buildings of the characteristic bayed form associated with cordite incorporators and press houses, one of which survives (Fig 5.51).[42] Neither the field remains nor the layout reveals the location of an acid section, though it was recorded as a manufacturer of acids by the outbreak of war.[43]

Other chemical explosives manufacturers with the necessary skills were keen to

Figure 5.51 Pitsea Hall Farm, Essex. Characteristically bayed explosives building. (BB94/8130)

Figure 5.52 Uplees near Faversham, Kent. Footings of acid factory adjacent to the river Swale; see Fig 5.7. (BB94/10464)

Figure 5.53 RGPF Waltham Abbey, North Site. Plan of acid and nitroglycerine factories, c 1900 (redrawn from WASC 900/79): 1 Shifting house; 2 Boiler house; 3 Engine house; 4 Glycerine and acid store; 5 Denitrating house; 6 Sulphuric acid concentration house; 7 Nitric acid factory; 8 Plumbers shop; 9 Egg house; 10 After separating house; 11 Nitrating house (Fig 5.24); 12 Washing house; 13 Washing house; 14 Wash-water settling house; 15 Mud-washing shed; 16 Mud-washing shed; 17 Soda store; 18 Dirty store; 19 Tower.

break into the cordite market. The New Explosives Company of Stowmarket more than quadrupled in area to accommodate a new cordite section. Its buildings were dug into the hillside on the opposite side of the railway line to the north of the original guncotton factory, and were linked to the new factory by a tramway beneath the main line.

By the late nineteenth century the Uplees explosives works at Faversham was one of the largest in the kingdom. In addition to guncotton, it expanded to manufacture a range of 35 varieties of explosives in about 150 buildings. It was a particularly well-equipped factory with an acid plant adjacent to the Swale (Fig 5.52) and its own gas works for light and heat; it had three sets of hydraulic accumulators, air compressors, and a high pressure water system to serve the fire-fighting hydrants. The scattered buildings were linked by a 3ft 3in (1m) gauge tramway. For cordite manufacture a nitroglycerine factory was built and the area of the factory expanded eastwards and away from the river to accommodate the new buildings.[44]

The raw materials – chemicals, plant, and people

Chemicals

One of the most important building blocks of the modern chemical industry is sulphuric acid. In explosives production it was doubly important in the manufacture of nitric acid and as a dehydrating agent in nitration processes. The inherited locational advantages for the explosives industry in the Thames Estuary area were reinforced by the long-standing chemical industry centred on the West Ham area, which was able to supply its basic needs for sulphuric and

nitric acid.[45] Though many factories manufactured their own nitric acid, sulphuric acid continued to be acquired commercially. At Hayle its manufacture proved to be an uneconomic venture and was discontinued. Kynoch's were exceptional in continuing to ensure an independence in the supply of raw materials.

The ground plans of early chemical explosives factories show few had their own chemical plants: they were reliant on external suppliers. Yards full of acid carboys in wire cages packed with straw and jars of nitric acid were a common feature of these works. The danger of storing nitric acid in large glass carboys was not inconsiderable: on a number of occasions they exploded with fatal results. Good communications either by rail or preferably water were vital for their safe transport. Nor is there any evidence in the early factories for facilities to recover the spent acids after the nitration processes, to form part of a two-way traffic with the originating chemical works.

From the 1880s the acid section became an indispensable feature of any chemical explosives factory. Acid handling facilities might typically include sulphuric and nitric acid production plants, mixing and storage facilities, waste acid receiving and storage facilities, de-nitration plant, and acid concentrators.[46] Acid factories are recognisable by their large concrete floor surfaces sited outside the danger area. In some cases,

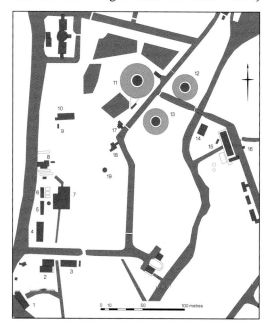

Figure 5.54 RGPF Waltham Abbey, North Site. Nitrate soda store. (BB92/26147)

often unremarkable field remains belie the technologically advanced processes these structures once housed (Fig 5.52). In other instances, the remains may be unravelled to reveal the positions of machine bases and the flow of liquids through the plant. Despite the unpromising appearance of these remains they contain invaluable information on the layout of early chemical plants in an era before the growth of the chemical engineering profession. Each plant was typically the product of the chemical engineer engaged by a company to build its factory.

At Waltham Abbey the factory remained dependent on the trade for its acid needs until the major reorganisation of the late 1890s. Two separate factories were then built to serve North (Fig 5.53) and South Sites, but the processes carried out appear to be similar. Sulphuric acid, acquired commercially, was brought up to the required concentration in plant installed in both factories. Here too, in the 1890s the 'fuming' grade of nitric acid, which was dangerous to transport, was produced for the first time within the factory. The process involved distilling sulphuric acid and potassium or sodium nitrate, which formed nitric acid and as a waste product nitre cake (a mixture of sodium sulphate and bisulphate). In addition to guaranteeing the quality of ingredients and securing supply, the acid factory

was important in the economy of explosives production for it contained a de-nitrification plant where the nitric and sulphuric acids were separated after the nitration process (see Fig 5.22).[47] The resulting sulphuric acid was commonly used in the manufacture of nitric acid.

The buildings of the Waltham Abbey acid factories were well constructed in brick with slated roofs; their blue brick floors were laid on concrete. Later additions included iron-framed stores with corrugated iron roofs to hold the waste nitre cake.

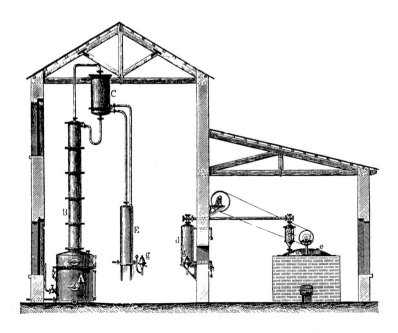

Figure 5.55 RGPF Waltham Abbey, North Site. Acetone factory, designed by Oscar Guttmann and supplied by Richard Luhn of Hapse (after Guttmann 1895).

Only the nitrate soda store, built around the outbreak of the Great War, remains standing (Fig 5.54). It is 68ft 6in × 44ft 6in (20.9m × 13.6m) with battered mass concrete walls and a self-supporting timber roof. At Hayle the nitrate store was also mass concrete but with a light metal single-pitch roof, perhaps originally covered by corrugated iron. Adjacent to it, the brick nitric acid factory is now roofless but its floor paved in acid-resistant bricks remains. This perhaps contrasts with elsewhere in the explosives and chemical industries where contemporary photographs show acid plant housed in corrugated iron or weather-boarded buildings.

Acetone, the solvent used in cordite production, resulted from the distillation of acetate of lime, which in turn came from a combination of pyroligneous acid resulting from the distillation of wood with lime. In the early years of cordite production, Britain imported acetone from Germany. This unsatisfactory situation was partly resolved by work at Woolwich in the early 1890s when an experimental plant was set up to take advantage of the waste wood from the sawmills and workshops. By 1895 an acetone factory was established at Waltham Abbey in the buildings of the redundant 1860s guncotton factory on North Site (Fig 5.55).[48] Elsewhere in the factory other buildings made redundant by the run-down of gunpowder production were used as acetate of lime and acetone stores, probably in part to create a strategic reserve.

Figure 5.56 Hayle, Cornwall. Dump of earthenware associated with acid handling. (BB94/16170)

Plant and materials

Vital supply links were also built up with less hazardous industries. Glycerine, a valuable by-product of soap and candle manufacture, and mineral jelly or vaseline, used as a stabiliser in cordite, were both acquired commercially. Such was the demand for cotton waste that a minor industry developed to convert mill waste into a product suitable for guncotton manufacture. Among machinery engineers, Easton, Anderson, and Goolden of Erith were suppliers to both Waltham Abbey and the National Explosives Company Hayle; elsewhere local engineering works were commissioned to supply the necessary machinery.

Makers of terracotta and industrial earthenware were particularly important before the development of acid-resistant metals around the outbreak of the Great War. Until then, earthenware and to a lesser extent glass remained the only practical materials to hold and handle acids. In many instances, the large dumps of intricately shaped and moulded earthenware around former acid factories will provide a clearer indication of the processes formerly undertaken than the associated vast concrete floor slabs (Fig 5.56). Well-known manufacturers included Doulton of Lambeth, whose products have been found at Waltham Abbey and Hayle; others were Jennings pottery at Poole in Dorset, and Hathernware from Hathern near Loughborough.[49]

The special acid-resistant bricks used as flooring in acid handling areas and sometimes in the first few courses of walls to guard against acid splashes were a similarly specialised product. At Hayle, well-fired dark-coloured bricks include those marked 'HANCOCK & CO/HAWARDEN', 'OBSIDIANITE/REGD/ACID ROOF', 'C.DAVIDSON & CO'S/ADAMANTINE', and 'TRADE MARK METALLINE'.[50] Here and elsewhere, too, acid-resistant bricks occur without any distinguishing marks. Their joints were sealed by a tough paste of asbestos powder, sodium silicate, and water, sometimes with ground barytes, and the same is found between the sections of acid earthenware.[51]

People

The new chemical explosives industry also required new people with the training and knowledge to construct and operate these plants. As in other areas of the chemical industry, many of the chemists were of continental origin. Foremost among the men who turned their research into practical explosives was Alfred Nobel (1833–96), whose invention of dynamite revolutionised the explosives industry. This was not an entirely one-way traffic: in particular Abel's work on the purification of guncotton was widely adopted abroad. Many continental chemists were instrumental in establishing new factories for the private companies. This happened with the Schultze powder factories at Eyeworth and Barwick (see above, Schultze powder). One of the most influential was the cosmopolitan Oscar Guttmann, a Hungarian later naturalised as British (Fig 5.57). He worked widely in the explosives industry as a consulting engineer and was responsible for the works at Hayle, and for plant at Waltham Abbey. He also published extensively and many of his designs were adopted by the industry.[52]

For the industry to function it was also necessary to have a tier of well-trained factory chemists, who were essential to oversee the analysis of raw materials and to monitor the nitrogen content and stability of finished explosives. The laboratory and small ancillary test huts for the factory chemist became a feature of all chemical explosives factories (Fig 5.58). At Waltham Abbey in the early years there was a preponderance of Scottish-trained chemists, who included James Thomson (formerly of Nobels), and his younger brother William Thomson, William Bennie, and Robert Robertson. William Rintoul, another Glasgow-trained chemist, worked in the laboratory and later assumed charge of the manufacture of nitroglycerine. Many of these men were more than factory chemists and contributed directly to the advances made in explosives manufacture, such as the Nathan-Thomson displacement process for guncotton manufacture and the Nathan-Thomson-Rintoul method of nitroglycerine manufacture (described above, Nathan-Thomson-Rintoul nitration process). Rintoul and Robertson later developed a process for recovering acetone vapour from drying cordite. Presiding over these revolutionary changes at Waltham Abbey was the monocled figure of Colonel Sir Frederic Nathan – a man who did not suffer fools gladly. A regular officer in the Royal Artillery, he was appointed as Assistant Superintendent in 1889 and Superintendent in 1900. As with Congreve a century earlier, he had great organisational skills, the ability to eliminate the unnecessary and simplify what remained, and,

Figure 5.58 RGPF Waltham Abbey, North Site. Laboratory, built 1897 and extended 1902. (BB92/26103)

Figure 5.57 Oscar Guttmann. (© Hagley Museum and Library PAM 87.417)

*Figure 5.59
RGPF Waltham
Abbey, North Site.
Earthenware
Guttmann balls,
used to pack acid
towers to produce a
large internal surface
area. (BB94/7992)*

although lacking a specialised chemical training, was unflagging in his interest in technical and experimental work. Such was the culture that placed Waltham Abbey at the forefront of explosives development at the end of the nineteenth century.[53]

Where the expertise was lacking among the resident staff, a wide range of experts was called upon. George McRoberts, former manager at Ardeer, advised on the erection of the first Quinton Hill nitroglycerine factory. Oscar Guttmann was consulted on a number of questions and was responsible for the erection of the acetone factories at Woolwich and Waltham Abbey. Archaeologically his influence is marked by small earthenware balls the size of golfballs

that occur as site finds at Waltham Abbey; they are so-called 'Guttmann balls' used to pack acid towers (Fig 5.59). Skills and knowledge flowed the other way to the private companies, too; notably Nathan and Rintoul transferred to Nobels at Ardeer.[54]

Housing

Like the contemporary powdermakers, manufacturers of chemical explosives were modest in their provision of housing. In a number of remote rural or coastal areas, however, it was a practical necessity, as in any greenfield development. Here many of the houses remain as a legacy of the explosives industry though the original reason for their siting has gone.

At Eyeworth in Hampshire there was a single lodge at the centre of the works when the site was acquired by the Schultze Powder Company. By the end of the century this was considerably extended and was occupied by the company's chemist, R W S Griffith. Though the workforce numbered around 100 by this date, the only other accommodation attached to the factory consisted of a foreman's house and six cottages. In Hertfordshire, the Smokeless Powder Company was responsible for the creation of the small factory hamlet of Barwick (see Fig 5.15).

*Figure 5.60 Hayle,
Cornwall, Factory
housing – 'Dongre'.*

Within the works perimeter were the manager's house and a bungalow. On the lane leading to the factory four pairs of cottages were built and a public house, originally the Factory Arms.[55]

Social stratification and the necessity to recruit and retain chemists and managers are reflected in the housing provided. At Hayle, imposing houses with pilasters and Corinthian capitals built for the senior officials (Fig 5.60) contrast with a more modest pair of cottages provided for lower grades of employees. But the majority of the workforce was recruited locally, including young girls for the dynamite sheds, and the factory's opening provided some relief for the nearby town of Hayle, beset by a declining engineering industry.[56] At the Cotton Powder Company's works on Uplees Marshes near Faversham, the factory absorbed the small former settlement of Upper Lees. At its entrance stood two symmetrically arranged managers' houses; other cottages were added, but too few to accommodate the entire workforce.

At Arklow, Kynoch's built three houses of a 'superior character' for the senior officials and 12 cottages let to foremen at the cost of half a crown (12fip) per week. Later more houses were built, a grocery shop,

and a social hall. A timber building named Kynoch Lodge was provided for entertaining important visitors and as a club for the senior management.[57] But the most ambitious housing scheme associated with a new explosives factory was by Kynoch's near Corringham. When work began on the factory in 1896, a collection of huts served for the workers. The remoteness of the site caused a decision in 1897 to build a small village adjacent to the factory, which was named Kynochtown. It consisted of 40 two- and three-bedroomed bungalows and houses, a school for over 60 children, and a shop. An Institute, forming the centre of social life for this isolated community, also acted as a church hall. The company also built the Hotel Kynoch on Canvey Island for visitors to the factory, who were originally ferried to it by rowing boat. Until the factory was linked to the main line by the Corringham Light Railway in 1901, the workforce was collected at Stanford-le-Hope station by horse brakes. The settlement of Kynochtown outlasted the closure of the works in the 1920s and was renamed Coryton, but after less than a century the name and settlement were lost when in 1970 the village was demolished to make way for the expansion of Mobil's oil refinery.[58]

Endnotes

1 For an up-to-date discussion of detonation and definitions, see Bailey and Murray 1989, 24–33; HMSO 1938, 1–2, 19–20; Read 1942, 57–61.
2 HMSO 1938, 86, 93.
3 For the history of guncotton, see Abel 1866 and 1867; Cavendish nd, 126–32 and 850–8; Vernidub 1996. Hogg 1963a, 749–50, gives a summary of Abel's career.
4 WASC 20, Younghusband, C W, 1873 Description of the manufacture of Abel's pulped and compressed guncotton at Waltham Abbey, November 1873.
5 Abel 1863.
6 New Explosives Company Ltd 1902 and 1906; Hodgetts 1909, 386–95.
7 Majendie 1872.
8 Explosives Inspectorate Report 45, 1882.
9 PRO Supp5/860, photo no 59.
10 Engelbach 1899, 405.
11 Fitzgerald 1895; Nathan 1909a.
12 Nathan 1909a.
13 Schultze 1865.
14 For Eyeworth, see Hodgetts 1909, 409–11; Pasmore 1993.
15 For Barwick, see Johnson 1970, 81; Storey 1971. NMR SU 21 SW 3; PRO BT 31/7899 Schultze Gunpowder Company Ltd; Explosives Inspectorate Report 104, 1893; 1891 Census Return RG12/1095 Barwick part Stanton Hertfordshire, 13.
16 See Bibliography, Selected legislation.
17 Nathan and Rintoul 1908; Reader 1970, 16–36; Dolan and Oglethorpe 1996.
18 Reader 1970, 67–89 and 125–62.
19 Earl 1978, 250–62.
20 Ibid, 264–94.
21 For an account of the career of Paul Vieille, see Medard 1995.
22 The Times 1893; Reader 1970, 138–43.
23 HMSO 1894a.
24 HMSO 1895, pl XIV opposite 81.
25 Fitzgerald 1895, 317.
26 HMSO 1895, 81–8; HMSO 1907, 88–94; Nathan and Rintoul 1908.
27 Nathan 1909b, 443.
28 Marshall 1917, 290.
29 HMSO 1938, 101.
30 Routledge 1995, 268.
31 Anderson 1898, 81.
32 Trebilcock 1966.
33 Earl 1978, 233; Wood 1977, 37.
34 Kelleher 1993, 91–160.
35 For Cliffe, see Hodgetts 1909, 364; Explosives Inspectorate Report 157, 1903; Explosives Inspectorate Report 166, 1904; Explosives Inspectorate

Report **167**, 1904; Explosives Inspectorate Annual Report 1905.

36 Obituary: *J Soc Chemical Industry* 1910.

37 For Hayle, see Earl 1978, 184–236; Earl and Smith 1991; Explosives Inspectorate Report **109**, 1894; Explosives Inspectorate Report **136**, 1899.

38 Kelleher 1993, 102.

39 Reader 1970, 148.

40 *Ibid*, 179–206.

41 Hodgetts 1909, 339; For plan see Ordnance Survey 25” Essex LXXXIX.3, LXXXIX.4, LXXXI.15, LXXXI.16.

42 Reader 1970, 184; RAF vertical aerial photograph, 58/647 Frame 5012, 23 April 1951.

43 PRO MUN 5/159/1122.7/28.

44 For Uplees, see Hodgetts 1909, 346–52; Percival 1985; Explosives Inspectorate Report **133**, 1899; Explosives Inspectorate Report **161**, 1903.

45 Davidson 1980, 43–5.

46 Levy 1920, 31.

47 For acids, see Guttmann 1895, 126–68; Earl 1978, 214–26.

48 Guttmann 1895, 117–21; Anderson 1898, 123–4.

49 Cooksey 1969.

50 Fergusson 1994, 18–19.

51 Earl 1978, 214–26.

52 *The Times* 1910; Earl 1978, 185.

53 HMSO 1894a, 40; Rintoul 1934, 564-5; Robertson 1937; Miles 1955, 48–51.

54 Miles 1955, 47–63.

55 Ordnance Survey 25” Herts XXII.9 1879, 1897, 1923.

56 1891 Census Return RG12/1852 Gwithian Cornwall.

57 Kelleher 1993, 124.

58 Scott 1981.

6
The Great War 1914–18

'A chemists' war', delivered by 'men of push and go'

Throughout Europe in the last decades of the nineteenth century chemical-based explosives had largely supplanted gunpowder as the principal military explosive. Industrialists and chemists thereby gave politicians and soldiers the power to unleash the most destructive war the world had yet seen. Though the technologies for manufacturing the majority of wartime explosives were fully developed, the problem for the combatant nations was to harness their industrial resources to feed the carnage of the battlefields. So important was the supply of explosives that the Great War has been dubbed 'a chemists' war'.[1] The skill of a nation's scientists was now as important as the valour of its soldiers in determining the outcome of a war. The size and sophistication of its chemical industry and research facilities were as critical as the size of its armies. The poor development of the British organic chemical industry in comparison with that of Germany was one reason for the faltering start Britain made to adapt its peacetime industries to those of war. Furthermore, the interdependence of the armaments industry and the rest of the economy became increasingly evident, as competing demands placed great strains on scarce raw materials and novel solutions were required to maintain the flow of explosives (Fig 6.1).

A crisis of supply: government control

On 8 August 1914, four days after the declaration of war, the government passed the first of the Defence of the Realm Acts (DORA). Under these it acquired sweeping powers to prosecute the war, including the authority to acquire land and control of everything necessary to make munitions.[2] In the first phase of the war, however, munitions procurement lacked a strong central lead, as pre-war administrative structures were overwhelmed by the demands of a new type of warfare characterised by almost continuous operations and punctuated by massive bombardments and futile attacks. This failure was brought to a head in the

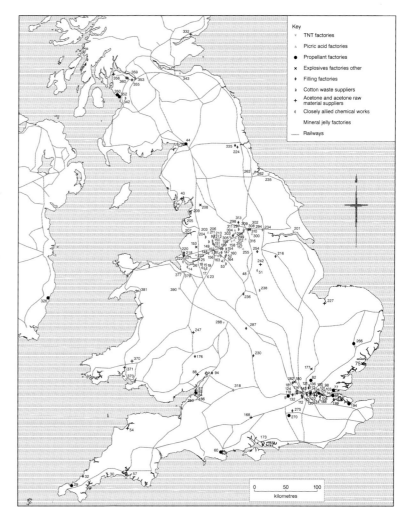

Figure 6.1 Distribution of Great War explosives factories, showing principal activities.

155

Figure 6.2 Lloyd George as Pharaoh. Cartoon from Punch, *16 June, 1915.*

DESIGN REPRESENTING THE DISTORTED VIEWS ENTERTAINED BY CERTAIN QUERULOUS SONS OF LIBERTY AS TO THE METHODS OF THE NEW MINISTER OF MUNITIONS.

so-called 'shells scandal'. An article in *The Times* on 14 May 1915 claimed, 'the want of an unlimited supply of high explosives was a fatal bar to our success', and for this want soldiers were dying in vain.[3] Mounting criticism of all aspects of the government's prosecution of the war led that same month to its fall and the formation of Asquith's coalition government.[4] Among its first acts was the creation of the Ministry of Munitions, with responsibility for all areas of munitions supply and manufacture.[5] The energetic Lloyd George was appointed as its first minister, and from his headquarters in No 6 Whitehall Gardens he set about replacing the pre-war bureaucracy with men of 'push and go'.[6]

The 1915 Munitions of War Act further tightened state control of armaments production (Fig 6.2).[7] Under its provisions the state could declare essential factories as controlled establishments. The profits of the owners were then regulated, lock-outs declared illegal, and plant could be removed to other locations. It also removed an employee's right to strike, provided badges for workers employed in munitions work (Fig 6.3; and see Fig 6.47), and through a system of leaving certificates restricted the movement of labour. The most conspicuous effect of the creation of the Ministry of Munitions were the 'National Factories'. These covered a wide range of activities besides explosives, including the manufacture

of aeroplanes, machine guns, and shells. The ministry also wrested control of the royal factories formerly administered by the War Office and Admiralty.[8] Elsewhere it took control of or converted private factories for war work, designating them *His Majesty's Factory.*

This unprecedented state intervention had many important consequences for factory design. The National Factories tended to be built on greenfield sites, and exhibited the regularity of layout associated with a scheme created at a single point in time and governed by the orderly flow of materials. A Welfare Section in the Ministry of Munitions was also instrumental in improving conditions within state and controlled establishments. The factory canteen, meal, rest, and wash rooms became commonplace, as did the provision of medical facilities. In areas with a dense concentration of munitions workers, the provision of housing and social facilities also became a feature of the wartime factory.

It is one of the ironies of the Great War that, despite its scale and the centralising influence of the new ministry, much of the success of explosives supply resulted from the talent and charisma of a small number of individuals. One of the earliest was Lord

Figure 6.3 Postcard 'On War Service', WASC 1027/2. (BB94/8005)

Moulton, an elderly Law Lord who chaired the War Office's Committee on High Explosives. Under him, high explosives supply was far better organised than many other areas of munitions manufacture, and planning for large new factories was begun.[9] Pragmatic early decisions promoted the expansion or adaptation of pre-existing factories. But the inability of this system to deliver the necessary munitions acted as the catalyst for change in production methods and factory design.

Raw materials

For all the international nature of chemical research and related industrial development in the previous half-century, at the outbreak of war Britain lagged far behind Germany in these fields, most notably in organic chemistry. Also, Britain was heavily dependent on imports for the manufacture of explosives. Sulphur and pyrites were required in large quantities to produce sulphuric acid and nitrates for nitric acid. It was only near the war's end that the government planned an ammonia-nitric acid factory at Billingham on Teeside, based on the synthesis of ammonia and its oxidation to nitric acid using the processes devised by the German chemists Haber and Ostwald, respectively. Construction began in 1918 but was unfinished at the Armistice.[10] By contrast, as coal tar by-products, including toluol, phenol, and aniline, became vital in high explosives manufacture, the British coal by-products industry was sufficiently well developed to be a supplier to Germany prior to the war. Another vital raw material, glycerine, was an important by-product of soap and candle manufacture. Thus, generally, the growing diversity of linkages with commercial chemical-industrial activity is characteristic of this period and leaves few monumental remains that can be isolated as specifically relevant to explosives production.

Acetone

Acetone illustrates the efforts – part ground-breaking research, part practical ingenuity – made to ensure a secure supply of an essential raw material.

For the production of cordite MD an assured supply of the solvent acetone was vital. There were large demands for it also for manufacturing dope (to tension aircraft fabric) and products such as tear gas. Pre-war supplies were imported from the great timber-growing countries – America, Canada and Austria. Erosion of this dependency began around the turn of the century when Oscar Guttmann installed acetone works at Waltham Abbey (see Chapter 5), Woolwich, Clapton, and Manchester.[11] In 1913 the Office of Forest and Woods erected an acetone plant of German design at Coleford in Gloucestershire. This plant and the others built by this agency early in the war relied on the destructive distillation of wood, which was reflected in the woodland distribution of the industry.[12] New plants of American design were constructed at Bideford in Devon and at Dundee in Angus, and Kynoch's established an acetate of lime factory at Longparish in Hampshire to supply an acetone plant at Kynochtown. The latter reflected usual practice, whereby a chemical firm remote from the supply plant undertook processing; the United Alkali Company's factory at Widnes in Cheshire was involved in this way, for example.[13] New factories at Carmarthen in Carmarthenshire, Ludlow in Shropshire, and Mid Lavant in West Sussex were planned in 1917, but were incomplete by 1918.[14] In plan (Fig 6.4), the factory area of

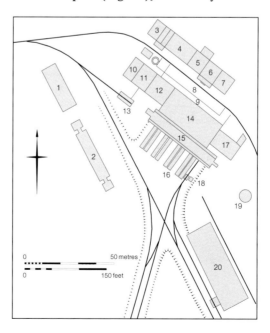

Figure 6.4 His Majesty's Wood Distillation Plant, Mid Lavant, Hampshire (plan redrawn from PRO MUN4/6187): 1 Offices and laboratory; 2 Mess rooms and lavatories; 3 Store; 4 Refinery; 5 Sludge vats; 6 Neutralising lime; 7 Settling vats; 8 Coal bunker; 9 Firing pit; 10 Workshop; 11 Power house; 12 Boiler house; 13 Locomotive shed; 14 Retorts; 15 Traverser; 16 Coolers; 17 Acetate store; 18 Weigh office; 19 Tank; 20 Charcoal store.

a distillation plant was relatively compact, but large open areas served by railways were necessary as stack yards to store wood awaiting distillation.

An alternative source for acetone lay in the infant science of biotechnology through zymotechnology or fermentation technology. In the years immediately preceding the war the Synthetic Products Company established plants at Rainham in London and Kings Lynn in Norfolk to produce acetone using a micro-organism discovered by Fernbach at the Pasteur Institute. Neither plant lived up to the expectations of their backers. A team based at Manchester working on the same problem included Chaim Weizmann, the future president of Israel. When he left to work on his own, he identified a bacterium which could ferment a starch source directly to ethanol, acetone, and butanol. After first approaching Nobel's, in early 1916 he was summoned to the Admiralty and directed by Winston Churchill to work the process up to an industrial scale. Research was moved to the

Lister Institute in London and a pilot plant was created at J & W Nicholson's gin distillery at Bromley-by-Bow in London.[15]

The first purpose-built plant to exploit the Weizmann process, using maize as a starch source, was constructed at the Royal Naval Cordite Factory Holton Heath, Dorset. This plant remains partially intact (Fig 6.5). It comprised a large barn (1 in Fig 6.5), 114ft 10in × 32ft 10in (35m × 10m), to store maize, with a cooker house (2) at its eastern end, where it was reduced to a mash. The mash was introduced into the fermentation vessels (3); six of the original eight of these survive. They are 37ft 9in (11.5m) in diameter, constructed from reinforced concrete, and their floors are raised off the ground on concrete pillars probably to aid heat retention. Internally they were lined with aluminium fermentation vats. The facility was also innovative in the laboratory-like sterility which it introduced into an industrial process, evident in the careful jointing and sealing in the surviving pipework. The plant was sited

Figure 6.5 RNCF Holton Heath, Dorset. Survey plan of acetone plant, July 1996: 1 Barn; 2 Cooker house; 3 Fermentation vessels. (© Crown copyright. NMR)

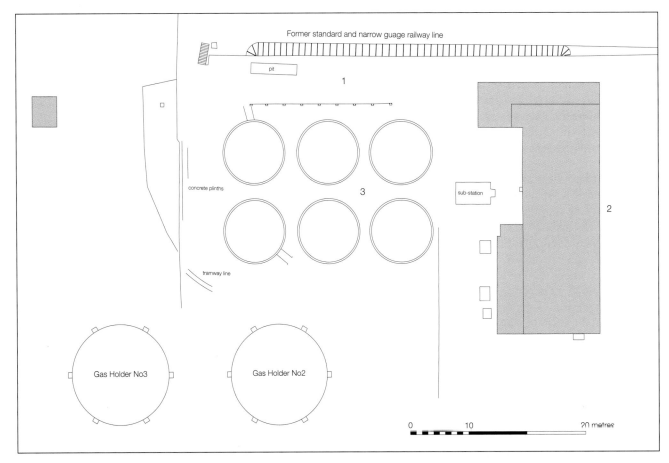

Figure 6.6 RNCF Holton Heath, Dorset. Demolition of the acetone plant in 1934, showing the fermentation vessels in place. (© Lesley Hayward/MoD)

conveniently close to the factory boiler house for a supply of high-pressure steam necessary for sterilisation. In the absence of contemporary drawings, it is only the chance survival of photographs of the demolition of the plant in 1934 that shows that the tanks were enclosed in a tall brick structure (Fig 6.6).[16]

Pressure from German U-boats restricted the supply of maize to Britain and in 1917 experiments were made to substitute artichokes as the starch source. Even more mysterious at the time was the request by the Admiralty for schoolchildren across the country to collect acorns and horse-chestnuts for the Director of Propellant Supplies at the Ministry of Munitions, destined for this plant. Elsewhere, two more distilleries were converted to use the process and further plants established at Terre Haute in Indiana, Toronto in Canada, and at Nazik in India.

Cotton waste

A reliable supply of cotton waste as the raw material for guncotton was another essential for the war effort. The trade was in the hands of small dealers, a group of whom, called the British and Foreign Supply Association Ltd, controlled nine-tenths of it, centred on the cotton mills of Manchester.

This was taken over by the government in 1917 and mills at Bury, Hadfield, Oldham (several mills including the Greenfield Mill) and Woodley in Manchester, Charlesworth and Whaley Bridge in Derbyshire, and Rawtenstall in Lancashire were designated as His Majesty's Cotton Waste Mills.[17]

Factory types – propellants manufacture

Cordite

Pre-existing factories expanded

On the declaration of war in August 1914 the government placed orders for 16,000 tons (16,256 tonnes) of cordite against a previous normal yearly average of 3600 tons (3657.6 tonnes), of which the government factory at Waltham Abbey had supplied one-third and seven trade factories the remainder.[18] This supply was dominated by Nobel's, though their ownership of many firms was effectively concealed.[19] To increase output, a short-term solution was to augment the workforces at the existing factories and run their plant around the clock; but to increase capacity new plant was needed. This is apparent in the site plans of nearly all the pre-existing cordite factories, as extensions were built and the firms expanded to meet the new demands.

Waltham Abbey itself, an already crowded and inefficiently organised factory, presented little opportunity for expansion. Nevertheless, new cordite incorporating and press houses were strung out along the canal to the north and south of the former pellet powder building. The new buildings were single-storeyed and utilitarian, and of a characteristic bayed form. The press houses at either end of the group were 216ft 6in and 200ft (66m and 61m) long and divided into eight and seven bays respectively, with large vents over each bay retained on the northern range. Between them were four cordite incorporating houses, each originally 105ft × 28ft 10in (32m × 8.8m) and divided into seven bays. The end gable walls and the bay walls were of brick, laid in English bond, and the bays had a metal-framed roof and light timber-framed outer walls. An overhead drive shaft powered the incorporating machines (see Fig 5.35), supported by bearing boxes in the bay walls which survive as blocked features, but there is no evidence for the location of the motor room. In the bay walls the cut-off ends of I-section girders are perhaps evidence of the former support for drenching tubs. The new plant was in operation by April 1915, and between the outbreak of war and August 1915 the capacity of the factory was raised from 70 tons (71.12 tonnes) per week to a, still modest, 140 tons (142.24 tonnes).[20]

The pressures on raw materials that were a feature of all wartime munitions manufacture especially affected the supply of acetone for cordite MD (see above, Acetone). The Research Department at Woolwich, therefore, sought to develop a new form of cordite for land service, dispensing with the need for acetone but retaining the same ballistic properties and employing the same manufacturing machinery as cordite MD. The result was cordite Research Department B, or cordite RDB, in which ether alcohol was substituted for acetone. As this was a less powerful solvent, it required a less highly nitrated form of nitrocellulose than guncotton. One of the few alterations made to the factory process was that ether was piped to the incorporating mills.[21] The mineral jelly store at Waltham Abbey, constructed in August 1918, was also used as an ether store when the ether pipeline was laid.[22]

At Stowmarket extensions were made to the existing factory and the workforce rose from a few hundred to a peak of around 3000, and at Ardeer a new cordite plant was laid out on a 122 acre (49.37ha) site at Misk, close to the existing factory.[23] At Chilworth the Admiralty created a new cordite section in 1915 to the south of the 1890s cordite factory. Traces of this survive as low earthworks and concrete bases with the impressions of corrugated iron walls.

Figure 6.7 Cliffe, Kent. Aerial photograph of the site of Curtis's and Harvey's explosives factory; cf Fig 5.43. To the right are the structures added during the Great War. (NMR 15033–25)

The westerly pair (Figs 6.8a and b) are 60m long, divided in two by a central spine wall, with 30 bays along either side. These very small bays suggest a design to handle small amounts of explosives far more sensitive than cordite. To their east are another pair of ranges, 167ft 4in (51m) long, each originally divided into nine bays. In a block between these and the Thames are 20 untraversed reinforced concrete magazines or stores. Each measures 52ft 6in × 45ft 11in (16m × 14m) and is cruciform in plan, divided into four separate compartments. The sites of other groups of structures erected at this time are marked by concrete floor slabs or earthwork traverses, but it is not possible to say with any certainty whether they were associated with manufacture or storage of explosives.

On the Uplees Marshes a comparable enlargement is evidenced by the spread of floor slabs across the marsh, with a similar difficulty of interpretation in the absence of contemporary mapping. At Hayle expansion included construction of a new press house, an acetone recovery plant, and canteens to feed the enlarged workforce, which rose to 1800. In order to cope with the greater requirements for raw materials the factory was connected by a standard-gauge line to the Great Western Railway at Hayle.[25]

Figure 6.8 Cliffe, Kent. Great War structures, (a) (left) from the air (NMR 15033/33); (b) (above) on the ground. (BB94/8736)

A more substantial solvent recovery stove, divided into four bays that had a barrel-shaped roof, is the only remaining standing building. A five-bay cordite press house remained standing until recently, converted into two-storey cottages, with traces of a curving roof visible in its end gable wall. A contemporary plan of the works indicates that it continued to specialise exclusively in finishing cordite from pre-prepared cordite paste.[24]

At Cliffe the open marshland gave considerable potential for enlargement eastwards (Fig 6.7). What the field evidence does not reveal is whether this marked an expansion in cordite manufacture or in handling other forms of explosives. At the centre of the new area were seven long reinforced concrete structures, of which four remain.

New factories created

This piecemeal expansion was insufficient to meet the increasing demands of the navy and Kitchener's 'new armies' on the western front; the solution was to build modern up-to-date propellant factories.

Royal Naval Cordite Factory (RNCF) Holton Heath

Before the war the Royal Navy was supplied with nearly all its cordite needs by Waltham Abbey RGPF. The Admiralty, however, wanted a factory under its sole control and

Figure 6.9 RNCF Holton Heath, Dorset. General factory plan of 1946, showing the structure of the site laid in the Great War.

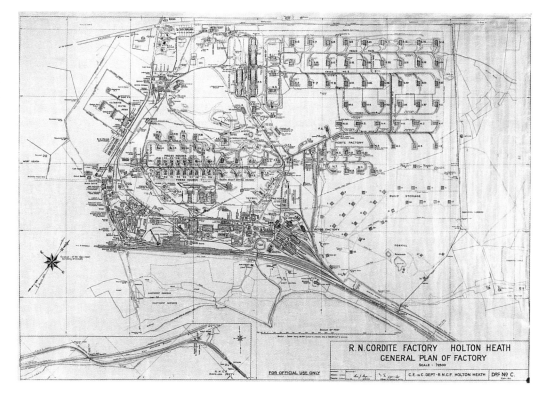

on 25 January 1914 Winston Churchill gave instructions as First Lord of the Admiralty that work should begin on a cordite factory.[26] Its design and erection was entrusted to Sir Frederic Nathan who, since leaving government employment in 1909, had joined Nobels as works' manager at Ardeer and early in 1914 was set the task of erecting a new TNT and propellant factory on the site of the former dynamite factory at Pembrey in Carmarthenshire. The details of the Admiralty cordite factory's layout and design of its buildings were carried through by the London engineering firm of Sir Douglas Fox and Partners.

The site chosen at Holton Heath in Dorset, 6km to the west of Poole, lay on sandy heathland between the Poole to Wareham road on the north and the railway connecting the two towns to its south (Fig 6.9). Additionally it was served by its own jetty, which eased the movement of raw materials and shipping the finished cordite to naval filling facilities. Holton Heath was laid out on a greenfield site, roughly rectangular in plan and covering 494 acres (just under 200ha), with the principal purpose of producing cordite MD. The relatively level heathland allowed a rectilinear plan to be adopted with few constraints imposed by

the natural topography. A characteristic feature of this factory was that many of its buildings were sunk to eaves height below the ground surface, though elsewhere conventional traverses were also used. At the western end, the gentle fall from Black Hill was utilised by the nitroglycerine factory and a large reservoir was constructed on top of the hill.

The factory was largely self-contained, with an independent power supply. It was equipped to be self-sufficient in acids (Fig 6.10), both in sulphuric, manufactured from pyrites, brought to the factory by ship, and in nitric acid. A trade later developed in the waste nitre cake, when it was sent to Hull as the raw material for the domestic cleaner, Harpic. The plant was also responsible for revivifying mixed acids from the nitration processes, the reworked sulphuric acid often being reprocessed to yield nitric acid, thereby adding to the economy of the acid section.[27] Weizmann's fermentation plant for acetone (see above, Acetone) added to these facilities.

The guncotton factory, as a heavy user of acids and producer of waste acids, was sited adjacent to the acid plant and close to the boiler house to supply steam (Fig 6.38). It was housed in four separate buildings,

Figure 6.10 RNCF Holton Heath, Dorset. Section of site model, showing the nitrocellulose section in the left foreground and to its right the acid plant. (BB94/17026)

two of which survive, with a production flow from east to west and the process buildings connected by short covered passages. The nitroglycerine section was situated to the north on the slope of Black Hill (Fig 6.10). Mixed acids, glycerine, cooling brine, and soda wash waters were pumped to store tanks at the top of the hill and then let down by gravity through one of two nitrator-separators and then down into the other process buildings.

The precise early arrangements of processes within the factory are unclear, as the field remains and surviving plans represent the factory as it was remodelled in the 1930s. Nevertheless, a logical production flow placed the guncotton stoves and mixing houses between the nitrocellulose plant and nitroglycerine factory, with the cordite incorporators and press houses in the long rectangular ranges to its north. From the press houses cordite was removed for solvent recovery and drying in groups of stoves in the north-eastern corner of the site.

The factory's design drew on Nathan's recent experience at Pembrey in Carmathenshire, which also influenced the design of Nobel's Misk extension at Ardeer and the new cordite factory at Gretna in Dumfriesshire.[28] Much of the plant followed the types he helped to develop at Waltham Abbey, including the guncotton displacement tanks and the Nathan-Thomson-Rintoul type of nitrator-separators.

Links with the production methods developed at Waltham Abbey were further strengthened by W T Thomson's appointment as the first manager and Deputy Superintendent, by the transfer of Waltham Abbey foremen to Holton Heath, and the training of new men at the RGPF.[29]

Gretna

The site selected for the new army cordite factory stretched for 7fi miles (12km), straddling the English and Scottish border between Dornock in Dumfries and Galloway in the west and Longtown in Cumbria in the east (Fig 6.11). Known as His Majesty's Factory Gretna (see Gazetteer entry 044, Rockcliffe, Cumbria), the factory covered 9000 acres (3642.3ha). It was the largest explosives factory in the empire, employing 19,772 people at its height in October 1917, with a projected capacity of 40,000 tons (40,640 tonnes) of cordite per year. It cost £9,295,000. Its location on the western coast was chosen to afford good protection from the threat of attack from the land, sea or air. It also lay astride excellent rail communications, used initially to bring in the building materials and later to supply raw materials, transport the workforce, and move the finished cordite to the filling factories. The factory was split between two main areas, at Dornock (1–3 in Fig 6.11) and Mossband (5 in Fig 6.11). Both were relatively level

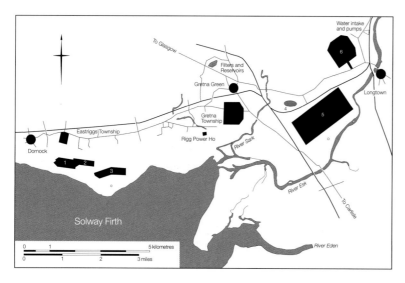

Figure 6.11 HM Factory Gretna, Cumbria (redrawn from PRO Supply 10/15): 1 Acids and guncotton section; 2 Guncotton drying stoves; 3 Nitroglycerine hills; 4 Ether section; 5 Mossband cordite section; 6 Storage magazines.

Figure 6.12 HM Factory Gretna, Cumbria. Quinan guncotton drying stove. (© RCAHMS, C64506)

greenfield sites, affording few topographical constraints and adequate spacing between the buildings.[30]

Gretna was a remarkable achievement not only in its scale but also in the successful design of plant for novel processes, for the decision to accept cordite RDB was taken only in May 1915 when planning was already under way.[31] The design of the new factories at Holton Heath and Gretna highlighted another problem in wartime munitions supply, namely the shortage of trained chemical engineers. Fortunately, the Ministry of Munitions secured the services of Kenneth B Quinan, an American and formerly the general manager of the Cape Explosives Works at Somerset West in South Africa.[32] He became the most influential chemical engineer in Britain during the war, responsible for the design not only of Gretna but of many other wartime explosives factories.

Like the majority of such factories, Gretna was self-sufficient in the manufacture of sulphuric and nitric acid; more unusually, it also had its own glycerine distillery. The acids section was located at the Dornock end of the factory, with raw material stores for sulphur, pyrites, and nitre.

The production flow moved from west to east. Adjacent was the guncotton section, which was similar in layout to the one at Holton Heath and formed the model for the majority of later nitrocellulose sections. It was divided into four principal units corresponding to the production stages of guncotton and they were connected by covered corridors. At the western end cotton was received from the stores into the picking, teasing, drying, and willowing building; from here it went to nitrating rooms using Nathan-Thomson type nitrating pans; then to the boiling house and on to a beating, potching, and screening building; and, finally, to the press house.

Drying the wet guncotton also took place on the Dornock site. The drying stoves here differed from those at Waltham Abbey and followed a design patented by Quinan a few years earlier.[33] Their principle was rapid drying of guncotton in small quantities. The advantage of this new system was that it greatly reduced the amount of guncotton in a stove at any one time, while maintaining an efficient through-put by a speedier drying time.

There were 41 of these drying houses spaced 200ft (61m) apart, grouped together in pairs in a large rectangular enclosure with the exception of a single stove on the eastern side. At the centre of each pair was a heater house, 26ft 3in × 18ft 9in (8m × 5.7m), where steam from the mains warmed air for blowing to the stoves. Along the sides of the stoves towards the heater were the air mains, probably originally covered by a lean-to structure, 5ft (1.5m) wide. The surviving drying houses are brick-built and measure 130ft long × 17ft wide (39.6m × 5.2m) (Fig 6.12). Internally they were divided into a wet porch, drying room, weighing room, and dry porch. The drying room was subdivided by thin walls into 15 bays, 6ft (1.8m) wide, with a working area to their rear. Each bay housed a metal pan, 4ft (1.2m) in diameter and 16in (0.4m) deep (Fig 6.13).[34] A parcel of wet guncotton on a cheese cloth was placed on a mesh within the pan and warm air was introduced from below to dry it. The warm air main was then closed and compressed air introduced, cooling the guncotton as it expanded. As only one small guncotton magazine

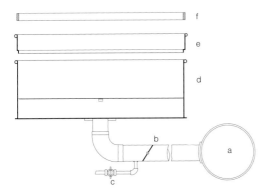

was provided, the dry guncotton was probably taken straight from the Quinan stoves to the mixing houses by trolley girls pushing 2ft (0.6m) gauge covered bogies.

Also on the Dornock site, the nitroglycerine section was laid out on the back-fall of a coastal ridge gently sloping back towards the factory. It comprised five almost identical nitroglycerine hills, traces of which have almost been removed by later development (Fig 6.14). Along the crest of the ridge were glycerine, mixed acid tanks, brine tanks for cooling waters, and soda stores for the washing waters. These were let into the nitrator-separators by gravity and flowed through the units in the standard manner. Below the nitrator-separators were three washing houses and two washing water settling houses. The nitroglycerine was run to one of six mixing houses and combined with guncotton to form cordite paste, for whose storage each unit was equipped with two paste magazines.

Cordite paste was moved 4.3 miles (7km) by standard-gauge line to the eastern part of the factory, to the cordite ranges at Mossband. These were laid out on low-lying level marshy ground on the floodplain of the river Esk. Though this section, too, covered a large area of approximately 1.5 miles

× 0.75 miles (2.5km × 1.2km) and comprised over 400 main process buildings, the range of activities undertaken was restricted. A plant immediately to the north produced ether-alcohol for gelatinising the cordite paste. Otherwise the section was divided into eight units, each comprising incorporating and press houses and eight pairs of drying stoves, along with blending houses. The stoves were untraversed and of brick with a curved roof covered in rubberoid. They were equipped to collect the solvent vapours by absorption in cresol; by this method around 36% of the ether and 83% of the alcohol was recovered through distillation.[35] The finished cordite was moved to a group of 25 storage magazines in a detached location to the north-east (6 in Fig 6.11). These were brick-built, with a rubberoid roof and asphalt floors laid on timber; they measured 80ft (24.38m) by 40ft (12.19m) and stood 8ft (2.44m) to the eaves, and each was protected by an L-shaped earthwork traverse.

The process was succinctly summed up in a contemporary pastiche, by A W Stevenson in *The Mossband Farewell Magazine* (1919), of the popular children's hymn, 'Daisies are our silver...'.

Gretna Victory Recipe
Little drops of solvent
Little bags of paste
Little tins of jelly
Twenty pounds of waste

Mix it all together
Press it through a die
Truck it to a stove bay
Leave it there to dry

Take it out and blend it
Send it to the guns
Pull the bloomin' trigger
Strafe the blasted Huns!

Today little remains of this great factory. It was largely demolished in the 1920s and the area reoccupied as an army storage depot in the 1930s. On the Dornock site, there are odd buildings and footings; at Mossband the principal survival is the main office block (Fig 6.35), some factory housing, a chimney, and footings of the ether plant.

Figure 6.13 Diagrammatic section of an early Quinan drying pan (redrawn from Fraser and Chalmers Ltd trade pamphlet 1908): a Warm air main; b Valve; c Compressed air main; d Basket supporter; e Basket; f Cover.

Figure 6.14 Dornock, Dumfries and Galloway. Remains of nitroglycerine hill no 1 and base of acids tower, looking towards the nitrator. (© RCAHMS, C64501)

Linking the two sites are the earthworks of the railway line, and widely dispersed across this vast factory landscape are scattered workers' housing, former police posts, and small factory buildings or their footings.

Nitrocellulose tubular and nitrocellulose

Cordite supplies were supplemented by the introduction of the single-base propellant, nitrocellulose tubular (NCT). Its manufacture employed a similar process to that of cordite, but omitted nitroglycerine. A brittle explosive, it was used in short lengths rather than in long strands. It was the standard American propellant and was imported in large quantities for use in small arms ammunition and howitzers, but not for guns larger

than 60lb. In addition, a new government factory was erected at Irvine in Ayrshire and managed by Nobels as an agency factory, which produced around 100 tons (101.6 tonnes) of ordnance NCT and 50 tons (50.8 tonnes) of rifle NCT per week. Work also began in December 1916 on another NCT plant at Henbury near Bristol, but this was abandoned in May 1917.[36]

In addition to these facilities, the new high explosives factory at Queensferry in Flintshire included a large guncotton section, the impressive brick buildings of which survive intact adapted to new uses. This supplied Gretna before its plant was in operation. The Chemical and Explosives Company at Colnbrook in Buckingham-shire, as His Majesty's Guncotton Factory, produced guncotton principally for export to Belgium.[37]

High explosive bursting charges

Gunpowder's role as a bursting charge for artillery shells (Fig 4.2) persisted until the closing decade of the nineteenth century, as few of the new chemical explosives met the stringent criteria for shell fillings. In principle they needed to be relatively economical to manufacture with readily accessible raw materials, to be stable in storage and transport, and to withstand the shock of firing yet to explode with great violence at the target. Some countries adopted guncotton as a shell filling, but in British service use it was restricted to filling mines and torpedoes. Manufacture of guncotton-filled shells in Britain was limited to those companies supplying foreign governments, notably the New Explosives Company at Stowmarket and the National Explosives Company at Hayle.[38]

High explosives (see above, Chapter 5, Definitions: explosives and propellants, high and low explosives) for shell fillings became dominant during the Great War. In the main they were coal-tar derivatives using phenol or carbolic acid, toluol, and aniline.[39] The chief sources of these substances were coke ovens, tar distillers, and town gas works. In the last case, they formed a small proportion of the volatile compounds driven off during gas production, and when special plant was installed to accelerate their production there was a corresponding loss in calorific value of the gas. The close link between the coal industry and its by-products is illustrated by the juxtaposition of collieries and by-product companies. A wartime example is the National Ammonium Perchlorate Factory established in 1916 adjacent to Langwith colliery in Derbyshire (Fig 6.15), where coal was processed using a secret process devised by Carlson's of Stockholm to obtain chlorates and perchlorates.[40] Such processing had direct analogues in the synthetic textile dye industry, in particular concerning the aniline dyes discovered by Perkins in 1856.

Lyddite was the primary high explosive filling for British shells from 1898 into the early part of the war (Fig 6.20). TNT was introduced at the outbreak of war and rapidly took a dominant role. Its derivative, amatol, was developed because it conserved precious stocks of toluol by using TNT in combination with ammonium nitrate, coupled with its reduced volatility in handling. TNT's introduction also had the effect of bringing to the fore as an initiator the sensitive explosive tetryl, for which there had been little demand when it was developed before the war.

Factory types – high explosives manufacture

Picric acid or lyddite

Picric acid (trinitrophenol) was discovered in the late eighteenth century, but only the work of Eugene Turpin in the 1880s realised its potential as an explosive. He also devised a method of casting it as a liquid in shells. In this guise it was first tested at Lydd in Kent, and in consequence took the name lyddite.

Picric acid is manufactured by converting phenol into phenol-sulphonic acid by means of concentrated sulphuric acid, then treating this compound with strong nitric acid. Before the discovery of its explosive properties it was used as a yellow dye in the textile industry. The distribution of its production sites reflects this, concentrating in West Yorkshire with an outlying factory at Reddish, near Stockport in Greater Manchester (see Fig 5.1). Its potential as an explosive was also frighteningly revealed in 1887 with the accidental destruction of a chemical works at Cornbrook, near Manchester. Perhaps as a result of this explosion its use as a dye declined. Nevertheless, a War Office contract for lyddite in 1898 led to the establishment of several new firms, and by the turn of the century seven licences had been issued for its manufacture as an explosive.[41]

Estimates in June 1915 of the production capacity for picric acid revealed that it was concentrated in the hands of nine producers, all except for Nobel's located around northern industrial conurbations (Fig 5.1). A later survey by the Ministry of Munitions identified 16 plants capable of

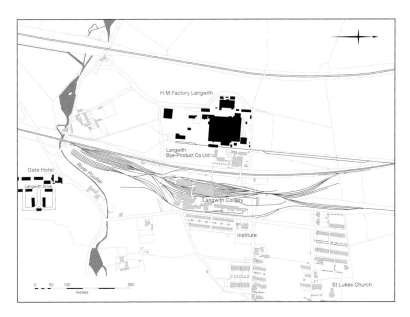

producing it and the concentration on the northern towns lessened as new state picric acid factories were built at Avonmouth near Bristol (Fig 6.16) and at Rainham in London, with an experimental plant nearby at Grays in Essex.[42] It was noted that delays in commissioning new capacity resulted from problems in erecting nitric acid plant, caused partly by delayed supply of acid-resisting earthenware from the two or three specialist suppliers.[43] Lyddite required a detonator to set it off as a main charge. Picric powder, a mixture of ammonium picrate and potassium nitrate, served this purpose. It was manufactured using a similar milling process to black powder and in the 1890s at least one of the water mills at Waltham Abbey was converted to its manufacture.[44]

As the war progressed, TNT became the standard filling for land shells, and lyddite remained important for naval shells.

Figure 6.15 HM Factory Langwith, Derbyshire. Site plan at date of sale in 1927 (redrawn from Derbyshire Record Office D996 Z/E54).

Figure 6.16 HM Factory Avonmouth. Main administrative building. (BB97/114)

It was later superseded by a related substance, shellite, a mixture of trinitrophenol and dinitrophenol.[45]

TNT and amatol

Lyddite's disadvantages as a shell filling were that it required a powerful detonator and reacted with any exposed metal to form potentially sensitive picrates. An alternative was trinitrotoluene (TNT or trotyl), introduced by the Germans as early as 1902. Pre-war manufacture of TNT was restricted to Ardeer and a small research plant at Woolwich. The immediate need was greatly to increase production capacity within Britain.

Britain was well placed for the acquisition of TNT's basic ingredient, toluol. It was a coal-tar derivative, but an additional source was toluol derived from the distillation of benzine from Shell Borneo petroleum. Shell possessed a distillation plant in Rotterdam, which was rapidly dismantled and brought by naval escort to London and then by rail to Portishead on the Severn Estuary, where it was re-erected (Fig 6.17). Shell also built a duplicate plant at Barrow-in-Furness in Cumbria close to their existing ocean bulk storage installation. The two facilities contributed about half of Britain's toluol needs throughout the war.[46]

TNT was regarded as a relatively safe explosive to manufacture in that it could not be exploded by flame or strong percussion. A rapid acceleration of production was most readily achieved by plant installed in existing chemical factories with the necessary infrastructure. The early distribution of the industry, therefore, clustered around Manchester, where chemical firms were already utilising coal-tar derivatives in manufacturing textile dyes.[47] At Hackney Wick in East London, too, the Phoenix Chemical Works was converted to TNT manufacture. Wartime need forced unsuitable premises into service. The Hooley Rubber and Chemical Company occupied a disused cotton mill in Ashton-under-Lyne in Greater Manchester.[48] Brunner Mond converted an idle caustic soda plant at Silvertown in the east end of London to TNT production (Fig 6.42). In an attempt to lessen the dangers, the production process was often split between two locations. Crude TNT manufactured at one plant was taken to another for the more hazardous purification stage, which initially was carried out by Brunner Mond at Northwich in Cheshire, Silvertown, and at H M Factory at Rainham in London.

Early in 1915 there were ten TNT plants in operation, producing an estimated 122 tons (123.952 tonnes); by June this was projected to rise to 16 factories with an output of 489 tons (496.824 tonnes).[49] By 1917 the new TNT plants were in operation which could produce it more economically and safely; the early plants were, therefore, mothballed.[50]

Short-term solutions gradually gave way to efficient purpose-built plant. One of the earliest was that laid out in 1914 by Sir Frederic Nathan at Pembrey in Carmarthenshire for Nobels.[51] While research into TNT manufacture was conducted at the Research Department at Woolwich, the first National Factory erected at government expense was at Oldbury in the West Midlands, operated by Messrs Chance and Hunt using toluol supplied by Shell in a plant designed by K B Quinan. A second was established at Penrhyndeudraeth in Gwynedd on the site of a former Ergite explosives works[52] followed by Queensferry in Flintshire on the floodplain of the Dee Estuary reusing the site of a derelict chemical plant. It, too, was designed by Quinan, and Stafford Cripps

Figure 6.17 Portishead near Bristol, Avon. Shell's toluol distillery brought from Rotterdam. (Smith nd).

SHELL Plant at Portishead, which maintained an output of 1,100 tons of toluol benzine per month—sufficient for about 1,300 tons of T.N.T.

was Assistant Superintendent for some time after receiving his initial training at Waltham Abbey.[53] This large and self-sufficient factory, with one of the largest and most efficient sulphuric acid plants in the world attached to it and an acids section also capable of producing nitric acid and denitrating spent acids, was divided into two sites. A smaller detached site at Sandycroft produced mono-nitro-toluene, which was taken to the main Queensferry site for further nitration to produce TNT. It had five TNT nitrators capable of producing 500 tons (508 tonnes) of TNT per week, in addition to a large nitrocellulose section and a small tetryl plant.[54] Scattered buildings of this great factory still survive within the modern chemical works.

Pure TNT was relatively expensive to produce, however, and consumed the scarce raw material toluol. By mixing ammonium nitrate with it a very effective explosive filling known as amatol could be produced.

Chemists at Brunner Mond took the lead in devising methods to manufacture ammonium nitrate, whose production was centred on a number of pre-existing plants in Cheshire where there was long experience in handling ammonia. A purpose-built plant was also constructed at Stratton near Swindon in Wiltshire, where a waste sodium sulphate hill formed a feature of the local landscape for many years.[55]

Tetryl

Trinitro-phenyl-methyl-nitramine or tetryl, more commonly known in the services as 'composition exploding' or CE, was first made by Mertens in 1877. Its sensitivity, cost, and difficulties in handling made it unsuitable as a shell filling, but it was widely used as an intermediary explosive. Demand increased greatly with the adoption of TNT and amatol as the principal British shell filling during the war. For whereas tetryl's

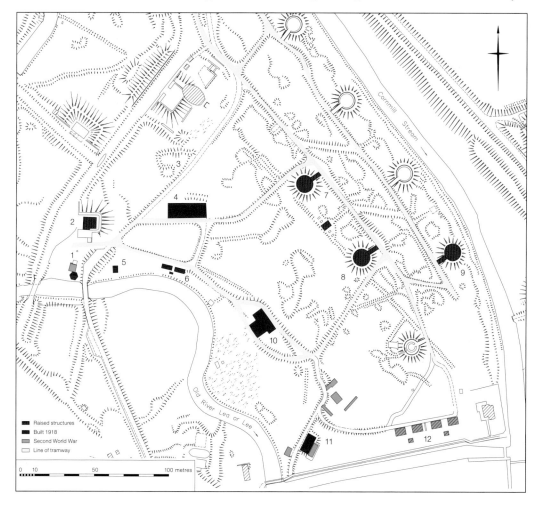

Figure 6.18 RGPF Waltham Abbey, North Site. 1918 tetryl factory (with additional Second World War buildings), based on RCHME site survey: 1 Still house and purification plant; 2 Packing house; 3 Traverse; 4 Corning house; 5 Fire-engine house; 6 Cleaning houses nos 1 and 2; 7 Stove no 1; 8 Stove no 2; 9 Stove no 3; 10 Incorporating house; 11 Shifting House; 12 Four drying stoves 1940. (© Crown copyright. NMR)

Figure 6.19 RGPF Waltham Abbey, North Site. The water purification plant of the new tetryl factory erected in 1918 (1 in Fig 6.18). To the right is the former Gunpowder Press House built in 1879; cf Fig 3.34. (BB94/8011; © MoD)

stability was affected by picric acid (lyddite), the new fillings caused no such difficulty yet needed the more powerful detonating qualities that tetryl provided.

The production facilities required for tetryl were modest, because only small amounts were required compared to bulk shell fillings. Its manufacture was based on the nitration of dimethyl aniline, another coal-tar derivative commonly used in dye manufacture. This was acquired from commercial sources, the Clayton Aniline Company being one of the most important suppliers. Nitration required facilities for the manufacture, concentration, and reworking of sulphuric and nitric acid; for this reason tetryl manufacture was usually placed near existing facilities within larger explosives factories.

Production began at Waltham Abbey North Site in 1910 on an area cleared by levelling an early nineteenth-century steam drying stove (Fig 2.35) at the northern end of the acid factory. Somewhat curiously for this potentially hazardous product, the facilities were housed in 20 or so closely spaced and unmounded sheds; only the purification house was placed on the opposite side of Millhead Stream. In 1916 to meet an increased demand for tetryl, the Waltham Abbey chemists with characteristic resourcefulness improvised, within 24 hours, a nitrating plant capable of producing 5000lb (2268kg) a week from scrap acetone barrels and lead.[56] This plant was cleared soon after the Second World War, leaving a legacy of contaminated soil and smashed process earthenware marking its site.

Throughout the Great War this early plant was beset by fires. Perhaps to lessen this risk, and to increase its capacity, an extension was built in early 1918 on the eastern side of the site (Fig 6.18). This concentrated on the purification and finishing of tetryl. Partly finished tetryl was brought by barge to a loading stage adjacent to the former gunpowder press house (see Fig 3.34), then in its fourth change of function as a tetryl packing house (2 in Fig 6.18). A new narrow-gauge tramway system (Fig 6.19) served the network of process buildings, including three circular former guncotton drying stoves converted to tetryl drying. These buildings, too, were untraversed, but they were widely spaced within woodland and an earthwork traverse (3 in Fig 6.18) was constructed between the tetryl corning house (4) and the gunpowder stove to its north.

Tetryl factories constructed during the war at Queensferry and Holton Heath had buildings that were small – a reflection of the small amounts and sensitivity of explosive handled in each building – and generally traversed.[57]

Factory types – National Filling Factories

High explosives: lyddite

At the outbreak of war the filling facilities for high explosives were limited to the Royal Arsenal Woolwich and factories at

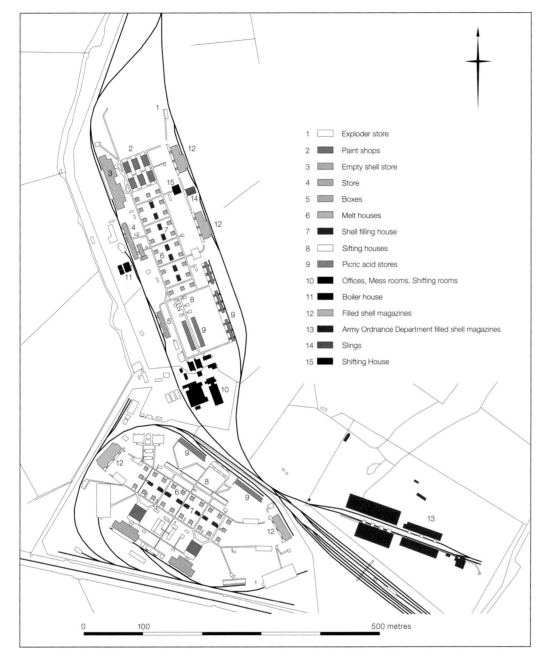

Figure 6.21 NFF no 9, Banbury, Warkworth, Northamptonshire. Plan redrawn from OS, Oxfordshire, Sheet VI.9, 25-inch, third edition, 1922; OS, Northamptonshire, Sheet LVIII.9, 25-inch, third edition, 1922.

1 ☐ Exploder store
2 ▨ Paint shops
3 ▨ Empty shell store
4 ▨ Store
5 ▨ Boxes
6 ▨ Melt houses
7 ■ Shell filling house
8 ☐ Sifting houses
9 ▨ Picric acid stores
10 ■ Offices, Mess rooms, Shifting rooms
11 ■ Boiler house
12 ▨ Filled shell magazines
13 ■ Army Ordnance Department filled shell magazines
14 ■ Slings
15 ■ Shifting House

0   100   500 metres

Lemington Point and Derwenthaugh (Newcastle upon Tyne) belonging to the armament manufacturers Armstrong Whitworth and Co. Ltd.[58] The first wartime lyddite filling factory was commissioned in November 1915 and by December a site at Banbury, Warkworth, had been selected (Figs 6.20 and 6.21). Responsibility for its construction and management was given to Mr Herbert Bing and the building contract was let in January 1916 to Messrs Willet of Sloane Square. The first lyddite was run on 25 April. Initially the factory comprised only the northerly No 1 unit, designed to fill 100 tons (101.6 tonnes) of lyddite per week. The layout of No 1 unit was based on Armstrong and Whitworth's factory at Lemington Point, and it survives relatively intact as earthworks and concrete floor slabs covering a rectangular area 450m × 140m. The basic operations of most filling factories are evident in the plan. Empty components were brought into one side of the unit and the explosives into the other side, and the filled shells were moved to a storage magazine before

Figure 6.20 (facing) NFF no 9, Banbury, Warkworth, Northamptonshire from the east; see Fig 6.21). (NMR 15442/15)

Filling before the Great War

The function of filling various types of munitions with explosives and assembling complete rounds for issue to the services was a historic one, whose origins lay in the artillerists' assembly of the variety of exploding projectiles depicted in early manuscripts. This activity became more formalised by the seventeenth century, and focused on the misleadingly named Royal Laboratory at Greenwich. This was not a laboratory in the modern sense, but a specialised manufactory engaged in filling cartridges and assembling other types of munitions. It moved to Woolwich at the end of the seventeenth century, and was located around a courtyard whose two mutilated pavilions are the oldest surviving buildings of the Arsenal complex.[59] As cased munitions increasingly replaced loose powder, more areas were devoted to filling, and until the outbreak of the Great War Woolwich remained the principal government filling factory. Private firms were also engaged in ammunition manufacture, principally of sporting cartridges or for export. Some, like the New Explosives Company at Stowmarket, had a cartridge section attached to their factory manufacturing sporting powders. Those filling small arms ammunition continued to be important suppliers throughout the war along with new agency firms, but only five firms were involved in shell filling.[60]

With the introduction of lyddite in the 1890s, the existing facilities at Woolwich became inadequate and a new, specialised, establishment was required. It was added to the east of the main Arsenal site on Plumstead Marshes, and on a compact site measuring 800ft (244m) × 300ft (91.5m) it comprised 43 buildings. These were generally small and constructed in corrugated iron; typical danger building features included external lights and lightning conductors. Picric acid supplied as crystals was taken to the melting house around 6am for use at around 11am. The molten picric acid was carried in 30lb (13.6kg) cans to the filling houses, where it was poured into the nose of the shell (Fig 6.22). Though the devastating potential of picric acid was well known, the close spacing and lack of traverses in the design of this establishment ignored many of the basic principles for explosives production. Work abruptly halted on 18 June 1903 in an explosion which claimed 16 lives.[61]

Construction of a new lyddite factory began almost immediately. It also was built on Plumstead Marshes, at Tripcock (also known as Margaret Ness), and cost £8000.[62]

The field remains consist of footings of around 60 structures. The larger buildings included shifting rooms, empty and filled shell stores, and melting stoves. The majority were small and generally subdivided into smaller units, both to minimise the amount of explosive within a building and the loss of life should one explode (Fig 6.23). They were sunk in at ground level so that perhaps only their roofs jutted above the surface, making them effectively traversed to eaves height. They handled shells up to 10in (0.25m) in diameter, which were moved by a tramway network set into a cutting.

National Filling Factories (NFF) were the distinctive creation of the new Ministry of Munitions; planned in the summer of 1915, with the British Army pinned down on the western front, they were an attempt to circumvent the bottleneck caused by the flow of empty shells vastly exceeding the filling capacity of the existing facilities and initial expectations. Like the explosives factories they were built for wartime need, to provide a capacity far beyond peacetime requirements. In their layout many elements of modern factory design emerged, especially the concept of the logical flow of materials and a production line through a building or groups of buildings. Principles of 'scientific management' were applied to the workforce, including the process of 'dilution' where skilled work was broken down into individual repetitive tasks which could be performed by unskilled or semi-skilled labour.

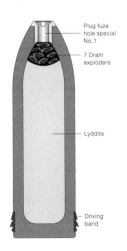

Figure 6.22 Section through a Lyddite shell, 1915 (redrawn from HMSO 1915 Textbook of Ammunition).

Plug fuze hole special No.1

7 Dram exploders

Lyddite

Driving band

This was less evident in explosives manufacture than in engineering, however, since each task was generally carried out in isolation for reasons of safety. In the National Factories, dilution usually meant the use of female labour, which reached over 90% of the total labour force in some factories.[63]

The filling factories were a vital link in a wartime network of production. It was here that the products of the complex and diverse networks of military explosives manufacture – of specialist suppliers, and factories large and small – focused. Here they came together with the output of equally complex networks of engineering or 'metal-bashing' workshops producing the receptacles for munitions of all sizes.[64] In most cases propellants, high explosives, and intermediaries were manufactured in different factories. The heavy machined shell was brought from shell works or, for larger types, from National Projectile Factories; the intricate fuze mechanism, often in brass, and ready-machined or recycled brass cartridge cases for quick-firing rounds were brought from other works (see Fig 4.2).

Though part of a national network financed by the government, considerable latitude was given in the design of factories. Certain principles were laid down following good practice at Woolwich, but many aspects of the Home Office guidelines were relaxed, especially regarding the spacing of buildings. There was no rigid template imposed on each site; plan form was influenced by topography and the design of the architect. Four factories – at Warkworth, Banbury (Northamptonshire), Chilwell (Nottinghamshire), Hayes, and Southwark (Greater London) – were designed, built, and managed by their managing directors; those at Hereford and Gainsborough (Lincolnshire) were designed by the Office of Works. Construction generally employed local firms, though the Office of Works erected those at Banbury and Perivale (London). Elsewhere, factories were administered by agency firms, as at Abbey Wood (London), Cardonald (North Lanarkshire), Morecambe (Lancashire), and Pembrey (Carmarthenshire), and design of the factory was their responsibility.[65]

Three main categories of shell filling factories may be recognised, with some subdivisions: (i) ammunition filling, including high explosives, cartridge, and small components; (ii) Trench Warfare Department stores; and (iii) gas filling. The broad groups depend on types of components or munitions, and plan forms and building types that mirror the factory's activities. Nevertheless, a range of filling activities might be undertaken within any one factory and as the war progressed buildings were adapted to fulfil unforeseen demands, for example, sea mines and aerial bombs.

they were either removed off-site or moved for temporary storage in an Army Ordnance Department (AOD) store. In detail, at the southern end of the unit, outside the danger area, were offices, changing rooms, messrooms, and lavatories, and to the west of the group a boiler house, loco shed, and oil store. On this side, inside the factory railway line, were box stores and the empty shell store, where on arrival the empty shells were cleaned and painted before they were issued to the filling houses. Within the danger area all the buildings were mounded. At the centre

Figure 6.23 Royal Arsenal Woolwich, new lyddite establishment on Plumstead Marshes, 1903. (BB95/954)

*Figure 6.24 NFF
no 9, Banbury,
Warkworth,
Northamptonshire.
Cross-section of Unit
1 in 1918 showing
consistent floor level
between buildings
(redrawn from PRO
MUN5/155/1122.3/
51): 1 Railway
wagon; 2 Empty
shell store; 3 Shell-
cleaning floor with
pit for workers;
4 Cap-inserting
house; 5 Charge-
typing house;
6 Shell-filling house;
7 Assembling shed;
8 Filled shell maga-
zine; 9 Railway
wagon.*

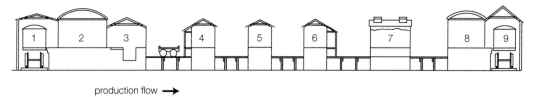

production flow ➜

of the group was a row of eight melting houses, 30ft × 20ft (9m × 6m), serving 22 filling sheds, each 20ft (6m) square. Picric acid for melting was held on the eastern side of the group in long sheds and, when ready for use, it was brought into the stores at the southern end of the group and then sifted before melting. After filling, the shells were moved by tramway to the two magazines, each 150ft × 40ft (45m × 12m), and surrounded by earth-work traverses, 8ft 2in (2.5m) high, which were entered from the production side through portals.

A schematic cross-section, drawn after the unit was converted to gas filling, reveals the careful arrangement of the work in the third dimension (Fig 6.24). The working surface across the unit was level between all the buildings, railway wagons, and tramway bogies, so that shells could be 'man-handled' at the same level throughout. When some buildings were later converted to shrapnel filling, the workers stood in a trench around the outside to fill the shells.

The buildings in the factory (Fig 6.25) were generally timber-framed and weather-boarded or covered in uralite (brown asbestos sheeting), set on brick foundations or concrete slabs. Larger buildings, generally stores with roof widths of no more than 40ft (12m), were spanned by Belfast trusses.

This factory's capacity was doubled with the construction of No 2 unit to the south (now nearly buried by the M40), giving a total area of 132 acres (53.42ha). Experience in operating the first unit brought modifications to improve the flow of materials through the second, including a clearer flow of materials from the empty shells stores on the south-western side, through the paint shops to the filling hous-es, and on the opposite side from the long picric acid stores through the sifting houses to the melting houses. When demand for lyddite declined by September 1917 as the army switched to TNT, sections of the fac-tory were converted to filling naval mines and shrapnel shells and, early in 1918, gas shells.[66]

A feature of most filling factories were AOD stores. These might physically be sep-arated from the production areas or demar-cated by a fence. They were under military command and formed a separate adminis-trative section outside civilian control. Until the point at which the shells were ready for delivery to the army, all raw materials were controlled by the civilian Ministry of Munitions. Finished shells after inspection became the responsibility of the AOD and from their stores were moved to other stor-age depots or directly to the main embarka-tion ports at Newhaven, Richborough, and Southampton.

The original arrangement of the second lyddite filling factory at Hereford (Fig 6.26) is less easy to reconstruct, as it was substan-tially rebuilt during the 1930s. The decision to build it was taken in April 1916, and the plans were prepared by Frank Baines, princi-pal architect of His Majesty's Office of Works.

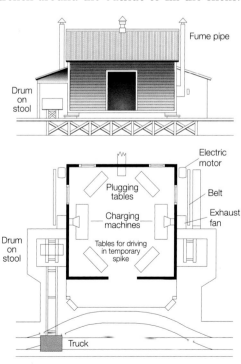

*Figure 6.25 NFF
no 9, Banbury,
Warkworth,
Northamptonshire.
Plan and elevation
of filling shed, after
conversion to gas
filling in 1918
(redrawn from PRO
MUN5/155/1222.3/
5).*

At 460 acres (186ha) it was far larger than Banbury and was originally designed to fill 400 tons (406.4 tonnes) of amatol and 100 tons (101.6 tonnes) of lyddite per week; this was later raised to 700 tons (711.2 tonnes) of amatol and 200 tons (203.2 tonnes) of lyddite. The division of the factory's production buildings matched these proportions – seven for amatol and two for lyddite.

A drawing of the later adaptation of the lyddite section for gas filling, as at Banbury, shows a group of 30 small untraversed filling sheds connected by a cleanway with tramway; there was a receiving shed for empty shells, with cleaning and painting tables, at one end and a fuzing, weighing, and boxing shed at the opposite end of the group. In the aerial photograph (Fig 6.26) the production group at the centre probably dates from the 1930s. However, six brick-built store houses in the lower part of the photograph, each around 21ft 4in (6.5m) long, divided into 24 bays and protected to their rear by earthwork traverses, are probably retained from the earlier phase. They may correspond to the long narrow stores at Banbury where picric acid was held before it was taken to melting houses.[67]

High explosives: TNT and amatol

TNT in a pure form is readily melted and, when adopted as the preferred shell filling, could thus be poured into a shell, mine, or aerial bomb using similar methods to lyddite. These properties were altered, however, by mixing TNT with ammonium nitrate to form amatol. With 60 parts TNT a melt process could still be employed, but the preferred composition of amatol at 80 parts ammonium nitrate to 20 parts TNT was too stiff to pour. New responses were required from the filling factories. Alternatives included pressing amatol into shaped blocks that could be packed into empty shells, a method previously employed by some private companies for filling guncotton shells. It was very slow, however, and the results variable. Another method was to heat the 80/20 mixture until it was plastic and use a screw feed to load the shells.[68] The most successful solution was to look for methods of dry mixing the ingredients and to fill the shells with powdered amatol.

Amatol was usually prepared at the filling factories using the two ingredients supplied from separate chemical factories. Extensions to existing filling facilities at Aintree (Merseyside), Barnbow (West Yorkshire), and Georgetown (Renfrewshire) may be recognised as distinct appendages to accommodate amatol sections. That at Barnbow was originally intended for Otley, also in West Yorkshire, where the earthwork remains of the unfinished factory survive. At Hereford an amatol section was designed from the outset alongside the lyddite section (Fig 6.26).[69]

At Barnbow a dry mixing process for the ammonium nitrate and TNT was devised using small edge-runner mills similar to those for milling gunpowder. Three mills were housed in large open sheds covered by Belfast truss roofs, but with no attempt to shield the machinery or the buildings. A similar edge-runner mill, believed to have been purchased from the Royal Arsenal Woolwich during the 1920s, survives in the restored Thwaite putty mill in Leeds. The milled amatol powder was at first filled or 'stemmed' into the empty shells by hand, and compacted using a wooden drift, the width of a broom handle, and a mallet. A press then created a cavity in the amatol filling, which was filled with pure TNT to aid detonation.[70] Photographic evidence suggests that hand-filling may have been replaced by a pressing process by the end of the war.[71]

One of the most innovative and idiosyncratic amatol filling factories of the war was designed by Viscount Chetwynd at Chilwell in Nottinghamshire (Figs 6.27 and 6.28). Chetwynd, who had no prior experience of

Figure 6.27 NFF no 6, Chilwell, Nottinghamshire. Factory layout, based on MoD plan: 1 No 1 store; 2 Ammonium nitrate drying shed; 3 TNT store; 4 Ammonium nitrate ?melt house; 5 TNT ?melt house; 6 Mixing house; 7 North and south press houses; 8 Filled shell store; 9 Canteen; 10 Shifting rooms; 11 Boiler house; 12 Power house; 13 Laboratory; 14 Loco shed; 15 Stores. This was 'Thunder Valley' – 'wherein death was compounded daily, and lightnings were chained and mighty earthquakes were reduced to a chemical formula' (Edgar Wallace, The real shell man, 1919).

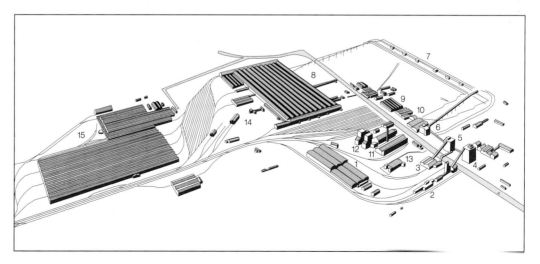

handling explosives, was an individualist – a man of 'push and go' – who would not be bridled by red tape and demanded a free hand in the design and running of his highly systematised shell factory. Against convention he adapted coal crushing, stone pulverising, sugar drying, paintmaking, and sugar sifting machinery to prepare the ingredients, even using the porcelain rollers of a flour mill to grind the TNT. Work began on the factory in September 1915; the contractors Holland, Hannen, and Cubitt worked to sketches made by Chetwynd, and its total cost was £3,000,000.

In operation, TNT and ammonium nitrate were brought into the factory (1 and 3 in Fig 6.27), and the hydroscopic ammonium nitrate was dried before milling (2). The mills (4 and 5), respectively six and seven storeys high, were modelled on flour mills where the ingredients were raised to the top floors and allowed to fall by gravity. The ammonium nitrate was crushed, heated, ground, dried, and sifted, and the TNT ground and sifted in a separate mill (5) before they were mixed together in the five-storey mixing house (6) in the proportion of 80 parts ammonium nitrate to 20 parts TNT to form amatol. The dry ingredients were then conveyed to the press houses (7) at the top of the site, where empty shells were carried along separate alleyways to the pressing rooms and were filled through the nose with powdered amatol. The filling was compacted under hydraulic pressure. Filled shells were moved downhill through a covered passageway to the filled shell store below (8), where shells were moved around by 72 overhead cranes (Figs 6.29 and 6.36). Covering 9 acres (3.6ha), it could hold 600,000 filled shells and 100,000 shells ready for filling. During the course of the war over 19,000,000 shells, 25,000 sea mines, and 2500 aerial bombs were filled with amatol at Chilwell.[72]

Another purpose-built amatol filling factory was constructed at Morecambe. Originally the majority of the process buildings were wooden with felted roofs, but the folly of this design was revealed when large parts of it were destroyed by fire in October 1917.[73] Surviving buildings of this factory are brick, some post-dating the fire.

Figure 6.28 NFF no 6, Chilwell, Nottinghamshire. Chetwynd monogram cast on factory lamp standard. (AA96/3560)

Figure 6.29 NFF no 6, Chilwell, Nottinghamshire. Interior of filled shell store, 17 May 1917. (AA96/3610; © MoD Chilwell)

Cartridges

Before the war, cartridge filling and the assembly of quick-firing ammunition by the government was carried out in the filling section at the Royal Arsenal Woolwich. This activity was split between four units scattered around this overcrowded establishment, which constrained their plan form. None can, therefore, be regarded as typical, though generally the filling sections were surrounded by magazines containing the requisite explosives and empty components, which were moved into the central area for filling and assembly. The filling sheds were fairly short: the longest, divided into three bays, was 34m long and the shorter single-room sheds 11m long. The whole group was arranged on a rectilinear layout connected by cleanways.

During the war, six new factories were erected specifically for filling cartridges. Two of the smaller ones, at Abbey Wood of 36 acres (14.57ha) and at Hayes of 152 acres (61.51ha), closely followed the layout of Woolwich. At both sites the filling was carried out in small untraversed rectangular sheds connected by cleanways. The other four, at Aintree, Barnbow, Georgetown, and Quedgeley, varied in size between 343 acres (138.81ha) and 520 acres (210.44ha). In these factories on greenfield sites there were few constraints to a layout of the desired form for the most efficient production, with the exception of Barnbow near Leeds where the factory site straddled a small brook. Quedgeley, near Gloucester, is a good example of a larger cartridge factory laid out on an almost clear site (Fig 6.30). It covered 343 acres (138.81ha) and in 1917 employed 4763 workers.[74] At its eastern end were explosives stores for TNT and cordite, and two smaller traversed magazines for black powder (B in Fig 6.30). At the opposite end of the factory lay the boiler house, administrative buildings, workers' shifting rooms, mess rooms, laundry, and box store (F, G, H, J). The flow line brought empty components by rail into long storage sheds (D) at the centre of two rows of filling sheds (A). At the north-eastern corner of the filling sheds, two were set aside for filling igniters with black powder. Twelve of the sheds, each divided into six bays, were devoted to cutting cordite to the correct length for making up into charges. Two smaller sheds, each divided into seven bays, were used for filling the shells with TNT. All of the components were then brought together in the four seven-bay assembly rooms at the western end of the ranges. Other smaller filled components – fuzes, gaines, and primers – were supplied from small storage sheds (E) to the west of the assembly rooms. Filled ammunition became the responsibility of the AOD, which controlled 12, 100 ton, magazines along the northern part of the site and eight along the south side (C), and a larger store. Slightly detached from the factory to the south was a buffer store, where ammunition might be stored if there was a delay moving it off site.

Georgetown in Renfrewshire, though a relatively level site, was arranged in a different pattern from Quedgeley. Here the filling and assembling sheds were surrounded on two sides by cordite and TNT magazines and three traversed black powder magazines, with filled ammunition stores at the periphery of the group.[75]

The filling sheds in these factories were sometimes over double the length of the longer three-bay sheds at Woolwich, and were divided into as many as seven bays. Buildings were generally of temporary construction, comprising brick foundations with timber-framed superstructures, usually with Belfast truss roofs. The Hayes factory had the distinction of being constructed almost entirely of corrugated iron; 20 store magazines were situated away from the factory at Northolt.[76] Because of the relatively small amount of explosive handled in any one building, all were untraversed except the black powder magazines. They were served by extensive internal tramway systems, connected to a standard-gauge line to transport the explosives, metal components, and finished ammunition.[77]

Small components

Small components included detonators, exploders, fuzes, gaines, and primers. Though the amount of explosive filled into any component was comparatively small, the types of explosives involved were often

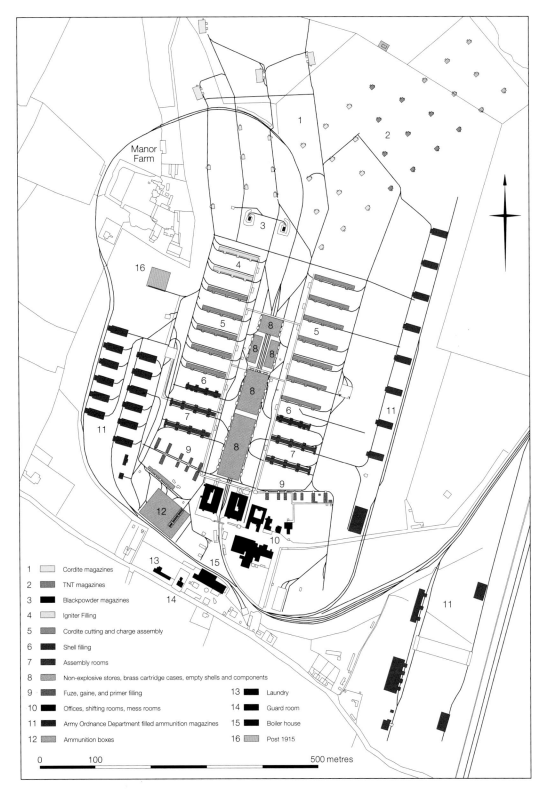

Figure 6.30 NFF no 5, Quedgeley, Gloucestershire. Site plan redrawn from OS, Gloucestershire, Sheet XXXIII.10, 25-inch, third edition 1923; OS, Gloucestershire, Sheet XXXIII.14, 25-inch, third edition, 1923.

1		Cordite magazines
2		TNT magazines
3		Blackpowder magazines
4		Igniter Filling
5		Cordite cutting and charge assembly
6		Shell filling
7		Assembly rooms
8		Non-explosive stores, brass cartridge cases, empty shells and components
9		Fuze, gaine, and primer filling
10		Offices, shifting rooms, mess rooms
11		Army Ordnance Department filled ammunition magazines
12		Ammunition boxes

13		Laundry
14		Guard room
15		Boiler house
16		Post 1915

0   100   500 metres

far more sensitive than the bulk fillings and could easily maim or kill if incorrectly handled. The larger filling factories where complete rounds were assembled might also contain small component filling sections.

One factory entirely dedicated to small components at Coventry was managed by White and Poppes Ltd, pre-war petrol engine manufacturers. It covered around 100 acres (40.47ha) and, in this case,

Figure 6.31 NFF no 21 Coventry. Site plan PRO MUN4/12. (BB94/11220; © PRO)

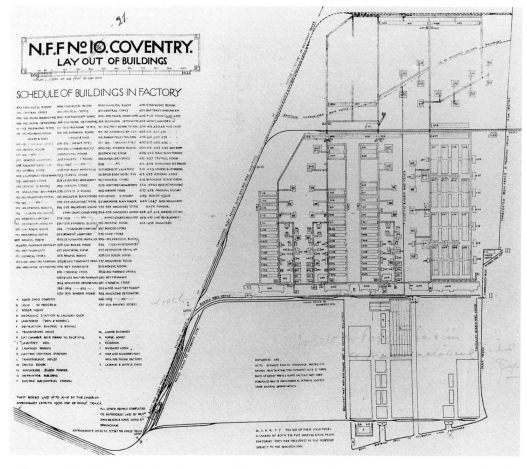

a factory sited immediately adjacent to the south made the components for filling on the spot. The main features of NFF Coventry were three almost identical north to south rows of sheds for filling detonators, fuzes, and gaines, and to the east a large group devoted entirely to fuzes (Fig 6.31). At the southern end of each row large shifting rooms, lavatories, and a surgery were provided within the danger area but all mess facilities were in the non-danger area to the south. The activities in each row were arranged in parallel, and served by small stores and magazines for black powder and tetryl. All the buildings were connected by raised cleanways. The fuze sheds to the east had four attendant black powder magazines. North of the filling sheds were brick-built black powder magazines, general magazines, and bonded stores for filled components. All filling sheds were rectangular in plan and undivided, built on brick foundations with a timber superstructure and gabled corrugated iron roofs. Work benches were set along the glazed side walls.

The tetryl press rooms were exceptionally divided into bays, with brick bay and end walls and timber panel infills.

NFF Coventry was relatively large for component filling. The factory at Perivale covered 138 acres (55.8ha), that at Cardonald only 21 acres (8.5ha), and Southwark was tiny at 1⅓ acres (0.5ha). Perivale, in West London, was similar in appearance to Coventry with gabled timber filling sheds of rectangular plan connected by raised cleanways, with covered hand-pushed narrow-gauge bogies. In contrast, Cardonald, under the management of the Nobel Explosives Company, was a mixture of brick and timber buildings, many with clerestories and roof lights, with detached and mounded powder magazines away from the filling sheds.[78]

Trench Warfare Department

In addition to requiring vast quantities of filled shells, operations on the western front called for many novel types of weapons, in particular grenades and mortar bombs.

Agency firms were commissioned to erect factories to fill these: British Westfalite at Denaby near Rotherham (South Yorkshire), the Thames Ammunition Company at Erith (London), W E Blake Explosives Loading Company at Fulham (London), and at Watford in Hertfordshire two factories were managed by the Watford Manufacturing Company Limited, formerly Dr Tibbles Vi-Cocoa. By the end of the war, two further sites were established at unidentified locations. All were in the range 3 to 40 acres (1.21 to 16.2ha).[79]

The factories at Watford were housed in temporary timber hutting, and the surviving photographs suggest that few of the precautions normally associated with explosives factories were in force. In one building filling aerial bombs weighing 112lb (50.8kg) and 336lb (152.4kg), amatol was let in down shutes along the shed walls.[80]

Gas filling

The release of 'the ghastly dew' of chlorine gas by the Germans in the Ypres salient in April 1915 marked a new phase in modern warfare.[81] It also further exposed the gulf between the British and German organic chemical industries, since German chemists and industrialists were able to respond quickly to these new demands on their skills. All poison gases were based on chlorine or chlorinated hydrocarbons gases, which placed them in the sphere of expertise of the chemists and plant of the dyestuffs industry.[82] The Manchester dyestuffs firm of Leveinstein's had the dubious distinction of manufacturing the only good quality British mustard gas.

Filling facilities were required for gas shells. Research reported on in June 1916 showed that the high concentrations of gas produced by shells could have tactical advantages over that produced by cylinder discharge. Like other experimental work, this was initially carried out at the Royal Arsenal Woolwich, but problems with leaking shells led to fears about the contamination of other areas of this vital factory.[83] These considerations led in July 1916 to the appointment of Mr A G M Chalmers to design, construct, and equip a purpose-built

gas shell filling factory at Greenford in Perivale (West London), an area with a long association with the chemical industry.[84]

NFF Greenford exhibited a similar rectilinear plan form to other filling factories (Fig 6.32). Its unity of purpose was reflected in the narrow range of building types and the identical form of the filling sheds. Its principal features were three rows of seven filling sheds, measuring 36ft × 10ft (11m × 3m), linked together by cleanways and a tramway, a large receiving and dispatching shed, 500ft × 90ft (152.5m × 27.5m), a box shed, large component store, three fuzing sheds, and three mounded magazines.

In operation, charged shells were received from either a contractor's or government factory for the insertion of bursting charge into the nose of the shell, in the process known as 'head filling'. In the case of chemical shells the filling was fumyl, a mixture of TNT, ammonium chloride, and ammonium nitrate. The quantities of explosives used were relatively small, with the largest exploder taking no more than 6oz (170g). Operations within the factory broke down into six distinct processes: unloading and stacking; cleaning; head filling; painting, stencilling, and banding; fuzing; and boxing and dispatch. In 1917, working around the clock, the normal weekly output was 42,000 shells, a figure which was pushed up to 83,000 during the German spring offensive on the western front in March 1918, following closely on Germany's peace with Russia. The total output of the factory was 3,500,000 shells.[85]

The almost universal adoption by the army of TNT as its standard shell filling rendered many of the lyddite manufacturing

Figure 6.32 NFF no 28 Greenford, West London. Site plan redrawn from Wootton and Lowry 1919.

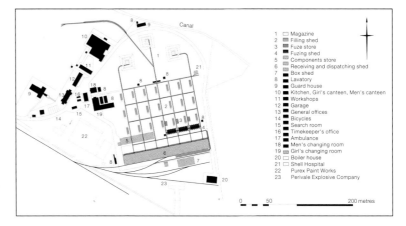

1	Magazine
2	Filling shed
3	Fuze store
4	Fuzing shed
5	Components store
6	Receiving and dispatching shed
7	Box shed
8	Lavatory
9	Guard house
10	Kitchen, Girl's canteen, Men's canteen
11	Workshops
12	Garage
13	General offices
14	Bicycles
15	Search room
16	Timekeeper's office
17	Ambulance
18	Men's changing room
19	Girl's changing room
20	Boiler house
21	Shell Hospital
22	Purex Paint Works
23	Perivale Explosive Company

0   50   200 metres

and filling facilities redundant. The picric acid factory at Avonmouth was converted to mustard gas production, and the two purpose-built lyddite filling factories at Banbury and Hereford were in part converted to gas filling.[86] They are good examples of plan and plant forms closely linked to a specialised product, where the obsolescence of the product also rendered the plant obsolete, yet they also illustrate how in modern warfare the unforeseen development of new weapons placed demands on factory plans that they were never designed to fulfil.

Though not designed for the purpose, both Banbury and Hereford proved relatively easy and effective conversions to handling gas shells, since they were laid out for the efficient movement of heavy empty shells and were divided up into many small units in case of leaks. Initially No 1 unit at Banbury was converted with minor alterations to head filling using a similar procedure to Greenford. By spring 1918 the army had yet to receive adequate operational supplies of HS or mustard gas. With a continued decline in demand for lyddite shells, sheds were also converted to fill shells with liquid mustard gas (Fig 6.25), an activity later extended to the former lyddite section at Hereford. Further capacity for gas filling was realised by converting part of the Trench Warfare Department at Watford. Work also began on a new factory at Chittening near Bristol, though after the appointment of Quinan in April it was abandoned in favour of the new plant at Avonmouth.

Naval facilities

Explosives factories supplying the navy stood to some extent apart from those supplying the other services. This separation was partly due to the specific need for the uniformity of ballistics offered as a propellant by cordite MD, which was supplied by a small number of propellant factories at Holton Heath, Hayle, and Chilworth.[87] The navy also retained the use of lyddite and later shellite as its principal shell filling after the army had switched to TNT. Not unsurprisingly, the majority of naval facilities were coastal or within easy access of a navigable river, though all the major ports were also well served by railways

Filling facilities were shared, as for example at Chilwell where mines were filled with amatol. Mine filling was also carried out at Woolwich, by the Explosives Loading Company at Faversham, and later by Vickers at NFF Banbury, Warkworth. The navy had exclusive use of a purpose-built filling factory at Gainsborough in Lincolnshire, devoted to filling what were described as 'sinkers' with TNT and mines with ammonium perchlorate. The factory was sited outside the town to the north-east and adjacent to the Gainsborough to Brigg railway line, served by a signal box and sidings at Thonock connecting to an internal standard-gauge line. Only constructed in November 1917, it had a very short life and, after employment in post-war ammunition breaking, it was closed by 1922 and demolished shortly afterwards. Two small buildings and a few concrete floor slabs are all that remain.[88] Another Admiralty filling station was sited at an unlocated factory at Stratford, probably East London, for shell filling with vincenite and also apparently for other chemical munitions for the navy.[89]

Close to most naval dockyards were naval armament depots for handling and maintaining explosives.[90] These acted as stores for the issue of explosives to ships putting out to sea and for the return of munitions when a ship returned to port for a refit. An armament depot at Upnor Castle served Chatham, and at Plymouth a filling factory was planned at Ocean Quay in Devonport, though little is known about its activities. The Royal Arsenal Woolwich remained an important supplier of naval munitions throughout the war, with part of its eastern area designated as a Royal Naval Armament Depot (RNAD).

At Portsmouth the main depot was Priddy's Hard (Fig 6.33). This dated back to the late eighteenth century, when it was built as a powder store, and was protected by a bastioned trace. In the late nineteenth century its area was extended west of the trace with the construction of a filling factory, with magazines surrounded by penannular tumps identical in form to those on the Erith Marshes at the Royal Arsenal Woolwich. This area was further extended during the war when three double rows of timber filling sheds and ancillary buildings were added.

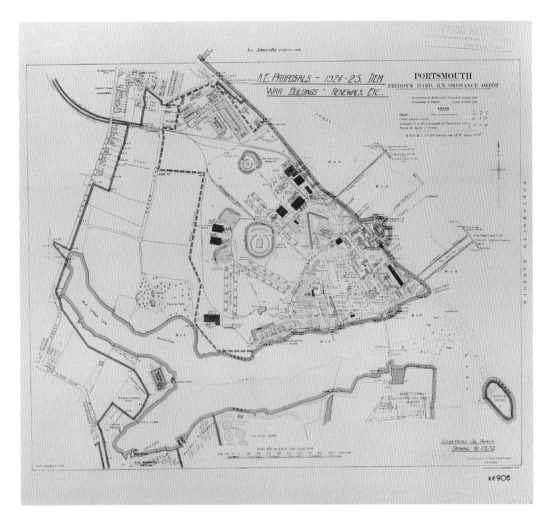

Figure 6.33 Royal Naval Armament Depot Priddy's Hard, Gosport, Hampshire. Site plan 1925, RCHME 95/5127 PTM-2481. (BB97/97413)

Factory architecture, materials, and infrastructure

The varieties of factory types reflect how the new factories were designed to meet their often very specialised tasks. Nonetheless, a range of buildings and functions might be encountered in varying combinations on all sites.

Construction

Even in peacetime the construction of the new factories would have been a considerable undertaking. Their scale, typically large, was sometimes huge, requiring the organised supply of large quantities of building materials, labour for their construction, and a wide range of plant to equip them. Contemporary photographs[91] reveal that manual labour still predominated even where earthmoving was required, though at

Gretna a tracked Bucyrus steam crane was employed in building mounds. Here during the period of construction 30,000 people were employed. Rail links were vital to bring in building materials, which arrived at a rate of 600 wagons per day. Usually the internal railway system of a factory was laid first and this was used to move the building materials around the site; alternatively temporary narrow-gauge lines were laid. The costs of an undertaking like Gretna were comparable with capital expenditure on other military installations such as naval dockyards and victualling stations.

Architecture and materials

The diversity of individuals, organisations, and building firms involved in the design and construction of munitions factories is reflected not only in their plan forms but also in the design of individual buildings.

Figure 6.34 RNCF, Holton Heath, Dorset. Main offices, designed by Sir Douglas Fox and Partners, 1915. (BB94/16969)

Figure 6.35 HM Factory Gretna, Cumbria. Main offices at Mossband. (© RCAHMS, C64518)

Figure 6.36 NFF no 6, Chilwell, Nottinghamshire. Interior of the former filled-shell store (see Fig 6.29). (AA96/3550)

Though all the factories were hastily erected, there were marked contrasts in their architectural treatment. At the larger government factories the administrative blocks and laboratories were often designed in a plain neo-Georgian style, embellished with overhanging bracketed eaves, dormer windows, and gauged-brick window-heads, some with tile keystones; the more distinguished were surmounted by ornate clock towers (Figs 6.16, 6.34, 6.35). These imposing structures towering over their single-storey factory often had a symbolic function as the backdrop to official ceremonies or to receive distinguished visitors.

In the production and danger areas a wide variety of building types were found. Temporary timber buildings were commonly used for their speed and ease of construction, and of reconstruction in case of a disaster. The Belfast truss roof was frequently employed. Originating in Irish bleach works in the late nineteenth century, it was a very adaptable form, economical in the use of timber and skilled labour. It could span large spaces, as in the case of aircraft hangers and canteens, but equally could be used for much smaller buildings. In acid handling areas or where there was a fire risk, brick was preferred, though in some instances local materials were used. At Gretna, the steel-framed pyrites store was infilled with cut stone.

Steel framing was not uncommon. At Hereford it was used in the amatol sections and in the AOD stores, infilled in brick with a rough-cast cement render and corrugated iron roofs.[92] The filled shell store at Chilwell had a steel framework, with steel stanchions to support the roof and the overhead travelling cranes (Figs 6.29 and 6.36). Here its use may have been more a matter of opportunity than design, for the steel was originally destined for a London hotel.[93] Steel framing was commonly found in the chemical processing areas of the factories, for example, in the tall single-storey guncotton factory sheds at Holton Heath, roofed with north lights and pitched spans. It often supported chemical plant, sometimes covered simply by corrugated iron sheeting. In taller buildings where materials were moved by gravity, a standard rectangular grid frame with relatively narrow floor areas was favoured, as in the mills at Chilwell and the process buildings at Langwith. In contrast, at Morecambe rolled steel joists supported the upper floor of process buildings.

Concrete figured most commonly in floor slabs and bases for steel framing, and as the core of traverses, which were often brick faced. It appeared little as a building material, with the notable exceptions of the reinforced concrete stores and process buildings at Cliffe (see Fig 6.7) and the reinforced concrete fermentation vessels at Holton Heath (see Fig 6.5).

Utilities

All the new national factories used electricity as their prime mover, though where heating was required in the production processes gas might also be employed. One of two options was available for such power supplies; it could either be generated on site or purchased from a local utility company. The major state factories all chose to generate their own power. They were equipped with large boiler houses to drive dynamos and produce steam for heating, which was carried around the sites in miles of lagged pipes. At Waltham Abbey the newly built boiler house (Fig 6.37) also provided power for an adjacent engine driving a hydraulic pump. At Holton Heath a massive boiler house, 340ft (104m) long, housed 24 boilers to generate electricity and provide steam heating (Fig 6.38). The boilers were fed from a semicircular coal transporter, and next to it was a gasworks. Queensferry and Gretna were also served by their own power houses.

Installation of such power-generating facilities was expensive and supply of the necessary plant could impose time delays. Many of the new filling factories, therefore, chose to make use of existing sources of power. At Hereford and Banbury electricity and gas were supplied from the local towns and Barnbow took electricity from the Yorkshire Electric Power Company.[94] By contrast, the Morecambe amatol filling factory, though less than 1km from the town, has an imposing power house that still survives alongside a disused railway line.

In those cases where power was taken from external sources, each factory generally had its own boiler house for steam heating and for manufacturing processes.

An adequate supply of water, too, was also a vital component in explosives manufacture, especially in the acid sections which were particularly heavy consumers. Considerable efforts were made to ensure an adequate supply. At Holton Heath, a pumping station was built at Corfe Mullen, 8km from the factory, to supply the large factory reservoir. Gretna required up to 10,000,000 gallons (45,460,000 litres) of water per day and had its own reservoir fed by water taken from the river Esk (Fig 6.11).[95] Other factories used the local town supply. Most new factories were also equipped with high pressure water mains for firefighting; the hoses were permanently attached to the hydrants, for the use of factory fire brigades or staff trained in firefighting and rescue.

Figure 6.37 RGPF Waltham Abbey, North Site. Power house; the projection to the engine room was added in 1916. (BB92/26070)

Figure 6.38 RNCF Holton Heath, Dorset. Boiler house. (BB94/17017)

Figure 6.39 RGPF Waltham Abbey. 1917 Rushton and Procter petrol-paraffin locomotive, southbound with a train of cordite trays for the drying stoves on South Site. (BB94/8009; © MoD)

Transport

No explosives factory stood alone: each was dependent on a range of suppliers and a reliable delivery of raw materials. From these factories explosives were conveyed to the filling factories where they were combined with the inert metal components brought there from engineering works. Delivery to users then followed. All factories and all stages were linked to the national railway network; good rail communications were one of the most important locating factors for new factories and the encircling loop of a railway line one of their most distinctive features. However, for some of the inherited late nineteenth-century factories, and for some naval facilities water transport remained dominant. Mechanised road transport also began to make an impact on communication patterns. It was often preferred where short journeys were involved, to relieve the pressure on the railways.

Within factories, movement of bulk supplies such as coal was generally on standard-gauge railway lines, while within the process areas narrow-gauge tracks were laid. At Waltham Abbey the existing tramway system was considerably expanded, including major engineering work to link North and South Sites, entailing the construction of three swing-bridges and a tunnel beneath Highbridge Street. Mechanical traction was introduced in 1917 with the purchase of four Rushton and Procter locomotives, and a two-road

locomotive shed was built on Great Hoppit to accommodate them. Battery locomotives were also used and more rarely ponies, but within the production areas hand-propelled wagons were preferred.[96] At Holton Heath steamless engines were employed and at Gretna electric tractor units powered from overhead wires. Contemporary photographs show that factory tramways were largely operated by the female workforce (Fig 6.39).

Security

Most pre-war explosives factories employed some form of security force to control access to their premises, but the war brought police and guard services to increased prominence. A police post controlled the gate and search rooms were placed nearby for searching workers entering and leaving the factories. Police were stationed at most explosives factories, including female constables. Larger factories also had military guard units, often provided by the Royal Defence Corps and made up of time-expired soldiers. The threat posed in Britain by revolutionary groups has yet to be assessed. An act of attempted sabotage by the Independent Workers Party of the World was certainly enough to prompt the Ministry to issue confidential intelligence to the filling factories in February 1917.[97]

Figure 6.40 German airship attacking a munitions works near London (Kriegs-Album Lustige Blatter, 2 Band, 1915, 26, 8): 'You English are short of munitions; here's some for you.' The bombs strike only military targets, which include the orderly layout of a munitions factory

Air defences

Only a few steps were taken before the war to provide protection for factories against attack from the air, in the first instance by airship (Fig 6.40). By April 1914 anti-aircraft guns were in place or planned for Waltham Abbey and the Royal Arsenal Woolwich and the magazines at Portsmouth, Purfleet, and Upnor. By early 1915 the explosives factories at Stowmarket, Pitsea, Kynochtown, and Chilworth had received guns, and the protection of munitions factories became an important factor in the location of later anti-aircraft defences.[98]

At Gretna the anti-aircraft defences comprised a height-finder station at Howend and a gun station at Battenbush.[99] Elsewhere, there is photographic evidence for passive air defence measures, including dapple-pattern camouflaged buildings at Chilwell (Fig 6.41) and sandbag surface shelters at Waltham Abbey, but no physical remains now survive.[100]

The social history of munitions

Accidental explosions

Given the large influx of inexperienced workers into the industry, supervised by equally green officials, a marked jump in the accident statistics might have been expected. Figures produced by the Explosives Inspectorate, however, show that in over four-and-a-quarter years of war the average loss of life was 1.25 per 1000 employees per annum, compared with 1 per 1000 in the five years prior to 1910. Arriving at a total figure for those killed manufacturing and handling explosives in the war is complicated by wartime censorship and the split in documentation between private licensed factories and those operated directly by the government. In those factories licensed by 1914 there were 325 deaths and within the National Filling Factories 218. Taking into account other directly controlled explosives factories, this might give a total figure of around 600 killed, of whom about a sixth were female employees and a further sixth civilians unconnected with explosives manufacture.[101]

However, such figures are distorted by a few explosions associated with TNT and picric acid. Before the war TNT was regarded as a comparatively safe explosive, whose main danger lay in a fire rather than detonation. Two serious explosions in 1917 illustrated the folly of hastily adapting unsuitable premises in built-up areas for TNT production. In one of the most notorious accidents of the war, large parts of Silvertown in East London were devastated when the TNT plant there exploded in January, killing 16 staff and 53 local residents (Figs 6.42 and 6.43).[102]

Figure 6.41 NFF no 6, Chilwell, Nottinghamshire. Reconstruction work underway after the disastrous explosion in July 1918. Note camouflaged ammonium nitrate mill, photographed 8 October 1918. (AA96/3595; © MoD Chilwell)

Figure 6.42 Silvertown, East London. Part of the devastation caused by the explosion of TNT plant on 19 January 1917. (NBR Print A)

Figure 6.43 Silvertown, East London. Monument to the employees who died in the explosion of TNT plant on 19 January 1917. (BB95/10093)

Figure 6.44 (below left) Faversham, Kent. Love Lane cemetery, mass grave of 69 out of 108 men killed in the Uplees explosion on 2 April 1916. (BB94/10451)

Figure 6.45 (below right) Chilwell, Nottinghamshire. Monument to the 134 workers killed in an explosion at the National Filling Factory on 1 July 1918. (AA96/3542)

Later the same year, another TNT plant constructed in a former mill amongst the terraced streets of Ashton-under-Lyne exploded, killing 24 employees and 19 residents.[103] A year earlier, a picric acid factory at Low Moor near Bradford in West Yorkshire exploded with the loss of 34 lives.[104]

The effects of TNT explosions in purpose-built factories could be just as devastating. An explosion at Ardeer in 1915 stopped the production of TNT for the duration of the war.[105] At the Explosives Loading Company's works on Uplees marshes, a fire in discarded TNT sacks spread to a neighbouring building which exploded, leaving a crater 46m in diameter and 3m to 4.5m deep, and in turn caused explosions in other buildings: 108 men were killed (Fig 6.44).[106] This loss of life was exceeded only in the explosion at the Chilwell Filling Factory (Fig 6.45) discussed below.

Generally the new filling factories were in remoter locations and casualties were restricted to employees. Out of the 218 fatalities that they sustained, over half occurred in the TNT-related explosion at Chilwell. Thirty-five female workers perished in serious explosions at Barnbow in 1916 and ten men were killed in a fire at Morecambe. In the design of filling factories, buildings were well spaced and small or divided into compartments. This ensured both that relatively small amounts of explosive were handled and that few workers were in any one area, which ensured that the loss of life only exceptionally exceeded three in any one accident. In fact, prodigious amounts of munitions were filled without fatality – more than 83 million grenades and 8000 million small arm cartridges. At Waltham Abbey cordite was manufactured without fatality; elsewhere the total loss of life attributed to cordite was 35, of whom 27 died at Arklow in 1917.[107]

Welfare

Potentially as dangerous as accidental explosions were the toxic effects of working with chemicals and explosives, though precise figures for those who were affected or died are difficult to ascertain. Before the war, the yellow colouration given to the skin by picric acid resulted in workers being nicknamed 'canary birds'; TNT had similar effects and its workers were known as 'canaries'. TNT could also induce toxic jaundice and at least 106 women died from its effects during the war.[108] As its effects became better understood they were mitigated by provision of overalls, caps and masks, good food, and washing facilities. Handling of tetryl could result in dermatitis, and severe headaches were associated with working with nitroglycerine-based explosives, though usually some tolerance was built up.

Medical facilities also became a feature of the wartime munitions factory (Fig 6.46). In addition to the effects of accidental explosions there were many minor accidents and illnesses to be dealt with. A more enlightened attitude to the dangers of working with explosives also ensured that the workforce were regularly examined for any injurious effects.

Resistance to the effects of handling explosives was partly a matter of personal constitution. The Welfare Section of the Ministry of Munitions recognised that a healthy and well-fed workforce was more productive than a poorly fed one. In many of the new factories the factory canteen became indispensable. Working hours were long: factories commonly operated around the clock on a pattern of either three 8-hour or two 12-hour shifts, leaving workers little time for food preparation. Where the factory was isolated, a large section of the workforce lived in purpose-built accommodation

or travelled from a great distance. In more built-up areas works canteens were encouraged to keep the workforce away from local public houses. At White and Poppes at Coventry three canteens were provided, each capable of accommodating 2500 people.[109] Canteens were commonly some of the largest buildings in the factory, with large clear floor areas spanned by Belfast truss roofs, and also doubled as concert or dance halls. They were usually segregated according to sex, and the standard of furnishings distinguished between the managerial, white collar, supervisory staff, and the workforce. At the Royal Arsenal Woolwich by 1917 there were 31 dining rooms and 14 coffee stalls, which in 1918 employed 1000 workers supplying 80,000 to 90,000 meals per day and processing between 20 and 25 tons (20.32 and 25.4 tonnes) of food.[110]

Many of the apparently open areas on factory plans also played an important part in the welfare of the workers, for in addition to being used for *ad hoc* storage they were vital for growing food. At Barnbow the factory had its own dairy, with a herd of 120 cows looked after by six girls; there were also vegetable plots, pigs fed on swill from the canteens, and a slaughter house. Vegetable plots sprang up at Banbury, Georgetown, and Hereford; pigs and cattle were kept, too, and at Gretna the workforce were involved in haymaking in their spare hours. Even a factory close to an urban area, like White and Poppes at Coventry, was able to grow practically all the greengrocery required for the canteen on its spare land.[111]

Women – the Munitionettes

One of the greatest social changes brought about by the war was the employment of women in roles traditionally associated with men.[112] The pattern of the uptake of women workers at Waltham Abbey was typical of many established pre-war factories (Fig 6.47). Recruitment of female labour began from April 1916 but was relatively slow; by June just 40 had been appointed. By the following May women and girls numbered 2144 out of a total workforce of 5259, which rose to a maximum of 3108 out of 6230 in March 1918.[113]

Figure 6.46 NFF no 6, Chilwell, Nottinghamshire. Medical centre. (AA96/3552)

Figure 6.47 RGPF Waltham Abbey. Women workers in factory clothing. Trousers and tunics were another novelty for women brought about by the war; cf Fig 6.56. On the right, Miss Kiddy wears a triangular war workers badge; cf Fig 6.3. (BB94/8006)

A Lady Superintendent was engaged to supervise them. The first, a Miss Hilda Walton of Somerville College, Oxford, resigned shortly afterwards, ostensibly because of the slow appointment of women; she was replaced by Miss Jessie O'Brien, formerly the superintendent of a nurses' institute.[114]

Beyond the bare statistics about the numbers of women employed in the explosives industry, contemporary photographs form an illuminating source for the range of activities carried out by women workers (eg Figs 5.35 and 6.47). The presence of women had other impacts on the facilities of factories. At Waltham Abbey North Site, a large new shifting and dining room was built for the female employees and a separate Y-shaped hospital (Fig 6.48). At the Marsh Works near Faversham the dining room was divided by a brick central wall to eaves height, and the porch was divided for separate entry to each section. Here it is uncertain whether this represented gender differentiation or a distinction between workers on the clean and dirty sides of the factory. Elsewhere, annotated plans noted distinct male and female changing, lavatory, and washing facilities (eg Fig 6.31).

Housing

A problem in managing these large workforces was in moving them to and from their place of work. Where possible factories were sited close to urban centres to draw upon the local labour pool. Most factories made use of rail communications, and halts were built to serve the new works. At Hereford workers were drawn from Hereford, Ross, and Leominster by free trains and a free breakfast before work. At Faversham the Admiralty built and operated the Davington Light Railway to move workers from the town to Uplees Marshes.[115] Its route may be traced across the marshes to a short tunnel with concrete-faced portals dated 1916; beyond this the line is lost beneath modern development. Those factories close to town centres were served by public trams, as at Aintree and the Royal Arsenal Woolwich.[116]

New workforces often numbering many thousands also caused accommodation problems. For factories close to market towns like Hereford and Banbury, enough accommodation was found through a billeting system; elsewhere purpose-built housing was provided. Wartime housing associated with the explosives' industry was only part of a wider programme for munitions workers, but generally it illustrates an interesting and typical range of designs.[117]

One of the earliest and most ambitious housing schemes was initiated in late 1914 to accommodate the ever-expanding workforce at the Royal Arsenal Woolwich. The housing estate at Well Hall was intended to be permanent and despite wartime pressures on materials and labour it followed 'best town planning lines'. Its designer was Frank Baines of the Office of Works;

Figure 6.48 RGPF Waltham Abbey, North Site. Women's Hospital, 1916; below the skylight was the operating room. (BB92/26040)

the estate's conception as an 'old English Village', with winding roads centred on an open green, reflected his Arts and Crafts background. Its groups of houses (Figs 6.49 and 6.50) exhibit a variety of designs, whose use of a wide range of materials was a response to wartime shortages, Baines argued, that made the best use of every material which came to hand.[118] Most features were in reality a direct continuation of pre-war practice, including weather-boarded or tile-hung gables, rough-cast finishes, and imposingly angled blocks at road junctions.

Later workers at the Royal Arsenal were not so fortunate and were housed in estates of regimented rows of wooden huts in the Woolwich area. The largest was the Corbett estate at Eltham, comprising 852 temporary houses, with street names including Amatol Avenue, Gaines Road, Mortar Gardens, and Lyddite Lane.[119] Most were standard single-storey timber hutments. In response to the timber shortage, one of the estates employed a novel A-frame or triangular section form of 'cottage bungalow', designed in 1915 by H E Pritchard (Fig 6.51). These 'cheap houses for the people' appear to have been built in rows of three. They were timber-framed and weather-boarded, with porches and slate covered roofs, some with brick end walls. All were provided with a living room and scullery; the smallest unit

with a 20ft (6m) frontage had one bedroom, while the largest with a 33ft 6in (10.2m) frontage had four bedrooms.[120]

Responsibility for the permanent housing schemes at Gretna and East Riggs near by was given to Raymond Unwin of the Local Government Board, with C M Crickmer acting as resident architect. Unwin and his colleagues had been associated with some of the large pre-war garden city schemes, including Letchworth, Hampstead, and estates for the London County Council.[121] These schemes marked a transition to a simplified neo-Georgian style in public housing, the majority with brick walls and slate roofs (Fig 6.52). The Gretna township of Longtown was roughly rectangular in plan, on a grid laid off a central avenue that was cut at its northern end by the main through route of Annan Road. This was fronted by the permanent public buildings and permanent housing. At the northern end of Central Avenue a tree-lined green had imposing two-storey hostels, dated 1916, to either side. Along the roads leading northwards off Annan Road the

Figure 6.49 Well Hall estate, Southeast London, 4 Prince Rupert Road. Angled corner block typical of best pre-war estate planning. (BB96/227)

Figure 6.50 Well Hall estate, Southeast London; 7–13 Prince Rupert Road. (BB96/228)

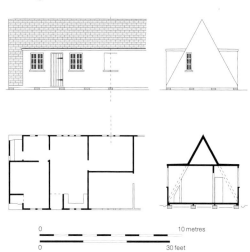

Figure 6.51 The BSB cottage bungalow, designed for explosives workers at Royal Arsenal Woolwich (redrawn from PRO MUN5/266).

Figure 6.52 Longtown, Cumbria. Factory housing at Blackbank for HM Factory Gretna. (© RCAHMS, C64522)

Figure 6.53 East Riggs, Dumfries and Galloway. Timber hut, 65 Pretoria Road. (© RCAHMS, C64439)

Figure 6.53 East Riggs, Dumfries and Galloway. Timber hut, 65 Pretoria Road. (© RCAHMS, C64439)

permanent housing was built. At the end, close to the main road, were placed semi-detached houses, some gabled, giving way northwards to less impressive hostels and simpler cottage-style accommodation. Despite the demolition of the blocks of timber hutments and hostels, the original layout south of Annan Road is preserved in the modern road pattern. The planned township was well served by public buildings, all in a neo-Georgian style, including shops, an institute, dance hall, cinema, medical facilities, post office, school, and a large police headquarters serving the factory complex. Along the southern side of the town were large communal kitchens, bakeries, and laundries. No pubs were provided, but no less than three churches, whose architecture varied with the denomination – Early Christian for the Episcopalians, Byzantine for the Catholics, and Italianate for the Presbyterians.[122]

The smaller township of East Riggs was laid out 3.75 miles (6km) to the west. Far fewer communal facilities were provided, principally a single row of shops and two churches, of which only St John the Evangelist remains standing. The most prestigious semi-detached housing in the township sat on a ridge overlooking the factory and lined The Rand, the main approach to the factory from the station. Cutting through the centre of the township, Melbourne Avenue also led to the factory gate and was lined along one side with hostels. Like the Gretna hostels these were designed to be converted into houses after the war. Behind these containing roads, the township was made up of more types of lower-class housing, typically in a three- or four-unit cottage style with hipped roofs. Temporary timber hutments were common, traces of which may still be found as earthworks and one of which, remarkably, is still inhabited (Fig 6.53).[123]

In both townships serving the Gretna factory many themes in contemporary estate planning are recognisable, including quadrangles and staggered building lines to break up the street frontage. Unwin's preference for curving roads is found in the areas of permanent housing; only in the hutment areas did a rigid grid plan dominate. Pre-war principles about a variety of house types, and about mixing the social classes, and attention to small design details also survived. The grouping of house types mirrored the factory hierarchy and subtle social distinctions were worked out in the provision of bay windows or a front door with cutaway brickwork. The most prestigious, detached housing lay away from the townships, however, on Rosetrees Lane within the Mossband factory area.[124]

Still, the overwhelming majority of the workforce was housed in standardised types of temporary hutments within the two townships. A type IV hostel to house 72 men, for example, consisted of a central block, measuring 80ft × 16ft × 9ft 6in to eaves (24.5m × 5m × 2.9m), that contained the kitchen and mess rooms with attached stores and four dormitories, measuring 60ft × 16ft × 8ft 6in to the eaves (18m × 5m × 2.6m).[125]

Another permanent housing scheme on a different scale was the government village at Langwith in Derbyshire, erected in 1916 for the chemists and workers of the chemical by-products factory. It consisted of 38 cottages and four larger managers' or chemists' houses (Fig 6.54) set at the top

Figure 6.54 Langwith, Derbyshire. Manager's or chemist's house in Langwith Drive associated with national byproducts factory (Fig 6.15). (AA96/4381)

of a rising drive. The cottages were built in three-, four- and six-row units, some of them organised around a quadrangle on one side of the drive.[126] Estates built in 1916 at Mancot and Sandycroft to house workers from the Queensferry factory consisted of four types of three-bedroom houses.[127] Their layout, too, incorporated design features such as quadrangles and staggered frontages. Groupings of houses exhibit a similar mixture of three- and four-unit terraces, and of hostels mixed with differing styles of semi-detached housing. The detailing of individual houses combined variations of bay windows, cutaway brickwork around front doors, and paired front doors separated by an arched alleyway leading to the rear. Dwellings were also built within or close to the factory perimeter to house essential workers, including cottages for the fireman, time keeper, and electrician, and close to the factory gates at Sandycroft a pair of staff villas and a row of six terraced cottages for the foremen.[128] Even where there was little need for mass housing, accommodation was often provided for key workers; a number of detached and semi-detached houses at Holton Heath, designed by Sir Douglas Fox and Partners, served this purpose. The works managers lived in some style: at both Quedgeley and Holton Heath their colonial-style bungalows with verandas were located adjacent to the factories.[129] Barrack accommodation for the military guard units and police quarters or barracks were generally separated from that of the workforce, sometimes lying within the factory areas as at Woolwich. Firemen might be treated similarly: at Hereford a row of houses known as 'Firemens' Quarters' lay within the factory perimeter.

In contrast to these well-built permanent houses, temporary accommodation was constructed at many factories. At Coventry 466 temporary cottages were built for workers at White and Poppes, at Abbey Wood five temporary hostels, at Hereford a single hostel, and at Erith accommodation for the employees of the Thames Ammunition Company.[130] A combination of hostels, cottages, and a manager's house was built at Georgetown.

The Carlisle experiment

There was concern about social disorder, particularly resulting from the influx of a numerous and comparatively well-paid workforce into a given area. This was addressed by a further amendment to DORA which gave the state powers to control, and if necessary acquire, the commercial premises associated with the drinks trade.[131] It was not a problem confined only to the explosives industry: for example, public houses close to the Royal Small Arms Factory Enfield were also brought under state control.[132] The most marked manifestation of such control was in Carlisle, one of the main dormitory towns for the Gretna factory. In 1916 the Central Control Board took over 119 licensed premises, and their regime resulted in a reduction by almost 50% by 1918 and closure of three of the four city breweries.[133] Pubs were also refurbished to meet the Board's aim to provide cheap and good food, so as to discourage the drinking of alcohol except with meals.[134] The principal architect responsible for this was Harry Redfern. In one of his earliest designs, he converted the former post office in Lowther Street in Carlisle into the Gretna Tavern. In the manner of modern pubs, large open rooms filled with tables and chairs for dining were formed creating an unconvivial atmosphere, in stark contrast to the cosiness of the Victorian snug. This was reinforced by a battleship-grey paint scheme. The Globe Tavern at Longtown, Gretna (Fig 6.55), was also redesigned by Redfern, as commemorated by the inscribed stone dated 5 October 1916 set on one side of the entrance.

Figure 6.55 Longtown, Cumbria, Globe Tavern. (© RCAHMS, C64584)

The inglenook and minstrel gallery were attributed to his assistant, C F A Voysey. Explosives manufacture with its demands for alcohol-based solvents also further drove up the availability and price of spirits.[135]

The impact of peace

After the Armistice on 11 November 1918, the government factories quickly began to shed labour; females and boys were rapidly dismissed in the following weeks (Fig 6.56).[136] The Ministry of Munitions was wound up by the Cessation Act 1921 and the majority of its assets passed to the Disposal and Liquidation Commission.[137] At the end of the war there were vast stocks of government stores. Many redundant filling factories were used to store this material, while others were turned to the task of breaking down and destroying unwanted ammunition.[138] This was in itself a hazardous activity, which between 1918 and 1924 claimed five lives at Banbury alone.[139] By the late 1920s the majority of the wartime factories had been sold and cleared of buildings and the land returned to agriculture; a few formed the basis of small trading estates. Because of their specialised nature the new explosives factories contributed less to the industrial infrastructure of the country than, for example, the more adaptable engineering works created during the war. Few of the large chemical plants survived. Gretna was closed and was auctioned off piecemeal. The old and inefficient plant at Waltham Abbey was retained, as it

Figure 6.56 'What might be done with the uniforms' (from The Mossband Farewell Magazine, *1919).*

was able to meet the reduced needs of the services. Its geographical links with the other remaining government factories and local lobbying were factors in its retention.[140] The modern Queensferry plant was also closed at the insistence of the trade, who regarded its plant as being too efficient. In contrast, the uncompleted artificial nitrate factory at Billingham, Stockton on Tees, was sold to Brunner Mond and Company and formed the basis of the present ICI chemical plant there.[141]

In the private factories there was a rapid rationalisation amongst the chemical explosives manufacturers and the consolidation into Nobel Industries Ltd, already described in Chapter 4 (above, Merger and Explosives Trades Ltd). One of the strangest schemes to find new uses for idle plant was the manufacture of macaroni at Kynochtown using cordite presses. It came to nothing but illustrates the close links between explosives manufacture and food processing.[142] Elsewhere, factories were closed and their contents and buildings auctioned. At Holton Heath the ministry was faced with the task of disposing of 39 tons (39.62 tonnes) of horse-chestnuts and 117 tons (118.87 tonnes) of acorns.[143] A number of the buildings from the Uplees factory were sold and found new uses in the Faversham area, one at least surviving as a house. At Chilworth many of the buildings of the cordite factory were simply reused agriculturally, though at least one was converted into a house and had a fireplace installed.

Endnotes

1   Armytage 1976, 251.
2   Public Statutes General 1914, **4 and 5 George V, c. 63**; Defence of the Realm No 2) Act, 1914; Public Statutes General 1915, **5 and 6 George V, c. 42**; Defence of the Realm (Amendment) (No 3) Act, 1915.
3   *The Times* 1915, 14 May.
4   James 1978, 317–23.
5   Public Statutes General 1915, **5 and 6 George V c. 51** Ministry of Munitions Act, 1915.

6   More detailed information on the Ministry of Munitions can be found in, for example, its *History of the Ministry of Munitions* (HMSO 1920–2), Lloyd George's memoirs (1933), and the voluminous archive of the Ministry at the PRO; see also Adams 1978.
7   Public Statutes General 1915, **c. 54** Munitions of War Act, 1915.
8   PRO MUN 5/10.
9   Hartcup 1988, 44–5.
10 Levy 1920, 28; Travis 1993; an original

Haber-Bosch reaction vessel from Ludwigshafen is on display at the Science Museum large object collection at Wroughton, Wiltshire.
11 *The Times* 1910.
12 For a description of the process, see Rae 1987.
13 HMSO 1920–2, **VII**(IV), 65.
14 *Ibid*, **VIII**(II), 83–5; Marshall 1917, 341–6; PRO MUN 4/6187.
15 For further information on the process, see Nathan 1919; HMSO 1920–2,

VII(IV), 65–72, and VIII(II), 85; Weizmann 1949, 218–22; Girling 1987; England 1993; and, for a recent discussion, see Bud 1992 and 1993, 37–45; Ministry of Munitions papers concerning Weizmann and the process are preserved in classes PRO MUN 7/235–8.

16 Site photographs in Lesley Hayward's private collection are copied in the NMR. I am also grateful to Dr Bud of the Science Museum for his comments on site about the vessels.

17 HMSO 1920–2, VII(IV), 84, and VIII(II), 86.

18 PRO MUN 7/555.

19 HMSO 1920–2, X(IV), 92; Reader 1970, 192.

20 HMSO 1920–2, VIII(II), 39.

21 Levy 1920, 57; Robertson 1921, 524.

22 Waltham Abbey Special Collection, WASC 901/300, 300A, 301.

23 Reader 1970, 300-1; Double 1988.

24 Crocker 1984, 16–17.

25 Earl 1978, 245–9.

26 HMSO 1920–2, X(IV), 28 for a detailed history of the factory, see Bowditch 1983; Bowditch and Hayward 1996.

27 Bowditch 1983, 23.

28 Rintoul 1934; Reader 1970, 301.

29 Bowditch 1983, 3.

30 For the history of Gretna, see HMSO 1920–2, VIII(II), 58–61; Rayner-Canham and Rayner-Canham 1996. For principal sources see PRO MUN 5/239 Photographs of H M Factories at Queensferry, Gretna and Langwith under construction and in operation; Quinan 1920 (copies in PRO MUN 5/285 and PRO Supp 10/15); PRO MUN 5/297; PRO MUN 5/436; Carlisle Library, Local History sales catalogues, accession number 17950.

31 HMSO 1920–2, X(IV), 3.

32 Cartwright 1964, 136–9. See PRO Supp 10 Quinan papers.

33 Fraser and Chalmers Ltd 1908; see also HMSO 1938, 101–2.

34 Quinan 1920, 138; PRO Supp 10/15.

35 HMSO 1938, 105.

36 HMSO 1920–2, X(IV), 111; Levy 1920, 55–6; HMSO 1938, 108–9; Reader 1970, 301; PRO MUN 7/555.

37 PRO EF 5/20.

38 New Explosives Company Ltd 1906; Hodgetts 1909, 386–95.

39 Marshall 1917, 245–76.

40 Personal communication Whaley Thorns Heritage Centre, Derbyshire; HMSO 1920–2, X(IV), 51; PRO 1801 [3] H M Factory Langwith, 1918, extracted from MUN 4/2061; PRO MUN 5/294 H M Explosives Factory, Langwith, Mansfield, Nottinghamshire.

41 Marshall 1917, 277–81; PRO Explosives Inspectorate Special Report LXXXI 1887; PRO Explosives Inspectorate Special Report CXXXIX 1900.

42 HMSO 1920–2, VIII(II), 49; HCRO 109M91/RM9; PRO MUN 5/159/1122.7/28; PRO MUN 7/40.

43 Ibid, VII(IV), 35.

44 HMSO 1938, 128.

45 HMSO 1926, 31.

46 Smith nd c 1920, 5–11.

47 Lewes 1915, 825–7; HMSO 1920–2, X(IV), 32–48; HMSO 1938, 129–43; MUN 7/36; PRO MUN 5/159/1122.7/28.

48 Billings and Copland 1992.

49 Hampshire Country Record Office, HCRO 109M91/RM9.

50 Billings and Copland 1992, 14.

51 Rintoul 1934, 564.

52 HMSO 1920–2, X(IV), 55.

53 Ibid, VIII(II), 43; Cooke 1957, 65–71.

54 Levy 1920, 92; PRO MUN 5/239.

55 Ibid, 78–81; Freeth 1964.

56 Simmons 1963, 59–60.

57 Levy 1920, 16–17, 72–3; HMSO 1938, 143–7; Bowditch 1983, 34–5; PRO Supp 5/861, S.32.B.01 22-4-1918.

58 PRO EF 5/20.

59 RCHME 1994, NMR Building Index No 92394.

60 HMSO 1920–2, VIII(II), 48.

61 PRO SUPP 5/148.

62 Hogg 1963a, 945; PRO Supp 5/148.

63 For a general history of the National Filling Factories, see Lloyd George 1933, 587–98; for a more detailed history and brief site histories, see HMSO 1920–2, X(V). For original records, site photographs and some plans of the National Filling Factories, see PRO MUN 5/154/1122.3/33; MUN 5/154/1122.2/34.

64 Cocroft and Leith 1996.

65 HMSO 1920–2, VIII(II), 150.

66 PRO MUN 5/155/1122.3.51.

67 Ministry of Munitions 1919; PRO MUN 5/154/1122.3/39.

68 Robertson 1921, 526

69 PRO MUN 5/154/1122.3/39.

70 Brooks 1990, 11, quoting Imperial War Museum oral history source; Leeds Central Library, Gummer R H, 1918 Barnbow No 1 (Leeds) NFF A short history and record of the factory, unpublished typescript LQ623.45 G953.

71 Collection of photographs in Leeds Central Library.

72 Anon c 1919; Wallace 1919; HMSO 1920–2, VIII(II), 160; Lloyd George 1933, 594–8; Haslam 1982, 1–70; PRO MUN 5/154/1122.3/33.

73 HMSO 1920–2, VIII(II), 171–2; PRO MR 1801 [5].

74 PRO MUN 4/1703; MUN 5/155/1122.3/50.

75 PRO MR 1802 [3].

76 PRO MUN 5/154/1122.2/34; MUN 5/157/1122.3/65; PRO MR 1801 [1].

77 PRO MUN 5/157/1122.3/65.

78 PRO MUN 5/157/1122.3/65.

79 HMSO 1920–2, XI(I), 121–30; PRO MUN 5/146/1122/8.

80 HMSO 1920–2, XI(I), 127–30; for Watford, see Watford Reference Library, Box J Munitions.

81 For recent discussion of gas warfare, see Haber 1986; Hartcup 1988, 94–117; Richter 1994.

82 Haber 1971, 208–9.

83 Hartcup 1988, 104.

84 HMSO 1920–2, VIII(II), 156–7.

85 Bing 1919; Ministry of Munitions 1919; Wootton and Lowry 1919; PRO MUN 5/154/1123.3/39.

86 HMSO 1920–2, VIII(II), 49.

87 Earl 1978, 245.

88 HMSO 1920–2, VIII(II), 63; personal communication Margaret Arbon of Gainsborough.

89 PRO MUN 4/2710.

90 For a discussion of the Ordnance Yards associated with the 'Sailing Navy', see Coad 1989, 245–68.

91 MUN 5/297.

92 PRO MUN 5/154/1122.3/36.

93 Haslam 1982, 16.

94 PRO MUN 5/154/1122.3/36; PRO MUN 5/155/1122.3/51; Leeds Central Library Gummer 1918, 4.

95 PRO Supp 10/15.

96 Jenkins 1989, 392–410; Edwards 1994, 39.

97 Watford Reference Library, Box J Munitions.

98 Hogg 1978, 28–36; Dobinson 1996a, 11–47.

99 Carlisle Library, Auction catalogue of Messrs Robert Dalton and Son, 11 May 1920.

100 PRO MUN 5/154/1122.3/33; PRO

Supp 5/861, Photographs 346 Air raid shelter 14-11-1918, 347 Air raid shelter 25-11-1918.

101 Explosives Inspectorate Annual Report 1920, 6–7; PRO MUN 5/155/1123.3/59 Oct 1919.

102 PRO MUN 7/36.

103 Billings and Copland 1992; PRO MUN 7/37.

104 Earnshaw 1990, 28.

105 HMSO 1920–2, Vol IX, 55, Pl IV.

106 Percival 1985, 434–8.

107 Kelleher 1993, 151–2; Explosives Inspectorate Annual Report 1920, 6–7; PRO MUN 5/155/1123.3/59.

108 Guttmann 1909, 13; The *Lancet* 1916; Livingstone-Learmouth and Cunningham 1916; Lloyd George 1933, 592.

109 The *Engineer* 1918.

110 See HMSO 1920–2, **V**(IV), 1–22; Hogg 1963a, 986–7.

111 Leeds Central Library, Gummer 1918, 43–4; PRO MUN 5/155/1122.3/51; MUN 5/154/1122.3/36.

112 See Marwick 1977; Woollacott 1994.

113 HMSO 1920–2, **VIII**(II), 38.

114 PRO MUN 7/554.

115 Taylor 1986.

116 PRO MUN 5/155/1122.3/50.

117 For a general discussion, see Pepper and Swenarton 1978.

118 *Ibid*, 368–9; Swenarton 1981, 53–8.

119 Kennett 1985, 4.

120 PRO MUN 5/266.

121 Beattie 1980, 85–120; Gray 1985, 359–60.

122 For a fuller description of the churches, see Gifford 1996, 331–2.

123 For a discussion of the architectural significance of these settlements, see Pepper and Swenarton 1978, 369–72; Swenarton 1981, 58–62; PRO MUN 5/297.

124 Harwood and Saint 1991, 104.

125 Carlisle Central Library, Auction catalogue.

126 PRO MUN 4/6131.

127 PRO MUN 4/6256.

128 PRO MUN 5/239.

129 Bowditch 1983, 9.

130 PRO MUN 4/6256; MUN 5/96/346/2/15.

131 Public Statutes General 1915, **5 and 6 George V, c. 42**; Defence of the Realm (Amendment) (No 3) Act, 1915.

132 Putnam and Weinbren 1992, 88–90.

133 Hunt 1971, 25.

134 *Ibid*, 19; Department of Culture Media and Sport (DCMS) Listed Building descriptions, The Globe Tavern, Longtown, and The Post Public House, Carlisle.

135 Levy 1920, 90.

136 HMSO 1920–2, **VIII**(II), 38; PRO MUN 7/555.

137 Public Acts General 1921, **11 George V, c. 8**; Ministries of Munitions and Shipping (Cessation) Act, 1921.

138 Haslam 1982, 70–2; Edwards 1994, 45–6.

139 Simpson 1978, 56.

140 PRO MUN 7/555.

141 HMSO 1920–2, **VII**(IV), 62.

142 Scott 1981, 26.

143 PRO MUN 4/5747.

7

Rearmament and the Second World War

The inter-war years: the 1920s and early 1930s

The material and financial cost for Britain of the Great War was immense. Post-war Britain experienced deep economic depression and massive unemployment, the General Strike of 1926, the financial crisis of 1931, and a National Government. There were vast stocks of munitions stored in ordnance depots at the end of the war and contemporary assessments saw little necessity to maintain a large manufacturing capacity. Despite the substantial number of Britain's significant military commitments in Europe in the aftermath of war, demand dropped catastrophically for the industry. In the 1920s and 1930s military activity was increasingly confined to training and to active operations characterised as policing of frontier tribesmen, which resulted in campaigns of small-scale infantry skirmishes, aided by the RAF, that required relatively small amounts of explosives.

Among the trade factories the end of the war was devastating. As with the traditional black powder makers, the private manufacturers of chemical explosives had merged, becoming part of Nobel Industries Ltd, and by the mid-1920s most had closed. Nobels concentrated their activities on Ardeer in Ayrshire, with a scatter of other factories across the country, principally manufacturing mining explosives (Fig 7.1). Of the government factories, only Waltham Abbey and Holton Heath remained open and filling was once again concentrated on the Royal Arsenal Woolwich. The explosives factory at Irvine in Ayrshire was kept on a care and maintenance basis, as was the filling factory at Hereford.[1] While generally pursuing their own agendas, the three active government establishments exchanged information about the development of new types of explosives.

Waltham Abbey RGPF

In the previously established pattern, small-scale laboratory research into explosives continued at the Research Department at Woolwich and throughout the inter-war period piecemeal building programmes continued in support of explosives research.[2] Where large-scale experimental work or pilot plants were needed, Waltham

Figure 7.1 Distribution of Second World War explosives factories, showing principal activities.

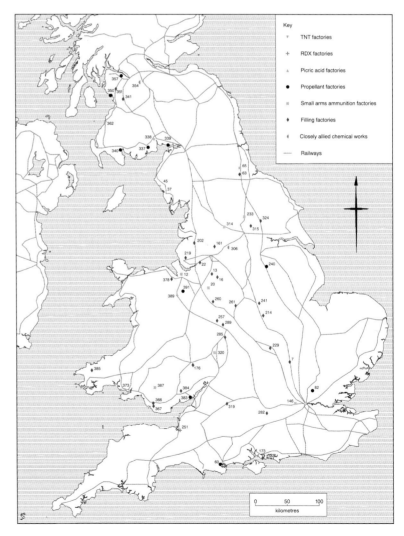

Abbey provided a convenient site. An early post-war example was the development of a flash suppressant for inclusion in cordite. This additive was nitroguanidine, also known as petrolite or picrite, and in 1925 a plant was installed in an unidentified location, probably within the Edmonsey Mead acid factory area at the northern end of North Site (Fig 5.53), for its manufacture. Field evidence of this research remains only in a modified guncotton stove converted to either a picrite store or stove, to which the surviving metal drying racks perhaps belong. No other buildings have been identified on the site from the 1920s, and it was not until the early 1930s that an experimental TNT plant was erected within the Edmonsey Mead acid factory. The focus of later activity moved to the northern part of South Site, where part was given over to the production of the fuze powder RD (Research Department) 202 by the mid-1920s.[3] In 1938 work also began on a pilot plant for RDX, an explosive 30–50% more powerful again than TNT but with the additional advantage that it required no imported raw materials.[4] For its manufacture a group of steel-framed sheds, sunk into the ground to eaves level, was built on South Site, served by the acid factory adjacent to the 1880s Guncotton Factory.

At the same time experiments took place in the design of structures to militate against the effects of accidental explosions. Work on a Quinan type guncotton drying stove began in 1934 and construction was under way by July 1935 (Fig 7.2). It presents a contradiction between its contemporary design

and the outmoded technology it housed, together with its continuing dependence on barge transport. It was built on the Hyrib construction principle, employing rail-pattern girders firmly anchored in the ground. Its roof members were lightly secured, so that in the event of an explosion the walls would offer considerable resistance and the pressure would be relieved through the roof. To reduce danger from flying debris the wall panels were infilled with wire mesh, rendered in pumice concrete. Other features were standard in explosives industry buildings, including external lighting, lightly wired glass windows, a gritless asphalt floor, and doors which opened outwards. Internally it was lined in painted calico. As with the Gretna stoves (Figs 6.11 and 6.12), it was divided internally into 15 bays and worked in a similar manner.[5] Elsewhere in the factory improvements were made by redesigning sulphuric acid concentrators. In place of the earlier towers using imported volvic stone, the Evans-Bowden tower was developed using Staffordshire blue bricks at a fraction of the cost, and was widely adopted elsewhere.[6]

RNCF Holton Heath

Despite its vulnerability to aerial attack, the RNCF at Holton Heath was also retained and, in spite of this being a period of reduced military spending, continuous updating is evident to its factoryscape. As early as 1919 a square enclosure was added on the western side of the factory to house Naval Ordnance Inspection Laboratories, including laboratories and climatic test cubicles to study explosives under different service conditions.

The most significant change was a remodelling to accommodate manufacture of solventless cordite or cordite SC, in a process introduced in 1927. For this, nitro-cellulose with a reduced nitrogen content was used, the ratio of nitroglycerine was altered and carbamite or centralite was used as a stabiliser in place of mineral jelly, which assisted in the gelatinisation of the cordite.[7] Although primarily introduced to rectify operational failures of British naval propellants during the Great War, it also brought benefits to the manufacturing process.

The need to dry the guncotton before mixing and the need for cordite drying were removed, thereby eliminating the handling of hazardous guncotton and saving the cost of fuel, in the process rendering drying buildings redundant. It also dispensed with acetone as a solvent, and in 1934 the acetone plant was demolished (Fig 6.5). Nitrocellulose was still prepared in the existing factory but, instead of being dried, it was moved as a paste to the mixing houses. In 1932 this process was altered and the nitrocellulose was pumped as a slurry to an intermediate house for distribution to the mixing houses. In a vessel known as a tundish, nitroglycerine was added and the resulting aqueous mixture was sent down a gutter to a mixing tank where carbamite was added. It was then pumped to a sheeting table where excess water was drained off under vacuum to produce a sheet up to fiin (12mm) thick. This product was loaded into hand-pushed tramway trucks and taken to paste sheet drying houses, which consisted of an open earthwork emplacement surrounded on three sides by earthwork traverses. Leading into the centre were six tramway lines with heater houses to either side; trucks were pushed into the emplacement and warm air pipes connected to their ends (Fig 7.3). After drying, the sheets were

taken to cordite rolling houses (Fig 7.4), where they were gelatinised by passing between heated rollers and then cut into 7in (180mm) squares and packed in aluminium containers holding 25lb (11.34kg). Still warm, these were moved to a charge forming house and pressed to form a 'cheese', then on in specially heated trucks to the press houses. The more hazardous pressing of cordite SC was reflected in the design of the press houses, within which the press in its own room was operated from a separate control room and was also separated from the motor and cutting rooms. An elaboration of this method was known as the 'semi-solvent process'. After pressing, the propellant was dried and then passed though heated rolls to form sheets. These were loaded into a press cylinder and extruded, producing cords with more flexibility and a smoother surface.

The factory suffered a major setback on 23 June 1931 when there was an explosion in the nitroglycerine factory with the loss of ten lives, including the chief chemist Mr Blair. As a result, modifications were made to the operating procedures within the remaining nitrator separating house. Most noticeably, the gutter link for running the nitroglycerine between the washing house and mixing houses was cut. Instead, it was moved in a hand-propelled bogie, thereby breaking the physical link between the buildings (Fig 7.5 and 7.6).

Figure 7.3 RNCF Holton Heath, Dorset. Paste drying stove 'F' House. (Source Lesley Hayward, 423; © MoD)

Figure 7.4 RNCF Holton Heath, Dorset. Cordite rolling house, with distinctive projecting corner porches and elaborate roof vents. (Source Lesley Hayward, 147; © MoD)

Figure 7.5 RNCF Holton Heath, Dorset. Part of the factory model. At the centre the rebuilt nitroglycerine factory, to its left the covered reservoir, in the foreground the mixing and paste sheet drying houses and to the rear the cordite ranges. (BB94/17031)

Figure 7.6 RNCF Holton Heath, Dorset. Asphalt runway tracks leading from washing house to mixing house. (Source Lesley Hayward, 96; © MoD)

Figure 7.7 RNCF Holton Heath, Dorset. Mound over nitroglycerine factory under construction. (Source Lesley Hayward, 325; © MoD)

The bogies were mounted on solid rubber wheels and pushed along grooves in an asphalt trackway set in a cutting between the houses, following practice previously associated with the German and American explosives industries.[8]

When it came to replacing the shattered nitrator, research from the late 1920s indicated a continuous nitration plant might form a more efficient option. Such plants also offered greater safety as there was less nitroglycerine in the plant at any one time and it was easier to control. Their development was a continental innovation, notably

Figure 7.8 RGPF Waltham Abbey, South Site. Horizontal extrusion press similar to the type installed at Holton Heath. (BB93/27112)

by a German engineer Schmid, and a Swiss engineer Dr Mario Biazzi. A Schmid plant produced by the Meissener organisation of Cologne was chosen, similar to one recently installed at Ardeer. Installation by German engineers began in 1936 and was complete early in the next year. It was housed in a reinforced concrete shell, with walls up to 2ft (0.6m) thick and the crown of the curving roof 12in thick (0.3m), lined internally with white glazed bricks and entered through two approach tunnels. The whole was covered by a massive earth mound, 210ft (64m) × 180ft 6in (55m) and standing around 39ft 5in (12m) in height (Fig 7.7). Adoption of a continuous nitration process for nitroglycerine manufacture was itself part of a wider development in the chemical industry in general to replace batch processes with continuous operations.

Another important innovation of the inter-war years was the substitution of paper for cotton in the production of nitrocellulose (Table 7.1). The change reflected experiments begun in Germany during the Great War to substitute wood pulp as a

Table 7.1 Revised flowline for modified paper nitrocellulose production, after HCRO 109M91/COL12

Paper
Scrolling Machines
Paper and Mixed Acids
Nitration Pans
Nitrocellulose
Boiling Vats
Beating Machines
Potchers
Grit Extractors
Dewaterer
Blending and Adjusting
Pulp Store

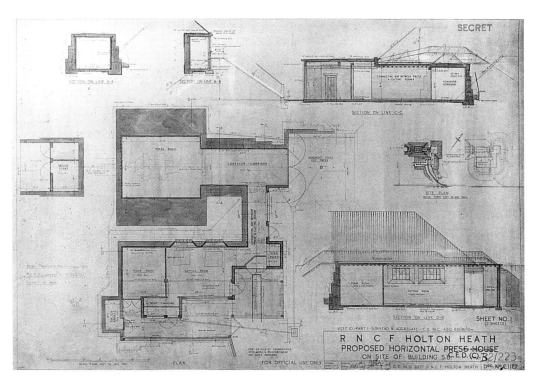

Figure 7.9 RNCF Holton Heath, Dorset. Design drawing of press house for horizontal press as Fig 7.8. (BB94/17027)

source of nitrocellulose, and this trend continued in Europe during the inter-war years to lessen dependence on American cotton supplies.[9] At first paper was simply nitrated in the Nathan-Thomson type nitrating pans (above, Chapter 5), but it tended to pack together with little of the surface exposed to the acids. The solution was to use scrolled paper with the appearance of corrugated cardboard, which ensured that a larger surface area was exposed to the acids. Apart from the provision of a paper store these innovations had little effect on the layout of the factory, although in the nitrating house the circular nitrating pans (Figs 5.12 and 5.13) were replaced by squares ones, each holding four rolls of paper.

Against this background of almost continuous innovation and reconstruction it is difficult to isolate specific changes brought about by the rearmament programme of the mid-1930s. In 1936 large horizontal presses were installed for extruding cordite charges up to 10fiin (0.27m) in diameter (Fig 7.8), for assembly into catapult charges to launch shipboard aircraft. They were housed in press rooms covered by an earth mound, whose associated control, pump, and cutting rooms occupied flimsy timber sheds separated from the press room by a concrete wall (Fig 7.9). The presses at Holton

Heath were supplied by Greenwood and Batley of Leeds, who supplied much of the machinery to the factory at this date.[10]

One of the drawbacks associated with the use of Cordite SC was excessive barrel flash. This could be overcome by the use of picrite or nitroguadine, but this was water soluble and manufacture of flashless cordite also required a return to a solvent-based process. Cordite paste was prepared in the same way as for Cordite SC but was then dried, and in this hazardous form conveyed to the incorporating houses. It was incorporated with picrite and acetone into a paste, and then carbamite and cryolite added. The cordite dough was pressed and then dried in stoves in the north-eastern corner of the factory. In 1937 work started on a Picrite factory at a cost of around £46,000 (Fig 7.10).

Figure 7.10 RNCF Holton Heath, Dorset. Picrite building under construction, showing typical building work of the rearmament period. (Source Lesley Hayward, 215; © MoD)

Figure 7.11 RNCF Holton Heath, Dorset. Picrite drying stove. (Source Lesley Hayward, 470; © MoD)

Figure 7.12 RNCF Holton Heath, Dorset. Field remains of picrite drying stove, cf Fig 7.11. (BB94/17001)

It was approached from a central tramway giving access to all the buildings, which were either set below the surface or surrounded by earthwork traverses. A similar drying method was adopted to that used for cordite SC, whereby warm air was blown into trucks loaded with picrite (Fig 7.11 and 7.12).[11]

Rearmament and the Royal Ordnance Factories (ROF)

In the early 1930s public opinion in Britain was strongly pacifist, rearmament a much-debated political issue, and foreign policy inert. In 1933 Adolf Hitler became Chancellor of Germany; Germany had been rearming secretly for some time, but Hitler now began a programme of open rearmament. In May 1934 the international Disarmament Conference adjourned indefinitely. Britain's rearmament programme of 1935 outlined the overhaul of the RAF and of the Navy, but in comparison neglected the Army, only partly modernising it. Until the Munich Agreement in September 1938

expenditure on defence was constrained by a combination of Treasury control, Parliamentary economies, Opposition distrust, and public opinion; thereafter the economy became geared to war production, with war formally declared on 3 September 1939.[12]

Planning the new programme
(Fig 7.1)

Responsibility for providing technical advice about all aspects of the rearmament programme fell to the Director of Ordnance Factories, a post re-established in 1926.[13] Progressively from 1936, as the programme gathered pace, the senior staff from Waltham Abbey and from the Research Department and filling factories at Woolwich spent increasing amounts of time sitting on technical committees to design modern factories and plant for explosives' manufacture and ammunition filling.[14] As during the Great War, the state factories provided a nucleus of expertise and a cadre of trained staff from which a much expanded national network could be formed. One of the earliest considerations was the relocation of the filling section away from the Royal Arsenal Woolwich. This problem was addressed by the Hacking Committee which met in 1934, but its findings were equally applicable to other war industries. Its principal concern was the threat of aerial bombardment and for this reason it favoured sites in the west of Britain. The subsequent Robinson Committee, reporting in 1936, was tempered by political considerations and emphasised the desirability of locating new factories in economically depressed areas. Other considerations included the necessity for large open sites for the spacing of buildings, good rail communications, water supply, and the provision of an adequate labour supply. The priorities of explosives also had to be balanced against the demands of the armament industries, all of whom were competing for sites, building materials, plant, and labour. The very large level sites needed for explosives manufacture also placed them in direct rivalry with airfields, which had very similar requirements.

Raw materials

Despite changes in manufacturing processes during the inter-war years, Britain still remained heavily reliant on imported raw materials for explosives manufacture. During the Great War pyrites was the principal raw material for sulphuric acid, but traditional sources in Norway were unavailable during the Second World War and Spain was an unreliable source.

Production directly from sulphur became more common, with supplies from Louisiana becoming the principal source. An indigenous supply also became available in 1930 when the ICI plant at Billingham, Stockton-on-Tees, began producing sulphuric acid from anhydrite.[15] It was also an important supplier of synthetic ammonia, which, using the Ostwald process, provided a crucial alternative route to the production of nitric acid.[16] The process was important as it freed nitric manufacture from reliance on imported sodium nitrate, reduced the amounts of sulphuric acid required, and, although technologically more complex, resulted in smaller and more compact units in comparison to the sprawling nitric acid plants of the Great War. Ammonia oxidation plants became the standard method for producing nitric acid in the wartime ROFs (Fig 7.13), though the ROF at Drigg, Cumbria, was also equipped with a stand-by sodium nitrate plant.[17]

The new explosives factories were all equipped with acids sections. All fulfilled four basic functions – manufacturing nitric acid, producing sulphuric acid and oleum, preparing mixed acids and recovering unconsumed acids – but generally only the largest factories such as RNCF Holton Heath and RNPF Caerwent produced their own sulphuric acid. Caerwent was equipped to receive its powdered sulphur from railway hoppers, which discharged their loads from the base of the wagons into the store. At the smaller factories, such as ROF Bridgwater and ROF Drigg, the sulphuric acid was secured from external sources and concentrated to the required strengths.

Salvage of apparently innocuous materials such as bones and paper also provided another source of essential raw materials (Fig 7.14 and 7.15). The exhortation that 'PAPER helps to make MUNITIONS' must have been a puzzling message to many in wartime Britain.

Factory types – propellants manufacture

Waltham Abbey RGPF

In contrast to the ten cordite factories operational in 1914, by 1935 there were just three – Waltham Abbey, Holton Heath, and a section at Ardeer.[18] Construction of a fourth propellants factory at Irvine, reusing the site of a Great War factory, was approved in 1936 and it was operational by January 1939.[19] The problem of their design was also more complex than at the outset of the Great War, as increasing variations of cordites were developed to meet specific propellant needs, for example for cordite rocket motors (see Chapter 8). This had led to an almost total remodelling of the factory at Holton Heath through the 1930s, and although the layout and flowlines of Waltham Abbey appeared little altered a new form of solventless cordite had been introduced here too, Cordite W ('W' for Waltham), using carbamite to gelatinise the cordite paste.[20]

Early in the war, when the output from Waltham Abbey was most needed, it suffered a major disaster, when on 18 January 1940 a cordite Mixing House exploded damaging buildings within a 0.5km radius. Just three months later, with reconstruction work well under way, another cordite Mixing House exploded on 20 April with a similar devastating effect.[21] This resulted in a considerable rebuilding of the process

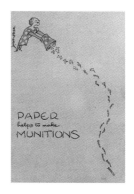

Figure 7.13 ROF Bridgwater, Somerset. Atmospheric oxidation process tanks for the production of weak nitric acid, within an unclad steel-frame structure. To the left the reclad building housing acid concentration towers is visible. (BB93/22236)

Figure 7.14 Wartime poster, 'PAPER helps to make MUNITIONS'. (BB95/11947; © PRO INF3/197)

Figure 7.15 Wartime poster, 'I need BONES for explosives'. (BB95/11946; © PRO INF3/216)

Figure 7.16 RGPF Waltham Abbey, North Site. Cordite mixing house, 1940. (BB92/26213)

Figure 7.17 RGPF Waltham Abbey, North Site. Surveyed plan of New Hill nitroglycerine factory. 1 Charge house; 2 Nitrator; 3 Wash house; 4 Mixing house; 5 Wash-water settling house; 6 Flume house. (© Crown copyright. NMR)

buildings around the Edmonsey nitroglycerine factory. The two devastated circular mixing houses were rebuilt as circular buildings on new sites to the east, while two mixing houses in reused gunpowder buildings rendered unusable by collateral damage were demolished. The one alongside Newton's Pool was rebuilt on its existing site (Fig 7.16), while the second in a reused Press House was moved to the opposite side of a newly dug canal. Construction work around this date was characterised by the

use of timber-framed buildings clad and lined in asbestos sheets and roofed in corrugated asbestos, and by revetment walls constructed from breeze block. Freestanding breeze block traverses, sometimes earth backed, were also positioned around the area to mitigate the effects of any further accidents.

The investigating committee into the April explosion recommended that an additional nitroglycerine factory should be constructed. The site chosen was on 29.7 acres (12ha) of farmland to the east of the factory. Its situation on gently falling ground towards Cornmill Stream was ideal for a traditional gravity-fed layout, which could also be planned without the constraints of earlier activity (Fig 7.17). Work on the new plant, known as New Hill, began in late 1940 and by August 1941 the buildings were ready for fitting out.[22] As a unit it was self-contained, with its own pump house, transformer station, shifting room, and transport section. Each process building was served by a separate plenum heater house to supply warm air. It was intended that the acids and wash waters would be piped from the acid factory lying along the western perimeter of North Site and an above-ground pipeline, 1805ft (550m) in length, was laid across the site. Waste acids were to be run back for reprocessing. Raised on a concrete platform above the mound of the nitrating house was the charge house containing storage tanks for the nitric and sulphuric acid, glycerine, and the wash waters, which were run down by gravity into the nitrating house and then on into the other process buildings. Dry guncotton for mixing was brought from the weighing house on the opposite side of Cornmill Stream by tramway forming a new line brought across the stream on a Bailey bridge. Although the production flow within the plant might therefore be understood by analogy with other plants, what the field evidence alone cannot reveal is the type of nitration technology in use. Mr Stanley Thomas, a wartime employee of the Woolwich Research Department, believes that a Biazzi continuous nitrate plant was installed similar to the one in use at Woolwich. In the event, the plant was evidently never put into production. It might

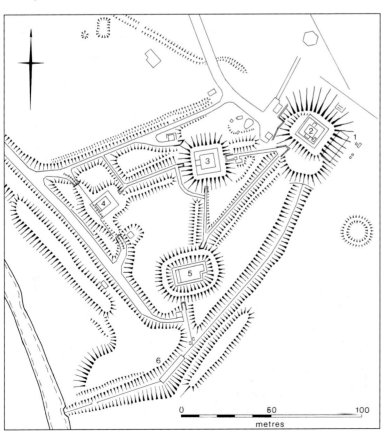

0   50   100
metres

be that events overtook its commissioning as new plants became operational elsewhere and brought an end to nitroglycerine production at Waltham Abbey in September 1943.[23]

New propellants factories at ROF Bishopton, ROF Wrexham, RNPF Caerwent and ROF Ranskill
(Table 7.2)

The outmoded and vulnerable factory at Waltham Abbey had long been recognised as inadequate to meet the requirements of any future war. Its lack of rail communications and the restructuring of the munitions industry left it geographically isolated. In 1937 approval was given for the construction of a new cordite factory to replace it, to be sited at Bishopton near Glasgow. Factors which favoured this location included the desire to alleviate unemployment, an abundant supply of good quality process water and an equable climate for nitroglycerine manufacture.[24] The perimeter fence at Bishopton enclosed 1910 acres (773ha) and, with 1500 buildings and a peak workforce of 20,000, it was one of the largest explosives factories. Within it were two distinct cordite manufacturing units, separately approved in 1937 and January 1939, to guard against loss by enemy action or accidental explosions. The first was in operation by March 1940. It was later expanded to operate as three factories to manufacture

solvent-based and solventless cordite, solventless and rocket cordite, and solvent-based cordite respectively. In contrast to the regimented layout of Holton Heath, Bishopton extended over the local rolling topography and full use was made of pre-existing belts of coniferous trees to break up the factory's outlines. Local eminences were typically selected for the siting of the nitroglycerine factories, three of which supplied each production unit. But in other respects it followed many of the features of the remodelled Holton Heath factory, including the layout of the nitrocellulose sections and in the use of Schmid-type continuous nitration plants, though here surrounded by a standard form of traverse. In the cordite production areas drying was similarly carried out with warm air blown through wagons parked in sidings. The total cost of the factory was £17.1 million.[25]

Table 7.2 Summary of explosive factory costs and first production dates, after Hornby 1958, 118

	Final cost £m	Date of first production
Propellant factories		
Bishopton	17.1	June 1940
Wrexham	10.9	March 1941
Ranskill	4.4	March 1942
Explosives factories		
Irvine	2.1	March 1939
Pembrey	2.9	November 1939
Drigg	2.5	April 1941
Sellafield	2.5	March 1943
Bridgwater	5.7	August 1941

Figure 7.18 ROF Wrexham, Clwyd. Cordite factory 1941. (RAF vertical air photograph, Sortie 106G/UK/1454 frame 4124. 2 May 1946; © MoD)

Figure 7.19 ROF Wrexham, Clwyd. Air photograph showing the former interconnected building of a nitrocellulose section adapted to new uses by 1970. The process (Table 7.1) probably worked from left to right, with a paper store at the extreme left leading to the paper scrolling room, then the nitrating room (large vented building), the stabilisation vats and on to the potchers, pulp-beating and blending rooms. (MAL/70015 frame 034, 25 March 1970, Library number 6959, © Reserved)

Figure 7.20 (right) RNPF Caerwent, Gwent. Western acids area from east. (© RCAHMW, 965074–54)

The second new cordite factory was approved in August 1939 and was sited at Marchwiel, west of Wrexham. This massive factory (Fig 7.18), which covered around 1730 acres (700ha) was built over relatively level farmland but was cut in two by the river Clywedog. Again, pre-existing field boundaries and woodland were left in an attempt to break up its outline. This siting was primarily governed by relief of local unemployment but it also fulfilled the other criteria of remoteness from the continent and good railway communications to the ROF filling factories in South Wales and the west of England. The cordite section was served by three nitroglycerine factories, and apparently two large nitrocellulose sections (Fig 7.19).[26] Two smaller and inter-connected mounded units in the south-western section of the factory perhaps represent a tetryl nitration plant.

In South Wales, the large new Royal Naval Propellant Factory was built to the north of the Roman town of Caerwent (Fig 7.20). This was selected from a choice of four sites. One of the deciding factors was the assured water supply from the Great Western Railway Severn tunnel pumphouse, which produced 7.5 million gallons (34,095,000 litres) of water per day. The 1977 acre (800ha) factory was situated in open farmland with relatively few houses and a natural fall at its rear, ideal for the construction of a nitroglycerine factory. The total cost was £7.2m, of which £4.7 million was spent on the buildings and roads, and £2.5 million on plant.[27]

RNPF Caerwent was intended to supplement the production of naval cordite and provide a reserve unit in the event of RNCF Holton Heath being put out of action. It was closely modelled on the RNCF Holton Heath and designed by the staff of the RNCF and the Admiralty's consulting engineers, Freeman, Fox, and Partners of London, who had designed Holton Heath a generation earlier.[28] The production areas for solventless cordites were directly comparable with those at Holton Heath but were able to conform to a more logical layout on this greenfield site. Its nitroglycerine factory followed the Holton Heath model. In it a Schmid continuous nitration plant was installed and the link between the weighing house and the mixing houses was also by an asphalt trackway. A feature of wartime factory design was the duplication of essential plant (see below, Passive Air Defence). The factory at Caerwent was no exception, as it was laid out as two principal units, each designed to produce 75 tons (76.2 tonnes) of cordite per week. The central services area including administrative buildings, search rooms, canteens, laboratories, and transit sheds was shared between the two units; production areas to the west and east, however, were almost self-contained. Each unit had its own power house supplied by rail with coal to generate steam heat and electricity. Despite the close links with Holton Heath, RNPF Caerwent was built to utilitarian wartime designs and shares few similarities even with the late 1930s buildings at the Dorset factory.

The last cordite factory to be built during the Second World War was at Ranskill in Nottinghamshire. It was the only one in England and was a relatively small plant covering some 494 acres (200ha; Fig 7.21).

Despite its almost complete loss by landscaping and the absence of an inventory of building functions, a clear understanding of the site's functioning may be reconstructed by analogy with building layouts elsewhere, in particular those at Holton Heath. To the north of the principal east to west road lay the buildings of the acid factory, a number of which remain incorporated into a derelict pre-stressed concrete works (Fig 7.22). To their east the distinctive interconnected buildings of a nitrocellulose plant were arranged as a double unit. In the southern corner of the factory the two-unit nitroglycerine factory was laid out on the high ground within the site formerly equipped with a Schmid continuous nitration plant. Arranged to its north, a logical pattern of buildings corresponds to the manufacturing flow for cordite. These include mixing houses, and adjacent to these, paste sheet drying houses surrounded by tear-shaped earthwork traverses, and, beyond these, the characteristic long rectangular rolling houses, their presence probably revealing the manufacture of Cordite SC. The remainder of the manufacturing processes were carried out in the small buildings to the west. Despite the provision of twin nitrocellulose and nitroglycerine factories, the advantages of doubling these facilities was diminished by their juxtaposition.

Among the most distinctive buildings in these explosives factories were those of the acids sections. They were the tallest, often standing three or four storeys high, though internally they were open to the roof, which might be vented by large circular metal vents typical of buildings of this date or by a louvred clerestory (Fig 7.20). Their function was to house the tall acid towers used in the concentration of sulphuric acid or denitrification of spent acids. These towers were supported by a massive steel framework, passing through its successive platforms. Crane gantries were also fitted for the periodic maintenance of the plant. The towers at this date were still composed of interlinked earthenware segments. Fragments of quartz or pottery Raschig rings used to pack these towers often litter their sites. In their simplest form they consisted of a steel framework clad in corrugated iron

as at ROF Bridgwater. Another form of steel-framed building survives at the wartime ROFs at Wrexham and Ranskill (Fig 7.22); here they are steel-framed with a brick infill. At Wrexham the building was roofed by a flat concrete slab while at Ranskill a standard A-frame truss covered with corrugated iron sheeting was employed. Floors were acid-resistant bricks. At RNPF Caerwent the steel frame was entirely concealed by a brick skin. Other plant within the acid sections, including towers, storage tanks, and timber-framed Bradford water coolers, remained exposed to the elements.

Characteristically the nitrocellulose or guncotton sections can be recognised as groups of large, single-storey buildings

Figure 7.21 ROF Ranskill, Nottinghamshire. Cordite factory 1942, photographed in 1954. (RAF vertical air photograph, Sortie 542/63 frame 0200 F22, 12 Oct 1954; © MoD)

Figure 7.22 ROF Ranskill, Nottinghamshire. One of the remaining buildings of the acids section, with large vents characteristic of factories of this period. (BB94/17439)

interconnected by covered corridors, following the model established at Holton Heath and Gretna during the Great War (Fig 7.19). The plan form of the nitroglycerine sections can also readily be identified, those at Wrexham sharing the same configuration as New Hill at Waltham Abbey (Fig 7.17). Other features which can be distinguished included embanked truck drying stoves, and the distinctive cordite rolling houses with projecting porches on each corner and large roof vents built at Caerwent and Ranskill betray a clear familial resemblance with those at Holton Heath (Fig 7.4). The functions of other buildings in the process areas of explosives factories are less easy to identify. Many were single-storey brick buildings with flat concrete roofs. Because of the hazardous processes, most were mounded and usually housed a restricted number of operations.

Trade factories and overseas production

To supplement the output of the ROFs, three new propellant factories were built in Dumfriesshire – at Dalbeattie, Dumfries itself, and at Powfoot – where single-base nitrocellulose propellants were manufactured.[29] They were built at government expense but were managed as agency factories by ICI; between January 1942 and June 1945 they produced around one-third of the cordite manufactured in Britain.[30] Differences in building forms between this group and the state factories result mainly from their concentration on single-base propellants, like the contemporary USA trade factories, rather than the double- or triple-base products of the ROFs and RNPFs. Though none has any architectural pretensions, resemblances in these utilitarian buildings show that they lay outside the responsibility of the ROF design office, their use of oversailing concrete roofs being one of the most noticeable features (Fig 7.23). Powfoot was a coastal site on the Solway Firth; its range of plant reflected the distinctive manufacturing process for nitrocellulose powders. Nitrocellulose in a wet state was received 'and the production process was h ly d ndent on the use of solvents in its uel .on and gelatinisation.

A feature of this factory was, therefore, a large solvents area devoted to preparing and handling ethyl alcohol, which was supplied in sealed railway tanks, and ethyl ether, which was manufactured on site (Fig 7.24). Other features of the plant included Baker Perkins incorporators and vertical presses, some dating from the Great War. After pressing and cutting the propellant was moved to drying and steeping houses, initially to remove remaining solvents and secondly excess moisture.[31]

Explosives supply to British forces was also partly met by factories overseas. Canada and America supplied Britain directly both with raw materials and finished explosives, while Allied forces in the Far East were equipped by government factories in India and Australia. In practice, Australian government factories adopted or modified recent developments in Britain. In 1935 the Maribyrnong cordite factory, established in 1910,

Figure 7.23 Powfoot, Dumfries and Galloway. Press house at ICI agency factory. (© RCAHMS, C37542)

Figure 7.24 Powfoot, Dumfries and Galloway. Recovered alcohol section at ICI agency factory, with still house in the background. (© RCAHMS, C37544)

began to manufacture the naval propellant, cordite SC, based on the wet mix process developed at Holton Heath. At the Albion explosives factory on the outskirts of Melbourne, laid out 1939–41, a combination of accepted Australian and British practice was followed, but in buildings with overhanging verandas typical of Indian explosives factories. The nitroglycerine factory followed Holton Heath in using hand-pushed vehicles running in asphalt grooves to move liquid nitroglycerine from the weighing house to the mixing houses. The nitroglycerine plant was of the Nathan-Thomson-Rintoul batch-production type, however, rather than the more up-to-date continuous nitration process. The Australian factories were heavily dependent on British plant, including large horizontal cordite presses manufactured by Greenwood and Batley of Leeds and cordite incorporators by Baker Perkins of Peterborough.[32]

Factory types – high explosives manufacture

(Table 7.2)

TNT

Britain's capacity to manufacture high explosives was just as run-down in the inter-war years as propellants manufacture. New state factories were required and their siting followed the principles of the other strategic industries by locating them in the west of Britain.

By bulk, TNT was the most important requirement, but, as in the Great War, it was usually diluted with ammonium nitrate to form amatol. The TNT plants were the smallest of the RO factories and seldom occupied more than 300 acres (121.4ha). The largest and earliest was at Pembrey, which included facilities for manufacturing ammonium nitrate and tetryl. More typically, ammonium nitrate was acquired commercially or through agency factories. Unusually this factory, approved in 1937, reused the site of a Great War explosives factory. Indeed the existence of the Great War water works was decisive in its choice; the only other notable survival were the administration buildings which had been used as a convalescent home for the children

of unemployed miners. In the new layout, the central office, police barracks, canteen, surgery, library, and administration buildings were grouped around its entrance. Away from this grouping, raw material stores, acid factory, nitration buildings, and magazines were laid out in a logical manner to follow the production flow. Buildings within the factory were linked by an extensive rail network, and it was connected to the Paddington to Fishguard mainline by two branch lines.[33]

A second TNT factory was approved in August 1939 at Drigg in Cumbria (Fig 7.25) and after the outbreak of the war two more were added, mainly to provide explosives for the heavy bomber offensive against Germany. That at Sellafield was an ROF and the second, perhaps at Dumfries, was an agency factory managed by ICI.[34] Unusually a TNT plant was also installed at the agency propellant factory at Powfoot.

The later TNT factories all followed a standardised plan, well exemplified at Drigg (Fig 7.25), with plant designed for the same maximum output. The workforces in the

Figure 7.25 ROF Drigg, Cumbria. TNT factory 1941, photographed in 1947. (RAF vertical air photograph, Sortie CPE/UK 1940 frame 4003, 18 Jan 1947; © MoD)

209

high explosives factories were relatively small and rarely exceeded 2000.[35] They were chosen as fairly level, open sites, with an assured water supply, which was essential; at Drigg it was piped from Wastwater over six miles away. A coastal location also provided for the minimum of site preparation, a ready supply of material for construction of traverses, and a convenient dump for the untreated acidic effluent. The sites at Sellafield and Drigg were almost self-selecting as the only open sites free from the threat of mining subsidence in Cumbria. Plant design followed the Great War continuous nitration process redeveloped at Woolwich and Waltham Abbey during the early 1930s.

RDX

At the outbreak of war, RDX – that is Research Department Composition X or 'Cyclonite', chemically cyclo-trimthylene-trinitramine – was a recently developed high explosive, whose production was restricted to pilot plants at Waltham Abbey and the Research Department at the Royal Arsenal Woolwich. In August 1939 a site was chosen for an industrial-scale RDX production plant at Puriton to the north of Bridgwater. Lying on the edge of the Somerset Levels, it offered the advantage of level ground with the minimum of ground preparation, although it suffered from poor drainage. The river Huntspell was dredged to the north of the site to provide a reservoir of water for the factory, with the additional benefit of improved drainage for the North Somerset Levels. The factory covered 700 acres (283.3ha), divided into uneven quadrants (Fig 7.26). In an attempt to conceal its outline from the air, a pre-existing droveway and drains and hedgerows were incorporated by the factory plan. It was linked by a short spur to the Great Western Railway mainline, with extensive exchange sidings along its western side. Transport within the factory was by narrow-gauge line and

Figure 7.26 ROF Bridgwater, Somerset. Photographed in 1995; to the right (north) are reed beds used to filter nitrates from the spent acid section waters, in the background the disused railway spur to the main line cut by the M5 motorway. (NMR 15306/56)

movement of materials between the two systems was managed through transit sheds. At the entrance to the factory (Fig 7.26 left) are the search rooms, administrative buildings, and factory laboratory. Dominating the central section is the acids section, with a formaldehyde plant adjacent to it. Ammonia when treated with formaldehyde produces hexamine, which is then nitrated to produce RDX. The northern section of the factory which housed these processes was originally divided into duplicate units to guard against accidental loss or bomb damage.

Tetryl

In the early years of the war the old and improvised tetryl plant on North Site at Waltham Abbey (see Chapter 6) played a vital role, since the only other tetryl plant in operation at this time was at Holton Heath. Repurification of tetryl dating from the Great War had continued there until 1935, and in that year the newer tetryl plant, mothballed since 1918, was brought into production (Fig 6.18).[36] In June 1940 these facilities were expanded at their southern

end with the construction of a new store, four drying stoves (Figs 7.27a and b; 12 in Fig 6.18), a number of small ancillary buildings, and linking tramways. So important was this plant that it was the last section of Waltham Abbey RGPF to close.[37] Manufacture of this important intermediary explosive was later established at Bishopton, Bridgwater, Caerwent, and Pembrey, but with around 16% of the war's output also produced by ICI agency factories.[38]

Factory types – filling factories

A technocratic approach

The filling factory system which had evolved during the Great War had been quickly dismantled at the end of that war. The core of filling activities had reverted to the Royal Arsenal Woolwich and the naval armament depots, with the factory at Hereford (Fig 6.26) retained on a care and maintenance basis. In planning the new munitions factories, the ROF organisation was challenged with designing some of the largest industrial undertakings in the United Kingdom. Indeed, at the height of war production in 1942 not only were the ROFs the largest group of factories, but of the 12 factories in the country employing more than 19,000 people seven were ROFs.[39] The number of people employed in the filling factories rose from just 800 at Woolwich and Hereford in 1936 to over 150,000 in 20 factories by 1943.[40]

Great War munitions factories were some of the earliest to adopt modern ideas about the organisation of factories and plant to correspond to the production flow and about splitting the manufacturing process into a series of semi-skilled or unskilled tasks, but each was left to local or individual initiative (Chapter 6). In the new filling factories a technocratic approach was applied, with all planning centralised on skilled staff of the Engineering Department (Filling) at Woolwich and a high degree of standardisation and unity of design across different factories. Planning began well before the outbreak of hostilities, and this allowed a measured expansion (Table 7.3).

Figure 7.27a RGPF Waltham Abbey, North Site. Tetryl drying stoves, built in June 1940 and formerly served by narrow-gauge railway with a spur passing into each stove. (BB92/26117)

Figure 7.27b RGPF Waltham Abbey, North Site. Interior of tetryl drying stove (Fig 7.27a). Drying lockers fill the right-hand wall; note the traces of the narrow-gauge line in the floor, toe-board marking division between dirty (left) and clean (right) areas, pegs for clothing and step for donning magazine shoes before crossing the boundary. (BB92/26118)

Table 7.3 Construction of the Filling Factories, after Hornby 1958, 101 and PRO CAB102/273.

factory	final cost £m	approved
No 1 Chorley	13.14	1936
No 2 Bridgend	9.58	1937
No 3 Glascoed	6.30	1937
No 5 Swynnerton	13.60	May 1939
No 6 Risley	13.39	by end 1939
No 7 Kirkby	8.63	by end 1939
No 8 Thorpe Arch	5.95	March 1940
No 9 Aycliffe	6.64	March 1940

Note: Filling Factory No 4 was the former Great War factory at Hereford

It was originally envisaged that Woolwich would be responsible for the design and construction of all the filling factories, but in August 1939 it was thought desirable to interpose an agent between the designers and contractors. In consequence, His Majesty's Office of Works was responsible for seven, the consulting engineers Sir Alexander Gibbs and Partners for six, and Rendel, Palmer, and Tritton for just one factory, that at Queniborough in Leicestershire.[41]

The factories were planned with scientific precision. At a primary level, their number was matched to the needs of the services, based on the number of projected divisions in the field force along with naval and RAF requirements. Then, the composition of these forces and estimated expenditure rates determined the variety of ammunition types and the total amounts required. With this information the Engineering Department (Filling) could begin work on the design of a factory. Ideally all filling factories were planned on a playing card shape but might vary to accommodate the local topography. Within them, operations were classified into eight main production groups (Table 7.4). The overall size of a factory could be assessed through the estimated load of Group 8, tasked with filling the main charge. With a predicted load within any particular group

Table 7.4 Summary of group functions, after PRO CAB102/630.

Group 1	**Initiators** – very sensitive includes cap filling, detonators required for primers and fuzes, primer and tracer filling.
Group 2	**Fuze Magazines** – pellets, exploder pellets, exploder bags includes powdered TNT and tetryl.
Group 3	**Fuze filling** – Includes pressing of time ring fuzes, filling of time and percussion fuzes and assembly of detonators produced on Group 1 and fuze magazines made on Group 2.
Group 4	**Gunpowder** – Blending of blackpowder of delay and time fuzes.
Group 4a	Only gunpowder handled, pressed into small pellets, used to link flash from the detonator with the powder in the delay mechanism and to the main magazine, filling of gunpowder into cloth bags for insertion into cartridges, the link between the primer and the main cordite charge.
Group 5	**Cartridge work** – Takes components from other groups for assembly and issues completed work.
	i) Filling cordite into cloth bags for breech loaders
	ii) Filling cordite into brass cartridges for separate loading ammunition
	iii) Filling cordite into brass cartridges for complete rounds
	iv) Cordite rocket assembly
Group 6	**Smoke producing compositions** – and tracer filling
Group 7	**Small arms filling** – subdivided into six groups A–F depending on type
Group 8	**Filling of main charge into shells or bombs** – High Explosives received, mixed and put into the shell or bomb; work is of a heavier nature, including grenade filling.
Group 9	**Filled storage magazines**
Group 10	**Infrastructure including Workshops & Proof range** – subdivided in groups A–R

it was possible to produce a statement of the explosive expense magazines, empty components stores, empty box stores, filling shops, and filled transit sheds required by that group. This in turn allowed the number of operatives to be allocated to a group and a schedule of the ancillary buildings including shifting houses, clocking stations, canteens, rest rooms, latrines, administrative buildings, and air-raid shelters to be calculated. With this information, the next stage was to produce a 'cut-out' of every building surrounded by a scaled circle representing the intra-factory or danger building distance. From these a 'pin-out' was produced with each building positioned according to the production flow, but in such a way that the circle of any building did not enclose another building. The plans of the projected groups could then be placed together to ensure a safe and efficient flow between groups, and the ancillary infrastructure could be added. Production experience at Woolwich itself had also shown that the safety distances between buildings particularly in Groups 1 and 5 could be safely cut, with a commensurate saving in factory area and materials.

A further factor in the planning of the new factories was the 1937 Factories Act. This set down new standards for conditions in factories, with regular provision for cleaning, washing, and painting. It also required reasonable working temperatures, adequate ventilation and light, whether artificial or natural, and for factories to be provided with 'sanitary conveniences', with separation according to sex, proper washing facilities, and areas to accommodate clothing. In the design and layout of machinery, it required all flywheels and transmission systems to be fenced or arranged in such a way as to present no danger. Crown factories were not exempt from this Act, though they might be freed from its provisions in a state of emergency. In their design the new ROFs met all these criteria. To the influx of wartime workers in the industry, used to the constant danger and dirt of coal mining, the grime of the potteries, or the incessant noise of the textile mills, the new ROFs epitomised the advantages of modern factory design in improving the working environment and welfare provision.

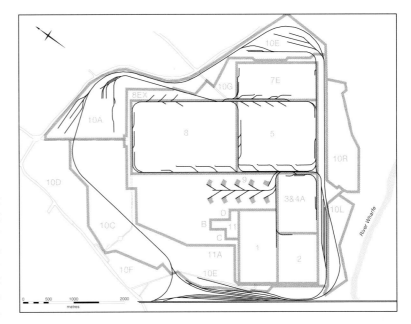

Internally the factories were divided by a grid road system between the production groups and these in turn were divided by a grid of smooth, gritless asphalt cleanways connecting the buildings (Fig 7.28). Each group within the factory formed a self-contained unit, with workers rarely moving between groups. Their typical arrangement was for one side of the group to be occupied by group offices and male and female shifting rooms, the second by explosive expense magazines, the third by empty components, and the fourth by filled ammunition stores, with the process buildings in the centre.

Figure 7.28 ROF Thorpe Arch, West Yorkshire. Block diagram illustrating the arrangement of production groups (based on Royal Ordnance plan).

Figure 7.29 ROF Chorley, Lancashire. Interior of shifting room. (AA93/5842)

This inner core of each group was usually classified as a clean, or danger, area, and all workers and visitors passed through a shifting room (Fig 7.29). Here workers changed into their buttonless and pocketless clothing and rubber safety shoes, leaving behind all contraband metal items before being searched and stepping over a toeboard into the clean area (see also Fig 7.27b). Components and explosives entering the group through the expense magazines and transit sheds passed from the dirty into the clean area, within which materials were moved about on small electric trolleys or 'dillies', or in the case of small explosive components might be carried by hand along the cleanways, these carriers having right of way. Within the later filling factories the magazines were set obliquely to the production groups in a characteristic way to lessen the effects of blast between buildings. Despite these common principles of factory form, no two production groups had identical plan forms, as the calculated throughput of individual factories varied or different types of ammunition were assembled.

Construction

In their construction the filling factories absorbed prodigious amounts of resources funded entirely by the state. ROF Chorley in Lancashire (Fig 7.30) took three years to build with a peak workforce of 15,000, using 20 million bricks, 15,000 steel window frames, half a million yards of steel

Figure 7.30 ROF Chorley, Lancashire from west. (NMR 12920/51)

reinforcing, and 10,000 tons (10,160 tonnes) of constructional steel. Concrete for the operation was supplied from the centre of the site by means of a mixer 120ft (36.5m) high, from which buckets suspended on cables delivered concrete to the place required at the rate of 5000 tons (5080 tonnes) per day.[42] The main building contractors at Chorley were Sir Lindsay Parkinson and Co, who from their base in Blackpool later built ROF Risley in Cheshire; other well-known firms included Bovis Ltd and Mowlem Ltd, who worked together to construct ROF Swynnerton in Staffordshire. Each also employed many subcontractors.[43]

The first of the new filling factories (Table 7.3) at Chorley, Bridgend in Bridgend UA, and Glascoed in Monmouthshire, in addition to the re-activated factory at Hereford, were conceived from 1936 to replace the filling capacity at Woolwich. The choice of South Wales for two of them arose from a deliberate policy to attempt to alleviate unemployment by siting rearmament in areas of high unemployment.[44] Despite the prospect of work which it brought to a Britain emerging from depression, this was one of the most contentious issues in the 1935 general election and was strongly opposed by many in the Labour movement, including Stafford Cripps.[45] The imposition of these large factories on the landscape, involving compulsory purchase and destruction of farmland, also had its critics. In the case of a proposed filling factory at Oswestry, the Ministry of Agriculture and the Council for the Protection of Rural England successfully lobbied against its construction.[46] The next phase of filling factory construction began with ROF Swynnerton, approved in May 1939, followed by factories at Risley (Cheshire) and Kirkby in Merseyside initiated after the declaration of war on 3 September 1939. In the siting of Thorpe Arch in West Yorkshire and Aycliffe in Durham in March 1940 the policy of locating in 'safe areas' was outweighed by targeting fresh sources of labour.

Unlike the Great War factories, these large new sites, some over 1235 acres (500ha), were designed to fill a variety of munitions, and all eight of the new factories

comprised between five and seven production groups (Table 7.5). A large factory such as Swynnerton had 1245 individual buildings while a medium-sized one such as Thorpe Arch had 619. They were rarely dedicated to providing the needs of one service and, with the standardisation of weapons, most served all three service arms. Nevertheless, in some there was greater emphasis on one particular service, and this might be overtly acknowledged and used to focus morale: Swynnerton's production for the RAF was recognised in the factory motto, *Per ardua ad victoriam*. The period of the 'phoney war' between September 1939 and the Battle of Britain in summer 1940 was critical in establishing these new factories, allowing Swynnerton, for example, to play a vital role in the supply of incendiary bullets for the Battle of Britain, with RAF lorries queuing to take supplies off the ends of the production lines to the fighter airfields in the south of England.[47] This factory alone filled an estimated 1000 million rounds between 1940 and November 1944.[48] Glascoed specialised in the assembly of naval cartridges and shells, including shellite filling; and the satellite to ROF Bridgend at Brackla in Bridgend UA functioned as a Royal Naval Armaments Depot, including a small fuze powder group.[49]

The failure of the Luftwaffe's air offensive and the perceived lessening of this threat as German forces became bogged down in Russia allowed the planners to redefine the safe areas and look further afield for labour pools to staff the new filling factories. The last group of six filling factories (Table 7.6) at Elstow in Bedfordshire), Walsall in West Midlands Metropolitan County, Burghfield in West Berkshire, Queniborough in Leicestershire, Ruddington in Nottinghamshire, and Featherstone in Staffordshire came into production between February and August 1942. They differed from the earlier factories in being smaller, with a restricted number of production groups to meet specific requirements (Table 7.5). Burghfield was the largest with a peak labour force of 3400; the others rarely exceeded 1000. The problem of creating local management teams to run these new factories, after the first group of factories

Table 7.5 Summary of groups present at all filling factories

no	factories					groups						
1.	Chorley	1	–	3	4	5	–	–	8	9	10	
2.	Bridgend	1	2 2a	3	4	5	6	7	–	–	10	
3.	Glascoed	1	–	–	4	5	6	–	8	9	10	Proof
4	Hereford	–	–	–	–	–	–	–	8	9	10	
5.	Swynnerton	1	2	–	4	–	6	7	8	9	10	Proof
6.	Risley	Information deficient										
7.	Kirkby	?1	2	–	4a	5	6	–	8	9	10	
8.	Thorpe Arch	1	2	3	4	5	–	7	8	9	10	Proof
9.	Aycliffe	–	–	–	–	?5	–	–	?8	9	10	
10.	Queniborough	–	–	–	–	–	–	–	8	9	10	
11.	Brackla	–	–	–	4	–	–	–	–	–	10	
12.	Tutbury	Not built										
13.	Chelford	Not built										
14.	Ruddington	–	2	–	–	–	6	7	8	9	10	
15.	Walsall	–	–	–	–	–	–	–	–	9	10	
16.	Elstow	–	–	–	–	5	–	–	8	9	10	Proof
17.	Featherstone	1	–	–	–	5	–	–	8	9	10	
18.	Burghfield	–	–	–	–	–	–	?7	–	9	10	
19.	Wootton Bassett	Not built										
20.	Northampton	Not built										

[1] Thorpe Arch and perhaps Brackla also had Group 11, of unknown function.

Table 7.6 Summary of the later filling factories, after PRO CAB 102/627, 13

factory	construction began	production began	managing agents	requirements
No 10 Queniborough	Jan 1941	April 1942	Unilevers	Fuzes & detonators
No 14 Ruddington	Dec 1940	June 1942	Co-Op Wholesale	Bombs
No 15 Walsall	Dec 1940	Dec 1940	Metal Closures	Phosphorous & smoke
No 16 Elstow	Dec 1940	Feb 1942	Lyons	Cartridges HE & bombs
No 17 Featherstone	Nov 1940	April 1942	Courtaulds	PIAT & caps
No 18 Burghfield	Nov 1940	Aug 1942	Imperial Tobacco	20mm Oerlikon

had absorbed the majority of pre-war ROF-trained personnel, was met by using agency companies (Table 7.6). Although none of them had previous experience of munitions manufacturing, they could offer trained management and administrative teams familiar with handling large workforces and mass production. Schemes for a further four factories already planned for Kirklington, Wootton Bassett, Macclesfield, and Tutbury were cut. Four of what were termed 'assisted factories' were established, two in under-used confectionery factories at York and at Bournville in Birmingham, a third in a disused mill at Healey Hall near Rochdale in Greater Manchester to act as a satellite of Chorley for filling trench mortar ammunition, and the fourth at Fereneze in Renfrewshire. Seven factories were also built specialising in the manufacture and filling of small arms ammunition at Blackpole in Worcestershire, Capenhurst and Radway Green in Cheshire, Hirwaun in Rhondda, Cynon, Taff UA, Spennymoor in Durham, Steeton in West Yorkshire, and Yeading near Hayes in London.[50]

At ROF Featherstone there were three production groups within the factory, namely Groups 1, 5, and 8 for filling PIAT anti-tank shells and caps, while Group 8 probably also undertook bomb filling. Here, aerial photographs reveal empty traverses only a year after the end of the war, suggesting that it may have been left unfinished as hostilities drew to a close.[51] Elstow in Bedfordshire, authorised in late 1940 and managed by the ice-cream and cake makers J Lyons and Co Ltd, was small at some 371 acres (150ha) (Fig 7.31).[52] The production area had a Group 5 and a Group 8 complex, with an area of unoccupied ground between them, perhaps intended for future expansion. Production began in February 1942 filling trench mortar bombs with 20/80 amatol; by the summer the pellet, high explosives, and cordite groups were also in operation. The pellet and cordite groups were relatively short-lived and closed in spring 1943; the buildings of the latter were soon converted for shell reconditioning and the storage of ammunition components and machine tools. 'In ten thousand years it is very likely that somebody will come along and excavate the ruins of Elstow rather as we now excavate the ruins of Egypt and Pompeii. They will piece together a pattern buried by earth, and they will try to decide what that strange town-like plan of roads and buildings was for, and if it had a name. They will wonder and guess and give their verdict perhaps, before the learned societies of the day.' (H E Bates, *The tinkers of Elstow*). As the war entered a new phase with the heavy bomber offensive against Germany, the bomb unit in Group 8 became particularly important (Fig 7.32).

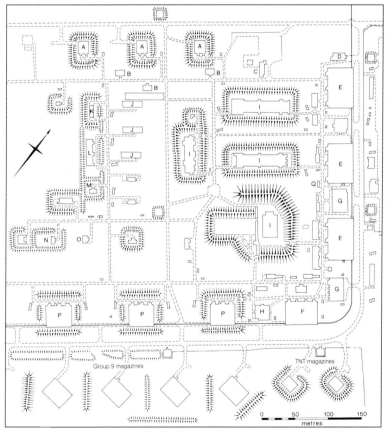

Figure 7.31 (top) NFF no 16 Elstow, Bedfordshire. Begun in December 1940, photographed 1962: 1 Hostels and canteens; 2 Administration, Police headquarters and barracks; 3 Workshop group; 4 Group 5 filling; 5 Group 8 filling; 6 Group 9 magazines. (RAF vertical air photograph, Sortie 58/5517 frame 0182 F21, 18 Oct 1962; © MoD)

Figure 7.32 NFF no 16 Elstow, Bedfordshire. Reconstruction of Group 8 functions (based on OS, Plan TL 0444, 1.2500, 1975; OS, Plan TL 0544, 1.2500, 1975): A TNT expense magazines; B Empty-box stores; C Ammonium nitrate crushing; D Garage; E Transit-in, empty-shell store; F Transit-in, empty-box store; G Shifting houses; H Canteen; I Group 8 filling houses; J Pellet pressing; K Tetryl crystal sifting; L Wrapping and pasting; M Varnishing bay; N Dry varnish; O Compressor; P Transit-out; Q Bath house; Unidentified buildings blank, air raid shelters green.

It pioneered the filling of the 4000lb (1814.4kg) 'blockbuster' bomb, and during the course of the war filled 24,225 of them, along with smaller bombs and naval mines. A distinctive feature of the factories filling large bombs were the cooling pits into which the bombs were lowered to allow their hot mixed contents to cool.

In addition to the Royal Ordnance organisation, a number of private contractors were engaged in filling work, including the Nobel Explosives Company Limited on behalf of the Air Ministry. The specialised factory facilities required for manufacturing and filling mustard gas munitions were met by Ministry of Supply factories at Randle in Cheshire and Rhydymwyn in Flintshire, both of which also contained small explosives areas for the final assembly of the weapons, complete with fuzes and bursting charges.[53]

The buildings of the filling factories

Each group had a characteristic range of building types. Some buildings were standard within all the groups, including shifting rooms, supervisor's offices, air-raid shelters, and transit sheds. Although each of the groups specialised in one part of the manufacturing process, a keynote of the buildings' design was flexibility. It was recognised that the needs of the armed forces would change as new types of munitions were developed and as the military campaign entered new phases. Where safety allowed, open workshops were preferred so that new internal layouts could be organised to meet changing demands (Fig 7.33).

In most groups the filling buildings at their centre were not traversed, though the group's expense magazines and filled ammunition stores were. The exception to this rule was Group 8 (main charge filling), where all the buildings were usually traversed. Of the smaller buildings, many were gabled, with light metal roof-ties, designed to lift if there was an internal explosion; a flat concrete roof was perhaps only preferred as a passive air defence measure (see below, Passive air defence). Although many of the assembly processes involved handling very sensitive explosives such as tetryl, fulminate of mercury, or powdered TNT, the amounts in hand were relatively small. By carefully regulating the total quantity of explosive in a building, the effects of any accidental explosion on a whole building could be controlled, though the danger of maiming or killing an individual was always present.

The design of individual structures exhibited general features common to all buildings where explosives handling took place. Most were relatively small and lit by natural light; in larger buildings roof monitors were often inserted to light the central part of the building. All artificial lighting was electric, and leads and switch boxes were attached to the exterior of the building and carried in small-bore metal pipes. Either the light shone in through the windows or bulbs were sealed in bulkhead units set into the walls or suspended from the ceiling. Internally, the walls were plastered and painted to produce a clean washable surface and floor coverings were either gritless asphalt or linoleum, which was regularly washed. Doors universally opened outwards for rapid egress and were closed

Figure 7.33 (left) ROF Thorpe Arch, West Yorkshire. Group 1 Primer Shop; note use of enclosed danger building lighting. (AA95/2733; © Royal Ordnance)

Figure 7.34 (right) ROF Thorpe Arch, West Yorkshire. Group 1 Cap Shop in operation; note danger building lighting and emergency pull. (AA96/2724; © Royal Ordnance)

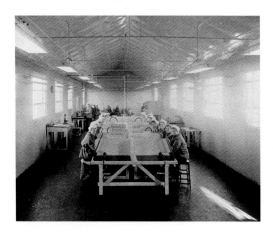

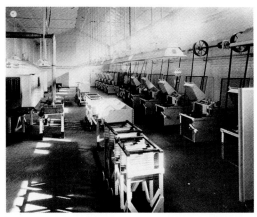

automatically by brass weights suspended in the door frame. Workers and visitors to the clean areas wore rubber galoshes, to prevent both ingress of grit and build-up of static electricity. All buildings were fitted with lightning conductors and copper strapping down their exteriors; internally all the process machinery was earthed and in some magazines a grid of copper straps was embedded beneath the asphalt. In the most sensitive buildings meters were fixed near the doors to monitor body static. Most process buildings were also equipped with an overhead drencher system connected to the factory's high pressure water main for firefighting. Buildings were all heated from a central boiler house or houses, and the steam was conveyed in a network of lagged pipes carried above the ground, which formed one of the most characteristic features of these sites. Within buildings the heat was sometimes simply radiated from an unlagged steam pipe; alternatively the steam was converted in a plenum heater house to warm air and blown through conduits into the buildings. Elsewhere flat radiators were mounted flush to the wall to prevent the accumulation of explosive-laden dust. Specific wartime features included provision of blackout blinds or shutters. At ROF Featherstone, for example, there were offset wall vents to prevent any light escaping.

Power for machinery was usually supplied by an external electric motor, attached to a single line shaft mounted within the building. The use of belt drives, although generally considered to be outdated in the 1930s, in this situation allowed the prime mover to be kept outside the building (Fig 7.34). Where there was less risk from very sensitive explosives or dust, the motor was attached directly to the machine (Fig 7.35). In processes using hydraulic power this was usually delivered from pumps and control gear housed in separate rooms also attached to the exterior of the building. With this system each building was a self-contained unit, not dependent on a centralised supply which was vulnerable to bomb damage. It also allowed the assembly rooms to be left as open shells, which could be arranged and rearranged as new demands dictated. To reduce the need for

and cost of heavily armoured buildings, shielding was given to individual pieces of dangerous process machinery by enclosing them within an armoured partition (Fig 7.36), behind which a single operative could work or could control the process remotely. Assembly of small sensitive components was often done sitting down at a bench, with the face and chest protected by an armoured glass screen.

Some of the most sensitive explosives were handled in Group 1. Here careful control of the handling procedures attempted to reduce the risk of accident. Caps were normally stored in trays on wheeled trolleys. At ROF Chorley, for example, when filled they were passed through a serving hatch to a separate room with small armoured cubicles for cap packing, and from there through another serving hatch to the handlers on the cleanway, all to prevent them from being accidentally knocked by a swinging door. Failure to use the hatches could result in immediate suspension. At Featherstone they were similarly passed through a serving hatch from the filling room to the cleanway.[54] The small size of components and the small amounts of explosives handled in Group 1 were reflected in its filling sheds tending to be small and untraversed. Surviving examples at ROF Chorley are rectangular and gabled with light metal roofs (Fig 7.37), while those at ROF Featherstone are small square buildings with flat concrete roofs.

By contrast, within Group 3 buildings dedicated to fuze filling, several activities were commonly located within a single larger building. At ROF Chorley, the filling sheds of this group were long rectangular buildings with small attached power rooms.

Figure 7.35 ROF Chorley, Lancashire. Directly driven Beken mixing machine. (AA93/5836)

Figure 7.36 ROF Chorley, Lancashire. Interior of a Group 3 building with screens around gunpowder presses. (AA93/5830)

*Figure 7.37 ROF
Chorley, Lancashire.
Group 1 cap shop.
(AA93/5814)*

Internally, several filling shops were linked by a side corridor, and time fuzes were pressed then taken for assembly using already filled products from Group 1. These sheds were separated from one another by concrete blast walls, between which the group's air-raid shelters or refuges were sited. Group 5 cartridging work was carried out at Chorley in relatively small filling sheds with projecting porches to either end, sunk to eaves height below ground level; at Aycliffe, Elstow, Featherstone, and Thorpe Arch the same task was housed in larger, untraversed, rectangular buildings, up to 243ft (74m) in length, which are easily recognisable by their serried entrance porches along one side and layout in opposing rows with the porches generally facing one another.

Some of the most distinctive buildings were found within Group 8, dedicated to

*Figure 7.38 ROF
Chorley, Lancashire.
Group 8 pressed
filling building
colloquially known
as a 'Queen Mary'.
Reconstruction from
HMOW drg 1/9/4B
Nov 1937.
(© Crown copyright.
NMR)*

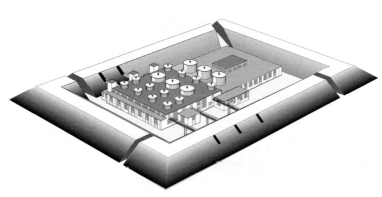

main charge filling. This group's bulk filling with high explosives varied from comparatively small items such as grenades or shells to heavy bomb filling, exceptionally up to 22,000lb (9979.2kg) by the end of the Second World War. One of the most unusual types comprised the pressed filling buildings designed in 1937 by H M Office of Works for the new filling factory at Chorley (Fig 7.38). Colloquially they were known as the 'Queen Mary' buildings on account of the projections like ship's funnels through their roofs. Originally designed for filling shells with amatol, they were later adapted to more powerful TNT/RDX mixes. They were of brick construction, with a large window area supplemented by a clerestory roof above the finishing bench area to maximize the natural light. The roof was boarded and covered by bituminous felt, with a slight fall away from the centre of the building, and was supported on a framework of steel stanchions and beams covered by a concrete casing. Much of the internal organisation and processes can in this case be discerned from the external appearances of the building. Its most distinctive features were the protruding funnel-like press cubicles, designed to isolate the most hazardous part of the process. The smaller cubicles were 12ft (3.6m) in diameter, formed of a mild steel inner and outer liner separated by a sand filling, 1ft (0.3m) in width, which shielded the press within the cubicle from the rest of the building in the event of an explosion. Entry into the cubicle was at ground level through a traversed door opening. To maintain the stiff, porridge-like amatol mixture in a malleable form it was continually stirred in a 'Harvey' mixer, clad in a hot-water jacket and powered by an overhead electrically driven line shaft (Fig 7.39). The lines of cubicles were serviced by high level filling corridors, where hot amatol was moved to the filling cubicles along a vibrating conveyor. The corridors' positions are marked by the lift shafts projecting above the roof line at one end and the escape bridges leading through the traverse for the workers in the corridors (Fig 7.38). After filling, the shells were taken to the larger press cubicles, 19ft (5.8m) in diameter with two flattened sides to economise on space, where the explosive was further compressed. Entry to these was

Figure 7.39 ROF Chorley, Lancashire. Interior of Group 8 pressed filling building, showing the belt-driven 'Harvey' mixers between the shrouded press cubicles. (AA93/5873)

Later this method was largely replaced by hand stemming. Other types of munitions, including anti-aircraft and semi-armour piercing bombs, required pure TNT.[55] The type of unit designed for this operation consisted of a central melt house flanked by two filling shops: their symmetrical arrangement earned them the nickname at Chorley of the 'Butterfly' buildings (Figs 7.40 and 7.41). There, the units were sunk below the artificial ground level to eaves height to minimise the risk from accidental explosion. In some versions the filling shops were divided into a characteristic bayed form, while elsewhere they were open. This resulted in an adaptable unit, where a variety of types of munition were filled, including bombs, shells, and rocket heads. An apparently similar plan form, therefore, does not necessarily enable confident interpretation of the type of plant it housed or the precise type of munition being filled. Typically (Fig 7.41) the TNT, arriving in a form resembling domestic soap flakes, was melted in a steam-heated hopper then pumped along steam-heated pipes to the filling sheds. Shells were filled at the end of the building and then placed in the stalling to cool and for finishing.

through the flattened sides with hydraulically operated lifting door. The insubstantial roofs of the cubicles, consisting of timber joists covered by timber boarding and a bituminous felt topped with an asbestos cement vent, provided the line of least resistance in the event of an explosion. After pressing, the shells passed to the finishing benches to be readied for dispatch to filled shell stores. These buildings also contained steam-heated kettle ranges, where kettles of molten explosive were kept to top up any underfilled shells, and on their exterior were self-contained rooms to house the power plant. These included the lift and motor room, motors for the overhead drive shafts, a hydraulic pumphouse, and a plenum heater house to blow warm air through overhead conduits to heat the building. 'Queen Mary House' at Thorpe Arch was of a similar design and function, though its single row of three circular cubicles may indicate it was used for bomb filling.

Other methods of filling shells with amatol also resulted in distinctive building types. At ROF Risley a screw filling process occupied a single building, subdivided internally into three by concrete blast walls. In the first room the amatol was mixed, in the second it was fed into the shell or bomb with a power-operated steel worm, and the third room was reserved for finishing procedures.

Figure 7.40 ROF Chorley, Lancashire. Section of Group 8 buildings. (NMR 12920/18)

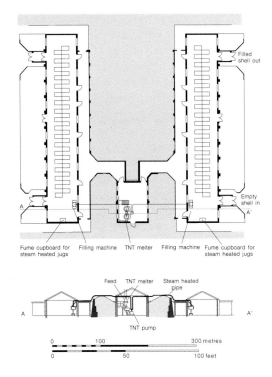

Fume cupboard for   Filling machine   TNT melter   Filling machine   Fume cupboard for
steam heated jugs   steam heated jugs

Feed   TNT melter   Steam heated
                               pipe

TNT pump

As the TNT cooled and solidified it was topped up from steam-heated kettles kept at the end of the shop. At ROF Thorpe Arch, a small section of five units used a similar arrangement of buildings within Group 8 to fill No 36 hand grenades with Baratol, a mechanical mixture of ammonium nitrate and TNT.[56] Each unit there consisted of a central mixing house surrounded by a concrete blast wall and two parallel six-bay, single-storey ranges (Figs 7.42 and 7.43). The detailed identification of the functions of this group and of the individual bays could be made in this instance from painted-over stencilled signs, a level of detail normally lacking.

Heavy bomb filling became an increasingly important function for the newer agency factories. This can be inferred at ROF Featherstone from the surviving remains of the factory, in the absence of documented building functions. At the centre of the Group 8 area (main charge filling) is a large, rectangular building, of two storeys but internally open to the roof, and surrounded by an earthwork traverse. Within, it is divided across into two by a freestanding wall, 4ft 3in (1.3m) wide and 8ft 2in (2.5m) in height. At either end heavy T-shaped concrete walls create compartments in the four corners of the building.

Peeling painted notices on the wall indicate that mixers were housed at one end of the building and melters at the other, consistent with the preparation of amatol by mixing TNT and ammonium nitrate or producing TNT/RDX fillings. A sign referring to steam kettles probably indicates a filling activity in the building, which required topping-up jugs. Within an adjacent traverse stands a timber-framed danger building which, although stripped of its plant, nevertheless, retains a covered lean-to along one side with entry holes similar to those associated with Quinan-type drying stoves (see Chapter 6). It was perhaps for drying ammonium nitrate before mixing with TNT. At ROF Elstow the only remains of the Group 8 filling buildings is a tall concrete wall, probably similarly representing a heavy bomb filling room. In that case, there is literary confirmation (see Fig 7.31).[57]

The Group 10 buildings included all those with functions needed to support the production facilities and encompassed a wide variety of other types, including the administration buildings, clocking and pay stations, shifting rooms, canteens, laundries, tailors' shops, laboratories, maintenance and motor transport sections, and effluent treatment, but also the factories' proof ranges. For efficiency many of these

buildings were usually grouped together near the main entrance. In the very large factories, however, they might be replicated to reduce travelling time, usually on foot or bicycle, between the production groups and the central services. Laboratories were a feature of all the explosives manufacturing and filling factories for testing raw materials and the products at different stages of manufacture. Most factories also had quality inspection laboratories. These were usually staffed by an independent agency such as the Naval Ordnance Inspection Department.[58] Like other buildings of central services they were single storey, but were distinguished by small detached stores for explosive samples, either connected by a short corridor or, as at ROF Swynnerton, a separate locker magazine. Part of the same process of testing finished products were factory proof ranges (Fig 7.44), used to test samples of small arms ammunition up to 20mm shells. They comprised a traversed expense magazine to store ammunition awaiting testing, administrative buildings, and shelters for the limited number of staff. The firing ranges generally consisted of a covered gunshed and a butt, the space between either open or totally enclosed in long brick chambers (Fig 7.44). The longest covered ranges at ROF Swynnerton were 722ft (220m) in length and the longest open range 2296ft 6in (700m); the longest at Thorpe Arch 1804ft 5in (550m), mounded as necessary to restrain stray shots. Butts took a number of forms but were usually mounted on rails within a shed, so when hit by a shell they could move back to absorb its impact. On the longest ranges, targets could be placed at measured intervals towed on an adjacent narrow gauge railway or at its maximum length were mounted on rails in a covered shed and could be pushed from side to side. The area of the butt was covered by high-speed camera positions. At Swynnerton there was also a smaller range only 52ft 6in (16m) in length, perhaps for pistol ammunition. Proof ranges were generally a feature of the earlier and larger filling factories, and, though distinctive in size and peripheral location, cannot be recognised from the plans or aerial photographs of the later factories. Such factory proof ranges were additional to the proof butts

at Woolwich, which were involved in the development of special propellants and whose concrete butts and earthwork traverses still remain. Other ranges were developed for research work during and after the war, including Inchterf near Glasgow, and the re-activated Great War range at Melton Mowbray.[59]

A feature of all filling factories that was often no more than a piece of remote and cleared space was the factory burning ground. Here factory waste of all sorts from unsalvageable paper and damaged packing crates to waste explosives were burnt, usually in the open, which makes it potentially the most contaminated area within any former factory complex.

Naval filling facilities

The Navy's filling requirements were partly met by the ROFs, for example through the refurbishment of the former NFF at Hereford during the 1930s for activities including naval mine filling. The Navy also retained its own filling facilities at Priddy's Hard at Portsmouth (Fig 6.33) and Lodge Hill at Upnor near Chatham. The filling sections in these establishments dated from the Great War or earlier, but unlike their counterparts elsewhere they were maintained in the inter-war period through piecemeal refurbishments and additions. The impact of the Second World War is

Figure 7.44 ROF Swynnerton, Staffordshire. Air photograph of proof range (NMR 15244/08)

difficult to assess. There were no major new extensions and the most obvious additions and alterations concern the passive air defence of these facilities, including the construction of refuges, decontamination centres, and protected water pump trailer houses. Many of the slated roofs of the storage magazines were replaced by flat concrete roofs in an attempt to make them more bomb resistant. At Lodge Hill a noticeable increase in its storage capacity was achieved by creating semi-permanent magazines out of Nissen huts, some set on concrete bases.[60] Other RNADs continued to contribute to filling activities, including RNAD Trecwn in west Wales specialising in filling mines.[61]

Factory architecture, materials, and infrastructure

Architectural standardisation and adaptability

As in the layout of factories, so too with buildings there was a wish to produce a range of near-standard types. In contrast to the Great War building programme little was left to personal initiative or local discretion and design drawings were issued centrally, for part of the war from the requisitioned Palace Hotel in Southport.[62] In the planning of each factory scientific principles were brought to bear to estimate the quantities of each component required and how its production could be logically ordered; similarly in the conception of each building there was an economy of design and use of materials. The large process buildings were well designed according to functional modern ideals with no extraneous decorative detailing (Fig 7.38). Unlike Ministry of Munitions factories of the Great War or the contemporary neo-Georgian of the expansion period airfields, there was little architectural embellishment of any of the factory buildings. Even in the treatment of administrative blocks, the symbolic focus of the factories: only in their scale do the larger ones stand out above the plainest of facades of the contemporary 'bypass factory' (Fig 7.45). At ROF Chorley, the main door surround of this prestigious factory was faced in stone with a wrought iron panel and the royal cypher above. At ROF Kirkby, the two-storey hostel block was relieved by raised stair towers projecting above the roof line at either end, each lit by a small circular window above a long rectangular light. Elsewhere only in the curving faces of the gate lodges at Chorley and Swynnerton were the architects allowed to indulge in details with contemporary art deco influences.

A higher standard of building construction is noticeable in the first three factories built at Bridgend, Chorley, and Glascoed. The factories commissioned after the outbreak of war lack even these pretensions to architectural embellishment. Most buildings were single-storey, dominated in only the largest factories by two-storey administration and canteen blocks. They were utilitarian, designed for speedy and economic erection using relatively unskilled labour with maximum economy in the use of buildings materials. Their drabness was compounded by a coating of camouflage

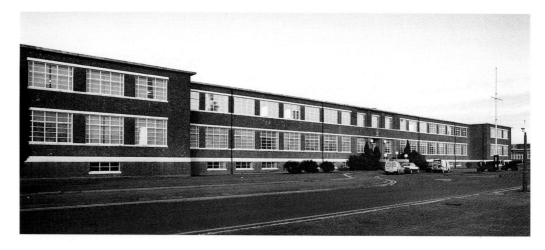

Figure 7.45 ROF Chorley, Lancashire. Main administrative block c 1937. (AA93/5893)

paint and the battleship grey or brown paint of the door- and window-frames. Interiors were a little brighter, generally painted in cream gloss and furnished with utility quality furniture, perhaps brightened by a Ministry of Information poster. Despite their functional outlook they made little use of new building materials, in particular reinforced concrete. Concrete was extensively used in foundations and for flat roofs, however, and in some buildings for giving extra protection to end walls or creating reinforced compartments in buildings, also for revetting traverse banks and for roads and cleanways. Most buildings were of brick. Some factories used hollow double bricks to economise on materials and time, for example at ROF Featherstone they formed the underside of the flat concrete roofs. The nature of the activity in filling factories, however, ensured that their buildings were more substantial than many others of the wartime and most of those in the process areas were built in strong English bond brick walls. It was generally only in ancillary buildings that typical wartime expedients of single thickness walls punctuated by thicker piers to carry roof trusses or of laying bricks side on were found. The flat concrete roofs that became common as a constructional expedient afforded some protection from incendiary bombs. Many of the smaller elements of buildings – doors, door frames, windows, and metal roof trusses – were standard components and could be specified by reference number and assembled in the desired combination. To economise in the use of metal and also afford some fire proofing, asbestos cement fittings were commonly used for guttering, downpipes, and roof vents. Corrugated asbestos sheeting served as a roofing material, particularly in ancillary buildings such as ablution blocks and bicycle sheds. Steel framing afforded speed of erection, and was typically used in the chemical plants, where multi-storey structures were needed to enclose process plant, but also for framing magazines, as at ROF Featherstone or the storage depots at Chelford and Dunham on the Hill, with the side walls infilled with brick and the roof generally of reinforced concrete. At ROF Featherstone there were quite small steel-framed buildings even in

Figure 7.46 ROF Thorpe Arch, West Yorkshire. Bomb store in transit shed. (AA96/2734; © Royal Ordnance)

the production areas, their walls infilled with standard or hollow bricks and their roofs generally a flat concrete slab.

Any explosives factory, with its well spaced and often traversed buildings, made a difficult target for enemy attack, though disruption to part of a plant could seriously diminish its efficiency. Minimising the risk to personnel and plant from enemy attack or accidental explosions, and diminishing the loss of production these might give rise to, were overriding principles governing the design of all buildings and plant.[63] As in the layout of the production groups, an aim was to build as much flexibility into a particular building as possible. In the less specialised and hazardous buildings large open floor areas were preferred, which could readily be modified to new uses. This adaptability of design was best exemplified in the transit sheds located at the sides of each group to receive the empty non-explosive components. They were generally brick-built, with standard-sized steel roof trusses. Transit sheds occurred in three-, four- and five-aisle versions (Fig 7.46), some with varying aisle widths of which the narrowest usually accommodated a railway line to deliver the goods at platform height. If extra capacity was needed, either a further aisle or bays could be added to the design. To economise in materials, they were covered by corrugated asbestos sheeting which required only light metal roof trusses supported internally

Figure 7.47 RNCF Holton Heath, Dorset. Changing room for stores section, illustrating typical design and materials of the 1930s rearmament period (redrawn from RNCF drg no C.1110 31.8.38).

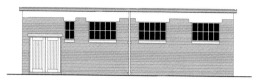

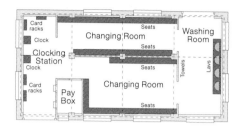

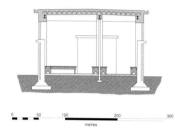

wire mesh and concrete to support the roof. Concrete was poured on top of asbestos troughing laid between the RSJs to form a gently sloping roof 10fiin (0.25m) thick (Fig 7.47), and finally sealed with bituproof. The method was apparently unique to Holton Heath. Another characteristic there was the use of white glazed bricks within the process buildings, with odd white bricks also cemented around the entrance to surface refuges to guide the workers to the door. Many buildings of this date are also characterised by large black roof vents.[64]

Utilities and factory infrastructure

As with the Great War factories it was the larger factories that had their own power plants, either to run independently or to provide emergency backup. The largest, such as the RNPF Caerwent, had two power houses each supplied by rail from massive semicircular coal storage pits with transporters. These generated a 6.6kv supply, which was transformed down by substations to provide a 400/230 volt, three phase, supply to the factory.[65] Smaller sites, such as ROF Featherstone, relied on local electricity sources, with on-site transformer houses to create the required voltage. Where gas was required, it was drawn from the local town gas supply. All the factories had boiler houses for raising steam for heating, both within the production cycle – for example, melting explosives in jacketed vessels – and more generally heating buildings, commonly via a plenum heat exchanger producing warm air. It was carried around the site in lagged pipes on a network of (usually concrete) stanchions: at ROF Swynnerton they stretched for 31 miles (50km).

Much of the infrastructure was invisible, buried beneath the ground or concealed within buildings. The statistics are, nevertheless, staggering. At ROF Swynnerton there were 62 miles (100km) of water mains, 17 miles (27.4km) of storm water sewer pipes, 17 miles (27.4km) of compressed air, hydraulic and gas mains, 220 miles (354km) of lighting cables, 95 miles (153km) of conduits, and 28 miles (45km) of motor cables.[66]

on regularly spaced brick piers. At Chorley and Risley among the earlier factories, north-light sheds are encountered in the storage areas. The filled transit stores on the edge of groups were more substantial brick buildings, usually with a flat concrete roof, often supported by rolled steel girders set on concrete piers. Only in engineering shops was a steel-framed interior commonly found where the columns were also used to support travelling cranes. The administrative separation between the ROF organisation and the Royal Naval factories was reflected in their architecture as well as their solution of problems of explosives factory design. Replanning of the RNCF at Holton Heath in the 1930s appears to have lain with the factory's own construction department, and many of its features were carried on to RNPF Caerwent. As with the ROFs, the expectation that the factory would be subject to aerial attack was a prime consideration. All the new or rebuilt buildings were in brick, both reflecting permanent status and offering greater protection from flying debris, with standard steel windows and glass bricks used for addition illumination. Above brickwork to window height, a framework of RSJs (reinforced steel joists) of differing sizes was covered in

Fire, whether started accidentally or by enemy incendiaries, was of particular concern in the presence of explosives. A high-pressure fire main connected along the roadways was standard equipment and the earlier factories had distinctive American-style hydrants (Fig 7.48) while later factories were supplied with plain stand-pipes. Pressure was maintained in the system by a pumping station and usually a reservoir was constructed to maintain the supply in an emergency. Additionally all the process buildings were equipped with an overhead drencher system, painted red. Emergency communications within the factory were by telephones housed in cast-iron pillars spaced along the cleanways or within the porches of marked buildings.

Munitions storage and maintenance

Within the factories finished munitions were stored in the Group 9 factory magazines. These were primarily to safeguard valuable finished munitions from accidental damage; they would probably have offered insufficient containment to withstand the full force of the whole magazine exploding. Some of the most substantial bombproof magazines were associated with the early factories at Chorley and Swynnerton (Fig 7.49), where they were covered by large earthen mounds. All were served by standard-gauge rail connections. At Chorley two corridors lay at right angles to the platform with separate storage bays between them, with access from either end. In later factories, such as Thorpe Arch and Elstow, the storage magazines were similar to transit sheds, with a rail platform and an undivided floor interior except for the roof piers, but with no overhead cover beyond the concrete roof slab. They were variously sunk below the surrounding ground level to eaves height, surrounded by an earthwork traverse with an entrance passage, or, as at Elstow, freestanding and separated from one another by a long earthwork bank. Storehouses were generally built with 14in (0.36m) brick walls and a 6in (0.15m) reinforced concrete roof. Buildings to these specifications were generally accepted as being able to withstand a direct hit by a 2.2lb (1kg) incendiary bomb

and the blast and splinters from a 500lb (225.8kg), medium-case bomb exploding 50yd (45.7m) away from a building, or closer if the store was also traversed.[67]

Many factories also had detached storage areas. At Aycliffe, Thorpe Arch, and Elstow the magazines were located adjacent to the perimeter or up to 1 mile (about 1.5km) away. These small magazines, each measuring 36ft × 23ft (11m × 7m), were arranged in blocks of four, surrounded by earthwork traverses; they were grouped together in varying numbers according to local requirements. At Kirkby the magazine area was over 1.2 miles (2km) distant and consisted of a block of nine untraversed transit sheds. Their structure was similar to magazines at other dispersed locations removed from the factories. At Dunham on the Hill near Helsby, steel-framed magazines with brick infill were scattered across the Cheshire landscape, linked by standard gauge lines but with the hedgerows left intact to break up the pattern of the establishment. The depot at Ulnes Walton in Lancashire was similar. Chelford, also in Cheshire and the site probably originally selected for filling factory No 13, is a good example of a magazine storage area set within the existing landscape to present a difficult target to locate or attack from the air (Fig 7.50).[68] The magazines were spaced at about 200yd (180m) intervals and were untraversed; they were of a standard size,

Figure 7.48 ROF Swynnerton, Staffordshire. Fire hydrant. (AA96/6517)

Figure 7.49 ROF Chorley, Lancashire. Storage magazines (NMR 12920/19)

DANGEROUS ENERGY

*Figure 7.50
Chelford, Cheshire.
Magazine storage
area, photographed
in 1966.
(© Ordnance
Survey OS/66106
frame 780 29 MAY
1966)*

90ft × 150ft (27.4m × 45.7m), and constructed of steel or reinforced concrete frames with brick infill, with corrugated iron roofs. Access was entirely by standard-gauge railway line from the main Crewe to Manchester line. Each magazine was served by a single line passing through the centre of the buildings to a dead end to allow for shunting. To simplify construction, loading and unloading was directly from the wagons, awkwardly necessitating heavy lifting. Completing the establishment were a military guard unit, fire station, and locomotive shed.

These establishments were passive storage magazines, where ammunition was received and stored before issue to service units. Naval storage depots were classified as Royal Naval Armament Depots (RNADs), and operated both for passive storage or also in the periodic examination of stored munitions. The 1200 acres (485.64ha) RNAD at Broughton Moor in Cumbria had around 150 explosives storehouses, a mixture of timber framed sheds covered by corrugated asbestos sheeting and larger brick buildings with flat concrete roofs, the latter probably constructed after the outbreak of war. The whole complex was served by a narrow-gauge tramway system. Additionally there were laboratories or

shell examination rooms for inspecting ammunition returned from sea or after long-term storage. These were small buildings located at the centre of the site, surrounded by concrete traverses in case of explosion. Other facilities dealt with decayed ammunition, including laboratories to steam out explosives, and also apparently a breaking facility. Within these buildings arrangements for the safe handling of explosives were similar to those in manufacturing contexts, including shifting rooms, dirty and clean areas, and danger building lighting. Many of the larger depots like Broughton Moor or RNAD Ditton Priors in Shropshire also had temporary sub-depots, many of which were little more than tarpaulin-covered dumps at the side of railway or road. Alternatively, temporary storage was sometimes created at the RNADs by assembling pre-fabricated Stanton air-raid shelter segments.[69] Similar storage facilities operated by the RAF were termed Maintenance Units (MUs). The periodic maintenance of stored bombs resulted in the largest detonation of conventional explosives during the war when on 27 November 1944 15,000 tons (15,240 tonnes) of explosives went up at the underground MU 21 at Fauld in Staffordshire, located in a former gypsum mine. Eighty-one people were killed and a crater 800ft 6in × 302ft × 121ft 4in deep (244m × 92m × 37m), which remains to this day, was created. The cause was thought to be the unauthorised removal of a CE exploder from a bomb in one of the storage areas rather than in the Ammunition Inspectorate Department compound.[70]

Transport

Proximity to a railway line was one of the principal locational factors, as in the Great War. Manufacturing munitions was a complex process bringing together different types of explosives and metal components at the filling factories and then distributing products to storage magazines before issue for service use. Logistically it was an immense task to ensure the correct quantities arrived at the right place at the right time, notwithstanding the disruption caused by air-raids. The railways were the vital link.

228

All the factories were joined to main lines by short spurs and loops and, where possible, alternative lines were provided. Within their perimeters they had marshalling sidings to receive goods and assemble trains of filled munitions. In all cases the filling factories were served by internal standard-gauge lines, which eliminated double handling onto an internal factory system; loading and unloading in the transit sheds was on the level, directly from wagon to platform. The railways were densest in those factory groups handling the heavier components (see Fig 7.28). Trucks were moved around by internal factory locomotives, usually of the steamless type or diesels to reduce the risk of fire. Engine sheds to house and carry out light maintenance work were a feature of all factories, which might also possess some rolling stock for internal use, usually antiquated mainline stock. Most other factories, too, relied entirely on standard-gauge lines, usually flatbed rails directly onto the sleepers to economise in steel; narrow-gauge tramways prevailed in the explosives factories at Bishopton, Bridgwater, and Powfoot, where material was transhipped from standard-gauge trucks. Waltham Abbey retained its barges as well until the end of manufacture, and at RNPF Caerwent electric road trolleys were used exclusively for moving explosives around the factory production areas. The field evidence of a stretch of narrow-gauge rail set in concrete near the bomb filling section suggests that ROF Featherstone may have been the only filling factory to have used tramways. Within the groups, material was normally moved around by small electric tractors known as 'dillies' running on the cleanways.

Security

The main threat to any munitions factory was from the air. Fifth columnists were also regarded as a very real danger, although in practice this threat never materialised. Similarly, groups of mobile, lightly armed German paratroopers were anticipated, mounting assaults against key targets, and it was this menace that the ring of pillboxes around Waltham Abbey RGPF and ROF Wrexham, for example, were designed to counter, rather than full-scale invasion.[71] Factory security was under the control of the War Department Constabulary, the local Home Guard (usually drawn from the factory's staff), and more rarely by detachments of regular troops. The last line of defence was the factory fence, which in most ROFs was simply a wirelink mesh capped with barbed wire. Naval facilities, however, generally employed pressed-steel fencing, wartime examples of which were usually ribbed to deflect machine gun bullets.[72] Occasionally projecting bastions were incorporated, large enough for one man to monitor the line of the fence, and more routinely observation or police posts were spaced along the interior of the fence for surveillance of the perimeter. All factory entrances were controlled by police posts, to issue passes to temporary visitors and inspect workers entering and leaving the factory. Nearby were search rooms, which the workers passed through and where they were subject to random searches for contraband items.

Air defence

In the early 1930s the certainty that in any future war the civilian population and industry would be subject to air attack (see Fig 6.40) was one of the prime factors in locating new munitions factories. Planners were concerned not only with the menace from Germany, but with a possible threat from France: they were apprehensive about the wisdom of siting factories in South Wales, less heavily defended than the south coast and therefore accessible to a fleet operating out of French ports. Surviving accounts indicate that in practice there was little systematic targeting of explosives factories by the Luftwaffe. Most actual attacks appear to have been opportunistic, like that on Waltham Abbey in October 1940 in which a single stove on South Site was destroyed and other minor damage caused, which appeared to be the work of a single aircraft. On other occasions it was hit by a parachute mine and two V2s. Attacks on Caerwent, Glascoed, and Swynnerton were similarly by single aircraft, either off course or tipping bombs on a secondary target.[73]

Figure 7.51 (above) RNCF Holton Heath, Dorset. Luftwaffe reconnaissance photograph, 12 8 1940. (© Nigel Clarke publications)

Figure 7.52 (top right) RNCF Holton Heath, Dorset. Observation post. (BB94/16995)

Figure 7.53 (below right) RNCF Holton Heath, Dorset. Elevated gun platform originally mounting a Bofors gun and range finder. (BB94/17035)

The Royal Arsenal Woolwich was an exception. It presented a large target, set against the river Thames and easily traced from the air, and suffered 25 raids by massed aircraft and later by V1s and V2s, in which 103 people were killed and 770 injured.[74] RNCF Holton Heath was in the same category (Fig 7.51), for it too was relatively easy to find by following the coastline and its layout was probably well known from the work of German engineers in the 1930s (see below). Ardeer, also a coastal site, was attacked on a single occasion in May 1941.[75]

Active air defence

The air defences of any factory usually fell within a wider pattern of need. Anti-aircraft batteries, therefore, tended to be pushed away from the factory perimeter, which also ensured that spent rounds were less likely to fall in the factory. Within RNCF Holton Heath there was a small observation post with a vertical steel ladder leading down into an underground shelter (Fig 7.52) that controlled the factory decoy sites. Sector boards for the south of England surviving *in situ* suggest that it was also a sub-station to the main gun observation room at Portland.

The importance of Holton Heath was recognised in its designation as 'vulnerable point 50', and it was eventually defended by six heavy anti-aircraft gunsites each with four 3.7in guns and two light anti-aircraft gunsites equipped with Bofors guns (Fig 7.53).[76] Surviving emplacements at Waltham Abbey, Priddy's Hard, and Thorpe Arch also show factories defended by light machine guns to counter attempts to strafe them at low level.

Passive air defence

Passive air defence (PAD) featured three principal activities: prevention of detection from the air, measures to stop the whole factory being put out of action, and defence of the factory when it was detected and attacked. Contemporary aerial photographs (Fig 7.51) reveal that little in reality could be done to hide these large rectilinear sites with freshly dug earthworks and ballasted railway lines. Most buildings were painted in camouflage patterns; while making target recognition more difficult at low level, the protection this offered was perhaps more psychological than actual. Pools of static water such as the large reservoir at Holton Heath were covered to prevent reflection; concrete paths and roadways were also tarred or painted. At night, the factories worked under strict blackout conditions and decoy sites were used in many cases to draw away enemy bombers. RNCF Holton Heath was protected by two, one on the Arne peninsula and the second at Decoy Heath near Wareham; that at Arne received 206 bombs on 3 June 1943.[77] ROF Swynnerton's decoy site at Whitgreave, 5km to its south, was carefully placed in a similar topographic position adjacent to the main railway line.[78]

In layout explosives factories were ideally designed to resist aerial attack, as the buildings were dispersed and often protected by traverses. Many of the key process areas were duplicated. Structurally buildings were usually sturdier than Great War examples, machinery was often encased in protective screens, and each building could operate as an independent unit. The widely used flat concrete roofs offered some protection against incendiary attacks, since most were at least 6in (0.15m) thick, which was the recommendation for resisting a light incendiary bomb and was capable of resisting a normal debris load.[79] In most munitions factories it became standard practice to work through local air-raid warnings and work would only cease if the factory was directly threatened. Observation posts for roof spotters were created on tall buildings, or, as at ROF Elstow, a specially constructed tower on top of a building, and many factories had brick observation posts, 8ft (2.5m) square, with pre-cast concrete observation loops and concrete roofs, from which the progress of a raid could be monitored. Though similar to pillboxes, they are distinguished by narrow observation loops not suitable for mounting a weapon.

Whereas air-raid shelters had been a rarity in the Great War, all munitions factories were provided with shelters or refuges. There were different types to suit local needs. Most were small surface shelters designed to accommodate between 25 and 50 people, usually placed between buildings in the production area. In addition, in places where crowds might be caught in the open, such as the railway station at Swynnerton or the approaches to the station at Holton Heath, larger shelters were provided. In the production areas at Holton Heath surface shelters were brick-built with flat concrete roofs; close to the main changing and mess rooms larger shelters, 131ft (40m) in length, were constructed from pre-cast oval section piping, partly buried by earth, forming a distinctive type encountered only there and at Caerwent. Also at Holton Heath the former fermentation vessels (Fig 6.5) were filled with earth and their basements used as refuges. Despite Waltham Abbey's predictably limited life once the new factories came on stream, provision was still necessary for the safety of its workforce, which already in the rearmament period increased from just 488 in 1935 to 819 in the following year.[80] Instant air-raid shelters or refuges were formed from semicircular Nissen type huts, covered with a layer of concrete just over 6in (0.15m) thick and capped in earth. The ends were sealed in timber, and entry was through a double gas-proof door protected by an earth-filled timber-framed blast screen and by sandbags. These were built in 33ft (10m) and 56ft (17m) lengths as refuges for 25 and 50 persons. Smaller reinforced concrete surface shelters were also built in the production areas, since this low-lying site made slit trenches impractical. At Priddy's Hard plans were prepared in the wake of the Munich crisis in September 1938 for hastily constructed timber-lined trenches covered in earth. It was not until 1941 that these were replaced by concrete-lined semi-sunken trenches and brick-built surface shelters.[81]

Gas bombs and sprays, perhaps lingering as pools of liquid, were another potential threat. Personal respirators gave some protection, or more heavy-duty versions for those required to perform strenuous activities. Shelter doors were designed to be gasproof and at Thorpe Arch were provided with sealable vents, measures intended to offer protection, along with personal respirators, until a raid was over and the gas dispersed. Sloping wooden guiderails to house a cloth cover provided an extra barrier at the entrance to some shelters. Gas decontamination stations afforded facilities where workers could strip off contaminated clothing, shower, and be issued with clean clothes. Factories generally had one such station for each production group or area.

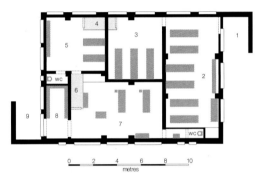

Figure 7.54 RNCF Holton Heath, Dorset. Ground plan of main decontamination station (redrawn from RNCF drg no R1199 12.4.39): 1 Entrance; 2 Waiting room with stretchers; 3 Undressing and inspection room with stretchers; 4 Airlock; 5 Decontamination room with stretchers; 6 Airlock; 7 Surgical room with operating tables; 8 Waiting room; 9 Exit.

Outwardly and in detail they exhibited a number of different styles, but all included a receiving room, ablution room with showers and wash basins, and a dressing room, and all had a tall tower above the shower room to hold the water tanks. One of a number at RNCF Holton Heath was fairly elaborate in including a surgery (Fig 7.54), and at ROF Featherstone separate doors were provided for walking and stretcher cases. There, too, the station had an emergency source of power comprising two bicycles connected to a dynamo! A simpler type at Priddy's Hard had just three rooms and entry and exit porches, employed either in a single row or double row for both sexes. At Waltham Abbey modified versions of the semicircular refuges served as decontamination centres.[82]

Firefighting was part of the normal provision of any explosives factory. All had firestations with tenders and firefighting personnel as well a high-pressure water main and internal drencher systems. The small number of full-time firefighters were supplemented by specially trained production personnel. Additional firefighting equipment was often deployed around the factory: at the naval factories at RNCF Holton Heath and Priddy's Hard water trailers were provided, and in the latter case were stored in dedicated double-doored shelters with benches for their crews.

The workforce, housing, and welfare

A ready pool of labour was one of the most critical requirements affecting the location of a factory. In the 1930s rearmament was a means of alleviating unemployment; after the outbreak of war ensuring an adequate labour supply became a pressing matter (Fig 7.55). The Second World War filling factories employed far more people than their equivalents in the Great War: at their peak the workforce at Bridgend numbered 29,000, at Chorley 28,000, at Glascoed 11,000, and at Swynnerton 21,450. The totals at explosives factories were generally lower, like Caerwent's 6000, though Bishopton exceptionally employed around 20,000.[83] All factories usually worked a two- or three-shift system, ensuring production was maintained around the clock. At the

Figure 7.55 Wartime recruiting poster, 'COME INTO THE FACTORIES'. (BB95/11949; © PRO INF3/403)

WOMEN OF BRITAIN
COME INTO THE FACTORIES
ASK AT ANY EMPLOYMENT EXCHANGE FOR ADVICE AND FULL DETAILS

Figure 7.56 (left) ROF Thorpe Arch, West Yorkshire. A worker scrubs up with special CE soap. (AA96/2729; © Royal Ordnance)

Figure 7.57 (right) ROF Kirkby, Merseyside. Small tea and rest room. (© National Museums on Merseyside, N96-0718)

largest, including Chorley, Kirkby, Risley, and Swynnerton, dedicated railway stations were built to bring the workforce to and from the factory. Outside the gates there were parking areas for buses and bicycle sheds and at Kirkby the tramline was extended out to the factory.

Facilities were required within the factory for managing these large workforces. On arrival and after passing through the search rooms, workers were often faced with a long walk to their production group. At the entrance to each group was a group office, a clocking station, and shifting rooms, usually in blocks of two, male and female. There, workers changed from their everyday clothes into overalls and protective shoes before entering the clean area. Within the production groups were ablution facilities, usually close to more shifting rooms with separate male and female blocks (Fig 7.56). At ROF Featherstone these were flimsy structures built to wartime utility standards with single-thickness brick walls and roofed in corrugated asbestos. They were divided into a central changing room with a shower room and wash basin room to either side. In some factories drinking water fountains were positioned along the cleanways. Admiralty establishments tended to be older and less well provided with welfare facilities. At Priddy's Hard it is difficult to disentangle whether the construction of new toilet blocks and washing facilities was prompted by the 1937 Factories Act or general refurbishment in the lead-up to war, though these new toilet blocks came into use only after 1940. Most naval yards were served only by mess rooms for heating pre-packed food or canteens run by workmen's societies. At Priddy's Hard it was not until

1941 that a Victorian building was converted into a central canteen and not until after the war that prefabricated canteens were installed.[84]

In the ROFs the larger production groups were served by canteens, which were usually separated into dirty and clean for workers on either side of that divide. What cannot be recovered from surviving black-and-white photographs and the derelict empty canteens with smashed windows and peeling floors is any sense of the social centres they once were and their role in fostering a strong camaraderie in the workforce (Fig 7.57). Despite their apparent uniformity of physical form, the character of individual factories was very different. At Glascoed many of the workers were drawn from the ranks of unemployed miners with a strong trade union background; the Glaswegian workforce at Bishopton was equally militant. Despite dilution by conscripted labour, the Liverpudlian accents at Kirkby, those of former Lancashire millworkers at Chorley, or Yorkshire accents at Thorpe Arch would have been easily discernible to any visitor, while the former Staffordshire potters at Swynnerton were enlivened by a large influx of Irish workers. As the largest communal buildings, canteens commonly doubled as social facilities for entertainments by ENSA (Entertainments National Service Association), for factory concert parties, dances, and parties (Fig 7.58), or for morale-boosting talks by visiting dignitaries.[85] The play, *I don't want to set the world on fire*, by Bob Eaton, staged in 1991 at the Newcastle New Vic theatre, on the 'roses' – female workers – of Swynnerton caught the mix of these functions well. The factory public address system was used to broadcast

Figure 7.58 ROF
Kirkby, Merseyside.
A dance, probably
held in one of the
communal canteens.
(© National
Museums on
Merseyside, N96-
0179)

Figure 7.59 Boston
Spa, West Yorkshire.
Factory housing.
(BB95/5024)

Figure 7.60 (right)
Swynnerton,
Staffordshire. Semi-
detached house in
South Road.
(AA96/6557)

'Workers' playtime', BBC news, and other radio series. Most factories also had tailors' shops, which in addition to repairing danger area clothing undertook the manufacture of the cloth and paper components of munitions. Cleaning the factory clothing was in itself an industrial undertaking: at Swynnerton the laundry handled around 110,000 articles per week with a dry weight of 20 tons (20.32 tonnes).[86]

Since many of the new factories were sited close to large conurbations, they were able to draw on local labour pools or billet workers within the towns. Characteristically, though, all the new factories had some attached housing. This usually took the form of a small estate just outside the factory perimeter for essential personnel and larger estates at a distance. At ROF Thorpe Arch, there was a detached estate at West End in Boston Spa, where semi-detached bungalows were the norm (Fig 7.59). The housing was utilitarian in character, lacking the architectural embellishments associated with the permanent Great War housing schemes. In the group of ROFs comprising Swynnerton, Kirkby, Risley, and Featherstone, where Alexander Gibb and Partners were the consulting engineers, there was a standard house type

with a single-pitch roof sloping from front to rear (Fig 7.60). Buildings of this type were used in a number of forms, including single-storey semi-detached bungalows at Swynnerton for the factory police and, more commonly, two-storey detached and semi-detached houses and hostel blocks. Typically these variations were found on mixed estates. Some of the most extensive and varied housing was associated with ROF Swynnerton. Though this factory at first recruited locally from the Potteries, it was later forced to look further afield to Bradford, Huddersfield, Northern Ireland, Lincolnshire, and Northamptonshire for workers. Conscription of female labour from December 1941 only added to the requirement for hostels, as such labour was conscripted to any location where it was needed.[87] Swynnerton was also a training centre for assistant managers and shop managers for the midland and north-eastern regions and therefore had a high transient population. As usual, some housing was provided adjacent to the factory, but with a large estate at Walton near Stone, 2½ miles (4km) from the factory, for 480 families.[88] These houses were built against air attack, with flat concrete roofs capable of withstanding a small incendiary and reinforced porches to act as an integral air-raid shelter.[89] There were also seven hostel complexes able to accommodate 6000 people within a 1¼ mile (2km) radius of the factory perimeter: each was termed a hall, patriotically named after the naval heroes Beatty, Drake, Duncan, Frobisher, Nelson, Howard, and Raleigh. Contemporary timber temporary accommodation has rarely survived. At Swynnerton the factory police were housed in typical wartime temporary hutting with single-thickness brick walls and metal roof trusses, and at Caerwent there was a large group of Nissen huts.[90] At Featherstone an enclosure beyond the eastern perimeter formerly contained hostel type accommodation which may still be traced as floor slabs.

Later agency factories were sited to make the best use of available local labour, but they too all had some accommodation attached. As with the Great War factories, the factory hierarchy was mirrored in the housing provision. At Elstow it was split into three sections. A block of 15 hostels for the female and male workers was grouped with two large canteens, recreation room, and assembly room, with air-raid shelters between the hostel blocks. Close to the factory gate and away from the workers were the police barracks. Along the factory's southern perimeter a small estate for the managers and superintendents was built around a green with an air-raid shelter at the centre, comprising four semi-detached bungalows, one detached bungalow, and two hostels or block of flats. The bungalows were HM Office of Works C type for warrant officers or chief instructors, each measuring 21ft 2in × 37ft (6.5m × 11.3m), and brick-built with a flat concrete roof, as also found at Burghfield, Featherstone and Thorpe Arch adjacent to the factory (Fig 7.61). They contained two bedrooms, a kitchen, bathroom, an entrance lobby, a living room which projected from the front of the building, and an integral ARP shelter protected by a 6in (0.15m) concrete roof slab. The bungalow at one end of the row additionally had bay windows, and its design drawing notes 'bay window for warrant officer type only'.[91] ROF Featherstone had a small estate of similar bungalows, and hostels identical to those found at other north-western ROFs. In remoter locations accommodation was even more essential: for ROF Drigg in Cumbria hostels were provided at Millom, Silecroft, and Holmbrook, while Stanley Ghyll youth hostel was requisitioned.[92]

The range of communal facilities provided alongside factory accommodation depended partly on the remoteness of the factory site and the proportion of the workforce housed there. At minimum they

Figure 7.61 Thorpe Arch, West Yorkshire. HM Office of Works C-type bungalow. (BB95/5018)

consisted of a canteen, assembly, and recreation rooms. With Swynnerton's high level of hostel accommodation, there was a cinema or theatre block at Raleigh Hall, recognisable from its raised end over the stage or screen; this was a common feature in wartime encampments where large groups of people were gathered together. RNPF Caerwent had facilities including a large welfare centre, grocery store, cafe, theatre with a lounge and foyer, quiet room, games room, dining room, central kitchen, canteens, hospital with a theatre, and surgery.[93] Hostel accommodation was generally unpopular; occupancy rates were often low and at some locations it was over-provided as projected numbers of workers tailed off.[94]

The 1937 Factories Act put in place new standards which the new ROFs met. Their planning from the outset included canteens, washrooms, sanitary facilities, surgeries, first aid posts, and rest rooms, and the nature of the work ensured adequate provision was made for heating and lighting. The peculiarities of the work also meant all employees within danger areas were supplied with factory clothing and spark-free footwear.

The safety record for explosives manufacture and handling was far better than during the Great War. Development of the new factories had followed a prepared plan, which did not include hastily converted plant in unsuitable areas. Better internal design and understanding of handling high explosives contributed to safer working conditions. Wartime and post-war secrecy surrounding these factories makes any assessment of the total numbers killed and injured difficult, but from readily available information 134 were killed in the filling factories and probably less than 20 in the explosives factories.[95]

Figure 7.62 ROF Bridgwater, Somerset. Control room for 1950s RDX plant. (BB93/22237)

Post-war, Korea, and after

There was no headlong rush to dispose of the newly created explosives factories. Production requirements actually peaked in 1943 and sufficient stocks were accumulated to act as a reserve for the invasion of Europe in 1944.[96] After the end of the war in Europe in May 1945, the munitions industries rapidly began to shed labour and reduce output. An early loss was the RGPF at Waltham Abbey, which ceased production in 1943. Production halted at RNCF Holton Heath in 1945, and the factory was placed on a care and maintenance basis, with naval production switched to RNPF Caerwent, where one unit worked intermittently.[97]

A little new construction work of the period is recognisable here, since a picrite plant was built to make it independent of supplies from Holton Heath and from the Welland Company of Canada. Shortly afterwards a rocket propellant section was added at the eastern end of the factory.[98] ROF Bishopton was retained as the principal supplier of propellants, while a redundant RDX plant from there was dismantled and shipped to the Albion explosives works in Australia.[99] Other factories were engaged in breaking up surplus ammunition, and this became the dominant activity at Pembrey until its closure in 1965.[100] Filling activities were centred on the three large factories at Chorley, Glascoed, and Swynnnerton with a further eight held as war reserve and used as storage by the Ministry of Supply or the services. In the factories that survived, the trend to mechanised filling led to a move away from smaller buildings and where possible the amalgamation of buildings to allow the installation of machinery.[101]

The explosives factories were less adaptable than the engineering ROFs to meeting pent-up peacetime demands, which led the Royal Arsenal engineering section, for example, to produce 16 ton (16.25 tonnes) steel mineral wagons for the railways and knitting frames.[102]

Some of the unspecialised buildings at ROF Chorley and ROF Swynnerton were converted to clothing manufacture, principally for the services. This not only allowed factories and working teams to find useful employment, but also freed civilian industry to produce for the home market and (more importantly at the time) for export. The ROFs at Bridgwater, Glascoed, and Chorley were also employed in manufacturing two-storey reinforced concrete prefabricated 'Airey' houses, contributing to the post-war housing programme.[103] When concern over American sulphur reserves led to restrictions in its export in the 'sulphur crisis' of the early 1950s, the explosives factory at Holton Heath played an important part by reactivating its old pyrites-burning plant, while the acid plant at Bishopton was employed producing sulphuric acid for the Board of Trade.[104]

Despite pressure in the home economy against military spending and the disengagement from the Empire, mounting anxiety in Europe, punctuated by periods of acute tension that culminated in the Berlin airlift of 1948, reinforced the wisdom of maintaining these up-to-date factories. The crisis when it came was not in Europe but in Korea. In August 1950 the British cabinet agreed to support the lead of the United States in its campaign to repel the invasion of South Korea by communist forces, and to consolidate the Anglo-American alliance by sanctioning additional defence expenditure of £3400 million over three years, increased to £4700 million in January 1951 – sums the post-war economy could not sustain.[105] Despite these large increases in defence spending, there is little physical evidence of this great rearmament programme. In many cases production could be resumed by reoccupying recently vacated buildings, many less than ten years old, as certainly happened at Thorpe Arch, for example. No major extensions to factories

Figure 7.63 ROF Bridgwater, Somerset. Nitration vessel in 1950s RDX plant. (BB93/22238)

presumption that any future major war would be fought with nuclear weapons heralded a steady erosion of the manufacturing capacity for conventional explosives. From the 1950s onwards the wartime factories began to close. Within the surviving factories enough flexibility was found in the surviving buildings to install new production processes, or with limited clearance to create new production groups. But the distinctive legacy of the Second World War explosives factories lies not only in this continuing selective adaptation, or in the residual or reused survival of buildings and sites, or even in the proud warm memories of those who made their contribution to the war effort in and through these factories. It lies also, and perhaps as importantly, in the successful experience and example of their state-led technological design. The significance of these exceptional military works for the history of factory development – in scale and predictive planning, in their functional refinement of layout, in their implementation of modern factory legislation, even in their incorporation and adaptation of the existing features of rural landscapes – is part of a wider topic. They undoubtedly both reflected changing concepts of industrial design and planning current in the inter-war years and the role of government policies on these matters, and gave those trends a new impetus, particularly in relation to the development of greenfield sites.

were required, therefore, required; evidence such as a test date of 29-9-52 stencilled on a press house lifting beam at Holton Heath affords the only indication that it was reoccupied. The RDX plant at Bridgwater was apparently remodelled around this time (Figs 7.62 and 7.63). Atypically, a section was also laid out on green fields at the northern end of ROF Ranskill to house a RDX section sometime during the 1950s.[106]

Continuing reduction in the size of Britain's armed forces and the underlying

Endnotes

1   Hay 1949, 16.
2   PRO WORK 43/1244–1301.
3   PRO Supp 5/334.
4   Admiralty 1945, 10; Simmons 1963, 59–63; PRO Supp 5/446; WASC 1451 and 1452,; PRO Supp 5/861, photographs 364–72.
5   PRO EF 5/19; Supp 5/861, photographs 364–72.
6   HMSO 1938, 72; Simmons 1963, 63.
7   HMSO 1938, 105–7.
8   Marshall 1917, 227–8.
9   Levy 1920, 6; HMSO 1938, 84–5; Lugosi 1996.
10 PRO Supp 5/854.
11 For developments at Holton Heath, see Bowditch 1983; Bowditch and Hayward 1996; PRO Supp 5/853.
12 See, for example, Thomson 1965, 177 and *passim.*
13 Hornby 1958, 83–4.
14 *Ibid*, 88.
15 ICI 1955, 33–5; Bowditch and Hayward 1996, 69–71.
16 HMSO 1938, 58–62; Harding 1959, 33; Hardie and Davidson Pratt 1966, 129; Reader 1975, 263.
17 PRO Supp 5/956.
18 Reader 1975, 253.
19 PRO CAB 102/273.
20 Simmons 1963, 57; HMSO 1938, 99–105.
21 Elliot 1996; PRO Supp 5/752; Supp 5/753.
22 PRO Supp 5/863.
23 Simmons 1963, 77.
24 PRO CAB 102/273.
25 PRO Supp 14/1030.
26 RAF vertical air photograph, sortie 106G/UK 1454 Frame 3170, 2 May 1946.
27 PRO Supp 14/1064; HCRO 109M91.PH25; HCRO 109M91 COL12.
28 HCRO 109M91/MP40.

29 For photographs of Dalbeattie, see HCRO 109M91/PH36.

30 Reader 1975, 274; PRO CAB 102/273.

31 Powfoot has been photographically recorded by RCAHMS, negatives C37529–C37586.

32 For the Albion explosives factory, and the Australian explosives industry generally, see Vines and Ward 1988 and Yelland 1989.

33 Pembrey Country Park nd.

34 HMSO 1938, 129–38; Hornby 1958, 113–17; PRO Supp 5/956.

35 Hornby 1958, 90.

36 PRO Supp 5/446.

37 Simmons 1963, 59–60.

38 Reader 1975, 274.

39 Hornby 1958, 90.

40 *Ibid*, 90.

41 Jeremy 1984, 529–36; PRO CAB 102/627.

42 *Profile* 1988.

43 Jeremy 1984, 535–9; PRO CAB 102/626.

44 PRO Supp 14/1063.

45 James 1978, 540, 563–5.

46 PRO CAB 102/627.

47 PRO CAB 102/626.

48 PRO CAB 102/626.

49 PRO Supp 14/1063.

50 PRO CAB 102/273, 2–3.

51 RAF vertical air photograph, sortie 106G/UK/1483 Frame 4009, 9 May 1946.

52 Bates 1946; additional information from a map in the possession of the site's current owners, National Power.

53 Toler 1993, 12–33.

54 Hay 1949, 61.

55 PRO CAB 102/630.

56 Admiralty 1945, 11.

57 Bates nd, 22–4.

58 McIntyre 1954, 260–4; Maber 1967.

59 Skentlebery 1975, 29, 58, 212–13.

60 HCRO 109M91/PH66; PH79.

61 Personal communication Medwyn Parry, RCAHMW.

62 Reference to the Palace Hotel on a drawing held by National Power's Elstow Storage Depot.

63 PRO Supp 5/1050.

64 Bowditch 1983, 12–35; PRO Supp 5/853; Supp 5/854.

65 HCRO 109M91 COL 12.

66 PRO CAB 102/626.

67 Home Office 1949, 17.

68 PRO CAB 102/630.

69 HCRO 109M91/PH42.

70 Jones 1988, 58–76.

71 Waltham Abbey defences: personal communication Fred Nash.

72 Personal communication Roger Thomas, RCHME York.

73 *Profile* 1994; PRO WASC 1333/3–7.

74 Hogg 1963a, 1024–5.

75 Dolan and Oglethorpe 1996, 21.

76 Perks 1992, 29–39.

77 Bowditch 1983, 17–19.

78 For a general discussion of decoy sites, see Dobinson 1996b; PRO AIR 20/4352.

79 Home Office 1949, 17.

80 PRO Supp 5/446.

81 HCRO 109M91/MP52.

82 PRO Supp 5/984.

83 Inman 1957, 183; PRO CAB/102/626; PRO Supp 14/1030.

84 Inman 1957, 239–42; HCRO 109M91/.

85 See, for example, Clark 1995.

86 PRO CAB/102/626.

87 Public General Acts and Measures 1941, c.4 National Service (No 2) Act, 1941.

88 Personal communication Bernard Lowry.

89 Public General Acts and Measures 1941, c.4 National Service (No 2) Act, 1941.

90 HCRO 109M91/PH25.

91 On-site records at National Power's Elstow Storage Depot, Type C Bungalow HM Office of Works 10 Apr 1941.

92 PRO Supp 5/956.

93 HCRO 109M91/PH25, 53.

94 For housing and hostels generally, see Inman 1957, 242–57.

95 Hay 1949, 63; PRO Supp 5/336.

96 HCRO 109M91/COL12.

97 Bowditch 1983, 36.

98 Bowditch and Hayward 1996, 107; HCRO 109M91/MP40 and MP41.

99 Yelland 1989, 52.

100 Pembrey Country Park nd.

101 Secret memo 'Closing factories' J E Jackson DPF/F 15-2-57.

102 Hogg 1963a, 1027.

103 Hay 1949, 69–75.

104 Imperial Chemical Industries 1955, 33–5; Bowditch 1983, 36; PRO Supp 14/1030.

105 Macdonald 1990, 5, 22–3, 49.

106 RAF vertical air photographs, sortie 542/63 frame 200, 12-OCT-54; sortie MAL/73007 frame 68, 24-FEB-73.

8

The archaeology of rocketry

Throughout their history, military explosives have been as important as a source of propellant energy as for their destructive force. Much of the development of the industry and its changes of plant and technology were fuelled by the propellant function of explosives. This propellant energy has been most spectacularly harnessed as a propulsive force for rockets.

What is a rocket?

The basic principle of the motion of a rocket is encapsulated in Newton's Third Law of Motion, 'to every action there is an equal and opposite reaction'. The propulsive force to propel a rocket forward is obtained by burning fuel to produce a stream of hot gases which produce a reactive force in the opposite direction (Fig 8.1a). The source of the energy to power the motor is chemical, but unlike other thermochemical propulsion systems a rocket carries with it the oxygen needed for the fuel to ignite and burn.[1]

Rocket propulsion systems may be generally classified into two groups, solid propellants and liquid propellants. Examples of suitable solid fuels include black powder or cordite: they combine the necessary fuel and oxidiser. In solid propellant rockets the rate at which the propellants burn and therefore generate pressure within the motor is principally controlled by the surface area of the charge. Simple motors, 'cigarette burning', burn only from the end; but to increase surface area, while ensuring that the pressure is kept near constant, the 'charge design' is often formed as a star-shape to maintain a constant burning surface area as the charge burns back towards the casing (Fig 8.1b). This shape may be modified to vary burning characteristics of the motor.

Rocket engines using liquid propellants (Fig 8.1c) are potentially more efficient, as they are able to develop more power for the same weight of propellant and also offer more adjustable control of the duration of burning. They are usually far more expensive to manufacture, however, because of the requirement for complex fuel delivery systems, and the propellants can be more hazardous to handle. Liquid systems may be *mono-propellants*, where the fuel and oxidiser are combined in a single material, or *bi-propellants*, where the fuel and oxidiser are stored in separate tanks and brought together in the combustion chamber. Many possible combinations of fuels and oxidants exist: fuels include alcohol and kerosene, and conventional oxidants include nitric acid, IRFNA (inhibited red fuming nitric acid), hydrazine, liquid oxygen, and highly concentrated hydrogen peroxide alias 'high test peroxide'.

The type of propellant system chosen will depend on the application to which the rocket is to be put. Solid-fuel rocket motors, although not as efficient as their liquid-fuel counterparts, offer many advantages to the designer of military missiles: they are generally cheaper; they are free of the hazards of handling liquid fuels; and they may be easily stored over long periods ready for immediate use. Recent advances, for example in aluminium-based solid propellants and hybrid propellants using a solid fuel and liquid oxidisers, are excluded from this historical narrative.[2]

Figure 8.1
(a) Diagram of
forces acting on an
ideal rocket motor,
from Lee et al *1983;*
(b) Section through
a solid propellant
rocket, from Lee et
al *1983;*
(c) Diagrammatic
bipropellant rocket
engine, from Lee et
al *1983.*
(© Brassey's)

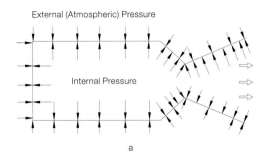

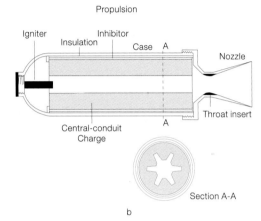

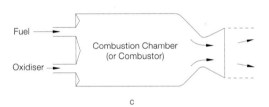

Origins

The origins of rockets as weapons of war are as obscure as those of gunpowder. Rocket-like fireworks appear to have been enjoyed at the Chinese court by the late twelfth century and their use by the Chinese in warfare is documented by the fourteenth century.[3] In Europe, rockets were first mentioned at the Battle of Chioggia between the Genoese and Venetians in 1380, and around 1400 Conrad Kyeser's manual of war, *Bellifortis*, described a rocket with a trough-shaped launcher.[4] Whether they functioned as flares, scares, or effective missiles is not clear. Contemporary depictions of rocket-like projectiles are less reliable and may easily be confused with firearrows, an incendiary composition tied to an arrow and fired from a crossbow.[5] The deployment of fireworks, including rockets, for triumphs and courtly display was regarded as one of the skills of the contemporary artillerists and firemasters; artillerists' manuals frequently concluded with a description of their manufacture.[6] Rocket-based flying fiery dragons were evidently a recurrent feature.[7] Abolition of the armoury at Greenwich in the late seventeenth century led to the Great Barn's being converted into a 'laboratory', as a specialised manufactory for the filling of munitions. It may also have produced fireworks for use in the adjacent park, which in 1695 contained a 'House for Fire Works'.[8] Throughout the seventeenth and eighteenth centuries, rockets formed an important part of courtly firework displays, often set against the backdrop of elaborate temporary architectural structures or within formal gardens.[9]

The Congreve rocket

European interest in the rocket as a weapon of war was rekindled in the late eighteenth century by reports of East India Company troops being attacked by Indian war rockets in the campaign against Hydar Ali, prince of Mysore, and his son Tippoo Sahib.[10] In place of the pasteboard tube of the firework rocket the Indian rocket corps used an iron casing or carcass. Resulting research in Europe saw one of the earliest and most successful systems developed by the younger William Congreve, son of William Congreve, the Comptroller of the Royal Laboratory (see Chapter 2).[11] Beginning in 1804, he quickly progressed from pasteboard rockets to the use of iron carcasses. Manufacture began at Woolwich in August 1805 in a workshop converted from a shed at the back of the old proof butts; part of the work previously carried out under canvas moved into temporary weather-boarded sheds in 1806.[12]

Detailed treatises describing the use of the Congreve rocket deliberately omitted any information on the manufacturing processes.[13] In appearance it resembled a modern firework rocket, consisting of a head up to 8in (0.20m) in diameter attached to a long guide stick.[14] In a later modification

Figure 8.2 (left) 'Monkey' press or small pile driver, as used for filling Congreve rockets. From Illustrated London News **26**, *28 April 1855, 411*

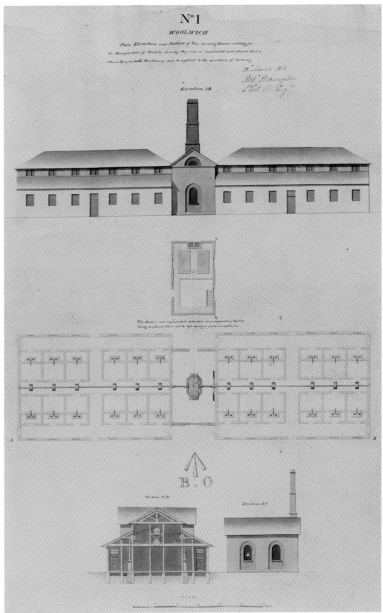

Figure 8.3 Royal Arsenal Woolwich. Design drawing of Driving Houses, 1814. PRO MPH 515. (BB95/11937; © PRO)

designed to improve the rocket's flight characteristics and, therefore, accuracy, the stick was repositioned to form a central tail. This also facilitated launching from a tube. Manufacture involved the production of the iron casing, and driving or ramming it full of black powder rocket composition, characterised principally by its low sulphur content to slow the rate of burn.[15] At first, this was carried out by hand or with a hand-cranked 'monkey' with rammers of wood or gunmetal (Fig 8.2). A design drawing of 1814 for a specialised building at Woolwich (Fig 8.3) shows the intention to move to an industrial scale. The identical pair of so-called driving houses were to be powered by a steam engine sited between them in a brick engine house, with a matching brick boiler house, detached by a few feet to lessen the danger of an explosion. The driving houses themselves were timber-framed and clad. The resultant T-shaped overall configuration is similar to that adopted from mid-century for the steam-powered incorporating mills at Waltham Abbey RGPF (Figs 3.5 and 3.11). Here the power was to be carried into the driving houses by overhead drive shafts and transmitted to the pile-driving 'monkey'

presses by belts. Each house contained 12 such presses, organised symmetrically in groups of three and each occupying a screened-off bay. The 'monkey' or weight of the press was used in conjunction with rammers, as in later practice, but was prone both to producing clouds of gunpowder dust and to causing occasional ignition of the charge.[16]

Figure 8.4 Congreve
Rocket Works at
Abbey Marsh, West
Ham, in 1869;
established in 1817
it worked until the
1870s. Extract from
OS, London, Sheet
XXIX, 25-inch, 1st
edition, 1869

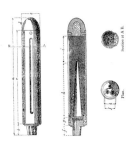

Figure 8.5 Hale war
rocket, from War
Office Notes on
Ammunition 1872.

Figure 8.6 Hale war
rockets deployed by
British expeditionary
force in Abyssinia
(now Ethiopia) in
1868 (from
Illustrated London
News 53, 11 July
1868, 32).

Congreve himself established a private rocket works in 1817 on the West Ham Marshes (Fig 8.4). Its isolated location was presumably deliberate and a reflection of the danger of what was essentially a specialised filling factory, initially comprising a cluster of detached timber sheds with a combustible store 300yd (274.5m) from the workshops. The plan form and layout of its buildings are not sufficiently distinctive to suggest functions. Rocket carcasses may have been fabricated there, but more probably they were brought in, like the rocket composition from the powdermakers of the nearby Lea Valley or the Thames Estuary. Here, war rockets were manufactured for the East India Company along with signal, whaling, and rescue rockets, and domestic fireworks.[17]

The Congreve rocket would in modern terminology be called a weapons system. It was manufactured in a variety of sizes between 6 and 42 pounds (2.72 and 19kg), and more rarely up to 100, 200, and 300 pounds (45.5, 91 and 136.5kg). They could be fitted with a range of different heads, including case shot, shells, or incendiary

compositions, and employed on land or at sea. Early successes included the firing of Boulogne in 1806 and Copenhagen in 1807, but, most memorably, in the attack against Fort McHenry in Baltimore, Maryland, in 1814, which inspired the line in the American national anthem, 'the rockets' red glare, the bomb bursting in air'.[18] These powerful demonstrations of the rocket's potential resulted in 14 foreign governments adopting the war rocket, some perhaps supplied from Congreve's West Ham factory.[19]

The Congreve rocket survived in service use until 1864, when it was replaced by a modified version designed by Captain Boxer. By 1867 this was formally superseded by the design of an independent inventor and entrepreneur called William Hale, though Hale's fundamental advance had been in production at least since 1855.[20] He did away with the long guidance stick and replaced it by a tail piece with three conical vents; these were cut away on one side, causing the rocket to spin along its axis as the gases escaped (Fig 8.5) – an effect that could be augmented by launching from a rifled tube (Fig 8.6). The Hale rocket had five hardware components – a head, case, base piece, tail piece, and safety cap; for its production at Woolwich the castings for the tops and bottoms were supplied by Messrs Fairbairn and Co. The rocket establishment at Woolwich mapped in 1866 on a site alongside the main canal of the Royal Arsenal (Fig 8.7) probably had its origin in expenditure of £5500 in 1855 on new buildings and machinery; it was equipped with hydraulic presses for the manufacture of the Hale rocket. In common with all filling operations, the 'dead' hardware components were brought to one side of the establishment and the explosive filling to the other. During assembly the ready prepared corrugated rocket casing, made of Atlas metal (from the Bessemer process) with a rivetted and brazed seam, was filled from the top with rocket composition. This was inserted as pellets and squeezed down under hydraulic pressure in one of the four cruciform-plan press rooms (21–4 in Fig 8.7), powered from a central engine house (14 in Fig 8.7). A millboard washer was put in place and the cast iron

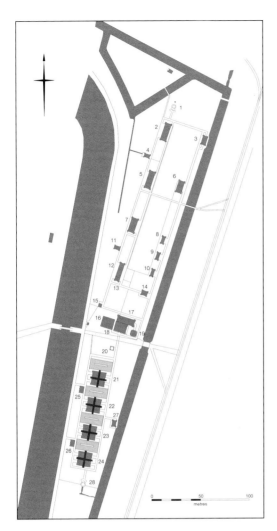

Figure 8.7 (left) Royal Arsenal Woolwich. Principal buildings of the Rocket Establishment in 1866 (redrawn from PRO, Supply 5/60): 1 Latrines; 2 Painting house; 3 Magazine; 4 Shifting house; 5 Material store; 6 Material store; 7 Heading rooms; 8 Mixing room; 9 Mixing room; 10 Mixing room; 11 Shifting house; 12 Boring room; 13 Engine room; 14 Engine house; 15 Iron shed; 16 Coal yard; 17 Boiler house; 18 Engine house; 19 Chimney; 20 Hydraulic accumulator; 21 Press rooms; 22 Press rooms; 23 Press rooms; 24 Press rooms; 25 Shifting house; 26 Shifting house; 27 Magazine; 28 Latrine.

Figure 8.8 (top right) Hale's Rocket Factory at Rotherhithe (from Illustrated London News *22, 23 April 1853, 297).*

Figure 8.9 (below right) Bramah-type hydraulic press introduced by William Hale to fill his rockets; cf Fig 8.2 (from Illustrated London News *26, 1855, 411).*

head rivetted to the body in the heading rooms (7 in Fig 8.7). A conical hollow was then bored out of the charge in the boring room (12 in Fig 8.7) to form a large burning surface on ignition, and a millboard washer was again inserted before the base piece was screwed in place and the tail piece and safety cap attached. Before leaving the establishment all the war rockets were painted red and marked with the date of manufacture.[21] Besides projectiles, signalling rockets, sound rounds, and (most importantly) life-saving rockets used to throw lines to stricken ships were manufactured.

The rocket establishment at Woolwich remained in use at least through the late nineteenth century, but by the Great War it had been re-located eastwards on the marshes. Other factories manufacturing war rockets included William Hale's private factory at Rotherhithe (Fig 8.8) and Macdonald's War Rocket Factory at

Whitehill near Gravesend in Kent, first licensed in 1876. This comprised a group of workshops and a magazine 150yd (137m) distant, and a similar manufacturing process to Woolwich was used, except that the rocket composition was inserted into the casing as loose powder. The casing then was placed on the table of a hydraulic ram, which was raised, pressing the head of the drift against a fixed piston on the upper part of the press, with progressively shorter drifts inserted as the casing was filled with powder (Fig 8.9). In this private concern, Bramah type hand presses were used, as opposed to the centralised hydraulic system in the state factory at Woolwich.[22]

In the Great War, the British use of rockets was restricted to signalling, carrying messages, and illuminating the night sky. Much of the requirement was supplied by commercial firework manufacturers.[23] After just over a century of use, black powder war rockets were removed from the list of warlike stores in 1919.[24]

The Second World War

Cordite rockets

In contrast to the United States of America and especially to Germany, in Britain there was little amateur interest in rocketry or in the romance of space travel in popular culture after the Great War. The British

Figure 8.10 Cordite rocket (from W H Wheeler 1945 British Rocket Equipment, Ministry of Supply).

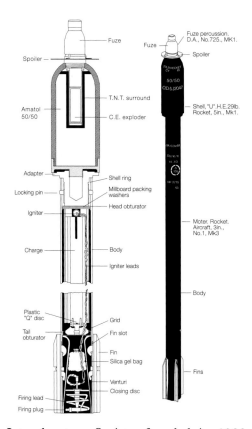

Figure 8.11 (left) ROF Chorley. View of the Group 5 filling sheds. (AA93/5822)

Figure 8.12 (right) ROF Chorley. Cordite rocket filling machine. Note the trolley used to move the rocket motors. AA93/5901

Interplanetary Society, founded in 1933, was a latecomer in comparison with the equivalent continental societies. Practical experimentation by this amateur group was perhaps constrained by the 1875 Explosives Act.[25] Government sponsored research into rocketry began in April 1935, when a team under Dr Alwyn Crow at the Explosives Research Department at Woolwich was set to investigate the development of rocket projectiles. The main objectives for intensive study, in order of priority, were anti-aircraft defence, long-range attack, air weapon against hostile aircraft, and assisted aircraft take-off.

Facilities for this research were *ad hoc*. Early static firing of 2in (50mm) diameter rockets was carried out in the 'white elephant', a domed concrete structure usually used to study the fragmentation patterns of shells. Later work on 3in (76mm) rockets was moved to Fort Halstead in Kent, where one of the underground casements of the disused Victorian fort was converted into a static firing chamber. Live firing trials were conducted at pre-existing ranges at Shoeburyness in Essex and Orford Ness in Suffolk, where the only specialised facilities were two parallel railway lines inclined at 15° and set in concrete. Coastal firing sites were also established at the Victorian forts at Blacknor on the Isle of Portland overlooking Lyme Bay in Dorset and at Brean Down in Somerset, where rails were installed to test rocket-propelled sea-launched bouncing bombs.[26]

For many practical reasons and economy of production, cordite was chosen as the propellant for these rockets. Initially it was supplied by the RNCF at Holton Heath in Dorset, which was already equipped with large horizontal presses (Fig 7.8) normally used to extrude naval catapult charges. This was later supplemented by production at the new propellant factories including ROF Bishopton, Renfrewshire, where a section was set aside for rocket propellant. The assembly of cordite rockets (Fig 8.10) was similar to any filling activity and was initially carried out in the filling section at Woolwich. Later this activity was moved to the new filling factories (see Chapter 7). At Chorley (Lancashire) and Thorpe Arch (West Yorkshire), for example, rocket assembly was carried out in the Group 5 buildings (Figs 8.11 and 8.12). The cordite

rocket was a versatile design and was produced in 2in, 3in, and 5in versions with a variety of heads. The 5in (130mm) version was originally developed to deliver a chemical-filled shell, but was later adapted for so-called 'mattress bombardments', a name which pays tribute to its softening effect on the enemy.[27] Though they were not used to deliver chemical weapons, there is circumstantial archaeological evidence, in the form of the demolished remains of a blockhouse, a series of radiating concrete posts, and rusting 5in rocket casings, that experiments by chemical warfare troops of the Royal Engineers took place on Brendon Common on Exmoor in Devon.[28] Cordite rockets also powered the experimental wartime guided weapons, 'Brakemine', 'Little Ben', and 'Stooge'.[29]

Liquid propellant rockets

In developing cordite rockets, Britain could claim for a few years to have taken a lead in the military application of rocketry. Yet in comparison with Germany Britain lagged a long way behind in the development of liquid propellant rockets. The earliest British liquid-fuel rocket, nicknamed 'Lizzy' or 'Lizzie', was developed as an assisted take-off unit for the Wellington bomber through the Asiatic Petroleum Co Ltd by a team led by Isaac Lubbock, under a contract from the Ministry of Supply. Work on the project began in February 1941 in makeshift surroundings at the Fuel Oil Technology Laboratory in Fulham in West London. It was later moved out to suburban Surrey at Cox Lane in Chessington, where the pit dug for the foundations of Shell's new laboratories was utilised as a crude test facility. In autumn 1941 work was transferred to the Flame Warfare Establishment at Langhurst in West Sussex, and here the first purpose-built facilities in Britain for testing liquid-fuel rocket engines were constructed (Fig 8.13). Compared with contemporary German facilities, the Langhurst establishment was rudimentary. The firing shed was a simple steel-framed Dutch barn structure covered in corrugated iron, with a low brick wall and an earth-dug flameway to direct away the efflux gases (Fig 8.14). Inside, the rocket motor was suspended in a trapeze,

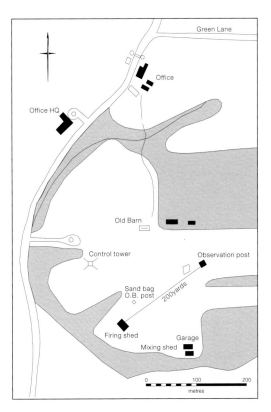

Figure 8.13 Langhurst, West Sussex. Sketch plan of layout of the Flame Warfare Establishment during the 'Lizzy' trials (1941–3). (Source Dr John Griffiths, Science Museum, London)

its front end attached to a hydraulic thrust measuring cylinder. Firing was controlled automatically from three positions – inside the shed, from a sandbag emplacement 70yd (64m) away, or from a concrete bunker 200yd (183m) away. Pressures in seven different areas of the motor were recorded using Dobbie McInnes indicators, and the ignition stages were recorded by a high-speed camera. The establishment otherwise included an observation post, control tower, garage, mixing shed, and administrative buildings.[30]

The only other significant British wartime project using liquid propellants was 'LOPGAP', a liquid oxygen petrol guided anti-aircraft projectile. Responsibility for this work originally lay with the Armament Research Department at Woolwich, but was later transferred to the Royal Aeronautical Establishment with its headquarters at Synehurst near Farnborough, Hampshire.[31] Towards the war's end, missile testing facilities were established among the coastal sand dunes of Ynyslas at the mouth of the river Dovey (or Dyfi), Ceredigion, in west-central Wales. The location is marked by a brick observation post looking out to sea, enigmatic concrete foundations, small

Figure 8.14 Langhurst, West Sussex. The firing shed at the Flame Warfare Establishment, 1942. (Source Dr John Griffiths, Science Museum, London)

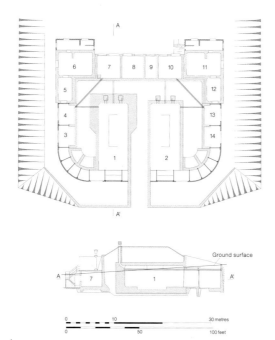

Figure 8.15 RGPF Waltham Abbey, South Site. Purpose-built research manufacturing facility, P716, built in 1954 as part of Project III. In contrast to full-scale manufacturing plant, all the principal production processes are housed in a single building (redrawn from Royal Ordnance Plan): 1 Large press house; 2 Small press house; 3 Special ovens; 4 Oven bay; 5 Control bay; 6 Cutting room; 7 Pump room; 8 De-waxing; 9 Die store; 10 Pump room; 11 Cutting room; 12 Control bay; 13 Oven bay; 14 Special ovens.

Figure 8.16 RGPF Waltham Abbey, North Site. Excavated K research round (BB94/7989)

camera huts, and a scatter of hutting typical of many derelict wartime establishments.[32] Other reminders of this activity include cordite booster motor casings which are occasionally washed up on the beach to local consternation.[33] Also in Wales, another missile range directed out to sea was established to the south at Aberporth, Ceredigion, as an out-station of the Royal Aeronautical Establishment, remote and away from the threat of air raids.

Post-war rockets

Waltham Abbey, Farnborough, and Cranfield

After the formal closure of the Royal Gunpowder Factory at Waltham Abbey on 28 July 1945 it reopened on 30 July 1945 as an experimental station of the Armament Research Department, redesignated the Chemical Research and Development Department (CRDD) in October 1946. High on the list of its priorities was the development of liquid- and solid-fuel rocket propellants. Extra urgency derived from mounting pressure from the other allied powers for the closure and dismantling of German research centres (see below, The German connection – people and know-how). To accommodate the new establishment, the former production buildings were

converted into laboratories or supporting facilities, often with minimal outward alteration (eg Fig 3.6). The most noticeable topographic change was the construction of roads where previously buildings were linked only by water or tramway. On South Site facilities were created for small-scale production of propellants or developing pilot plants, the most significant designated Projects I, II, and III in the early 1950s. These typically combined adapted pre-existing buildings with new purpose-built structures (Fig 8.15).

British scientists lacked the experience of designing suitable test stands and many of the early post-war designs drew on German practice, in particular incorporating direct observation. At Waltham Abbey a test stand was required to support the research work on the ignition and combustion of novel propellants with thrusts

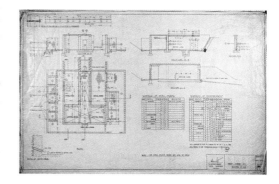

Figure 8.17 RGPF Waltham Abbey, North Site. Design drawing for proof stand no 1, 12-4-1946. (BB92/26357; © MoD)

Figure 8.18 RGPF Waltham Abbey, North Site. Western firing pit of proof stand no 1. (BB92/26048)

varying between 100 and 1000lb (45.5 and 453.6kg) (Fig 8.16). Beginning early in 1946, work began to convert a former cordite reel magazine into a proof stand (Fig 8.17). All but one of the magazine's external brick walls were retained, and in the centre a T-shaped reinforced concrete command and control room was constructed with firing pits to either side, viewed through armoured glass windows (Fig 8.18). Early work in this stand is known to have included investigations into bi-propellant systems, using nitric acid and a variety of fuels, and into mono-propellants, using the hazardous liquid explosive dithekite developed during the war. A detached and mounded magazine was built for this 33yd (30m) away from the stand. It is unclear, however, whether each firing bay was served with fuel and oxidant from the adjacent storage tanks, or if the liquids were more effectively separated by placing them either side of the stand to prevent accidental mixing.[34]

A comparable arrangement was adopted at Farnborough in a purpose-built rocket test bed with a central control room and test beds to either side (Fig 8.19). The fuel and oxidant bays were similarly placed adjacent to one another next to the test bed. Instructions on the design drawing indicate that this stand was used for firing hydrogen/liquid oxygen rockets.[35] Recording was typically by a multi-channel recorder or by high-speed camera photographing the gauge readings during firing; the gauges were mounted close together for this reason.[36]

The small test stand built at Cranfield College of Aeronautics, Bedfordshire, in the mounded bomb dump of the former RAF station, has many of the features typical of a liquid propellant stand (Fig 8.20). Tests were controlled and directly observed from a small reinforced concrete blockhouse. The oxidant and fuels were stored in pressurised tanks in separate bays at the rear of the stand (Fig 8.21). Above the propellant bays is a Braithwaite tank for storing water to douse the firing stand during its operation and to wash away unspent fuel into the grilled soakaway. The firing bay is in the angle between the control room and fuel bays: during firing, a rocket engine was

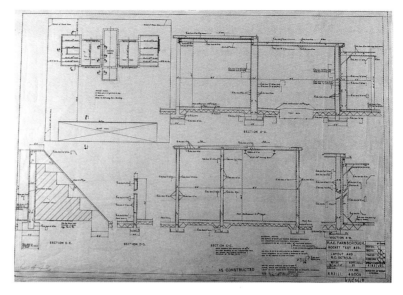

mounted on a steel frame and the fuel and oxidant were fed to it from the rear. A safety feature typical of most liquid propellant test stands is the bath tub where technicians could plunge if they spilt any oxidant on their clothing. An additional feature of this establishment, where aeronautical engineers were trained, was the facility for a small group of observers to watch test firings from the safety of a concrete-lined trench to the south of the stand. In this, the observers stood with their backs to the stand, beneath an overhanging parapet, and viewed the firing through a mirror.

Rocket Propulsion Department, Westcott

The site at Waltham Abbey was far too constricted for rocket test stands to be constructed with adequate spacing to ensure their safety. So in April 1946, under the auspices of the Ministry of Supply, the Guided Projectile Establishment was set up at a disused wartime airfield at Westcott in Buckinghamshire. Departmental politics

Figure 8.19 (above) RAE Farnborough, Hampshire. Design drawing for rocket test stand, July 1946. (BB95/11945; © PRO WORK 44/48)

Figure 8.20 (left) Cranfield College of Aeronautics. Rocket test stand. (BB93/27458)

Figure 8.21 Cranfield College of Aeronautics. Pressurised oxidant tanks serving rocket test stand (Fig 8.20). (BB93/27461)

The German connection – people and know-how

Two contrasting aspects of Britain's attempt to draw on German personnel and rocketry expertise characterise the immediate post-war period. One, 'Operation Backfire', was directed at the technology of large ballistic missiles and was essentially a dead end. The second focused on the use and handling of liquid propellants and related test stand design. This shaped the future direction of British rocket technology.

'Operation Backfire'

The alarming and psychologically devastating V1 and V2 campaigns against Britain in 1944 and 1945 highlighted the role rockets might play in any future war. Britain's backwardness in this field was confirmed by the capture of German rockets and scientists and the study of research materials and documents removed as war booty.[37] Britain took an early lead in the evaluation of German rockets by establishing 'Operation Backfire' soon after the German capitulation to test captured A-4 rockets, as the V2 was officially designated.[38] The site selected for this work was Krupp's former naval gun proving ground at Altenwalde near Cuxhaven. Ground clearance was under way by June and in July design drawings for the necessary installations were prepared.[39] After material was gathered together and assembled, three rockets were launched in October 1945. Supervision was by the British but nearly 600 German personnel were employed; and this was reflected in the design of the ground installations, including the reinforced concrete observation post and control post, whose solid concrete hipped roofs were of characteristic German design (Fig 8.22). Elsewhere, research institutes were kept open and work continued under British supervision to produce summaries of wartime work and carry out small-scale experiments.

In the popular imagination, the research on the V2 by Dornberger and Von Braun at Peenemunde on the Baltic coast has overshadowed many other important German rocket programmes.[40] Yet, it is these smaller projects that set the direction of post-war British rocketry. In the aftermath of war, Britain's economy was on the verge of bankruptcy and could not sustain research into large ballistic missiles, with the result that work on an A-4 derivative, code-named 'Hammer', was suspended by the late 1940s.[41] The chiefs-of-staff nevertheless gave a high priority to the development of rockets for anti-aircraft defence, to counter the perceived threat of jet bombers carrying nuclear weapons.

Liquid propellants

Little practical use appears to have been made of German designs or propellant types for solid-fuel rockets. However, Britain did need to acquire German technical know-how about liquid propellants. In particular, it was research by Hermann Walter at Kiel into the use of hydrogen peroxide as an oxidant and by Bayrische Motoren-Werke (BMW), who pioneered the use of oxygen-rich nitric acid, which determined the future direction of British rocket research.[42]

The lack of British expertise in this area was partly solved by the arrival of ten German rocket engineers at the Rocket Propulsion Department at Westcott in Buckinghamshire in November 1946. They were later joined by six more, to form the largest contingent of German rocket engineers in Britain. Significantly for the development of British rocket technology, the majority were from the Walter Werke, bringing knowledge of the pioneering use of hydrogen peroxide as an oxidant. Another so-called 'draughtsman' named Zumpe may have been responsible for test stand design and instrumentation, a subject he later published on.[43] He was from Peenemunde, but importantly he had also worked on the anti-aircraft rocket code-named *Wasserfall*, which used nitric acid as an oxidiser.[44]

Work at the new establishment at Westcott was organised into sections dealing with heat transfer, combustion chamber design, fuel supply, materials, and instrumentation.[45] Details of the facilities required to support these activities are sketchy, however. Initial lists refer to eight small emplacements for engines with a thrust of up to half a ton, and facilities for testing monofuel, hydrogen peroxide, and nitric acid fuel systems, along with the necessary engineering and other support. An inspection in December 1947 – perhaps prompted by an accident a month earlier when a German RATO (rocket assisted take-off) unit exploded killing the leader of the German team, Dr Johannes Schmidt, and two British technicians – named one of the test stands as the 'temporary German emplacement'; but beyond saying that the walls were of brick, between 12in and 13.5in (0.30m and 0.32m) wide, and recommending it should be strengthened with reinforced concrete, it gave no details of its plan form.[46]

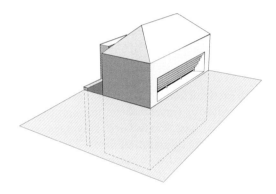

saw the main responsibility for guided weapons research transferred to the Royal Aeronautical Establishment at Farnborough, and Westcott was renamed the Rocket Propulsion Department (RPD) and assumed responsibility for 'research and development on all aspects of rocket propulsion for civil and military applications'.[47]

In the early years research concentrated on development of liquid propellant engines. Important programmes in the late 1940s included Research Test Vehicles I and II, the former developed from LOPGAP and the latter using kerosene and hydrogen peroxide.

The physical facilities at Westcott were at first characteristically rudimentary, adapting former airfield structures to new uses, though by 1949 a small housing estate had been added. The corrugated iron structure used for test firing 'Lizzie' was also

apparently moved from Langhurst to Westcott, for an inspection in 1947 found it unsafe and suggested it should be surrounded by a traverse.[48] But other, more important, inputs were necessary for such a complex technological research programme, and these were in short supply in post-war Britain. It needed an industrial infrastructure to manufacture the scientific instrumentation and metals required to withstand the high temperatures and pressures in rocket engines, and trained scientists and technicians. German rocket engineers were imported (see above, The German connection – people and know-how). Some instrumentation was available from disposal stores in Britain, and other gaps were filled by war 'booty', and later by acquisition or purchase from Germany, in particular from Walter Werke at Kiel.[49]

Probably in response to the accident in 1947 that cost lives from the combined German and British research team, the new Jury or 'P' site emplacements designed by J C Clavering of the Ministry of Works in 1948 for component and rocket testing exhibit far greater care (Fig 8.23).[50] The different elements of the test beds were separated by a traverse or earth cushion. At the centre was the firing bay with an effluent drain to carry away any unspent fuel, and on two sides separate fuel and oxidant bays. The firing bay was viewed through periscopes from the observation room and

Figure 8.22
Altenwalde near Cuxhaven, northern Germany. Reconstruction drawing of observation post, based on design drawing of July 1945. (Source Royal Ordnance, Westcott)

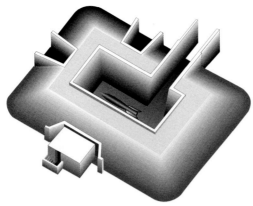

Figure 8.24 RPD Westcott. Test Cubicles built in 1949. In these examples the safety baths contained warm water. (BB94/4857)

Figure 8.26 RPD Westcott. Pug mill used for filling rocket casings. In the foreground is the Raven motor used in the Skylark rocket. (BB94/4845)

Figure 8.25 Rocket Motor Facility at RPD Westcott. (NMR 4859/51)

technical data were recorded in a detached recording room adjacent to the entrance ramp. Four small test cubicles added in 1949 at Westcott appear less safety-conscious (Fig 8.24). In these, probably because of the smaller amounts of fuel and oxidant handled, the different elements were clustered together in a single structure with a detached rear control room. They were without traverses, too, though nearby examples had earthwork traverses surrounding the direction of firing. Their safety baths were filled with warm water.

In 1949 research also began into the use of solid propellants, especially new types of plastic propellants for use in booster motors. In the following year a small experimental filling section was established in the south-western corner of the site, to test new filling methods and to operate as a small-scale production unit (Fig 8.25). In layout and operation the rocket motor facility was similar to a section within a filling factory, with the explosive propellant and metal components brought together for assembly. It was designated a danger area and entry was through a shifting room to don safety footwear and clothing. As with a filling section, it comprised a series of small scattered production buildings which were generally of flimsy construction. Those where the more hazardous processes were carried out had traverses and the operations were controlled remotely from a separate control room. They were connected by asphalt cleanways and protected by the usual array of lightning conductors and a fire main.

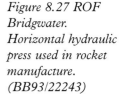

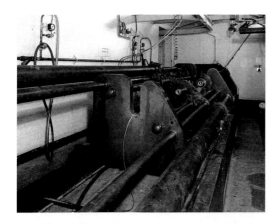

Most operations were carried out with rockets in a horizontal position, so buildings are generally low. An exception was the building used to fix the ethyl cellulose inhibitor between the casing and the charge, where the rocket was held vertically with a raised platform and, hence, a double-storey building was required. For filling, the rocket casing was held horizontally and propellant was fed into it using a pug mill (Fig 8.26). In a separate operation, the propellant was then compacted into the casing, and the conduit shape formed using a long horizontal hydraulic press (Fig 8.27).

The test stands required for static firing of solid propellant motors were generally less specialised than those handling liquid fuels and could accommodate a range of motors, size being the principal constraint. As with liquid fuels, the danger of the motors exploding during firing made it essential that firing took place within a confined space with adequate protection for the test personnel. The earliest surviving solid propellant test stand, built in the 1950s, consists of a central firing bay enclosed in sheet piling, covered by railway lines and

enclosed in an earth mound (Fig 8.28). In 1958, solid propellant test beds were built on a former runway at Westcott, and included the tall K1 test stand (Fig 8.29a), which allowed rockets to be inverted and fired vertically to make thrust measurements. The adjacent K2 site (Fig 8.29b) was designed for horizontal firing of rockets. Firings were overseen from a control room and recorded from three high-speed camera bays in each of the side walls. The firing bay was covered by water sparges. The rocket's efflux gases were directed away along a flameway surfaced in refractory concrete, through a blast wall 38ft 6in (11.7m) high, and into an earth flameway, where the gases scoured a deep trench.[51]

As at other specialised defence research establishments, many unusual and often unique facilities were constructed, in this case to investigate rocket propulsion. These include the test beds already described, a radio attenuation tower constructed in the

Figure 8.27 ROF Bridgwater. Horizontal hydraulic press used in rocket manufacture. (BB93/22243)

Figure 8.28 RPD Westcott. Early 1950s test stand for solid propellant rockets. (BB94/4871)

Figure 8.29 RPD Westcott. Solid propellant test stands, 1958. (a) (above) K1 site used for vertical firing and (b) (below) K2 site for the horizontal firing. (BB94/4860 and BB94/4862 respectively)

late 1940s by adapting Bailey bridge sections, a centrifuge, vacuum tanks for simulating upper atmosphere, and pressure vessels for underwater firing.[52] The site's infrastructure had a high-pressure nitrogen main used to pressurise fuel and oxidant tanks, and filtration beds to neutralise contaminants in the cooling water. Climatic test cubicles and non-destructive test facilities including X-ray and ultrasound might be found at other explosives research centres, while administration buildings, workshops, a steam-raising boiler house, library, photographic section, and canteen are typical of any large defence site.

A new industry

In the years immediately after the war, the development of rockets and guided weapons rested firmly with the government establishments. By the late 1940s it was realised that, on their own, they did not possess the

necessary resources or facilities to develop the ambitious arsenal of rocket-propelled missiles and guided weapons then planned.[53] The natural commercial collaborator was the aircraft industry, and the new rocket industry reflected its names and geographical distribution (Fig 8.30). There was the same split, too, between plants which primarily produced the airframes and those that manufactured aero-engines.

Some firms were involved in rocket and guided weapons work from the end of the war, notably Fairey Aviation on a missile named 'Stooge'. Armstrong Siddeley worked at their engine works at Ansty near Coventry, Warwickshire, in cooperation with Westcott on an assisted take-off unit, 'Snarler', whose initial design was based on a stripped-down Walter Werke 109-510 rocket.[54] The six leading aircraft companies of Vickers-Armstrong, Hawker-Siddeley, Rolls-Royce, Bristol Aeroplane Co Ltd English Electric, and de Havilland also dominated the manufacture of guided weapons.[55] These were the tip of the pyramid, however, and it is estimated that around 400 firms were involved in missile-related work.[56] Spending on missile systems also encouraged the growth of new companies to produce the complex electronics and guidance systems needed to support this programme; for example, it largely underpinned Ferranti's establishment of their computer department at Wythenshawe.[57] Invariably the production of any one missile involved a consortium of companies, often geographically dispersed. For the anti-aircraft missile 'Bloodhound' in the 1950s Bristol Aeroplane Co Ltd took the lead, but among six main contractors Ferranti produced the guidance control, Bristol Aerojet produced the booster rocket motors, and Bristol Siddeley produced the ramjet sustainer engines.[58]

Most companies chose to locate their new guided weapons or rocket motor sections within existing plants – the Bristol Aeroplane Company at Filton, Gloucestershire, and English Electric at Luton, Bedfordshire. None of these can be regarded as architecturally distinctive of the industry since they either reused existing buildings, perhaps with temporary accommodation added, or occupied anonymous

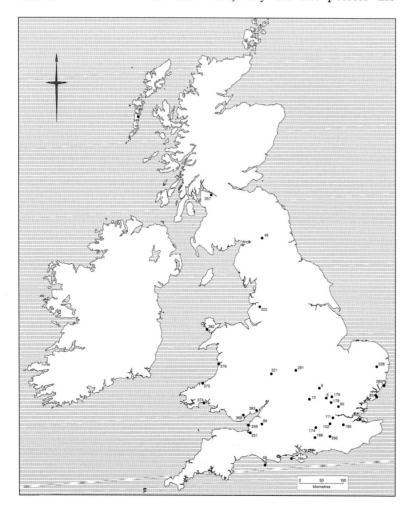

Figure 8.30 Map of principal British twentieth-century rocket manufacturing and research centres.

premises on industrial estates. When the Bristol Aeroplane Co Ltd needed additional space for Bloodhound, they converted a former electric motor factory at Birch Grove in Cardiff. Despite the long lead-in times of research and development, production runs for these technologically complex products were usually measured in the hundreds, although of high unit value.[59] Only rarely did the level of production create new factories. It was exceptional, for example, when de Havilland established one in Stevenage, Hertfordshire. Production of the anti-aircraft missile 'Thunderbird' for the army and later the anti-tank missiles 'Swingfire' and 'Vigilant' made that factory the largest single employer in the town, and an important factor in its success as a new town.[60]

Where a development contract was placed with a private company, close links were maintained with government establishments. This was especially true of the Rocket Propulsion Department at Westcott, which was involved in the majority of British rocket motors after the war. Manufacturers were able to make use of fundamental research carried out there and also its specialised facilities, although most built small test stands near their engine works. At Ansty these initially consisted of merely a small sandbagged emplacement; de Havilland also set up test facilities at their Hatfield, Hertfordshire, works.[61]

The most distinctive monuments created by the new industry, therefore, were those associated with research and development sites, and in particular the test stands concerned with the handling of explosive propellants.[62] The comment that 'the history of the post-war aircraft industry is the history of R[esearch] and D[evelopment] rather than the history of the production of aircraft' is equally applicable to the rocket industry.[63] The importance of surviving structures may lie principally in the specific project developed in them. Yet additionally, the lack of information about failed, unsuccessful, unworkable, and cancelled defence technology shrouds them in a cloak of invisibility.[64] Of the 20 or so British guided weapons projects using rocket propulsion proposed in the late 1940s, less than half entered service or reached sizeable production runs.[65] In many cases the reasons for failure were political,

Figure 8.31 RGPF Waltham Abbey, South Site. Propellant mixing-house built for the aborted Blue Water missile project. In the centre was the weighing room, with propellant mixers to either side. (BB93/27107)

through withdrawal of funding, rather than technological shortcomings. Despite their recent date, many of these projects are now little more than names; official secrecy and the destruction of prototypes and blueprints have efficiently erased nearly all trace of their existence or their locational associations. Attrition of identifiable monuments associated with failure is even greater than those associated with successful technological projects. A rare survival was the mixing house at Waltham Abbey (Fig 8.31), built to produce the propellant for the tactical surface-to-surface missile, 'Blue Water'. Developed by English Electric, this promising system was cancelled by the Minister of Defence, Peter Thorneycroft, in 1962.[66]

Manufacture and handling of rocket propellants

For solid-fuel rockets, a considerable amount of expertise was already available in the manufacture and handling of propellants. Cordite production was well understood and some plant was readily adaptable (Fig 7.8). Research into new types of solid propellants was concentrated at Waltham Abbey, while their manufacture and filling of rockets remained within the existing Royal Ordnance Factories (cf Chapter 7), with groups of buildings being converted for this new activity.

Developing rocket technology in the late 1940s, in particular the 'Red Duster' anti-aircraft missile project, demanded larger diameter motors and existing British extrusion technology was limited to diameters of up to 10in (0.25m). At the RNPF at Caerwent, captured German presses were evaluated which could extrude a charge 20.6in (0.52m) in diameter and development started on a press of 22.5in (0.57m) diameter, at least one of which was installed at ROF Bishopton.[67]

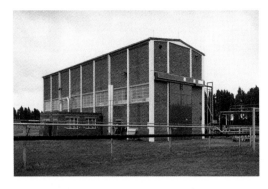

buildings with high access doors (Figs 8.32 and 8.33). As an alternative, in the motor assembly building pits were sunk into the floor. Supplies of liquid nitroglycerine for the casting operation posed a particular problem. It was at first solved by moving it by road from Caerwent, after the addition of the desensitiser triacetin (Fig 8.34). Later Summerfield was equipped with its own nitroglycerine factory (Fig 8.35).[68] Characteristically, much research and development took place within the factory. Facilities included laboratories for routine control and inspection of manufacturing processes in addition to development of new products. Also, along the western boundary of the factory was a range for test firing motors, and off-site in the Wyre Forest a centrifuge.

A particular feature of this post-war phase was that earlier functional distinctions between factories began to break down. At factories previously dedicated to manufacturing explosives, as at Bishopton, Bridgwater, and Caerwent, sections were adapted and new buildings constructed to manufacture rocket motors.[69]

An alternative method of manufacturing large rocket motors developed at this time was the cast double-base method. In essence, this involved filling a rocket casing with a nitrocellulose casting powder, into which a casting liquid, nitroglycerine, was then introduced, initially under vacuum but later pressurised using nitrogen. Casting gave advantages in allowing more flexibility in the configuration of the charge design and the ability to bond the propellant to the casing. The process had at first been suggested in Britain, but it was developed to a production scale in the United States and reintroduced at trial plants set up at Woolwich and Waltham Abbey. Full-scale facilities were established by Imperial Metal Industries in a former wartime small arms factory at Summerfield near Kidderminster, Worcestershire, and later at the RNPF at Caerwent and ROF Bishopton. Work to adapt existing structures and erect new buildings began in September 1951. In contrast to Westcott, where the rockets were handled horizontally, at Summerfield they were held vertically during manufacture. This, combined with the need for access to the top of the rockets from raised platforms inside the filling sheds, demanded tall

Supply of fuel and oxidants for liquid propellant engines remained with the companies already active in this area. Kerosene came from the petroleum companies. The principal supplier of pressurised gases was the British Oxygen Corporation. British Oxygen Wimpey Ltd was also one of the few contractors able to undertake installation of the complex pump and pipe arrangements needed to supply the rockets with fuel and oxidants during test firing. The demand for concentrated hydrogen peroxide was met by Laporte Chemicals Ltd's autoxidation plant at Warrington in Cheshire, an area with a long association with the chemical industry.[70]

The culmination of all this post-war research and industrial activity was the 1957 defence White Paper.[71] This firm technological base established in the preceding decade gave the defence minister, Duncan Sandys, the confidence to state that the most effective deterrent to war was the maintenance and development of Britain's nuclear weapons. Delivery was then by free-fall bombs from the V-bombers, but they were to be supplemented by ballistic rockets. The decision not to proceed with the development of a supersonic bomber indicated that the future was seen to lie with rockets. In the meantime the life of the bombers was to be extended by the introduction of the rocket-powered Avro 'Blue Steel' stand-off bomb, which could be launched from outside the range of Soviet air defences.[72] The White Paper also foresaw that the manned fighter force would be reduced and the remaining aircraft fitted with air-to-air missiles, but would be replaced in due course by ground-to-air guided missiles like Bloodhound and Thunderbird, which were about to enter service in 1958. It is probably no coincidence that Duncan Sandys, Winston Churchill's son-in-law, had a long association with rockets, first as the commander of the first experimental cordite rocket battery and later as head of the committee set up to investigate the threat from the German V weapons.

'Blue Streak'

In the mid- to late 1950s a high political priority was given to developing an intercontinental ballistic missile delivery system for Britain's independent nuclear deterrent.[73]

In 1955 a specification was drawn up for such a missile, to be called 'Blue Streak'. Responsibility for coordination of the project was given to de Havilland Propeller Company, overseeing the work of three principal contractors, the de Havilland Aircraft Company for the airframe, Rolls Royce for the engines, and Sperry Gyroscope Company for the inertial guidance system, with Marconi supplying the ground radar and communications.[74] In the decade since the firing of captured V2s, Britain had not kept pace with the technology necessary to manufacture large ballistic missiles. It was longstanding agreements with the Americans that allowed the British contractors to obtain assistance from General Dynamics for the airframe and from the Rocketdyne Division of North American Aviation Incorporated in engine and test stand design. They were already important manufacturers of aircraft or their components, and were able to adapt existing plant for rocket manufacture. Construction of the airframe was centred on the de Havilland factory at Hatfield, but for final assembly the rocket, comprising 30,000 or so components, was moved to de Havilland's Stevenage factory.

Just as challenging as the design of the rocket was the development of test facilities, with their demands on the skills of civil, mechanical, and electrical engineers. These were necessary to test all the components of the rocket individually and assembled into a prototype launch vehicle, and to ensure that the vehicle systems were compatible with the ground control systems. Using these facilities, after the initial design stage, each vehicle was proved before it was shipped for launch. Although all large rocket launch sites exhibit many generic similarities, all are unique to an individual rocket system to ensure the correct delivery of propellants, gas supplies, and correct launch sequencing. Study of the technology of any rocket programme therefore cannot be divorced from consideration of the supporting ground facilities, and vice versa.[75]

Spadeadam

The site selected in 1955 for the Blue Streak static firing trials was Spadeadam Waste in Cumbria, covering approximately

Figure 8.36 Core of the Spadeadam Rocket Establishment, Cumbria, showing dispersal of principal rocket test areas: 1 Administrative and launch vehicle assembly area; 2 British Oxygen Liquid Oxygen production plant; 3 Electricity sub-station; 4 Component test area; 5 Priorlancy Rigg engine test area; 6 Greymare Hill main rocket test area; R Reservoir. (© OS Plans NY 57 SE and NY 67 SW)

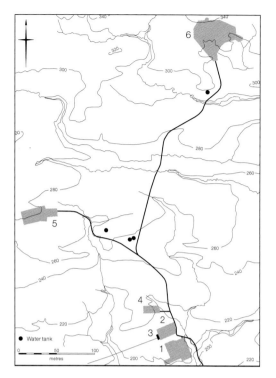

8006 acres (3240ha) of desolate moorland (Fig 8.36). Surveying started in 1956 and in January 1957 construction work began. Over 2000 men were employed on this, 600 of whom lived in a temporary work camp close to the site. To accommodate the site's permanent workforce of around 1000 people, two housing estates were built six miles (10km) away at Brampton and an on-site hostel provided for single staff. The site was managed by Rolls Royce on behalf of the Ministry of Aviation; the main contractors responsible for construction were British Oxygen Wimpey Ltd, with the electrical instrumentation subcontracted to Pye Ltd. The cost of the establishment was estimated at around £20 million out of a total development cost to April 1960 of £84 million.[76] On completion these were the most advanced testing facilities in Europe, although modest by comparison with those of the principal superpowers.

The establishment was divided into five principal areas; administration, liquid oxygen factory, component testing, engine testing, and rocket testing. Within the administrative area were workshops for the assembly and checking of the airframe and engines when they arrived on the site. Also in this area were support services including transport, a surgery, and fire and ambulance stations.

The component test area lay 547yd (500m) to the north, and here the smaller parts of the rocket were tested, including pumps and valves. Though less dangerous than firing the rocket motors, testing of these pieces involved simulating their working conditions at high pressure using potentially explosive mixtures of fuel and oxidants. Experiments were supervised from a large reinforced concrete control room, surrounded by nine attached test cubicles and three detached cells for turbo-pump testing.

Nearly 1¼ miles (2km) to its north were the Priorlancy Rigg engine test stands (Fig 8.37). One of the first principles in their design was that an accident was almost inevitable. The four test stands were therefore well spaced at 250ft (76m) intervals, and the servicing facilities, including propellant tanks and pump houses, were placed away from the stands. Their design placed many demands on the engineers. They needed to be massive to withstand the rocket engines' thrust, which from a single engine could be in excess of 50 tons (50.8 tonnes). They had also to be accessible for the positioning of engines and required cranes and walkways for the technicians to handle the engines. Characteristically, access was from the top, which reduced the amount of lifting and separated these 'clean' operations from the disposal of spent propellants at the base of the stand. Following typical American practice they were dug into an escarpment, which

Figure 8.37 Spadeadam Rocket Establishment, Cumbria. Foundations of engine test stand and flameway at Priorlancy Rigg. (AA94/1953)

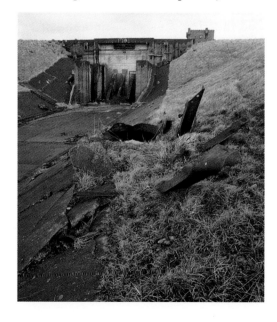

allowed the flameway to fall away from the stands, to carry away the efflux jet, waste propellant, and cooling waters. These were led to a lagoon, where any unspent fuel was floated off. Also typical of large engine test stands, the engines were fired in the vertical position. This both simulated their position during flight and ensured no potentially explosive gels formed in the combustion chamber, as all unspent fuel should fall and be washed away. The stands were set on massive concrete foundations to support the heavy steel framework needed to withstand the force of the engine. Beneath this framework sat the deflector to turn the efflux jet from the engine through 90°. The design of this deflector had to be able to withstand the sudden load of the efflux jet emerging at around 8000–10,000ft/sec and the thermal shock of a temperature of between 2780 and 3320°C. The solution was to design an elbow-shaped, mild steel bucket into which water was pumped at a rate of 20,000 gallons (90,920 litres) per minute during firing. An assured supply of water was in consequence a further essential requirement of the site's infrastructure, and was pumped from the river Irthing three miles away and stored in four one million gallon (4,546,000 litre) circular storage tanks.

Also in contrast to the earlier test stands in Britain, the firings were controlled and observed remotely. The control room was a reinforced concrete blockhouse, surrounded on three sides by an earthwork traverse and sited 186yd (170m) to the east of the nearest stand. Firings were controlled and monitored from consoles in this building linked to the stands by 8000 instrument and electrical control cables passing in a duct 7ft square and 361yd long (2.1 × 330m) beneath the stands. Typical values measured were thrust, propellant flow rates, and temperatures and pressures through the system. Firings were viewed from periscopes and episcopes set in the roof and from black-and-white and colour television monitors.

Another problem facing the designers of the test stands was handling the cryogenic supercool oxidant liquid oxygen with a boiling point of −183°C. At these temperatures the physical properties of metals alter:

they contract and can become brittle and more susceptible to shock, and problems also occur with icing and condensation. To eliminate transport and storage problems, the range was equipped with its own liquid oxygen plant, managed by the British Oxygen Corporation and capable of producing 100 tons (101.6 tonnes) of liquid oxygen per day, in addition to liquid and gaseous nitrogen. The gaseous nitrogen was pumped around the site by pipeline to pressurise fuel and oxidant tanks. Liquid oxygen was moved by tankers to the test stands, where up to 160 tons (162.56 tonnes) was stored in tanks ready for use. To minimise the lengths of pipes that needed pre-cooling before the liquid oxygen was pumped into the vehicle, its store tank and pump house (15 in Fig 8.39) were placed as close to the test stand as possible.

The facilities at Priorlancy Rigg were designed solely for test firing engines. Full testing of the fully assembled vehicle was carried out at Greymare Hill, 1fl miles (3km) to the north-east of Priorlancy Rigg. This complex consisted of two stands, C2 (Fig 8.38) and C3, though only C3 was ever brought into operation (Fig 8.39). Many of the design problems encountered in the engine test beds were also evident here, but in addition to testing the compatibility of the engines and vehicle systems it was used to prove the ground launching and monitoring equipment.

Before firing, the assembled test vehicle was brought by transporter in its handling frame to the multi-storey servicing tower,

Figure 8.38
Spadeadam Rocket
Establishment,
Cumbria. C2 test
stand at Greymare
Hill. (AA94/2010)

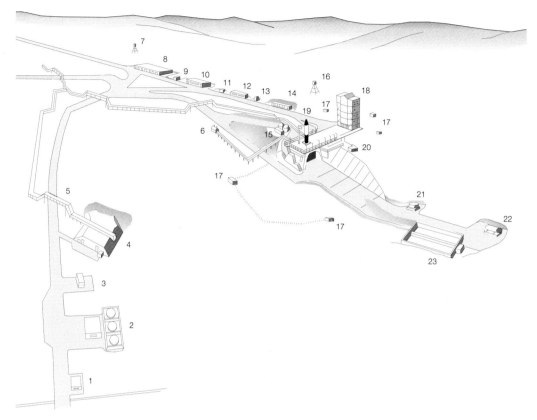

*Figure 8.39
Spadeadam Rocket
Establishment,
Cumbria. C3 static
firing station at
Greymare Hill (from
Williams and Hume
1963; source J Brit
Interplanetary Soc,
19, no 5, 188).*

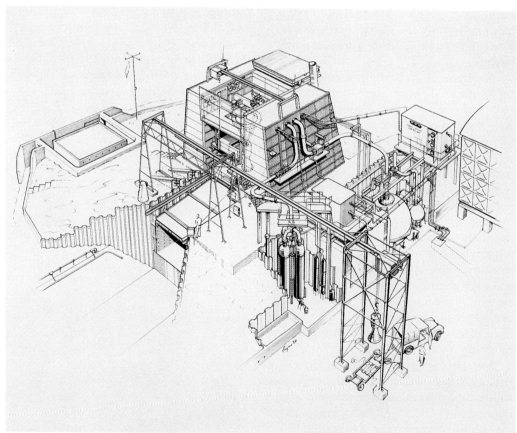

*Figure 8.40 RPD
Westcott. 'P' site test
stand (Fig 8.23)
remodelled for Blue
Streak's RZ2
engine. (© Royal
Ordnance)*

weighing 400 tons (406.4 tonnes) and standing 110ft (33.5m) high (19 in Fig 8.39). Still in its handling frame, it was raised into a vertical position on its launcher and the whole servicing tower moved on rails to the end of the causeway of the test stand, 50ft (15m) above the ground, ready for firing. Beneath the causeway was a series of rooms known as the test post (20 in Fig 8.39), which housed launch facilities including equipment for the ground pressurisation of tanks, pumping propellants, electrical power supply, and cooling air for the vehicle. In position, the vehicle was filled with an explosive combination of 60 tons (60.96 tonnes) of liquid oxygen and 27 tons (27.432 tonnes) of kerosene. This loading of fuel and preliminary tests were run from the test post beneath the launcher. Thereafter firings were controlled from the safety of the control centre (4 in Fig 8.39), 273yd (250m) to the south of the stand, since mishap could result in a devastating fireball. The walls of this blockhouse were nearly 3ft 3in (1m) thick and surrounded by an earthwork embankment on the three sides facing the stand. As with the engine test stands, operations were remotely controlled by wires carried along ducts to relays beneath the stand; visually the firing was watched with episcopes and four observation periscopes set into the roof of the control centre, closed-circuit television, and from remote-controlled camera huts (17 in Fig 8.39) close to the stand. During firing, the flame deflector was continually cooled with water flowing down the spillway to the lagoon (23 in Fig 8.39), where any unspent kerosene was removed. Dump tanks for the liquid oxygen and kerosene were also sited beneath the stand (6 and 21 in Fig 8.39), in case the vehicle had to be rapidly unloaded.[77]

In support of this programme, as early as December 1954 proposals were put forward at the Rocket Propulsion Department at Westcott to modify the late 1940s P site test stand (Fig 8.23) to accommodate the RZ2 engine for Blue Streak (Fig 8.40). By 1960 over 500 static firings tests had been made. Westcott was also involved in the next phase of the project, developing the underground silos from which Blue Streak would be launched. One-sixth scale trials were conducted using an above-ground emplacement and full-scale tests were planned for Spadeadam.[78] At Hatfield three test stands were erected for low-power engine tests, flow testing, and development of launcher release gear using a static development vehicle. Other work included pressure testing of tanks at Farnborough and experiments at Luton into the heat differential between the fuel and oxidant tanks caused by aerodynamic heating.

Totland, West High Down, Isle of Wight

As part of the Blue Streak programme, an experimental test vehicle was required to study the ballistic properties of a warhead re-entering the earth's atmosphere. The design study was carried out by the Royal Aircraft Establishment at Farnborough, and the industrial contract was let to Saunders Roe Ltd at their Osborne works at East Cowes on the Isle of Wight. The rocket was called 'Black Knight'. Propulsion was provided by an Armstrong Siddeley Gamma engine, developed at Westcott using the propellant mixture of kerosene and high test peroxide.

The site chosen for the test facilities was on War Department land adjacent to the late nineteenth-century Needles Battery, set on top of chalk cliffs facing out to sea (Figs 8.41 and 8.42). The facility was split into two sections. The test area comprised two servicing towers (1 and 2 in Fig 8.42) at either end of a curving roadway, with a blockhouse and pump room (4 in Fig 8.42) and storage for kerosene, demineralised water, high pressure air, and nitrogen (5 in Fig 8.42) at the centre. Although the oxidant high test peroxide was easier to handle than liquid oxygen, special precautions were taken. It was held in a bulk storage tank on the site and then pumped by underground pipeline to the test stands prior to firing. During filling, the technicians wore protective clothing and worked in pairs in case of accident and the oxidant area was kept flooded by a constant stream of water. Design of the test facilities was undertaken by Saunders Roe, with the ground control and monitoring equipment regarded as an extension of the vehicle systems design and

Figure 8.41 High Down, Isle of Wight. Remains of Black Knight and Black Arrow static test facilities. (BB94/16349)

Figure 8.42 High Down, Isle of Wight. Layout of static test facilities (redrawn from British Hovercraft Corporation 1971): 1 Servicing tower; 2 Servicing tower; 3 Test posts; 4 Blockhouse and pump room; 5 Storage for kerosene, demineralised water, high pressure air and nitrogen; 6 Oxidant laboratory; 7 Offices, conference room, first aid, and canteen; 8 Main building; 9 Laboratories and mechanical workshop; 10 Battery room; 11 Recording room; 12 Store; 13 Garage and maintenance workshop; 14 Fore station with reservoir; 15 Transformer and sub station; RF (Radio Frequency) laboratory 16 RF site; 17 Old lookout tower; 18 Police cottages, shelter, and office; 19 Police post and RF laboratory; 20 Lower gatehouse.

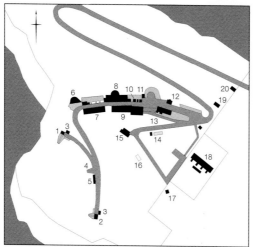

identical to that used at Woomera (see below), except that at High Down the servicing towers were static and the release jack inoperable. The support services lay above the test area. They included offices, laboratories, workshops, and general storage areas – some reused buildings converted by a firm of architects, John Strube. The estimated cost of the work was £45,000. The stands were used for the rocket's initial development and for the acceptance tests for each vehicle before it made the six-week journey by sea to Woomera for launch.[79]

Weapons Research Establishment, Woomera, Australia

Crucial to the progress of the British missile programmes was the Weapons Research Establishment at Woomera in South Australia. Development of the Long Range Weapons Establishment began in 1947, with supporting facilities at Salisbury near Adelaide reusing the idle wartime Salisbury explosives factory. By the late 1950s and before the arrival of Blue Streak, Woomera had already played an important part in Britain's missile research. The ranges in the United Kingdom capable of use for live firing, Aberporth in Ceredigion and Ty Croes on Anglesey, principally faced out to sea, which made the recovery of spent rounds difficult. Smaller land ranges such as Larkhill in Wiltshire were too constricted for large rockets. In contrast, Woomera offered live firing over a range approximately 1200 miles (1930km) long over some of the most sparsely populated land in Australia, a climate which ensured work could carry on throughout the year, good visual observation, and ready recovery of test rounds.[80] For Blue Streak, Black Knight, and then 'Black Arrow' (see below) almost identical facilities were constructed to those at Spadeadam and High Down (Fig 8.43). Because of the remote desert situation, cooling of the stands with vast quantities of water was impractical and, instead, a longer flame drop was used and an efflux deflector of refractory concrete. As a launch site, Woomera lacked component and engine test areas, but had facilities absent from British static test sites, including optical and radar tracking equipment and telemetry receivers to monitor the rocket after launch.

An end

Even before the completion of the Spadeadam facilities, the Blue Streak missile programme was cancelled on 13 April 1960.[81] As a silo-based missile it was thought vulnerable to a pre-emptive strike by the Soviet Union and to lack the flexibility of air- or submarine-launched weapons. There was also a necessity to reduce defence expenditure. Symbolically, this marked an end of Britain as a manufacturer of superpower technology and the end of the country's military independence.

Development on Blue Streak continued, however, as the first stage launch vehicle for the European Launcher Development Organisation's (ELDO) rocket, Europa I. During its lifetime ELDO launched 11 Europa rockets. In all cases the success of the Blue Streak first stage was let

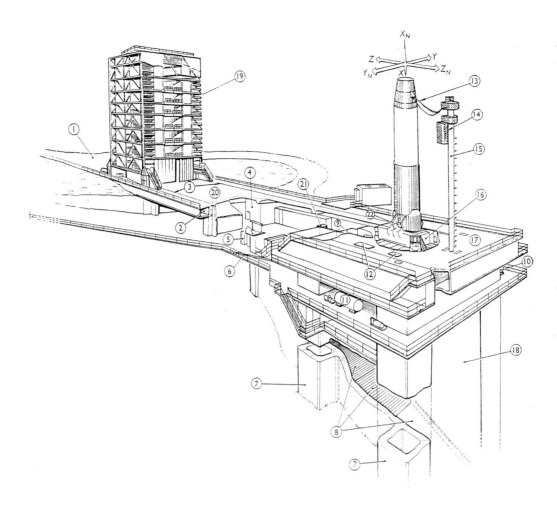

8.43 Woomera, Australia. Launching site no 6A, almost identical to static test stands at Spadeadam (Figs 8.38, 8.39) (from Williams and Hume 1963; 1 Access road; 2 Cable duct; 3 Servicing tower rails; 4 AC electrical switch room; 5 Equipment racks; 6 LOX supply pipe; 7 Emplacement supports; 8 Refractory concrete slots; 9 Hydraulic and pneumatic equipment; 10 Liquid nitrogen storage tank; 11 Trico tank; 12 Stub-ups; 13 Catenary; 14 Catenary arrester net; 15 Cable mast. Source J Brit Interplanetary Soc **19,** *no 5, 187).*

down by malfunctions in the upper stages. Britain withdrew from the development of a satellite launcher in 1969 and the last launch of a Europa rocket took place in 1973.[82] Work on the Black Knight rocket was halted, too, but its technology was transferred into the development of Black Arrow, which was built and tested on the Isle of Wight. On 28 October 1971 a Black Arrow successfully launched the British satellite 'Prospero', the only all-British launching system to place a satellite in orbit.[83] By then it too had already been cancelled, on 29 July 1971.

Endnotes

1   For a basic description of a rocket motor, see Lee *et al* 1983, 5–23; Bailey and Murray 1989, 99–114.

2   Bailey and Murray 1989, 107–8; Bottaro 1996.

3   Needham 1980, 41; *ibid* 1986, 472–516; Pan 1996.

4   Needham 1986, 516; see also the Science Museum's Exploration of Space gallery for the most accessible introduction to British rocket technology, and Baker 1978 for a history of rocketry worldwide.

5   See, for example, Royal Armouries Library, Anon, mid-fifteenth century Firework Manuscript, ref 1–34.

6   Norton 1628, 150–2; 'W T' 1672, 14–23.

7   Anglo 1969, 157 and references cited there.

8   Greenwich Local History Library 'A Survey of the King's lordship or manor of East Greenwich' by Samuel Travers, 1695.

9   Canby nd, 13–24.

10 Ley 1951, 67–8.

11 See Winter 1990, 1–79, for the most recent discussion of the introduction and deployment of the Congreve rocket system.

12 Hogg 1963a, 517–20.

13 RAHIL, Woolwich Congreve 1814.

14 *Ibid,* pl 13.

15 HMSO 1938, 174.
16 *Illus London News* 1855; Hogg 1963a, 590–1; Winter 1972; Horner nd, 51.
17 RAHIL, Kaestlin J P, manuscript notes MS 213 Box II.
18 Hogg 1963a, 1376–9.
19 *Gentleman's Magazine* 1828.
20 See Winter 1990, 179–224, for a discussion of the invention and introduction of the Hale rocket.
21 Admiralty 1905, 134–5; Hogg 1963a, 751 and 1376–9.
22 Majendie 1878; PRO WORK 44/627/354.
23 See the Imperial War Museum, London, galleries for examples of trench rockets, some by Pain and Sons.
24 Hogg 1963a, 1379.
25 See Bibliography, Selected legislation; Becklake 1984; for a discussion of rocket pioneers, see Neufeld 1995, 5–39.
26 Windibank 1979; Hawkins 1988, 112; Pooley 1994; NMR ST 25 NE 33.
27 Crow 1947b, 532.
28 NMR SS 74 SE 109.
29 Becklake 1984; see also Maxwell 1993 for post-war use of cordite.
30 Griffiths 1985; the rocket is referred to as 'Lizzie' in PRO AVIA 48/37.
31 Twigge 1993, 246–7.
32 Becklake 1984; Twigge 1993, 99, 109.
33 *Western Mail* 1995.
34 Johnson 1965; WASC 35, CRDD, 1947.
35 PRO WORK 44/48.
36 Zumpe 1950, 118.
37 PRO AVIA 54/2226.
38 For 'Operation Backfire', see War Office

39 1946; Becklake 1998, 160–1. Royal Ordnance site records at Westcott, Drg No. 5003 9 July 1945 — Cuxhaven.
40 For a recent discussion of the V2 project, see Neufeld 1995.
41 Twigge 1993, 65, 137, 246.
42 Zborowski 1957, 302–5.
43 Zumpe 1950.
44 Becklake 1998, 165.
45 Maxwell 1993, 286.
46 Bower 1988, 200–2.
47 Maxwell 1993, 286.
48 PRO AVIA 48/37.
49 PRO AVIA 48/37.
50 RO site records at Westcott, drawings AK 303/3, AL303/7 and XB303/9.
51 RO site records at Westcott, drawing AB 397/5.
52 RO site records at Westcott, drawing 5022/15, Experimental Bridging Establishment.
53 Adams 1976, 5–8; Twigge 1993, 213–20.
54 Hurden 1955; *Bristol Siddeley J* 1964; *Spaceflight* 1967.
55 Edgerton 1991, 96.
56 Sherwood 1989, 34; Twigge 1993, 215–16.
57 *Ibid*, 215.
58 *Bristol Siddeley J* 1962.
59 For example, the order for Bloodhound II for the RAF was put at 534 rounds and for Thunderbird II 200 rounds for the army (this of course excludes export orders); a Thunderbird missile cost £56,000 in the early 1960s: see PRO DEFE 7/1338; PRO DEFE 7/1846.

60 Adams 1976, 58–63, 108, 114.
61 Hurden 1955, 220 fig 4.
62 For an international perspective on the preservation of space-related sites, see London 1993.
63 Edgerton 1991, 92.
64 Hacker 1995.
65 Twigge 1993, 15, 136–7.
66 Adams 1976, 56–7, 95–6.
67 Dr G Bulloch personal communication; PRO SUPP 14/1166.
68 Gordon 1987.
69 *Ibid*, 322.
70 *Bristol Siddeley J* 1964, 110.
71 HMSO 1957.
72 Twigge 1993, 204–10.
73 Wynn 1994, esp 373–402.
74 *Ibid*, 328.
75 Lofts 1963, 77.
76 Wynn 1994, 328.
77 Forster and Breen 1962; Pollock 1962; *Spaceflight* 1962; Hume 1963; Robinson 1963; Samson 1963; Williams and Hume 1963; Carter 1965.
78 Robinson 1965; Maxwell 1993, 287; Wynn 1994, 383; RO site records at Westcott, drawings AK359/1, Proposed modifications to P2 site for large thrust chamber firings 22-12-1954; XB359/1 Feb 1955.
79 Tharratt 1963a and 1963b; British Hovercraft Corporation 1971; Scragg 1990; PRO AVIA 48/57.
80 Carter 1950, 1–3.
81 Wynn 1994, 398; PRO CAB 21/4453–6.
82 Massey and Robins 1986, 228.
83 *Ibid*, 73.

9

Survival and reuse

The legacy of powder works and their contribution to the modern landscape

A number of factors relating to their 'after-life' contribute distinctively to a study of the physical remains of gunpowder and explosives works. On closure, the fixtures and fittings were generally auctioned. Some of the machinery might be sold to other manufacturers and reused elsewhere, in a process that might not uncommonly go through several cycles,[1] while the remainder went for scrap. Of the standing structures, specialised danger buildings were particularly vulnerable: in addition to any inherent awkwardness for reuse arising from their distinctive forms, they would typically be fired to remove any residual traces of explosives. After firing, any salvageable metal and brickwork was removed, and only the structures that were the most difficult to demolish were left standing. Associated housing, administrative buildings, and the less specialised manufacturing buildings (eg open sheds) tended to survive better, as they were more easily adaptable for other uses; former saltpetre production buildings at the Marsh Works in Faversham are notable early examples (Figs 2.12 and 2.13). The capacity for creative assimilation and adaptation nevertheless continues to reveal unexpected survivals (Figs 2.19 and 2.20), and raises the prospect of further discoveries.

In contrast to the poor survival of individual buildings of powder works, the layout of many factories is still traceable and exerts an influence on the modern landscape. In many instances, as notably at Oare (Fig 4.3), the narrow and often water-logged valleys which attracted the early powder makers are today marginal and unattractive for large-scale redevelopment.

In many instances these overgrown sites, dissected by a network of watercourses, act formally or informally as wildlife refuges or havens within or on the fringe of urban and suburban development. This combination of ecological and amenity value with archaeological and historic interest makes individual former powder works valuable assets, capable of benign and informative management for their local communities – as at Crane Park in west London, whose riverside extent encompasses the former Hounslow Gunpowder Mills (cf Fig 3.44), or at Chilworth (Fig 9.1).

The afterlife of the factories constructed for the Second World War exhibits a contrasting variety. On disposal, some sites presented large self-contained and often self-sufficient units, ideally located to form the basis of trading estates. Bridgend in South Wales, Aycliffe in County Durham, Kirkby on Merseyside, and the explosives factory at Wrexham were quickly converted in this way (Figs 7.17 and 7.18). The pattern

Figure 9.1
Chilworth, Surrey, here a popular trail has been laid through the former gunpowder works by Guildford Borough Council.
(BB94/10129)

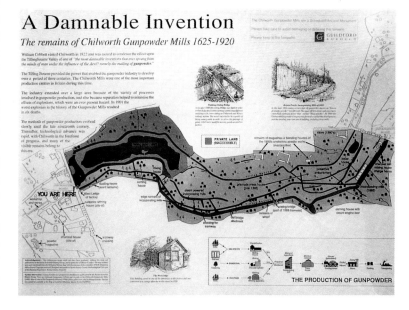

263

of building reuse varied from site to site. At Elstow in Bedfordshire and Thorpe Arch in West Yorkshire many of the wartime structures proved acceptable; even bunkered magazines at Thorpe Arch have been converted to retail units. Other sites or parts of sites were retained in government hands but substantially modified: the filling factory at Burghfield in Berkshire was converted for nuclear warhead production at a cost of £3 million in 1953 and the Small Arms Ammunition factory at Capenhurst in Cheshire for use for plutonium enrichment.[2] The former TNT plant at Sellafield in Cumbria and the filling factory at Risley in Cheshire were also absorbed by Britain's nuclear programme. At ROF Featherstone in Staffordshire part of the site was occupied by a prison, and the detached hostel accommodation at Thorpe Arch and at Swynnerton in Staffordshire became open prisons. Virtually no trace remains at Queniborough in Leicestershire despite the large size of that factory,[3] and at Ranskill and Ruddington, both in Nottinghamshire, the sites have been landscaped, with little more than a scatter of unremarkable single-storey buildings surviving.

As with any complex industrial site, the processes of decontamination and demolition make it difficult, if not impossible, to reconstruct the production processes carried out in a particular factory without reference to documentary material. Alongside the destruction of physical remains, the written and drawn paperwork relating to the plant, buildings, and manufacturing processes are also particularly vulnerable at the time of closure. The legal documents concerned with landholding often survive better, because they have a continuing commercial significance.

In the midst of these destructive factors, the site of the former Royal Gunpowder Mills at Waltham Abbey stands out as a uniquely remarkable monument of the British explosives industry. In both private and government hands, it was important for military powder production in the service of the state. Government ownership ensured that the site archive has remained intact to an exceptional degree, even if historically there was a tendency to favour the written administrative records at the expense of

drawn and technical records relating to plant and processes. The overriding factor in the survival of this site, however, was its reuse as a defence research establishment for nearly half a century following the Second World War; new uses were found for many of the specialised buildings and within the secure perimeter large areas were left to return to nature without interference. A striking resultant survival is the small flotilla of powder barges formerly used to transport the product around the works (Fig 3.41).

In 1991, following the end of the Cold War and a new round of contraction in the state-supported United Kingdom defence industry, it was this history of use and reuse that delivered the site, intact, at the beginning of a search for beneficial reuse within the framework of modern conservation policies. This process has proved to be a remarkably positive and instructive case of dynamic compromise.

Waltham Abbey: the conservation of the site

Pre-history

In 1979, the Ministry of Defence (MoD), faced with severe financial stringencies, began to rationalise its estate. One of the sites earmarked for disposal was the old Waltham Abbey Royal Gunpowder Factory (RGPF), as it was still quaintly known, gunpowder manufacture on a large scale having ceased there by the end of the Great War. In a letter from the Department of the Environment (DoE), a member of the Ancient Monuments Secretariat wrote: 'The site... has probably the longest continuous association with explosives in the country... Surviving historic remains are extensive both intrinsically and as part of a valuable complex illustrating a number of manufacturing processes... Of exceptional importance is a group of well-preserved and inter-related structures [and] we consider the national significance of this group...in industrial archaeology terms is demonstrably very great.' A little later, after a further site visit, the same official wrote to the Defence Land Agent in London forewarning him that 'Our Scheduling Section will be writing to you formally in due course with plans showing the areas proposed for scheduling', going on to explain that, although Crown Exemption freed the MoD from the legal obligations of scheduling, agreements obtaining between the two departments meant that the MoD would give the DoE prior notice if there were proposals that might affect important structures.[4]

In the event very little happened. Nothing was afforded statutory protection. The list of archaeologically sensitive structures formed the basis of a guidance note for site managers. Even so, impressive traverses and magazines on Lower Island (identified as being of importance in correspondence in May and October 1979) were demolished when the M25 was constructed in the early 1980s, and another 14 years passed before a full appraisal was carried out and any scheduling and listing took place. Why should this have been? The answer is a complex one. The recent history of Waltham Abbey encapsulates the experience of many important military sites and is worth probing in a little detail for the light it sheds on the wider picture.

The most obvious inhibition was national security. The Cold War heightened the tension between operational requirements and wider access to working sites, and increasing economic pressures on the armed forces constantly pushed the maintenance of redundant historic buildings well down the list of spending priorities. Public access to the Waltham Abbey factory, home in the 1970s to the Propellants, Explosives and Rocket Motor Establishment (PERME), one of the most sensitive defence institutions, had been denied for 200 years. Few people knew what went on there. The presence of historic buildings and sensitive archaeology on sites such as this presented a number of dilemmas. If they were listed or scheduled, then there was an expectation that despite Crown Exemption they would be maintained and protected. The only statutorily protected building at the gunpowder factory in 1979 was the former officers' quarters at the perimeter of the site (listed at grade II). If statutory protection had to take place on sensitive military sites then scheduling was preferred. This was not because it was the most appropriate designation. On the contrary, it was often the least appropriate; designed to protect archaeological sites and ruined buildings with little or no viable use, scheduling could be slow and cumbersome when applied to buildings in use. The preference for scheduling was based on security considerations: scheduling procedures, from identification to consent, were carried out by government staff who had signed the Official Secrets Act; the granting of listed building consent, in the main, was the concern of local planning officers who had not.

In the absence of available documentation, it is tempting to develop conspiracy theories about why no listing or scheduling took place at that time, but such a theory would be difficult to sustain. The 1979 option to dispose of the Waltham Abbey site was shelved, and though a territorial split in 1984 placed Lower Island and South Site in the hands of Royal Ordnance plc, the more ancient North Site remained in use as an official research establishment (RARDE) until 1991. A gentleman's agreement to take note of the archaeologically sensitive areas was put in place and the absence of formal constraints certainly removed the need for external surveillance from Ancient Monuments Inspectors and this may have been a consideration, if not an overriding one. But the reluctance to schedule may well have been mutual. The passing of the Ancient Monuments and Archaeological Areas Act of 1979 highlighted inconsistencies in the operation of Scheduled Monument legislation and, in particular, the new Scheduled Monument Consent procedures made a thoroughgoing review of the Schedule of Ancient Monuments an urgent priority. The newly formed English Heritage inaugurated a programme of review of the Schedule, which in 1987 became the Monuments Protection Programme. It was not until 1992 that work began on the review of industrial monuments, but when it did, the Waltham Abbey RARDE site was one of the earliest major complexes to be processed.

The lack of progress towards scheduling on the site was less damaging than might have been the case had it continued in intensive use or passed into private hands. Its research function made little use of most of the site, which continued to decline gently into wilderness. Its state when disposal finally became a reality was described evocatively by Andrew Mead: '...the sense of enclosure is strong. You feel that you are trespassing in a private domain, a sensation doubtless more intense because of the secrecy that so long surrounded all activity here; the site has a powerful hold on the imagination...a world of derelict industry, narrow-gauged railways, choked pathways and malign woods...you remember stories of ruined cities discovered in Central American jungles.'[5] It is this sense of mystery and wonderment – one shared by almost everyone who visits the site for the first time – that it will be most difficult to sustain as the current proposals for use as an interpreted landscape unfold, but it remains, nevertheless, a central and welcome element in those proposals.

The secrecy, the lack of access, the dereliction, and the high levels of contamination provided a test-bed upon which to measure the effects of benign neglect on archaeological sites. It also attracted birds and newts. The heronry and the alders (grown originally to provide the high-quality charcoal necessary for the production of gunpowder) were of great interest and a protected Site of Special Scientific Interest (SSSI) was designated in 1986 – a reflection of nature conservation's more successful infiltration into official consciousness at a time when the internationally significant archaeology remained unprotected and effectively unknown (a point made in Everson 1998).

The opening-up of the defence estate

The 1991 decision to dispose of the site was made in a very different political climate to that when the proposals of 1979 were drawn up. The end of the Cold War led to a radical rethink about defence policy and the level of resources required by the armed forces in a less threatening world. This culminated in the government's 1991 discussion paper, *UK defence policy: options for change*. The large-scale disposals on the defence estate that the strategy outlined in this document would involve had immense implications for the long-term future of

many highly significant historic buildings and archaeological sites. The ensuing debate also served to throw light on the parlous state of some of these monuments, victims of minimal maintenance and neglect. SAVE's campaigning exhibition and book, *Deserted bastions* (1993), and some well-targeted criticism from other quarters helped bring about a change of heart on the part of the MoD. This new mood was expressed with great clarity in 1994 by Lord Cranborne, the Under-Secretary of State for Defence, in the first annual report.[6]

Options for change also created major challenges for conservation. One was the relative lack of detailed information and understanding of certain important parts of the historic defence estate. For example, while the buildings that served the sailing navy were well enough understood, those supporting the ships of the steam fleet remained pretty well a closed book. It quickly became apparent that much work also needed to be done on aviation structures and airfields and on the archaeology of the Cold War. Similar blind spots surrounded what is termed in defence parlance the 'tail' of the services (as opposed to the 'teeth'), which included buildings such as barracks and ordnance stores. Given the potentially rapid rate of disposal of the defence estate, full appraisal and designation (where appropriate) were seen to be a matter of urgency. Where large-scale listing and scheduling programmes were envisaged, the need to know was paralleled by the need to explain and justify to owners and the wider public alike. This became an increasingly important factor after the Secretary of State for National Heritage introduced consultation into the listing procedures in February 1995. Both English Heritage and the Royal Commission on the Historical Monuments of England (RCHME) embarked on programmes of assessment on the defence estate, complementing each other in the main, but from time to time working in close partnership as at Waltham Abbey.

Towards a conservation strategy

There were a number of options open to the MoD when the Waltham Abbey site fell out of use. Given government pressures to maximise the value of a site earmarked for disposal, the 'do nothing' option was not really an option at all: no income would be raised and an unending commitment to security and the problem of liability would have involved a continual and unquantifiable outlay. Selling it on 'as found' would have been unlikely to attract commercial buyers prepared to take either the risk or the financial burden. Even if those with experience of contaminated sites, such as chemical operations, had shown an interest, they would not have been welcome residents within the Green Belt. Green Belt, Conservation Area Status, and other constraints also meant that its full potential commercial value was unlikely to be attainable.

The decision by English Heritage to reopen the case for listing and scheduling on the Waltham Abbey site was taken at the eleventh hour. Preparations for disposal were well under way, and in order to make the site safe for any use radical decontamination programmes were also in progress. These involved the removal of up to two metres of soil in certain areas and burning the combustible material of the buildings within the shell of the buildings themselves. A procedure less sympathetic to archaeological deposits and historic structures could not be imagined. Anything more elaborate, however, would be (and indeed turned out to be) hugely more expensive. While recognising that the archaeology and historic buildings were considerations that had to an extent to be taken into account, the MoD's brief to CIVIX, the consultants charged with the job of finding a beneficial reuse for the site, did not envisage carrying out further substantial work on these. The prospect of additional constraints such as listing or scheduling was not a welcome one to those who were seeking a viable future for the site, yet, in the event, the extensive heritage designations when they did take place provided one of the keys to the ultimate success of the site's transition from military to civilian use.[7]

The RCHME had decided that the remains at Waltham Abbey were a high priority for recording. Likewise, English Heritage recognised the importance of the site, but was at first uncertain how best to proceed in the face of its extraordinary complexity and the large number of components, the functions of which remained barely (if at all) understood. The political and economic pressures driving the search for a change of use also meant that any recommendations for scheduling or listing would come under the closest scrutiny. Unless the case for designation was compelling it would most likely be rejected. The 1979 proposals were no longer considered to be self-evident; they would require further research and contextualisation before arriving at a fit state to present to ministers. The obvious solution was for English Heritage and the Royal Commission to join forces. The Commission agreed to adapt its survey to meet the urgent need to inform decisions about listing and scheduling. This close collaboration, of which the present book is also a product, provided the solid basis of fact that the Secretary of State for National Heritage needed in order to schedule an area of 100 acres and list 21 buildings (including one in grade I and seven in grade II*) on a site which was known to be of immense sensitivity. These designations took effect in the autumn of 1993.

The listing and scheduling designations were an important stage in determining the shape of development at Waltham Abbey. It is likely that the success of the final outcome in terms of archaeological sustainability would not have been secured without them; most planning commentators acknowledge that 'sustainability needs to be implemented via regulation – ie that it is the planning system that has to control the activities of developers along an environmentally sensitive route'.[8] The designations were not in themselves sufficient to ensure a viable future: as is often the case, it was a mix of factors, including the mix of people involved, that successfully resolved the conflicting interests of those with responsibility for the site and that finally secured substantial sums of public money for its imaginative development as a cultural and educational centre and an interpreted landscape of the explosives industry. These factors are worth exploring in greater detail because, by and large, they all need to be present if complex heritage sites of this kind are to find a long-term future.

Conservation and management planning at Waltham Abbey

In order to achieve its goal, the conservation and development plan for Waltham Abbey had to pass five tests.

(i) The archaeology of the site needed to be fully understood and its importance made readily intelligible; appropriate designations and controls had to be put in place, designed where possible to complement other environmental sensitivities and designations.

(ii) All those with an interest in the management of the site needed to be brought together, areas of conflicting and complementary interests identified, and an operational consensus achieved; this required flexibility and compromise.

(iii) Lines of communication needed to be kept open at all times to ensure rapid resolution of problems, and consultation with the wider public (both the general public and 'opinion formers') was made effective.

(iv) An imaginative set of long-term objectives needed to be established that balanced conservation (sustainability) with economic viability, and that was realistically timetabled, deliverable, and financially certain.

(v) Adequate public and private funding needed to be secured to meet these objectives.

Understanding and protecting the historic resource

The detailed archaeological survey of the site carried out by the RCHME began with a number of handicaps. (The following account is based largely on Everson 1998, where further technical problems are discussed at greater length.) The low level of awareness of the importance of the site and the high security and difficulties of access had led to its virtual abandonment in conservation terms. In effect, it had no planning history. Although a substantial amount of the site lay within a Conservation Area, the lack of detailed information about the archaeology and its significance limited the local planning authority's scope for intervention. Nor had the normal good practice guidelines enshrined in the government's Planning Policy Guidance note 16, *Archaeology and planning*,[9] which requires full archaeological appraisals of a site to be made prior to development, been adhered to. Consequently some field evidence such as steam-pipe runs and a number of standing structures had already been lost.

The survey work confirmed the views of those who had assessed the site in 1979, especially regarding its earlier history, but also – critically – provided what had been lacking then: the incontrovertible and detailed evidence that permitted the remains to be placed securely in an international context. Here was a site that enabled the continuous development of gunpowder manufacturing to be observed from the early phases, using traditional water-powered technology (situated around Millhead), through to the major expansion period of the steam-powered incorporating mills in the 1850s with the parallel development of moulded and prismatic powders. The survey also brought out the significance of the physical remains on the site in other, less expected, ways as a centre of the manufacture of chemical-based explosives such as guncotton (from the 1860s), nitroglycerine, and cordite, and later still as a centre of research in the field of propellants for missiles and rockets.

The Royal Commission's detailed analyses of these and other findings and their significance form the principal subject of this book.[10] But in the short term they provided English Heritage with the data it needed to recommend (and defend) its listing and scheduling recommendations.

The primary purpose of both scheduling and listing is, of course, to afford the below-ground and standing remains adequate legal protection. The practical effect of each, however, is different and it was important to get the designations right. Two principal issues informed the approach to designation: sustainability and appropriateness. The below-ground archaeology, the machinery, much

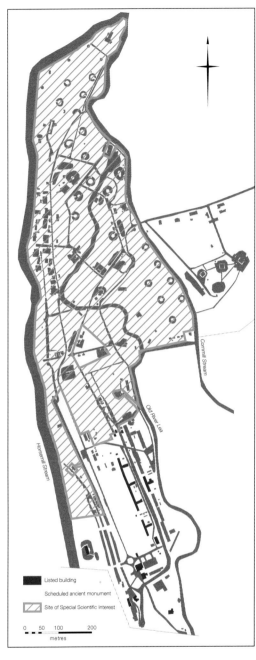

Scheduled Ancient Monuments extend more widely. It is presumed that change in a Scheduled Monument will be very limited in nature and that the monument's survival intact will be a dominant consideration in its future management. Scheduled Monument Consent favours management regimes which involve minimal change and it exerts control over aspects of setting, repair and maintenance as well as over new works. As Figure 9.2 shows, much of the scheduled area is coterminous with the SSSI.

Listing, on the other hand, forms part of the Town and Country Planning legislation and shares with planning generally the objective of managing (rather than inhibiting) change. Where buildings on the site that were of special architectural or historic interest were currently in use or clearly had a potential for reuse that could be realised without compromising their special character, it was considered more appropriate to list than to schedule. Listing controls allow greater flexibility, balancing the needs of the historic building with those of the owner, and operate on the assumption that the long-term interests of a building are best served by its remaining in beneficial use. The 21 buildings that were listed, including the eight distinguished by high grades, were considered to be amenable to the greater flexibility afforded by listing.

Managing conflicting interests and objectives

With poor management and an absence of goodwill, the numerous and varied competing interests of those involved in the site could easily have come into conflict, resulting in a dissipation of resources, a clouding of issues, fudged decisions, and slow progress. Conflicting interests would have been exploited rather than resolved – nature conservation versus good archaeological management, housing development against amenity, heritage gain against the spiralling costs of decontamination, and so forth. In the event, the project succeeded on the basis of cooperation and flexibility. Without this, it is difficult to see how the large injection of public money, notably from the MoD and the Heritage Lottery Fund, could have been secured.

of the canal network and many of the ruinous structures were considered to be so sensitive and vulnerable that even minor interventions would be damaging. There was little potential for viable uses being found that would not in themselves destroy or seriously damage those features that gave the site its national importance. While the presence of archaeological sites is recognised as a constraint on development within the planning process and within other legislation affecting land management, the powers assumed by the Secretary of State over

There were a number of factors that helped the project gel at an early stage. First, ministers and senior staff within the MoD were alert to the heritage significance of the site, not only through the existence of the SSSI (which did not enjoy Crown Immunity), but also through the mediation of Malcolm Maclaren, the site's Head of Library Services – whose understanding of the archaeological significance of the site and the details of its recent history was unsurpassed – and the MoD's Principal Surveyor, David Stanners. The MoD was also fortunate in its choice of Project Coordinator (CIVIX), who performed with great success the critical task of facilitator, bringing all the players in the game together for monthly meetings to monitor progress and identify and resolve problems (from January 1993 on), as well as developing an imaginative and realistic development brief and outline planning proposals.

Decontamination work and planning could not hang fire while the survey was under way and it was necessary to find a way of feeding in the RCHME's early findings to help inform the practical work in progress. The MoD's site managers (W S Atkins working for the Environmental Services Group of Royal Ordnance) adapted their decontamination techniques to minimise damage. On those parts of the site where the archaeological interest was marginal or of no great significance, English Heritage decided to state clearly at an early stage and ahead of completion of the RCHME's full survey that it would be taking no further action. Consequently, rapid clearance and radical decontamination could be carried out on the western flank (the Horsemill Stream area) thereby clearing the path to prepare it for housing – a private finance initiative with John Laing Construction Ltd as development partner. This pragmatic approach by the key conservation agency to freeing up a sector of the site that had some (but not irresistible) heritage interest for enabling development expedited the formulation of a more convincing business case for the overall development of the site and the securing of public funds which, it had always been accepted, depended upon a level of cross-subsidy.[11]

Wider consultation

Consultation beyond those directly involved in the day-to-day management of the site needed to target three groups: the decision-makers within the bodies that held the purse strings; local politicians and opinion-formers; and the public at large. Senior MoD managers and, ultimately, ministers had to feel comfortable with the justifications made for escalating remediation costs and the plans for vesting the site in a trust which would need a substantial dowry if its long-term heritage objectives were to be met. Local politicians were concerned principally with questions of safety, access, and amenity, and the implications of permitting even fairly small housing developments on the edge of Waltham Abbey, which was within the Green Belt and would require an adjustment to the local plan. Full consultation was seen as essential if the two key components of the proposals for the future of the site were to gain widespread support: the need for some enabling development to cross-subsidise the amenity and heritage objectives and the setting up of a local development trust to assume ownership of the site and to realise the transition from obsolescence to beneficial new use.

The details of the consultation process are fully documented by Keeping and Comerford (1997). A series of structured forums and public meetings was organised in 1991 by the MoD's land use consultant (CIVIX). These meetings involved the widest range of local interest groups (including representatives from the local councils, local residents' groups, industrial history and nature conservation societies, etc) and were impartially monitored by academic staff from the University of London and supported by expert advisers. The decisions and preferences that emerged from these meetings were clear. The priority was to make the site safe for public access and this access should be as free as was possible within the conservation constraints. The sensitivities of the SSSI were fully appreciated and it was during these meetings that the full significance of the site as the most important for the history of explosives in Europe became apparent. It was also clear that while the need for cross-subsidy was understood there was a strong desire to limit development on the edge of the town. Further public consultation was carried out the following year and this resulted in an amendment to the Draft Local Plan (itself at the consultation stage) which was presented at an exhibition attended by the minister at the Department of National Heritage, Lord Astor.

The business case

By the winter of 1993–4, after the listing and scheduling designations were put in place and a consensus had emerged from the public consultations, Lord Cranborne, the Under-Secretary of State at the MoD, decided to fund a steering committee whose task was the preparation of a detailed business plan for the site. The plan was drawn up by Prince Research Consultants. The primary objective was to establish the viability of any future heritage proposals for the site in order both to secure planning permission from the local authority and give the MoD the confidence it needed before passing the freehold to a trust and establishing that trust by means of an endowment.

The long-term aim of the steering committee was to plan for the establishment of a major educational and research resource for the interpretation of the site and the explosives industry and, at the same time, secure the fullest possible public access. It was agreed that the site needed to be managed and interpreted holistically and accepted that such an objective would take time to accomplish. It was not considered 'necessary, or indeed, desirable to undertake a "big-bang" development of the site':[12] initial planning assumed a nine-year development strategy and allowed for the possibility that the site would not be fully developed within 20 years. This 'long-fuse' approach to the site's development was a significant factor in the plan winning financial backing.

Because any endowment (provided in the form of a dowry from the MoD with additional funds from other public sources) would be unlikely in itself to be sufficient to develop a national educational and interpretation resource, it was essential to build into the business plan the capacity for raising additional revenue. The proposed organisational structure was designed, therefore, to minimise the financial risks to the project and the endowment upon which it would depend by creating a secure buffer between its charitable functions and its trading arm, a procedure now becoming widely adopted by charitable bodies. The proposal was for the establishment of a foundation to hold the estate and a capital fund as a permanent endowment. The foundation would then grant an operating lease to a charitable company set up to run the site as an interpreted historic landscape. This company would in turn operate commercially and legitimately through a wholly-owned trading company.

Winning the prize

The business plan was accepted by the MoD in January 1995 and £5.5 million was committed in principle as a dowry for the project. This in itself was not sufficient to meet the capital required to conserve the site in perpetuity as a public facility and national interpretation centre and educational foundation which was estimated at around £14.8 million. The MoD required substantial private sector involvement.

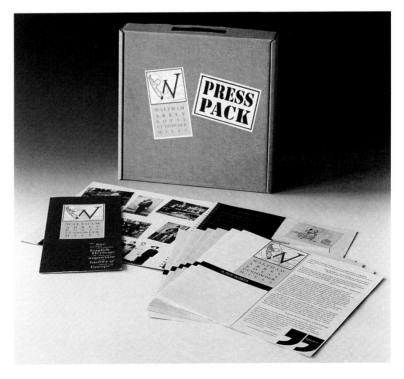

Figure 9.3 Display of presentation material prepared in support of the lottery bid for Waltham Abbey Royal Gunpowder Mills. (BB98/30010)

Figure 9.4 Ballincollig, near Cork, Republic of Ireland, reconstructed gunpowder mill. (© Cork County Council)

Figure 9.5 La Poudrérie Nationale de Sevran-Livry, near Paris, France. Engine house, 1873, two engines housed within this building powered an extensive cable drive system that criss-crossed the factory. (© W D Cocroft)

Figure 9.6 A Fábrica da Pólvora de Barcarena, near Lisbon, Portugal. Restored early eighteenth century Caldeira dos Engenhos, a header pool that was used to power incorporating mills in the building to the right. (© W D Cocroft)

This was secured, John Laing Construction bringing a further £1 million on the back of a housing development on the western flank of the site – the area identified by English Heritage as being dispensable in heritage terms, thereby releasing it for enabling development at an early stage. Much of the shortfall was made up in a spectacular Heritage Lottery Fund grant of £6.3 million in 1996, one of the largest ever given by that body (Fig 9.3). The next chapter – setting up and developing the site and realising the vision of the steering committee – is history in the making, about which it is too early to make any judgement.

Public access

The remarkable site of the former Waltham Abbey RGPF is set to become an interpreted landscape of the social, political, and technological history of military explosives manufacture and research in England. It joins an international array. The heightened awareness of the importance of the industry and its archaeology has led to the statutory protection of a number of sites worldwide and the dissemination of information more widely through museums and preserved sites. A notable early example was the preservation through local initiative of the single mill building of the Chart Mills at Faversham, Kent (Figs 2.9 and 2.10). Recent discussions about the display of gunpowder works such as the Oare Works, also at Faversham, have tended to follow a site-based approach. For the wider black-powder industry in England, a greater number of Scheduled Ancient Monuments are positively managed as amenities, including examples on Dartmoor and in the Lake District related to the local mining industries, as well as the site at Chilworth that combines both black powder and later explosives production (Fig 9.1).

In Europe, the preference has been for open-air museums encompassing whole sites. At Ballincollig, County Cork, in Ireland, a tour area comprises an interpretation centre, reconstructed mill and restored powder magazine, within a public park (Fig 9.4). Others include Frederiksvaerk (Denmark), the Musée de la Poudrérie Nationale at Sevran Livry near Paris

(Fig 9.5), and the outdoor Museum of Water Power at Ai Yannis Dimitsana, Greece. A new scheme is also under way to develop the Bacarena powderworks near Lisbon, Portugal (Fig 9.6), as an interpreted site rather than as a museum. Pride of place, both as a preserved site, museum, and an international study centre is occupied by the Hagley Museum, Wilmington, Delaware (USA). Here, remains of the DuPont Company's gunpowder factory on the banks of the Brandywine River are displayed as an extensive outdoor museum (Fig 9.7). It includes a full range of nineteenth-century waterpowered process buildings with restored or reconstructed machinery, plus remains of one of several workers' communities built by the company within walking distance of the works. In many instances these centres were designated for

preservation before production ended, so that associated machinery remained in place. But nearly all have also developed into repositories for related artefacts.

Similar positive display of sites related to the chemical explosives industry is less common. In Norway, a complete nitroglycerine factory has been preserved and displayed at Engene, about 40km south of Oslo,[13] and within the town at Sevran Livry

buildings and artefacts associated with the work of Alfred Nobel survive, though with limited attempts to convey their significance. In Britain, an association has been formed at Holton Heath in Dorset to develop a small museum devoted to the Royal Naval Cordite Factory, but the site itself is beyond its scope. At Pitsea Hall Farm, near Basildon in Essex, the site of a late nineteenth-century factory is preserved as splendid earthworks within a country park (Fig 5.51): it is designated as a SSSI and is not protected as an industrial monument as such; there is limited interpretation.

With its complex history, rich yet well-understood field remains, and secure operating basis, the site at Waltham Abbey offers the prospect of public access and interpretation explaining its international context in the history of explosives and how they have shaped the world.

Figure 9.7 Hagley Museum, Wilmington, Delaware, USA. Restored Birkenhead mills, 1822–4, these were the first edge-runner gunpowder incorporating mills erected in the United States. (© W D Cocroft)

Endnotes

1   eg Cocroft 1994, figs 22–3.
2   Norris *et al* 1994, 67, fig 2.33.
3   cf vertical air photographs NMR Swindon RAF 106G/UK/829 23-SEP-45 frame 3014; OS/68-023 8-APR-1968 frame 132).
4   WASC 1544: letters of 31 October 1979 and 4 May 1979.
5   Mead 1997.

6   1994, *Defending our heritage Historic military buildings on the defence estate.*
7   Keeping and Comerford (1997) discuss these issues in greater detail.
8   *Ibid*, 126.
9   Department of the Environment 1990.
10 RCHME 1994; Cocroft 1996; Everson and Cocroft 1996.
11 Planning permission had already been

granted for housing development on a five-acre site at Powder Mill Lane, just within the Waltham Abbey conservation area but outside the Green Belt, as part of the overall development strategy for the site.
12 Bone and Prince 1995, 362.
13 Dr Björn Ivar Berg, Norsk Bergverksmuseum, personal communication.

Gazetteer

Information in the gazetteer is divided into a maximum of nine fields:

1   a unique number, which equates with the numbers on the maps
2   site location
3   site name if different from 2
4   postal address
5   the controlling company or companies in chronological order
6   national grid reference: where the precise location of a site is unknown this is indicated by an asterisk (*)
7   period or dates of activity related to explosives production
8   preferred term describing site type
9   narrow term or note describing its function more precisely

Abbreviations used in the gazetteer:

FF	filling factory
MNT	mononitrotoluene
NFF	National Filling Factory
ROF	Royal Ordnance Factory
TNT	trinitrotoluene
UA	Unitary Authority
WW2	Second World War

The principal sources used to compile this list are: for gunpowder works Crocker (1988), for late nineteenth-century factories Hodgetts (1909), for Great War factories the unpublished papers of Ministry of Munitions in the PRO, and for the Second World War the Cabinet Office papers also in the PRO.

Each gazetteer entry for England equates to a primary record created and available for consultation within the National Monuments Record, through which bibliographical references and any supporting material can be obtained. Enquiries to the NMR Public Services, NMRC, Great Western Village, Kemble Drive, Swindon, SN2 2GZ; 01793 414600; http://www.rchme.gov.uk. Gazetteer entries for Scotland and Wales have been supplied and validated by staff of RCAHMS and RCHAMW: supporting information is similarly available from their respective National Monuments Records.

The gazeetter is not comprehensive for every location mentioned in the text, but rather contains only sites mentioned in the text where gunpowder and/or other explosive materials were made. Sites are listed under the headings England, Ireland, the Isle of Man, Northern Ireland, Scotland, and Wales, *in that order*. These areas are further subdivided into counties and unitary authorities in alphabetical order; and within these the sites are listed alphabetically.

The most up-to-date *OS Gazetteer of Great Britain* (4 edn; Macmillan Reference/Ordnance Survey, London, 1999) was used for spellings and for counties and unitary authorities. For convenience, however, the older groupings 'Greater London', 'Greater Manchester', 'Merseyside', and North, South, and West Yorkshire have been retained, with appropriate 1999 unitary authorities listed and cross-referenced.

England

Barking and Dagenham UA, see Greater London

Barnsley UA, see South Yorkshire

Bath and North East Somerset UA

001   Bath,*ST 74 64, early seventeenth century, saltpetre works
002   Littleton, ST 5575 6369, c1750–by 1839, gunpowder works
003   Middleton, ST 561 595, 1799–by 1850, gunpowder works
004   Woolley, ST 749 688, c1722–c1803, gunpowder works

Bedfordshire

005   Bedford, *TL05 49, seventeenth century, gunpowder works
006   Cranfield, SP 93613 42073, 1950s–70s, rocket test facility
007   Elstow, ROF FF no 16, TL 045 441, WW2 1942–5, explosives factory – filling factory
008   Luton, English Electric, *TL 10 20, 1950s–70s, munitions factory – Thunderbird rocket manufacture

Berkshire, see West Berkshire

Bexley UA, see Greater London

Birmingham UA, see West Midlands

Blackburn, see Lancashire

Bolton UA, see Greater Manchester

Bradford UA, see West Yorkshire

Bristol, see City of Bristol

Buckinghamshire

009   Colnbrook, Colnbrook Chemical and Explosives Co, H M Guncotton Factory, *TQ 02 77, Great War 1916–18, explosives factory – guncotton
010   Westcott, SP 710 170, 1946–present, rocket motor factory and rocket test facility
011   Wooburn, SU 898 872, c1665, gunpowder works

Calderdale UA, see West Yorkshire

Cheshire, Halton UA, and Warrington UA

012   Capenhurst, ROF, SJ 365 745, WW2, explosives factory – small arms ammunition
013   Chelford, ROF FF No 13, SJ 83 75, WW2 194?–60s, armament store, explosives factory, projected filling factory not built
014   Ellesmere Port, H M Factory, *SJ 41 76, Great War 1915–?, chemical works – synthetic phenol and arsenic compounds
015   Lostock Gralam, Northwich Brunner Mond and Co, Ammonia Soda Co, SJ 683 741, Great War, chemical works – phenol, ammonium nitrate
016   Macclesfield, ROF, *SJ 92 71, WW2, explosives factory – filling factory not built
017   Northwich, Gadbrook Works, Brunner Mond and Co Ltd, *SJ 689 716, Great War 1916–18, explosives factory – TNT purification
018   Northwich, Victoria Works, Victoria Salt Works, Brunner Mond and Co Ltd H M Factory, *SJ 646 750, Great War 1916–18, chemical works, ammonium nitrate, calcium nitrate tetrahydrate
019   Plumley, Ammonia Soda Company, Brunner Mond and Co Ltd, *SJ 720 743, Great War, chemical works – calcium nitrate for Lostock
020   Radway Green, ROF, SJ 783 543, WW2–present, explosives factory – small arms ammunition
021   Randle, Wigg Island Runcorn, Ministry of Supply operated by ICI, SJ 543 842, WW2, explosives factory – filling factory gas munitions
022   Risley, ROF FF No 6, SJ 653 925, WW2 1940–60s, explosives factory – filling factory

023　Sandbach, * SJ 736 612, Great War, chemical works – ammonium nitrate
024　Thelwall, SJ 65 88, 1758–1855, gunpowder works
025　Warrington Bank Quay, Crosfield and Sons, SJ 598 881, Great War, chemical works – glycerine
026　Widnes, United Alkali Co, *SJ 50 84, Great War, chemical works – ammonium nitrate and acetone

City of Bristol UA, see Gloucestershire

City of Derby UA, see Derbyshire

City of Leicester UA, see Leicestershire

City of London UA, see Greater London

City of Nottingham UA, see Nottinghamshire

City of Plymouth UA, see Devon

Cornwall

027　Bishops Wood, SW 83 49, 1863–87, gunpowder works
028　Cowsawes, SW 77 38, 1809–98, gunpowder works
029　Hayle, National Explosives Company, SW 572 395, 1889–1920, explosives factory – cordite, dynamite, gelignite, and guncotton
030　Herodsfoot, SX 205 609, 1845–74 East Cornwall Gunpowder Company; 1874–98 East Cornwall Gunpowder Company Ltd; 1898 Curtis's and Harvey, gunpowder works; 1900–02 Safety Explosives Company; 1902–14 Ammonal Explosives Ltd, 1914–18 Ministry of Munitions, explosives factory – ammonal explosives; 1938–1963/5 Burrowite Explosives, explosives factory – burrowite
031　Kennall Vale, SW 751 374, 1811–c1910, gunpowder works
032　Perranporth, SW 7513 5435, 1889 British and Colonial Co Ltd, 1893 Nobel Explosives Co Ltd, explosives factory – dynamite, guncotton, gelatinous explosives; Great War explosives factory – filling factory
033　Trago, SX 1777 6481, 1850–98 East Cornwall Gunpowder Company, 1898 Curtis's and Harvey, gunpowder works; 1902 Ammonal Explosives Ltd, 1908 Marpal Ltd, closed 1919 by Nobel Industries Ltd, explosives factory – ammonal explosives; 1931–60 explosives factory – burrowite

Coventry UA, see West Midlands

Cumbria

034　Barrow-in-Furness, *SD 194 737, Great War, chemical works – toluol
035　Bassingill, SD 51 87, 1790–1935, gunpowder works
036　Black Beck, SD 333 856, 1860–1928, gunpowder works
037　Drigg, ROF, SD 055 990, WW2 194?–5, explosives factory – TNT
038　Elterwater, NY 33 05, 1824–1928, gunpowder works
039　Gatebeck, High and Low Works, SD 55 86, 1850–1936, gunpowder works
040　Greenodd, Furness Chemical Co, *SD 31 82, Great War, wood chemical works – acetate of lime
041　Low Wood, SD 346 836, 1798–1935, gunpowder works
042　New Sedgwick, SD 51 88, 1857–1935, gunpowder works
043　Old Sedgwick, SD 51 87, 1764–1850, gunpowder works
044　Rockcliffe, H M Factory Gretna, NY 36 67, Great War 1915–18, explosives factory – cordite
045　Sellafield, ROF, NY 025 038, WW2 194?–5, explosives factory – TNT
046　Spadeadam, NY 62 74, 1957–70s, rocket test facility – Blue Streak missile testing

Darwen UA, see Lancashire and Blackburn

Derbyshire and City of Derby UA

047　Charlesworth Mill, H M Cotton Waste Mill, *SK 00 92, Great War burnt down April 1918, cotton mill – cotton waste mill
048　Chesterfield, The White Lee Chemical Co, ICI, *SK 38 70, late nineteenth century, explosives factory – picric acid
049　Derby, *SK 354 573, Civil War, gunpowder works
050　Fernilee, SK 01 76, 1801–1920, gunpowder works

051 Langwith, National Ammonium Perchlorate Factory, H M Factory, SK 527 710, Great War 1915–18, chemical works – ammonium perchlorate

052 Lee Valley near Dinting Vale, Greenfield Mill Co Ltd, *SK 01 94, Great War, cotton mill – cotton waste mill

053 Whaley Bridge, Edward Hall and Bros Ltd, H M Cotton Waste Mill, *SK 01 81, Great War, cotton mill – cotton waste mill

Derwen UA, see Lancashire

Devon and City of Plymouth UA

054 Bideford, Office of Woods, H M Wood Distillation Factory, *SS 45 27, 1915–18, wood chemical works – acetate of lime for acetone

055 Brendon Common, ST 7727 4403, WW2, rocket test facility

056 Cherry Brook, SX 627 773, 1844–c 1897, gunpowder works

057 Devonport, Ocean Quay NFF No 14, *SX 450 555, explosives factory – filling factory (probably not active and used as a store)

058 Plymouth St Budeaux, Royal Powder Works, SX 444 619, 1804–?, gunpowder works – reworking gunpowder

Doncaster UA, see South Yorkshire

Dorset

059 Fort Blacknor, *SY 67 71, 1930s, rocket test facility

060 Holton Heath, Royal Naval Cordite Factory, SY 946 906, 1915–7, explosives factory – cordite

061 Sherborne, *ST 63 16, early seventeenth century, saltpetre works

062 Stockwood, *ST 584 068, late sixteenth century–seventeenth century, gunpowder works

Durham

063 Aycliffe, ROF FF No 9, NZ 280 235, WW2 1941–?, explosives factory – filling factory

064 Haswell, Sabulite ICI, *NZ 38 42, c 1939–62, explosives factory – sabulite

065 Spennymoor, ROF, NZ 276 333, WW2, explosives factory – small arms ammunition

Ealing UA, see Greater London

East Sussex

066 Battle, Crowhurst, TQ 7580 1197, 1676–1874, gunpowder works

067 Battle, Farthing, TQ 7370 1465, gunpowder works

068 Battle, House Mills, TQ 7421 1462, late seventeenth century–1874, gunpowder works

069 Battle, Peppering Eye, TQ 7435 1399, 1676–1874, gunpowder works

070 Brede, TQ 8002 1913, 1769–1825, gunpowder works

071 Maresfield, TQ 46 23, 1849–59, gunpowder works

072 Sedlescombe, TQ 781 176, by 1750–1874, gunpowder works

Enfield UA, see Greater London

Essex, Southend-on-Sea UA, and Thurrock UA

073 Colchester, *TL 99 25, Civil War, gunpowder works

074 Grays, Grays Chemical Works Ltd, H M Experimental Picric Acid Plant, *TQ 60 78, Great War, explosives factory – picric acid

075 Great Oakley, Bramble Island, Harwich, The High Explosives Co Ltd, Standard Explosives Company, The Explosives and Chemical Products Co, Ex Chem Industries, TM 215 265, 1899–present, explosives factory – dynamite, gelignite, gelatine, and permitted explosives, Great War – ?tetryl

076 Kynochtown, Kynoch's, TQ 745 825, 1897–192?, explosives factory – cordite, gunpowder works; near Corringham

077 Pitsea Hall Farm, British Explosives Syndicate, TQ 745 862, 1891–192?, explosives factory – cordite, dynamite, gelignite, and gelatine

078 Purfleet, TQ 5490 7860, 1760s–1950s, magazine

079 Sewardstone, TQ 373 963, 164?–1715–20, gunpowder works

080 Shoeburyness, *TQ 95 86, nineteenth century and 1930s, rocket test facility

081 Stanford-le-Hope, Curry Marsh, The Miners' Safety Explosives Co Ltd, TQ 710 815, late nineteenth century, explosives factory – ammonite, ammonium nitrate

082   Waltham Abbey, Royal Gunpowder Factory, TL 376 015, 1664?–1945, gunpowder works; explosives factory – cordite, guncotton, picric acid, tetryl; 1945–91 Government Research Establishment, rocket test facility
083   Walton-on-the-Naze, *TM 26 23, 1944-6, rocket test facility – testing Brakemine

Gloucestershire, South Gloucestershire UA, and City of Bristol UA

084   Avonmouth, St Andrews Road, H M Factory Avonmouth, ST 520 797, Great War 1916–18, explosives factory – picric acid, later mustard gas
085   Bristol, *ST 58 72, early seventeenth century, gunpowder works
086   Bristol, Netham Works United Alkali Co, *ST 61 72, Great War, chemical works – ammonium nitrate
087   Chittening, near Bristol, NFF No 23, *ST 54 83, Great War 1916–18, explosives factory – filling factory for mustard gas
088   Coleford, Monmouth Road/Speech House Road, Office of Forest and Woods, H M Acetone Factory, *SO 57 10, opened 1913 Great War, wood chemical works – acetate of lime for acetone
089   Filton, Bristol Aviation, *ST 60 61, 1950s–80s?, aircraft factory – Bloodhound rocket manufacture
090   Gloucester, *SO 83 18, early seventeenth century, saltpetre works
091   Gloucester, Cathedral Precinct, *SO 831 188, Civil War, gunpowder works
092   Gloucester, Quay, *SO 827 188, Civil War, gunpowder works
093   Henbury, H M Factory, *ST 54 82, Great War 1916–abandoned 1917, explosives factory – nitrocellulose powder
094   Quedgeley, NFF No 5, SO 815 132, Great War 1915–18, explosives factory – filling factory
095   Thornbury, *ST 64 90, early seventeenth century, saltpetre works

Greater London

096   Abbey Wood, NFF No 11, Kings Norton Metal Co, *TQ 473 790, Great War 1915–18, explosives factory – filling factory
097   Balham, TQ 29 74, 1701–24, gunpowder works
098   Beckton, Gaslight and Coke Co, TQ 44 81, Great War, chemical works – ammonium nitrate
099   Bedfont, TQ 11 75, c 1609–1926, gunpowder works
100   Bromley-by-Bow, J and W Nicholson's Three Mills Distillery, TQ 384 828, Great War, distillery – acetone
101   Carshalton, TQ 28 66, c1650–by 1740, gunpowder works
102   Chessington, Cox Lane, *TQ 18 63, WW2 1941, rocket test facility – testing 'Lizzy'
103   Dagenham, Nitrogen Products and Carbide Co, *TQ 49 82, Great War, chemical works – ammonium nitrate
104   Enfield, *TL 37 96, 1697, gunpowder works
105   Enfield Lock, TQ 374 991, 1653–late seventeenth century, gunpowder works
106   Enfield Mill, TQ 362 955, 1653–by 1691, gunpowder works
107   Enfield Naked Hall, *TQ 374 993, 1663–late seventeenth century, gunpowder works
108   Erith, Thames Ammunition Works, Crayford Marshes, *TQ 53 77, Great War 1915–18, explosives factory – Trench Warfare Department filling factory
109   Fetter Lane, *TQ 313 813, by 1583, gunpowder works
110   Fleet Lane, *TQ 317 813, late sixteenth century, gunpowder works
111   Fulham, 22 Bagley's Lane, Fuel Oil Technical Laboratory, *TQ 25 76, WW2 1941, rocket test facility – engine research
112   Fulham, Putney Bridge Hurlingham Avenue, W E Blake Explosives Loading Co, TQ 244 758, Great War, explosives factory – filling factory
113   Fulham, Stevenage Road, Trench Warfare Department NFF No 27, *TQ 236 766, Great War, explosives factory – filling factory
114   Greenford, Greenford Chemical Company, *TQ 15 83, Great War, explosives factory – picric acid
115   Greenford, Perivale, NFF No 28, *TQ 157 838, Great War 1916–18, explosives factory – filling factory gas shells
116   Hackney and Clapton, *TL 36 84, 1652–late seventeenth century, gunpowder works
117   Hackney Wick, White Post Lane/Wallis Road, Donald Bagley Phoenix Chemical Works, H M Factory, *TQ 371 846, Great War 1915–18, explosives factory – TNT
118   Hayes, National Emergency Filling Factory NFF No 7, TQ 10 79, Great War 1916–18, explosives factory – filling factory
119   Hounslow, TQ 125 730, 1757–1926, gunpowder works
120   Leyton, Temple Mills, *TQ 376 854, 1641/9–c 1690, gunpowder works
121   Lower Edmonton, Balham Road, Snowden Fibre Machining Co Ltd, *TQ 34 93, Great War, cotton waste works
122   Millwall, Vacuum Oil Co Ltd, *TQ 37 79, Great War, oil distillery – mineral jelly
123   North Feltham, TQ 11 74, 1668–1752, gunpowder works
124   Perivale, Willesden Lane Park Royal Acton, NFF No 3, *TQ 16 83, Great War 1915–18, explosives factory – filling factory
125   Rainham, C Betrand Fields Soap Works, *TQ 51 82, Great War 1915–?, explosives factory – picric acid
126   Rainham, Rainham Chemical Works Synthetic Products Co, H M Factory, *TQ 51 81, Great War 1914–18, chemical works – acetone; explosives factory – picric acid, tetryl, TNT purification

127   Ratcliff, *TQ 362 808, late sixteenth century–early seventeenth century, gunpowder works
128   Rotherhithe, TQ 36 80, c1540–1600, gunpowder works
129   Rotherhithe, *TQ 36 79, late nineteenth century, rocket motor factory – Hale rockets
130   Royal Arsenal Woolwich, TQ 440 793, 1671–1994, arsenal/explosives factory – filling factory
131   Silvertown, Crescent Wharf/Venesta Wharf North Woolwich Road, Brunner Mond and Co Ltd, TQ 4085 8000, Great War 1915–17, explosives factory – TNT
132   Southall, London Chemical Company, *TQ 13 79, Great War, explosives factory – TNT
133   Southwark, *TQ 31 80, 1630, gunpowder works
134   Southwark, Sumner Street, National Emergency Filling Factory, NFF no 8, *TQ 320 803, Great War 1915–18, explosives factory – filling factory
135   Stratford, *TQ 38 84, early seventeenth century, gunpowder works
136   Stratford, Admiralty Filling Station, *TQ 381 841, Great War 1917–18, explosives factory – filling factory for vincenite and prussic acid
137   Stratford, St Thomas Mills, *TQ 379 835, 1597–early seventeenth century, gunpowder works
138   Stratford, Three Mills, TQ 383 829, 1588–late sixteenth century, gunpowder works
139   The Tower of London, TQ 336 806, fourteenth to sixteenth century, gunpowder works
140   Tolworth/Worcester Park, TQ 210 653, 1560–1854, gunpowder works
141   Tottenham, TQ 348 896, 1656–by 1698, gunpowder works
142   Walthamstow, TQ 3507 8829, 1659–c90, gunpowder works
143   Walthamstow, Baird and Tatlock, Blackhorse Lane, H M Factory Trench Warfare Supply Department, *TQ 35 90, Great War 1915, explosives factory – filling factory lachrymatory shells
144   West Ham, Abbey Marsh, Congreve's Rocket Works, TQ 3857 8239, early nineteenth century, rocket motor factory – Congreve rockets
145   Wimbledon, TQ 26 72, by 1666–late eighteenth century, gunpowder works
146   Yeading near Hayes, ROF, *TQ 12 82, WW2, explosives factory – small arms ammunition

Greater Manchester

147   Ashton-Under-Lyne, William Street, Hooley Hill Rubber and Chemical Company, SJ 92 97, Great War 1915–17, explosives factory – TNT
148   Barton, Trafford Park, H M Factory, *SJ 75 97, Great War 1915–18, chemical works – toluol refinery
149   Bolton, Quarton Vale Turton, T E Clarke, *SD 73 15, Great War, cotton mill – cotton waste works
150   Bury, Calrows Mill, H M Cotton Waste Mill, *SD 81 11, Great War, cotton mill, cotton waste mill
151   Bury, Higher Woodhills Works, Waste Bleachers Ltd, *SD 80 12, Great War, cotton mill, cotton waste works
152   Clayton, Clayton Aniline Co, *SJ 88 99, Great War 1915–?, explosives factory – TNT, picric acid
153   Gathurst, Wigan, Roburite Explosives Co Ltd, Ammonal Explosives Ltd, ICI, *SD 545 075, 1887–present, explosives factory – ammonal explosives roburite
154   Hadfield, Waterside Mills, near Dinting Vale, by 1915, Greenfield Mill Co Ltd, H M Cotton Waste Mill, *SJ 944 985, Great War, cotton mill – cotton waste mill
155   Lees, Holts Mill near Oldham, Greenfield Mill Co Ltd, H M Cotton Waste Mill, *SD 95 04, Great War, cotton mill – cotton waste mill
156   Manchester, Bridgewater House, Whitworth Street, Dugdale Everton and Co, *SJ 83 98, Great War, cotton waste works
157   Oldham, Export Mills, B Dyson and Sons Ltd, *SD 94 04, Great War, cotton mill – cotton waste mill
158   Oldham, Greenfield Mill, Greenfield Mill Co Ltd, H M Cotton Waste Mill, SE 0088 0365, Great War, cotton mill – cotton waste mill
159   Oldham, Hoyle and Jackson Ltd, *SD 93 04, Great War, cotton waste works
160   Reddish, Stockport, Chas Lowe and Co, *SJ 90 93, late nineteenth century, explosives factory – picric acid
161   Rochdale Healey Hall, ROF assisted factory, *SD 88 16, WW2 1941–?5, explosives factory – filling factory
162   Weaste, Cresol Chemicals, *SJ 80 98, Great War, explosives factory – picric acid
163   West Gorton, Gorton Brook, M N Morris and Co Ltd, H M Factory, *SJ 87 97, Great War, chemical works – synthetic phenol, MNT; explosives factory – TNT
164   Woodley Arden Mills near Stockport, Greenfield Mill Co Ltd, H M Cotton Waste Mill, SJ 9270 9337, Great War, cotton mill – cotton waste mill

Greenwich UA, see Greater London

Halton UA, see Cheshire

Hammersmith UA, see Greater London

Hampshire

165   Ashurst, SU 3294 0968, late sixteenth–early seventeenth century, saltpetre works

166   Bramshott, Royal Aeronautical Establishment Guided Weapons Division, *SU 84 32, WW2 1940s?, rocket test facility

167   Eyeworth, Bramshaw, 1860-9 gunpowder works; 1869 Schultze Powder Company, 1898-192? New Schultze Gunpowder Company, SU 226 145, explosives factory – nitrocellulose powders (Schultze Powder)

168   Longparish near Andover, Kynoch's, *SU 43 44, Great War 1917, wood chemical works – acetate of lime for acetone

169   Marchwood, SU 396 112, 1814-?, magazine

170   Portchester Castle, SU 625 046, 1512, gunpowder works

171   Portsmouth, Horsea Island, Royal Powder Works, SU 632 048, 1804-?, gunpowder works – stoving gunpowder

172   Portsmouth, Stampshaw Point, Royal Powder Works, SU 636 033, 1804-?, gunpowder works – dusting and mixing gunpowder

173   Priddy's Hard, Royal Naval Armament Depot, SU 619 012, Magazine, explosives factory – filling factory

174   Synehurst near Farnborough, Royal Aeronautical Establishment-Vickers, SU 86 54, 1946-?, rocket test facility

Haringey UA, see Greater London

Havering UA, see Greater London

Herefordshire

175   Hereford, *SO 51 39, Civil War, gunpowder works

176   Hereford, NFF No 16 (was 14?), SO 53 38, Great War 1916-18, filling factory; WW2 ROF FF No 4, explosives factory – filling factory

Hertfordshire

177   Barwick, 1889 Smokeless Powder and Ammunition Co Ltd, 1898 New Schultze Powder Co, TL 388 193, explosives factory – nitrocellulose powders

178   Hatfield, de Havilland, TL 209 096, 1950s-60s, aircraft factory – Blue Streak rocket assembly and testing

179   Stevenage, de Havilland, TL 235 230, 1950s-60s, munitions factory – Blue Streak rocket assembly

180   Watford, H M Factory National Ammonal Factory, *TQ 119 989, Great War 1915-18, explosives factory – ammonal (adjacent Watford No 2)

181   Watford, Balmoral Road, Trench Warfare Department Watford No 1, NFF No 24, TQ 115 980, Great War, explosives factory – filling factory

182   Watford, Callowland Bushey Mill Lane, Trench Warfare Department Watford No 2, NFF No 25, TQ 116 987, explosives factory – filling factory

Hillingdon UA, see Greater London

Hounslow UA, see Greater London

Kirklees UA, see West Yorkshire

Isle of Wight UA

183   Isle of Wight, *SZ 50 86, early seventeenth century, saltpetre works

184   Totland, West High Down, Saunders Roe, SZ 299 848, 1950s-60s, rocket test facility – testing Black Knight and Black Arrow

Kent and Medway UA

185   Cliffe, Lower Hope Point, 1891 Roslin Powder Company, gunpowder works – blending, dusting and packing gunpowder; 1898 Curtis's and Harvey, TQ 730 785, explosives factory – cordite, dynamite

186   Dartford, Curtis's and Harvey, *TQ 54 73, 1890-?, explosives factory – guncotton

187   Dartford, Green Street Green, E C Powder Co, *TQ 57 74, 1884-?, explosives factory – guncotton, nitrocellulose powders

188   Dartford, Hills and Hutchin, *TQ 54 72, Great War, chemical works – ammonium nitrate

189   Dartford, Powder Mill Lane, TQ 548 729, 1732-c1920, gunpowder works

190   Faversham, Home Works Royal Gunpowder Factory, 1759-1825, TR 0096 6124, 1650-1934, gunpowder works

191   Faversham, Marsh Works Royal Gunpowder Factory, 1786-1854, TR 013 626, 1786-1934, gunpowder works; 1846-7 explosives factory – guncotton first guncotton factory in the world

192   Faversham, Oare Works, TR 0035 6245, 17??-1934, gunpowder works

193   Faversham, The Abbey Works, 1924 Mexco Ltd, 1931 Heaters Ltd, 1991 Long Airdox (Cardox Ltd), TR 0266 6225, 1924-present, explosives factory

194   Faversham, Uplees, Cotton Powder Co Ltd and Curtis's and Harvey, TQ 990 650, 1873–192?, explosives factories – guncotton, tonite, cordite
195   Fort Halstead Projectile Development Establishment, *TQ 49 61, 1930s–present, rocket test facility
196   Maidstone, TQ 75 54, 1698–1704/c1750, gunpowder works
197   Royal Tunbridge Wells, Old Forge Mills, TQ 5944 4285, 1768–by 1835, gunpowder works
198   Tonbridge, Leigh Mills, TQ 57 47, 1811–193?, gunpowder works; 1890s Smokeless Sporting Powders, Curtis's and Harvey, explosives factory – nitrocellulose powders
199   Upnor Castle, Lodge Hill Upnor near Chatham, Royal Naval Armament Depot, TQ 758 732, Great War–WW2, explosives factory – filling factory
200   Whitehill, Gravesend, Macdonald's War Rocket Factory, TQ 64 74, nineteenth century, rocket motor factory

Kingston upon Hull UA

201   Hull, Sculacoates, Major and Co Ltd, *TA 09 31, Great War, explosives factory – TNT

Kingston upon Thames UA, see Greater London

Knowsley UA, see Merseyside

Lancashire and Blackburn, with Derwen UA

202   Chorley, ROF FF No 1, SD 563 208, 1938–present, explosives factory – filling factory
203   Church, W Blythe and Co Ltd, *SD 73 28, Great War, explosives factory – picric acid
204   Darwen, Springvale Mill, Darwen Paper Mills Co Ltd, *SD 68 22, Great War, cotton mill – cotton waste mill
205   Fleetwood, United Alkali Co, *SD 33 46, Great War, chemical works – ammonium nitrate
206   Haslingden, I W Mitchell, *SD 78 23, Great War, cotton waste works
207   Lytham, H M Factory, *SD 36 27, Great War January 1917–March 1918, explosives factory – picric acid
208   Melling, Cotton Powder Co Ltd, *SD 60 71, 1880–?, explosives factory – potentite, tonite and permitted mining explosives
209   Morecambe, White Lund, NFF no 13, SD 45 63, Great War, explosives factory – filling factory
210   Rawtenstall, Albert Works Cloughfold, Cotton Cellulose Co Ltd, *SD 81 22, Great War, cotton waste works
211   Rawtenstall, Constable Lee Works, Cotton Cellulose Co Ltd, *SD 81 23, Great War, cotton waste works
212   Rawtenstall, Holme Mill, Waste Bleachers Ltd, H M Cotton Waste Mill, *SD 792 163, Great War, cotton mill – cotton waste mill

Leeds UA, see West Yorkshire

Leicestershire and City of Leicester UA

213   Asfordby, SK 718 196, Great War, reopened 1938–69, proof range
214   Leicester, *SK 58 04, Civil War, gunpowder works
215   Queniborough, ROF FF no 10, SK 640 134, WW2 1940–?, explosives factory – filling factory

Lincolnshire

216   Gainsborough, NFF no 22, SK 825 930, Great War 1917–18, explosives factory – filling factory, for naval mines
217   Stamford, *TF 03 07, early seventeenth century, saltpetre works

Liverpool UA, see Merseyside

London, see Greater London

Manchester, see Greater Manchester

Medway UA, see Kent

Merseyside

218   Aintree, Bland Park Farm Sefton, NFF No 2, *SJ 36 98, Great War, explosives factory – filling factory
219   Kirkby, ROF FF No 7, SJ 432 988, WW2 1940–5, explosives factory – filling factory

220 Liverpool, Litherland, Brotherton and Co, H M Factory, *SJ 33 97, Great War 1914–18, explosives factory – TNT, ?picric acid
221 Liverpool, NFF No 2a, *SJ 35 98, Great War, explosives factory – filling factory
222 Port Sunlight, Lever Brothers, SJ 34 84, Great War, soap factory – glycerine
223 Sutton Oak, St Helens, UK Chemical Products Company, H M Factory, *SJ 53 93, Great War 1915–18, explosives factory – picric acid, phenol, arsenic compounds

Merton UA, see Greater London

Middlesex, see Greater London

Newcastle upon Tyne UA

224 Derwenthaugh, Sir W G Armstrong Whitworth and Co Ltd, *NZ 20 63, early twentieth century–Great War, explosives factory – filling factory
225 Lemington Point, Sir W G Armstrong Whitworth and Co Ltd, *NZ 17 64, early twentieth century–Great War, explosives factory – filling factory

Newham UA, see Geater London

Norfolk

226 Hardwick, TM 265 905, 1960s, rocket test facility unfinished
227 Kings Lynn, Alexandra Dock Synthetic Products Company Ltd H M Acetone Factory, *TF 612 213, Great War, chemical works – acetone

Northamptonshire

228 Northampton, *SP 75 60, Civil War, gunpowder works
229 Northampton, ROF FF No 20, *SP 73 63, WW2, ROF, explosives factory – filling factory not built
230 Warkworth, NFF Banbury, No 9, SP 47 40, Great War 1916–24, explosives factory – filling factory
231 Weedon Bec Royal Military Depot, SP 625 595, 1804–1965, ordnance store/magazine

North East Somerset UA, see Bath

North Somerset UA, see Somerset

North Yorkshire and Redcar and Clevelend UA

232 Allerston, SE 878 830, seventeenth century, gunpowder works
233 Farnham, Greenwood and Batley Ltd, SE 351 598, WW2, explosives factory – small arms ammunition, post-war sporting powders also
234 Selby, Watson, Joseph and Sons, *SE 61 32, Great War, chemical works – glycerine
235 Skinningrove, Skinningrove Iron Co Ltd, *NZ 70 19, Great War, explosives factory – TNT

Nottinghamshire and City of Nottingham UA

236 Chilwell, Longeaton, NFF No 6, SK 509 352, Great War 1915–18, explosives factory – filling factory
237 Newark-on-Trent, *SK 79 54, Civil War, gunpowder works
238 Nottingham, Old Radford Canterbury Road Mills, J C Ley and Sons, *SK 55 40, Great War, cotton mill – cotton waste mill
239 Nottingham Castle, SK 569 394, Civil War, gunpowder works
240 Ranskill, ROF, SK 678 862, WW2 194?–5?, explosives factory – cordite
241 Ruddington, ROF FF No 14, SK 575 320, WW2 1942–?, explosives factory – filling factory
242 Worksop, Anglo Shirley Aldred and Co, *SK 57 80, Great War, wood chemical works – acetate of lime

Oxfordshire

243 Banbury, *SP 45 40, Civil War, gunpowder works
244 Oxford, *SP 51 06, early seventeenth century, saltpetre works
245 Oxford, Oseney Mill, SP 5040 0589, Civil War, gunpowder works

Reading UA, see West Berkshire

Redcar and Cleveland UA, see North Yorkshire

Rotherham UA, see South Yorkshire

Sefton UA, see Merseyside

Shropshire

246   Ludlow, *SO 50 74, Civil War, gunpowder works
247   Ludlow, *SO 50 75, Great War 1918, unfinished, wood chemical works – acetate of lime for acetone
248   Shrewsbury, *SJ 49 12, Civil War, gunpowder works

Somerset and North Somerset UA

249   Brean Down Fort, ST 281 592, WW2, rocket test facility
250   Portishead, Shell, *ST 474 769, Great War, chemical works
233   Farnham, Greenwood and Batley Ltd, SE 351 598, WW2, explosives factory – small arms ammunition, post-war sporting powders also
234   Selby, Watson, Joseph and Sons, *SE 61 32, Great War, chemical works – glycerine
235   Skinningrove, Skinningrove Iron Co Ltd, *NZ 70 19, Great War, explosives factory – TNT

Nottinghamshire and City of Nottingham UA

236   Chilwell, Longeaton, NFF No 6, SK 509 352, Great War 1915–18, explosives factory – filling factory
237   Newark-on-Trent, *SK 79 54, Civil War, gunpowder works
238   Nottingham, Old Radford Canterbury Road Mills, J C Ley and Sons, *SK 55 40, Great War, cotton mill – cotton waste mill
239   Nottingham Castle, SK 569 394, Civil War, gunpowder works
240   Ranskill, ROF, SK 678 862, WW2 194?–5?, explosives factory – cordite
241   Ruddington, ROF FF No 14, SK 575 320, WW2 1942–?, explosives factory – filling factory
242   Worksop, Anglo Shirley Aldred and Co, *SK 57 80, Great War, wood chemical works – acetate of lime

Oxfordshire

243   Banbury, *SP 45 40, Civil War, gunpowder works
244   Oxford, *SP 51 06, early seventeenth century, saltpetre works
245   Oxford, Oseney Mill, SP 5040 0589, Civil War, gunpowder works

Reading UA, see West Berkshire

Redcar and Cleveland UA, see North Yorkshire

Rotherham UA, see South Yorkshire

Sefton UA, see Merseyside

Shropshire

246   Ludlow, *SO 50 74, Civil War, gunpowder works
247   Ludlow, *SO 50 75, Great War 1918, unfinished, wood chemical works – acetate of lime for acetone
248   Shrewsbury, *SJ 49 12, Civil War, gunpowder works

Somerset and North Somerset UA

249   Brean Down Fort, ST 281 592, WW2, rocket test facility
250   Portishead, Shell, *ST 474 769, Great War, chemical works – toluol
251   Puriton, ROF Bridgwater, ST 332 424, WW2 1939–present, explosives factory – RDX, tetryl, rocket motors
252   Taunton, *ST 22 24, early seventeenth century, gunpowder works
253   Wells, *ST 54 55, Civil War, gunpowder works

Southend-on-Sea, see Essex

South Gloucestershire UA, see Gloucestershire

Southwark UA, see Greater London

South Yorkshire

254 Denaby near Rotherham, British Westfalite, *SE 524 001, Great War 1915–?, explosives factory – filling factory ammonal explosives and Trench Warfare Department filling factory
255 Silkstone, Chemical and Dyewares Ltd, *SE 29 04, Great War, explosives factory – picric acid
256 Worsborough Dale, SE 35 03, 1849–1911, gunpowder works

Staffordshire

257 Featherstone ROF FF No 17, SJ 925 050, WW2 1942–5, explosives factory – filling factory
258 Lichfield, *SK 116 098, Civil War, gunpowder works
259 Stafford, *SJ 92 23, Civil War, gunpowder works
260 Swynnerton, ROF FF No 5, SJ 850 338, WW2 1940–50?, explosives factory – filling factory
261 Tutbury, ROF FF No 19, *SK 20 28, explosives factory – filling factory not built

Stockton on Tees UA

262 Billingham, H M Nitrate Factory, *NZ 47 22, Great War, chemical works – unfinished
263 Stockton-on-Tees, Power Gas Corporation, *NZ 43 20, Great War, explosives factory – TNT

Suffolk

264 Ipswich, *TM 16 44, late sixteenth century, saltpetre works
265 Orford Ness, TM 437 490, WW2, rocket test facility
266 Stowmarket, Patent Safety Gun-Cotton Company; New Explosives Co Ltd, TM 06 58, 1861–192?, explosives factory – cordite, sporting powders and other explosives
267 Trimley near Ipswich, the War and Sporting Smokeless Powder Syndicate Ltd, Curtis's and Harvey, *TM 272 340, 1891–190?, explosives factory – smokeless sporting powders, cannonite nos 1 and 2

Surrey

268 Abinger, TQ 11 47, 1589–mid-seventeenth century, gunpowder works
269 Abinger Hammer, TQ 10 47, c1790, gunpowder works
270 Chilworth, 1885 Chilworth Gunpowder Company, TQ 029 473, 1626–1920, gunpowder works; explosives factory – cordite
271 East Molesey Lower Stert, TQ 15 68, 1650s–60s, gunpowder works
272 East Molesey Upper Stert, TQ 14 68, 1650s–1780, gunpowder works
273 Ewell, TQ 210 636, 1750–c1875, gunpowder works
274 Godstone, TQ 3176 5083, 1589–1635, gunpowder works
275 Horley, NFF No 17, *TQ 28 43, Great War, explosives factory – filling factory (?used as a store, also addressed as NFF No 16)
276 Stanwell, TQ 03 74, by 1791–late nineteenth century, gunpowder works
277 Thorpe, *TQ 02 68, 1625, gunpowder works
278 Wandsworth, *TQ 27 75, late seventeenth century, gunpowder works
279 Wotton, TQ 117 470, ?late sixteenth century–seventeenth century, gunpowder works
280 Wotton, Pigeon House Farm, TQ 124 471, ?late sixteenth–seventeenth century, gunpowder works

Sussex, see East Sussex; West Sussex

Sutton UA, see Greater London

Swindon UA, see Wiltshire

Tower Hamlets UA, see Greater London

Thurrock UA, see Essex

Tyne and Wear, see Newcastle upon Tyne UA

Wakefield UA, see West Yorshire

Walsall UA, see West Midlands

Waltham Forest UA, see Greater London

Wandsworth UA, see Surrey

Warrington UA, see Cheshire

Warwickshire

281   Ansty, Armstrong Siddeley Rolls Royce, SP 404 815 1940–?, rocket test facility and rocket motor factory

West Berkshire and Reading UA

282   Burghfield, ROF FF no 18, SU 68 68, WW2 1942–present, explosives factory – filling factory; post-war munitions factory – missiles
283   Reading, *SU 72 73, early seventeenth century, saltpetre works

West Midlands Metropolitan County

284   Birmingham, *SP 07 86, 1827, gunpowder works
285   Bournville, *SP 04 81, WW2, explosives factory – filling factory ROF assisted
286   Coventry, *SP 33 79, Civil War, gunpowder works
287   Coventry, Foleshill, White and Poppes NFF No 21 (was 10), *SP 35 82, Great War 1915–18, explosives factory – filling factory
288   Oldbury, Tat Bank, Chance and Hunt, *SP 993 888, Great War 1915–18, explosives factory – TNT, ammonium nitrate
289   Walsall, ROF FF No 15, *SP 01 99, WW2 1942–?, explosives factory – filling factory

West Sussex

290   Fernhurst, SU 895 281, 1796–early nineteenth century, wood chemical works – charcoal cylinder works
291   Fisherstreet, SU 948 314, 1795–early nineteenth century, wood chemical works – charcoal cylinder works
292   Langhurst, Flame Warfare Establishment, TQ 179 352, WW2, rocket test facility – testing 'Lizzy'
293   Mid Lavant, Chichester, His Majesty's Wood Distillation Plant, SU 85 08, Great War 1918 unfinished, wood chemical works – acetate of lime for acetone

West Yorkshire

294   Barnbow, NFF No 1, SE 38 34, Great War 1915–?, explosives factory – filling factory
295   Bradford, Bradford Dyers Association Ltd, *SE 15 28, late nineteenth century, explosives factory – picric acid
296   Bradford, Low Moor Chemical Co, *SE 16 28, late nineteenth century–Great War, explosives factory – picric acid
297   Bradford, Wyke, S Breaks and Sons Ltd, *SE 16 32, late nineteenth century–Great War, explosives factory – picric acid
298   Bradford, Wyke, T F Hoare, *SE 15 26, Great War, explosives factory – picric acid
299   Bradley near Deighton, H M Factory managed by L B Holliday, *SE 17 20, Great War 1915–?, explosives factory – picric acid
300   Castleford Ings, Ings Lane, Hickson and Partners Ltd, *SE 43 26, Great War 1915–?, explosives factory – TNT
301   Cleakheaton, The White Lee Chemical Company, *SE 19 25, late nineteenth century, explosives factory – picric acid
302   Garforth, NFF No 1a, *SE 393 345, Great War, explosives factory – filling factory
303   Greetland, H M Factory managed by Sharp and Mallet, *SE 096 211, Great War 1917–18, explosives factory – picric acid
304   Halifax, Brookes Chemical Ltd, *SE 09 22, Great War, explosives factory – picric acid
305   Halifax, Copley Sharp and Mallet, *SE 08 22, late nineteenth century–Great War, explosives factory – picric acid
306   Huddersfield, ICI, *SE 11 14, 1938–?, explosives factory – ammonium nitrate
307   Huddersfield, Turnbridge Works, Read Holliday and Sons Ltd, *SE 15 17, late nineteenth century–Great War, explosives factory – picric acid, TNT
308   Leeds, Brotherton and Co Ltd, *SE 30 33, Great War, explosives factory – picric acid
309   Leeds, Marsh Pudsey, R Peel and Co, *SE 21 34, Great War, cotton waste

310   Leeds, Whitehall Soap Works, Watson Joseph and Sons, *SE 31 32, Great War, soap factory – glycerine

311   Lightcliffe, NFF No 15, *SE 14 25, Great War, explosives factory – filling factory

312   Milnsbridge Coln Valley, J W Leitch and Co Ltd, *SE 11 15, Great War, explosives factory – TNT

313   Otley, Midgley Farm, NFF, SE 222 455, Great War 1915, explosives factory – filling factory unfinished

314   Steeton, ROF, SE 032 448, WW2, explosives factory – small arms ammunition

315   Thorpe Arch, ROF FF No 8, SE 450 465, WW2 1941–?, explosives factory – filling factory

316   Wakefield, Calder Vale Works, Brotherton and Co Ltd, *SE 33 19, Great War, explosives factory – picric acid

Wiltshire and Swindon UA

317   Salisbury, *SU 14 30, early seventeenth century, saltpetre works

318   Swindon, Stratton Works, Brunner Mond and Co Ltd, *SU 16 86, Great War 1917–18, chemical works – ammonium nitrate

319   Wootton Bassett, ROF FF No 12, *SU 06 82, WW2, explosives factory – filling factory not built

Wirral UA, see Merseyside

Worcestershire

320   Blackpole, ROF, SO 857 577, WW2, explosives factory – small arms ammunition

321   Summerfield, Imperial Metal Industries, SO 835 735, 1950s–to present, explosives factory – filling factory, rocket motor manufacture

322   Worcester, *SO 85 54, Civil War, gunpowder works

Yorkshire, see North Yorkshire; South Yorkshire; West Yorkshire; York UA

York UA

323   York, castle mills and bridge, SE 606 513, Civil War, gunpowder works

324   York, Rowntree Factory County Industries Ltd, *SE 605 538, WW2 1940–?, explosives factory – filling factory ROF assisted

Ireland

County Cork

325   Ballincollig, WS 59 71, 1794–1903, gunpowder works

County Wicklow

326   Arklow, Kynoch's, Explosives Trades, Nobel Industries, T 22 74, 1895–192?, explosives factory – cordite, picric acid

Dublin

327   Clondalkin, River Camac, O 07 31, 1717–by 1822, gunpowder works

328   River Poodle, *O 15 34, c1590–by 1600, gunpowder works

Unlocated

329   Metheglin, late nineteenth century

Isle of Man

330   Port Cornaa, Maughold, *SC 470 884, 1890–2 unfinished, explosives factory – bellite

Northern Ireland

Belfast

331   Belfast, 1796, gunpowder works

Scotland

Angus

332   Dundee, Graham Street, Office of Forest and Woods, H M Wood Distillation Factory, *NO 40 32, Great War 1915–18, wood chemical works – acetate of lime for acetone

Argyl and Bute

333   Clachaig, Glen Lean, NS 122 814, 1832–1903, gunpowder works
334   Furnace, Loch Fyne, NN 023 004, 1841–87, gunpowder works
335   Melfort, NM 839 143, 1853–by 1874, gunpowder works
336   Millhouse, Kames, NR 958 706, 1839–1921, gunpowder works

Ayrshire, see East Ayrshire; North Ayrshire; South Ayrshire

Dumfries and Galloway

337   Dalbeattie, Ministry of Supply operated by Nobel Explosives Co Ltd/ICI, NX 848 632, WW2, explosives factory – cordite
338   Dumfries, Ministry of Supply operated by Nobel Explosives Co Ltd/ICI, *NX 94 74, WW2, explosives factory – nitrocellulose, TNT
339   Powfoot, Ministry of Supply operated by Nobel Explosives Co Ltd/ICI, NY 1610 6564, WW2, explosives factory – propellants, TNT
340   Wigtown, Ministry of Supply operated by Nobel Explosives Co Ltd/ICI, NX 425 594, WW2 1940–5, gunpowder works

East Ayrshire

341   Bowhouse, Air Ministry Factory, NS 467 348, 1940–5, filling factory – incendiary bombs and pyrotechnic devices
342   Kilmarnock, Bonington Road, H M Cotton Waste Mill, *NS 41 38, Great War, cotton mill – cotton waste mill

Edinburgh UA, see Midlothian

Glasgow UA, see North Lanarkshire

Inverclyde, see Renfrewshire

Kirkcudbright, see Dumfries and Galloway

Midlothian and City of Edinburgh UA

343   Craigleith Quarry, Lothian Chemical Company H M Factory, NT 266 746, Great War 1915–18, explosives factory – TNT
344   Edinburgh Castle, NT 251 735, 1541, gunpowder works
345   Gorebridge, NT 343 612, 1794–c1865, gunpowder works
346   Marfield, NT 1829 5640, 1812–by 1853, gunpowder works
347   Roslin, NT 265 624, c1805–1954, gunpowder works
348   Water of Leith, 1701, unlocated, gunpowder works

Na h-Eileanan an Iar

349   South Uist, NF 76 42, 1960s, rocket test facility – launch site for Skua and Petrel rockets

North Ayrshire

350   Ardeer, Stevenston, Nobel Explosives Co Ltd, NS 28 40, 1872–present, explosives factory – dynamite, TNT and a wide range of other blasting explosives, propellants including ballistite, cordite, ?tetryl; 1930s–70s gunpowder works

351   Giffen, Nobel Explosives Co Ltd/ICI, NS 359 505, 1941–3, explosives factory – mortar and anti-tank munitions

352   Irvine, Nobel Explosives Co Ltd, *NS 310 380, Great War 1916–18, explosives factory – nitrocellulose powder; 1936–45 ROF explosives factory – TNT

North Lanarkshire and Glasgow UA

353   Cardonald, NFF No 12 managed by Nobel Explosive Co Ltd, *NS 515 652, Great War, explosives – filling factory

354   Mossend near Motherwell, ICI, *NS 743 604, WW2, chemical works – ammonia

355   Whiteinch, Glasgow, H M Cotton Waste Mill, *NS 54 66, Great War, cotton mill – cotton waste mill

Renfrewshire and Inverclyde

356   Ardgowan, Greenock, H M Distillery, *NS 208 730, Great War, distillery – acetone

357   Bishopton, ROF, NS 44 69, 1937–present, explosives factory – cordite, tetryl, RDX and rocket motors

358   Fereneze, *NS 502 598, WW2 194?, explosives factory – filling factory ROF assisted

359   Georgetown, Fulwood Erskine, NFF No 4, NS 448 676, Great War 1915–18, explosives factory – filling factory

360   Georgetown, NFF No 4a, NS 448 676, Great War 1915–18, explosives factory – filling factory

Roxburghshire, see Scottish Borders

Scottish Borders

361   St Boswells, Ministry of Aircraft Production operated by Nobel Explosives Co Ltd/ICI, NT 585 295, WW2, filling factory – incendiary bombs

South Ayrshire

362   Girvan, Grangeston, Ministry of Supply operated by Nobel Explosives Co Ltd/ICI, NX 204 997, WW2, explosives factory – TNT

West Lothian

363   Camilty, NT 0627 6160, 1889–1931, gunpowder works

364   Fauldhouse, NS 95 63, 1812–by 1837, gunpowder works

365   Linlithgow, Regent Factory, Nobel Explosives Co Ltd/ICI, 1901–?, NT 005 771, fuse factory, WW2 filling factory – fuse and bomb filling for Air Ministry

Western Isles/Inverness-shire, see Na h-Eileanan an Iar

Wigtown, see Dumfries and Galloway

Wales

Anglesey, see Isle of Anglesey

Bridgend UA

366   Brackla, ROF FF No 11, SS 916 810, WW2 1941–?, explosives factory – filling factory satellite to Bridgend

367   Bridgend, ROF FF No 2, SS 92 79, WW2 1940–?, explosives factory – filling factory

Cardiff UA

368   Llanishen, ST 168 812, post-war, rocket motor factory

369   Whitchurch, Curtis's and Harvey, *ST 1428 8010, WW2, explosives factory

Carmarthenshire

370   Brechfa, Anglo French Nickel Co, *SN 52 30, Great War, wood chemical works – acetate of lime

371   Carmarthen, SN 4141 1961, Great War, wood chemical works – acetone unfinished

372   Pantyffynnon Ammanford Carmarthen Chemical Works, SN 6228 1167, 1871–80s, ?gunpowder works

373   Pembrey Burrows, SN 415 005, 1882–by 1906 Explosives Company of Stowmarket, explosives factory – dynamite; Great War 1915–18 Nobel Explosives Co Ltd, explosives factory – TNT, tetryl and propellants also NFF No 18; 1937–65 ROF explosives factory – TNT, ammonium nitrate, tetryl

374   Pendine, SN 26 08, WW2 1940s–present, rocket test facility

Ceredigion

375   Aberporth, SN 243 518, WW2 1940–present, rocket test facility

376   Ynyslas, SN 61 94, WW2, rocket test facility

Flintshire

377   Queensferry, H M Factory, SJ 328 680, Great War 1915–18, explosives factory – guncotton, TNT, MNT, tetryl

378   Rhydymwyn, Ministry of Supply operated by ICI, SJ 206 666, WW2, explosives factory – filling factory gas munitions

379   Sandycroft, Asiatic Petroleum Co, SJ 339 673, Great War 1915–18, explosives factory – mono nitro toluene

Gwynedd

380   Dolgellau Tyddyn Gwladys, SH 735 274, 1887–1901, gunpowder works

381   Penrhyndeudraeth, SH 618 389, 187? Patent Safety Gun-Cotton Company; New Explosives Co Ltd, explosives factory – guncotton; 1908 Steelite Explosives Co Ltd, explosives factory – steelite; H M Factory Great War 1915–18 Ergite and Co and Cooks Miners Safety, explosives factory – picric acid, TNT

Isle of Anglesey

382   Ty Croes, SH 3350 6925, post-war, rocket test facility

Monmouthshire

383   Caerwent, Royal Naval Propellant Factory, ST 477 907, 1940–67, explosives factory – cordite, tetryl; post-war – naval rocket motors

384   Glascoed, ROF FF No 3, SO 348 012, WW2 1940–present, explosives factory – filling factory

Pembrokeshire

385   Trecwn, Royal Naval Armament Depot, SM 978 321, WW2–1993, naval filling factory

Powys

386   Glyn-neath, SN 91 08, 1857–1931, gunpowder works

Rhondda, Cynon, Taff UA

387   Hirwaun, ROF, *SN 940 061, WW2, explosives factory – small arms ammunition

Wrexham UA

388   Glyn Ceiriog, Hendre, *SJ 189 343, 1870–?79, gunpowder works

389   Plas Bennion, SJ 2887 4421, 1916–19, 1936–?45, explosives factory – picric acid

390   Ruabon, Robert Graesser, SJ 2750 4271, late nineteenth century–Great War, explosives factory – picric acid

391   Wrexham, ROF, SJ 38 49, WW2

Glossary and abbreviations

The glossary amplifies many of the specialist terms used in the book, and the abbreviations which the general reader may encounter when studying historic explosives factories. Terms in italics appear elsewhere in the glossary.

Acetone Solvent, used in the gelatinisation of some forms of *cordite*.

Amatol Mixture of *TNT* and *ammonium nitrate*, used for bomb and shell filling.

Ammonium nitrate Produced by the neutralisation of nitric acid by ammonia, commonly used as diluter with *TNT* to form *amatol*.

Anhydrite Sedimentary rock associated with gypsum, used as a source of sulphur.

Ball mill Wooden barrel or cylinder containing wooden or metal balls, used to pulverise ingredients or in the *incorporation* of gunpowder, also used to produce meal powder by pulverising corned powder. Also known as *moulins à tonneaux*.

Ballistite *Propellant* invented by Alfred Nobel in 1888 consisting of *nitrocellulose*, *nitroglycerine*, potassium nitrate and chalk.

Baratol Mixture of *TNT* and barium nitrate, generally used for filling grenades and anti-tank mines.

Bipropellant Name given to *propellant* systems where the fuel and *oxidant* are stored in separate tanks, generally applied to rocket propulsion.

Black powder Term current from the late nineteenth century for *gunpowder*, to distinguish the traditional mechanical mixture of saltpetre, charcoal, and sulphur, from the newer *smokeless* and *brown powders*.

Blasting gelatine Mixture of 7–8% nitrated cellulose and *nitroglycerine*, forming a plastic mass.

Blasting oil Late nineteenth-century term used to describe liquid *nitroglycerine*.

Brown powder Mechanical mixture of *saltpetre*, carbonised straw (usually rye straw), and sulphur. Developed in the late nineteenth century as slow-burning powder for use in large bore guns. Also known as *cocoa powder*.

Carbamite Also known as *centralite* and diphenyldiethylurea, used as a stabiliser in solventless cordites.

CDB Cast double base, a rocket motor *propellant* formed from a *nitrocellulose* casting powder and *nitroglycerine*-based casting liquid.

CE Composition exploding, see *tetryl*.

Centralite See *carbamite*.

Cheese See *runner*.

Clean area Designated section of an explosives factory or building where loose explosives may be encountered. Usually marked by toeboards or a painted line, and floor surfaces which may be easily kept clean and free from explosive dust. Also referred to as the *danger area*.

Cocoa powder See *brown powder*.

Cordite Double base *propellant* produced by combining *nitrocellulose* with *nitroglycerine*; a number of different forms are found.

Cordite paste Intermediate form of *cordite* produced by mixing *nitrocellulose* with *nitroglycerine* prior to incorporation.

Cordite SC Solventless *cordite*.

Cordite W Type of *cordite* developed in the inter-war period at Waltham Abbey, where *carbamite* was used in place of *mineral jelly* as a stabiliser.

Corning Process whereby *millcake* or pressed *gunpowder* is reduced to grains of a consistent size by the use of a *corning sieve*. The term is also used more loosely to describe the *granulation* process using rollers. It may also be used to describe the *granulation* of other types of explosives

Corning sieve Usually a wooden sieve with holes of a given size punched in its base, into which is placed a *runner* or *cheese* which forces the powder through the holes to produce a uniform sized grain.

Cracker house Building dedicated to an intermediate process between *pressing* and *granulation* to reduce the size of the *press cake*. Only example known is from Ardeer in the 1930s.

Cryogenic Exceptionally low temperature.

Cryolite Additive to certain types of *cordite* to reduce barrel flash.

Cyclonite See *RDX*.

Danger area See *clean area*.

Deflagatory Burning.

Dirty area All parts of an explosives factory outside the *clean area*.

Dithekite Liquid high explosive based on benzene, developed during the Second World War

Dynamite Explosive formed by mixing *nitroglycerine* with an inert siliceous earth.

Edge runner Vertically mounted millstone or *runner*.

ELDO European Launcher Development Organisation.

Engine Propulsion unit of a liquid *propellant* rocket.

ENSA Entertainments National Service Association.

Eprouvette Powder trier, a device to test the strength of gunpowder. A measured amount of powder was inserted into it and inflamed; this raised its lid or cover, the higher it went the stronger the powder.

EXE Type of *prismatic powder* which used a blend of carbonaceous substances.

Expense magazine Magazine in a factory where part-manufactured explosives are stored between manufacturing processes.

Explosive train Series of decreasingly sensitive explosives arranged in a sequence to ensure the detonation of the *main charge*.

FG Fine grain (gunpowder).

Flashing house Building where *gunpowder* was tested; named after the flashing plates on which a sample of gunpowder was ignited.

Filling factory Factory where explosives and the inert components of munitions are brought together for assembly.

Foul grain Term used to describe powder after the *granulation* process.

Fuze Device for initiating the explosion or detonation of an explosive at a given time. Readers should note that the spelling 'fuze' has been used throughout, as the standard form found in British service literature: see Bailey and Murray 1989, 177.

Gaine Device filled with high explosive used to transmit the initial shock from the detonator to the *main charge*.

Gelatine dynamite 80% *nitroglycerine*, 20% mixture of *saltpetre*, and woodmeal.

Gelignite 65% *nitroglycerine*, 35% mixture of *saltpetre*, and woodmeal.

Glazing house Building where *gunpowder* was glazed by placing it in a drum or cylinder mounted on a central horizontal axis; the glaze was imparted by the grains rubbing together, graphite may also be added.

Gloom stove A stove used for drying *gunpowder*; it usually comprised two separate rooms, one containing a stoke hole to heat a cast iron fireback or cockle, which protruded into the drying room. Gunpowder to be dried was then laid out on racks in the drying room.

Granulation Process of reducing *presscake* to grains of specified sizes by use of a granulating machine with serrated rollers. See also *corning*.

Green charge Charge of *gunpowder* mixed together in the correct proportions prior to *incorporation*.

Guncotton An explosive produced by the nitration of cotton. See *nitrocellulose*.

Gunpowder A mechanical mixture of saltpetre, charcoal and sulphur. See *black powder*.

Gutta-percha Tough, rubber-like substance.

Guttmann balls Small, hollow, pierced, and serrated earthenware balls used to pack acid towers to increase the available surface area within the tower. Named after their inventor Oscar Guttmann. See Figure 5.59.

HE High Explosive

Heading Term used to describe the fixing and sealing of the lid of a gunpowder barrel; 'unheading' opening a barrel.

Hexamine HMX, hexamethylenetetranitramine, a high explosive.

HS Mustard gas.

HTP High test peroxide, used as an *oxidant* in liquid fuelled rocket motors.

Igniter Explosive used to set light to the main *propellant* charge or rocket motor, see *primer*.

Incorporation Term used to describe the intimate mixing of the ingredients of *gunpowder*; it might be achieved by a number of processes including by a pestle and mortar, *ball mills*, *edge runners*, and stamp mills. The term is also used in the chemical explosives industry to describe the mixing of ingredients, for example the mixing of *guncotton* and *nitroglycerine* with a solvent in the manufacture of *cordite*.

Incorporator Mixing machine similar to that used for making bread dough, used in the manufacture of *cordite*.

Kieselguhr Exceedingly fine grained and absorbent siliceous earth, formed from the skeletal remains of microscopic plants, diatoms. Used in conjunction with *nitroglycerine* to form *dynamite*.

LG Large grain (gunpowder).

Lignum vitae Tree native to the American tropics; it yields a very hard, heavy wood, brownish green in colour. It is used to make pulleys, shafts, axles, bowls, balls etc. Used in owder manufacture for runners in *corning sieves* and for the balls in *ball mills*.

LOX Liquid oxygen, commonly used as an *oxidant* in liquid fuel rocket engines.

Lyddite British term for the high explosive trinitrophenol (*picric acid*); after Lydd in Kent, where it was first tested.

Main charge Principal bulk filling of a high explosive shell.

Meal powder Produced in breaking down machine by breaking *millcake* between rollers. Carried out in normal production immediately prior to pressing or to produce powder for shell filling.

Mealed powder Finely pulverised powder produced by crushing corned powder in a *ball mill*.

Mill cake Term given to powder at the end of *incorporation*.

Mineral jelly Initially added to *cordite* to lubricate the shell during its passage along the gun barrel, though ineffective in this role it was found to be a useful chemical stabiliser.

Mixing The process by which the three ingredients of *gunpowder* were mixed in their correct proportions prior to *incorporation*.

Mixing house Building in which the ingredients of an explosive charge are carefully weighed into the correct proportions prior to processing.

MNT Mononitrotoluene.

Monopropellant Usually a liquid chemical substance which can be made to evolve hot gases under certain conditions; a term commonly associated with rocket *propellants*.

Motor Propulsion unit of a solid *propellant* rocket.

Moulins à pilons *Stamp mills*.

Moulins à tonneaux *Ball mills*, where the mixing and grinding action is achieved by rotating a substance in a barrel partly filled with balls.

NFF National Filling Factory (Great War).

Nitrator Chemical plant used to treat a variety of substances with nitric acid.

Nitrocellulose An explosive produced from cellulose, either cotton or wood pulp, under the action of strong nitric acid (usually with sulphuric acid as a dehydrating agent). Where cotton is the cellulose the result is guncotton.

Nitroglycerine Colourless, transparent, liquid, oxygen-rich explosive substance.

Nitroguanidine Also known as petrolite or *picrite*, anti-flash agent and cooler for gun *cordite*.

Nitro-lignin Nitrated substance produced from wood products.

Observation post Small protected shelter (Second World War) which was used to observe the progress of an air raid over a factory and to report this to a central control room. These posts were not designed to be defended and should not be confused with pill boxes.

Oleum Solution of sulphur trioxide in sulphuric acid; used either to fortify sulphuric acid or in strong nitrating solutions.

Oxidant The component of a *bipropellant* fuel which supports the combustion of the fuel.

PAD Passive air defence (Second World War).

Pebble powder Large grains of powder, or powder cut into varying sized cubes, for use in large bore guns.

Pellet powder Pressed powder, used in large bore guns and for mining charges.

Percussion cap Small, steel or usually copper cap filled with a sensitive cap composition, which when struck by the firing mechanism of a gun will explode to ignite the main *propellant* charge.

Phenol Raw material for the production of *picric acid*, traditionally produced by the fractional distillation of coal tar.

PIAT Projector infantry anti tank; portable anti-tank weapon.

Picric acid Trinitrophenol, more generally known as *lyddite*.

Picric powder A mixture of ammonium picrate and potassium nitrate; used as a boosting composition for picric acid.

Picrite See *nitroguanidine*.

Poaching machines Less commonly used alternative name for a *potcher*.

Potcher Large tank in which nitrocellulose is energetically agitated in water as part of the final washing process.

Poudre B *Nitrocellulose* based *propellant* developed in the 1880s by the French government chemist, Paul Vieille; adopted by the French government for rifle *propellants*.

Press cake Powder which has been pressed.

Primer Explosive placed between the *percussion cap* and the *main charge*.

Prismatic powder Pressed powder introduced in the late nineteenth century. The prisms were formed in either a cam or hydraulic press from either *black* or *brown powders*. Prismatic powders were used in large bore guns and for mining, where it was important to control the rate of burning.

Propellant Explosive substance which, when burnt in a regulated manner, will produce gases that can be controlled to do work.

Pyrocollodion See *nitrocellulose*.

Pyroligneous acid Acid produced during the destructive distillation of wood.

Raschig rings Hollow, unglazed earthenware cylinders used to create a large surface area within acid towers. To further increase the surface area the rings may have a partition down their centres, or have a ceramic insert placed in the middle. Modern types are normally made of glass. See also *Guttmann balls*.

RAE Royal Aircraft Establishment

RATO Rocket assisted take-off.

RD 202 Research Department composition No 202. *Fuze* powder consisting of ammonium perchlorate 77%, charcoal 20%, and starch 3%.

RDX Research Department composition X Cyclotrimethylenetrinitramine, also called cyclonite (USA), hexogen (Germany) and T4 (Italy). A high explosive discovered around 1899 but not successfully developed until the 1930s.

Refuge Term applied to an air-raid shelter within a factory complex (Second World War).

RFG Rifle fine grain (gunpowder).

RGPF Royal Gun Powder Factory.

RNAD Royal Naval Armament Depot.

RNCF Royal Naval Cordite Factory.

RNPF Royal Naval Propellant Factory.

ROF Royal Ordnance Factory.

Round Single, ready-assembled piece of ammunition comprising *propellant* and projectile.

RPD Rocket Propulsion Department

Runner Hard circular piece of wood, sometimes *lignum vitae*, in a *corning sieve*, also referred to as a *cheese*.

Saltpetre Generic name given to three naturally occurring nitrates; ordinary saltpetre or potassium nitrate, chile saltpetre or sodium nitrate, and lime saltpetre or calcium nitrate. Saltpetre is the principal ingredient of gunpowder and certain types were also important in the manufacture of nitric acid.

SAP bombs Semi armour piercing bombs.

SBC Slow burning cocoa, a type of brown *prismatic powder*.

SC Solventless *cordite*.

Schultze powder Nitrocellulose *propellant* powder invented by a German, Eduard Schultze.

Serpentine powder Loosely, usually hand mixed, *gunpowder*; term usually applied to early forms of *gunpowder*.

Shellite High explosive shell filling, a mixture of *picric acid* and dinitrophenol.

Shifting house Building or room where workers change into special clothing before entering a factory *clean area* or magazine.

SM Short milled, *gunpowder* milled for a shorter time than normal government powders; used as a bursting charge in shells.

Smokeless powder Late nineteenth-century term to describe the new chemical propellants developed to replace the traditional *gunpowder* or *black powder*.

Stamp mill A mill using pestles or stamps to *incorporate gunpowder*. See *moulins à pilons*.

Subliming kiln or furnace Building used in the refining of sulphur, in use in Britain from at least the late eighteenth century.

Tetryl Trinitro-phenyl-methyl nitramine, also known as *CE*, used as a booster in *explosive trains*.

TNT Trinitrotoluene, produced by the nitration of *toluene*.

Toluene By-product of the fractional distillation of coal tar and certain crude petroleums.

Tonite Blasting explosive comprising thoroughly purified *guncotton* mixed or impregnated with a nitrate or nitrates.

Torpex High explosive mixture of *TNT*, *RDX*, and aluminium.

Traverse Protective wall, mound or screen surrounding an explosives building.

Triacetin Desensitiser added to liquid *nitroglycerine* to enable it to be moved safely.

TWD Trench Warfare Department (Great War).

Uralite Brown asbestos sheeting.

Bibliography

Abbreviations used in the bibliography

BCL Bolton Central Library
BL British Library
CSPD Calendar of State Papers Domestic published by the PRO
DNB Dictionary of National Biography
DNH Department of National Heritage
HCRO Hampshire County Record Office
ICI Imperial Chemical Industries
ILN Illustrated London News
LPFD Letters and Papers Foreign and Domestic, published by the PRO
NMR National Monuments Record
PRO Public Record Office
RAHIL Royal Artillery Historical Institution Library
VCH Victoria County History
WASC Waltham Abbey Special Collection

Sources

A wide variety of historical sources have been used in this study. Some of them are so extensive that they have only been sampled: no reference to them should be taken to indicate an exhaustive search. Others are not properly in the public domain. They may be confidential: they may survive on site, disregarded or forming part of working site records: they may be in private hands. At best their future may be uncertain and liable to change in location or ownership.

For the early history of gunpowder and saltpetre manufacture the Calendars of State Papers Domestic (CSPD) and the Letters and Papers Foreign and Domestic (LPFD), published by the Public Record Office, are a rich source of information. For the eighteenth- and early nineteenth-century state establishments the papers of the Board of Ordnance preserved at the PRO form the most accessible source. The PRO collections are also vital for all aspects of munitions production during the Great War, in particular the voluminous archives of the Ministry of Munitions. Among these, the albums of photographs compiled during the construction of factories could be singled out as a direct and invaluable access route to a given factory. Their content is patchy as far as site plans and buildings drawings are

concerned, however. The Imperial War Museum is a second major source of information about Great War factories and conditions within them, specifically through their collections of oral histories and photographs. Of equal importance for more recent factories are the papers and reports of the Explosives Inspectorate, housed in the PRO. Information on individual Second World War factories is less abundant and less predictable in its classification; for example, the organisation of the system of Royal Ordnance Factory may be found in the Cabinet Office papers. For twentieth-century naval facilities, some records may be found at the PRO, but the most comprehensive archive relating to twentieth-century explosives, manufacturing, and handling sites is held at the Hampshire County Record Office (HCRO).

The National Monuments Record (NMR) of the Royal Commission on the Historical Monuments of England (RCHME), and now of English Heritage, contains the national collection of air photographs, comprising both historic verticals and specialist obliques. These are especially helpful for Second World War military manufacturing sites where contemporary site plans no longer exist. The NMR in England and the Royal Commissions in Scotland and Wales also hold archives on the explosives industry donated by the late Mr E M Patterson, including manufacturing method books from the 1930s.

More specifically, information about the Royal Gunpowder Factory at Waltham Abbey, Essex, is divided between the holding of the Waltham Abbey Royal Gunpowder Mills Charitable Foundation (part on site and part forming the Waltham Abbey Special Collection (WASC) in Epping Forest District Museum), and a further deposit of Waltham Abbey material in the PRO. Elsewhere, local record offices will often contain information about factories in their area, and are frequently a good starting point to explore the social history of the industry, which this book has addressed in only a limited way.

In addition to the sources cited in the endnotes, the bibliography also contains references to other general works and articles on individual sites.

This bibliography is divided into three sections: selected legislation, published works and reports in the public domain, and unpublished material listed under the location of the library or repository in which it is to be found, arranged alphabetically.

Selected legislation

Statutes at Large 1756, **29 George II, c. 16**; An Act to impower His Majesty to prohibit the export of saltpetre; and to enforce the law for impowering His Majesty to prohibit the exportation of gunpowder, or any sort of arms and ammunition, and also to impower His Majesty to restrain the carrying coastwise of saltpetre, gunpowder, or any sort of arms or ammunition.

Statutes at Large 1772, **12 George III, c. 61**; An Act to regulate the making, keeping and carriage of gunpowder within Great Britain, and to repeal the laws hereto made for any of those purposes.

Public Statutes General 1860, **23 and 24 Victoria, c. 139**; An Act to amend the law concerning the making, keeping, and carriage of gunpowder and compositions of an explosive nature, and concerning the manufacture, sale and use of fireworks.

Public Statutes General 1861, **24 and 25 Victoria, c. 130**; An Act for amending an Act passed in the last session of Parliament to amend the law concerning the making, keeping, and carriage of gunpowder and compositions of an explosive nature, and concerning the manufacture, sale and use of fireworks.

Public Statutes General 1862, **25 and 26 Victoria, c. 98**; An Act for the amendment of an Act of the session of the twenty-third and twenty-fourth years of the reign of her present Majesty, Chapter one hundred and thirty-nine, intituled An Act for amending an Act passed in the last session of Parliament to amend the law concerning the making, keeping, and carriage of gunpowder and compositions of an explosive nature, and concerning the manufacture, sale and use of fireworks, and of an Act amending the last-mentioned Act.

Public Statutes General 1866, **29 and 30 Victoria, c. 69**; An Act for the amendment of the law with respect to the carriage and deposit of dangerous goods.

Public Statutes General 1869, **32 and 33 Victoria, c. 113**; An Act for a limited period the importation, and to restrict and regulate the carriage, of nitro-glycerine.

Public Statutes General 1875, **38 Victoria, c. 17**; An Act to amend the law with respect to the manufacturing, keeping, selling, carrying, and importing gunpowder, nitro-glycerine, and other explosive substances.

Public Statutes General 1914, **4 and 5 George V, c. 29**; Defence of the Realm Act 1914.

Public Statutes General 1914, **4 and 5 George V, c. 63**; Defence of the Realm (No 2) Act, 1914.

Public Statutes General 1915, **5 and 6 George V, c. 42**; Defence of the Realm (Amendment) (No 3) Act, 1915.

Public Statutes General 1915, **5 and 6 George V, c.51**; Ministry of Munitions Act, 1915

Public Statutes General 1915, **5 and 6 George V, c. 54**; Munitions of War Act, 1915.

Public Acts General 1921, **11 George V, c. 8**; An Act to make provision for the cessation of the Ministry of Munitions and the Ministry of Shipping.

Public Acts General 1923 **13 and 14 George V, c. 17**; An Act to amend the Explosives Act, 1875.

Public General Acts and Measures 1937 **1 Edw VIII and 1 Geo VI, c. 67**; An Act to consolidate, with amendments, the factory and Workshop Acts, 1901–1929, and other enactments relating to factories; and for purposes connected with the aforesaid.

Public General Acts and Measures 1941 **5 and 6 George VI, c. 4**; An Act to amend the law as to the liability to national service, 1941.

Published works

Abel, F, 1863 On the application of gun-cotton to warlike purposes, *Reports, British association for the advancement of science*, 16–25

——, 1866 Researches on guncotton — on the manufacture of and composition of guncotton, *Roy Philosophical Soc Trans*, **156**, 269–308

——, 1867 Researches on guncotton — second memoir on the stability of guncotton, *Roy Philosophical Soc Trans*, **157**, 181–253

——, 1890 Smokeless explosives 1, *Nature*, **61**, February 6, 328–30

Adams, A R, 1976 *Good company: the story of the Guided Weapons Division of British Aircraft Corporation*, Stevenage

Adams, R J Q, 1978 *Arms and the wizard*, London

Admiralty, 1905 *Handbook on ammunition*, London

——, 1915 *Handbook on ammunition*, London

——, 1945 *Handbook on ammunition* London

Agricola, G, 1556 *De re metallica*, eds H C Hoover and L H Hoover, 1912

Anderson, E W, 1898 The machinery used in the manufacture of cordite, *Proc Inst Civil Engineers*, **123**(2), 69–129

Anglo, S, 1969 *Spectacle, pageantry and early Tudor policy*, Oxford

Anon, c 1919 *A short history of the National Shell Filling Factory Chilwell, Notts 1915–1918* Place of publication unknown

Armytage, W H G, 1976 *A social history of engineering*, London

Atkin, M, and Howes, R, 1993 The use of archaeology and documentary sources in identifying the civil war defences of Gloucester, *Post-medieval Archaeol*, **27**, 15–41

Aubrey, J, 1718 *The natural history and antiquities of the county of Surrey*, **4**, London

Baddeley, F, 1857 *Pamphlet on the manufacture of gunpowder as carried on at the Government Factory Waltham Abbey*, privately printed Waltham Abbey

Bailey, S, 1996 The Royal Armouries 'Firework Book', in Buchanan 1996a, 57–86

Bailey, A, and Murray, S G, 1989 *Explosives, propellants and pyrotechnics*, London

Baker, D, 1978 *The rocket: the history of and development of rocket and missile technology*, London

——, 1991 *Potworks: the industrial architecture of the Staffordshire potteries*, London

Barlow, T W, 1855 *Cheshire and its historical and literary associations*, Manchester

Barron, C, 1990 A powder house in Holborn, *Gunpowder Mills Study Group Newsletter*, **8**, 6

Barter Bailey, S, 1996 The Royal Armouries 'Firework Book', in Buchanan 1996a, 57–86

Bates, H E, 1946, *The tinkers of Elstow*, London

Beattie, S, 1980 *A revolution in London housing: LCC housing architects and their work 1893–1914*, London

Becklake, J, 1984 British rocketry during World War II *International Aerospace Abstracts*, Abstract A85–13157

——, 1998 German engineers: their contribution to British rocket technology after World War II, *American Astronautical Soc History Ser*, **22**, 157–72

Benecke, T, and Quick, A W, 1957 *History of German guided missile development*, Germany

Billings, J, and Copland, D, 1992 *The Ashton munitions explosion 1917*, Tameside Leisure Services, Tameside MBC

Bing, H, 1919 *Report on the development of the vacuum charging machine for H.S.*, Ministry of Munitions, London

Biringuccio, V, c 1540 *The Pirotechnia of Vannoccio Biringuccio*, eds C M Smith and M T Gaudi, 1959, New York

Blackman, H, 1923 The story of the old gunpowder works at Battle, *Sussex Archaeol Coll*, **64**, 109–22

Bone, D and Prince, D, 1995 Beneficial reuse of the Waltham Abbey Royal Gunpowder Mills, in Coulson and Baldwin 1995, 359–66

Bottaro, J C, 1996 Recent advances in explosives and solid propellants, *Chemistry and Industry* **7**, April, 249–52

Bower, T, 1988 *The paperclip conspiracy*, London

Bowditch, M R, 1983 *Cordite-Poole: a short account of the Royal Naval Cordite Factory*, MOD PR

Bowditch, M R, and Hayward, L, 1996 *A pictorial record of the Royal Naval Cordite Factory Holton Heath*, Wareham

Braddock, J, 1829 *A memoir of gunpowder in which are discussed the principles of its manufacture and proof*, Madras

Bret, P, 1994 *Lavoisier a la Régie des Poudres: le savant, le financier, l'administrateur et le pédagogue, La vie des sciences: comptes rendus de l'Academie des Sciences, serie generale*, **11**(4), 297–317, Paris

——, 1996 The organisation of gunpowder production in France, 1775–1830, in Buchanan 1996a, 261–74

Bristol Siddeley Journal, 1962 Bloodhound, **3**(3), 58–62

Bristol Siddeley Journal, 1964 Rocket engines for piloted aircraft, **5**(4), 109–12

British Hovercraft Corporation, 1971 *The High Down industrial test facilities*, BHC Cowes trade pamphlet, Cowes

Brooks, M, 1990 Women in munitions 1914–1918: the oral record, *Imperial War Museum Rev*, **5**, 4–17

Brown, G I, 1998 *The Big Bang: a history of explosives*, Stroud

Buchanan, B J, 1976 A comment on the manufacture of black powder *J Soc Ind Archaeol* (West Virginia University) **2**(1), 75–80

——, (ed), 1996a *Gunpowder: the history of an international technology*, Bath

——, 1996b Meeting standards: Bristol powdermakers in the eighteenth century, in Buchanan 1996a, 237–52

——, 1996c The technology of gunpowder making in the eighteenth century: evidence from the Bristol region, *Trans Newcomen Soc*, **67**, 125–59

Buchanan, B J, and Tucker, M T, 1981 The manufacture of gunpowder: a study of the documentary and physical evidence relating to the Woolley powder works near Bath, *Ind Archaeol Rev*, **5**, No 3, 185–202

Bud, R, 1992 The zymotechnic roots of biotechnology, *Brit J Hist Science*, **25**, 127–44

——, 1993 *The uses of life: a history of biotechnology*, Cambridge

Canby, C, nd *A history of rockets and space*, Lausanne

Carlton, C, 1992 *Going to the wars: the experience of the British Civil Wars 1638–51*, London

Carter, L J, 1950 Anglo-Australian Long Range Weapon Project, *J Brit Interplanetary Soc*, **9**(1), 1–3

——, 1965 The Spadeadam Rocket Establishment, *Spaceflight*, **7**(5), 176–80

Cartwright, A P, 1964 *The dynamite company*, London

Cattell, J, and Falconer, K, 1995 *Swindon: the legacy of a railway town*, London

Cavendish, nd c 1878 *Chemistry theoretical, practical, and analytical as applied to the arts and manufactures*, London

Cherry, J, 1974 Essex: Waltham Abbey, Post-medieval Britain in 1973, *Post-medieval Archaeol*, **8**, 132

Chitty, G, 1996 *Monuments Protection Programme: gunpowder industry, recommendations for protection (Step 4)*, unpublished consultancy report for English Heritage

City of Coventry, 1992 *Coventry in the Civil War 1642–1651*, City of Coventry leaflet

Clark, A, 1995 *R.O.F. Kirkby 1940–1946: a photographic history*, Kirkby

Clay, C G A, 1984 *Economic expansion and social change: England 1500–1700 Vol 2 Industry, trade and government*, Cambridge

Clayton, H, 1992, *Loyal and ancient city: Lichfield in the Civil Wars*, Lichfield

Coad, J G, 1989 *The Royal Dockyards 1690–1850*, Aldershot

Cocroft, W D, 1994 *Oare Gunpowder Works Faversham Kent*, Faversham Paper No 39, Faversham

——, 1995 A methodology for recording complex industrial/military sites; the example of RCHME's survey of the Royal Gunpowder Factory, Essex, in Coulson and Baldwin 1995, 367–76

Cocroft, W D, and Leith, I, 1996 Cunard's shellworks, Liverpool, *Archive*, **11**, 53–64

Coleman, R, 1801 On the manufacture and constituent parts of gunpowder, *Philosophical Magazine*, **9**, 355–65

Colver, E de W S, 1918 *High explosives*, London

Colvin, H M, Ransome, D R, and Summerton, H (eds) 1975 *The history of the King's works, Volume III 1485–1660 (Pt 1)*, London

Congreve, W, 1783 *Experiments with several sorts of powder manufactured in England and Holland etc by firing shells and brass balls from mortars*, London

——, 1785 *Abstract of experiments tried at the Royal Powder Mills at Faversham under the direction of Major William Congreve*, London

——, nd 178? *Method of extracting saltpetre from damaged powders with a press invented by Major Congreve for that purpose*, London

Cooke, C, 1957 *The life of Richard Stafford Cripps*, London

Cooksey, A J A, 1969 Jennings south western pottery, Parkstone, *Industrial Archaeol*, **6**(2), 164–171

Coulson, M and Baldwin, H (eds), 1995 *Pilot study on defence environmental expectations*, NATO CCMS Report No 211, University of Wales, Swansea

Crocker, A, 1986 Carshalton gunpowder mill in 1661, *Gunpowder mills study group newsletter*, **2**, 3

——, 1989 The 1796 Faversham drawings, *Gunpowder mills study group newsletter*, **6**, 12–13

——, 1997 The gunpowder mill at Radcliffe near Nottingham, *Gunpowder mills study group newsletter*, **21**, 22–23

Crocker, G, 1984 *Chilworth gunpowder*, Surrey Industrial History Group, Old Woking

——, 1986 *The gunpowder industry*, Aylesbury

——, 1988a *Gunpowder mills gazetteer*, London

——, 1988b *The Lowwood gunpowder works*, Cartmel

——, 1994 *A guide to the Chilworth gunpowder mills*, Surrey Industrial History Group, 2nd ed, Old Woking

Crocker, G, and Fairclough, K R, 1998 The introduction of edge-runner incorporating mills in the British gunpowder industry, *Ind Archaeol Rev*, **20**, 23–36

Crocker, A, Crocker, G, Fairclough, K R, and Wilks, M, forthcoming *Gunpowder mills documents of the seventeenth and eighteenth centuries*, Surrey Record Society, Woking

Crow, A D, 1947a The rocket as a weapon of war in the British forces No. I, *Engineering*, 28 November 1947, 510–12

——, 1947b The rocket as a weapon of war in the British forces No. II, *Engineering*, 5 December 1947, 532–3

Crozier, R D, 1998 *Guns, gunpowder and saltpetre: a short history*, Faversham Papers No. 58, the Faversham Society

Davidson, J S, 1980 A history of chemistry in Essex, *Essex J*, **15**(2), 38–46

Department of the Environment, 1990 *Planning policy guidance note 16, archaeology and planning*, London

——, 1995 *Chemical works explosives, propellants and pyrotechnics manufacturing works*, Department of the Environment Industry Profile, London

Dickinson, H W, 1945 A study of galvanised and corrugated sheet metal, *Trans Newcomen Soc*, **24**, 27–35

Dickinson, H W, and Straker, E, 1938 Charcoal and pyroligneous acid making in Sussex, *Trans Newcomen Soc*, **18**, 61–6

Diderot, D, 1771 *Encyclopédie, ou dictionnaire raisonné des sciences, des arts et des métiers* Paris

DNB, 1930 *The dictionary of national biography*, **4**, London

Dobinson, C S, 1996a *Twentieth century fortifications in England* **1.1** *Anti-aircraft artillery England's air defences gunsites 1914–46*, York

——, 1996b *Twentieth century fortifications in England* **3** *Bombing decoys of WWII*, York

Dolan, J E, and Oglethorpe, M K, 1996 *Explosives in the service of man: Ardeer and the Nobel heritage*, Edinburgh

Double, H, 1988 Petticoat workers of secrets factory, *Bury Free Press* (26 August, No 9)

——, 1991 *Stowmarket — the march of time*, Stowmarket Town Council

Earl, B, 1978 *Cornish Explosives*, Penzance

Earl, B, and Smith, J R, 1991 *National Explosives, Upton Towans, Hayle*, Cornwall Archaeological Unit, Truro

Earnshaw, A, 1990 *Britain's railways at war 1914–1918*, Penryn

Edgerton, D, 1991 *England and the aeroplane*, London

Edwards, B, 1994 National Filling Factory No.5 Quedgley, *J Gloucestershire Soc Ind Archaeol*, 32–52

Edwards, P, 1995 Gunpowder and the English civil war, *J Arms and Armour*, **15**(2), 109–31

Elliot, B, 1996 The Royal Gunpowder Factory Explosions 1940, *After the Battle*, **93**, 34–49

Engelbach, F G, 1899 Her Majesty's Ordnance Factories, *The Navy and Army Illustrated*, 30 December 1899, 405–7

The Engineer, 1918 Birmingham and the production of munitions No. II, 5 April, 288–9

Engineering, 1894 The first patent of saltpetre, *Engineering*, **57**, 773

England, J, 1993 Acetone production at RNCF Holton Heath: acorns urgently needed, *J Naval Sci*, **18**(3), 189–222

Essex County Council Planning Department, 1994 *RARDE North Site, Area P, Waltham Abbey Essex Archaeological Excavation*, unpublished report

Everson, P, 1998 Waltham Abbey RGPF: a case study of exemplary reconciliation? in Jones *et al* 1998, 79–86

Everson, P, and Cocroft, W, 1996 The Royal Gunpowder Factory at Waltham Abbey: the field archaeology of gunpowder manufacture, in Buchanan 1996a, 377–94

Explosives Inspectorate, 1879 *The circumstances attending to the destruction by explosion of the Press House of Mr S. Sharp's Gunpowder Factory at Chilworth, near Guildford, on 10th February 1879*. Report 21, HMSO London

——, 1882 *Circumstances attending an accident which occurred in the factory of the Potentite Company (Limited), at Melling, near Liverpool, on the 15th July 1882*. Report 45, HMSO London

——, 1883 *The circumstances attending an explosion which occurred at the Chilworth Gunpowder Factory, on the 15th November 1883*. Report 57, HMSO London

——, 1884 *Circumstances attending an explosion which occurred in the Worsborough Dale Gunpowder Factory on the 15th October 1884*. Report 66, HMSO London

——, 1887 *Circumstances attending a fire and explosion at Messrs. Roberts, Dale, and Company's Chemical Works, Cornbrook, near Manchester, on the 22nd June 1887*. Report 81, HMSO London

——, 1890 *Circumstances attending an explosion of gunpowder, which occurred at the Roslin Gunpowder Factory, near Edinburgh, on the 22nd January 1890*. Report 91, HMSO London

——, 1893 *Circumstances attending the destruction by explosion and fire of a Drying-house at the factory of the Smokeless Powder Company (Limited) at Barwick, Hertfordshire, on the 26th May 1893*. Report 104, HMSO London

——, 1894 *Circumstances attending an explosion which occurred in the Mixing House at the factory of the National Explosives Company, Limited, at Upton Towans, Gwithian, near Hayle, Cornwall on the 4th September 1894*. Report 109, HMSO London

——, 1899 *Circumstances attending an explosion of Carbo-gelatine in course of manufacture which occurred at the factory of the Cotton Powder Company, Limited, at Uplees Marshes, near Faversham, on 5th May 1899*. Report 133, HMSO London

——, 1899 *Circumstances attending an explosion of blasting gelatine which occurred in a Mixing House at the factory of the National*

Explosives Company, Limited, at Upton Towans, Gwithian, near Hayle, Cornwall, on 19th May 1899. Report 136, HMSO London

——, 1900 Circumstances attending an explosion of Picric Acid which occurred at the factory of Messrs. Read, Holliday and Sons, Limited, at Huddersfield, on May 30th, 1900. Report 139, HMSO London

——, 1903 Circumstances attending an explosion of partly mixed Cordite Paste which occurred at the factory of Messrs. Curtis' and Harvey, Limited, at Lower Point, near Cliffe, Kent, on the 15th December, 1902. Report 157, HMSO London

——, 1903 Circumstances attending an explosion of nitroglycerine which occurred in the Final Washing House of the Cotton Powder Company, Limited, at Uplees Marshes, near Faversham, in the County of Kent, on the 23rd August 1903. Report 161, HMSO London

——, 1904 Circumstances attending an accident which occurred in the Drying House for Nitro-cotton, at the factory of Messrs. Curtis's and Harvey, Limited, at Cliffe, in the county of Kent, on the 18th February, 1904. Report 166, HMSO London

——, 1904 Circumstances attending an explosion of Nitro-glycerine in the Separating House of the factory of Messrs. Curtis's Harvey, Limited, at Cliffe, in the county of Kent, on, on the 23rd August 1903. Report 167, HMSO London

——, 1891 Fifteenth Annual Report of Her Majesty's Inspectors of Explosives; being their report for the year 1890. HMSO PRO LAB 59/4

——, 1895 Nineteenth Annual Report of Her Majesty's Inspectors of Explosives; being their report for the year 1894. HMSO PRO LAB 59/4

——, 1905 Twenty-ninth Annual Report of Her Majesty's Inspectors of Explosives; being their report for the year 1904. HMSO PRO LAB 59/6

——, 1906 Thirtieth Annual Report of Her Majesty's Inspectors of Explosives; being their report for the year 1905. HMSO PRO LAB 59/7

——, 1907 Thirty-first Annual Report of Her Majesty's Inspectors of Explosives; being their report for the year 1960. HMSO PRO LAB 59/7

——, 1920 Forty-fourth Annual Report of Her Majesty's Inspectors of Explosives; being their report for the year 1919. HMSO PRO LAB 59/12

Fairbairn, W, 1861 Treatise on mills and millwork. Part 1. On the principles of mechanism and on prime movers, 2, London

Fairclough, K, 1985 Early gunpowder at Waltham Abbey, Essex J, 20, 11–16

Falconer, K A, 1993 Fireproof mills — the widening perspectives, Ind Archaeol Rev, 16(1), 11–26

Farmer, J, 1735 History of the ancient town, and once famous abbey, of Waltham, in the county of Essex, London

Fergusson, J, 1994 Brick imports into Hayle, Cornwall, Information (newsletter of the British Brick Society), 62, 15–23

Ferris, J P, 1964 The saltpetremen in Dorset, 1635, Proc Dorset Nat Hist Archaeol Soc, 85, 158–63

Ferro-concrete, 1910 New cordite magazine, Purfleet, 1, 10

Fitzgerald, W G, 1895 How explosives are made, Strand Magazine, 11, 307–18

Foard, G, 1995 The Civil War defences of Northampton, Northamptonshire Past and Present, 9(1), 4–44

Forster, R II B, and Breen, L, 1962 Some problems encountered in the design of large rocket engine test beds, J Brit Interplanetary Soc, 18, 55–69

Fox, M R, 1987 Dye-makers of Great Britain 1856–1976 – a history of chemists, companies, products and change, ICI Orpington

Francis, G H F, 1852 Opinions and policy of the Right Honourable Viscount Palmerston, London

Fraser, A, 1996 The Gunpowder Plot: terror and faith in 1603, London

Fraser and Chalmers Ltd, 1908 The Quinan system of drying gun-cotton, trade pamphlet

Freeth, F A, 1964 Explosives for the first world war, New Sci, 402, 274–6

Fuller, T, 1662 The worthies of England, (reprinted by George Allen and Unwin London, 1952)

Garrad, S, 1980 Bellite Factory, Port Cornaa, Maughold, Isle of Man, Ind Archaeol, 15, 313–7

The Gentleman's Magazine, 1828 Obituary Sir William Congreve, 98(2), 178–9

The Gentleman's Magazine, 1843 Domestic occurrences, NS 19, 525

Gifford, J, 1996 The buildings of Scotland: Dumfries and Galloway, Harmondsworth

Giles, C, and Goodall, I H, 1992 Yorkshire textile mills 1770–1930, London

Gimpel, J, 1977 The medieval machine, London

Girling, R B, 1987 Conkering heroes, Chemistry in Britain, 20(6), 324–5

Gordon, S, 1987 IMI Summerfield rocket motors and propellants history and development, J Brit Interplanetary Soc, 40, 311–22

Gould, S, 1993 Monuments Protection Programme: the gunpowder industry combined steps 1–3, unpublished consultancy report for English Heritage, London

Gray, A S, 1985 Edwardian architecture: a biographical dictionary, London

Gray, E, Marsh, H, and Maclaren, M, 1982 A short history of gunpowder and the role of charcoal in its manufacture, J Materials Sci, 17, 3385–400

Greener, W W, 1910 The gun and its development, ninth edition, reprinted by the Arms and Armour Press, London

Griffiths, J, 1985 Lizzy: the first British liquid propellant rocket motor, J Brit Interplanetary Soc, 38, 531–6

Guedalla, P, 1926 Palmerston, London

Guillery, P, and Pattison, P, 1996 The powder magazines at Purfleet, Georgian Group J, 6, 37–52

Gunpowder Mills Study Group News, 1989a The civil war powder mills Hereford, 5, 8

Gunpowder Mills Study Group News, 1989b The Derby powder mills, 6, 11

Gunpowder Mills Study Group News, 1989c Barges found at Littleton, Somerset, 6, 13

Guttmann, O, 1883 Die englische Explosivstoff-Industrie; von Fabriksdirector Oscar Guttmann, Dingler's Polytechnisches Journal, 249, 455–515

——, 1895 The manufacture of explosives, 1, London

——, 1906 Monumenta Pulveris Pyrii, London

——, 1908 Explosions and the buildings of explosives works, J Soc Chemical Ind, 27(13), 669–73

——, 1909 The manufacture of explosives: twenty years' progress, London

——, 1910 Buildings for explosives works, J Soc Chemical Ind, 29(15), 930–1

Haber, L F, 1971 *The chemical industry 1900–1930*, Oxford

——, 1986 *The poisonous cloud: chemical warfare in the first world war*, Oxford

Hacker, B C, 1995 Whoever heard of nuclear powered ramjets? Project Pluto at Livermore and the Nevada Test Site, 1957–64, *Icon*, **1**, 85–98

Hall, B S, 1996 Gunpowder and early gunpowder weapons in Buchanan 1996a, 87–120

——, 1997 *Weapons and warfare in renaissance Europe*, Baltimore and London

Hardie, D W F, and Davidson Pratt, J, 1966 *A history of the modern British chemical industry*, Oxford

Harding, A J, 1959 *Ammonia manufacture and uses*, London

Hartcup, G, 1988 *The war of invention: scientific developments, 1914–18*, London

Harwood, E, and Saint, A, 1991 *Exploring England's heritage*, London

Haslam, M J, 1982 *The Chilwell story VC factory and ordnance depot*, the Boots Company PLC, Nottingham

Hassenstein, W, 1941 *Das Feuerwerkbuch von 1420 — 600 Jahre deutsche Pulverwaffen und Büshsenmeisterei*, Munich

Hawkins, M, 1988 *Somerset at war*, Wimborne

Hay, I, (*alias* Beith J H), 1949 *R.O.F.: the story of the Royal Ordnance Factories 1939–1948*, London

Hay, J, 1878, The manufacture of gunpowder, *Engineering*, **25**, 1–2, 37–8, 95–6, 137–8, 197–8, 235–6

Hime, H W L, 1904 *Gunpowder and ammunition, their origins and progress*, London

HMSO, 1894a *Report on the committee appointed to enquire into the explosion of the 7th May, 1894 at the nitro-glycerine factory Waltham Abbey*, London

——, 1894b *First report of the committee appointed to enquire into the accident of the 13th December 1893, at the Royal Gunpowder Factory, Waltham Abbey*, London

——, 1895 *Treatise on service explosives*, London

——, 1907 *Treatise on service explosives*, London

——, 1920–2 *History of the Ministry of Munitions*, 12 vols, London

——, 1926 *Text book of ammunition*, London

——, 1938 *Text book of explosives used in the services*, London

——, 1957 *Defence: outline of future policy*, London

Hobsbawm, E J, 1969 *Industry and empire*, Pelican Econ Hist Britain, **3**, Harmondsworth

Hodgetts, E A B, 1909 *The rise and progress of the British explosives industry*, London

Hogg, I V, 1978 *Anti-aircraft a history of air defence*, London

Hogg, O F G, 1944 Gunpowder and its association with the Crown, *J Roy Artillery*, **91**, 178–90

——, 1963a *The Royal Arsenal*, London

——, 1963b *English artillery 1326–1716*, London

Hollister-Short, G J, 1985 Gunpowder and mining in sixteenth- and seventeenth-century Europe, *History of technology*, **10**, 31–66

Home Office, 1949 *Manual of basic training*, **2**, *Basic methods of protection against high explosive missiles*, Pamphlet No 5, London

Hornby, W, 1958 *Factories and plant*, London

Horner, J G, nd *The encyclopaedia of practical engineering and allied trades*, London

Hume, C R, 1963 A ballistic vehicle launching site; its development and operation, in Samson 1963, 95–112

Hunt, J, 1971 *A city under the influence*, Carlisle

Hurden, D, 1955 The development of the Armstrong Siddeley 'Snarler' rocket motor, *J Brit Interplanetary Soc*, **14**(4), 215–29

Hurte, J, 1989 A powder mill in Dorset in the late sixteenth century and Civil War period, *Gunpowder Mills Study Group News*, **6**, 9–10

Hutton, C, 1778 The force of fired gunpowder and the initial velocities of cannon balls, *Philosophical Trans Roy Soc*, **68**, 50–85

Imperial Chemical Industries, 1955 *Sulphuric acid manufacture and uses*, London

The Illustrated London News, 1843 The explosion at Waltham Abbey, **2**, 275

The Illustrated London News, 1853 Hale's Rocket Factory at Rotherhithe, **22** (23 April), 297–8

The Illustrated London News, 1854 Her Majesty's gunpowder mills at Waltham Abbey, **25** (11 November), 478–9

The Illustrated London News, 1855 War-rockets and their manufacture, **26** (28 April), 411

The Illustrated London News, 1861 Gunpowder explosion near Waltham Abbey, **38** (8 June), 519, 537

The Illustrated London News, 1868 The Abyssinian expedition, **53** (11 July), 28, 32

The Illustrated London News, 1875 Cotton gunpowder, **66** (13 February), 157–8

Ingenhousz, J, 1779 Account of a new kind of inflammable air or gas a new theory of gunpowder, *Philosophical Trans Roy Soc*, **69**, 376–418

Inman, P, 1957 *Labour in the munitions industries*, London

James, R R, 1978 *The British Revolution British Politics 1880–1939*, London

Jenkins, C F, 1891 The electric lighting of danger buildings, *Proc Inst Civil Engineers*, **110**, 367–79

Jenkins, J M, 1989 The railways of the Royal Gunpowder Factory, Waltham Abbey, *Ind Railway Record*, **117**, 385–415

Jeremy, D J, 1984 *Dictionary of business biography*, London

Johnson, B, 1970 *Industrial archaeology of Hertfordshire*, Newton Abbot

Johnson, C H, 1965 The Explosives Research and Development Establishment, Waltham Abbey, *Chem and Ind*, **8**, 320–27

Jones, M, and Rotherham, I D (eds), 1998 *Landscapes — perception, recognition and management: reconciling the impossible?*, Landscape archaeology and ecology 3, Sheffield

Jones, T, 1988 The great Fauld explosion, *Staffordshire Studies*, **1**, 58–76

J Soc Chem Ind, 1910 Obituary: Oscar Guttmann, **29**(16), 995–6

Keeping, M, and Comerford, J, 1997 Sustainable development and public participation: the benefits for property developers *J Property Development* **I**, No 3, 125–37

Kelleher, G D, 1993 *Gunpowder to guided missiles Ireland's war industries*, Ireland

Kelleher, B, 1996 The Royal gunpowder mills, Ballincollig, County Cork, in Buchanan 1996a, 359–75

Kelway, A C, 1907 A great explosives factory on the Essex marshes, *Essex Rev*, **16**, 112–21

Kennedy, P M, 1976 *The rise and fall of British naval mastery*, 2nd edn 1983, London

Kennett, J, 1985 *The Eltham Hutments*, London

Kramer, G W, 1995 *Berthold Schwarz — Chemie und Waffentechnik in 15 Jahrhundert*, Munich

——, 1996 *Das Feuerwerkbuch*: its importance in the early history of blackpowder, in Buchanan 1996a, 45–56

Lampson, M, nd *A history of the Maresfield 'Powder mills'*, privately published

The Lancet, 1916 The effects of tri-nitro-toluene on women workers, 12 August 1916, **2**, 286–7

Lee, R G, Garland-Collins, T K, Garnell, P, Halsey, B H T, Moss, G M and Mowat, A W, 1983 *Guided weapons including light, unguided anti-tank weapons*, London

LPFD Henry VIII *Letters and papers, foreign and domestic, of the reign of Henry VIII* (eds J S Brewer, J Gairdner and R H Brodie), 21 vols in 35, 1862–1932, London

Levy, S I, 1920 *Modern explosives*, London

Lewes, V B, 1915 Modern munitions of war, *J Royal Soc Arts*, **63**, 821–31

Ley, W, 1951 *Rockets, missiles and space travel*, London

Livingstone-Learmouth, A, and Cunningham, B M, 1916 The effects of trinitrotoluene on women workers, *The Lancet*, 12 August 1916, 261–3

Lloyd George, D, 1933 *War memoirs*, London

Lofts, D L, 1963 Blue Streak propulsion and pressurization systems, in Samson 1963, 77–94

London, J R, 1993 The preservation of space-related historic sites, *J Brit Interplanetary Soc*, **46**, 279–85

Lugosi, J, 1996 *The 'Gyori Programme' and the production of gunpowder in Hungary*, unpublished conference paper delivered at International Conference for the history of technology, Budapest 1996

Maber, W F, 1967 Naval ordnance inspection laboratory, Caerwent — R.I.P, *J Roy Naval Sci Soc*, **22**(4), 202–3

Macdonald, C, 1990 *Britain and the Korean War*, Oxford

Majendie, V D, 1872 *Report on the explosion of guncotton at Stowmarket on the 11th August 1871*, London

——, 1874 *Reports on the necessity for the amendment of the law relating to gunpowder and other explosives with the suggestions for a new Act*, London

——, 1878 *The circumstances attending an accident by explosion, which occurred in Mr Macdonald's war rocket factory, at Whitehill, near Gravesend, on the 13th September 1878*, London

Marshall, A, 1915 *Explosives — their manufacture, properties, tests and history*, London

——, 1917 *Explosives, 1, History and manufacture*, London

Marshall, G, 1995 Redressing the balance — an archaeological evaluation of North Yorkshire's coastal alum industry, *Ind Archaeol Review*, **18**, no 1, 39–62

Marwick, A, 1977 *Women at war 1914–1918*, London

Massey, H, and Robins, M O, 1986 *History of British space science*, Cambridge

Mauskopf, S H, 1990 Chemistry and cannon: J-L Proust and gunpowder analysis, *Technology and Culture*, **31**(3), 398–426

——, 1996 From Rumford to Rodman: the scientific study of the physical characteristics of gunpowder in the first part of the nineteenth century, in Buchanan 1996a, 277–93

Maxwell, W R, 1993 A note on the history of the Westcott establishment 1946–1977, *J Brit Interplanetary Soc*, **46**, 286–8

McIntyre, R, 1954 Naval Ordnance inspection Laboratory Caerwent, *J Roy Naval Sci*, **9**(6), 260–4

McLaren, M, 1975, The Explosives Research and Development Establishment, its historical background, *J Naval Sci*, **1**(2), 176–83

Mead, A, 1997 Secret world on the edge of London, *Architects' J*, 5 June 1997, 28–33

Medard, L, 1995 *L'oeuvre scientifique de Paul Vieille (1854–1934)*, *Rev Hist Sci*, **47**(3–4), 381–404

Melton, M, 1973 A grand assemblage, George W Rains and the Augusta powder works, *Civil War Times*, **11**(9), 28–37

Miles, F D, 1955 *A history of research in the Nobel Division of I.C.I.*, ICI Nobel Division, Birmingham

Ministry of Munitions, 1919 *H.S. Gas charging at No. 14 N.F.F. Hereford*, London

Morgan, S P, 1875 Recent improvements in the manufacture of pebble powder, *Proc Roy Artillery Inst*, **9**(2), 1–28

Napier, G, 1788 Observations on fired gunpowder, *Trans Roy Irish Academy*, **2**, 97–117

Nathan, F L, 1909a Guncotton and its manufacture, *J Soc Chem Ind*, **28**, 177–87

——, 1909b Guncotton and nitroglycerin; improvements in production and manufacture and application of, *J Soc Chem Ind*, **28**, 443–4

——, 1919 The manufacture of acetone, *J Soc Chem Ind*, **38**, 271–82

Nathan, F L, and Rintoul, W, 1908 Nitroglycerine and its manufacture, *J Soc Chem Ind*, **27**, 193–205

Needham, J, 1980 The guns of Khaifeng-fu, *Times Lit Supp*, 11 January 1980, 39–42

——, 1985 *Gunpowder as the fourth power, east and west*, Hong Kong

——, 1986 *Science and civilisation in China*, **5**, *Chemistry and chemical technology*, (7), *Military technology; the gunpowder epic*, Cambridge

Nef, J U, 1932 *The rise of the British coal industry*, London

——, 1934 The progress of technology and the growth of large-scale industry in Great Britain, 1540–1640, *Econ Hist Rev*, 1 ser, **5**, 3–24

Neufeld, M J, 1995 *The rocket and the Reich: Peenemunde and the coming of the ballistic missile era*, New York

New Explosives Company Ltd, 1902 *Guncotton as the bursting charge for shells*, pamphlet, Stowmarket

New Explosives Company Ltd, 1906 *Guncotton, its history, properties, manufacture and uses*, pamphlet, Stowmarket

Newbold, J T W, 1916 *How Europe armed for war 1871–1914*, London

Norris, R S, Burrows, A S, and Fieldhouse, R W, 1994 *Nuclear weapons databook*, **5**, *British, French and Chinese nuclear weapons*, Boulder

Norton, R, 1628 *The gunner: the making of fireworks*, London

Nye, N, 1670 *The art of gunnery*, London

Over, L, 1984 *The gunpowder mills at Hounslow*, Richmond-upon-Thames Friends of the Earth

Palmer, A, 1998 *The Low Wood Gunpowder Company: its inception and early growth 1798–1808*, London

Pan, J, 1996 The origin of rockets in China, in Buchanan 1996a, 25–32

Partington, J R, 1960 *A history of Greek Fire and gunpowder*, Cambridge

Pasmore, A (ed), 1993 *New Forest explosives — an account of the Schultze Powder Company of Eyeworth and the Armaments Research Department, Millersford*, Hampshire Field Club and Archaeological Society

Patterson, E D, 1986a *Gunpowder terminology and incorporation*, Faversham Paper No 27, Faversham

——, 1986b A gunpowder vocabulary, *Ind Archaeol Rev* **8**(2) 215–6

——, 1995a *Gunpowder manufacture at Faversham*, Faversham Papers No 42, Faversham

——, 1995b *Blackpowder manufacture in Cumbria*, Faversham Papers No 43, Faversham

Pembrey Country Park, nd *The history of the Pembrey Royal Ordnance factory*, leaflet

Pepper, S, and Swenarton, M, 1978 Home front: garden suburbs for munitions workers, *Architectural Rev*, **163**, 366–76

Percival, A, 1968 The Faversham gunpowder industry, *Ind Archaeol*, 5, 1–134

——, 1985 The great explosion at Faversham 2 April 1916, *Archaeologia Cantiana*, **100**, 425–63

——, 1986 *The Faversham gunpowder industry and its development*, Faversham Paper No 4, Faversham

Perks, J, 1992 *Dorset's Anti-Aircraft Defences*, Upton Press, Upton

Philo, P, and Mills, J, 1985 The Bedfont gunpowder mills, *London Archaeol*, 5(4), 95–102

Philp, B, 1984 *The Dartford gunpowder mills*, Kent Archaeological Rescue Unit

Plot, R, 1686 *The natural history of Staffordshire*, Oxford

Pluck, D, 1989 The gunpowder mill at Wooburn, Buckinghamshire *Gunpowder Mills Study Group Newsletter*, **6**, 10

Pollock, D B, 1962 Testing Blue Streak, *Flight International*, **82**, September, 539–42

Pooley, S J, 1994 The development of the 3-inch British military rocket, *J Brit Interplanetary Soc*, **47**, 123–4

Pritchard, T, Evans, J, and Johnson, S, 1985 *The old gunpowder factory at Glynneath*, Merthyr Tydfil and District Naturalist's Society

Profile, 1988 Chorley — fifty years ago, November, 6–7

Profile, 1994 Folly of war rises again, September

Punch, 1915, Design representing the distorted views entertained by certain querulous sons of liberty as to the methods of the new Minister of Munitions [cartoon], 16 June, **148**, 473

Putnam, T, and Weinbren, D, 1992 *A short history of the Royal Small Arms Factory Enfield*, Centre for Applied Historical Studies, Middlesex University

Pye, A R, and Robinson, R, 1990 *An archaeological survey of the gunpowder factory at Powdermills farm, Postbridge, Devon*, Exeter Museums Archaeological Field Unit

Quinan, K B, 1920 *H M Gretna: a description of the plant and processes*, Ministry of the Munitions of War

Quinan, W R, 1912 *High explosives*, London

Rae, I D, 1987 Wood distillation in Australia: adventures in Arcadian chemistry, *Historical Records of Australian Science*, 6(4), 469–84

Rains, G W, 1882 *History of the Confederate powder works*, Augusta, Georgia, USA

Ravenshill, W, 1974 *250 years of map making in Surrey*

Rayner-Canham, M, and Rayner-Canham, G, 1996 The Gretna garrison, *Chemistry in Britain*, 32(3), 37–41

Read, J, 1942 *Explosives*, Harmondsworth

Reader, W J, 1970 *Imperial Chemical Industries: a history, Vol 1: the forerunners*, London

——, 1975 *Imperial Chemical Industries: a history, Vol 2: the first quarter-century*, London

Rees, A, 1819 *The cyclopedia or universal dictionary of the arts, sciences and literature*, London (reprinted 1972, David and Charles, Newton Abbot)

Richie-Noakes, N, 1984 *Liverpool's historic waterfront the world's first mercantile dock system*, London

Richter, D, 1994 *Chemical soldiers*, London

Rimington, F C, 1966 Excavations at the Allerston manor site 1962–4, *Trans Scarborough and District Archaeol Soc*, 2(9), 19–28

Rintoul, W, 1934 Frederic Lewis Nathan 1861–1933 Obituary Notice, *J Chem Soc*, Part 1, 564–5

Robertson, R, 1921 Some war developments of explosives, *Nature*, **107**, 524–7

——, 1937 William Rintoul 1870–1936: Obituary Notice, *J Chem Soc*, 183–4

Robertson, W B, c 1900 Where gunpowder is made, in *Britain at work*, Cassell and Co, London, 281–5

Robins, B, 1742 *New principles of gunnery*, London

Robinson, H G R, 1963 A review of range SUPPort equipment, *J Brit Interplanetary Soc*, **17**, 174–8

——, 1965 The development of 'Blue Streak': the first stage of Europa I, *J Brit Interplanetary Soc*, **21**, 98–115

Routledge, G L, 1995 Boom town at Gretna, *Scots Magazine*, **142(3)**, 265–76

Roy, I, 1964 *The Royalist Ordnance Papers 1642–1646 Part I*, Oxford Record Society, **43**

Royal Commission on the Historical Monuments of England, 1964 *Newark on Trent: the Civil War siegeworks*, London

——, 1994 *The Royal Gunpowder Factory, Waltham Abbey, Essex: an RCHME Survey*, London

——, 1994 *Historic Buildings Report: the Royal Arsenal Woolwich*, unpublished typescript report, NMR Building Index No 92394

Ruhmann, J, 1996 Gunpowder for the defence of a city: Sopron from the sixteenth century, in Buchanan 1996a, 157–62

Samson, D R (ed), 1963 *Development of the Blue Streak satellite launcher*, Oxford

Saunders, A D, 1989 *Fortress Britain*, Liphook

SAVE, 1993 *Deserted bastions: historic naval and military architecture*, London

Schultze, E, 1865 *The new chemical gunpowder and its advantages over the old blackpowder and its substitutes*, pamphlet, London

Schulze, M P, 1996 The gunpowder mill at Spandau, in Buchanan 1996a, 351–8

Scott, W N, 1981 *Coryton: the history of a village*, Mobil Oil Company Limited

Scragg, J, 1990 A contractor's view of the Black Knight programme, *J Brit Interplanetary Soc*, **43**, 297–300

Sherwood, R, 1989 *Superpower Britain*, Cambridge

Silberrad, O, and Simpson, W S, 1906 Note on gunpowder and bullets, made about 1641, recently discovered in Durham Castle, *Chem Soc Proc*, **22**, 172–3

Simmons, W H, 1963 *A short history of the Royal Gunpowder Factory at Waltham Abbey*, Controllerate of Ordnance Factories, London

Simpson, W, 1978 *The Banbury to Verney Junction Branch*, Oxford

Skentlebery, N, 1975 *Arrows to atoms: a history of the Ordnance Board*, London

Sladen, D (ed), 1898 *Who's Who*, London

Smith, F M, 1868 Gunpowder, *Quarterly Rev*, **125**, 106–33

——, 1870 *A handbook on the manufacture of gunpowder as carried on at the Royal Gunpowder Factory, Waltham Abbey*, London

Smith, J R, 1986 *The Kemnall Vale Company, Kemnall Vale, Pensanooth*, Truro

Smith, P G A, no date but c 1920 *The shell that hit Germany the hardest*, London

Smith, T, 1991 Hydraulic power in the Port of London, *Ind Archaeol Rev*, **14**, 64–88

Snape, C, 1989 The Derby powder mill, *Gunpowder Mills Study Group Newsletter*, **6**, 11

Snow Harris, W, 1858a Lightning conductors, principles and instructions relative to their application to powder magazines and other buildings, *Roy Artillery Inst Occ Pap*, **1**, 55–63

——, 1858b On a system of lightning conductors, for Waltham Abbey, *Roy Artillery Inst Occ Pap*, **1**, 129–32

Spaceflight, 1962 The Blue Streak Booster, **4**(1), 2–5

Spaceflight, 1967 Rocketry at Ansty, **9**(9), 311–13

Sporting Goods Review, 1896 The Hounslow powder factory, 16 March, 61–3

Sprat, T, 1667 *History of the Royal Society*, (reprinted 1959), London

Steele, B D, 1994 Muskets and pendulums: Benjamin Robins, Leonhard Euler, and the ballistics revolution, *Technology and Culture*, **35**(2), 348–82

Stevenson, A W, 1919, Gretna victory recipe, *Mossband Farewell Mag*, 45

Stocker, D A, 1995 Industrial archaeology and the Monuments Protection Programme in *Managing the industrial heritage* (eds M Palmer and P Neavison), Leicester, 105–13

Storey, R, 1971 Barwick gunpowder works: a note, *Ind Archaeol*, **8**(3), August, 275–7

Sweetman, J, 1984 *War and administration: the significance of the Crimean War for the British army*, Edinburgh

Swenarton, M, 1981 *Homes fit for heroes*, London

Taylor, M M, 1986 *The Davington Light Railway*, Oxford

Tharratt, C E, 1963a, Black Knight Support facilities, *J Brit Interplanetary Soc*, **17**, 178–84

——, 1963b, Black Knight, *J Brit Interplanetary Soc*, **19**, 248–62

Thirsk, J, 1978 *Economic policy and projects: the development of a consumer society in early modern England*, Oxford

Thomson, D, 1965 *World history from 1914–1968*, London

Thomson, J H, 1941 *Guide to the explosives act, 1875*, London

Thompson, B, 1782 New experiments upon gunpowder with occasional observations and practical inferences: to which are added an account of new methods of determining the velocities of any kind of military projectiles and the description of a very accurate eprouvette for gunpowder, *Philosophical Trans Roy Soc London*, **71**(2), 229–328

The Times, 1879 Prismatic Powder, 18 November 1879, 8

The Times, 1886 New Gunpowder, 6 July 1886, 5

The Times, 1890 Explosives and cannon powders, 4 September 1890, 14

The Times, 1893 Supply, 12 September 1893, 4

The Times, 1910 Oscar Guttmann, 4 August 1910, 1

The Times, 1915 Shell and the great battle, 14 May 1915, 9

Toler, T I J, 1993 Poison gas manufacture in the UK, *After the Battle*, **79**, 12–33

Tomlinson, H C, 1979 *Guns and government: the Ordnance Office under the later Stuarts*, London

Tooley, P, 1971 *Fuels, explosives and dyestuffs*, London

Toynbee, M, and Young, P, 1973 *Strangers in Oxford*, Chichester

Travis, T, 1993 The Haber-Bosch process: exemplar of the 20th century chemical industry, *Chem and Ind*, **15**, 581–5

Trebilcock, R C, 1966 A 'special relationship' – government, rearmament, and the cordite firms, *Econ Hist Rev*, 2 ser, **19**, 364–79

Twigge, S R, 1993 *The early development of guided weapons in the United Kingdom, 1940–60*, Chur, Switzerland

Vernidub, I I, 1996 One hundred years of the Russian smokeless (nitrocellulose) powder industry, in Buchanan 1996a, 395–400

VCH, 1905 *A history of Surrey*, **2**, London

VCH, 1905 *A history of Sussex*, **1**, London

VCH, 1907 *A history of Essex*, **2**, London

VCH, 1966 *A history of Essex*, **5**, London

VCH, 1972 *A history of Oxford*, **10**, London

VCH, 1979 *A history of Oxford*, **4**, London

Vines, G, and Ward, A C, 1988 *Albion Explosives Factory heritage study*, for the Ministry for Planning and Environment, Melbourne

Wallace, E, 1919 *The real shell man*, John Waddington pamphlet

Wardell, W H, 1888 *Handbook of gunpowder and guncotton*, London

Warner, D W, 1975 The early history of gunpowder manufacture at Chilworth *Surrey Hist* **1**(3), 95–105, **1**(4), 131–57

War Office, 1872 *Notes on ammunition*, London

——, 1900 *Treatise on service explosives*, London

——, 1915 *Text book of ammunition*, London

——, 1925 *Report of the committee on the manufacture of gunpowder at the Royal Gunpowder Factory, Waltham Abbey*, London

——, 1946 *Report on Operation Backfire*, 5 vols, London

Watson, R, 1818 *Anecdotes of the life of Richard Watson, Bishop of Llandaff*, **1**, 2 edn, London

Weaver, E M, 1917 *Notes on military explosives*, New York

Weizmann, C, 1949 *Trial and error*, London

Wenham, P, 1970 *The great and close siege of York 1644*, Kineton

West, J, 1991 *Gunpowder, government and war in the mid-eighteenth century*, Royal Historical Soc Studies in Hist **63**, Woodbridge

Western Mail, 1995 Beach explosion, 18 August, 1

Wheeler, W H, 1945 *British rocket equipment*, London

——, 1946 Rocket development, *Nature*, **158**, 464–9

Whitehorne, P, 1562, *Certain waies for the orderyng of souldiers in battlray and settyng of battailes, after divers fashions, with their maner of marchyng: and also fygures of certaine new plattes for fortofications of townes*, London, Nicholas Englande reprint New York 1969

Wild, H W, 1996 Blackpowder in mining – its introduction, early use, and diffusion over Europe, in Buchanan 1996a, 203–17

Williams, A R, 1975 The production of saltpetre in the Middle Ages, *Ambix*, **22**(2), 125–33

Williams, C C, and Hume, C R, 1963 Blue Streak ground Support equipment, *J Brit Interplanetary Soc*, **19**, 185–95

Wilkinson, N B, 1975 An American powdermaker in Great Britain: Lammot du Pont's journal, 1858, *Trans Newcomen Soc*, **47**, 85–96

Wilson, P N, 1957 The waterwheels of John Smeaton, *Trans Newcomen Soc*, **30**, 25–48

——, 1963–4 The gunpowder mills of Westmorland and Furness, *Trans Newcomen Soc*, **34**, 47–65

Windibank, M P, 1979 Shoeburyness: a centre of Britain's rocket testing in the 19th century, *J Brit Interplanetary Soc*, **32**, 471–6

Winfield, J, 1996 *The gunpowder mills of Fernilee*, privately published, Whaley Bridge

Winter, F H, 1972 Sir William Congreve: a bi-centennial memorial, *Spaceflight*, **14**(9), 333–4

——, 1990 *The first golden age of rocketry*, Washington DC

Winters, W, 1887 *Centenary memorial of the Royal Gunpowder Factory,*

Waltham Abbey, compiled from original sources, private publication, Waltham Abbey

Wolper, R S, 1970 The rhetoric of gunpowder and the idea of progress, *J Hist Ideas*, **31**(4), 589–98

Wood, J, 1977 *Powderbarge WD*, Society for Spritsail Barge Research, Twickenham

Woollacott, A, 1994 *On her their lives depend*, Berkeley Ca, USA

Wootton, H A, and Lowry, T M, 1919 *Report on the head filling of chemical shells*, Ministry of Munitions, London

Wrey, E C, 1953 Saltpetre House, Ashurst Wood, Colbury, *Proc Hampshire Fld Club*, **18**, 335–7

W T, 1672 *The compleat gunner* (reprinted 1971, S R Publishers, London)

Wynn, H, 1994 *The RAF strategic nuclear deterrent forces: their origins, roles, and deployment 1946–1969, a documentary history*, London

Yelland, S, 1989 *Heritage survey of the Albion Explosives Factory*, unpublished MA thesis, Monash University, Australia

Young, A, 1808 *Agriculture of Sussex*, London

Zborowski, H von, 1957 BMW — Developments, in *History of German guided missile development* (eds T Benecke, and A W Quick, 1957), 297–324, Brunswick, Germany

Zumpe, H F, 1950 The testing of rocket motors, *J Brit Interplanetary Soc*, **9**(3), 108–30

Manuscript sources

Birmingham Central Library, West Midlands
Boulton and Watt Collection, portfolio 383

Bolton Central Library, Lancashire (BCL)
Benjamin Hick and Son Archive, Drawing 1856/9 Waltham Abbey, incorporating mills
Benjamin Hick and Son Archive, Drawing 1857/95 Waltham Abbey, gearing and hoist
Benjamin Hick and Son Archive, Drawing 1857/106 Waltham Abbey, crank and links
Benjamin Hick and Son Archive, Drawing 1860/184 Curtis and Harvey, Hounslow, incorporating mills
Benjamin Hick and Son Archive, Drawing 1856/74 Waltham Abbey, machine details

Carlisle Central Library, Cumbria
Local History sale catalogues, accession number 17950
Auction catalogue of Messrs Robert Dalton and Son, 11 May 1920

Chelmsford, Essex County Record Office
T/M125, copy of *c* 1590 map of Waltham Holy Cross, Epping and Loughton (original at Hatfield House)

Elstow, National Power's Storage Depot, Bedfordshire
Map in possession of the site's current owners, National Power, Elstow Storage Depot
On-site records at National Power's Elstow Storage Depot, Type C Bungalow H M Office of Works 10 April 1941

Epping Forest District Museum, Waltham Abbey, Essex
Waltham Abbey Special Collection (WASC)

WASC 20, Younghusband, C W, 1873 Description of the manufacture of Abel's pulped and compressed guncotton at Waltham Abbey, November 1873
WASC 35, CRDD, 1947 The Chemical Research and Development Department. Its programme and facilities
WASC 106, Excavation of Smeaton's Mill, 5 March 1975
WASC 176, ERDE North Site. Two circular brick structures uncovered during demolition of stores building, December 1963. Thought to be foundations of horse mills
WASC 518, Notes on the records of the RGPF.
WASC 540, Biderman, A, *c* 1838 Notes on Waltham Abbey
WASC 557, Faraday, M, 1843 Letter from Michael Faraday 20 June 1843.
WASC 791, Plans of buildings at Ballincollig.
WASC 900/79, Royal Gunpowder factory, map scale 1:2500, *c* 1910
WASC 901/106, Drawing No C10, Ground plan and elevations shewing six incorporating mills...to be driven by one steam engine for the Honourable Board of Ordnance, Waltham Abbey. Seen in PRO Hayes Store
WASC 901/300, 300A, 301, Drawings of August and September 1918 – ether pipeline to Mineral Jelly Store No 2. Details of pump house and trestles. Seen in PRO Hayes Store
WASC 1333/3–7 Photographs of bomb damage 5 October 1940
WASC 1375, Letter from the Royal Powder Mills, Faversham, dated 3 February 1792, to Major Congreve, comptroller, conveying news of an explosion that morning of No 3 and 4 pairs of runners at the Horse and Chart Mill
WASC 1376, Letter from the Royal Powder Mills, Faversham, conveying news of the Horse and Chart Mill explosion of 3 February 1792, addressed to His Grace the Master General and Honourable Board of Ordnance
WASC 1396, Demand from the Royal Powder Mills, Waltham Abbey, dated 1 January 1788 for 'materials and stores, necessary for carrying on the service of this place, on its first establishment and for the present year'
WASC 1451 and 1452, Photographs of RDX plant, Royal Gunpowder Factory
WASC 1479, Smeaton's Mill. Excavations, September 1973
WASC 1482, Evans, C C, Blackpowder manufacture at Nobels Explosive Company, Ardeer 13 July 1978. Report following a visit on 30 June 1978 by C C Evans and E Steel
WASC 1509, Royal Gunpowder Factory Buildings Ledger 1909
WASC 1544, Correspondence relating to Ancient Monument Inspectorate visits 1978–9

Greenwich Local History Library, Greater London
A survey of the King's lordship or manor of East Greenwich by Samuel Travers, 1695

Guildford Muniment Room, Surrey
132/3 Prospectus for the Chilworth Gunpowder Company Limited, 1885
132/5/2 The Chilworth Gunpowder Co. Ltd, trade pamphlet for Royal Naval Exhibition 1891

Leeds Central Library, West Yorkshire
LQ623.45 G953 Gummer R H, 1918 Barnbow No 1 (Leeds) NFF. A short history and record of the factory, unpublished typescript
Collection of photography

London, British Library, Department of Manuscripts (BL)
Althorp Papers, 12
Sloan MSS 2156 Roger Bacon *c* 1249

London, House of Commons
UK defence policy: options for change, Background paper, October 1991

Kew, Public Record Office (PRO)
AIR 20/4352 Schedule of 'Q' sites, 1941 Aug–1943 Dec
AVIA 48/37 Facilities at Westcott 1945–48
AVIA 48/57 Black Knight – entry test vehicle, 1955–57
AVIA 54/2226 Circular on employment of German scientists, 1946–50
BT 31/7899 Schultze Gunpowder Company Ltd
CAB 21/4453–6 Space research and Blue Streak
CAB 102/273 Munitions factories, locations and siting
CAB 102/626 History of the Royal Filling Factory Swynnerton, D Mack Smith unpublished narrative
CAB 102/627 Construction of Filling Factories, D Mack Smith unpublished narrative
CAB 102/630 The Filling Factory Organisation, P E Masters unpublished narrative
DEFE 7/1338 RAF production programme for guided weapons: Bloodhound
DEFE 7/1846 War Office production guided weapons: Thunderbird and Redshoes, 1962–3
EF 5/18 Royal Gunpowder Factory, Waltham Abbey: correspondence and notes 1878–1934
EF 5/19 Royal Gunpowder Factory, Waltham Abbey: correspondence and notes 1893–1940
EF 5/20 Government factories established during the war 1914–18
INF 3/197 'Paper helps to make munitions', artist Fougasse
INF 3/216 'I need bones for explosives', artist E Oliver
INF 3/403 'Women of Britain. Come into the factories...', artist Zec
MP 11/15 Maps and plans extracted from SUPP 5/762
MPH 189 [10] Faversham, Plan of Home and Marsh Works, 5 November 1790, extracted from WO 78/1131
MPH 189 [7] Faversham, Plan of the Marsh Works, 17 April 1810, extracted from WO 78/1131
MPH 206 [5] Ballincollig, Co Cork 1806, extracted from WO 78/1159
MPH 206 [6] Ballincollig, Co Cork 1806, extracted from WO 78/1159
MPH 250 Faversham, Kent, Plan of certain lands to be purchased, 1781, extracted from WO 78/1212
MPH 311 Sketch of Ordnance lands and buildings at Ballincollig, 1825, extracted from WO 78/1347
MPH 409 Faversham, Saltpetre 28 March 1798, extracted from WO 78/1533
MPH 410 Faversham, Clerk of Cheques and first clerk's houses, 1811, extracted from WO 78/1536
MPH 426 Faversham, General plan of the new buildings erected also shewing proposed willow plantations and ground for respective officers, 31 January 1790, extracted from WO 78/1554
MPH 515 Royal Arsenal Woolwich, Proposed driving-house for rockets with steam engines, extracted from WO 78/1718
MPH 555 Faversham, Construction of cylinders for charring wood, extracted from WO 78/1808

MPHH 271 Royal Gunpowder Manufactory Waltham Abbey, Essex, c 1827, extracted from WO 78/1865
MPHH 590 Ordnance lands and buildings at Tipner and Stampshaw Points, extracted from WO 78/2591
MPHH 597 Design for fitting up the ovens for subliming furnaces, 21 July 1790, extracted from WO 78/2713
MPHH 677 [12] Plan of Ordnance lands at St Budeaux, no scale, extracted from WO 55/2331
MR 580 [2] Plan describing the whole of the land and its situation at Waltham Abbey belonging to the Board of Ordnance, 1801, extracted from WO 78/2591
MR 580 [3] Waltham Abbey, 1806, extracted from WO 78/2591
MR 593 Waltham Abbey: Powdermills and fishery in the River Lea, 1783, extracted from WO 78/1408
MR 909 Faversham, Ordnance land and powder mills, 10 April 1789, extracted from WO 78/1517
MR 910 Faversham, Plan of powder mills and other Ordnance property, 1784, extracted from WO 78/1519
MR 914 Faversham, Ordnance powder mills, shewing freehold lane, also buildings since demolished, extracted from WO 78/1555
MR 1801 [1] Plan of Northolt Magazines
MR 1801 [3] H M Factory Langwith, 1918, extracted from MUN 4/2061
MR 1801 [5] Plan of National Filling Factory, Morecambe
MR 1801 [13] Scottish Filling Factory, Georgetown, site plan, 1918, extracted from MUN 4/2061
MR 1802 [3] Plan of National Filling Factory Georgetown
MR 1810 [4] Ministry of Munitions National Filling Factory No 7 Northolt Magazines, site plan, 1917, extracted from MUN 4/2061
MUN 4/1703 Summary of National Filling Factories, 29 August 1918
MUN 4/2710 Admiralty Filling Station at Stratford, 14 March–30 May 1917
MUN 4/3186 Gunpowder Supplies, 12 March–2 May 1917
MUN 4/5747 Disposal of horsechestnuts and acorns, 10–16 April 1918
MUN 4/6131 Transfer of housing schemes, H M Office of Works, schedules and plans, June 1921
MUN 4/6187 H M Wood Distillation Factories: disposal 13 March 1922–28 June 1923
MUN 4/6256 Government housing estates: sale of houses 31 July 1923–3 December 1930
MUN 5/10 Transfer of functions from War Office
MUN 5/10/180/43 Notes and correspondence on the issue of badges to munition workers, 15–23 April 1915
MUN 5/96/346/2/15 Copy of correspondence November 1915 to February 1916 on provision of accommodation for employees of Thames Ammunition Co
MUN 5/146/1122/8 List of factories operated by the Ministry in March 1918
MUN 5/154/1122.2/34 Pamphlet. *A short history of National Filling Factory No 7, Hayes, Middlesex* printed post January 1919
MUN 5/154/1122.3/33 Photographs of National Filling Factory Chilwell
MUN 5/154/1122.3/36 Memorandum on history of No 14 National Filling Factory Hereford, post November 1918
MUN 5/154/1123.3/39 Historical note No 28 Factory, Greenford, Middlesex, post November 1918
MUN 5/155/1123.3/59 Memorandum on danger building practice

and duties of danger building officers in National Filling Factories, 15 November 1915–29 October 1919

MUN 5/155/1122.3/50 Historical note, with plans and graphs, on No 2 Factory, Aintree, Liverpool, Lancs

MUN 5/155/1122.3/51 Historical note, with plans and graphs, on No 9 Factory, Banbury, Oxon

MUN 5/157/1122.3/65 Photographs taken in December 1915 and January 1916 of Abbey Wood, Cardonald, Chilwell, Coventry, Georgetown, Gloucester, Hayes, Leeds, Liverpool, Morecambe and Perivale factories

MUN 5/159/1122.7/28 *List of factories, etc, at which explosives are manufactured and stored* Harrison and Sons 1915, printed

MUN 5/239 Photographs of H M Factories at Queensferry, Gretna and Langwith under construction and in operation

MUN 5/266 Letters on, and plans and photographs of, bungalows to be erected at Woolwich, SE London for munition workers

MUN 5/285 Volume *H M Factory, Gretna, Description of plant and process*, HMSO, December 1918, printed

MUN 5/294 H M Explosives Factory, Lanwith, Mansfield, Nottinghamshire

MUN 5/297 Photographs of H M Factory, Gretna, Dumfries January 1916–March 1919

MUN 5/436 Gretna-Waltham Abbey Committee 1919–1920

MUN 7/36 Minister's queries on the report of the Committee on the Silvertown explosion 23 February 1917–9 October 1919

MUN 7/37 Report and other papers on explosion at Hooley Hill Rubber and Chemical Co at Ashton-under-Lyne, Lancs, 13 June 1917 14 June 1917–14 February 1919

MUN 7/40 Claims against contractors for plant, etc, destroyed in explosion at Range Works, Rainham, Essex 9 November 1917–12 January 1923

MUN 7/235 Miscellaneous papers about the appointment and working for Admiralty and the Ministry of Dr Charles Weizmann on experiments in the manufacture of acetone 18 July 1915–9 July 1917

MUN 7/236 Reports by Dr Charles Weizmann on experiments in production of acetone 23 Sept 1915–1 July 1916

MUN 7/237 Reports by W J Bush and Co Ltd, on working of industrial plant in manufacture of acetone 4 January–8 March 1916

MUN 7/238 Reports on Weizmann acetone process carried out at the Royal Naval Cordite Factory, Poole, Dorset 20 December 1915

MUN 7/554 Lady Superintendent at Waltham Abbey

MUN 7/555 Reduction in output at Royal Gunpowder Factory Waltham Abbey and question of future of factory

RG 12/573/2 St Martha, Surrey, Census Return 1891

RG 12/1095 Barwick part Stanton, Hertfordshire, Census Return 1891

RG 12/1715 Waltham Abbey, Essex, Census Return 1891

RG 12/1852 Gwithian, Cornwall, Census Return, 1891

SUPP 5/65 Faversham In-Letter Book 6 February 1778–25 May 1785

SUPP 5/148 Explosion at the Lyddite Establishment, Report of the Report of Enquiry 1903

SUPP 5/334 Explosion in RD Composition 202 Milling Houses 1925–6

SUPP 5/336 Explosion at ROF Bishopton 1941

SUPP 5/446 Royal Gunpowder Factory Waltham Abbey Annual Report 1935–6

SUPP 5/510 Powder Pellet 1869–1871, 1881

SUPP 5/559 Powder Prismatic December 1875–December 1880

SUPP 5/595 Special Materials November 1885–June 1888

SUPP 5/577 Brown Powder 1889–February 1903

SUPP 5/752 Proceedings of court of enquiry into explosion which occurred on 18th January 1940

SUPP 5/753 Proceedings of court of enquiry into explosion which occurred on 20th April 1940

SUPP 5/762 A treatise on gunpowder by Frederick Drayson, 1830 [drawings extracted to MP 11/15]

SUPP 5/853 Progress reports from Royal Naval Cordite Factory, Holton Heath 1927–34

SUPP 5/854 Progress reports from Royal Naval Cordite Factory, Holton Heath 1935–38

SUPP 5/860 Volume of plans of Ordnance establishments, 1864–67

SUPP 5/860 Photograph album, Vol 1 (explosions and plant)

SUPP 5/861 Photograph album, Vol 2 (explosions, plant, women war workers)

SUPP 5/863 Photograph album, 1940–1 (damage by enemy action)

SUPP 5/866 Copies to and from the Comptroller relating to the quality of gunpowder and proving of gunpowder, c 1781–1809

SUPP 5/867 Copies of reports to and from Comptroller relating to plant, etc at Waltham Abbey, 1789–1811

SUPP 5/868 Copies of reports to and from Comptroller relating to plant, etc at Faversham, 1795–1811

SUPP 5/869 Copies of miscellaneous correspondence, etc relating principally to plans for laboratories at Portsmouth and Plymouth, c1804–1810

SUPP 5/870 Incomplete copies of a report made by the Deputy Comptroller of the Ordnance Board in 1788 relating to the grounds on which the late and present Master General had reasons to doubt the goodness and durability of gunpowder delivered to the Royal Magazine, January 1788

SUPP 5/956 History of ROF Drigg 1945

SUPP 5/984 Principles and practice of passive air defence for explosive factories: Reports 1937–8

SUPP 5/1050 Notes and designs and construction of Ordnance factories, 1915

SUPP 10 Quinan papers, Kenneth B Quinan

SUPP 10/15 *Gretna: Description of plant and processes* printed

SUPP 14/1030 Visit to ROF Bishopton by E.D.P.C. 1949

SUPP 14/1063 Visit to ROF Glascoed 1949

SUPP 14/1064 Visit to Royal Naval Propellant Factory Caerwent

SUPP 14/1166 Cordite charges for guided weapons: proposed installation in ROFs

WO 47/60 Surveyor General's minutes July–December 1762

WO 55/425 Warrants 1660–8

WO 55/2331 Statements of lands and buildings owned and hired by the Ordnance with plans and reports, Plymouth 1807

WO 55/2334 Statements of lands and buildings owned and hired by the Ordnance with plans and reports, Purfleet 1806

WO 55/2351 Statements of lands and buildings owned and hired by the Ordnance with plans and reports, Waltham Abbey 1807

WO 55/2425 Statements of lands and buildings owned and hired by the Ordnance with plans and reports, Portsmouth Division 1811

WO 55/2425 Statements of lands and buildings owned and hired by the Ordnance with plans and reports, Purfleet

WO 55/2694 Statements of lands and buildings owned and hired by the Ordnance with plans and reports, Waltham Abbey 1830

WO 78/1533 Saltpetre store 1789

WORK 43/1244–1301 Royal Arsenal Woolwich, Research Department building drawings

WORK 44/48 Royal Aeronautical Establishment, Farnborough, Rocket test bed: lay-out and details 1946
WORK 44/627/354 Invention Wm Hale rockets 1853

London, Royal Armouries Library, Tower of London
Anon, Mid fifteenth century Firework Manuscript Royal Armouries Library ref 1.34

London, Science Museum Library
MS 412 *An American powder maker in Europe: Lammot du Pont's Journal, 1858* unpublished typescript in MS 412: see Wilkinson 1975

Swindon, Royal Commission on the Historical Monuments of England, National Monuments Record (NMR)
RCHME architectural survey reports, Fisherstreet (NMR Building Index No 94771) and Fernhurst (NMR Building Index No 94772)
SS 74 SE 109
ST 25 NE 33
SU 21 SW 3

Watford Reference Library, Herts
Box J Munitions

Winchester, Hampshire County Record Office (HCRO)
109M91/COL12 Caerwent training notes
109M91/MP40 and MP41, RNPF Caerwent.

109M91/MP52, Priddy's Hard: passive defence structures, Trench 38 Drawings 846/38 3-10-38, PD3120/41 31-7-41, and PD 3227/41
109M91/MP74 1941, Priddy's Hard: stores, kitchens, WCs, surgery
109M91/PH25, RNPF Caerwent (Monmouth)
109M91/PH36, RNAD Dalbeattie (Kirkudbright)
109M91/PH42, RNAD Ditton Priors (Shropshire)
109M91/PH66, RNAD Lodge Hill, Upnor (Kent)
109M91/PH79, RNAD Upnor and Grain (Kent)
109M91/RM9, Memo on HE by Lord Moulton 16 June 1915

Woolwich, Royal Artillery Historical Institution Library (RAHIL)
Congreve, W, 1788 *A statement of facts relative to the grounds on which the late and present Master General have had so much reason to doubt the goodness and durability of the gunpowder which was delivered into the Royal Magazine for the King's service*, Military Documents 13 Box 1, also PRO SUPP 5/870
Congreve, W, 1811 *A statement of facts relative to the savings which has arisen for manufacturing gunpowder in the Royal Powder Mills and of the improvements which have been made in its strength and durability since the year 1783*, London (pamphlet) G3L/18
Congreve, W (jun), 1814 *The details of the rocket system*, London (pamphlet)
Congreve, W, (jun) 1818 *A short account of the improvements in gunpowder made by Sir William Congreve*, London (pamphlet) G32/18
Kaestlin, J P, manuscript notes MS 213 Box II

Index